A Sheep's Song

A Writer's Reminiscences
of Japan and the World

KATŌ SHŪICHI

Translated and Annotated by
CHIA-NING CHANG

University of California Press
BERKELEY   LOS ANGELES   LONDON

University of California Press
Berkeley and Los Angeles, California

University of California Press, Ltd.
London, England

Library of Congress Cataloging-in-Publication Data

Katō, Shūichi, 1919–
   [Hitsuji no uta. English]
   A sheep's song : a writer's reminiscences of Japan and the world /
Katō, Shūichi ; translated and annotated by Chia-ning Chang.
     p.   cm.
   Includes bibliographical references and index.
   ISBN 0-520-20138-8 (alk. paper). — ISBN 0-520-21979-1 (alk. paper)
   1. Katō, Shūichi, 1919– . 2. Intellectuals—Japan—Biography.
3. Critics—Japan—Biography. I. Chang, Chia-ning. II. Title.
CT1838.K35A313   1999
952.03'3'092—dc21   98-49027

Printed in the United States of America
9 8 7 6 5 4 3 2 1

Contents

Translator's Preface

After presenting an autobiographical account of the first forty years of his extraordinary intellectual journey, Katō Shūichi surprised and bewildered many of his readers when, without any prior warning, he compared his personal experiences to "those of an average contemporary Japanese."[1] Whether Katō's proclamation represents willful posturing, self-mockery, or genuine self-perception, the epistemological dynamics between Katō the autobiographer and Katō the autobiographical subject tellingly reveal the nature of rhetorical engagement in the autobiographical enterprise. In the interest of self-knowledge, it is not only expedient but even inevitable that memory, imagination, and past and present consciousness should agree to suspend contesting visions of experience in favor of creative collaboration after a greater truth. Far from being a frivolous game of hide and seek, autobiographical self-representation, when seriously pursued, is nothing less than a spiritual movement toward self-discovery.

Twentieth-century Japanese autobiographers, like their international cousins—Jawaharlal Nehru, Pu-yi, Mary McCarthy, and Jean-Paul Sartre—engage in the act of self-portraiture by answering to both artistic and historical imperatives, to what Paul John Eakin has described as "the freedoms of imaginative creation on the one hand and the con-

---

1. See Katō's epilogue to *A Sheep's Song*, 409–10. It is "preposterous" (*tondemonai machigai*), said the novelist Fukunaga Takehiko, for his longtime friend Katō to assign such improbable thoughts to himself, a "custom-made intellectual" (*tokubetsusei no interi*). See Fukunaga's "Kyōretsu na ichi kosei no jiden: Katō Shūichi cho *Hitsuji no uta*," *Nihon Keizai Shimbun*, September 2, 1968.

straints of biographical fact on the other."[2] The results are often a med-
itative adventure between and across interacting layers of biographical
experiences before the authors acquire a new awareness of self and identity, turning themselves into artisans and choreographers as they reimag-
ine the journeys of their souls—even if the actual journeys are only par-
tially completed. Autobiographers and memoirists as diverse in style and
taste as Hirotsu Kazuo, Uno Chiyo, and Nakamura Shin'ichirō all in effect proclaim the improbability—or, more frankly in the case of Uno,
the futility—of arriving at absolute autobiographical truth.[3] And as in
the more manifestly fictional experiences of Futabatei Shimei's Utsumi
Bunzō and Mori Ōgai's Ōta Toyotarō that epitomize the moral dilemmas of an emerging modern intelligentsia, the self-portraits of Uchimura
Kanzō and Kinoshita Naoe in the Meiji period and of Kamei Katsuichirō
and Fukunaga Misao after the Pacific War bear equal witness to the continuing quest for self-redefinition.[4]

Ōoka Shōhei once declared that any individual in the public limelight
can scarcely resist the temptation to entertain multiple self-images: an
"objective" self that exists inviolate; a self-perceived self; a self believed
to be so publicly perceived; and the most frightening of all for a writer, a
secret self formed in muted silence among readers.[5] Although Ōoka was
discussing Natsume Sōseki's autobiographical novel *Michikusa* (Grass
on the wayside, 1915)—not Katō's *Hitsuji no uta: waga kaisō* (A sheep's

2. Paul John Eakin, *Fictions in Autobiography: Studies in the Art of Self-Invention* (Princeton: Princeton University Press, 1985), 3.

3. Hirotsu Kazuo, *Toshitsuki no ashioto* (Footsteps from times long past, 2 vols. [Kōdansha, 1963–67]); Uno Chiyo, *Watashi no bungakuteki kaisōki* (My literary reminiscences [Chūō kōronsha, 1972]); Nakamura Shin'ichirō, *Ai to bi to bungaku: waga kaisō* (Love, beauty, and literature: my reminiscences [Iwanami shoten, 1989]). Most effectively, Nakamura evokes the French say-ing, "You may be right, but I am not wrong" (232).

4. The best known autobiographical sketches by Uchimura Kanzō are *How I Became a Christian: Out of My Diary* (1895, trans. into Japanese [1935] as *Yo wa ikani shite Kirisuto shinto to narishi ka*) and *Kirisuto shinto no nagusame* (So-lace for a Christian convert, 1893). Kinoshita Naoe wrote *Zange* (Confessions, 1906), a masterpiece of late Meiji autobiographical literature, after his surprising public withdrawal from the Meiji socialist movement. Those by Kamei Katsuichirō and Fukunaga Misao are *Waga seishin no henreki* (My spiritual wanderings [Sō-gensha, 1951]) and *Aru onna kyōsanshugisha no kaisō* (Reminiscences of a woman Communist [Renga shobō shinsha, 1982]). My thinking about the auto-biographer's art is indebted to Eakin, *Fictions*, and James Olney, *Metaphors of Self: The Meaning of Autobiography* (Princeton: Princeton University Press, 1972).

5. Ōoka Shōhei, *Kantsū no kigōgaku* (Bungei shunjūsha, 1984), 41.

song: my reminiscences, 1968)—this awareness of the plurality of the self at any one time deepens our appreciation of Katō's attempts at self-revelation and demonstrates how imagination and memory collude in autobiographical self-reconstruction.[6] The final product takes its current form, a contemporary narrative with the rare combination of imaginative authority to dramatize private vicissitudes and the cultural breadth to encompass the experiences of a generation of early and mid-Shōwa Japanese intellectuals. Invigorating in its self-awareness and cultural metaphors, spiced with ironies and witticisms, Katō's work epitomizes the literary autobiography as both an imaginative art and a private dialogue.

Cultural critic, intellectual historian, social and political commentator, essayist, playwright, novelist, poet, and medical doctor, Katō Shūichi (1919–) is widely recognized as one of postwar Japan's eminent men of letters. He has been called Japan's "moral conscience" and "the quintessential postwar Japanese intellectual" or—by detractors at various stages of his career—a "Karuizawa Communist" and an eccentric literary historian.[7] Most commentators, admirers and critics alike, have been

6. "Hitsuji no uta" was serialized from October 1966 to December 1967 in *Asahi Jānaru*, published the next year in 2 vols. (Iwanami shoten, 1968), and included in Katō's 24-vol. selected works *Katō Shūichi chosakushū* (Heibonsha, 1978–) as vol. 14; its postscript, *Hitsuji no uta sono go*, is in vol. 23. On Katō's rhetoric of self-invention, see my "Jiga no saiteigi: Katō Shūichi no jiden *Hitsuji no uta*," in the collection's *Geppō* (1997), 20:2–8.

7. On Katō's place among the postwar Japanese intelligentsia, see Christine Chapman, "Shūichi Katō: Japan's Wandering Professor and Conscience," *International Herald Tribune*, June 9, 1986; Senuma Shigeki, "Shisō shōsetsu no tanjō," *Sengo bundan seikatsu nōto jō* (Kawade shobō shinsha, 1975), 159; and the Heibonsha pamphlet in fall 1978 announcing the publication of his selected works and describing the author as "*sengo Nihon o daihyō suru chisei to mo iubeki sonzai.*" • Among Katō's critics, Ara Masahito ("Tateito no nintai," *Kindai bungaku*, November 1947) and Honda Shūgo (*Monogatari sengo bungakushi* [Shinchōsha, 1960]) pointed out the wartime Europeanist intellectual elitism of the Matinée Poétique group, and Ara referred to Katō and the coauthors of *1946: Bungakuteki kōsatsu* (Nakamura Shin'ichirō and Fukunaga Takehiko) as "Karuizawa Communists." The poet Miyoshi Tatsuji gave a negative review of the group's innovative attempts at rhymed verse in Japanese ("Machine Poetiku no shisaku ni tsuite," *Sekai bungaku*, April 1948). See Kokubo Minoru, "Katō Shūichi, Nakamura Shin'ichirō, Fukunaga Takehiko kenkyū an'nai," in *Gendai Nihon bungaku taikei* (Chikuma shobō, 1971), 82:6; and Satō Shizuo, *Sengo bungaku ronsō shiron* (Shin Nihon shuppansha, 1985), 67–93. On Katō's works, see the survey of studies by Noguchi Takehiko, Ienaga Saburō, Maruyama Masao, and Kondō Jun'ichi in Yano Masakuni, "Kenkyū dōkō: Katō Shūichi," *Shōwa bungaku kenkyū* 24 (February 1992): 133–34.

impressed with his wide knowledge in both the natural sciences and the humanities as well as his broad erudition in the Japanese and Western European intellectual and literary traditions. Along with Nakamura Shin'ichirō and Fukunaga Takehiko and the critics associated with the literary coterie Kindai bungaku (modern literature), Katō has had an important role in remapping the postwar Japanese intellectual landscape decades after 1945.[8] His works in Japanese as well as in French and German range from theories of art in Japan and Europe to discussions of both intellectual traditions, from his thesis on the "hybrid" nature of Japanese culture to commentaries on contemporary Japanese politics and society. The last thirty years of his career have been marked by a tenacious commitment to revisit and reinterpret Japanese literature, art, and cultural and intellectual history.

His major publications during the last decade, for example, include reflections on contemporary Japanese history and politics, an interpretation of the images of women in Japanese and Western art, and a collection of essays ranging from discussions on Chen Kaige and Jean Marboeuf's films to contemplations on the *kyōgen* performances of the Nomura brothers at the National Nō Theater. Still active today, he most recently debuted as an innovative playwright and continues to write on a wide variety of subjects, as evidenced by his long-running essay serialization "Sekiyō mōgo" (Untempered utterances, *Asahi Shimbun*). In the words of the British sociologist Ronald P. Dore, Katō is "above all a citizen of the world with an insatiable curiosity about all things human."[9]

8. See Chia-ning Chang, "Katō Shūichi: hito to bungaku," *Karaki Junzō, Yasuda Yojūrō, Kamei Katsuichirō, Takeyama Michio, Katō Shūichi, Saeki Shōichi, Shinoda Hajime, Ōoka Makoto, and Yamazaki Masakazu, Shōwa bungaku zenshū* (Shōgakukan, 1989), 28:1072–75.

9. Essays collected into *Gendai Nihon shichū* (Personal interpretations of contemporary Japan [Heibonsha, 1987]) include his analysis of the Japanese government's textbook censorship system and postwar Japanese politics, with studies on writers and critics (Futabatei Shimei, Ishikawa Jun, Ōoka Shōhei, Hayashi Tatsuo, and others). • In *E no naka no onna tachi* (Images of women in painting [Heibonsha, 1993]), Katō discusses picture scrolls based on the eleventh-century *Tale of Genji* and on the works of Utamaro, Fra Angelico, Amedeo Modigliani, Käthe Kollwitz, Picasso, and others. • His essays on film artists and nō performers are collected in *Sekiyō mōgo* (Untempered utterances, 4 [Asahi shimbunsha, 1994]). • Katō's play *Kieta hangi Tominaga Nakamoto ibun* (The missing printing block: the strange tale of Tominaga Nakamoto) was staged in Tokyo in March 1998. • In his foreword to Katō's *History of Japanese Literature: The First Thousand Years* (trans. David Chibbett [Kodansha

Among the major works of Katō's voluminous oeuvre, only his autobiography addresses his private life and evolving sense of self against
the diverse cultural landscapes of Japan and Europe over the last seven
and a half decades. It begins with his grandparents' generation, his sheltered upper-middle-class childhood in the 1920s as the only son of a
Tokyo physician, and his burgeoning sense of self-identity as a young
child. Katō reminisces about his early attraction to the printed word—
in the natural sciences and then in Japanese and Western literature, from
the *Man'yōshū* to the works of Akutagawa Ryūnosuke, Pascal, Baudelaire, Valéry, and Proust. He recalls his formative years at the First Higher
School, his medical and literary training at Tokyo Imperial University,
and the dynamics among the elitist students and their many charismatic
teachers, offering vivid portraits of leading contemporary intellectuals
and literary figures such as Watanabe Kazuo, Nakajima Kenzō, Tachihara Michizō, Kobayashi Hideo, Yokomitsu Riichi, Nakano Yoshio, and
Yanaihara Tadao. He registers his reactions to the rise of fascism in Japan,
the February 26 Incident, and the surprise attack on Pearl Harbor against
the background of declining family fortunes in the depression that followed World War I. He recalls his rebelliousness against the jingoistic
political fanaticism during the late 1930s and early 1940s as he sought
refuge in the world of the *nō* and *bunraku* theaters, and new intellectual stimulation in modern French novels and symbolic poetry. He re-
captures his experiences as a founding member of a poetry recital gathering, Matinée Poétique, and its bold but ill-fated experiments to create
rhymed verse in Japanese. The first part of his work ends with a reflective chapter on the significance of Japan's defeat in August 1945 as the
author stands amidst the rubble of a devastated Tokyo and all its "lies
and duplicities, anachronisms and megalomaniac delusions." And yet
there is hope for the modernist in Katō amidst the spiritual wasteland
of postwar Japan: "I had never felt more optimistic about Japan's future
or more encouraged to rise to the occasion."

Continuing his narrative into the postwar period, he describes the
chaos as well as the exuberant energy he saw among the Japanese people

---

International, 1979], xi–xii), Ronald P. Dore writes, "Japan's post-war intellectual ferment has sometimes been dubbed a cultural renaissance, but . . . [few
other participants have] quite the renaissance-man breadth of interests and ac-
complishments of Shuichi Kato."

and their tragicomic encounters with the American Occupation forces. One chapter describes his experiences as a member of a joint U.S.-Japan medical team to investigate the effects of the atomic explosion in Hiroshima. And, as novelist and critic, he effectively conveys the sense of intellectual excitement shared by many Japanese literary figures after the oppressive years of thought control and spiritual deprivation. In 1951 he left for France on a French government scholarship and stayed in Europe until early 1955, a sojourn that would change not only his intellectual directions but indeed his entire life. Working as a medical researcher at the University of Paris, he was at the same time a fervent observer of European culture—its human dynamics, architectural forms, literature, music, opera, politics, and aesthetics. The balance of the autobiography offers cultural comparisons between Japan and Western Europe and observations from the author's travels in France, England, Italy, and Russia; some of its most engaging chapters consist of reflections on the ways his European experiences influenced his reinterpretations of Japanese art and the relations between imagination, art, and politics. Shortly after returning to Japan, Katō continued his literary career while working as a physician and a university lecturer on French literature. In 1958, on the occasion of his participation in the second Asian-African Writers' Conference in Tashkent, he made a firm resolution to leave the medical profession, not to transform himself this time into a literary specialist but "to obliterate the very idea of specialization." The original 1968 autobiography ends with a memorable chapter on the tumultuous student riots over the renewal of the Japan-U.S. Security Treaty in 1960 and an introspective assessment of his position vis-à-vis the power structure of the Japanese state.

The postscript to his work extends the autobiographical narrative from the original cut-off date of 1960 to the present decade. Beyond giving us an account of Katō's private life and his reflections for nearly four decades, it looks back at his experiences as a visiting professor at various foreign universities and registers his observations on the cultural and political landscapes in the many countries he visited. In particular, it goes into some detail about his life in Vancouver, in Berlin before the German reunification, as well as in New Haven, Mexico, China, and Eastern Europe, juxtaposing private memories with Katō's thoughts on the Vietnam War, the assassination of President Kennedy, the events of the Prague Spring, and the collapse of the Soviet Union.

Japanese critics have generally greeted Katō's work with enthusiasm.

Yamazumi Masami's view that he was "overwhelmed" by Katō's "personality" (*kosei*) probably reflects the reactions of *A Sheep's Song*'s many other readers, who helped make it a best-seller for many years after its first publication in 1968. Kataoka Yutaka characterizes Katō's endeavor as "the spiritual dissection of an intellectual living in a tumultuous time. . . . This book is not merely an autobiography. Not only does it provide a key to the understanding of the author's far-ranging endeavors, it must be remembered as one of the most celebrated achievements of autobiographical literature."[10]

I supplement the translation with annotations that may be of help to general readers and, in a few instances, to Japan specialists as well. I balance the risk of cluttering the text with copious notes against my hope of giving readers contextual and biographical information and perhaps even a small degree of intellectual stimulus as well. To preserve the narrative movement and structural integrity of the original, I translate its entire text and limit any intrusive editing to the bare minimum. Because the author's postscript was finished in the spring of 1997, his autobiography appears here in its complete form.

A number of colleagues and friends have read earlier drafts of my translation and offered useful suggestions. I particularly wish to thank Donald Gibbs and Carole Hinckle for their care and encouragement when my project was underway, and Edith Gladstone at the University of California Press for her conscientious editing. I fondly remember recent conversations about my work in Japan, particularly with Kano Masanao, Takemori Tenyū, and Tan'o Yasunori at Waseda University, as well as with the enthusiastic members of Meiji University's Bungei riron kenkyūkai. My wife, Tsui, has been my supportive friend and relentless critic, taking on her dual roles with sensitivity, patience, and insight. Editors at Heibonsha and the owner of Tsuchiya Photography Shop in Karuizawa have all kindly agreed to grant permission rights on the photographs reprinted here. I also wish to thank the Fulbright Program for

10. Yamazumi Masami, "Attōteki na kosei no miryoku," *Asahi Jānaru* (November 17, 1968): 83. Iwanami shoten's December 1997 edition shows that *Hitsuji no uta* is at its 41th printing. • Kataoka Yutaka's assessment is in *Nihonjin no jiden* (comp. Saeki Shōichi and Kano Masanao [Heibonsha, 1980–82]), *Bekkan 2,* 45. Kataoka appears most impressed with Katō's description of his childhood years in the Tokyo neighborhood of Shibuya, comparing his account of the city's *yamanote* life to Ōoka Shōhei's autobiographical renderings in *Yōnen* (Childhood) and *Shōnen* (Adolescence).

a research grant during my sabbatical year in Japan (1997–98) and the Office of the Dean, College of Letters and Science, University of California at Davis, for a subvention to help defray the publication costs.

Mr. Katō himself deserves a very special word of gratitude for providing rare family and private photographs and for graciously agreeing to the request for a new postscript. I appreciate his always prompt replies to my queries despite his usually pressing schedule, the ever pleasant and inspiring discussions we have had over many years in Tokyo, Shinano Oiwake, Honolulu, and Davis, and most of all, his personal warmth and uncompromising humanity.

This translation is dedicated to my father, who was born in the same year of the sheep and would have enjoyed meeting Mr. Katō in print if only fate had been a little kinder to him.

Chia-ning Chang
Summer 1998, Tokyo

Chronology
Major Events and Publications, 1919–1997

1919
Born in Tokyo on September 19 as the only son of Katō Shin'ichi (1885–1974) and [Masuda] Oriko (1897–1949). Shin'ichi, then thirty-four and a medical doctor, was a graduate of the First Higher School and the Medical Faculty of Tokyo Imperial University. Oriko, twenty-two, was a graduate of Saint Maur Girl's School.

1920   AGE 1
His sister, Hisako, was born.

1923–25 AGE 4–6
Briefly attended Saint Maur Kindergarten.

1926–30 AGE 7–11
Attended Tokiwamatsu Primary School in Shibuya Ward (Matsumoto Kenji was his fourth-grade science teacher).

1931   AGE 12
Attended First Tokyo Metropolitan Middle School; soon afterwards, spent an entire year's allowance on the collected works of Akutagawa Ryūno-suke, which—along with the *Man'yōshū* in his father's collection—engrossed him.

1935   AGE 16
Failed an entrance examination to the First Higher School during his

fourth year at middle school; summer: went to Shinano Oiwake, where he met the poet Tachihara Michizō.

1936   AGE 17
March: graduated from middle school; April: entered First Higher School's Science Division in Komaba and began residence in its dormitory (among his teachers were Yanaihara Tadao, Katayama Toshihiko, and Gomi Tomohide; among his schoolmates, Nakamura Shin'ichirō, Fukunaga Takehiko, Kojima Nobuo, Kubota Keisaku, and Hasegawa Izumi). Joined the *Man'yōshū* reading circle formed by fellow students, including Ōno Susumu and Koyama Hiroshi, developed an interest in *nō*, kabuki, and *kyōgen*, and frequented the Kabukiza and the Tsukiji Little Theater; played on the school's tennis team from 1936–37.

1937–38 AGE 18–19
Began to publish under the pseudonym Fujisawa Tadashi; became an editor of a school journal and a member of its literary committee.

1939   AGE 20
February: began to publish works in prose and verse such as "Sensō to bungaku to ni kansuru dansō" (Fragmentary thoughts on war and literature); March: graduated from First Higher School; June: published a coterie journal, *Gake* (Cliff), with Kojima Nobuo and Yanaihara Isaku.

1940   AGE 21
Translated works by Hans Carossa and Rilke and published essays in *Gake*; enrolled in the Medical Faculty at Tokyo Imperial University while attending classes in the Department of French Literature (among his teachers of French literature were Watanabe Kazuo, Suzuki Shintarō, and Nakajima Kenzō); critically ill for a time with moist pleurisy.

1941   AGE 22
Family moved to Akatsutsumi in Setagaya Ward; frequented the Nō Theater at Suidōbashi and on December 8, 1941, watched a *bunraku* play at the Shimbashi Theater.

1942   AGE 23
Formed the literary group Matinée Poétique with Nakamura Shin'ichirō, Fukunaga Takehiko, Kubota Keisaku, Harada Yoshito, and others.

1943   AGE 24
Graduated from the Medical Faculty at Tokyo Imperial University and
started working at Tokyo University Hospital as an unsalaried assistant
specializing in hematology. November: published poem "Imōto ni" (To
my little sister) and learned Latin during his daily three-hour commute
on the train.

1945   AGE 26
Spring: evacuated along with the Department of Internal Medicine
to Ueda, Nagano Prefecture; September: returned to Tokyo and witnessed its devastation; spent several months in Hiroshima as a member of the joint U.S.-Japan medical team to investigate the effects of
atomic explosion.

1946   AGE 27
July 1946–January 1947: serialized critical essays in the journal *Sedai*
(Generation) with Nakamura and Fukunaga in the column "Camera Eyes."
WORKS ~ March: "Tennōsei o ronzu—Fugōrishugi no gensen" (On
the emperor system: the origin of irrationalism) under the pseudonym
Arai Sakunosuke; April: "Yokomitsu Riichi" and "Furansu no sayoku
sakka" (Left-wing French writers); June: "Tōhiteki bungaku o sare!" (Escapist literature, out you go!); September: "Ankoku o hirake!" (Lift the
curtain of darkness!) and "Jan Geno ni tsuite" (On Jean Guéhenno); October: "Hyūmanizumu to shakaishugi" (Humanism and socialism);
November: "Yakeato no bigaku" (The aesthetics of burned-down ruins).

1947   AGE 28
July: joined the Kindai Bungaku (modern literature) coterie and began
a literary debate with its principal member, Ara Masahito (who was then
involved in the "politics vis-à-vis literature" debate with Nakano Shigeharu). Received his first manuscript fees from his contribution to the
journal *Ningen* (Humanity).
WORKS ~ January: "Sarutoru no gokai" (Misunderstandings of
Sartre); April: "Machine Poetiku to sono sakuhin ni tsuite" (On the Matinée Poétique group and its works) and "Riarizumu to shōsetsu" (Realism and the novel); May: with Nakamura Shin'ichirō and Fukunaga
Takehiko, coauthored *1946: Bungakuteki kōsatsu* (1946: a literary en-
quiry); May–June: "Valerī shō" (In praise of Valéry); June: "Iwayuru
dekadansu ni tsuite" (On "decadence"); July: "Amerika ni manabi risei

o motomeru tame no hōhō josetsu" (Methodology for acquiring the American sense of reason) and "Shinkō no seiki to shichinin no senkusha" (Century of faith and seven precursors); August: "*Nō* to kindaigeki no kanōsei" (Possibilities of *nō* and modern drama) and "Sarutoru to kakumei no tetsugaku" (Sartre and the philosophy of revolution); September: "Kakumei no bungaku to bungaku no kakumei" (Revolutionary literature and literary revolution); November: "Shōchōshugiteki fūdo" (Landscape of symbolism); December: "Nihon bungaku no dentō" (Traditions in Japanese literature).

1948   AGE 29
July: founded the coterie journal *Hakobune* (The Ark) with Mori Arimasa and Harada Yoshito et al.
WORKS ~ January: "Fujiwara Teika *Shūi gusō* no shōchōshugi" (Symbolism of Fujiwara Teika's *Meager Gleanings*) and "Shinpishugi kaigi" (Interpretation of mysticism); February: "Andore Jīdo to bungei hihyō no mondai" (André Gide and the question of literary criticism) and "Kondiyakku no *Kankakuron* ni tsuite" (On Condillac's *Traité des sensations*); March: "Bōdoreeru ni kansuru kōgi sōan" (Lecture draft on Baudelaire); March–April: "Sōseki ni okeru genjitsu" (Sōseki's idea of reality); April: "Bungei hihyō to shūjigaku" (Literary criticism and rhetoric); June: "Kāru Yasupāsu no seishin byōrigaku" (Karl Jaspers's psychopathology) and "Gendai Furansu bungaku no mondai" (Issues in contemporary French literature); June–August: cotranslated Condillac's *Traité des sensations* (Kankakuron [2 vols.]); July: coauthored *Machine Poetiku shishū* (Poetry collection of Matinée Poétique); September: *Dōkeshi no asa no uta* (Morning song of a clown[short stories]), *Bungaku to genjitsu* (Literature and reality), "Buntai ni tsuite" (On literary style), and coauthored "Re-sen tairyō ichiji shōsha no ketsueki narabi ni zōketsuki ni oyobosu eikyō" (Impact of one-time massive x-ray irradiation on blood and hematogenous tissues); October: *Gendai Furansu bungaku ron I* (On contemporary French literature [vol. 1]); December: "Kodoku no ishiki to hiroba no ishiki" (Idea of solitude and the idea of the plaza).

1949   AGE 30
His mother, Oriko, died in May.
WORKS ~ January–August: serialized his novel *Aru hareta hi ni* (One fine day [published in a single volume in 1950]). Coauthored "Ke-

tsuekigaku no shimpo 1941–48" (Advancements in hematology 1941–48). February: "Iwayuru Apure-gēruha to wa nani ka" (What is the so-called *après-guerre* school?) and "Orudasu Hakkusuri no saishinsaku *Jikan wa tomaranakereba naranai* ni tsuite" (On Aldous Huxley's most recent work *Time Must Have a Stop*); March: "Kinoshita Mokutarō no hōhō ni tsuite" (On the Methodology of Kinoshita Mokutarō) and "Sengo no Furansu eiga" (Postwar French films); July: "Sarutoru no ichizuke" (Positioning Sartre); August: "Watakushi-shōsetsu no eiko-seisui" (Rise and decline of the I-novel); September: "Gendaishi daini geijutsu ron" (Contemporary poetry as second-class art); October: "Shokuminchi bunka ni tsuite" (On colonial culture); November: "Kyōsanshugi to shimpoteki Kirisutosha" (Communism and progressive Christians); December: "Nihongo no unmei" (Destiny of the Japanese language) and "Bungei zasshi no urenai wake" (Why literary magazines don't sell).

1950   AGE 31

February: received his Doctorate in Medicine from Tokyo University. WORKS ~ January: "Sengo no Katorishizumu" (Postwar Catholicism); February: "Nihon no niwa" (Japanese gardens); March: "Ōgai to yōgaku" (Ōgai and Western learning) and "Minshushugi bungaku ron" (On democratic literature); April: "Miyagi Otoya cho *Kindaiteki ningen*" (On Miyagi Otoya's *Modern Man*); May: "Engeki no runessansu" (The renaissance of drama); August: *Bungaku to wa nani ka* (What is literature?), "Genjitsushugi to iu koto no imi" (Meaning of realism), and "Jitsuzonshugi no dentō ni tsuite" (On the traditions of existentialism); September: "Mittsu no shōsetsu ron" (Three views on the novel) and "Jean Guéhenno"; November: coauthored *Gendai Furansu bungaku* (Contemporary French literature); December: "Nagai Kafū" and entries on André Malraux, Jean Guéhenno, Jean Cocteau, Jean-Richard Bloch, Ramon Fernandez, Romain Rolland for *Furansu bungaku jiten* (Dictionary of French literature).

1951   AGE 32

Departed for France as a recipient of a French government scholarship to do medical research at the Institut Pasteur and at the Université de Paris. WORKS ~ January: "Rosserīni no Itaria" (Rossellini's Italy); February: *Utsukushii Nihon* (Beautiful Japan), "Burūno Tauto to Nihon" (Bruno Taut and Japan), "Ryūnosuke to hanzokuteki seishin" (Ryūnosuke's anticonventional spirit), "Furansu kokumin no teikō no rekishi" (History of the French people's resistance), and "Rōmanshugi no bungaku undō" (The romantic movement in literature); March: *Teikō no bungaku* (Literature of resistance); April: "Gendai Furansu shijin gaisetsu" (Brief discussions on contemporary French poets) and cotranslated (with Kōno Yoichi) Vercors's *Le Silence de la mer* and *La Marche à l'étoile* as *Umi no chinmoku* (Kōno) and *Hoshi e no ayumi* (Katō); May: "Bungaku to hihyō" (Literature and criticism) and "Shijin no taido—Rainā Maria Riruke no baai" (The poet's attitude: the case of Rainer Maria Rilke); June: "Sensō bungaku ni tsuite" (On war literature), "Engeki no tanjō" (The birth of plays), and "Bungakusha no seijiteki hatsugen" (Political statements by literary intellectuals); July: "Reisen no unda higeki" (Tragedy created by the Cold War); August: "Katei shōsetsu no mondai" (The question of domestic novels); September: essays on Rabelais, Rousseau, Flaubert, Anatole France, André Malraux, Jean-Paul Sartre, Jean de La Fontaine and others in *Furansu bungaku tokuhon* (French literature reader) and *Gendai shijin ron* (On contemporary poets); October: *Gendai Furansu bungaku ron* (On contemporary French literature).

1952   AGE 33
WORKS ~ January: cotranslated Jean-Paul Sartre's "Qu'est-ce que la littérature?" (Bungaku to wa nani ka) and "Jitsuzonshugisha no kafē" (The existentialists' café); March: "Pari no ongakukai" (Concerts in Paris); May: coauthored and cotranslated *Eryuāru shishū* (The poetry of [Paul] Eluard); June: "Kakeidaijō no Jannu Daruku" ([Paul Claudel's] *Jeanne d'Arc au bûcher*); July: *Teikō no bunka* (Culture of resistance); August: "Furansujin no shinsetsu ni tsuite" (On the kindness of the French people); September: "Nihon kara mita Furansu to Furansu kara mita Nihon" (France as seen from Japan and Japan as seen from France); October: *Sengo no Furansu: Watashi no mita Furansu* (Postwar France: the France I saw), "Mirano no annaisha" (A guide in Milan), and "Ruō no geijutsu" (The art of Rouault); November: "Furansu no jūtaku mondai" (Housing problems in France).

1953   AGE 34
WORKS ~ "Zur Situation der modernen japanischen Literatur" and "Etude morphologique des leucocytes dans l'anti-sérum contre la rate myéloide." January: "Yoshida Hidekazu cho *Ongakuka no sekai* kaisetsu" (Commentary on Yoshida Hidekazu's *The Musician's World*);

March: "Shopan no tegami" (Letters of Chopin) and "Gaikokugo kyō-iku no mondai ni tsuite" (On foreign-language education); July: "Gosho Heinosuke shi no iken" (Views of Mr. Gosho Heinosuke); August: "Pari no shibai" (The Parisian theater); December: "Pari no Nihonjin" (The Japanese in Paris).

1954   AGE 35

WORKS ~ January: "Aru kansō: Seiyō kenbutsu tochū de kangaeta Nihon bungaku no koto" (Some reflections on Japanese literature during my journey in the West); March: "Furansu no Katorishizumu" (French Catholicism); May: "Suisu no ukiyo-e ten" (*Ukiyo-e* exhibition in Switzerland); June: "Aruban Beruku *Votsekku*" (Alban Berg's *Wozzeck* [by Georg Büchner]); July: "Goya no sobyō to hanga" (Goya's sketches and prints); October: "Igirisujin no taido" (The attitude of the British) and "Pikaso no saikin no saku" (Recent works by Picasso); December: "Kurōderu ni tsuite" (On Claudel) and "Pari kara" (From Paris [a letter to Nakano Shigeharu]).

1955   AGE 36

February: returned to Japan and resumed work at Tokyo University Hospital; also worked as a physician at Mitsui Mining Company and as a lecturer of French literature at Meiji University; July–September: served as literary critic for the literary journal *Gunzō*.

WORKS ~ January: "Kamyu hōmon" (Interviewing Camus); March: "Chēhofu *Sakura no sono* sono ta" (Chekhov's *The Cherry Orchard* and others); May: "Igirisu to kyōsanshugi" (England and communism); June: "Nihon bunka no zasshusei" (Hybrid nature of Japanese culture); July: "Zasshuteki Nihon bunka no kadai" (Question about the hybrid nature of Japanese culture); September: "Tānā: Bijutsushi no shukuzu" (Turner: art history in epitome) and "Jindō no eiyū" (Hero of humanity); October: "Shibungaku no fukkō" (Revival of privatized literature), "Nakamura Minoru cho *Miyazawa Kenji*" (Nakamura Minoru's *Miyazawa Kenji*), "Kaisetsu Ishikawa Jun shōron" (Commentary: a short discussion of Ishikawa Jun), and "Jan Jirodō shōron" (Short discussion of Jean Giraudoux); November: "Shōzōga ni tsuite: Fan Aiku o megutte" (On portraits: focusing on Van Eyck); December: *Aru ryokōsha no shisō: Seiyō kenbutsu shimatsuki* (A traveler's thoughts: an account of my journey to the West), "Fukunaga Takehiko," "Shinshū no tabi kara" (From my trip to Shinshū), and "Vīn no omoide" (Memories of Vienna).

1956 AGE 37

WORKS ~ January–April: serialized the novel *Unmei* (Destiny); May: "Futsuin sensō to Gurahamu Gurīn" (The French-Indochina war and Graham Greene); June: "Hon'yaku no idai to hisan" (Greatness and pathos of translation); July: "Sakoku no shinri" (Psychology of national seclusion); August: "Shakaishugisha to kyōsanshugi" (Socialists and communism); September: *Zasshu bunka: Nihon no chiisana kibō* (Hybrid culture: a small hope for Japan), "Sekai bungaku kara mita Nihon bungaku" (Japanese literature as seen from world literature), and "Kinoshita Junji shōron" (Short discussion on Kinoshita Junji); October: "*Machine Poetikku* no kōzai" (Merits and shortcomings of the Matinée Poétique group); November: "Yōroppa shisō: Atarashii genjitsu to no taiketsu" (European thought: confronting a new reality); December: "Burehito no shi ni tsuite" (On Brecht's poetry).

1957 AGE 38

WORKS ~ January: "Kenryoku seiji to shakai seigi" (Power politics and social justice); March: "Kindai Nihon no bunmeishiteki ichi" (Modern Japan's position in cultural history); May: *Shirarezaru Nihon* (The unknown Japan), "Sarutoru to kyōsanshugi" (Sartre and communism), and "Seiō no chishikijin to Nihon no chishikijin" (Intellectuals in Western Europe and intellectuals in Japan); June: translated Bosch's *Enfants de l'absurde* (Warera fujōri no ko); July: "Eiga ni okeru kotenshugi no tanjō" (The birth of classicism in film), "Gottofurīto Ben to gendai Doitsu no seishin" (Gottfried Benn and the spirit of contemporary Germany), and "Gendai Yōroppa ni okeru handō no ronri" (The reactionary logic in contemporary Europe); September: "Isha no shigoto to bunshi no shigoto" (The work of a physician and the work of a writer) and "Gureamu Gurīn to Katorishizumu no ichimen" (Graham Greene and an aspect of Catholicism); November: "*Shukumei* to yobareta eiga" (A film called Destiny [*Celui qui doit mourir*]) and "Fukō hodo shiru koto no konnanna mono wa nai" (Nothing is more difficult than realizing one's misfortune); December: translated *Pītā Buryūgeru* (Pieter Brueghel).

1958 AGE 39

January–March: served as literary critic for *Gunzō*; September: took part in planning the second Asian-African Writers' Conference held in Tashkent, U.S.S.R., and decided on this occasion to leave the medical profession and devote himself to writing.

WORKS ~ February: "Kāru Baruto to Purotesutantizumu no ronri" (Karl Barth and the logic of Protestantism) and "Gendaishi ni nozomu" (My hopes in contemporary poetry); March: *Seiji to bungaku* (Politics and literature) and "Bungaku no gainen to chūseiteki ningen" (Idea of literature and the medieval man); August: *Seiyō sanbi* (In praise of the West) and "Gendai no shakai to ningen no mondai" (The question of contemporary society and humankind); November: "Chūgoku shōnin mondai" (On the recognition of China) and "Sorenpō nikagetsu no tabi" (Two-month trip in the Soviet Union); December: "Sorenpō no inshō" (Impressions of the Soviet Union).

1959   AGE 40
January: returned to Japan via Europe and India; October: participated in the symposium "Seifu no Anpo kaitei kōsō o hihan suru" (Criticizing the government's design to revise the U.S.-Japan Security Treaty). WORKS ~ February: *Gendai Yōroppa no seishin* (The spirit of contemporary Europe) and "E. M. Fōsutā to hyūmanizumu" (E. M. Forster and humanism) and "Shakaishugi no mittsu no kao" (Three faces of socialism); March: *Jinkōsai* (Festival of the gods) and "Vīn konjaku" (Vienna past and present); April: "Chūritsu to Anpo jōyaku to Chūgoku shōnin" (Neutrality, U.S.-Japan Security Treaty, and the recognition of China), "Seiō to wa nani ka" (What does Western Europe mean?), and "Minzokushugi to kokkashugi" (Nationalism and statism); May: "Masu komi wa yoron o tsukuru ka" (Does the mass media create public opinion?), "Nihon no geijutsuteki fūdo" (Japan's artistic landscape), and "Ishikawa Jun oboegaki" (Note on Ishikawa Jun); June: "Kafū et la littérature française"; August: *Ōgai: Iwanami kōza Nihon bungakushi* (vol. 15) and a travelogue, *Uzubekku Kuroachia Kerara kikō* (Travels in Uzbekistan, Croatia, and Kerala); September: coedited *Chishikijin no seisei to yakuwari, Kindai Nihon shisōshi kōza 4* (The formation and role of the intelligentsia, Lectures on modern Japanese thought [vol. 4]) in which he published "Sensō to chishikijin" (War and intellectuals); October: coauthored *Yakushiji: Nihon no tera 8* (Yakushiji temple [vol. 8]) and "Bungakuteki jiden no tame no danpen" (Fragmentary piece on literary autobiographies).

1960   AGE 41
February: participated in the symposium "Futatabi Anpo kaitei ni tsuite" (Once again on the revision of the U.S.-Japan Security Treaty);

April–July: became lecturer of modern European thought in the Department of French Literature, Tokyo University, and Assistant Professor of Japanese Literature at the University of British Columbia, Canada. WORKS ~ February: "Berunāru Byuffe to wareware no jidai" (Bernard Buffet and our time) and "Motoori Norinaga oboegaki" (Note on Motoori Norinaga); April: "Geijutsuka no kosei" (The artist's personality); May–July: "Gaikoku bungaku no uketorikata to sengo" (Reception of foreign literature and the postwar era); June: "Anpo jōyaku to chishikijin" (The U.S.-Japan Security Treaty and intellectuals); June–August: "Mono to ningen to shakai" (Things, people, and society), including the segment "Kafū to iu genshō" (The Kafū phenomenon); July: *Shinran: Jūsanseiki shisō no ichimen* (Shinran: one aspect of thirteenth-century thought); August: "Seijika no mono no kangaekata" (The politicians' way of thinking); September: *Futatsu no kyoku no aida de* (Between two extremes), *Tokyo nikki: Gaikoku no tomo e* (Tokyo diary: to my foreign friends), and "Bungakuteki Amerika ron" (Discussion of literary America); December: "Konnichi ni okeru geijutsu kyōiku no imi to mondai" (The significance of and issues in contemporary art education).

1961   AGE 42
WORKS ~ January: "Soto kara mita Nihon" (Japan as seen from the outside); February: edited *Sengo: Gaikokujin no mita Nihon 5* (Postwar era: Japan as seen by foreigners [vol. 5]); May: "Nihon no eigo kyōiku" (English education in Japan); June "Nihonjin no sekaizō" (The Japanese world view).

1962   AGE 43
WORKS ~ January–February: "Amerika inshōki" (Impressions of America); May: "Ninen buri no Nihon" (Japan I haven't seen for two years); August: "Nihonjin no gaikokukan" (The Japanese view of the outside world); September: "Gendai Nihon bungaku no jōkyō—Seikatsu no geijutsuka to geijutsu no seikatsuka" (The state of contemporary Japanese literature: the artification of life and the domestication of art) and "Subarashii kuni" (Wonderful country); October: *Atama no kaiten o yoku suru dokusho-jutsu* (Reading strategies for quick thinking), "Nihon bungaku no kakikae—Gaikoku bungaku no eikyō to kanren shite" (Rewriting Japanese literature: in connection with the impact of foreign literatures), and "Geijutsuron oboegaki" (Note on art).

1963   AGE 44

WORKS ~ January–December: "Katō Shūichi no sekai shūyūki" (Katō Shūichi's world travels) serialized weekly in the *Mainichi gurafu;* May: "Mori Ōgai"; June: "Aspects de la littérature japonaise contemporaine"; October: "Cha no bigaku—Futatsu no kasetsu" (The aesthetics of tea: two assumptions); December: "Kenedi shigo no sekai" (The world after Kennedy's death).

1964   AGE 45

May–July: served as visiting professor at the University of Munich.

WORKS ~ "Political Modernization and Mass Media." February: "Gendai no geijutsuteki sōzō" (The creation of contemporary art); May: *Katō Shūichi sekai manyūki* (Katō Shūichi's world wanderings) and *"Gengo to bungaku* ni tsuite no ron ni tsuite no ron" (About [Nishio Minoru's] "A Discussion of *Language and Literature*"); August: "Amerika 1964" and "Karuru Kurausu—*Jinrui saigo no hibi* ni tsuite" (Karl Kraus: On *Die letzten Tage der Menschheit*); October: "Zuisō dokusho" (Random thoughts on reading); November: "Shisendō shi" (Account of the hall of poetry immortals); December: *Umibe no machi nite: kasetsu to iken* (At a seaside town: hypotheses and opinions).

1965   AGE 46

WORKS ~ "Japanese Writers and Modernization." January: "Sōzōryoku no yukue—Nihon bunka no kanōsei" (Creativity's whereabouts: the possibility of Japanese culture) and "Nihon bunka no kihonteki kōzō— *Genji monogatari emaki* ni tsuite" (The fundamental structure of Japanese culture: on *The Genji Scrolls*); February: "Kurui gumo mori no harusame" (Wild clouds and spring rain in the woods), "Nomura Manzō no gei—bunka no fuhensei ni tsuite" (The art of Nomura Manzō: on the universality of culture), and "Betonamu sensō to Nihon" (The Vietnam War and Japan); April: "Nakamoto *Kōgo*" ([Tominaga] Nakamoto's [*Shutsujō*] *kōgo*), "Fukuzawa Yukichi *Bunmeiron no gairyaku*" (On Fukuzawa Yukichi's *A Brief Outline of Civilization*) and "Geijutsu to keishiki—Gendai Furansu no sōzōryoku" (Art and form: the creativity of contemporary France); June: "Gendai Nihongo to shakai" (Contemporary Japanese and society), "Nikkō Tōshōgū ron" (On Nikkō's Tōshōgū), "Yamatogokoro saisetsu" (More on the Japanese spirit), and "Kanada kara mita Betonamu sensō" (The Vietnam War as seen from

Canada); July: "Gendai ni okeru chishiki no keitai" (The configuration of contemporary knowledge); August: "Chūritsushugi no nijūnen" (Twenty years of neutrality), "Gendai shakai ni okeru geijutsuka no yakuwari" (The artist's role in contemporary society), and "Rekishi to bungaku to hihyō seishin" (History, literature, and the critical spirit).

1966   AGE 47
WORKS ~ February: "Gendai Chūgoku o meguru sobokuna gimon" (Some plain questions about contemporary China); September: "Nihon bungaku no dentō to 'warai' no yōso" (The Japanese literary tradition and the comic element) and "Chishikijin de aru jōken" (Qualifications of an intellectual); November: "Takeuchi Yoshimi no hihyō sōchi" (The critical apparatus of Takeuchi Yoshimi); November–April 1967: serialized "Hitsuji no uta" in the *Asahi Jānaru*.

1967   AGE 48
WORKS ~ January: "Tominaga Nakamoto: A Tokugawa Iconoclast"; May: "Betonamu to Zen to Anpo ni tsuite" (On Vietnam, Zen, and the Japan-U.S. Security Treaty); July–December: serialized "Hitsuji no uta" in the *Asahi Jānaru;* September: *Geijutsu ronshū* (Collected essays on art) and "Butsuzō no yōshiki" (Styles of Buddhist sculpture); November: "Takamaru Beichū sensō no ashioto" (War clouds gathering between the United States and China) and "Nihon no bigaku—Sono kōzō ni tsuite" (Design of Japanese aesthetics).

1968   AGE 49
WORKS ~ July: "Tawaraya Sōtatsu"; August: "Yonaoshi kotohajime" (The beginnings of social reform); August–September: *Hitsuji no uta: Waga kaisō* (A sheep's song: my reminiscences [2 vols.]); November: "Kotoba to sensha" (Words and tanks).

1969   AGE 50
September 1969–August 1973: served as professor at the Free University of Berlin and director of its East Asian Institute.
WORKS ~ February: "Problèmes des écrivains japonais d'aujourd'hui"; February–March: "Bunka Daikakumei kikigaki" (What I heard about the Cultural Revolution); March: "Beikoku saihō" (Revisiting the United States) and coedited *Geijutsu: Iwanami kōza tetsugaku 14* (Art: Iwanami lectures on philosophy [vol. 14]); July: "Bungaku no shakaiteki kōka"

(The social effects of literature); October: *Nihon no uchi to soto* (Perspectives on Japan).

1970   AGE 51

WORK ~ April: "Jakometti mata wa junsui geijutsuka" (Giacometti the pure artist).

1971   AGE 52

September: visited China for about three weeks as a member of the Association for Japan-China Cultural Exchange.

WORKS ~ *Form, Style, Tradition: Reflections on Japanese Art and Society* (University of California Press) and "Ein Beitrag zur Methodologie der japanischen Literaturgeschichte." January: "Ongaku no gendai" (The contemporary age of music); March: *Shi oyobi shijin* (Poetry and poets); May: "kaisetsu" (commentary) for *Hayashi Tatsuo chosakushū I* (Selected writings of Hayashi Tatsuo [vol. 1]); June: coedited *Gakumon no shisō: Sengo Nihon shisōshi taikei 10* (Ideas of learning: a comprehensive collection on postwar Japanese thought [vol. 10]); July: *Shimpan sekai man'yūki* (World travels: new edition); September: *Bungaku to wa nanika* (What is literature? [new ed.]), "Beichū sekkin—kansō mittsu" (The U.S.-China rapprochement: three thoughts), and "Oitsuki katei no kōzō ni tsuite—kotoni Nichi Doku kindaishi no baai" (Climbing on the bandwagon [of modernity]—with special reference to modern Japanese and German history); October: "Chūgoku mata wa hansekai" (China: against world trends); November: "Chūgoku—futatsu no kao" (Two faces of China).

1972   AGE 53

September 1972–August 1973: spent his sabbatical leave from the Free University of Berlin in Japan.

WORKS ~ January: "Uchikomi to sotokomi no mondai" (Intra-group and inter-group communication), "Ongaku no shisō" (Ideas in music), and "Waga shisaku waga fūdo" (My meditations, my landscapes); January–February: "Shōshiminteki hannō ni tsuite" (On the reactions of the petty bourgeoisie); March: "Shi no mikata—Edo jidai to kindai" (Views on death: the Tokugawa and the modern periods); May: "Edo shisō no kanōsei to jitsugen" (The possibilities of Edo thought and their realization); August: *Chūgoku ōkan* (A traveler in China); September: *Shōshin dokugo* (*Gratifying Monologues*) and "Saraba Kawabata Yasunari"

(Goodbye, Kawabata Yasunari); November: "Dōgijō no mondai futatsu" (Two moral questions), "Toshi no kosei" (The individuality of cities), and "Betonamu sensō to heiwa" (Vietnam: war and peace).

1973   AGE 54

January 1973–September 1979: served as a guest editorial writer for the *Asahi Shimbun.*

WORKS ~ January 1973–August 1974: serialized "Nihon bungakushi josetsu" (Introduction to a history of Japanese literature) in the *Asahi Jānaru;* March: *Rekishi, Kagaku, Gendai—Katō Shūichi taidanshū* (History, science, and modernity: conversations of Katō Shūichi) and "Kyoshō Tomioka Tessai" (The great master Tomioka Tessai); April: "Etsunan jiaibun" (Personal statement on the tragedy of Vietnam); May: a short-story collection, *Maboroshi no bara no machi nite* (The illusory city of roses); October: "Sōtatsu no sekai" (The world of [Tawaraya] Sōtatsu) and "Fukunaga Takehiko o ronzu" (On Fukunaga Takehiko).

1974   AGE 55

September 1974–August 1976: served as visiting lecturer at Yale University.

WORKS ~ *The Japan-China Phenomenon: Conflict or Compatibility?* (Paul Norbury Publications) and "Taishō Democracy as the Pre-Stage for Japanese Militarism." April: "Zeami no senjutsu mata wa nōgakuron" (Zeami's strategy: treatises on Nō) and "Sekaishi no tenkanten to shite no Vetonamu sensō" (The Vietnam War as a transitional point in world history); May: "Gakumon no hōkatsusei to ningen no shutaisei" (The comprehensiveness of knowledge and the subjectivity of man); June: "Hi-Rin Hi-Kō shichū" (Personal intrepretation of the anti-Lin [Biao] and anti-Confucius campaigns); July: coauthored *Nihon no koten* (Japanese classics); September: a new edition of *Zasshu bunka— Nihon no chiisana kibō* (Hybrid culture: a small hope for Japan).

1975   AGE 56

April 1975–March 1985: served as professor of Japanese literature and intellectual history at Tokyo's Sophia University.

WORKS ~ Coannotated *Arai Hakuseki.* February: *Nihon bungakushi josetsu jō* (Introduction to a history of Japanese literature [vol. 1]); March 1975–October 1976: wrote a series of seventy-seven essays under the collective title "Kotoba to ningen" (Words and human beings) in the evening edition of the *Asahi Shimbun;* July: "Arai Hakuseki no sekai" (The world of Arai Hakuseki); August: "Yokubō to iu na no densha to yokubō to iu na de nai densha" (*A Streetcar Named Desire* and a streetcar not named desire); October: "Geijutsu to gendai" (Art and the contemporary age); November: "On the Emperor" and "Giryū zuihitsu" (Random thoughts on Gion Nankai and Yanagisawa Kien); December: *Katō Shūichi shishū* (A poetry collection of Katō Shūichi).

1976   AGE 57

WORKS ~ March: *Katō Shūichi kashū* (The poetry collection of Katō Shūichi); April: coauthored *Rekishi o miru me—Mata wa rekishi ni okeru "nichijō" no hakken* (Viewing history: the discovery of mundanity in history); June: "Bungaku no yōgo—Kyōgi no bungaku gainen kara kōgi no bungaku gainen e" (In support of literature: from a narrow to a broad definition of literature); June 1976–July 1979: wrote a series of essays under the collective title "Majimena jōdan" (Serious jokes) in the *Mainichi Shimbun;* July: *Nihonjin to wa nani ka* (What is a Japanese?); October: *Genzai no naka no rekishi* (History in the present).

1977   AGE 58

September: visited China as a member of the Association for Japan-China Cultural Exchange.

WORKS ~ January–December: "Bungei jihyō 1977" (Criticism of current works, 1977); February: *Kotoba to ningen;* April: "E. H. Nōman—sono ichimen" (E. H. Norman: one aspect of him) and "Kōetsu oboegaki" (Note on [Hon'ami] Kōetsu); May–October: coauthored *Nihonjin no shiseikan* (The Japanese view on life and death [2 vols.]).

1978   AGE 59

April 1978–April 1979: served as a visiting professor at the University of Geneva.

WORKS ~ January 1978–October 1979: serialized "Zoku Nihon bungakushi josetsu" (Introduction to a history of Japanese literature, a sequel) in the *Asahi Jānaru;* April: "Koten no imi" (The meaning of classics) and coauthored *Chūgoku to tsukiau hō* (How to keep company with China); July: edited (with Ronald P. Dore) *Kokusai shimpojiumu—Sengo no Nihon: Tenkanki o mukaete* (International symposium—postwar

Japan in the face of transition); October: "Ikkyū to iu genshō" (The phenomenon of Ikkyū) and Heibonsha began publishing *Katō Shūichi chosakushū* (Selected works of Katō Shūichi [1978–May 1980; total 15 vols.]).

1979   AGE 60
January 1979–March 1982: served as editorial adviser to the journal *Shisō*; October 1979–April 1980: presented the NHK series *Daigaku kōza: Kagaku to bungaku* (NHK university lectures: science and literature) and its published version with the same title.
WORKS ～ *A History of Japanese Literature: The First Thousand Years*, trans. David Chibbett (vol. 1; Macmillan and Paul Norbury Publications); coauthored *Six Lives Six Deaths: Portraits from Modern Japan* (Yale University Press). July: "Dare ga hoshi no sora o mita ka—*Shigosen no matsuri* o megutte" (Who saw the starry sky: focusing on [Kinoshita Junji's] *The Meridian Festival*); August: "Fukunaga Takehiko no shi" (The death of Fukunaga Takehiko); October: "Sarutoru ron izen" (Before discussing Sartre); December: "Ishikawa Jun: Kotoba no chikara" (Ishikawa Jun: the power of words) and coauthored *Tenkeiki hachijū nendai e* (Into the eighties as a time of transformation).

1980   AGE 61
Received the seventh Osaragi Jirō Prize for his two-volume *Nihon bungakushi josetsu*.
WORKS ～ April: *Nihon bungakushi josetsu ge* (Introduction to a history of Japanese literature [vol. 2]); July 1980–May 1984: serialized "Sanchūjin kanwa" (Idle talks by a mountain recluse) in the evening edition of the *Asahi Shimbun*.

1981   AGE 62
September–December: served as visiting professor in the Department of History, Brown University.
WORK ～ May: coauthored *Erosu no bigaku* (The aesthetics of eroticism) with Ikeda Masuo.

1982   AGE 63
WORKS ～ January 1982–December 1983: serialized "E no naka no onna tachi" (Images of women in painting) for *Madamu*; October: "Kyōkasho ken'etsu no byōri" (The pathology of textbook censorship).

1983   AGE 64

January–June: served as visiting professor, Department of Asian Studies, Cambridge University, and, October 1983–July 1984, as visiting professor, Seminario di Lingua e Letteratura Giapponese, Università degli Studi di Venezia.

WORKS ~ Vols. 2–3 of *A History of Japanese Literature* (*The Years of Isolation* and *The Modern Years* [Kodansha International]). September: *Sanchūjin kanwa* (Idle talks by a mountain recluse).

1984   AGE 65

November 1984–June 1985: served as editor-in-chief for *Heibonsha daihyakka-jiten* (Heibonsha encyclopedia [16 vols.]).

WORKS ~ January–December: serialized "E—Kakusareta imi" (The hidden meaning in painting) for *Taiyō;* April: *Jinrui no chiteki isan—Sarutoru* (The intellectual heritage for humankind: Sartre) and "Hayashi Tatsuo o omou" (Remembering Hayashi Tatsuo); July: coauthored *Nihon bunka no kakureta kata* (Hidden forms in Japanese culture) and began serializing "Sekiyō mōgo" (Untempered utterances) in the evening edition of the *Asahi Shimbun.*

1985   AGE 66

Participated in various conferences in France and Italy and was named Chevalier des Arts et Lettres by the government of France.

WORKS ~ January: coedited *Yoshimitsu Yoshihiko zenshū 5* (The collected works of Yoshimitsu Yoshihiko [vol. 5]); March: "Tomioka Tessai"; May: *E no naka no onna tachi* (Images of women in painting); June: "Nihon bungaku" (Japanese literature).

1986   AGE 67

April–July: served as visiting professor at the Centro de Estudios de Asia y Africa del Norte at the Colegio de México.

WORKS ~ January: "Sengo yonjūnen—Nani ga kawari nani ga kawaranakatta ka" (Forty years after the war: what has changed and what hasn't); February: *Koten o yomu 23: Ryōjin hishō* (Reading the classics: the dance of dust on the rafters [vol. 23]); July: "Sengo to Nihon" (The postwar period and Japan); December: coauthored *Yōroppa futatsu no mado—Toredo to Venetia* (Two windows to Europe—Toledo and Venice) and coedited *Dainiji sekai taisen to gendai* (The Second World War and the contemporary period).

1987   AGE 68
April: served as visiting professor at Princeton University and, November 1987–March 1988, as the commentator of the NHK program "Nihon: Sono kokoro to katachi" (Japan: its essence and forms).
WORKS ~ February: "Gunkaku no mekanizumu" (The mechanism of military expansion); April: *Sekiyō mōgo 1* (Untempered utterances [vol. 1]) and "Kabuki zatsudan" (Miscellaneous thoughts on kabuki); August: *Gendai Nihon shichū* (Personal interpretations of contemporary Japan); October: *Sanchūjin kanwa zōho* (Idle talks by a mountain recluse [rev. ed.]). November 1987–March 1988: coauthored 10-vol. series *Nihon: Sono kokoro to katachi* (Japan: its essence and forms [an edited English translation appeared in 1994 as *Japan: Spirit and Form*]).

1988   AGE 69
March–April: served as editor-in-chief of *Sekai daihyakka-jiten* (World encyclopedia [31 vols.]); April: began serving as a professor at Ritsumeikan University in Kyoto and, from October 1988–March 1996, as head of the Tokyo Central Metropolitan Library.
WORKS ~ Coauthored *Das klassische Japan.* November: edited *Watashi no Shōwa shi* (A personal Shōwa history).

1989   AGE 70
January–March: served as Regents' Professor at the University of California, Davis. Also served (1989–91) on the editorial board for Iwanami shoten's multivolume series *Nihon kindai shisō taikei* (Comprehensive collection of modern Japanese thought [23 vols.]).
WORKS ~ January: "Meiji shoki no buntai" (Literary style in the early Meiji period) in *Nihon kindai shisō taikei 16: Buntai* (Comprehensive collection of modern Japanese thought: literary style [vol. 16]), which he coedited; August: *Kenpō wa oshitsukerareta ka* (Was the constitution forced upon Japan? [Kyoto]); October: edited *Yukawa Hideki chosakushū 7* (Selected works of Yukawa Hideki [vol. 7]).

1990   AGE 71
WORKS ~ January: *Sekiyō mōgo 2* (Untempered utterances [vol. 2]); November: *Nihongo o kangaeru* (Thoughts on the Japanese language [Kyoto]).

1991   AGE 72

January: joined in a public announcement with Ōe Kenzaburō and other literary figures regarding Japan's role in the Gulf War; October: began to serve on the Yoshida Hidekazu Prize Awards Committee with Yoshida and the composer Takemitsu Tōru; November: served as commentator for the Public Broadcasting System in a *Frontline* program on Japanese business practices in the United States.

WORKS ~ "Mechanisms of Ideas: Society, Intellectuals, and Literature in the Postwar Period in Japan," in *Legacies and Ambiguities: Postwar Fiction and Culture in West Germany and Japan*; April: "Bungaku no kōyō" (The uses of literature) and "Kodai Naijeriya no chōkoku" (Ancient Nigerian sculpture); May: "Hon'yaku koten bungaku shimatsu" (Translating classical literature); September: "Meiji shoki no hon'yaku—Naze nani o ikani yakushita ka" (Translations in the early Meiji period: the whys, whats, and hows) in *Nihon kindai shisō taikei 15: Hon'yaku no shisō* (Comprehensive collection of modern Japanese thought: the ideology of translation [vol. 15]), which he coedited; November: "Nakahara Chūya no Nihongo" (Nakahara Chūya's Japanese) in *Kindai no shijin 10: Nakahara Chūya* (Modern poets: Nakahara Chūya [vol. 10]), which he edited; December: *Izakaya no Katō Shūichi* (Katō Shūichi's conversations at a tavern [Kyoto]).

1992   AGE 73

April–July: served as guest professor at the Free University of Berlin; April 1992–March 1995: head of the International Museum for Peace at Ritsumeikan University.

WORKS ~ January: "Koto hozon" (Preservation of the ancient capital); February: *Sekiyō mōgo 3* (Untempered utterances [vol. 3]); summer: "Postmodernism and Asia"; November: commentary on Watsuji Tetsurō's *Nihon seishinshi kenkyū* (Study of the spiritual history of Japan) entitled "Sakuhin, hōhō, kanjusei oyobi jidai" (Creative works, methodology, sensibility, and time).

1993   AGE 74

April–August: served as visiting professor at the University of Zurich.

WORKS ~ "Tokyo et le nouvel ordre mondial." January: *Gendai sekai o yomu* (Interpreting the contemporary world [Kyoto]); March: "Shakaishugi saihō" (Revisiting socialism); April: "Sabetsu no kokusaika" (The internationalization of discrimination) and "Reisen no shūen o dō miru ka" (How to assess the end of the Cold War); June: *Izakaya no Katō Shūichi II* (Katō Shūichi's conversations at a tavern [vol. 2; Kyoto]); July: edited *Saitō Mokichi: Kindai no shijin III* with a commentary "Saitō Mokichi no sekai" (The world of Saitō Mokichi); August: "Sōseki shōron" (Short discussion of Sōseki).

1994   AGE 75
January: awarded the Asahi Prize; March–April: served as visiting professor at Beijing University and an adviser to the Institute of Japanese Studies at Beijing University.
WORKS ~ *Japan: Spirit and Form.* January: "Hotta Yoshie shiki" (My private account of Hotta Yoshie); March: *Sengo sedai no sensō sekinin* (War responsibility of the postwar generation [Kyoto]); June: "Nihon no kokusai 'kōken'" (Japan's international "contribution") and "Tsuru wa shinazu" (The crane will not die); August: "Shijin keizaigakusha" (Poet and economist); September: *Sekiyō mōgo 4* (Untempered utterances [vol. 4]).

1995   AGE 76
January–March: served as the commentator for the twelve-segment television series on NHK, *Ningen Daigaku,* in which he gave lectures on Mori Ōgai, Saitō Mokichi, and Kinoshita Mokutarō; the May edition of a leading Chinese literary journal, *Shijie Wenxue* (World literature), was dedicated to Katō; November: received the degree of Doctorat Honoris Causa from the Université Stendhal, France.
WORKS ~ May: *Tenkanki: Ima to mukashi* (Transitional period: past and present [Kyoto]); June: "Masuko Jun'ichi soshite reddo pāji" (Masuko Jun'ichi and the red purge); August: "Minshushugi no gojūnen" (Fifty years of democracy); September: "Taisei no jizoku to danzetsu" (Continuities and discontinuities in the established structure); October: "Seishin no ōfuku undō" (The revolution of the spirit) and coauthored *Gendai Kankoku jijō* (Contemporary Korea [Kyoto]); November: "'Kako no kokufuku' oboegaki" (Some comments on *Vergangenheitsbewältigung* [overcoming the past]) and coauthored *Ajia kenchiku no genzai* (Asian architecture today).

1996   AGE 77
March: resigned his positon as head of Tokyo Central Metropolitan Library.

WORKS ~ May: *Katō Shūichi Kōenshū I: Dōjidai to wa nani ka* (Lectures by Katō Shūichi: the question of contemporaneity [vol. 1; Kyoto]); August: "Nicchū kankei no mirai" (The future of Sino-Japanese relations); September: *Katō Shūichi Kōenshū II: Dentō to gendai* (Lectures by Katō Shūichi: tradition and the present [vol. 2, Kyoto]), *Nihon wa doko e yuku no ka* (Where is Japan heading?), and "Yakushi zatsudan" (Miscellaneous topics on the translation of poetry).

1997   AGE 78
Spring: served as visiting professor at Pomona College, U.S.A.
WORKS ~ *A History of Japanese Literature: From the Man'yōshū to Modern Times* (abridged ed., Curzon Press). March: *Hitsuji no uta: sono go* (Postscript to *A Sheep's Song*); May: coauthored *Jidai o yomu* (Interpreting the present); July: *Sekiyō mōgo 5* (Untempered utterances [vol. 5]) and "Nakano Shigeharu danpen" (Fragmentary piece on Nakano Shigeharu).

At the time of this compilation, the author's post-1979 books, essays, and other writings have been published in eight volumes under the title *Katō Shūichi chosakushū Dai'niki* (Heibonsha, 1996–97), with a ninth volume planned (date unknown), which will bring the selected works to a total of twenty-four volumes (and an appending volume).

SOURCES

Yano Masakuni, comp., "Katō Shūichi chosho mokuroku—waei taiyaku," *Ronkyū* 13 (March 1998): 87–120; "Katō Shūichi nenpukō," *Ronkyū* 11 Bessatsu (February 1991); and four manuscripts that Yano compiled: "Katō Shūichi nenpukō hotei" (1992), "Katō Shūichi nenpukō tsuika" (1994), "Katō Shūichi chosho mokuroku" (1995), and "Katō Shūichi nenpukō tsuika" (1996); "Chosaku nenpu," *Katō Shūichi chosakushū*, vol. 15 (Heibonsha, 1979), 328–76 and individual volumes in the same fifteen-volume collection (1978–80); individual volumes in *Katō Shūichi chosakushū dai'niki* (1996–); and Katō's chronology contained in Heibonsha's advertisement pamphlet for *Katō Shūichi chosakushū*; Kokubo Minoru, ed., "Katō Shūichi nenpu," in *Shōwa bungaku zenshū* (Shōgakukan, 1989), 28:1108–11; "Chosho ichiran," "Shuyō ronbun ichiran," "Shuyō igaku ronbun ichiran," and "Shuyō gaikokugo ronbun ichiran," in *Nihon no uchi to soto*, by Katō Shūichi

(Bungei shunjū, 1971), 488–94; private correspondence from Mr. Katō; Ichiko Teiji, Kubota Jun, and Miyoshi Yukio, eds., *Nihon bunka sōgō nenpyō* (Iwanami shoten, 1990); Matsubara Shin'ichi, Isoda Kōichi, and Akiyama Shun, *Zōho kaitei sengo Nihon bungakushi/nenpyō* (Kōdansha, 1985), 463–529. For a comprehensive list of Katō's public lectures as well as his participation in symposia and round-table discussions (both *zadankai* and *taidan*) from 1946–88, see Yano Masakuni, comp., "Katō Shūichi danwa mokuroku oboegaki," *Ronkyū* 9 (December 1988): 45–57. For a comprehensive list of Katō's translations, his edited works, and those edited under his supervision (*kanshū*), see Yano, "Katō Shūichi chosho mokuroku—waei taiyaku," 88–95. I am very grateful to Mr. Yano for his time and care in verifying the accuracy of this chronology during the last stages of its compilation. Any errors that remain are mine and mine alone.

In order to suggest the area of Katō's intellectual interest at specific dates, I cite the titles of his works at their first appearance rather than those in new editions or collections such as the *Katō Shūichi chosakushū*. One example is the much-discussed essay "Zasshuteki Nihon bunka no kadai" (July 1955), whose title was later changed to "Zasshuteki Nihon bunka no kibō." For serialized writings in journals or newspaper columns, I record only the collective titles, as in "Katō Shūichi no sekai shūyūki" (*Mainichi gurafu*) or "Kotoba to ningen" and "Sekiyō mōgo" (*Asahi Shimbun*). And with this translation's intended audience in mind, I list major English (but not Chinese, Korean, French, German, or Italian) translations of Katō's works and their publishers. Works with Japanese-language titles in the chronology and following text annotations are published in Tokyo (unless indicated otherwise).

VOLUME ONE

1 Grandfather's House

Toward the end of the last century, the only son of a wealthy family in
Saga became a cavalry officer in the Meiji army. Before he enlisted at
the time of the Sino-Japanese War, he spent his family fortune on two
horses and a groom and went on lavish sprees with the famous geisha
Manryū in Tokyo's Shimbashi district.[1] During his study tour of Italy,
he visited Milan's La Scala and heard Caruso's renditions of Verdi and
Puccini. This was my grandfather. Apparently during this time he acquainted himself with Western epicurean tastes and learned the etiquette
for social interaction between the sexes. A colonel by the time of the
Russo-Japanese War, he traveled to Australia to procure war horses for
the Japanese Imperial Army.[2] After he left the military at the end of the
war, he started a trading business and made some profits during World
War I. But the postwar depression wiped out most of his possessions,
leaving him without much affluence in his remaining years.

His early marriage to the daughter of a Saga governor's concubine
produced a son and three daughters. The son graduated from the Faculty of Medicine at the Imperial University but died soon afterwards.
The eldest of the three daughters was sent to the Peer's School and was
later married to the eldest son of a rich Saga family, a man who in time
became a Seiyūkai Diet member.[3] The remaining two daughters were

1. Parts of old Shimbashi, such as Karasumori, had been known for their
pleasure quarters since the Edo period.
2. The war occurred in 1904–5.
3. Before 1945 children from the imperial family, the aristocracy, and even
former samurai families were educated at the Peer's School (Gakushūin). • The

sent to Saint Maur Girls' Higher School and were even baptized, though both later married non-Christians. The husband of the second daughter, my father, was the second son of a large landowner in Saitama Prefecture and a medical doctor by profession. The youngest daughter's husband, a company employee, came from an Osaka merchant family. As Grandfather's family fortune began to decline, so did the economic status of his daughters' marriage prospects. During the Minseitō administration, the Diet politician found himself outside the arena of power and apparently spent his time drinking at home with his underlings.[4] But when the Seiyūkai seized political power, he was appointed as a prefectural governor, and suddenly he became a more influential figure. Before he was able to secure his political position, however, he died from a stroke on the way to a campaign speech. The physician did open a private practice, but since he sought no worldly success, he achieved none. Instead, he chose to lead a quiet life in Shibuya. On the other hand, the company employee in Osaka longed to make a name for himself and worked zealously, but tuberculosis overtook him before his ambitions were realized. These three sons-in-law were apparently not of much help in resurrecting Grandfather's declining fortunes.

All three daughters were married in the latter half of the 1910s, and immediately after World War I all of them gave him grandchildren. The eldest daughter had only one son, a future diplomat. The second daughter had a son and a daughter, myself and my younger sister. The youngest daughter also had a son and a daughter, who became a university professor and a company employee, respectively.

My childhood recollections do not extend beyond the Great Kantō Earthquake.[5] Grandfather's house, as I remember it from about the late 1920s, was on the left-hand side midway up the Miyamasuzaka on the way towards Aoyama 7-chōme from Shibuya Station. Granite pillars and an iron gate that opened sideways were erected a little further in from the Miyamasuzaka sidewalk. A straight gravel pathway with

---

Seiyūkai (formally Rikken Seiyūkai) was founded in 1900 by Itō Hirobumi, Saionji Kimmochi, and Hara Kei; the party formed five separate cabinets during the Taishō and early Shōwa period until internal dissension contributed to its dissolution in 1940.

4. The Minseitō (formally Rikken Minseitō) was formed in 1927. Along with the Seiyūkai, it ushered in a brief period of party government that ended in 1940.

5. September 1, 1923.

plants on both sides continued for some distance from the gate to the vestibule at the end. The vestibule and a number of its "Western-style" rooms were modeled after the Victorian style popular during the Meiji and Taishō eras, with tall ceilings and narrow windows, and were furnished with heavy leather armchairs. There was a pair of antlers hanging on the wall, a rug made from a tiger's skin, an old-fashioned cut-glass lantern, an embroidered Egyptian camel, and a tablecloth from Paris. In short, with the exception of the many framed photographs of horses to suggest something about Grandfather's past, these things were what any traveler might have brought back from the West and displayed like an antique shop's show window. These rooms did not seem to have any specific use. For everyday life, Grandfather and Grandmother, along with a student lodger and three maids, used only a few of the many Japanese-style rooms adjoining the Western ones at the back of the house.

It struck me as a child that all the events that took place at Grandfather's house had the air of a strange religious ceremony. Seating himself behind a large table in the living room, Grandfather would simply gesture with his chin, and Grandmother and two of the housemaids would instantaneously respond to his desire for things like cigarettes, tea, or the letter file. The kitchen maid and the student helper almost never appeared in the living room. A ridiculously large number of dishes were served at his meals, but not all of them were necessarily meant for consumption. They were often there just for Grandfather to poke with his chopsticks and brush aside. One time, he reportedly blurted out, "This is what you expect me to eat?" and hurled the dish out into the garden. But since I always went to his house in Mother's company, I never witnessed such a scene. In Mother's presence, Grandfather was always in a good mood, and even if something was bothering him, he tried to conceal it. I watched as the three intimidated women catered to the whims of the sole master of the house with unfailing attention, and I could sense the air of omnipotence emanating from Grandfather. I felt the same way about Mother for her ability to chitchat with a figure of such unapproachable authority, even though a small child like myself did not quite understand the nature of that omnipotence.

The strange ritual reached its apex when Grandfather was about to leave home on some business. Drawing her small frame close to Grandfather's huge upright body, Grandmother would help him dress in the undergarments and the Western clothing the two maids passed out piece by piece. Grandfather would put a folded white cambric handkerchief in his breast pocket, scrutinize himself in a big mirror, and fix his thinning hair. He would then spray on some imported perfume from a large bottle with a golden nozzle. Watching all the goings-on, Mother would say something like, "It looks like Father is going to have a good time again." Grandfather would respond with something humorous, his hands still preoccupied with his perfume bottle. Meanwhile, Grandmother would give out orders to the maids: "Are the shoes ready? No, these won't do for today. Quickly, go get another pair!" It was a boisterous scene. I could not understand at that time why so many people had to make such a fuss just to prepare one man to leave his house.

Grandfather did not put on his shoes in the vestibule. Instead, he preferred to do it on the stepping-stone at the porch facing the garden. From there he could walk straight down into the garden, stand before the shrine for the god of harvests at the corner, and clap his hands in worship. All these had become an indispensable part of the ceremony. Although he had sent two of his daughters to a Catholic girls' school, Grandfather would ask a Shintō priest to preside over such ceremonies as marriages, funerals, and memorial services. If he ever had any religious faith, he probably pledged his most heartfelt allegiance to the god of harvests in his own garden.

The shrine was situated in the shade of some small trees and was not visible from the porch. A flight of stone steps lined with plants led to a small red *torii*. The shrine was built on a stone pedestal about shoulder height with a stone fox on each side. I remember they were crafted by the fine hands of an artisan. The shrine was always in good repair with offerings in place. No one in the family except Grandfather believed in the deity, but everybody, even a confirmed atheist like my father, or a child like myself, knew how serious Grandfather was about his rituals. In his later years, every morning before he left home, he would go there to pray for the success of his business, for peace in his family, and, presumably, for the women he loved as well.

Grandfather had many female friends, one of whom was a Westerner. Sometimes, undeterred by our presence, Grandfather would pick up the telephone and speak with her in French. Since nobody else in the family understood French, he would explain away such conversation as a business call or something else. My mother would see through all his pretense and say, "Even though Grandma may not know what is going on, it's awful of him to do this right in her face!" This did not mean, however, that Mother was totally on "Grandma's" side. She once remarked that the linguistic barrier was not the only reason why Grandma had no idea what her husband was doing in her presence; rather, she did not want to know in the first place. Grandma considered debauchery as something natural for men, and this thinking of hers had something to do with the fact that she herself was a concubine's child. But as far as Grandfather's telephone conversation was concerned, she simply convinced herself that it was just a business call. This was what Mother told us. I have never met the Western woman in question, but I did meet another one of Grandfather's lady friends.

At that time, Grandfather owned a small Italian restaurant in the West Ginza district. A bar occupied the first floor, from whence a narrow and steep stairway led up to the dining area on the second floor. Sometimes Grandfather would bring his grandchildren to the restaurant for meals. He would announce something like "Here, I brought my family today," and then call out to his friends at the other end of the bar or crack jokes with his male acquaintances. They spoke Italian or French, with expressive intonations and dramatic body gestures. At these times I got the impression that Grandfather was an entirely different person from the one we knew at home surrounded by his family members. To me, it was like watching a scene in a play whose plot I could not understand. In it, there was no bond between the grandfather and the children. As we stood at the bottom of the stairway leading up to the second floor, I realized that the main character had momentarily forgotten our existence, and the children's role in this short scene was reduced to that of mere spectators.

The proprietress of the restaurant was already waiting for us on the second floor. In a voice somewhat ostentatiously cheerful, she would say something like, "Oh, my, what a rare pleasure it is to see you! Welcome!"

"Well. I guess I could say the same to you."

"Really, it's been a while, hasn't it?"

"You know my work has been keeping me busy."

"I wonder what kind of work that might be," she laughed teasingly.

"It isn't what you're thinking. I just returned from Osaka yesterday." Grandfather's tone of voice changed.

"How were things over there?" The woman's tone also changed abruptly.

"Oh well, they're still the same . . ."

"Hmm, you never say anything more than that!" She cast a sidelong glance at him with a coquettish manner impossible to describe. At least that was how it struck me.

Grandfather's scene with the proprietress belonged to yet another world, one different from his exchanges with the men at the bar. The woman and Grandfather seemed to speak a secret language, with unpredictable shifts from awkward seriousness to familiar chattiness, producing a mood that swung from the subdued to the light-hearted. It was immediately apparent to me that the relationship between Grandfather and this woman existed on a different level of intimacy than the one between him and Grandmother or my mother. I could also sense the unmistakable immediacy of this intimacy, as if it were a tangible object into which outsiders could scarcely hope to intrude. But at any moment at their discretion, they could always allow my sister, my cousin, or myself to merge into their dialogue as an excuse to change the direction of their conversation.

"What fine children you have!" the proprietress would say.

"You must be joking. They're my grandchildren."

"Well, I bet anyone would believe they were your children."

I couldn't comprehend why Grandfather should feel pleased when he was told he looked younger than his age, but I could tell he was happy even though he knew it was mere flattery. That was the grandfather I was so fond of. To be sure, he might clap his hands in worship before the shrine at one moment, exchange jokes with his Italian friends at another, or berate Grandmother even without any particular provocation on her part. And yet for all his amazing inscrutability—I thought at moments like this—there was at least one side of him I could understand. And this comprehensible aspect of his personality emerged only when he was with his female friends.

My father was no fan of Grandfather's and was often critical of his "licentiousness." For Father, any intimacy with women other than one's wife was the vice of all vices. Mother, educated as she was in a Catholic school, would probably concur with Father in denouncing licentiousness, but she tended not so much to criticize Grandfather's behavior as to rationalize it. Had it not been for the premature death of his eldest son in whom he had placed so many hopes, so she reasoned, Grandfather would not have spent his later years in such excesses. Or if only Grandmother had not acted against Grandfather's wish at every turn, he surely would have spent more time at home. Abhor the sin but not the sinner. But I wonder if it could really be called a "sin." For a long time I couldn't accept the logic of associating the Grandfather I knew with the notion of "the vice of all vices." But I was not even conscious of this incongruity, to say nothing of trying to resolve these irreconcilable associations by determining for myself when and how licentiousness was or wasn't a sin. I was a child. On the one hand, I accepted the idea of sin as it was imparted to me by my parents. On the other, I just had an inkling, nothing more, that maybe I could understand Grandfather the next time he was with his lady friends, even though in fact I never did. It was only years later that this inkling was realized within myself, after I looked into the eyes of a woman and found everything, after I experienced that flashing moment which was more valuable than the entire world: how completely meaningless it was to speak of such experiences in terms of good or evil . . .

I thought back about Grandfather, and I wondered who could say that Grandfather himself had not come to the same realization. It was apparent to me that the arbitrary application of the label "licentious" could shed little light on the person in question. The word means different things to different people, just as different well behaved children from good families all lead different lives. But our age difference was far too great for me to grasp the substance of Grandfather's life, assuming it could be known. Perhaps his "licentiousness" did not mean much, but then perhaps it did. It is just that there is no reason now for me to think that it did not. Have I indeed inherited Grandfather's blood? Yet I am totally skeptical about this business of blood lineage beyond the acquisition of certain physical traits through heredity. Other determinants might be involved, but if they are impossible to verify, one must be compelled to obliterate the possibility. Surely, what is more meaningful to me is the fact that a man described as "licentious" existed in my childhood, and even though one might think of his many failings, it is difficult to imagine that he did anything evil.

With his grandchildren, Grandfather was indulgent and generous with money. He was somewhat capricious but sincere in his own way. He would not lightly break a promise he had made, even with the children. For example, one time after he told me he would buy me anything I wanted, as he often did, I said I wanted a live horse. Surprised, Grandfather explained to me that live horses were not for sale, that even if he could manage to get one it was not something a child could handle, that when he promised to buy me anything I wanted what he meant was anything he could buy at a shop. Tirelessly, he went on and on, trying his best to reason with me. What moved me above and beyond the desire for a live horse was Grandfather himself, for sparing no effort in his earnest attempt to convince a mere child. And I held on even more tightly to my hope for a live horse, if only for the sake of reaffirming that experience.

The food at Grandfather's Italian restaurant was superb. Before I knew it, however, Grandfather sold the restaurant, and now not a trace of it remains. Even in today's so-called Western restaurants in Tokyo, I don't believe there is any food quite so delicious. Perhaps it is because when I was a child I knew nothing about any other delicacies. In any case, Grandfather preferred only the best in everything, and in this respect he treated the children no differently. He would order us the same Italian dishes he ordered for adult guests, and he also taught us table manners. Whether we understood it or not, he spoke to us as if we were grown-ups. For instance, once after taking my sister and me to a movie, he asked what we thought about it. Though I was already attending elementary school, I did not even understand what the story was about. Frightened by the noise and tumult in the movie, my sister had burst into tears. All I could do was to keep reminding myself that what was happening on the screen wasn't real; this was the only way I could endure my emotional turmoil in the darkness of the cinema. When Grandfather asked us about the movie, it was apparent that he did not appreciate our frightened confusion. But it was also true that his failure to show empathy for our feelings was no more than a somewhat impetuous expression of his desire to seek some common ground for communication with us. While I thought of him as inconsiderate, I was also drawn to a certain charm he had. If I had been older, I might even have been able to appreciate why certain women were attracted to him.

When I was a child, I found "the West" in his Italian restaurant. It was not because of the men at the bar or the foreign language Grandfather spoke. It was because of the delicate flavor of the food as well as the tunes from the Italian operas Grandfather hummed along with when he was in a good mood. The food there was unlike any I tasted at home, and the Italian melodies were radically different from those of the koto or the *shakuhachi* I heard at home or even from the songs we sang at my elementary school. There was a different sensory order at work. The next time I encountered the same sensory experience with the same intensity was twenty years later, when I first saw with my own eyes the purple tides of the Mediterranean and cities laid out in marble. In an old office in London's financial district, I found the leather armchair of Grandfather's room; in the streets of Rome I discovered the intonations and body gestures of the men in Grandfather's bar; and in the opera houses in Salzburg, songs sung by the guest singers from Italy reminded me of some of the tunes Grandfather hummed to himself. I rediscovered my long-forgotten childhood world in the Europe I saw for the first time. Western Europe in my first impression was not a destination reached after a long journey, but a place to which I returned at the end of a long vacation. But that was merely my first impression. Later, when I lived in Paris and managed to speak French perhaps more fluently than Grandfather, I came to realize how "the West" I had known as a child was only a small piece in a huge jigsaw puzzle. I also learned where my own piece fit into the overall canvas of "the West." I was beginning to learn about the origins of my origin.

I often visited Grandfather's house with Mother, with Father coming along occasionally. Grandfather's house was not far from where we lived, and it was also almost the only place where I had the opportunity to meet with the children of my other relatives. Grandfather had many excuses for calling family gatherings. One day it was a marriage ceremony or an anniversary, another day a farewell party or a memorial service. I looked forward to all these occasions. His big garden was a perfect playground and had everything the children needed. We would run around the yard, which was bordered by a hedge planted where the incline grew steeper. Immediately below the hedge was a low stone wall. Along a narrow road running parallel to the stone wall was a row of tenement houses with outward-facing doorways. The people there—women in front of their doorways cradling their babies or boys about our age kicking stones along the road—lived in a different world. They were so close to us that we could almost touch them, but there was no interaction of any kind between us. As a matter of fact, we could not even imagine having any possible interaction with them. I did not find anything at all strange about this until one day I learned that in fact Grandfather owned all the tenements, and that almost all the small shops along the left-hand side of Miyamasuzaka—from where it rises to just below Grandfather's front gate—were his rental properties. I was deeply shocked. And so it was not true that the people in the tenements were unrelated to us; we had a direct relationship whenever Grandfather's agents went around every month to collect rent from them. It was just that I didn't know the details of that relationship, nor its wider implications. The existence of people with whom we had a close relationship and yet no connection at all was not something I could explain to myself. I suppose this question represents a big black spot in my otherwise bright and transparent sky. Before I knew it, I was beginning to form the habit of not looking at the tenement dwellers whenever I went to Grandfather's house.

2   Fragrance of the Earth

I have never lived in the countryside, but that does not mean I had no connections with it at all.

The house in which Father grew up was in a village near Kumagaya in the Kantō plain.[1] In the Tokugawa era the head of the family assumed the title of *na'nushi*, or village chief, a position that allowed him to wear swords. In the 1920s my father's family owned most of the farmlands and forests in the village. Life there was prosperous; family members farmed their own land while keeping a large number of tenant farmers under their supervision. But the elders of the family, that is to say my grandfather and grandmother, seemed to be getting increasingly apprehensive about finding a suitable successor to continue the family tradition as they grew older. They had three children. The eldest was a daughter who had left the family house at an early age to marry a rich farmer in a neighboring village. Their third child—my father—left the village when he went to middle school in Urawa.[2] Since he set up his own medical practice in Tokyo, he was never considered to be a serious candidate to carry on the family's farming tradition. Their second child, a son, had no particular work to do after graduating from a higher school for commerce. Still, he had little desire to return to his family house unless events such as a marriage or funeral made his presence imperative. If pressed, he would send his wife instead. In time, when it became increasingly ap-

1. Kumagaya is a city in the northern part of Saitama Prefecture.
2. The school he attended, Urawa Chūgakkō, was the predecessor of today's Saitama Prefectural High School of Urawa (Saitama Kenritsu Urawa Kōtō Gakkō).

parent that somebody had to take care of both the old people and the farmwork, his wife was the one who took up the responsibility. She brought along their many children and made her permanent home in the countryside, returning only occasionally to her husband's house in Tokyo. My uncle remained in Tokyo by himself, hired a maid, and hardly ever went out of his house, withdrawing almost entirely from any social interaction and passing his days wearing a *dotera* and drinking sake.[3]

Until this day, I still cannot forget this enigmatic figure. When he was young, he was taken up with the then novel art of photography and taught the subject for a while. Beyond that, however, during some forty years from his graduation to the time of his death, he had no employment to speak of. He had not acquired any enthusiasm for calligraphy or painting, any fascination with ceramics, or any craving for fine food. He probably did not know any woman other than his own wife, nor was he likely to have even a single close friend. "How repulsive!" Mother used to say. "With an able body like that and not doing any work. And he calls himself a man?" But I never found him repulsive. He never took the initiative to visit us, but on the rare occasion when we went to his place, he was always in high spirits and would greet us with a "Hey, how nice of you to come!" I could feel a certain warmth in the way he uttered those words. Yet beyond that, I never developed any emotional bond with him or reached any better understanding of him. I felt bored at his house, and as soon as I left, I always felt distinctly refreshed by the surrounding brisk vivacity of downtown Tokyo.

I don't suppose this uncle of mine held the kind of philosophy about life that one could properly call misanthropy. Much less could his abandoning all worldly pleasures, except sake and tobacco, be attributed to enlightenment about life's transience. The truth of the matter is that this man who could live his life comfortably without having to work chose to do just that. And it was precisely because of this that there was no trace of obsequiousness about him. He did not have the vulgarity of the Osaka merchant's son who craved worldly success but failed to achieve any, or the petty cunning of his own hardworking wife, who had the knack of craftily maneuvering behind other people's backs. He did not speak with the arrogance of the elitist government bureaucrat minted by Tokyo Imperial University or display the pontifical manners of the swashbuckling Diet politician when he was surrounded by his under-

3. A *dotera* is a padded kimono worn in the winter.

lings. In short, he had nothing of what I as a child considered repulsive. At the time, the thought that he might not be of any use to society never entered my mind, and I certainly did not connect his lack of social worth to the absence of any disagreeable traits in his personality. Yet I had a very distinct feeling, even in my young mind, that there was not going to be any close association between us in our future. No man in his lifetime can realistically hope to know everything there is to know about another person. I wonder if it was through my uncle that I first began to appreciate this lesson.

Father did not bring his family to visit his country home very often— perhaps because of his work as a medical doctor, or perhaps because Sister and I had already started elementary school. At that time, there were only a few runs a day on the Shin'etsu Main Line, and for us to go from our house in Shibuya, change trains at Ueno, travel to Kumagaya, and return on the same day would have been too strenuous an itinerary.[4] Besides, we had to hire a car to take us to the village after we got off the train, and from there we had to walk for some time through the village before reaching Father's house, a rather time-consuming journey. So when we did travel to the countryside, we usually stayed overnight for two or three days. As a child, I always looked forward to taking these short trips, a source of unsurpassed pleasure. Perhaps the excitement they generated in me was not much different from that inspired by the trips I took years later across the Pacific or the Indian Ocean. As the train passed over the iron bridge over the Arakawa River, my journey into another world began.[5] When the rhythmic clatter of the train's wheels abruptly increased in volume as it passed over the bridge, I felt totally emancipated from my daily routine. From the train window, images of houses and people gave way to the water glittering between the expansive sky and the river banks. A new spatial cosmos completely different from that of the city I knew was opening up right before my eyes. Tokyo was completely behind me now, but the countryside was yet to be reached. My departure from a conventional routine had become final, while my contact with another was yet to begin. The train's reverberating whistles evoked more a feeling of total emancipation than a sense of anticipation

4. The Shin'etsu Main Line runs from Takasaki in Gumma Prefecture through Ueda and Nagano in Nagano Prefecture and Naoetsu on the Japan Sea coast to Niigata.

5. The Arakawa runs from Western Saitama Prefecture through the Kantō plain into Tokyo Bay.

about my destination. The Arakawa River and its banks are smaller than the Pacific Ocean. But the train was slow, and I was a small child.

There isn't the slightest difference between the sensation I feel today when I am aboard a passenger plane just after takeoff and the experience I had as a child on the Arakawa bridge. The city below quickly retreats into a boundless expanse of clouds, and the rhythm of the engine announces an end to the temporal order on land. Without thinking about my destination, I light up a cigarette after the no-smoking sign goes off. I think about my life, not in terms of my relationships with others but simply about myself; and I contemplate why I am here today. I want to savor myself at the moment when all my social ties have been severed.

We would get off at a small station on the Shin'etsu Main Line and wait for a long time for the car to take us to the village. A jolting ride finally brought us to a narrow path through the wheat fields where the larks were singing. As we started walking, my feeling was totally different from the way I feel today when I arrive at airports in large foreign cities. At the airports—with the exception of a few V.I.P.s—everyone is an alien anonymous to everyone else, minding his own business. The space where duty-free items are displayed belongs to no one, and therefore to everyone. But in a Japanese village, there is absolutely no question about who belongs there and who doesn't.

The country road wound its way through the fields and curved when it encountered a bamboo grove. Then it cut through a thick wooded area, and no sooner had it passed the mud walls of some farmhouses than it turned into a small crossroad. Larks could be heard in the wheat fields and bush warblers in the bamboo grove. Sometimes, as the wind rustled through the golden rice fields, the dry echoes of the clappers on the scarecrows could be heard. Sometimes after a rain small frogs would jump out onto the muddy road. At other times huge columns of clouds glinted dazzlingly over the horizon under a bright summer sky. And there was the peculiar and unchanging fragrance of the earth, probably produced by the mixture of straw and fertilizer. That was precisely the smell of a Japanese farm. Even today, no matter where I might be, this fragrance instantly comes to my mind as representing everything about the countryside. I always took a deep breath and ran to my heart's content amid the mulberry fields. On reaching the fork, I stopped to wait for my parents and got ready to dash out to the left or right. In those days, aside from elementary schoolyards, Tokyo already had fewer and fewer places where children could run free.

Certainly the country road was not ours alone. The children in the village would appear from nowhere and gather at the roadside, waiting for "the people from Tokyo" to pass by. Sometimes a few nursemaids carrying babies on their backs were among them, but mostly they were just small children with dirty hands and feet and tanned faces, wearing thongs and village smocks. They did not call out to us, nor did they talk or whisper among themselves. They would just stand there quietly watching us go by. While there were no welcoming or friendly gestures on their part, still less were there expressions of animosity or resentment. I suppose it was just plain curiosity. The village children were there because and only because they wanted to look at us. It was their gaze that turned me into "a person from Tokyo." What I learned at Father's country home was not about the countryside; instead I discovered that I was "a person from Tokyo."

The countryside did not belong to me but to the children who grew up there. After following us with their steady gaze—very rarely did they actually walk behind us—they scampered off and quickly dispersed and disappeared. For a while, we were left all by ourselves on the road between the fields. But a little further down the road as it curved behind the bamboo grove and the woods, they were again waiting for us. They watched as we approached, studying our movements as we passed before their eyes. Shortly after we walked past them, they would again disperse and repeat their act further down the road. Like guerrillas appearing and disappearing at will, they were thoroughly familiar with the territory, knowing each and every shortcut unbeknownst to me. Father might have had some knowledge of these shortcuts from the past when he grew up in the village. All I could do was follow the path Father picked, and even then I was not entirely sure where and how I should turn next. The village children knew everything, and I knew nothing. The world was there for them, not for me. That explains why I was not their observer but rather the object of their observation. I might have constituted a small part of their world, but I didn't know of any world in which they could form a part. Secretly, I couldn't help hoping to become one of them. Yet at the same time I had to admit to myself that, whether I liked it or not, that was only wishful thinking on my part.

In those days, I could not imagine that some of the village children might wish to become "Tokyo people" themselves. It was not until much later that I learned about country people's tenacious interest in the city, about their custom to name a Ginza district in every rural town, about young country girls' yearning for big city mannerisms and customs, and about the mixture of envy and disgust with which young people who grew up in the countryside look on their Tokyo counterparts. At the time, I was too proud to admit to myself that I longed to be one of the village children, and that attitude blocked any opportunity to observe them or imagine their inner thoughts or appreciate their side of things. Father and Mother, like any other proud parents, probably read in the village children's eyes only admiration for their own offspring. Accordingly, it did not even occur to them to speculate about what their son might really be thinking. They were totally indifferent to the movements of the village's ambush troops; their only concern was to make sure that their own children running ahead of them did not stumble into the wet rice fields.

The main structure of Grandfather's house was a two-story building constructed next to the tallest stand of cedars in the village. Its spacious lot was enclosed by a tall mud wall. Inside the wall and along it was a barn, a storage shed for farm equipment, a stable, and a chicken coop. A storehouse with white walls on four sides was built near the edge of the cedars. The second floor of the main structure was used for raising silkworms. During the right season, by climbing up the dark, steep stairs I could hear the silkworms nibbling on the mulberry leaves, a sound like a late autumn shower falling on a thicket of trees.

The family lived on the first floor with a spacious earth-floored *doma* separating the kitchen and the bath room on one side and six rooms with eight or ten mats on the other. The three rooms facing the garden on the south side were bright, whereas the north-facing ones were dark even during daytime. At that time there was no electricity in the house, and at night we used both kerosene lamps and candles. They only had two kerosene lamps—the old-fashioned kind with a glass chimney—one for the *doma* and the other for the living room. To go to the toilet we had to carry a candle, sheltering the flame from the wind with one hand as we walked down to the other end of the long corridor. Because the kitchen stove had no chimney, the smoke turned the room sooty black before escaping through the windows. With only the light from one candle, we would fumble in the dark when we got ready to take a bath. As I watched the flickering shadows on the walls with my entire body immersed in the hot water, the smell of the smouldering firewood and the fragrance of the cedar bathtub assailed my nose with the rising steam. In the darkness, they evoked a delicate sensual pleasure.

This, however, does not mean that as a small child I was not afraid of the dark. But the fear was not sufficiently intimidating to deter me from going to the bath room or to the toilet by myself. "How brave of you to go by yourself!" Grandmother once said as I began to walk toward the toilet holding a candle. "Aren't you afraid a ghost might come out?" Yet I did not believe that ghosts really existed. The way I was educated did not lead me to believe in this business of "ghosts" I had never seen, and that certainly was more convincing than any speculation that they might actually exist. More than anything else, this education might have turned me into what others call an "audacious" or "self-conceited" child. Yet thanks to it, darkness and graveyards, spirits of the dead and apparitions induced no fear in me. Even today, I derive no pleasure from talking about supernatural forces or ravaging gods.

During our visit, Grandfather himself would go to the yard to catch a chicken from the little coop, strangle it, pull off its feathers, and cut it up to serve us at dinner. Although I had no fear of ghosts, the strangling of a live chicken was too horrifying to watch. Not knowing how I felt, Grandfather cut off the dead chicken's head at the base of its neck, squeezed out the blood, and pulled the exposed tendons in such a way that the chicken's head began to move. He was only doing it to please me, and after his demonstration, he asked me to hold the chicken's neck in one hand and pull the tendons with the other. The chicken had been killed just a moment earlier, its head still looked alive, and its eyes shone with a strange brightness. The mere sight of it, to say nothing of the idea of playing with its movable head, sickened me unbearably. That I continued to watch with fascination as Grandfather showed me his trick was not because I found it interesting, but because I could scarcely suppress my curiosity aroused by the moving head of a dead animal. As curiosity and revulsion waged a fierce battle within me, the expression on my face probably gave the impression that I couldn't wait another moment to perform the trick myself. Meanwhile, Grandfather could not understand why I hesitated to go ahead with the game. In an attempt to please his grandson, the old man was displaying a sensitivity totally different from my own. And I, on the other hand, did not yet know how to protect my own feelings without acting discourteously toward him. Under the circumstances, a perplexed child like me could only react by starting to cry. Coming to my rescue was Mother, who comforted me by saying, "I know, it's pretty scary, isn't it?" She was certainly correct, although what she said was only part of the story. Yet to me, the kindness in her voice was a hundred times more important than the accuracy of her interpretation.

Facing the main structure to the left was a connecting corridor leading to another building that we called the "new annex," a bungalow with two ten-mat rooms and an alcove. Around it was a wide veranda that had the only urban-style glass doors in the house. Although the storm shutters were opened every morning and shut every night, it appeared that these two rooms were not normally used at all. In front of these quiet rooms was a courtyard with a fountain and some plants, an area secluded from the inner court in front of the main building where traffic was heavier. In the summer afternoons a chorus of cicadas would descend on these rooms that still held the fresh scent of new mats. I had learned to read at elementary school, and I would spend many long hours reading alone in the big twenty-mat room (the sliding doors separating the two rooms were always open). Though we had made a special trip to the countryside, I found the world in the books I was reading much more interesting than looking for mushrooms in the cedar forest, digging up bamboo shoots in the bamboo grove, or catching frogs along the furrows in the fields. But of course the new annex was not built for my reading pleasures.

Various ceremonies and festivities were held at Grandfather's house. Especially after Grandmother died, Buddhist services were held periodically in her name. On such occasions, people who were total strangers to me would fill both the main house and the annex. Children almost never came. But there were men with sun-weathered faces and heavy knuckles sitting cross-legged in every room drinking the sake served by women in mourning clothes. Lunch boxes prepared by a caterer from Kumagaya would pile up like a mountain, and when they were served, the men would untie the boxes, nibble on the cold braised fish and other items, and then continue with their drinking. From time to time, one man would leave the room while others would enter. On every such occasion, they put their hands on the tatami floor and exchanged their respectful bows and formal greetings. One of the women there would rewrap the lunch box left behind by the departing guest and hand it over to him along with another paper box containing two enormous *manjū* buns as a gift from the family. Some guests who were too drunk to walk had to wait out the effects of sake until late at night before they could leave. And there were others who simply stayed overnight in the new annex. For relatives who had come from nearby villages, it still was too far away for them to return home during the night.

Be it a Buddhist service or a wedding ceremony, these parties were conducted in more or less the same way. In other words, whether a Buddhist monk or a Shintō priest presided over the rituals, their roles were of negligible significance. The drinking party began from around noon and went on late into the night, while memories about the deceased or the well-being of the new couple were totally immaterial to the festivities as a whole. The vociferous noises among those who were drunk betrayed a kind of cheerful, exuberant energy. At a funeral or a memorial service, the living seemed totally preoccupied with their own affairs—drinking, eating, perspiring, or giving birth. And yet the men never danced and almost never sang. They would not socialize with the women serving sake, and certainly nobody exhibited any unruly behavior. Perhaps a drinking party hosted by the big landlord was not the kind of occasion that could inspire the tenant farmers to loosen up into a wild escapade. It represented quite a stark contrast to the scene depicted in Pieter Brueghel's *Wedding Banquet,* in which European farmers drink and sing, men and women all jumbled together in a wild dance, seemingly having the time of their lives.⁶

Whether it was a memorial service or a marriage ceremony, I would watch from a corner, a totally detached observer. The men were busy talking among themselves, and the women were even busier, running around preparing the sake and then the tea. Nobody was paying any attention to a child; never again could I be such an unobserved observer. But at the same time, I cannot recall observing anything that was more meaningless to me. I did not find the atmosphere of a country dinner party distasteful, but a child had no role to play in it other than to observe, and the events being observed were beyond his ability to comprehend. The fact that they took place in the countryside was just a matter of coincidence. In my childhood, these were the only occasions when I could attend a grown-up dinner party. Thus my connection with the countryside began with me being at once the object of observation by the village children and the observer of the men and women at the dinner party. This might be a matter of some importance. From the outset there was no interaction between the observers and the observed. I was an outsider, and I am afraid I shall forever live as one. But this does not

6. Pieter Brueghel the Elder's famous work was dated about 1565.

necessarily mean, as far as I am concerned, that my connection with the countryside was inconsequential.

Party etiquette naturally extends beyond the countryside. In the many social gatherings I later attended, I was no longer an observer by circumstance but by my own volition. And yet, just as in my childhood days, the object of my observation in many instances failed to evoke any particular interest in me. One time in Mexico City I found myself being dragged into what the local people call a fiesta, held at the house of a friend of a friend. There is no other way to describe the scene other than to say that everyone was literally swallowed up in the party's fever. People were drinking, gobbling, dancing, laughing, yelling, shrieking, and getting excited over their own excitement. They say when you are in Rome, do as the Romans do. So I too began drinking, talking, telling jokes, making superficial remarks, and passing out empty compliments in four different languages. Then it suddenly occurred to me in a strangely acute and most emphatic way—and quite without any special reason or motivation—that everything there was completely meaningless to me. On the instant all the people in the room, their excitement, their utterances, and their commotion receded into the infinite distance and turned into something totally irrelevant to me. I promptly left the crowd and went out by myself into a dark garden. The night breeze brought a faint fragrance of flowers and refreshed my cheeks flushed with wine. Although it was not quite the same as the peculiar smell of my countryside, it vividly reminded me of the chilly night air decades earlier in the garden of Father's country home during a dinner party. At the same time, everything in my countryside revived in my mind, and I could even hear the sound of the Japanese cicadas descending on the new annex in the late summer. For a moment, I seemed to be living in my original self again, unchanged over many decades, transcending the vast distance of the Pacific. When I came round—and presumably left my original identity behind—I wondered whether my authentic self might not always remain an outsider in all types of social gatherings. This realization did not evoke any remorse, regret, or sadness in me, just a compelling feeling that I needed to arrive at a resolution within myself.

3   Life in Shibuya's Konnō-chō

I mentioned earlier that the second son of a Saitama landlord left home at an early age to study in a middle school in Urawa. From there he entered Tokyo's First Higher School as a boarding student and learned to sing such songs as "Flowers in a Jade Cup" and to read German.[1] After that he entered the Faculty of Medicine of Tokyo Imperial University and spent four more years as a student in the Hongō area before joining the internal medicine division at the university hospital. Among his university classmates were Saitō Mokichi with his original Yamagata accent and Masaki Fujokyū, later the founder of the Fujimi Sanitarium and a literary figure as well.[2] Although Father did compose short verses himself and made many acquaintances among the poets associated with the *Myōjō* school, I don't think his association with Saitō and Masaki

1. "Aa gyokuhai ni hana ukete" was the First Higher School's famous *ryōka,* or dormitory song, composed by Kusunoki Masakazu with lyrics by Yano Kanji. For a partial translation of its lyrics, see chapter 11, note 3.
2. Saitō Mokichi (1882–1953), distinguished *tanka* poet, psychiatrist, and critic, was the most celebrated poet of the Araragi school and prominent in the history of modern *tanka;* he developed his predecessor Masaoka Shiki's idea of *shasei* (painting sketches) in *tanka* composition in his critical work *Dōba mango* (Random words on a young horse, 1919), and his most critically acclaimed *tanka* collections include *Shakkō* (Red radiance, 1913), *Aratama* (Unpolished gem, 1921), and *Tomoshibi* (Light, 1950). • Masaki Fujokyū (1887–1962) was a minor novelist and professor of medicine at Keiō University. Among his best known novels were *Shinryōbo yohaku* (The blank in the diagnosis notebook, 1922) and *Sanjūmae* (Before thirty, 1923).

involved any serious literary matters, mainly because Father's interest in this area was, as far as I can tell, merely avocational.[3]

After Father became Chief of Medical Staff for Internal Medicine at the university hospital, the head professor passed away and a conflict of opinion developed between the university authorities and the medical staff over the selection process for his successor. When the replacement candidate was subsequently chosen in accordance with the university's wishes, my father, who had represented the views of the medical staff, left the university to start his own practice. He was already married before all this happened, and his young wife, as I learned later, stood by her husband's bold determination in making his career decision. They did not need to worry about the expenses for starting his clinic, for Father's family was quite affluent. For his second son, whom he regarded as the pride of the village, Grandfather first acquired a piece of land in the Konnō-chō neighborhood of Shibuya Ward, then purchased an elaborate house on the market, disassembled it, and had it transported and rebuilt at the site.

Father had hoped to work at the university for a long time and was therefore not in a hurry to get his degree. He was not yet a doctor of medicine at that time, and his thinking was that clinical diagnosis and the ability to treat patients were different from doing the basic medical research required to get a degree. He probably never considered the fact that a successful private practice depends not only on the physician's ability to diagnose cases and treat patients but also on his academic qualifications. Still less could he imagine that oftentimes it might also depend on offering false diagnoses or concocting treatment methods, on handling people with tact, as well as on back-breaking hard work.

As a medical clinic doubling as a private residence, our house at Shibuya's Konnō-chō was an extraordinarily peculiar structure. It was surrounded by a tall board fence and, through the trees planted inside,

3. *Myōjō* (1900–1908) was a leading turn-of-the-century literary magazine edited by the poet Yosano Tekkan and published by Tokyo's Shinshisha. Among its prominent contributors were Kubota Utsubo, Ishikawa Takuboku, Sōma Gyofū, Yoshii Isamu, Kinoshita Mokutarō, Kitahara Hakushū, and Osanai Kaoru. Above all, the journal was dominated by the works of the Yosano couple Akiko and Tekkan and soon became a breeding ground for modern Japanese romantic poetry. The second and third runs of *Myōjō* were from 1921–27 and 1947–49, with contributors such as Mori Ōgai, Satō Haruo, and Nagai Kafū.

part of the second floor was visible to passers-by. The storm shutters, however, were closed even during the day. The front gate was open, to be sure; and on entering one came immediately into the vestibule. The sliding door at the vestibule on the north side was shut tight, creating a cold, uninviting appearance that would discourage any prospective visitor. A business sign was nowhere to be seen, and if one missed the ceramic doorplate with the words "Clinic of Internal Medicine" nailed to the gate pillar, one could easily mistake it for the residence of a retired government official. In a day, only one or two patients came through the door, and the neighborhood was usually dead quiet. What happened here was not the unfortunate case of a town doctor running out of luck. The fact of the matter was that this young man with a reclusive temperament simply endeavored to practice medicine as his heart pleased. In those days, the idea of setting professional boundaries between the doctor and the pharmacist had not yet turned into a controversy. A cordial and tactful town doctor could frequently make his living by selling medicine to a large clientele he had assembled without charging diagnostic fees. It was only natural for those accustomed to such doctors to be surprised to hear a physician declare all too bluntly that what they needed was not any immediate medication but just some rest. That was not the way the former samurai conducted business. I suppose the self-pride of this landlord's son and potential scholar could very well be described as a form of luxury built on his indifference to the mundane world and its conventions.

I was born and raised in this household after World War I. When I was a child, I often heard Father say, "A doctor is not a pharmacist!" and I also heard him say, "The difficult part is in the diagnosis. Once you've got the diagnosis, you can find out about the treatment in the books." When Mother said, "Don't you also have to consider the patients' feelings?" Father would reply, "A doctor is not a buffoon!" When a patient complained about the taste of his medicine, Father would say, "Sweet or bitter, you'd better take it because that's what you need."

"But it has such a bitter taste, so I skipped taking it two or three times . . ."

"Now that's too bad! If you don't follow my instructions, I'm not going to take any responsibility."

"I'm terribly sorry."

This was how the conversation would go. Later I even heard one of Father's patients complain, "I felt as though I was being reprimanded."

I can hardly remember seeing Father go into his office when a patient visited. I am quite sure that it happened, but it was not frequent enough to leave a strong impression in a child's mind. I do remember Father going out on house calls. When the telephone rang, Mother would answer it first and tell Father who it was. Father would then inquire about the patient's condition before deciding to pay a visit. He would call for the same old ricksha man, put into his black leather bag things like his stethoscope, reflex mirror, and syringe, and then walk out through the seldom-used vestibule door.

Among his house-call patients were some unusual individuals who had faith in this grumpy doctor with no flair for business. One of them was Tatsuno Kingo, the man who built Tokyo Station and made unique contributions in the history of Meiji architecture.[4] His eldest son was Professor Tatsuno Yutaka, who revitalized the Department of French Literature at Tokyo Imperial University. For two generations, Father was their family physician. I remember hearing Father speak proudly of Tatsuno the architect. "During the Great Earthquake, all the brick buildings in Tokyo and Yokohama collapsed, all except the structures Mr. Tatsuno built. Only his stood intact in the burned ruins. What a great accomplishment!" I never had the pleasure of meeting Mr. Tatsuno, but I did get to know Professor Tatsuno of the Department of French Literature. Not only did I attend his lectures on "Nineteenth-Century Literary Thinking," I also came to know him outside the classroom as an eloquent and high-spirited conversationalist with an endless flow of ideas. "Your father's a great physician," Professor Tatsuno said with his downtown Tokyo twang. "You know he's a direct disciple of Aoyama [Tanemichi], don't you? When he quit the university, they simply couldn't find anyone who could take Aoyama's place. Serves them right! Your father is a very good doctor, just a little testy, I'd say."[5] While I pondered his words, I wondered if they did not also impart his delicate

4. Tatsuno Kingo (1854–1919) worked in the office of William Burges in London after graduating from the Kōbu Daigakkō. Appointed as the first Japanese professor of architecture at the same college on his return in 1883, he designed the Bank of Japan's headquarters (1896) and the National Railway's Central Tokyo Station (1914). He was noted for his use of contrasting brick and stone and for his design of domes, a feature that came to be known as Tatsuno style.

5. Aoyama Tanemichi (1859–1917) was an eminent medical researcher, professor at Tokyo Imperial University from 1887 to 1917, and head of the medical faculty from 1901 to 1917. And in chapter 17 Katō reminisces about Professor Tatsuno.

compassion for a man whom the world could not accommodate. If indeed I did not misread his intention, I know of no one else who could, without unduly embarrassing the listener, deliver this subtle message with such flawless tact.

Among Father's frequent house calls were those to the main branch of a *zaibatsu* family. I remember they had three American-made automobiles, each with a different style, each with a chauffeur. One of them would always come to pick up Father. Sometimes, instead of the automobile, they would send a coach drawn by two horses. I was fascinated by the coach, and sometimes I would ride along with Father to the patient's house and wait until their meeting ended, when we returned by car. When the coach left our house, it went slowly up Miyamasuzaka, and once the road started its descent, the horses would start to pick up speed along the main street of Aoyama. On the paved road, the trotting sound grew louder as the coach began to shake. I would hold on to Father with one hand and gaze in fascination out the window at the buildings along Aoyama-dōri as if I were seeing them for the first time in my life: the original Eitarō shop, the depot at 7-chōme, the Aoyama Academy, the lanterns lining the front approach to the Meiji Shrine, and the endless row of small bungalows on both sides of the street.[6]

Father's association with the *zaibatsu* family continued after I entered middle school. For a doctor with only a small clientele, it appeared to be his main source of income. I did not know anyone from the main branch of that family. However, I was once invited to the house of the second or the third son of the second generation who maintained a separate household. The host was much younger than Father himself, and I heard that he was a painter. He lived in what looked like a palace with a wife who seemed to me young and beautiful.

"How do you feel these days?"

"Well, doctor, I still don't feel too well."

I listened to their exchanges by their side.

"If you continue to go out, I'm afraid you won't get well," Father said.

"Well, I'm used to going out every night."

---

6. The Eitarō shop was a famous confectionery, city streetcars stopped at the depot, and the academy was a private institution established in 1878 that developed into a university (Aoyama Gakuin Daigaku) in 1949. The Meiji Shrine was completed in 1920 in Shibuya's Yoyogi area and dedicated to the Meiji emperor and his mother.

"Are you that busy?"

"Oh no, I'm just busy having fun."

At that time I suppose I had just entered elementary school, and I was surprised to learn that anyone would be so set on a lifestyle that risked his own health just to have fun every night.

On our way home, Father said, "The head of the family told me he would rather see his son having fun with painting or music than meddling in business. That way, their wealth will grow naturally. He said the amount of money needed to support his son's habits is only minimal."

The defeat in the war and the Occupation changed those circumstances. Yet even before that, after the death of the head of the family, the second generation no longer cared anything about their father's old family physician. Father's relationship with this family thus came to a natural end.

My sister was born soon after me in the Konnō-chō house.[7] As Father and Mother had little work or socializing to occupy them, both were enthusiastic about educating their children. In order to prevent discriminatory behavior in any one child, they treated their son and daughter equally. Judgment after a quarrel would be handed down only after they had listened fully to both sides. Punishment was harsh considering the nature of the offense. Although they never hit us, they would sometimes lock us out of the house at night, refuse us a meal, or shut us up in a closet. Nevertheless, no punishment would befall us without a good reason, and they would always make sure that we understood what the reason was. They would never compromise their position and give in to our willfulness, nor would they make sweet promises to appease us. We had to follow our parents' instructions unconditionally, and they never allowed us to tell lies. Even today I can remember the gloomy darkness inside the closet in the Konnō-chō house and our sense of helplessness as we stood outside the storm shutters with the deepening shadows of the evening closing in on us. But I cannot remember getting any unfair punishment because of my parents' displeasure. Nor do I recall my parents' ever scaring us into submission by evoking an external authority such as, "If you do this, the policeman will come and get you" or "You'll be tormented in hell by King Enma." To me as a child, my family was a completely self-contained and secluded world in which I fully accepted the rules governing good and bad behavior. As long as I did not commit

7. Shūichi's sister, Hisako, was born in 1920.

a wrong deed, I did not have to worry about any impending punishment. But if I did do something wrong, then I could not expect to get away with it. I lived in a small, rational world, one I could comprehend. Things I could not understand belonged to the world outside.

On rare occasions, our relatives or Father's former classmates would bring their families to visit our Konnō-chō house. When their own children were crying and clamoring for candies, some mothers would look at Sister and me, saying, "How well-behaved your children are!" Needless to say, my parents were very pleased to hear that. As for me, I would look at the crying children around my age as if they were some exotic animals. And then there was this incident. On one occasion, our relatives had some sort of gathering at Grandfather's house on Miyama-suzaka. I was playing in the garden with cousins about my own age. Somehow I got into a squabble with one of them and I struck him. My uncle came out of the house and defended his own son without allowing me to explain myself. Not being accustomed to this kind of treatment, I looked on his action as a total miscarriage of justice perpetrated by a grown man armed with overwhelming physical strength against a child who was not yet old enough to go to elementary school. I abhorred this injustice. I soon forgot the reason for the fight, but for ten years I could not forget my sense of disgust. And until my uncle died of tuberculosis, I did not have the slightest goodwill toward him. Without his ever knowing it, his behavior challenged the very order of my universe. If I had been more exposed to the outside world during my childhood, I would surely have come across many similar challenges many times in many places. But before I went to elementary school, I had almost no such exposure. I grew up under the protection of my parents and knew less about the realities of the outside world than most other children my age. I was defenseless against malicious intent and intrigues, and I was sensitive to even the slightest breach of justice.

While both of my parents were enthusiastic about our education, they did not always concur when it came to educational philosophy. It was Mother who got worried about our staying home all the time with too little contact with other children. Out of this concern, she thought of the kindergarten at the Catholic girls' school that she herself had attended and where she had quite a few acquaintances. Once she got that idea, she tried to convince Father to let her take us there. Father, a stubborn atheist, did not welcome the idea of mixing his children's education with Christianity. On top of that, he had serious doubts about the effectiveness of kindergarten education itself. In the final analysis, their difference of opinion could perhaps be ascribed to their mutual dissatisfaction with each other's lifestyle. Mother was a city girl, and although she was not the flamboyant type, she enjoyed socializing with people. Father, on the other hand, had acquired the unpretentious mannerisms of his rural family despite its grand landholding status. He had no liking for wine or cigarettes and would rather spend his time reading at home. In any case, leaving aside my sister who was too young to go, they finally decided to let me try out the kindergarten experience. But for me, the new environment was not easy to get used to. With so many children, it was impossible for the Western nuns to give the same scrupulous attention I was used to with my parents. Since the nuns did not bother to secure my understanding—What a difficult child I must have been!—and when I could not get the nuns to understand my position, it meant, in effect, the breakdown of any negotiations. The school's playground was equipped with sandboxes and wisteria trellises for the kindergartners and I would stand in a corner and watch the girls in uniforms running about during recess time as the black-robed nuns moved among them. I would also listen curiously to the strange sound of the church bells echoing under the blue sky.

"I'm afraid he doesn't like to play with his friends!" one of the nuns told Mother in her accented Japanese when she came to pick me up. "He is just shy among strangers, Sister Ann. He will get used to it before long," Mother said. As I listened to their conversation, I wondered why it was necessary for me to get used to the other children and to join their ranks when I was not the least unhappy in my present situation. In the end I did not stay at the kindergarten for a long time, nor did I discover anything about the complexities of the world from the children there. I can fairly say that my kindergarten experience left in me only a series of strange and acute sensory impressions of Westerners in black attire, church bells, and young girls in uniforms swarming around the schoolyard.

It would be incorrect, however, for me to say that until the time I went to elementary school, the world of my sheltered childhood always revolved in a rational orbit. During my childhood I often suffered from swollen tonsils and fever. When the fever ran high, I would be besieged with nightmares. There was never any color or sound in them, and even the shapes of things became blurred. Although it was difficult to tell exactly what it was, there was something that resembled a gigantic wheel coming my way, slowly and noiselessly, and about to crush me. It was clear to me that if crushed, I would cease to exist and every bit of my world would be lost forever. But there was no way to escape regardless of how desperately I tried. The wheel-like object was so enormous that it nearly blocked out the sky. Even the gray sky itself turned entirely into a ponderous mass, looming and pressing closer every minute. The horror is impossible to describe, and just when I thought my entire body and soul were drained of any strength to resist, I would awaken from my dream. My whole body would be drenched in a cold sweat and I would be totally exhausted, and yet the dream remained real. Because the same nightmare recurred whenever I had a fever, I could even feel a premonition of the dream unfolding as I began to doze off. Sometimes, instead of being crushed by the wheel-like object, I found myself descending deeper and deeper into a whirlpool. The whole universe was turning in its vortex. I couldn't tell whether it was made up of a gas, a liquid, or some other substance. In any case, as it swirled, it sucked me into the depths of its bottomless abyss. I did not know what lay at the bottom. Probably nothing. But as my infinite descent continued, I was further and further removed from my world, a world which I could comprehend. The horror was exactly the same as when I was about to be crushed by the huge wheel-like object.

To be sure, I had other dreams as well. But as far as I can remember, they were no more than somewhat inauthentic reenactments of minor incidents in my everyday experience. These episodes were sometimes pleasant and sometimes not; but supernatural events did not occur, and neither did they cause me any great emotional disturbance. However, the horror in the two types of nightmares—I'll just call them that—was for a long time the only thing that terrified me both in my real life and in my dreams. What was it that horrified me so much in those nightmares? Was it death? Or was it the human society that stretched infinitely beyond the confines of my family? Or was it rather the unknown world, general matters beyond my comprehension? In any event, the horror seemed inseparable from the premonition of total destruction. Perhaps it signified the destruction of the rational order and, accordingly, of a world I could comprehend. If so, I have to say that the dark, turbulent, and opaque abyss of the irrational reality lurking beneath the rational order had already opened wide during my younger days, though it manifested itself only when I was suffering from high fever. But it was not until much later that I peered down into the abyss of real life.

When I awoke from my nightmares, Mother would wipe away my cold sweat and say, "So you had a bad dream again. Don't worry, it was only a dream." Her gentle voice delivered me from the world of terror to the routine everyday world under the quiet morning sun. Routine: that was how I felt as a child. Although I was not pampered, I was carefully sheltered, not only from the menacing realities of the outside world, but also from any problems inside the family, or even from questions a child might have about himself. Reality for me existed only in a faraway world. This is probably the only viewpoint of what people call "children from good families." Although assaulted again and again by nightmares, the child held tightly in the embrace of his parents was finally safe from being snatched away by the Prince of Darkness. I grew up as a sickly but well-disciplined child, sensitive to expressions of love, and filled with a peculiar sense of justice. On the other hand, I was at a complete loss when it came to interacting with other people. I had a strong sense of self-respect, but probably none of the charms of a child. With that I embarked on my journey.

4 Days of Illness

I was plagued by high fever and terrified by nightmares, and the bitter medicine and castor oil Father prescribed were near torture for me to take. The few days after my temperature had gone down, however, were not totally joyless. Father was careful to prevent relapse by forbidding me to go outdoors even long after I was on my way to recovery. Yet it was also during this time that I was able to monopolize Mother's scrupulous attentiveness, the source of my unsurpassed happiness. Moreover, I was permitted to eat my favorite foods during my recuperation.

My sickbed was in a small six-mat room at the western end of our Konnō-chō house. When the sliding door was opened, plenty of sunshine filtered in through the glass window over the veranda. Father would come in to check me once a day. Mother, on the other hand, would come more often, bringing me such things as food or medicine. Sometimes she would sit beside my pillow and read children's tales to me. This was how I heard such stories as "The Fight between the Monkey and the Crab" and "Urashima Tarō," as well as "Red Riding Hood," "Sleeping Beauty," and "The Little Prince." When she was gone and silence settled over my immediate surroundings, I would idle away the time watching the day go by. Lying in bed, I would begin to imagine how the unfinished story would unfold; I would look out through the window into the small yard and watch the sunrise, the sunset, and the changing contours of the stone lantern's shadow in front of the shrubbery. Sometimes, I could hear Mother playing the koto in a room at the other end of the house. We had a small crystal radio set in our house, but even deft manipulation of its controls would succeed only in making it produce just barely audible sound. Therefore, it never occurred to anyone to use it to listen to music. Grandfather, fond as he was of Western things, did have a hand-operated gramophone with a large trumpet-shaped speaker, the kind not many families had at the time. My encounter with music probably began with Mother's koto. Though its flowing notes did not stir my emotions, I liked its timbre and still do. Father played the *shakuhachi*, but its sound did not resonate with any joy or sadness in my heart. I think it was only when I got to know what was popularly known as *kayōkyoku*, or popular song-ballads, after I entered elementary school that I began to discover the connection between music and my own emotional life. Songs such as "Wine of Tears or Grief" and "Withered Eulalia Grass" moved me deeply. It was perhaps at that time that the name Yamada Kōsaku also began to surface in my world.[1] But I did not feel his impact until somewhat later.

The notes of the koto were not the only thing I heard as I lay in bed. Perhaps it is fair to say that my experience with music began with what Westerners today would call *la musique concrète*. When I was restricted to my sickbed, I would listen to children's tales and fantasize their ongoing plots. I would watch the same shrubbery in the garden over and over again or even gaze at all the minute details in the grain of the ceiling board. But I still had too much time on my hands. I listened intently to all the sounds that came into my six-mat room from the world outside. Even though I was not living in music, I was at least living in a world of sound. The sound of Mother's footsteps in the corridor as she ap-

---

1. "Sake wa namida ka tameiki ka" (Wine of tears or grief, 1931), by Koga Masao with lyrics by Takahashi Kikutarō and sung by Fujiyama Ichirō, ostensibly deals with lost love but reflects disillusionment with life (see Mita Munesuke's sociological study *Kindai Nihon no shinjō no rekishi* [Kōdansha gakujutsu bunko, 1978], 122); the song made a comeback after 1945. "Kare susuki" (Withered eulalia grass), or more accurately "Sendō kouta" (A ferryman's ballad, 1921), with lyrics by the poet Noguchi Ujō and music by Nakayama Shimpei, became a national hit in the early 1920s and inspired a Shōchiku Kamata movie (1923) starring Kurishima Sumiko and Iwata Yūkichi. • Yamada Kōsaku (1886–1965), one of Japan's most celebrated modern composers, fused elements of traditional Japanese music with techniques of composition he learned in Germany and tried to correlate melody to the intonation of Japanese. The contemporary composer Dan Ikuma maintains that Yamada and the poet-lyricist Kitahara Hakushū together made it possible for the Japanese to sing "the modern" for the first time ("Hakushū Kōsaku to Nihon no kakyoku," in *Utsukushii Nihon no jōjō* [Nihon Disk Library, n.d.], 16). Apart from his opera *Kurofune* (Black ships), his best-known works include "Aka tonbo" (Red dragonfly), "Pechika" (Stove), "Karatachi no hana" (Wild orange blossoms), and "Kono michi" (This trail). On the last two songs, see chapter 32.

proached my room filled me with anticipation; the noises coming from the kitchen at the other end of the house evoked all kinds of associations with food; and the sound of the vestibule door announced Father's departure on his house calls or his return from the outside.

And not a single day went by without my hearing the noise of the *nattō* peddler or the horn of the beancurd vendor from the outside.[2] Even men peddling things like *shijimi* clams, bamboo poles, and bread would all troll their voices with distinct rhythmic intonations as they walked past our residence. Into the six-mat room of our unusually quiet and fenced-in house, the noise from these peddlers conveyed with extraordinary vividness the varied rhythms of these working men. Today, the only sound that can be heard on opening the window in a suburban Tokyo home is the roar of traffic. In those days, however, Tokyo was still filled with the voices of living people. On a cold winter night, the approaching melody from the flute of the noodle vendor could be heard until its crisp notes gradually faded away into the distance. In an instant its melancholy tunes awakened the frosty roads, the clatter of geta as people hurried away with hands tucked inside their kimono, the warm glow coming through the window of the neighborhood bathhouse, and the crescent moon hanging high above the telegraph poles. And then there was the rattling sound of the storm shutters in the wintry wind and the distant whistle of the freight train passing through Shibuya Station. The notes from Mother's koto formed a part of my world of sound, a world perhaps not intrinsically different from what Verlaine called "the murmur of the street."[3] It was not music yet, but it certainly prepared me for it.

The child who seldom went out to play quickly learned to read. With this ability, my recuperation began to assume an entirely different meaning for me. I no longer felt bored even when I had to lie in bed for several days. When my parents bought me books, they did not seem to worry about my not reading them; instead, their worry was that I was reading too much. "Now, haven't you done enough reading already? Why don't you get a little more rest?" Mother would say. But as soon as she left, I would start to read again. This habit turned into a character trait, and even now, I sometimes have to remind myself, "Reading just takes away from

---

2. *Nattō* are fermented soybeans.

3. From the poem "Le ciel est, par-dessus le toit" in Verlaine's *Sagesse* (1881), bk. 3. The particular stanza reads, "Mon Dieu, mon Dieu, la vie est là, / Simple et tranquille. / Cette paisible rumeur-là / Vient de la ville."

writing time!" Needless to say, when I was well and could move freely about, reading was not my only source of pleasure. It became so only when I was sick in bed and couldn't find any other enjoyable things to do. Had I not been a sickly child, I would probably not have been so fondly attached to the printed word or thought of becoming a writer later on.

At that time, the eldest son of Father's elder sister was living in a room on the second floor of our Konnō-chō house. He was from the countryside and a student at Waseda University. The captain of the university's *kendō* club, he was heavily built and had extraordinary physical strength. While he seemed to be ill at ease with Father, he was very relaxed with Mother. If he returned early from the university, he would have a long conversation with Mother over a cup of tea before finally going off to his room. He was fond of children, and when we went out for a walk, he would let me and Sister each hang onto a finger and lift us off the ground. "Now, stop it! You'll exhaust him," Mother would say. "No, that's quite all right. It's really nothing," my cousin would say. With that, Sister and I would repeatedly pester him for more, and he would play along with us until he got tired. I suppose he was really fond of children. But perhaps he was even more fond of Mother. For a long time I idolized him. He was by far stronger than anyone I knew; he was nice to Mother, and he was the best playmate we could ever hope for.

In those days we often went shopping or took a walk after dinner to Dōgenzaka, then Shibuya's busiest spot. One time Mother took me, Sister, and my cousin along while Father, as I remember, was still out on a house call. At Dōgenzaka, Mother bumped into some drunks. She paid no attention to them. My cousin, as usual, was entertaining us with both his hands and had a nonchalant look on his face, but I am sure he was taking stock of the situation. As soon as he saw that the drunks' behavior was getting out of hand, he quickly let go our hands and stepped in between them and Mother. Pushing the drunks aside, he demanded sharply, "Go away!" The drunks were two middle-aged men. One of them shouted something and tried to grab my cousin's shoulder with one hand, only to find his arm twisted high behind his back, which immobilized him. The other drunk had already made good his escape. Releasing the man's right arm and pushing him away, my cousin said to Mother, "Let's go." After we returned home, Mother told Father the whole story, saying, "These people might have been carrying knives. I was really worried." "I'd say they should worry about themselves. When the man tried to

attack me, I was thinking of roughing him up, but then I decided not to,"
my cousin said with a smile. Although he was in the fourth rank in *kendō*,
he always said that he was not very good at judo. But considering his
physical prowess, I suppose he could easily handle two or three ordinary
men. And if he should decide to rough them up, there was no predict-
ing what would become of his challengers. After his graduation from
the university, my cousin returned to the countryside, got married, and
carried on the family's farming tradition. I seldom got to see him afterwards, but on the rare occasions when we visited him, we found that he
had turned completely into a young country gentleman and was busy
running a farming co-op.

"I'm not a big shot or anything, but now that I'm back in the countryside, people keep telling me how learned I am. Come to think of it, I
can read and write and nobody else here can. But at Waseda I spent almost all of my time practicing *kendō* and your father often scolded me
for that." Perhaps Father did scold him every now and then, but he
definitely did not dislike my cousin. Everyone in our family enjoyed his
company while he was living with us. During World War II when Tokyo
was devastated by fire, the first place we sought shelter was at his house.
At that time, my paternal grandfather and grandmother had already
passed away, and their house had ceased to be a possible asylum for us
in the midst of the war. My cousin and his wife never gave Mother any
cause for anxiety while she was attending my sister, who gave birth to
her second child at their house. When we were children, my cousin physically protected us when necessary; and after we became adults, we could
still always count on him if we found ourselves in trouble.

While I admired my cousin, I never imagined that I could one day
become as strong as he was. I was prone to illness and more frail than
other children my age. Perhaps I should say that my cousin's great physical strength made it possible for me to ignore the physical difference
between me and the other children. Naturally, it was expedient for me
to think like that.

Physical prowess was not the only thing we didn't have. When it
came to power, Father had absolutely none. When my Dietman uncle
became a prefectural governor, I was absolutely dumbfounded to see so
many government bureaucrats prostrating themselves before him.
Men with titles like section chief would treat even my aunt like a queen,
and some would even tie the shoelaces for their son, who was about my

age. To be sure, Grandfather also behaved like an emperor in his own house, ordering Grandmother and his maids around with his chin. But the character of their behavior was different. My uncle's entire family could give orders at will throughout the entire organization of the prefectural office. Although I could sense my uncle's vast authority, I only looked at his extraordinary behavior with detachment and without the slightest envy. I grew up without developing any particular attraction to what might be called masculine attributes, whether they were measured in terms of physical strength or worldly authority. I had no aspirations for the power of coercion or for a grandiose character. Rather, I yearned for the gentler and more delicate things in life, qualities others would, I suppose, describe as effeminate. I will have more to say about this later.

What kind of books did I mostly read as a child in my sickbed? Today, I can remember only the names of two authors. One of them was Harada Mitsuo, and the other was Kanetsune Kiyosuke.[4] Harada Mitsuo spent his career writing commentaries on subjects concerning the natural sciences, and he wrote many books for children. Thanks to him, by the time I started elementary school, I already knew that the human body was made up of cells, that many illnesses were caused by bacteria, and that human beings and monkeys probably shared a common ancestry. My first hero was not a celebrated Japanese warrior or Siegfried, but an Englishman named Charles Darwin. The first Latin word I learned was *Pithecanthropus erectus* (Java man). Harada Mitsuo talked about a myriad of phenomena in the universe, from the structure of the galactic system to an atomic model, from the experiments of Archimedes to those of Michelson and Morley. I was filled with curiosity, and I had no communication whatsoever with the world around me. The world was there not for me to change but only to interpret. Perhaps the books of Harada that I read did not provide accurate interpretations of the world,

4. Harada Mitsuo (1890–1977), a Tokyo Imperial University–trained botanist, popularized science subjects among children from the 1920s to the war years and founded journals such as *Kodomo to kagaku* (1917) and *Kagaku gahō* (1923). • Kanetsune Kiyosuke (1885–1957), musicologist and music critic and a graduate of Kyoto Imperial University's Department of Philosophy, did postgraduate work in classical Japanese music and the psychology of music before studying under Carl Stumpf at the University of Berlin in 1922–24. Among his major works were *Nihon no ongaku* (Japanese music, 1913) and *Nihon ongaku kyōikushi* (A history of Japanese music education, 1932).

but they gave at least the illusion that the interpretations were accurate. To me, that was almost analogous to poetic inspiration, something no children's tale could come close to having. With regard to the origin of human beings, only a long historical process could convince those who believed in the Bible to accept the theory of evolution. As someone who started off with the theory of evolution, it would probably take me a long time to recognize the significance of myths.

It was only coincidental that the books I read were concerned with the natural sciences and not with psychology, history, or the social sciences. Had I encountered another Harada Mitsuo of the social sciences, my curiosity in the organization of black African tribes might well have been stimulated in exactly the same way as my interest in the structure of the galaxies. The first foreign word I learned—for me it had the reverberation and mysterious aura of an incantation—might not have been the Latin word for the Java man but perhaps the contemporary German word *Gemeinschaft*, meaning a "closely knit kinship community." But I don't think there is much difference in these cases. As a child, I did not learn about the natural sciences from the books I read; rather I discovered the excitement in interpreting the world. For a long time afterwards, I never entertained any doubt that the world was capable of interpretation and that its structure evolved from a rational order.

I still remember the content of Harada Mitsuo's writings, but not anything about his literary style. With Kanetsune Kiyosuke, on the contrary, I have forgotten just about everything he said, but I can still remember very vividly the profound impression I had when I first came across his unique narrative style. In those days, almost all the authors of children's books would address their audience as "boys and girls." They would say something like "I am going to explain it in a simple way so that even boys and girls like you can understand." The style can be compared to that of someone who knows just about everything there is to know about the world and who allows himself to condescend to the level of children and speaks in a soft, coaxing voice. Of course, no one could expect to discover in such writings the kind of questions the authors themselves privately cherished, or their own thinking processes, or the real excitement and frustrations of their experience. That is to say, the authors' individual personalities were not revealed to their readers. But Kanetsune Kiyosuke alone did away with "boys and girls"; he addressed us as "my readers." He would say, "My readers! I am sure you have learned some of the elementary school songs at school.[5] It would be a big mistake if you think they are real music. Just listen to *Die Winterreise.*" In his writings, you won't find any coaxing narratives imparting harmless facts already universally known. He stood on the premise that there was no such thing as universal truth and appealed to his audience on what he himself truly believed. While I found myself almost at a total loss about what he was saying, I could nonetheless see that he was trying to make his case, that he had personally been moved by his experience, and that he had contemplated on his own accord. In the process, he displayed his wit and attacked with his sarcastic stings, taking the offensive and the defensive by turns. In short, he lives in his writings. It was in the writings of Kanetsune Kiyosuke that I discovered literature. And because I could not even remotely understand the content, perhaps I could even say that what I discovered was literature in its pure form.

Kanetsune Kiyosuke was the man who later stirred up quite a controversy in Japan for suggesting that "the pianist is expendable." Incidentally, Kanetsune Kiyosuke himself did not advocate this idea at the time. What he actually said was that "the piano will produce the same timbre whether it is played by Iguchi [Motonari] or walked across by a cat." And, notably, he also said, "I wish Japanese musicians would not just play Western piano pieces. I wish they would represent in their music the hearts of young Japanese in love in the same way Chopin infuses his own feelings of love into his compositions."[6]

I never met Kanetsune Kiyosuke in person, but I saw him a number of times near Shinano Oiwake Station on the Shin'etsu Main Line at the beginning of World War II. Perhaps Kanetsune had already evacuated from Tokyo, or perhaps he was only there for the summer to escape from the sweltering Tokyo heat. With disheveled hair the color of snow, the scrawny old man was wearing an informal kimono with a piece of string instead of an obi around his waist. The plumes of the tall

---

5. *Shōgaku shōka* refers to songs from the prewar elementary school curriculum since 1880 and specifically to the six volumes (1892–93) put together by Izawa Shūji, which consisted of Japanese folksongs, children's and Western songs, and Izawa's own compositions.

6. Iguchi Motonari (1908–83), renowned pianist and professor at Tokyo University of Arts from 1934 to 1946, was president of Tōhō Gakuen Daigaku, the founder of the League of Japanese Performers (Nihon Ensō Remmei) in 1965, and the author of *Waga piano waga jinsei* (My piano my life, 1977). • Kanetsune's rather sensational "Pianisuto muyōron" was published in 1935.

eulalia grass were swaying in the wind as dragonflies danced under the clear, blue Asama sky. It was near autumn, and the old man was strolling buoyantly along in the wind with a bamboo cane in his hand. It was unmistakably Kanetsune Kiyosuke I saw; but at the time I seemed to be looking at Hanshan and Shide in a Zen painting.[7]

The more I read and learned, the more questions I ended up having. The only person around me that I could talk with in an effort to dispel my doubts was Father. As our conversations grew more frequent, I naturally found myself strongly influenced by his way of thinking. The fact that he enjoyed chatting with his little son—for lack of other people to talk with—also contributed to the situation. "I wonder if it's appropriate to talk with a child about everything," Mother would say. But a vicious cycle had already begun. When I started elementary school, I realized right away that other children did not have the slightest interest in the kind of topics Father and I talked about. When I discovered that no other children had developed any capacity for inquiry, I enjoyed my conversations with Father even more. But the more often we talked, the more difficult it was for me to get satisfaction from talking with children my own age. And that was not all.

A scholar might apply positivistic thinking only in his study or laboratory, but Father—the potential scholar—went beyond that and applied it in his everyday life as well. According to him, spirits and ghosts were merely illusions. Grandfather's worship of the god of harvests was just a pitiable form of superstition. Mother's idea about the immortality of the soul seemed improbable, but even if the idea were true, the inability to verify it rendered any contemplation on the subject a waste of time. The deeds of larger-than-life heroes in legends and tales were simply embellished exaggerations. Nobody could possibly tell exactly what had happened since they took place so long ago. The love stories depicted in novels were totally unrealistic; only adolescent boys and girls who knew nothing about life would take them seriously. The competitive

7. Both celebrated and legendary T'ang dynasty Ch'an monks at Guo-qing Temple in Mount Tian-tai in the early seventh century, Hanshan (Kanzan in Japanese) and Shide (Jittoku) were thought to have been the human forms of Mañjuśrī (Monju bosatsu), Buddha's attendant on the left, and Samantabhadra (Fugen bosatsu), Buddha's attendant on the right. Their learning and literary talents, with their unworldly appearance and unconventional behavior, inspired drawings and portraits in China and Japan as well as a famous short story by Mori Ōgai in 1916.

instinct in human beings was already too strong, and the dynamics of group psychology could only intensify it. As a consequence, nothing could be more ludicrous than to deliberately divide elementary school-children into separate teams to make them compete. As a child, though I could only barely understand these ideas, I kept hearing them. It was not that I was precocious; I just learned the language of adults before I became an adult. And I had absolutely no doubt that adult language was a far more powerful tool than the utterances of children in any attempt to explain the world in a coherent way. Even if a child can adapt to adult language, it is not easy to go in the opposite direction. All adults have their own share of disillusionment, but most people are too preoccupied with their work to confront theirs. But Father was not a busy man, and instead of glossing over his disillusionments, he tried to theorize about them. As for me, I would say that under Father's overwhelming influence, I did not begin life by first romanticizing it and then gradually realizing its disillusionments. Rather, I anticipated disillusionment from the very start and then I gradually created my own romances. I have never felt more strongly about the utter silliness and naïveté of children's behavior than when I myself was a small child. I was considered "bashful among strangers" when I did not mix well with the other children at kindergarten. That I had no desire to join them in their games at the elementary schoolyard was because I couldn't endure the stupidity of children's play. But since a child has only a child's role to perform, I myself had to confront and deal with such childish behavior. That drove me to the brink of self-hatred. Naturally, I could not appreciate this situation, nor, I am afraid, could Father. It was Mother, and Mother alone, who did.

5   Life on Cherry Lane

Among my relatives' children, almost none went to the district elementary schools. Instead, they were sent to the "special" schools. The boys would go to places like L'Ecole de l'Etoile du Matin, Keiō Elementary School, or the elementary school affiliated with the Aoyama Normal School. The girls would attend Saint Maur or Sacred Heart.[1] That most of these schools had close Christian affiliations was probably not a matter of great relevance. The reason they were considered "special" was that their students came exclusively from middle-class families. Most of my relatives in Tokyo thought it unbecoming for "children from good families" to mix with the local city kids. But Father did not share that view. Quite the contrary, he thought that mixing with these children was anything but unbecoming. Indeed, the reason he did not hesitate to send his only son to the conventional district school was that he thought such interaction would be most valuable. His belief that money does not determine a person's worth, I suppose, also reflected his status as the second and not the eldest son of a landlord, a position that made it impossible for him to inherit the family fortune. Although I have no idea where he might have acquired it, he also held a kind of rational egalitarianism, an idea Mother could also accept because it did not conflict with her Catholic faith. No matter how poor the families of their son's schoolmates might be, when they came over to play, my parents would do everything they could not to make

---

1. The original Japanese name of the Ecole de l'Etoile du Matin is Gyōsei and of Keiō Elementary School, Yōchisha. For the girls' schools, the original Japanese name of Saint Maur is Futaba and of Sacred Heart, Seishin.

them self-conscious. But, of course, their very solicitous attention it-self only had the effect of sensitizing them to the disparities between their families and ours.

The classmates I played and fought with just like anyone else in the schoolyard underwent a subtle change in demeanor once they arrived at our gate. I would dash through the gate to get in, only to discover that my friends were not following. Looking back in surprise, I would see that some of them were about to run back home, while others were hesitant to come in. Since these were the same children who would al-ways fight to get into the classroom first, I was at a total loss as to why they had become so reluctant to come through our gate unless I went in first. "What a big house you have!" they would say. But it never oc-curred to me that we had a big house. All the other houses I knew at that time, be it Grandfather's on Miyamasuzaka or Father's country house, were much bigger than ours in Konnō-chō. Of course I was not ignorant of the fact that there were smaller houses in town, but the people who lived in those houses seemed so totally unrelated to my life. I was also surprised at the extraordinary astonishment on the part of my school chums over the light refreshments Mother prepared for us when we returned home. One time, one of them said in an impressed voice, "Wow, your mom's really nice!" To me, however, it was some-thing that I simply took for granted. In any case, it was difficult to play with those kids who ran away from my house without telling me why. Soon, I grew weary of their strange uneasiness, a complete and puz-zling departure from the way they acted when we were playing in the schoolyard. And so I met my classmates less and less often outside school.

That doesn't mean, however, that there were no exceptions. I doubt if I will ever forget a boy in my class who always did poorly at school and who was often scolded by our teachers. He was a big but skinny boy with clumsy movements and an oddly large head. Everybody was chummy with him because he had a likable personality. I once chanced on him at a place I would never have dreamed of.

One summer evening I went out for a walk along Dōgenzaka with Father and Mother in their casual kimono. In those days there were many night stalls in that area, and the smell of acetylene lamps filled the air along the narrow sidewalks. Jostling our way through the crowd, we stopped by the goldfish stall, peeked inside the shop selling wind-bells and potted morning glory, and watched the bargain sale by the banana

vendor and people playing *gomoku narabe*.[2] Stacking bananas into
piles on a crudely made wooden pedestal, the banana vendor was wearing a headband and waving an iron rod as he rattled away, "One pile is
only this much," he showed his outstretched fingers on his left hand,
"Cheaper than cheap! Folks, if you ain't buyin', it's your loss!" he
shouted as he hit the board with his iron rod. "Okay! Okay! I'll make
it an even better deal! Only this much!" Again he stretched out his
fingers. "I'm gonna lose money on this. Now this ain't no fair business
deal for me! But I'm desperate and I don't care any more!" Thereupon,
he would again proceed to cut his price by another half. Some customers
bought a whole pile, while others bought less, but the place was always
filled with an uproarious activity.

At the *gomoku narabe* stall, a middle-aged man was quietly waiting
for customers behind the chessboards set up with black and white pieces.
Every now and then, he would cry out to the passers-by, "Two more
moves on the black pieces and you can win!" as if he had just hit on the
idea. "How about it, Mister? You can win by just making two moves!
It's so easy! Just two moves. If you win, I won't charge you anything.
How about it? Hey, the young student over there! How about a game?"
But his young patron here and the student there were hesitant about
making their move. But then they just continued to stare at the chessboards with little intention of leaving soon. Even after Father had urged
me to keep going, I wanted to stay until somebody made his move so
that I could see whether my reading of the game was correct. At first
glance, the strategy seemed easy to unravel but actually was, I gather,
rather complicated.

Naturally, Dōgenzaka had other things besides night stalls. On both
sides of the street, brightly lit stores were bustling with crowds of shoppers going in and out. In addition, there were many eating places, all
jammed with people. I wanted to go into one of these places to see what
it was like. Perhaps it was because this particular night was very hot, and
I felt thirsty. We went into an ice shop for some shaved ice. The boy who
happened to take our order was none other than my classmate with the
big head. He had noticed me from afar, and even though we saw each

---

2. Dōgenzaka is a bustling area immediately west of Shibuya Station. • In
the chess game *gomoku narabe,* also known as *renju,* players try to outmaneuver
each other to be the first to arrange five in a row with black and white chess
pieces on a *go* chessboard.

other at school every day, he still wove his way nimbly through the crowd to come and greet me with a cheerful smile. Not only could the clumsy boy from school move with an agility one would never have imagined, but, compared with the wide-eyed child taken into the restaurant by his parents, my friend was already a full-grown adult who could maneuver his way with total ease in the cramped restaurant, handle his many customers, take their orders, and deftly bring them shaved ice. "I'm busy now. I'll talk to you later," he said in a friendly voice. "Busy now!" That's what he said. I, on the other hand, had never in my entire life experienced what it meant to be busy! The boy took the money from Father for our drinks. The world was actually revolving around the transaction between Father and the big-headed kid, and I was merely an onlooker. To me, this meant a rediscovery not only of my classmate, but also of my own place and my own role. I didn't know how to react to such a sudden and overwhelming discovery. The shaved ice with bright red, yellow, and green colors looked delicious on the outside, but it didn't taste good when I actually put it into my mouth.

Among the some fifty male and female students in my grade was a carpenter's son who had distinguished himself academically. Even during recess, he often spent his time studying. He was not very close to the other kids, but I was his friend as well as his rival in class. One day on our way home, he invited me to go to his place. The carpenter's home was on a rather wide street close to the school. It was so cramped with lumber, half-made storm shutters, and desks that some overflowed onto the sidewalk. The *doma* was littered everywhere with wood shavings, leaving no space to walk. In front of his house, my classroom rival suddenly said courteously, "Please wait here for a moment," and went inside himself. As there was no other entrance, passing through the work area seemed to be the only way to get in and out of his house. But he had no intention of showing me the inside. After a while, he reappeared and sat down on a wooden block on the sidewalk and said, "Here's fine." It was probably an autumn day with few pedestrians on the street, and the sun shone softly on the sidewalk. We saw neighborhood housewives and some students from Kokugakuin University in formal attire, their geta reverberating sharply as they strolled by. I can no longer remember what we talked about or what we did. At any rate, what took me by surprise after a while was a sharp voice from his house, calling my friend's name. It was a woman's voice, probably his mother's. He seemed quite used to this and slowly stood up without a disconcerted look on his face. "I've got to take care of the baby. You can stay longer, you know. You don't have to go. I just need to carry the baby on my back for a while." But the baby strapped on his back did not stop crying easily, making it almost impossible for us to continue our conversation. "When I'm at home, I just can't study," he said with a hint of melancholy in his voice. By then I had come to realize that our classroom rivalry was predicated on totally different circumstances, and I felt almost guilty about it.

Kokugakuin University was quite far away from my elementary school, but Jissen Girls' School was right next to us. From the corridor windows on the second floor, I could often see girl students practicing with their long swords (*chōtō*) in their gymnasium. For a long time, the image I had of female students was that of girls running around waving their *chōtō*, their sleeves held up with a cord, shrilling "Eh-i-i-i."

Not far across the street was the residence of the royal Korean Yi family. The place was always so very quiet that one could hardly tell whether people actually lived in it. A little further down the road from the Yi residence was a rather large vacant lot surrounded by tall wild orange shrubbery. A madman clad in rags used to frequent the place. He would approach the children with a thin smile and then expose himself. The kids would all jeer at him, but I only found the experience unpleasant. When I was a child, I learned from Kitahara Hakushū and Yamada Kōsaku to appreciate the beauty of wild orange blossoms, not from that empty lot.[3]

Near our school was a Hachiman shrine where many students went to play sham baseball, wrestle, spin tops, fly kites, or play *menko* cards.[4] It was on my way to and from school, but I never participated in their

---

3. Kitahara Hakushū (1885–1942), a celebrated and versatile modern poet who wrote free verse, *tanka, haiku, zuihitsu* (random essays), and lyrics for folk and children's songs, was one of the brightest stars in Yosano Tekkan's poetry group, Shinshisha. The music for some of his nine hundred lyrics for children's songs came from such talented composers as Nakayama Shimpei ("Sunayama," or Sand dunes) and Yamada Kōsaku ("Karatachi no hana," or Wild orange blossoms; "Kono michi," or This trail). He started *Pan no kai* (The society of Pan) with Yoshii Isamu and Kinoshita Mokutarō in 1908 with an impressionistic, lyrical style that contrasted with the prevailing naturalistic mode. His works include *Jashūmon* (The heretics, 1909), *Omoide* (Remembrance, 1911), *Kiri no hana* (Paulownia blossoms, 1913), and *Shirahae* (Southerly wind, 1934) (see Margaret B. Fukasawa, *Kitahara Hakushū: His Life and Poetry* [Ithaca: Cornell East Asia Series, 1993]). On Yamada Kōsaku see chapter 4, note 1.

4. The Hachiman shrine is dedicated to the Ōjin emperor, the fifteenth in the

games. They knew a lot of words and phrases that I had never even heard of before, not from my parents nor from school. They knew how to do battle with their tops equipped with iron wheels; they were experts in the game of *menko;* and they took no notice of children like me. Among them was a strong, muscular boy who acted as the leader of the group, with all the other kids following his whimsical orders as his subordinates. I was not particularly eager to join their company, partly because it was they who chose to ignore me and partly because I knew that in their world I was a nobody. In the classroom, the applause went to the children who could read the state-approved readers, not those who excelled in the game of *menko.* On the premises of the Hachiman shrine, however, those giving orders were the expert *menko* players, while the ability to read state-approved readers was not worth a penny. I did not have to make a choice between the two because, more accurately put, I had already made it from the start. Perhaps what I did not understand was that the society I chose and the values it embodied were in fact totally different from those in the children's world.

I had no real interactions with the local city kids at the district elementary school. If initiating such interactions was difficult for me, it was even more so for the local children. To begin with, as the only son of a doctor, the clothes I wore were different from theirs. When I opened my lunch box, not only did I have pickled *ume* and salted parched sesame seeds, I also had an egg and some meat for supplements. I lived in a house with a gate, and I knew how to read before I entered school. On the other hand, I knew nothing about the latest popular movie, about what my parents did when they went to bed, or even how to play the *menko* game. Far from being a habitual absentee from school and the object of the teachers' fury, I was treated with great attentiveness. In short, I was merely an outsider who happened to have strayed into their world by mistake, and there was little doubt that the other children would never think of treating me as one of their own.

However, I was not the only middle-class student at school, and I did

---

line, as the primary deity (and to his mother, Empress Jingū, and Hime Ōkami; they form its trinity of war gods). It was the earliest to incorporate both Shintō and Buddhist practices, giving rise to the title *Hachiman daibosatsu* for the Hachiman deity. • *Menko* is a children's game using round or square pieces of cards with different illustrations on one side. The idea is to strike at your opponent's card on the ground with your own or try to overturn it.

manage to make some friends. One of my classmates was the daughter of a captain from Japan Steamship Company, and she was the same age as I. The captain was away at sea most of the year. Without him at home, his wife probably found her young daughter a good conversation partner. This girl knew a lot of things I had never heard of before. She had a habit of saying, "You are so dumb! You don't even know that?" She would tell me all sorts of things like, "The reason why that teacher doesn't come to school is that she's pregnant," or "Looks like our principal is going to go abroad this time. But this is the election year, so it must be hard on him." Of course, I had never heard of the word "election," much less imagined any relation between the election for the district's council membership and the business of an elementary school principal. "You are so dumb! You don't even know that? Well, come to think of it, I don't quite understand it myself," she said nonchalantly. Her words could be pungent when it came to personality appraisals— things like, "That kid talks big, but, you know, he really doesn't quite know what he's talking about. After all, it's just all baby talk," or "Your dad's nice; but why does he have to look so sullen all the time? But then if he drinks and becomes all too jolly, that's no good either."

She was high-spirited, chatty, and sharp-tongued, but there was no meanness or the slightest trace of sentimentalism in her. Our friendship lasted a long time. It was she who introduced me to Akutagawa Ryūnosuke soon after I entered middle school.[5] "Oh, you are so ignorant! You mean you haven't even read Akutagawa Ryūnosuke yet?" She then loaned me a thick anthology of Akutagawa's works. After I finished reading it, I still wanted more, and so I saved a year's allowance and bought

---

5. Akutagawa Ryūnosuke (1892–1927) is one of modern Japan's preeminent short-story writers whose career epitomized the intellectual ambiguities, moral skepticism, and literary itinerary of many intellectuals in his generation. Many of his haunting and carefully crafted stories, at once witty, imaginative, and sarcastic, are inspired by his wide reading of classical Chinese and Japanese literature as well as Western writers from Pascal, Flaubert, Maupassant, France, and Baudelaire to Tolstoy, Dostoyevsky, Strindberg, Swift, and Shaw. Witness his innovative parodies "Aru hi no Ōishi Kuranosuke" (A day in the life of Ōishi Kuranosuke, 1917) and "Yabu no naka" (In the grove, 1922), as well as the trenchant social satire *Kappa* (1927) or extended aphorisms such as *Shuju no kotoba* (Words of a dwarf, 1923–25) and "Aru ahō no isshō" (The life of a certain fool, 1927). Other writings focus on representations of his life, such as *Daidōji Shinsuke no hansei* (The early life of Daidōji Shinsuke, 1925), or his disturbed mental state before his suicide at the age of thirty-five, an act he himself attributed to his "vague sense of anxiety" about the future.

a set of Akutagawa's collected works. She later became a good friend of Sister's, and they continued their friendship after both of them got married. As time went by, I seldom saw her, but whenever we did meet, she was always her cheerful and acrimonious self. Once when I returned to Japan after spending some years in Europe, she met me at my sister's house and told me something about a friend of mine in Tokyo. This was the first time I had heard anything about him for a long time. "Oh, you're such a dunce! Oops! Pardon me. But, mind you, you might be having what's called the Occidental dementia syndrome." "Right! You know, he *has* been away for three long years!" Sister said.

The road from the Hachiman shrine to school was lined with old cherry trees. In the spring, they had exquisite blossoms. Along Cherry Lane[6]—that was what people called it—there were a few shops here and there among the residential houses. Students would go there to buy pencils or notepads or to play and kill time if school finished early. Unlike the vacant lot with the wild orange shrubberies, the street was not far away from the downtown area, and unlike the precincts at the Hachiman shrine, it was not a playground exclusively for boys. On Cherry Lane there were boys, girls, housewives running the stationery shops, delivery boys from noodle shops passing by on their bicycles, and postmen making their route. Because of its proximity to the school and unlike places such as Dōgenzaka, Cherry Lane was both an extension of the school campus and, unlike the school campus, a link to the activities in town. I cherished the time I spent on Cherry Lane, that intersection between two worlds, a place where children and grown-ups coexisted and where the world unknown to me provided just the right kind of stimulus to my familiar surroundings.

In those days, I used to take Cherry Lane, pass through the Hachiman shrine, and follow the chain fence surrounding the Nagai residence before coming close to our house in Konnō-chō. The Nagai residence was built on a huge lot with several Western-style wooden buildings. At the end of the 1920s, they were leased to a Western family. Through the chain fence and between the Western-style buildings I could see carefully manicured lawns and flower beds, and foreign children playing. On one occasion a huge dog appeared, and on another an old woman was pushing a baby buggy. I also saw a big convertible carrying several men and women to the front of the house before scurrying away. The way

6. The Japanese name of Cherry Lane was Sakura Yokochō.

the people inside exchanged greetings, their clothes, their movements, and their facial expressions were all totally different from those of the world outside. Since we could not hear their conversations, we had the impression that we were watching an incredible pantomime. I used to observe them on my way to and from school. Even though several children clutching the chain fence were peeking in from the outside, the foreigners, on their part, paid absolutely no attention to us and never looked at us. The chain fence was not that tall, and if we had wanted to climb over it, we could have done so. That nobody ever attempted to do so had to do with the fact that it was not just a physical barrier but also a psychological one. The Westerners never cast a glance at us. For them, we did not exist. The chain fence at the Nagai residence was the symbol of the impossibility of any mutual communication.[7] It was true that Grandfather used to joke around with his Italian friends, but he was not me. Speaking for myself, I was firmly convinced that not only was there absolutely no point of contact between the lawn at the Nagai residence and the rain-soaked muddy road on Cherry Lane, but there was no conceivable way of establishing any relationship in the first place.

In one of the houses on Cherry Lane lived a girl who went to my elementary school. She was tall and elegant, prettier than anyone else I could imagine. But we never had even a single conversation. She was like a queen, always surrounded by her admirers. As I was looking at her from a distance, I dreamed of how wonderful it would be if I could be alone with her. But I also realized that even if I could be with her, there was nothing we could talk about, and in the end, it would just be impossible for her to like me. The sharp-tongued daughter of the sea captain said, "You are so stupid! What's so great about her? She's just a blockhead putting on airs!" I had to confess that the same thought had crossed my mind, and what she said could well be true. But it hardly changed my heart at all for the queen on Cherry Lane. On my way back from school, I couldn't help feeling somewhat disappointed if I didn't see her frolicking with her entourage of admirers halfway down the road and waving good-bye to them when she went up the stone steps in front of her house.

7. The writer Yasuoka Shōtarō reminisces that as a young boy he too used to walk past the Nagai residence on his way home after elementary school and remarks on the total absence of communication between himself and the foreign children inside it. Even if the latter had taken the initiative to talk to him, Yasuoka confesses, he would have run away (see his "Saru kara mita *Hitsuji no uta*," in *Geppō 12, Katō Shūichi chosakushū* [Heibonsha, 1979], 14: 4–5).

Many years later, in the middle of the war, Cherry Lane often came to my mind. In those days I was occupied with writing rhymed verses in Japanese, and I composed several poems about Cherry Lane following the rhyming pattern of the rondel popular in sixteenth-century France. Among them, "Cherry Lane," "My Love of Yesterday," and "We Could Meet No More" were composed in rhymed verses. But was that love? I suppose the answer would partly depend on how one defines "love"; and of course one's definition is necessarily shaped by one's experiences. Speaking from my own, I don't think I can call it that. But undoubtedly the experience tells a great deal about me at that time, and perhaps even much about me afterwards. I was too timid to approach the object of my desire, and what I wanted often belonged to a world in which I could never play a part. At my district elementary school, what I was learning about was not society, but my own position in it.

6 Honor Student

Elementary school was not a place that required a great deal of intellectual effort. I was already accustomed to reading, and none of the many new things we had to learn was particularly difficult to understand. On the other hand, I was sadly lacking in physical dexterity. I was completely hopeless when it came to gymnastics, and I had no hope of becoming a skillful painter or a good singer. The human head I made with clay bore absolutely no resemblance to what it was supposed to be.

"What's this?" said my teacher. "Whose head could it be? It doesn't seem to look like anybody's . . ." The class burst out laughing.

"Tell me, what is this?" the teacher again demanded, satisfied that he had made the class laugh.

"That's a Neanderthal man." At a loss for an answer, I said whatever came to mind.

"A what?"

"A Neanderthal man."

"What on earth is that Neander thing you're talking about?"

"I think it was the progenitor of modern man at a more advanced stage than *Pithecanthropus erectus.*"

"Is that right?" he muttered, looking displeased. "In any case, try to make a human head!"

To the teachers, I was probably one of the easiest students to teach but also, I fear, one of the most presumptuous.

Although an elementary schoolteacher had to teach everything on the curriculum, each had his or her own favorite subject. I could not develop a close rapport with teachers who liked gymnastics or emphasized drawing and calligraphy. But I felt blessed if my class teacher was someone interested in the sciences. Matsumoto *sensei* was certified by the old middle school system as a biology teacher.[1] Like a magician, he demonstrated before us how a thin wire ignited like fireworks in a glass jar filled with oxygen, how a small chip of sodium spun in water like a fish, and how the heart taken from a frog beat in Ringer's solution. I was totally fascinated by these experiments. Because he was patient with whatever questions we children might have, I would stay behind after the other students had scattered to the playground and listen to him as he talked about things like chemical reactions, the combination of molecules, and osmotic pressure. Once when he was using a diagram to explain the structure of the heart to me, he remarked, "On this subject, your father is the expert." He had a pale complexion and a small build, and his manners were always gentle. He spoke slowly and never shouted at us. There was an aura of loneliness about him, but I liked his personality and respected his knowledge. He had a habit of saying, "We must always look carefully at the facts." The superficial knowledge I had acquired from Harada Mitsuo's popular science books was utterly inadequate to explain everyday phenomena, I realized, no matter how simple they might at first appear. "That is not quite correct. The correct answer is a little more complex, though," Matsumoto *sensei* would say. In quite a few instances the factual explanation was too difficult for me to follow. Yet I was eager to find out the answers, and I suppose Matsumoto *sensei* could appreciate that as well. Often, the two of us would continue to talk in the empty classroom until dusk surprised us.

I knew the experiment on the frog's heart was not particularly stimulating to the other children in the class, nor did Matsumoto *sensei's* colleagues exhibit any special interest in the subject. This probably explains why there was a dispassionate, almost resigned tone in Matsumoto *sensei's* manner of instruction. Perhaps my rapport with him had something to do with our awareness that the two of us cherished different interests than the people around us. I was, to borrow a Western word, my teacher's "protégé," and I was well aware of it. In the children's world, being a teacher's protégé—a teacher's pet—was probably a disgusting thing. What I did not understand was why it was so.

Once there was a small incident. In those days there was a small bakery in front of the school gate next to a stationery shop. Children who had not brought their lunch to school were allowed to purchase bread

1. Matsumoto Kenji.

from the bakery during lunch break, but otherwise we were strictly forbidden to go outside. Some of us thought if we dashed out to get the bread and hurried back while our teacher was not looking, there was a good chance we might not get caught. Certainly we also calculated that we could take advantage of a class teacher who had never given his students a rough scolding. But our forbidden excursions were discovered and Matsumoto *sensei,* who saw through our intent, took an unprecedentedly severe stand. Those of us who had gone outside the gate were ordered to step forward. That made up the majority of the male students in our grade. Then each of us was grilled with questions, such as "Who suggested it first?" or "Why did you go along?" While some of the students did manage to keep their composure, the majority turned pale. My own knees were trembling. I could think of no way to explain away my behavior, and I had no idea what punishment was in store for me. "Who suggested it first?" I answered that I didn't know and I had only followed the crowd out.

"You knew the regulations, didn't you?"

"Yes, I did."

"When the crowd was running out, why didn't you try to stop them?"

"..."

"Didn't you try to stop them but couldn't?"

"..."

"Didn't you follow the crowd out in order to try to stop them?"

When the interrogation got to this point, it suddenly dawned on me—the apparent harshness of the questions notwithstanding—that a possible avenue of rescue was being pointed out to me. If I answered "yes," I could immediately go free. But that answer was contrary to the truth. But if I said, "No, I wasn't trying to stop the crowd," there was no telling what punishment might lie ahead. In addition, I'd be admitting either that I hadn't been smart enough to grasp the purpose of this line of questioning or that I was too stubborn to accept a helping hand even when I recognized it. I didn't want to acknowledge either. I was confused and didn't know what to do. A moment passed. Then I said in a low voice, "Yes, I did."

"I'm done with you now. You may go." At the time the words almost did not register with me. As I walked away emancipated, the only thing I could feel behind me was the gaze of the other lined-up students who had committed the same offense. Their invisible gaze did not censure me for having lied but rather conveyed their contempt for my betrayal. Meanwhile I was filled with intense self-disgust and self-hatred. The teacher in those days was authority itself. On the contrary, whatever the cause of their punishment or the nature of our friendship, those lined-up students were my comrades who stood powerless in the face of authority. Years later on several occasions—for instance in 1960, when I encountered groups of students coming out of the university main gate at Hongō-dōri holding up signs reading "Opposition to the Japan-U.S. Security Treaty!"[2]—I was reminded of the children dashing out of the elementary school for bread and my self-hatred for collaborating with the teacher.

Toward the end of the 1920s Shibuya was not only served by the Tokyo Loop Line and the city-run trains, it was also the terminal for such newly constructed subway routes as the Tamagawa line and the Tokyo-Yokohama Express Line. Tokyo was beginning to expand beyond the Tokyo Loop Line and Shibuya was on its way to becoming one of the busy shopping areas on Tokyo's periphery. The school I went to was one of those newly built to accommodate the growing population in Shibuya Ward. The buildings on campus were constructed with reinforced concrete, a rarity for elementary schools. The new principal was a politician who apparently was also very good at the art of budget negotiations. Later on, he resigned to become a council member of the ward. The school put those of us who had reached school age into the first grade, while second to sixth graders were transferred from Shibuya's other heavily enrolled elementary schools. That was how the school got started. The transferred students aside, our principal, a shrewd operator, had apparently thought of boosting the school's reputation by raising the academic performance of his first class of graduates. What this meant became apparent to me as I advanced from the fourth to the fifth grade.

Toward the end of fourth grade, we were divided into two groups: those who would advance to middle school and those who would not. Because there were parents who, for economic reasons, did not wish their children to advance in their studies, this division was not necessarily based on the students' academic performance. Boys and girls who did not intend to go on to middle schools were combined into a single class, whereas those contemplating advancement were divided according to sex into two classes. During the last two academic years, the class with male

2. Details about the 1960 student demonstrations against the security treaty's renewal are described in chapter 40.

students was assigned young and newly appointed teachers. The principal entrusted the students to these energetic, up-and-coming professionals for two years of rigorous training in the hope that some could get into the elite middle schools. These young teachers who had just graduated with distinction from normal schools were bursting with self-confidence and ambition. They became deeply committed to their assigned mission and immediately turned themselves into superb animal trainers in the competitive game of entrance examinations.

When we advanced to fifth grade, we were quickly shown the neatly established rankings of middle schools according to the difficulty of their entrance examinations. The first-rate schools were the middle school division of the seven-year higher schools and the First Tokyo Metropolitan Middle School (Tokyo Furitsu Daiichi Chūgakkō); the second-rate schools were the Army Junior School and others; whereas the third-rate schools and below weren't even worth mentioning. Elementary schools had rankings too. Schools such as Seiji Elementary in Hongō and the one affiliated with the Aoyama Normal School sent many of their graduates each year to the first-rate middle schools and were regarded as first-rate elementary schools. Our aim was to catch up with and surpass the performance of Seiji or Aoyama. It was completely out of the question to wait until the sixth grade to begin studying for the examinations. Preparation had to start that very minute, so our animal trainers declared, and if necessary, instruction could continue during the summer vacation. The times assigned for gymnastics or drawing were frequently switched in favor of the required subjects for entrance examinations. Even after the official school hours, instruction would continue until dark. By nightfall, the only people who remained in the large school buildings were the custodian on duty and us. Not a soul was to be seen in the spacious schoolyard where the children had been playing earlier in the day.

Inside the classroom, however, a vibrant energy filled the air. A sense of solidarity spread through the whole group as we focused our best efforts toward a single goal, however peculiar that goal might be. To be sure, that solidarity included only those who could perform to the satisfaction of their trainers. Half the students became exhausted in the course of the vigorous training, lost interest, or perhaps grew skeptical about the very purpose of the whole enterprise. Nonetheless, the merciless and feverishly enthusiastic teachers did not waste their energy with those who in their judgment were unlikely to do well in the competitive entrance examinations. They neither asked them questions nor even bothered to scold them. Their fury was not directed at students who did not understand their questions, only at those who offered the wrong answers. The former were nothing more than shadows; it was us, the serious competitors, who really mattered. And we were fully aware of it. On one occasion, an animal trainer said, "Today's supplementary instruction is going to take some time. Those who wish to go home may go!" As the cornered Henry the Fifth called out on horseback, "He which hath no stomach to this fight, Let him depart."

By the time I passed through the school gate after the supplementary session and walked down Cherry Lane on my way home, the air was already filled with the smell of dinners being prepared. There were lights in the windows of several houses. There were no children on Cherry Lane at this hour. Instead I passed people returning home from work, the beancurd man blowing his flute as he walked by, and young girls hurrying on their way to the neighborhood bathhouse. During the course of my solitary walks home I discovered the intricate web of leafless cherry branches stretching out into the early evening sky. (Twenty years later I would again encounter this enchanting world of leafless branches against the evening sky in a foreign city along the banks of the River Valmy.) What I got in my supplementary lesson might have been unimportant, but at least I developed a profound affection for Cherry Lane in the evening twilight.

On the grounds of the Hachiman shrine, the children who had been playing baseball or *menko* cards were about to call it a day since it had become too dark to see. When I quickly passed the children, I no longer had any interest in the things they were doing. On festival days, however, the Hachiman shrine was the scene of unusual activity from evening on. The stall vendors had already finished setting things up. Some were going to sell multicolored candies or *oden*, some were spit-roasting, others were busily making preparations for the night, taking cheap necklaces and paper crafts out of boxes or adjusting their acetylene lamps.[3] Inside the show tent, gaudy drawings of long-necked monsters, dwarfs, and Siamese twins had already been posted in place; only the noisy touting for customers had not yet started. On the platform

3. *Oden* is a popular Japanese hotchpotch with such ingredients as taro, boiled eggs, tofu, fish cakes, and daikon.

wrapped with red and white cloth, the drums alone had been put in place earlier, and men wearing headbands had been taking turns beating them since daytime. There was also a magician's booth and a big tent for equestrian acrobatics. Several coaches were parked there, while a few men were stretching ropes or driving piles around the tent. The crowd that was expected to swarm the place after sundown had not yet appeared. As I walked through a festival that was about to begin, the sense of anticipation gave me much more satisfaction than the actual hustle and bustle of the festival itself could. After my supplementary lesson, I felt satisfied with myself for having accomplished more than the average student. The world of the festival did not concern me or give me any sense of oppressive anxiety. My preoccupation was to pass the middle school entrance examination. The festival, the drums, and the Hachiman shrine were none of my concern. I was completely focused on my primary mission.

Competitive examinations seemed to inspire in me the same interest that a sports meet would for many other children. As a sickly and inept child, competing in examinations certainly put me in a more favorable position than any sports event. However, when I entered fifth grade, I was by no means entirely satisfied with the policies of my school, run as it was like a preparatory school for examinations. For example, I thought it unfair that the carpenter's son, who until then had been my worthy classroom rival, was assigned to a class that would not advance any further. Once, at a gathering of Father's friends at our house, I mentioned how I felt about it. One of Father's friends was an army doctor who enjoyed a good argument.

"I am afraid this can't be helped," he said.

"But that boy has been doing better than me. Don't you think it's odd that he's not allowed to go on with his studies?"

"No, it's not that the school prohibits him from continuing with his studies. The school opens its door to everyone fair and square."

"Then who did?"

"I'd say it's his father. It takes money to send your kid to school."

"Does that mean it's his father's fault because he is poor?"

"No, I don't mean that. But you have to know that there are many poor people in this world. If you're willing to work, then you can lift yourself above poverty. Look at me. I was poor once, but I worked really hard in school. The poor will continue to be poor because they don't try to break away from their poverty."

Since my friend and I went to different classes, we gradually saw less and less of each other. Sometimes when I chanced on him on my way home and invited him to do something with me, he would try to decline, saying, "I'm different from you. My family needs my help at home."

It also pained me when I had to leave Matsumoto *sensei's* class. When the time came for class promotion, I was secretly hoping that I could have Matsumoto *sensei* as my class teacher for both my fifth and sixth grades. As it turned out, he was assigned to teach the non-advancing class consisting of both male and female students. "Well, it's too bad for *sensei*," the daughter of the sea captain remarked. Yet Matsumoto *sensei* himself continued to conduct his experiments in his own quiet way, and when I came to see him, he was happy to explain his work to me. "You look busy with your study for exams," he once said to me with a smile. "Sometimes, it's also fun teaching a class with boys and girls, you know. I don't have to worry about the pressure as much." However, before I knew it, an unexpected turn of events enabled me to have Matsumoto *sensei* as my teacher once again.

By the time I was midway through the fifth grade, Father came up with a curious idea. In principle, the elementary school took six academic years to complete, but it was possible to advance to middle school if one passed an aptitude test at the end of the fifth year. I do not really know the reason why Father chose to skip one year of my education, but apparently he wanted his son to at least try. In order to take the aptitude test, a child had to study the sixth-grade curriculum at home while doing the fifth-grade at school. It was impossible to accomplish this alone, so Father decided to ask Matsumoto *sensei* to be my private tutor. "Is it really necessary to go this far?" Mother asked. But I did not feel miserable at all. If I could please Father and Matsumoto *sensei* just by doing that, I was willing to try. When I showed him that I could memorize the names of all the Japanese emperors, Matsumoto *sensei* was amazed. Perhaps never since that time have I devoted myself to such an unrewarding and pointless intellectual pastime. I did not know what life was all about. For a long time, I had no interest in most of what others called "children's games." There was no reason for me not to concentrate my efforts on playing the examination game. My parents would do everything they could to help their son. Father even taught me elementary algebra himself. I was able to apply the secret techniques I learned from him in class and had fun instantly solving difficult mathematical problems.

When my elementary school life ended one year sooner than usual, Father, Mother, and I could see how happy Matsumoto *sensei* was for having accomplished his mission as my private tutor. But I was saddened to leave my old school, my classmates, Cherry Lane, and Matsumoto *sensei*. While I was not dissatisfied with myself for having passed the examination, my satisfaction was a hollow one. I had been well prepared for the entrance examination to middle school, but I was not well prepared to be a middle-school student.

7 Five Blank Years

In the early 1930s, the First Tokyo Metropolitan Middle School had just moved its Hibiya campus to its new site in Hirakawa-chō. The new campus consisted of not only the original middle school but also the newly created seven-year Metropolitan Higher School, which did not yet have a campus of its own. Also attached to the five-year middle school was the Division of Supplementary Instruction, a kind of preparatory school where students studied for another two years. The number of classrooms was insufficient to meet the demands of the new campus, and even the gymnasium was filled with students. During recess students in black, close-buttoned uniforms created a clamorous scene in the schoolyard. Youths in their late teens mingled and jostled with students who had just come out of elementary school. It was so crowded that even teachers with business at hand had difficulty passing through. Naturally, freshmen like us were often squeezed into corners. No one bothered to pay any attention to us; in fact, we were looked on by the upper-class students as little more than a nuisance.

At the elementary school, I had the impression that our class was the center around which the whole school revolved. Moreover, in my case at least, even the whole family revolved around the children. That had given rise to my Ptolemaic view of the world. The middle school and its schoolyard dynamics compelled me to adopt a Copernican world view, so to speak. The sun no longer revolved around me. In those days, First Metropolitan Middle was already well known for feeding many of its graduates into the First Higher School. The new district elementary school's emphasis on entrance examinations could not even approach First Metropolitan Middle's fervor as a preparatory school. If preparation for entrance examinations at the former could be compared to an artisan handcrafting an object, that of the latter might be likened to production with industrial technology and corporate management. Among the teachers, a number of veteran specialists for entrance examinations would train the upper-class students, while the lower division students were left to the newly appointed teachers or oddball types who did not quite make it into the specialist rank. Our classroom instruction lacked enthusiasm, and the curriculum was boring. There was not even a place for us to play during recess. Ignored half the time, the freshman students could not help but feel that they were looked on as little more than a necessary evil.

In such an environment, I noticed two different reactions among my classmates. Some would devote themselves to sports and ignore their school work. After these students got into the upper division, some of them received their first rank in *kendō* or judo, while others became active in basketball competitions. There was also a boy who became so engrossed in the game of *go* that he would read a *go* book while walking along the corridor or under the cover of his desk in class. Once when his name was called by the teacher, he stood up looking startled. "Continue reading and see if you can translate it," the teacher said. But because he did not even know where he was supposed to start from, there was no way for him to continue, let alone translate it.

And there were quite a few young lads known in those days as *nanpa,* or "softies." They were avid fans of the musicals performed by the Takarazuka Girls' Troupe and constantly hummed their theme songs.[1] Even their movements were effeminate, and they talked only about women. I had never seen a musical by the Takarazuka Girls' Troupe, and it was only through them that I got to know the names of a few popular stars along with the melodies and fragmentary lyrics of a few songs. Back home, when I told Father that the lyrics of a song went "What is big with Mama is her rear end; what is big with Papa are the holes in his socks," Father's flat reply was, "How silly!" Generally speaking, a *nanpa* struck me as being at once too much an adult and too much a child. I was not mature enough to enjoy role reversals where a woman would take on a male role and a man the mannerisms of a woman. I was impressed by those who could, but when I saw how they failed to handle even simple questions in class, I had to conclude that their naïveté

1. This troupe formed in the city of Takarazuka in Hyōgo Prefecture in 1913 was the first all-female performance troupe in Japan.

would preclude any friendship between us. While I continued some degree of socializing with them, it was quite impossible for me to establish any real friendship with any one of them.

Of course, many students took the teachers' words as sacred. They unthinkingly accepted the school's credo, "Aiming at the First Higher School and Tokyo University." They were conscientious in their studies and played only moderately. Among them, we even had a "perfect student" who scored exemplary grades in all subjects. At the end of every academic year—there were five classes within each grade and about fifty students in each class—the school listed the student rankings based on their overall scores. I heard that the perfect student always maintained the best scores throughout his five years in middle school. I don't know what happened to him later. All I could remember was his demeanor when, as an upper-class man, he gave directions to our separate marching columns in a military drill. As we all lined up with rifles on our shoulders, he stood in front of us with great seriousness, his whole body stiff with tension. He then raised his sword above his head and gave us his commands. It was a ridiculously comical spectacle.

There were also some intelligent and academically distinguished students who studied and played as their interests led them. Yanaihara Isaku must also have been in our grade; but at that time the Yanaihara I knew directly was not Isaku my future friend, but another student called Gorilla who grew up in a Protestant family.[2] To be sure, he was called Gorilla because of his physique. But he was also intellectually endowed, stoic, and had a stern sense of justice. He was critical of the students who liked to hum the Takarazuka songs all the time, and he even resented the songs themselves. I myself had no dislike for those students or the songs they sang, much less anger toward them. I respected Gorilla, but I don't think in the end we succeeded in developing any real friendship. He entered high school a year ahead of me, and there he immediately distinguished himself. A little later, despite his strong physique, he died of a sudden illness one night before anybody knew what had happened.

2. Yanaihara Isaku (1918–89), philosopher, critic, and the eldest son of the educator and colonial economist Yanaihara Tadao, later taught at Osaka University and Dōshisha University before becoming professor of philosophy at Hōsei University. After World War II he helped found many important literary journals, including *Sōgō bunka* and *Hakobune,* with which Katō was also associated. Among his most notable works are *Geijutsuka to no taiwa* (A conversation with an artist, 1958), *Kyoto no niwa* (Kyoto gardens, 1962), and *Sarutoru* (Sartre, 1968).

When I was at the Metropolitan First Middle School, I got to know many classmates, and through them, I learned many different things. Yet, I found it difficult to find a close friend. Socializing among students was limited to the time spent at school, or rather, to the few minutes during recess. Any sense of camaraderie was entirely nonexistent. The world I lived in allowed almost no space for close human interactions, whether with my classmates or with my teachers. I told myself that life was a stage where everyone appeared with a mask. "Life" to me at that time meant the Tokyo Metropolitan Middle School. If there is indeed such a thing as a blank period in a person's life, I would say mine was the years I spent commuting between my Shibuya home and my Hirakawa-chō school. Those were five blank years. And as far I can remember, it was the only time in my life that I ever felt that way.

It was a great irony that a line in Metropolitan First's school song, one meant to exhort students to embrace high aspirations, went "As we look up respectfully at the high tower of the Diet building." The year in which I enrolled was the same year the Great Japanese Empire began its invasion of Manchuria. It is true that the school did not go to such an extreme as to teach its students, if they were to cherish any lofty aspirations, to ignore the Diet. At the same time, they never encouraged us to become Diet members either. While they taught us loyalty toward the emperor and patriotism for the country, they did not even mention the phrase "fundamental human rights." In class, we heard stories about Saigō Takamori and Admiral Tōgō, but not a word about the history of the Freedom and Popular Rights Movement or the history of popular elections.[3] To be sure, when our principal made his speeches to the stu-

3. Saigō Takamori (1827–77), a lower Satsuma samurai who became a leader of the Meiji Restoration through his pivotal role in causing the collapse of the Tokugawa shogunate. In 1873, a disagreement over government policy toward Korea led to Saigō's resignation from the new government and return to Kagoshima with his loyal followers. In September 1877, conflicts with the government's new conscript army ended with Saigō's defeat and suicide, though he was widely admired for his failed heroism. • Tōgō Heihachirō (1847–1934), a former Satsuma samurai best known for his role as Commander of the Japanese Combined Fleet during the Russo-Japanese War, in which he scored a decisive victory over the Russian Baltic fleet in the Straits of Tsushima on May 27, 1905. • The Freedom and Popular Rights Movement (Jiyū minken undō), an extensive early Meiji political movement (1874–89) whose supporters included discontented former samurai, peasants, merchants, and other commoners, demanded that the government produce a constitution and a national

dents assembled in the auditorium, he was fond of quoting Gladstone: "As the British prime minister Gladstone said. . . ." But what he was telling us was not the story known to every Englishman, that Gladstone prevailed over Queen Victoria as the representative of the British people. He was merely giving us snippets of worldly advice, for example, that one must act according to one's beliefs. Regardless of who might have uttered those words, by itself the statement had absolutely nothing to do with parliamentary politics. And even if it had had some relevance to British parliamentary politics, it clearly had nothing to do with the Diet building visible through the classroom window at our Hirakawa-chō school.

Once when I was totally bored in class, I did look up at the "high tower of the Diet building." The autumn sky outside the window was a clear blue and the deciduous trees in the schoolyard had taken on beautiful tints of yellow and gold. "Ah! Autumn is here again," I kept thinking about this trivial fact. Suddenly, I heard the teacher's angry voice descending on me. "Why do you keep looking out the window?" Astonished, I quickly collected myself. Meanwhile, for some strange reason, I was seized with a reckless impulse to say exactly what was on my mind. "Because you asked us to scrutinize the text before we come to class and I did. I think it is meaningless to listen to something I already know."

"Do you really understand everything?"

"I'll do the translation for you to judge." Thus said, I began to translate my English textbook.

"Your translation is not incorrect, but you may not look outside during class," the young English teacher said calmly in a sympathetic voice. "You do have to give some consideration to the other students, don't you?"

The teacher was a recent graduate from the English Department of Tokyo Imperial University and was an admirer of Professor Ichikawa

---

assembly. At its peak in 1880, 64 member-delegates to the League for the Establishment of a National Assembly represented some 130,000 members from various grass-roots organizations. A political crisis in 1881 forced the government to promise to convene a parliament nine years later. The movement's internal weakness, coupled with government action, forced the dissolution of its political parties, and the movement collapsed in 1889 with the promulgation of the Meiji Constitution. See Roger W. Bowen, *Rebellion and Democracy in Meiji Japan: A Study of Commoners in the Popular Rights Movement* (Berkeley: University of California Press, 1980).

Sanki.[4] He himself appeared to be bored at having to explain the all too obvious antecedents for this or that relative pronoun.

Enami Bunzō, a *tanka* and free-style poet originally associated with the Myōjō school, was also teaching English at our school.[5] To relieve tedium, he had a unique teaching method. He would bring caramel candies to class, distribute them to his students, and then proceed to explain simple English grammar using sample sentences about caramel.

The white-haired teacher of Chinese classics was more candid. "From now on we are going to read the *Analects*," he said. "But," he went on to declare, "this is not a work you students can understand." Every time he finished reading a line from the text, he would give us his almost impenetrable thoughts on the subject as if he were delivering a monologue. "This is what Kanno has to say about this word, but this is not something people like Kanno can understand." If Kanno Dōmei could not understand it, there was no reason to expect us to.[6] It was during lessons on Chinese classics that the study of *go* was pursued with particular enthusiasm. Fully convinced that the students could not possibly understand the text anyway, the old man did not care in the least what his students were doing as long as they did not whisper among themselves.

Almost all the teachers at the middle school were called by nicknames. The bald military officer attached to our school was "the Henchman," while the red-nosed art teacher was "the Onion." Simple nicknames though they were, it was not easy to explain their origin. Some nicknames splendidly captured the personality traits of their designated individuals. For example, the head teacher at the time was called *Dobu-ra*, presumably meaning *dobunezumi*, the sewer rat, the *ra* deriving, I suppose, from the first syllable of the English word "rat." As a matter of fact, that head teacher did have something of a sewer-rat air about him. Like folktales, these nicknames were apparently not casually invented

4. Ichikawa Sanki (1886–1970), a prominent scholar of English linguistics and a professor at Tokyo Imperial University. His *Eibunpō kenkyū* (Study of English grammar, 1912) first introduced the methodology of historical and comparative linguistics into the study of English in Japan.

5. Enami Bunzō (1887–1946), a graduate in English from Tokyo Imperial University and an editor of the literary journal *Subaru* in its heyday after 1910. He wrote critical essays, novels, and poems, but none of his works earned conspicuous critical attention.

6. Kanno Dōmei (1865–1938), a noted Sinologist. Among his works were *Jigen*, an etymological dictionary (1923), and commentaries on Confucius's *Analects* and on T'ang poetry.

by any one person. Although a nickname was immediately bestowed on any new teacher, many of those names were fleeting and quickly forgotten. Ones that stood the test of time epitomized the keen linguistic sense of middle-school students, just as the deep-seated sentiments of ethnic groups manifest themselves in folktales but not in the work of any single writer.

"Sewer Rat" was a slightly built, middle-aged man who always wore heavily tinted glasses. His voice was soft and effeminate, and his gold tooth glittered when he talked. Once he got angry, he could be quite merciless in inflicting punishment. Since rumor had it that he would flunk or expel students who incurred his wrath, we were terrified of him. He was responsible for English instruction, but in those days he hardly did anything beyond making his students from the first to the fifth grades use the five-volume reader he himself had compiled. That reader began with such elementary English sentences as "This is a pen," and progressed to excerpts of Victorian prose to be read in the upper-division classes. The selections consisted only of pieces like moral sermons which did neither good nor harm to the students. Nowhere could we find a love story, a line of witticism, a sarcastic remark, a paradox, or even a sample of that famous English humor. We all agreed that we had never seen Sewer Rat smile. His eyes always shone in the darkness, ever alert to catch us in any misconduct. When he attacked, his bite was vicious. He moved nimbly and insidiously without making the slightest sound, and nobody ever had any idea of what was going on in his mind.

In contrast to Sewer Rat, another English teacher was wonderful when he was in a good mood. But when he became angry, even the roots of his ears would turn red. He would snatch up the resisting student and shove him out of the classroom. While Sewer Rat was loathed, this teacher was well liked and even respected. He earned our respect because, as the rumor went, he was the only person capable of having a conversation in English with the foreign teachers he met in the corridor. To us, the ability to converse in English had a mysterious aura about it, something no ordinary person could ever be expected to accomplish, something totally different from reading an English textbook in class.

The students were quick to identify the power structure among the teachers, and they would immediately try to take advantage of the weaker ones. But we were totally wrong about what we had perceived as the weakness of Takagi *sensei,* the Onion. It was true that an art teacher did not have much clout in school, but that was certainly not the reason why Takagi *sensei* was always so even-tempered with us. Takagi *sensei* said to us once, "I am going to treat you not as children but as responsible human beings. Therefore, I am not going to monitor your examination. I hope you will not resort to any unfair practices. I hope you will act honestly even if you are not being watched. The purpose of education is not to prevent students from cheating, but to nurture people in a way that they will not cheat even when they can. I cannot tell you how much more important that is than your examination scores."

But the students weren't used to unmonitored examinations, nor was the sense of solidarity among them strong enough to bring an unfamiliar enterprise to a successful finish. The result of the examination revealed that some cheating had occurred. To this day, I cannot forget the white-haired Takagi *sensei* coming into the classroom with a bundle of examination papers with him. "You betrayed my trust in you. It is so unfortunate." His subdued voice echoed through the room. There was no anger or even the slightest threat of punishment in his voice. But there was something in it that caused a dead silence to settle over the whole classroom. "The kind of education where you have to monitor examinations is not true education. Not only did a few of you betray my trust in you, you also betrayed your friends who answered the questions honestly. I will not continue to subject the honest students to such a disadvantage. My only alternative is to monitor your next examination. As for today, I am not going to teach." Having said that, Takagi *sensei* left the classroom. A moment later, we heard the upper-class students shouting "The Onion! The Onion!" from the schoolyard. But for a while, nobody in the classroom stood up to leave or made a sound.

At the beginning of the 1930s low-ranking officers on reserve were attached to the middle schools to teach students how to use a rifle and how to march in separate columns during military drills. The Henchman was one of these officers. Because he had been working at the school for a long time, he was by then less a military man than a kind of educator. He understood the feelings of his students well, and he never asked us to do the impossible. But among the Takarazuka *nanpa,* there was one boy who could not maneuver his rifle briskly. "Can't you do any better? Try again!" the Henchman shouted angrily. But the boy's next attempt was not much of an improvement. The onlooking students burst out laughing, and the student himself looked at the Henchman with a bitter smile. "Stop grinning! Try again!" he demanded. Eventually, however, it was the Henchman who finally gave up. He never struck his students, nor did he ever lose his warm compassion. For this reason, we also felt a certain affection toward him.

In those days, a real officer from the Army Command Division would come to the middle school once a year to supervise our military drills. As the day of the so-called inspection drew near, we could feel very distinctly the mounting agitation on the Henchman's part. "How do you expect to pass the inspection with this kind of sloppy performance?" he would exclaim. We were totally fed up with the trivial and meaningless rituals he taught us and thought it ridiculous that we had to waste our time in such activities. But during the inspection, for the sake of maintaining the Henchman's reputation, we would earnestly apply ourselves for just one day and do our best as we were put through our paces in the marching drills. By the time the inspecting officer congratulated the Henchman on his achievement and left, it was already dusk. With us assembled in the courtyard, rifles in hand, he said sincerely, "Thanks for your hard work! Tell you the truth,"—that was his favorite phrase— "when I was watching you, I was a little worried. But if you put your heart in it, you can do it. After all, you are from First Metropolitan Middle. Well, tell you the truth, even I didn't expect to receive such a good review." By that time, the Henchman was so emotional that he was close to tears. We hardly cared about the review by the professional soldier, but we, too, were satisfied to see the jubilation of the Henchman.

I met many teachers at the Hirakawa-chō middle school. Most of them were very competent experts, and some were without doubt likable people. Perhaps with the exception of Takagi *sensei* at the moment described earlier, none of them exerted any real influence on me with respect to the development of my interests, my character, or, to put it a little more grandly, the way I looked at the world. While the extent of my interaction with my classmates was typical for a middle-school student, in the end I did not find the kind of friends with whom I could sit up all night to share my thoughts. When I left elementary school, I felt as if my heart had been left behind. When I finished middle school, I experienced something close to a sense of emancipation. But it was still too early to talk about it.

8   The Mitake-chō House

When I was in middle school, my family moved from the right side of Miyamasuzaka to the left and up the slope. Our old house in Konnō-chō, a resurrected part of a grand house, was not convenient to live in, nor was it suited to a doctor's private practice. So we leased a parcel of Grandfather's land in Mitake-chō and built a new house on it.

The site was on a steep incline above Grandfather's residence. The other side was connected to the fence of a Hikawa shrine.[1] The land had been used as a private tennis court; it was where I used to ride around on the bicycle Grandfather bought me and learned to play softball tennis from Father. We got rid of the tennis court and built a new two-story white wooden house in its place. Our new family house was even smaller than our old Konnō-chō house, but it was designed with easy living in mind. Clearly separated from the family living quarters was an internal medicine clinic with all the necessary facilities; besides the consultation room, it had a waiting room, a sterilizing room, and a small pharmacy.

Yet these new facilities did not bring in many new patients. Our family's financial situation changed considerably after we moved, but not because Father had a more prosperous practice. About the only thing that made any difference was that in addition to the income from the clinic, we also received rent from the lease of our old Konnō-chō house. Our

1. Dedicated to the mythical figures of Susanoo no mikoto, Ōnamuchi no mikoto, and Kushinada hime no mikoto. There are over 160 of these shrines in Saitama Prefecture alone, and in Tokyo the Hikawa Shrine in Akasaka is particularly famous.

daily livelihood was even more hard-pressed than before. Father was no longer closely associated with the *zaibatsu* family. Living costs had increased, and as the children grew older, their education became more costly. In those days we seldom went on a trip and almost never went out for a play or a movie, nor do I recall our ever having a fancy meal in a restaurant. Father himself did not smoke or drink and, other than growing roses in his garden, had no particular hobby, contented as he was with a thoroughly modest life. Perhaps it was because he did not feel the need for money that he had no enthusiasm for making it. He described his own lifestyle as "unpretentious and solid living."

Father's relatives in the countryside sent us rice and miso, and during the New Year they would also deliver to us more rice cakes than we could eat. During the week of the New Year, we would boil some of them with vegetables and store the rest, either in a sake cask filled with water or dried for future consumption. As a result, no matter how tight our family's financial situation was, we did not have to worry about food; we had only to curtail our other material expenses. Mother explained the budget clearly to me and Sister, who had started going to Saint Maur Higher Girls' School. Because we realized that buying one item would mean doing without another, I don't think we ever pestered our parents unreasonably about buying us things.

In those days aggressive peddlers and beggars sometimes stopped by our Mitake-chō house. Mother would make up various excuses for not buying from the peddlers, and she would only give the beggars a bare minimum. Most of them would accept what they were given and leave, but some would hurl the money on the ground. I remember hearing an angry beggar saying things like, "Is this all you are going to give me? I hope you die in your next childbirth and don't you forget it!" Probably not even a beggar could imagine that a doctor's family with a big fancy gate in front of their house could be living as austerely as we did.

After we moved into the Mitake-chō house, our family lived even closer to Grandfather's residence. With more frequent contact between the two households, we soon learned about all sorts of events, big and small, at Grandfather's house. When my uncle in Osaka died of tuberculosis, my aunt returned to her parents' house with her daughter. Because my uncle was an adopted son, there was no need for her to change her surname. The older of her two children, a boy my age who had long been entrusted to my grandparents' care, was attending the elementary school attached to Tokyo's Normal School. But finding a new school for her daughter, who was a year younger than Sister, was a somewhat difficult task. While my aunt and grandparents had had a hectic time deciding on the boy's school, it appeared that they were ready to settle for any in the daughter's case.

Throughout the 1930s Grandfather's business did not recover easily from the severe blow it had suffered during the depression. Some of his many rental properties had to be disposed of in order to pay off his debt. But Grandfather was not the type of person who would change his lifestyle easily, even when he had to mortgage his own estate. He continued to pay very scrupulous attention to his personal appearance whenever he went out, applying his imported perfume lavishly. His relationships with his female friends, contrary to what might be expected, became all the more active. As a result, Grandmother would sometimes erupt in frantic outbursts, tearing her clothes to pieces and throwing dishes at the garden rocks. My aunt who was living with them was a mild-tempered and timid woman, and when matters got out of hand, she would come up to our house to seek Mother's help. "Father just wouldn't listen to me," she would say. It was true that even when Grandfather was shouting at Grandmother and my aunt, he would behave in front of Mother as if he were trying to solicit sympathy from her. "It looks like he only listens to you," Father used to say. Sister and I, however, did not want Mother to venture out alone to deal with the domestic troubles in Grandfather's household. We were worried about her when we saw our aunt's agitation and Mother's unusual expressions. Sometimes, at the end of our long wait, Mother would return home crying. We wanted to comfort her in some way, but there was nothing we could do. "It's all right. You don't have to worry. Everything is all right." Mother ended up having to comfort us. "Why are you crying?" Sister would say. "Tell me why." And Mother repeated, "It's really nothing. It's just something you children don't have to know." But we always wondered why Father never came to comfort Mother when she was crying. We imagined that what made her cry was not simply what had happened at Grandfather's house; we thought it probably also had something to do with Father's attitude toward the matter as well.

After listening to the story about Grandmother breaking her dishes, Father's remark was "No need to worry; she'll be all right. A patient with hysteria won't hurt herself. And I doubt if the dishes she broke were the most expensive kind." Regarding Grandfather, he kept repeating the same criticism not only at times when trouble began to boil but on quieter days as well. If Grandfather's trouble with money was so serious that he had to mortgage his own estate, so went his first criticism, why didn't he economize? His second criticism was that it was a shameful act of decadence for a married man like Grandfather to spend time with other women. Mother defended Grandfather by saying, "He is trying to economize in his own way by laying off some of his maids and by not keeping a houseboy."

"That's not economizing! That's only a matter of course."

"I don't think he could live the way you do. People are different, you know."

"I'd say he's in no position to make such a claim."

Quite simply, Father's "unpretentious and solid living" was not so much a result of dire necessity as a lifestyle suited to his temperament. But that was not true for Grandfather. "At his age, he's too old to be a ladies' man," Father said. But I wonder if Father himself had ever been the object of a woman's infatuation, or if he had ever experienced falling head over heels in love. He did not womanize not because he thought it was inexcusable; I suspect rather that he came to think of womanizing as inexcusable because he himself was not a womanizer. Mother privately explained to us about Grandfather in this way: "You see, Grandma must bear some responsibility for Grandpa's behavior. She does exactly the kinds of things she knows perfectly well will provoke Grandpa's anger. You can just see how insensitive she is. Grandpa is a human being too, and in a situation like this, who can blame him for not staying home?" And so, Mother cherished Grandfather's "human quality," while Father emphasized his "moral decadence."

"Loving two women is equivalent to loving no one. It's just womanizing pure and simple," Father stated.

"Well, I'm not so sure. Christians love God as well as their husbands, don't they?"

"I wonder about that. If they truly loved God, wouldn't they diminish the love they have for their husbands?"

"But isn't love something that will not diminish no matter how much it is bestowed on others?"

"People are just saying that."

"But isn't a man who loves one woman deeply also capable of loving another the same way?"

Father was always the one who provoked this kind of endless argument between them. As for myself, having no experience with any woman to speak of, it seemed expedient for me to adopt Father's arguments in order to justify my own position.

Except for the marriages and marital relationships between couples from "well-matched" middle-class families, Father was very critical of relationships between the sexes, including even romances between young men and women. Nothing, he said, struck him quite as ludicrous as when pimple-faced middle-school students—that is to say, me and my classmates—started chasing after female students. That sort of behavior, he said, was not love or anything, just an emulation of love. It was the height of foolishness to accept love stories depicted in novels as genuine truth. The kind of love story depicted in *Konjiki yasha* (The golden demon) was not something that could happen in real life.[2] Novelists embellished such stories only to ingratiate themselves with women and girls and to turn their novels into commercial successes. Or else they were just trying to gloss over their own penchant for illicit affairs in the guise of lofty sentiments about love. Feelings of love were based on lust, and lust, like the desire for food, was an instinct common to animals. Far from being a noble sentiment, it was not even a defining human attribute. That was how his argument went. If Father had had the wit of an eighteenth-century Frenchman, he probably would have said, "Love begins with the contact of two people's souls and ends with the contact of their mucous membranes." His words taught me the condemnation of love before I knew love itself and the imminent disillusionment of a dream before I could indulge myself in one. Before I saw the play *Chūshingura* (The forty-six *rōnin*), I had already read Akutagawa Ryūnosuke's "Ōishi Kuranosuke."[3] Before I knew about knight-errantry in Western medieval

2. An unfinished novel (1897–1902) by the Meiji novelist Ozaki Kōyō (1867–1903). A celebrated melodrama of love and betrayal between Kan'ichi and his fiancée, Miya, the story was a phenomenal success among Meiji readers of the time.

3. *Chūshingura*, also popularly translated as *The Treasury of Loyal Retainers*, is the collective name for kabuki and *jōruri* plays based on the 1702 vendetta of forty-seven *rōnin* against Lord Kira of Kōzuke in revenge for their former master Lord Asano of Akō (the leader, Ōishi Kuranosuke, and his followers committed *seppuku* in 1703 by the order of the Tokugawa authorities); the most celebrated work in this genre was *Kanadehon chūshingura* (or simply *Chūshingura*) by the second Takeda Izumo in 1748.

Akutagawa's story "Aru hi no Ōishi Kuranosuke" (One day in the life of Ōishi Kuranosuke, *Chūō kōron*, 1917), turns Ōishi's selfless heroism on its head by presenting the image of a lone protagonist reflecting on how future generations will look upon his actions. Whether or not Akutagawa was drawing a

tales, I had already known its trenchant critique in *Don Quixote*. The road from knight-errant stories leads naturally to *Don Quixote,* but the road from *Don Quixote* to knight-errant stories requires, I am afraid, a long and winding detour.

When I was a middle-school student, of course I could not be an Akutagawa Ryūnosuke, much less a Cervantes. Intellectually, I might have emulated them in some way, but emotionally, I was their exact opposite, totally naive and inexperienced. In the eyes of a third person, I must have been one of the most unappealing of young men. Mother was putting it mildly when she observed, "Getting too contentious about things might not be good for you." She was, no doubt, worried about Father's influence on me. But she too did not understand the situation very well. I was no longer an elementary school student. I was not molded by Father's opinions; instead, I adopted his arguments. They were two completely different things. I was utterly bored with my daily routine going back and forth between my extraordinarily ascetic family and my middle school, that exemplary example of elitist militaristic education. On the other hand, I was not in a position to create any alternative lifestyle of my own choosing. Even though I might be attracted to Grandfather's lifestyle, it was something infinitely removed from my realm of possibilities. I simply accepted my own life the way it was and tried to rationalize it. Thereupon I adopted Father's views. But in the process, I also realized that there were discrepancies between his views and my own feelings.

The financial circumstances at Grandfather's household got worse with time. Hoping desperately to remedy the situation, he started to mortgage whatever property that could be mortgaged and began to invest in new ventures, only to hasten his own downfall. "It's such a shame. He's been working so hard to make it work. I just wish his efforts would pay off sometime," Mother said. Whenever his business showed some slight signs of improvement and made him feel hopeful about the future, Grandfather would instantly return to his old energetic self, exuberant and cheerful. But as time went by, this happened less and less frequently. Despite his attentiveness to his impeccable personal appearance,

---

"portrait of his own spiritual life" through Kuranosuke (Yoshida Seiichi, *Akutagawa Ryūnosuke* [Sanseidō, 1942]), Akutagawa's new interpretation goes beyond conventional form and probes the inner world of his hero.

we could see the darkening shadow of age and fatigue creeping over him. The repercussions of his business failure were soon felt in his daily life. His rental properties were almost entirely gone; what remained was only his own estate and the land on which our house was built. Before long, only one housemaid remained, and to cover the deficit in the family budget, Grandmother and my aunt sometimes had to call for the secondhand store to sell off some of the family belongings. "It's terrible to have to sell off the things we've known since we were children," Mother said. "Even though they may not be worth anything, they all have sentimental value." Years later, when I watched Higashiyama Chieko and Senda Koreya's performance of *The Cherry Orchard* and heard the chopping down of the cherry trees in the last scene, I was reminded of the noise of the carrier's horse-drawn cart hauling away the old furniture from Grandfather's house.[4] Grandfather was not home the day the secondhand-store owner came. Perhaps he could not bring himself to witness the scene.

While Grandfather's family was steadily declining, my relatives on Grandmother's side were doing better and better. At that time her older brother, a successful industrialist, was the vice president of a big monopolistic fuel company. Her younger brother in the navy had been promoted first to the rank of rear admiral and then to vice admiral. As the war that began in Manchuria in the late 1930s continued to spread, the big fuel company, needless to say, was doing a brisk business, while high-ranking naval officers commanded increasing authority. The vice president was good at looking after his relatives. Many of his family members were working as employees in every division in his company. But

4. Higashiyama Chieko (1890–1980), a distinguished *shingeki* actor who made her debut at the Tsukiji Little Theater in 1925 and performed with the New Tsukiji Troupe and the Bungakuza before joining the Haiyūza at its founding in 1944. She was best known for her role as Madame Ranevskaya in Anton Chekhov's *The Cherry Orchard* and in 1958 became the director of the Association of Shingeki Performers (Nihon shingeki haiyū kyōkai). • Senda Koreya (1904–94), a celebrated *shingeki* actor who appeared in or produced plays ranging from Maksim Gorky's *The Lower Depths*, Chekhov's *The Cherry Orchard*, Shakespeare's *Hamlet*, Bertolt Brecht's *The Three-Penny Opera* to those based on the works of Tanaka Chikao, Abe Kōbō, and Ishikawa Jun, founded the Haiyūza in 1944 and became one of the leading figures of the postwar *shingeki* movement. His writings include *Senda Koreya engeki ronshū* (Critical works on dramatic performance by Senda Koreya; 9 vols. [Miraisha, 1980–92]) and his autobiography, *Mō hitotsu no Shingekishi* (Another history of the *shingeki* movement [Chikuma Shobō, 1975]).

his helping hand did not extend all the way to his sister's—that is to say, Grandfather's—declining household. Even if he had hoped to do so, it was probably beyond his means. Although he was a vice president, he was promoted from his former position as a member of the technical staff, not as a big shareholder. He had one daughter, and his son-in-law later became the vice president of the same company. A man with a cheerful personality, he treated everyone alike. That was true even with Father: I say "even" because few among Father's own relatives could talk openly with the irascible doctor. Whenever they met, they never grew tired of talking and laughing with each other. When I was a middle-school student, I very seldom socialized with the vice president's family. Some years after the Pacific War, when I was eking out a scanty living in Paris, the second-generation vice president quite unexpectedly called on me one night. His letter suddenly arrived at my lodging, announcing simply that he would be coming to Paris on such and such a date and asking for my assistance. When I arrived at the airport, he emerged with two briefcase-carrying employees and greeted me with a brisk "Hey! How're things going for you?" His jolly demeanor revived in me memories from the prewar days and made me forget that he was the vice president of a big company.

The rear admiral studied in England in his younger days and served as a military attaché to the Japanese Embassy around the time of the London Disarmament Conference. An Anglophile, he frequently talked about things like British customs and history at the gatherings of our relatives. Because there was little interaction between naval officers and foreigners in Japan in the latter half of the 1930s, I had no idea how well he spoke English. But he often read English books and was the one who introduced the game of auction bridge to our family. He was, at various stages of his career, captain of a battle cruiser, commanding officer of the Yangtze fleet, and head of the Department of Naval Affairs. I still remember very well my visit to a battle cruiser when I was a child. It was totally different from the impression I got from witnessing for the first time the way my other uncle, the prefectural governor, exercised his authority. The behavior of bootlicking bureaucrats in the prefectural office was so degradingly servile that it bordered on the pathetic. The sailors on the battle cruiser, on the other hand, were not the least bit obsequious. They did not pass out empty compliments and spoke only when necessary, without a single superfluous word. Alert, precise, and efficient, they treated their captain's guests with flawless attention. There I saw an organization of men operating like a piece of machinery, and the impression it evoked could almost be described as aesthetic. The experience was so overpowering that I could hardly remember anything else on my trip: the size of the cruiser, who the other guests were, the color of the sea, the seagulls in flight, or the cruiser's flag fluttering in the wind on what might well have been a clear day. I sometimes called this naval officer "Uncle" and sometimes "Admiral." From before the Pacific War through its aftermath, the admiral always maintained a discerning position from which he never wavered: that fanatical ultranationalism would only bring destruction to the country.

The relationship between the admiral and our family continued for a long time. As to the kind of relationship that was, I might get into that later. He had two daughters and two sons. The older daughter was in the upper division of the same girls' school Sister went to, and the younger daughter was in a grade or two below hers. They were both pretty girls whom I secretly admired. But the older daughter must have thought of me as a younger friend, and I didn't have any real conversation with the younger one. The older daughter later married an architect and lived in the Hongō district, and her sister lived in Nagoya after she married an employee of the fuel company where many of her relatives worked. The air of vivacity and gaiety in the admiral's and the vice president's families only served to accentuate the decline of Grandfather's household.

Our family quarters in Mitake-chō were on the second floor above the clinic, and the room at the southwest corner was used as Father's study. Since he rarely used it during the day, I frequently spent my time there after school and before dinner. Across the south-facing window a giant pine tree spread its branches far and wide, and in the summer, the droning of the brown cicadas produced quite an annoying chorus. The west-facing window was directly exposed to the evening sun and, even with the sunshade, the room was unbearably hot in midsummer. Yet looking across a narrow strip of open space from the second-floor window perched atop a high cliff, one could see beyond the valley in the vicinity of Shibuya Station all the way to Dōgenzaka's incline until it merged with the horizon. Tall buildings—though nothing taller than four stories—were to be found only in the valley. The incline that extended all the way to the horizon lay under a blanket of low, black-tiled roofs. Below them yellow lights would pop up here and there in the evening. On a clear day, Mount Fuji was clearly visible over Dōgenzaka, and by the time the mountain turned to pure white, I knew that late autumn had arrived.

When the warm March winds raised clouds of dust on the Yoyogi drill ground, the snow on Mount Fuji had not yet thawed. Hakone spread out below it in a light purple haze along the horizon. Slender chimneys of the bathhouses pierced the air from the horizon like silhouettes, sending streaks of black smoke into the sky before they were scattered by the winds. Evening clouds sometimes glowed in a dreamy rose pink and sometimes in an ominous tint reminiscent of old, dry blood. At still other times, their lustrous golden linings filled the sky with a banquet of elegant colors, only to fade abruptly into a chilly gray. A cloudless evening had all the tonality of the western sky from a Hiroshige print, and before its colors completely faded away, evening stars would begin to twinkle in the night sky. All through those five years, except on rainy days, watching the evening sky was a daily routine I almost never missed. Of all the sensory impressions I gathered in those years, the western sky over Dōgenzaka was the most beautiful and quite possibly had the most profound effect on me. I had yet to encounter Bonnard's rosy pink or Tintoretto's dramatic red. In fact, I did not even know what an oil painting was like.

The emptiness I felt during those five years was not confined to my experiences at my Hirakawa-chō school. But then something unexpected began to creep into this numbing emptiness from an equally unexpected source.

9 Early Signs of Rebellion

My parents strictly forbade their children to go to a motion picture on their own. Because they themselves had little interest in this kind of entertainment, they almost never took me or Sister to see one. I had my maternal grandfather to thank for my initiation into motion pictures. He enjoyed taking us to a movie, followed by a meal in some famous Western restaurant. The pictures we saw were all made in the West, never in Japan. Now that I think about it, I still do not quite understand the reason. Perhaps he was drawn to the lure of their exotic images that in turn brought back happy memories of his younger days in the West. The fragrance of perfume, the taste of wine, the sensuousness of a woman's hair, the expressions on people's faces, and the intonation of their utterances . . . I suppose the more elusive these experiences became in his immediate Tokyo surroundings, the more precious and unforgettable they were to him at that time. Apparently, even the dizzy play of light and shadow in the darkness of the theater could impart a significance he alone could appreciate. Often in the middle of a movie, just when Sister and I became totally captivated by the plot and mesmerized by its images, Grandfather would rise and say, "Okay, that's enough for us." As to how the plot might unfold, he couldn't have cared less.

Before the advent of the "talkies," movie houses in Shibuya always had a small band to provide appropriate background music to synchronize with developments on the screen.[1] The charging of the cavalry would call for an overture from a Rossini opera; the gathering of momentum before a tumultuous climax would usher in the exuberant mu-

1. The talkies started to take over Japanese cinema around 1937.

sic of Offenbach of cancan fame; a tender scene of budding romance would inspire *Träumerei* performed on the violin. Anyone even slightly familiar with the limited repertoire of their melodies could very well tell, even without explanation, not only what was happening on the screen at the moment but what was going to happen next. Although I did not know it at the time—I was only an elementary school student—the bands at Shibuya's movie theaters were trying to accomplish what the musical accompaniment in the *nō* or the kabuki theater has been doing since the old days, only in a more contemporary and less refined style.

To make doubly sure that the audience with little familiarity with Western customs could readily understand what was happening on the screen, movie theaters also provided the service of commentators known as *katsuben*.[2] It worked very much like today's radio stations during the broadcast of an opera, where an announcer comes on the air to explain the plot while the orchestral music is switched off. But the *katsuben* in the bygone days were far more creative than today's radio commentators in terms of developing memorable stylizations in their delivery. In a *kyōgen* play, characters are often designated to play three different roles: the master, the manservant, and the second manservant. Likewise, the *katsuben* had their own system of categorization. Instead of calling each character in Western action films by his or her individual name, all leading females were called "Merii" (Mary), all good guys were "Jōji" (George), and all bad guys were "Jakku" (Jack). "Now, the villain Jakku is moving closer and closer behind Merii," the *katsuben* would explain the setting. "'Oh, Jōji-san! Jōji-san!' Her desperate crying and calling to no avail, the door is tightly shut; and at the top of her voice, Merii cries 'Jōji-san! Help meee . . . !' Aah! What's going to be the fate of poor Merii?" As soon as he finished, the scene would abruptly change to that of Jōji charging on horseback through the wilderness to come to the res-

2. The number of *katsuben*, short for *katsudō benshi* (movie interpreter), started to grow in the early 1910s with the production of dramatic films and peaked at around 7,000 in the 1920s. Some of them, most notably Tokugawa Musei (1894–1971), became quite famous. Part of their raison d'être had to do with the way they enchanted the audience with their storytelling and imaginative improvisation. Misono Kyōhei's study *Katsuben jidai* (The age of *katsuben* [Iwanami shoten, 1990]) is richly illustrated. For two studies in English, see Arthur Nolletti, Jr., and David Desser, eds., *Reframing Japanese Cinema: Authorship, Genre, History* (Bloomington: Indiana University Press, 1992); and Hiroshi Komatsu and Charles Musser, "Benshi Search," *Wide Angle* 9, no. 2 (1987): 73–90.

cue. The majority of Hollywood movies in the past were well serve by these three roles alone, as they are in the present.

While I did enjoy watching these action films, their dualistic demarcation of good and evil had no effect on my ethical values or on my world view. My visits to Shibuya's movie theaters were not frequent enough for me to be so influenced, and years later when I did watch many more Westerns, I was already too old to be affected. My moral and ethical values were not cultivated by the motion pictures.

The motion pictures I saw with Grandfather did play a role—and not a small one—in helping me discover a world independent of matters of right and wrong. One such picture imported by Tōwa Trading Company enacted the meeting and separation of two destitute lovers on the night of July 14.[3] Another depicted a Russian grand duke with a local town girl in a scurrying coach in a late-night scene at an ancient capital where an international congress was being held.[4] Yet another brought the scene of a still-unknown composer dallying with a beautiful maiden in the middle of a wheat field in central Europe.[5] In the fogged-in English capital, an elusive thief who has effortlessly outfoxed the police now finds himself doublecrossed by a prostitute. As he is being arrested, he mutters that poor people must stand by each other lest the whole world collapse on them.[6] There is little question that these story lines had little social relevance to the realities of any European city. Yet to a middle-school student like me, Europe was too infinitely far away to elicit the

3. Established in 1928, Tōwa Trading Company was instrumental in introducing a large number of European art films to the Japanese audience before 1945. Such activities continued into the postwar period, until overseas distribution rights for European films fell into the hands of American companies.
• The meeting occurs in René Claire's 1932 film *Quatorze Juillet,* which depicts a few hours in the life of a flower girl in Paris's Montmartre district on the eve of the country's annual holiday celebrating the storming of the Bastille on July 14, 1789.
4. A reference to Erik Charell's *Der Kongress tanzt* (The congress dances, 1931), set against the background of the Congress of Vienna and reputed to have been one of the best early European musicals. The Russian grand duke outsmarted his opponent by having a double take his place at the congress while he assumed a secret identity.
5. A reference to Willi Forst's *Leise flehen meine Lieder* (Unfinished symphony, 1933).
6. A reference to G. W. Pabst's *Die Dreigroschenoper* (Three-penny opera, 1931), his second sound film based on the play by Bertolt Brecht and derived from *The Beggar's Opera* by John Gay. The photography of Fritz Arno Wagner records this Soho underworld of the 1890s.

slightest misgivings on my part. To be sure, the black and white images that I saw were nothing more than a silhouette of reality, but I could actually hear the noise of the coach as it ran along the stone pavement in the old European capital, and I could feel the sun and the blue sky over the expansive wheat fields of central Europe. For me, the melodies played on the accordion, the faces of young girls peeking out from the windows of their homes in the alleys, and the swirling skirts of dancing women all existed in a real, substantive way. In my early childhood, Harada Mitsuo's popular science books nourished me; after I became a middle-school student, their role fell to the fairy tales I saw in the movies.

In the world of fairy tales, all kinds of things could happen: love, ambition, betrayal, fateful encounters, and irrevocable separations. But nothing ever happened in the real world I lived in, a world consisting only of going back and forth on the city train between my Mitake-chō home in Shibuya and my middle school in Hirakawa-chō. Since I did not have any dramatic encounters with anyone, I could not throw myself into the flames of love or, consequently, experience the agony of separation. Although the war on the Chinese continent had begun, its impact was not felt in my immediate surroundings, and revolution was nothing more than a distant myth. The only thing I knew about was my middle school, and I was totally fed up with it and myself. The movie theater taught me a way to escape into a world of fantasy in the darkness.

The movie theater was not the only place where I could indulge myself in a world of fantasy. Returning home from school, I would go up to Father's study on the second floor, not to study my textbooks but rather to look for poetry or other literary works to read. On his bookshelves thick with German medical reference books, only a few literary works—several books of *waka*—could be found in some inconspicuous corner. Moreover, the majority of them were old annotations on the *Man'yōshū*.[7] The first work of Japanese literature I read was the

7. *Man'yōshū* (Collection of ten thousand leaves), a late Nara or early Heian compilation of Japanese lyric poetry and the oldest collection known today, with 4,207 *tanka*, 265 *chōka*, and other forms including 4 Chinese poems and 22 Chinese prose passages. Some critics consider it the quintessential manifestation of the "pure Japanese spirit." For Katō's assessment of the *Man'yōshū*, see his *History of Japanese Literature*, 1:59–87. For a translation see Ian Hideo Levy, *The Ten Thousand Leaves: A Translation of the Man'yōshū* (Princeton: Princeton University Press, 1981).

Man'yōshū, but how that happened had nothing to do with my own critical judgment. When I was a middle-school student, I felt the need for a world of imagination; since watching movies could not always fulfill this need, literature became the only other avenue open to me. Fortunately— but unfortunately for me at the time—the *Man'yōshū* was about the only book I could lay my hands on. That was the simple explanation.

The *Man'yōshū* more than opened up a world of imagination for me, though in that sense the works of Hitomaro and Okura could hardly rival the films of René Clair or G. W. Pabst.[8] More significantly, it also opened my eyes to the world of literary expression. The language of the *Man'yōshū* was so radically different from the Japanese I had read so far that if I had not relied on the annotations, in many instances I could not have even imagined what the text meant at all. I discovered for the first time a language divorced from its semantic component, and I also began to notice other nonsemantic aspects of language and the possibilities they suggest.

> Plovers skimming the evening waves
> on the Ōmi Sea
> When you cry
> so my heart trails
> like dwarf bamboo
> down to the past.[9]

I was beginning to discover what could well be called the music of the *Man'yōshū* along with the subtleties and the indescribable magic of poetry. A number of Man'yō poems I memorized at that time have become

8. Kakinomoto no Hitomaro (dates unknown), one of the major Man'yō poets and considered to be one of the greatest in Japan, whose official eulogies and elegies have been compared to epics, though the emotional intensity in Hitomaro's private poems, such as his elegies on the death of his wife, are most admired (see Ian Hideo Levy, *Hitomaro and the Birth of Japanese Lyricism* [Princeton: Princeton University Press, 1984]). • Yamanoue no Okura (660–ca. 733), a major and remarkably versatile Man'yō poet who felt equally at home composing in Japanese and Chinese, has been especially noted for the social concern and humanism in some of his works as well as for his expression of Buddhist ideas about the precariousness of the human condition. Katō in *A History of Japanese Literature* also highlights the thematic originality in Okura's poems, which address topics such as the misery of old age and the destitution of a harsh life (1:76–77).

9. Katō's original text cites only the first half of the celebrated Man'yō poem no. 266 by Kakinomoto no Hitomaro. The English translation by Levy is *Ten Thousand Leaves*, 162.

an integral part of me. Meanwhile, I also read the poetry collections by Tōson and Bansui.[10] In terms of poetic diction, however, their language was too similar to our everyday speech to have any decisive impact on me. On the other hand, the language in the John Keats poetry collection Mother owned was too far removed from the Japanese I knew. Whenever I contemplate the nature of poetry, my frame of reference is neither Tōson or Bansui nor any foreign poet. The Man'yō poets come to mind before anybody else. That "poetry" has come to mean something special to me is a result of the countless evening hours I spent with the *Man'yōshū* on the second floor of my Mitake-chō home. Yet the world of the *Man'yōshū*, just like the world of René Clair and G. W. Pabst, was infinitely removed from the intolerably boring reality I faced every day. The first literary figure to speak coherently to me about this boredom, about this intolerable burden, and about the origin and the implications of my sense of self-disgust—even though he might not have all the answers—was Akutagawa Ryūnosuke.[11]

I had never contemplated suicide, but I was moved by Akutagawa Ryūnosuke's writings. A friend of mine from elementary-school days was then a student at a girls' school and an avid reader of novels. "Oh, you are so ignorant! You mean you haven't even read Akutagawa yet?" she said. "I'll let you borrow some of mine. See what you think. I don't know if he's the type for you, though." I admired his short stories, and, more than that, I was astounded by his *Words of a Dwarf.*[12] It was in

---

10. During the Meiji-Taishō period only Natsume Sōseki and Mori Ōgai achieved literary eminence comparable to that of Shimazaki Tōson (1872–1943); his works include novels (*Hakai* [The broken commandment, 1906], *Ie* [The family, 1910–11)], *Shinsei* [New life, 1918–19], and *Yoake mae* [Before the dawn, 1929–35]) as well as many verse and verse-prose collections, short stories, commentaries, and children's tales. • Often paired with him as modern Japan's leading poets, Doi Bansui (1871–1952) has also been compared to Schiller and Swinburne; his major poetry collections include *Tenchi ujō* (The sentimental heaven and earth, 1899) and *Gyōshō* (The bell at dawn, 1901).

11. On Akutagawa see chapter 5, note 5.

12. *Shuju no kotoba* (1923–27) is a collection of Akutagawa's aphorisms spiced with paradoxes and ironies. With no coherent plot or systematic organization to speak of, Akutagawa comments on contemporary culture, art, society, life, and thought. The writer and critic Nakamura Shin'ichirō praises its "very high literary value" and Akutagawa's "lucid logic, clever allegories, and the richness and originality of his ideas" (*Akutagawa Ryūnosuke no sekai* [Kadokawa shoten, 1974], 134), while other critics note his witty frivolity and generally cynical perspective.

the 1920s that Akutagawa wrote: "A military man is just like an infant."
But when I read it in the mid-1930s, these words struck me as an utterance from my contemporary. Every value that had until then been held sacred in schools, at homes, and by the public at large all of a sudden crumbled before my eyes under Akutagawa's single blow. Yesterday's heroes became ordinary mortals; patriotism became self-aggrandizement; absolute obedience became irresponsibility; and virtue became cowardice if not ignorance. My eyes were opened to the possibility that the same social phenomena could inspire diametrically opposite interpretations from those offered by the newspapers, by the middle schools, and by the general public as a whole. I was filled with such jubilation that I was beside myself in a moment of frenzied excitement. In the end, I bought the ten volumes of Akutagawa's complete works from a secondhand bookstore in Shibuya and immersed myself in them. I even ended up memorizing almost all the names of numerous literary figures quoted in his writings. By my fourth year in middle school, I had finished reading all the books I could borrow from my friend, the novel enthusiast. By then I had turned into a zealous reader of Japanese and foreign novels, devouring everything I could find at home as well as at Grandfather's house. Even when my higher-school entrance examination was approaching, I was not the least motivated to spend more than the minimum time preparing for it.

Father was not happy with his son for being so taken up with "trashy novels." He argued how socially worthless this idle business of literature was to begin with, how despicable the writers' morality was—with the exception of Sōseki[13]—and how foolish it was for me to waste my time reading novels when my higher-school entrance examination was just around the corner. But his arguments could no longer convince me. Mother came to her son's defense, saying that even if literature had no social relevance, it had its own aesthetic value. She pointed out that Father himself had once enjoyed reading the *Man'yōshū* and composing *waka*. She also said that as long as I could pass the higher-school entrance examination, she thought it was best for them not to be too critical. My position was that since I had already reduced my elementary-school education from its formal six years to five, I did not feel obligated to again shorten my middle-school years from five to four. At the same time, I was optimistic about my chances of passing the entrance exam-

13. On Natsume Sōseki see chapter 12, note 1.

ination and thought nothing could be more gratifying than passing it without working particularly hard. But things did not work out the way I expected. When I failed the examination, I realized it was much tougher than I had anticipated. I felt apologetic to Mother since she had defended my reading habits against Father's objections. Meanwhile, the thought of having to spend another year—my fifth year—in middle school nauseated me. I thought to myself that at the end of my fifth year, I would take the same examination again, and luck or no luck, I would have to pass it. That would not be particularly difficult to accomplish since during the fifth year nothing new was taught. Instead, we just went over what we had learned in the last four years. While I was preparing for the examination, I would still from time to time dig out literary materials to read. I explained to Father that passing the examination did not actually require as much time studying as he thought.

"But didn't you fail the examination because you were reading novels?"

"That was because I was down on my luck," I replied.

The reason for the distance now developing between Father and me went beyond the question of the entrance examination itself. It was tied, I think, to his expectation that I would become a scientist in the future. That would explain his elation at my interest in popular science when I was in elementary school and his disaffection at my addiction to literary works during my middle-school years. Father was a *Man'yōshū* fan and an amateur poet, an atheist and a thorough positivist, but not only did he despise the "literary youth," he considered them to be pests. And up until that time, I myself had never met one.

The first time I met a real literary youth was in the last summer of my middle-school years when I went to Shinano Oiwake.[14] It was the first time Sister and I had left our parents to go by ourselves to the highlands of Shinshū to escape the midsummer heat in Tokyo. Probably financial reasons kept our parents from coming along.

We took up lodging at an oil shop then situated on the south side of the Nakasendō.[15] It had served as a *wakihonjin,* or a subsidiary lodging

---

14. A summer resort in Nagano Prefecture's Karuizawa-chō, Shinano Oiwake served in the Edo period as a lodging station (*shukuba*) between Kutsukake on the Nakasendō and Odai in eastern Nagano. Its prewar popularity with writers and poets such as Hori Tatsuo and Tachihara Michizō gave the locale a literary flavor, and a number of writers including Katō still make regular summer visits there. See Kondō Tomie, *Shinano Oiwake bungakufu* (Chūō Kōronsha, 1990).

15. Sometimes known as the Tōsandō (road through the Eastern mountains)

house for travelers, in the old days. Its structure dated back to the Edo period and it still had many traces of its former self as a prosperous lodging station before the opening of the Shin'etsu Main Line. Overhanging its wide frontage facing the Nakasendō was its second floor with grid-lattice windows. In the Edo period courtesans presumably waited behind those windows for travelers passing through town, just as Saikaku and others have chronicled.[16]

Along the streets of Oiwake today, there remain only two or three houses with the same design dating back to the Edo period. But it is no exaggeration to say that at the time we were there, there were rows and rows of these structures, the largest one being the oil shop. The passing years had given the heavy pillars and the interior floorboards a black luster, and even when the shoji screen doors were closed, a gap was formed with the supporting columns. The house had electricity, but there were no lights along the corridor. In order to go to the toilet at night, it was necessary to carry a candle for light. Because there were few attendants at the lodging house, all the lodgers would gather in a spacious room for their three meals. Sightseeing attractions in the vicinity were limited to Mount Asama alone, so nearly all of the guests stayed only for the two summer months. Most of them were university students preparing for the senior civil service examinations, or higher-school students waiting to take their university entrance examinations. No one

---

as opposed to the coastal route along the Tōkaidō, the Nakasendō was the main road between Nihonbashi in Edo through Ueno, Shinano, and Mino (now southern part of Gifu Prefecture) to Kusatsu in the southwestern part of present-day Shiga Prefecture, where it merged into the Tōkaidō; some famous lodging stations along the way were Ōmiya, Karuizawa, Tsumago, Magome, Sekigahara, and Echigawa.

In the Edo period magistrates (*bugyō*), the chief retainers, or councillors of *daimyōs* stayed in the *wakihonjin;* the more imposing and elaborate *honjin* (main lodge) was for the *daimyōs* themselves along with members of the aristocratic *kuge* class and important *bakufu* officials.

16. Ihara Saikaku (1642–93), a *haikai* poet, perceptive chronicler of the mannerisms of the merchant class in the Edo period, and highly accomplished pioneer of realist fiction in the *ukiyo- zōshi* (floating-world fiction) genre. Saikaku's works include *Kōshoku ichidai otoko* (The life of an amorous man, 1682), *Kōshoku gonin onna* (Five women who loved love, 1686), *Budō denraiki* (The transmission of the martial arts, 1687), *Nanshoku Ōkagami* (The great mirror of manly love, 1687), and *Nippon Eitaigura* (The Japanese family storehouse, 1688). See Howard Hibbett, *The Floating World in Japanese Fiction* (New York: Grove Press, 1960).

brought his family along, and the local farmers did not hold banquets there, preferring the restaurants in Komoro.[17]

The student lodgers at the oil shop would sometimes go hiking together, and sometimes they would walk for about half an hour to play tennis near the train station. But ordinarily, after taking a short walk, they would shut themselves in their rooms and "hit the books" until late into the night. Through the sliding door, any talking in the next room was clearly audible, but almost none of them stayed for any long conversation. I suppose my parents must have somehow heard about the reputation of the oil shop and thought it would be a good place for their son to study.

As a matter of fact, there was nothing to do except study. After living together under the same roof for over a month, I got acquainted with a number of the university students. From them, I heard stories about fellow lodgers such as the poet Tachihara Michizō and a "literary youth," as the law students sarcastically called him. Tachihara Michizō was a student of architecture; he wrote poetry and was recognized by Hori Tatsuo.[18] The literary youth was reading the collected works of Shestov and generally refused to recognize the talents of any Japanese writer other

17. An old castle town a short distance west of Shinano Oiwake on the Shin'etsu Main Line, Komoro was also known in the Edo period as a lodging station on the Nakasendō. As Katō notes below, the Oiwake oil shop was destroyed by fire, but a remarkably well preserved Edo period *honjin* and a *wakihonjin* still remain, a short walk from the Komoro train station. The poet-writer Shimazaki Tōson spent six years in Komoro as an elementary school teacher (1899–1905), and the town fondly remembers him today with a Shimazaki Tōson Memorial Museum (Shimazaki Tōson Ki'nenkan).

18. Tachihara Michizō (1914–39), a member of the coterie poetry journal *Shiki* (Four seasons) founded by Hori Tatsuo in 1933, was known for the delicate lyricism and musical quality of his sonnetlike poems in fourteen irregular lines, many of them inspired by his experiences in Shinano Oiwake; his three poetry collections were *Wasuregusa ni yosu* (Dedications to the day-lilies, 1937), *Akatsuki to yūbe no shi* (Poems of dawn and dusk, 1937), and *Yasashiki uta* (Gentle songs, 1947). • Hori Tatsuo (1904–53) was a renowned early Shōwa novelist noted for his melancholy lyricism. A disciple of Akutagawa Ryūnosuke and the poet Murō Saisei, Hori also avidly read modern French poets, including Guillaume Apollinaire and Jean Cocteau, whose translations he published in the literary journal *Roba* (Donkey), before turning to Radiguet, Proust, Mauriac, and Rilke. *Kaze tachinu* (The wind has risen, 1936–38), Hori's most celebrated work, brilliantly evokes a young couple's subtle reactions to death at a sanatorium. During the war Hori's growing interest in the Japanese classics inspired his *Kagerō no nikki* (The gossamer diary, 1937) and *Arano* (Wilderness, 1941).

than Hori. While listening to their stories, I realized that my own knowledge of literature was not good enough to follow even the main thrust of their conversation. I hadn't read any of Hori Tatsuo's works, and as for Shestov, I hadn't even heard of him before. I already felt a sense of inferiority toward the literary youth before I ever saw him. But very soon my opportunity came.

He was a young man with a pale complexion and a thin, small build. He slouched like an old man, and his stroll on the street was punctuated by occasional coughs. When we passed each other, my companion, a law student, said, "You look really awful! You'd better not rack your brains too much composing poems. That's not good for your health, you know!"

The young man raised his head abruptly, mumbled something to the university student in a voice too low to be audible and didn't even bother to cast a glance at me. What an arrogant man, I thought. But that was not the incident that led to my understanding of what Father might have in mind when he used the expression "literary youth." That came later, when I saw the same young man who had acted with such discriminating arrogance then behave like an errand boy in front of Hori Tatsuo. I also witnessed how completely he changed his demeanor toward me after he learned that I was acquainted with Hori. Or rather it was the time when I read his poems before he died of tuberculosis. His garbled diction was filled with such saccharine expressions as "gods" and "angels," words that by themselves had nothing to do with Shestov or with Christianity. It was certainly not ideals loftier than the senior civil service examination that made this literary youth contemptuous of the law students in the Oiwake lodge. It was simply his illusion that honeyed words vaguely represented something superior to the subject of civil law. For this he had his intellect to thank, an intellect that would have disqualified him from even preparing for the senior civil service examination. This, I suppose, was precisely what Father had in mind when he talked about literary youths.

Only once during that summer did I have an occasion to talk with the poet Tachihara Michizō. One afternoon while I was taking a stroll on the Nakasendō toward Kutsukake, I saw a tall, lanky young man heading in the same direction. We fell into conversation with each other, and as we walked along, the young man said, "I am Tachihara." Along the way he picked a feathery cluster of eulalia, twirling it playfully in his hands. He said he was on his way to Mr. Hori's house in Karuizawa and inquired whether I was going to study science or the arts when I en-

tered higher school. Then he talked with me about architecture and poetry, and he even told me that he did not know what to pursue in the
future. At that time I had not yet read his poetry and so had not yet
been captivated by its magic. But I was impressed by the lucidity of his
thought and found an unpretentious charm in his personality. After I
returned to Tokyo in the autumn, I heard that the oil shop had been destroyed in a fire and that Tachihara, then living by himself on the second floor, had almost been killed but that the firemen had finally rescued him by sawing open the lattice window. The news brought back
memories of him: the young man in a straw hat twirling the silky white
crown of eulalia as we walked along the Nakasendō on a sunny summer afternoon. I remembered fragments of his incessant flow of quiet
conversation, and his large, curiously impressive eyes. Large not because
they betrayed anxiety or because they were overflowing with vitality
or burning with ambition. On the contrary, his wide-open eyes almost
had a frightened look about them, a fragility bordering on the morbid.
When I went back again to the village in Oiwake the following summer,
Tachihara was no longer there.

10 The February 26 Incident

I entered middle school in 1931, the year of the Manchurian Incident, and completed it in 1936, the year of the February 26 Incident.[1] During the interim, even though I read the newspaper and listened to the radio every day, I had no idea whatsoever about where Japan was heading. The middle school, or at least the community of middle-school students, was totally removed from the world of cabinet ministers, *zaibatsu* directors, and young army officers. To us, even assassinations committed by one party against another were nothing more than insignificant

1. The Manchurian Incident began fifteen years of war between China and Japan until Japan's defeat in 1945: growing Japanese strategic and economic interests in northeastern China, along with the rising tide of Chinese nationalism, prompted junior officers of the Japanese Kwantung Army (with the General Staff's tacit approval) to stage a coup on September 18, 1931, with the aim of turning the region into a Japanese protectorate; faced with this fait accompli and powerless to stop the runaway Kwantung Army, the Japanese government ended up endorsing its actions until nearly all Manchuria was in Japanese hands by January 1932.

The February 26 Incident, the last of a series of direct military actions in the 1930s by extremist army and civilian groups, began in early dawn when twenty-two young officers from the army's ultranationalist *Kōdō* (imperial way) faction and 1,400 troops occupied major government buildings such as the Diet, the Army Ministry, and the General Staff Headquarters and assassinated several cabinet ministers and high-ranking officials. The uprising was suppressed within three days, after initial sympathy for the young insurgent officers turned to widespread condemnation of their attempt at national reconstruction. The chief conspirators and ideological leaders of the uprising, including Kita Ikki and Nishida Zei, were quickly given death sentences, but the failed coup d'état ironically strengthened the army's political influence within the government, and its *Tōsei* (control) faction, the rival of the rebellious *Kōdō* group, became the predominant force.

episodes buried among more important matters such as term examina-tions, sports meets, and summer vacations. The son of Army Minister Araki was in my grade, but he was just an ordinary student and received no special treatment from anyone.[2] All these incidents took place out of the blue as if completely by accident, and after our momentary shock had subsided, they were quickly forgotten. Such was the case with the assassinations of Finance Minister Inoue, Dan Takuma, and Prime Min-ister Inukai, the recognition of Manchukuo, the conclusion of the Japan-Manchuria Agreement, and the withdrawal of Japan from the League of Nations.[3] Since none of these incidents had any immediate impact on our daily life, we did not even pause to ponder what significant changes they might bring to our lives in the future.

Father read the newspaper religiously every morning, and when a cer-tain incident took place, he would tell us his views over dinner. As his audience consisted only of members of his own family, he was un-doubtedly *free* to express his views without any fear of censorship or social pressure of any kind. However, the material that informed his opin-ion was restricted to the kind of information selectively reported by the newspapers and radio stations after they had gone through a process of

2. Araki Sadao (1877–1966), army minister under the Inukai Tsuyoshi and Saitō Makoto administrations and a leader of the army's radical *Kōdō* faction, became minister of education in the first Konoe Fumimaro cabinet (1937–39); sentenced to life imprisonment as a Class-A war criminal after Japan's defeat, he was paroled in 1954 because of ill health.

3. Inoue Junnosuke (1869–1932), a Minseitō politician, served as director of the Bank of Japan in 1919 and 1927 as well as finance minister in the second Ya-mamoto Gonnohyōe and Hamaguchi Osachi cabinets; he was assassinated by a member of an ultranationalist terrorist group called the Ketsumeidan (league of blood) in February 1932. • Dan Takuma (1858–1932), a former Fukuoka samurai who rose through the ranks to become the leader of the Mitsui *zai-batsu* and director of the Japan Economic League, was assassinated by a mem-ber of the Ketsumeidan in March 1932. • Inukai Tsuyoshi (1855–1932), a lead-ing party politician and a major voice for constitutional democracy in prewar Japan, was elected eighteen times to the House of Representatives; during his distinguished career he was education minister (Ōkuma Shigenobu cabinet, 1898), minister of communications (Katō Takaaki cabinet, 1924), president of the Seiyūkai (1929), and prime minister (1931–32), but his conciliatory policy toward China after the Manchurian Incident and his insistence on democratic principles led to his assassination by military officers in the May 15 Incident in 1932. • Japan's recognition of Manchukuo under its hand-picked ruler, Pu-yi, the last Qing emperor, came in September 1932 from the Saitō Makoto admin-istration. The Japan-Manchuria Agreement was ratified the same month, and Japan withdrew from the League of Nations in March 1933.

official and voluntary censorship. This was a time when freedom of the press *did not exist*. When Father expressed his thoughts freely about the fall of Nanjing, he—like perhaps the majority of the Japanese people— lacked free access to the facts about the Nanjing Massacre. "Lantern processions are fine, but it really appears we're going to have a tough time ahead" was what he said. If only he had known that the Japanese "imperial army" had massacred tens of thousands of Chinese citizens, including women and children, all in the name of "eternal peace in the Orient" and "friendship with our neighbors," I don't suppose he would have said the same thing about the lantern processions. People who believed they had the greatest freedom even though they had not been informed of anything in fact had the least freedom, just like the many Germans who "had not been told" about the concentration camps for the Jews, or the many Americans who "had not been told" about many Vietnamese towns reduced to rubble because of American bombardment of "military targets."

The commission sent by the League of Nations and headed by England's Earl of Lytton toured China, "Manchukuo," and Japan before producing a compromising report in the fall of 1932. Father thought that the report distorted the intention of the Great Japanese Empire with the aim of exerting unjust pressure on Japan. In the following year, the Japanese representative, Matsuoka, walked out of the General Assembly of the League of Nations in opposition to the passage of a remonstration bill against Japan, thus ensuring Japan's international isolation.[4] Yet to Father, nothing could be more gratifying. On the other hand, Father was critical of the increasing political influence of the army within the country, and when Saitō Takao presented his famous speech in the Japanese Diet urging greater army discipline, Father praised him in the highest terms.[5] However, when Father the atheist spoke of the Japanese emperor,

---

4. Called the hero of Geneva by Japan's military and right-wing groups, Matsuoka Yōsuke (1880–1946) became the president of the South Manchurian Railway (1935–39) and a close ally of Japan's fascist establishment. As foreign minister in the second Konoe cabinet, he signed the Tripartite Pact with Germany and Italy in 1940 and the Japan-Soviet Neutrality Pact in 1941. After the war, he was named a Class-A war criminal.

5. Saitō Takao (1870–1949), a Kenseikai and later Minseitō politician first elected to the Lower House in 1912 and a notable liberal during the Taishō period. In February 1940 Saitō's sharp criticism of Japan's China policy and the high moral rhetoric of Japanese expansionism on the continent led to his expulsion from the Diet (see Gordon Mark Berger, *Parties Out of Power in Japan:*

he always used the expression "His Majesty" with great reverence. His emotional attachment to the emperor was so strong that he would go to the Yoyogi drill ground on the day of the military parade and wait for a long time in the blustery wind just to catch a glimpse of His Majesty from afar. But when the House of Peers attacked Dr. Minobe's theory of the emperor as an organ of the state, Father was impressed with Dr. Minobe's coherent logic while severely criticizing the views of his attackers as totally inconsistent and utterly stupid.[6] "Don't you think it's better not to say too much in front of the children?" Mother said. "No!" Father responded. "Who knows if those incompetent self-proclaimed patriots and the House of Peers wouldn't bring harm to the country and to His Majesty? I'd say it's a mighty good idea to let the children know a thing or two about this."

However, Father's views had made almost no impact on me. Sometimes his views on certain incidents struck me as the only natural thing to say, while at other times I thought they were merely peculiar emotional reactions from someone who belonged to a different generation. Very seldom did his views elucidate the relationship between one incident and another. Causality played no role in Father's world, for to him things just happened haphazardly without any prior warning. His vision of the world was made up of a large number of villains coexisting with a few heroes, and they waged furious battles with one another. But in the final analysis, it was impossible to anticipate when, where, or what these elusive villains were conspiring. One knows not what tomorrow will bring: That was the crux of Father's world.

It seems to me that regardless of time and space, the majority of the

---

1931–1941 [Princeton: Princeton University Press, 1977], 245–48). After the war Saitō served under the first Yoshida Shigeru and Katayama Tetsu cabinets.

6. Minobe Tatsukichi (1873–1948), eminent constitutional scholar, law professor at Tokyo Imperial University from 1902–32, and a member of the House of Peers who recognized official *kokutai* (national polity) ideology and saw the emperor as "the highest organ of the state" but "clearly less than the state and subordinate to [its] laws." As a bulwark against Uesugi Shinkichi's more absolutist interpretation of the emperor's position under the Meiji constitution, Minobe's theory was "the dominant legal interpretation of the constitution from World War I until 1935"—the year Minobe's views were denounced in the Diet (John K. Fairbank, Edwin O. Reischauer, and Albert M. Craig, *East Asia: The Modern Transformation* [Boston: Houghton Mifflin, 1965], 533). For a detailed study of Minobe in English see Frank O. Miller, *Minobe Tatsukichi: Interpreter of Constitutionalism in Japan* (Berkeley: University of California Press, 1965).

citizens in a warring state will always try to align their own position with that of their government. When it came to Japan's foreign policy, Father, a supporter of Japan's withdrawal from the League of Nations, was no exception. But in his case, his intense dissatisfaction was directed at the existing power establishment and at the general conditions of his time. Perhaps such sentiments only served to heighten his psychological need to support his own government's foreign policy. During my middle-school years, Father no longer maintained much connection with the medical department of his alma mater nor with the local medical society, and the *tonari-gumi* had not yet been formed.[7] And with the exception of Grandfather's household nearby, Father's social interaction with our relatives was very limited as well. Our family had chosen to live in isolation and was totally powerless in society. Father's medical practice could hardly be called a success, and he himself derived neither satisfaction nor pleasure in his work. He was an honest man with a strong sense of responsibility, but generosity of spirit was definitely not one of his character traits. No one escaped his scathing criticism. To be sure, his criticisms were often very perceptive, though frequently they were also biased. "What good does it do to speak ill of everyone like that?" Mother used to grumble, to which Father would reply, "I'm not saying I'm the smartest man alive. But whether I am or not, it doesn't change the fact that those attacking Minobe's theory are incompetent." He surely had a point there. "Fellows who make a fortune by giving useless injections do not deserve to be called doctors. Giving vitamin shots to patients with no symptoms of vitamin deficiency is cheating." He was right about that one as well. If only the world did not have so many incompetent people and if only deception had not prevailed, surely the enterprise of Japan's wars could not have materialized, sending tens of thousands of young men to the battlefield and driving millions of Japanese into a frenzy just in the name of some short-lived and totally variable goals or ideals.

As I think about them now, most of Father's criticisms were not wide of the mark and most of his arguments were logically sound. However, Mother was concerned not so much with the substance of his criticisms

---

7. The *tonari-gumi*, neighborhood associations for every five to ten households, were formed in 1940 by the Home Ministry to coordinate mobilization at the city and village level and exercise greater supervisory control over its citizens as local indoctrination organs. They also distributed rations and organized anti-air raid drills. The system was abolished in 1947 (see Berger, *Parties Out of Power*, 282–83).

as with the psychological motivation behind them. It was not in spite of, but rather precisely because of, Father's dissatisfaction with every aspect of society around him that he felt compelled to worship "His Majesty" and to support Japan's international position. I suppose the reason why a great many fervent patriots love their country is that they cannot love their neighbors. And Father also had this fervent, patriotic side to his character. Mother, on the other hand, knew the English nuns only too well during her five years of close association with them to rebuke the Lytton Report and to curse the British people as a whole. And she was too deeply concerned with the lives of her son and his friends to accept the rhetoric of a "sacred war."

While a part of Father betrayed his impassioned patriotism, he did not allow himself to turn into a fanatic. He lacked the attributes necessary to be one. There was nothing in his character that would induce him to become supralogically possessed by some "divine spirit." His thorough, positivistic skepticism would not let him accept any frenzied ideology. As the war progressed, the more fanatical the behavior of the "clowns" in the army—that was what Father scornfully called them—the more frosty and brusquely sardonic his attitude became toward war propaganda. "All this rubbish about the divine wind and stuff like that! Total nonsense!" But this happened later on. When he supported Japan's withdrawal from the League of Nations, he was at the same time in favor of Saitō's speech demanding the tightening of army discipline. I wonder what he thought about the relationship between those two positions. In the 1930s when he supported the foreign policy of the Japanese government on the one hand and opposed the military's interference in domestic politics on the other, I wonder what he thought of the role of the military in the making of Japanese foreign policy. He probably hadn't thought through these issues adequately.

There was only one substantial difference between Father's thinking at that time and mine after the outbreak of the Pacific War during the early 1940s. I remembered how difficult it was to establish any logical coherence in the various views he expressed over dinner when I was still a middle-school student. I tried to interpret the multitude of events taking place in the aftermath of the Manchurian Incident as a movement within Japanese society toward a particular direction. My understanding was indisputably naive, but there were no logical inconsistencies in it. I detested militarism and considered the propaganda by fanatical patriots ridiculously anachronistic, and I never sanctioned the war aims as enunciated by the government of the Great Japanese Empire. Needless to say, whether I approved or disapproved of the war, my views were strictly private. No one threatened me because of my ideas and they didn't influence anyone, much less affect what I was doing at the time. In this sense, my attitude toward the war in the 1940s was not the least different from Father's attitude toward Japan's aggression against China.

Every now and then my relatives would gather at Grandfather's house, and sometimes somebody would say, "Here's something for your ears only," and then proceed to relate an insider story—or what sounded like one. They talked about rumors like such-and-such army division would leave Japan in the coming month, about Mazaki as the one behind such-and-such an incident and not Araki, or how His Majesty had said this and that to the prime minister.[8] Regardless of where these rumors might have originated, they somehow managed to filter into Grandfather's household. My uncle from Osaka loved to tell these insider stories, although he most certainly had no way of really knowing them. On the other hand, my uncle in the navy surely did have access to secret information, but even on the rare occasions when he appeared among our relatives, he never allowed anything to slip from his lips. But in most cases, one's assessment of any situation, whether it turns out to be right or wrong, seldom ever changes as a result of some secret information, to say nothing of words "for your ears only." That I had absolutely no idea of where Japan was heading when I was in middle school had nothing to do with any scarcity of information, but instead with my inability to analyze and synthesize it. Such a skill was not something I could learn from Father or from anyone around me. I could not think of anyone among my secondary school teachers, or among my relatives (including the industrialist, the top naval officer, the doctor, the merchant, and other men and women), who in this respect was any more capable than a middle-school student. And so in this way, we spoke of the war in a calm and leisurely manner without understanding what it meant. Even though we might occasionally hear about "dreadful" or "important" insider stories, never in our dreams could we imagine that dreadful things would ever come our way. In

8. General Mazaki Jinzaburō (1876–1956), a leader of the army's *Kōdō* faction and inspector general of military education in 1934. Although his role in the February 26 Incident was suspected, he was subsequently cleared of any complicity.

short, we, as good citizens, were awaiting the coming of February 26, 1936, without knowing it.

In that February of 1936, I was preparing for the entrance examination scheduled in March and did practically nothing except go over the intolerably boring reference books again and again. I cannot even remember whether I commuted to school every day. Most likely, the school was closed for holidays, in which case I must have kept myself at home most of the time. Each day was just like another. At times like that, watching the sunset from the window of the study on the second floor was the major event of the day. Sometimes the wind rattled the windows, and sometimes raindrops fell on the outside of the clouded glass. A raindrop might slowly glide down the surface, then come to a virtual stop at a certain point before continuing down again with a spirited dash. I thought of writing the name of my loved one on the clouded window, but since I didn't have a loved one and didn't even know a young girl I could pretend was my love, all I could do was write my own name, only to give up halfway through.

In those days, the place we called our dining room was next to the kitchen on the north side of the first floor. With our coal-burning stove, the room was warm even on wintry nights. After we finished dinner there, Father would read his newspaper, while Mother would clear the table and wash the dishes with Sister. When I was through with the newspaper, I would turn to my reference books. Our family would spend the evening there reading, writing letters, or having a quiet conversation. Sometimes after my parents and sister had retired to their chilly bedrooms, I would stay by myself in the room for a while. Since the stove had been filled with coal and started before dinnertime, the fire burned vigorously throughout the evening and into the middle of the night. Before it completely died out, I would warm my pajamas by the stove and then go to bed. From the outside I could hear the flute of the noodle peddler and the sound of freight trains as they ran over the short iron bridge at Shibuya Station, their rumbling noises echoing in the late night air. So went another day, I thought. Tomorrow would begin and end just like this, and the pattern would repeat itself until the end of my entrance examination. My life would—and could only—begin after I had escaped from the clutch of my cursed middle school that had prepared me for nothing except examinations. But of course history marched on irrespective of my entrance examination.

One snowy morning, Father heard on the radio's morning broadcast about the coup d'état by army officers. "It's probably not a good idea to send the children to school today," he remarked. The family gathering in front of the radio soon learned that Finance Minister Takahashi Ko-rekiyo, Minister of the Interior Saitō Makoto, Inspector General of Army Education Watanabe Jōtarō, and possibly Prime Minister Okada Keisuke had all been killed and that the rebellious troops had now occupied the vicinity of Nagata-chō, where the prime minister's residence and the Diet building were located.[9] "I'm so glad you didn't go to school today," Mother said. But as it became evident soon afterwards, even if we had gone to our school near Nagata-chō, we would have had nothing to fear for our personal safety. Since the occupation troops had blocked off traffic at Akasaka Mitsuke, students going to school that morning found them-selves chatting and smiling with armed soldiers, and when they were told to go home in any case, they all did. No one was as safe as a middle-school student. Although the soldiers had killed cabinet ministers, at-tacked the Metropolitan Police Headquarters, and thrown sand into the rotary machines at the Asahi newspaper company, they did not regard Tokyo citizens as their enemies.

This of course does not mean that they regarded the citizens as their allies either. Father did not like the coup d'état from the beginning. He thought that Takahashi Korekiyo and Saitō Makoto, unlike the corrupt politicians of the time, were exceptional men who had no desire for per-sonal gain. To have them killed in order to "purify" politics hardly seemed logical to him. In his eyes, the rebellion and assassinations were just manifestations of the army's uncontrollable ambitions. When he

9. Takahashi Korekiyo (1854–1936) was president of the Bank of Japan in 1911, finance minister in six separate cabinets, prime minister (1921–22), and president of the Seiyūkai (1921–25); his moderate fiscal policy antagonized the radical factions in the army that demanded greater military spending. • Saitō Makoto (1858–1936) was an admiral who served as governor general of Korea (1919–27, 1929–31) and as prime minister (1932–34) his administration rec-ognized Manchukuo in 1932 and withdrew Japan from the League of Nations in 1933. • Watanabe Jōtarō (1874–1936) was a moderate army general of the Tōsei faction who served as inspector general of military education from 1935. • Okada Keisuke (1868–1952) was an admiral and a former naval minister in the Tanaka Giichi and Saitō Makoto administrations and prime minister (1934–36); his administration could not restrain the army's radical faction in disputes over the constitutional status of the emperor and aggressive military involvement on the Chinese continent. He barely escaped assassination in the February 26 Incident, but rumors about his death led to his cabinet's resigna-tion the following March.

learned that the navy was gathering its combined fleet in Tokyo Bay in opposition to the army, Father said happily, "Looks like not everything is going the way the army wishes." When he heard on the radio Martial Law Commander Kashii Kōhei's appeal to the rebellious troops, "It's not too late yet. Return to your original units!" he thought that the incident would soon come to an end.[10] It would be best if the rebellious troops would surrender; if not, a short skirmish would settle everything. The matter did not concern us one way or the other.

While listening to the radio broadcast over dinner, we also talked about the kitten somebody had given to Sister, what to feed it, in which room to make its bed, and how to train it. From the moment it became clear that the failed rebellion had come to an end, the whole incident became even less real to us than a small kitten. "Since it has been fed milk before, I think we should also let it drink milk," Sister said.

"Now, that's a little extravagant, isn't it?" somebody said.

"No, we'll do that only for a short time."

Nevertheless, I cannot say that the February 26 Incident did not leave marks on me. I was strongly impressed, first of all, by the fact that army officers who had risen in rebellion in the name of the emperor were later indicted by the emperor himself as "traitors." Secondly, the army leaders who had initially praised the army officers as "troops rising in a high spirit of indignation" subsequently condemned them as "rebels" and began to prepare for their suppression. I don't mean to say that I was sympathetic with the rebellious officers, but in their betrayal I witnessed the unspeakable ruthlessness in the exercise of political power. Wise is the man who keeps politics at arm's length, for the political world is one in which sincerity is met with betrayal, idealism met with exploitation, and yesterday's loyalty construed as today's conspiracy as soon as one has outlived his usefulness. I had no intention of going into politics in the first place, and even if I had, I did not have the means to do so. My conclusion about politics did not change my views in the slightest. On the contrary, it only confirmed what I had believed all along. But beyond that, I would soon find out what the February 26 Incident meant in Japanese history.

When I entered First Higher School, I attended Professor Yanaihara

---

10. Kashii Kōhei (1881–1954), a member of the imperial faction and sympathetic to the rebellious troops, was then the commanding officer for the security of Tokyo.

Tadao's lectures on "Legal Systems in Societies" that were offered to science students at the time.[11] The lecture class met only once a week for an hour, making it impossible to discuss in detail the technical aspects of social systems. Perhaps for this reason, Professor Yanaihara wished to speak about the spirit of parliamentary democracy as it was breathing its last breath in Japan. He said that by exploiting the stipulation that cabinet ministers for the armed forces be chosen only from officers on active duty, the army could in effect paralyze the system of responsible cabinets.

"I see. Without the army minister, no cabinet can be formed," a student remarked. "But I suppose this also means that if the Diet refuses to make any compromise, the army can't create a cabinet either. After the army has aborted a cabinet, I wonder if it isn't impossible to continue without one while making no compromise with the army in policy decisions?"

Professor Yanaihara had been listening attentively to the question with downcast eyes. At that point, he suddenly lifted up his face and spoke in a calm but firm voice: "If that should happen, I am afraid that the army would come and surround the Diet with their machine guns." For a moment the classroom fell into a dead silence. We could see how the path toward military dictatorship would lead us straight into a desolate future. At that very moment and in that very room, we had a distinct feeling that we were listening to the final words of Japan's last liberal thinker. The meaning of the February 26 Incident was clear. At the same time, it also became clear to me what courage and nobility of spirit meant.

11. Yanaihara Tadao (1893–1961), an ardent Christian profoundly influenced by Nitobe Inazō and Uchimura Kanzō during his student days at the First Higher School and by Yoshino Sakuzō's liberal ideas when he was a student of politics at Tokyo Imperial University. Yanaihara taught economics at the latter institution from 1920 and wrote empirical and critical studies of Japanese colonialism: *Shokumin oyobi shokumin seisaku* (Colonization and colonization policy, 1926), *Teikokushugika no Taiwan* (Taiwan under imperialism, 1929), and *Manshū mondai* (The Manchurian question, 1934). His thoughtful September 1937 article "Kokka no risō" (The ideals of the nation; in *Chūō Kōron*), written immediately after the Marco Polo Bridge Incident, was attacked for its pacifist message, leading to his resignation from the university in December 1937. Despite government pressure, Yanaihara continued his Christian faith and antiwar position during the war years. He returned to Tokyo University in November 1945 and was its president from 1951 to 1957.

11 The First Higher School in Komaba

I know nothing about the First Higher School's Hongō dormitory where Father once resided.[1] I went to the same school a year after it had moved its campus to Komaba, and the dormitory I stayed in for three years was a building used after the war by the Faculty of Liberal Education of Tokyo University. Built of concrete, the structure was still new at the time. The neighborhood around Komaba, too, must have been a new environment for the students and teachers who had been used to Hongō. It did not have any of Hongō's secondhand bookstores, or their favorite *oden* shops, or the kind of sukiyaki places where they could have sake and get rowdy. Besides, Komaba did not have Tokyo Imperial University as its neighbor. Indeed, one had to go as far as Shibuya to find a good shopping area. In spite of this, or rather because of this, at Ichikō—that was what the First Higher School used to be called—the students tried hard to transplant the long-cherished customs their Hongō predecessors had created into this new setting. If there is ever such a thing as school spirit, perhaps that was the time when the residents of Ichikō's dormitories were

1. The higher schools prepared students for advancement into the imperial universities. The First Higher School (or Ichikō, short for Daiichi Kōtō Gakkō), established in 1886 in Tokyo's Bunkyō Ward and moved in 1935 to Komaba in Meguro Ward, had highest rank and was the stepping-stone to Tokyo Imperial University—the most prestigious institution of higher learning. Ranking second and third in prestige were the Third Higher School in Kyoto (or Sankō, mentioned below) and the Second Higher School (Nikō) in Sendai, respectively. In 1949 the First Higher School became the Faculty of Liberal Education (Kyōyō gakubu) of Tokyo University. On Ichikō see Donald Roden, *Schooldays in Imperial Japan: A Study in the Culture of a Student Elite* (Berkeley: University of California Press, 1980).

most conscious of it and the school's traditions. That a tradition or set of conventions needs to be consciously advocated, supported, and perpetuated may seem odd to an outsider. Being new to the dormitory, with no idea what life was like in Hongō, I found many things there that were worthy of my respect. At the same time, some of the things I encountered were so ludicrous that it was hard for me to take them seriously.

The First Higher School had long been proud of its system of self-governing dormitories.[2] With only a few exceptions, commuters were not allowed. In principle, all students had to live in the dormitories and share a communal life governed by regulations stipulated by the residents themselves. Elected committee members were responsible for maintaining discipline, and they answered to the dormitories' general assembly. Apart from budgetary matters, neither the school administration nor the teachers would interfere in any way with the residents' self-government. When students broke the rules, those they feared were not the teachers or the dormitory superintendents, but the generally elected committee members who had the residents' public opinion behind them. While the legacies of Taishō democracy were rapidly disintegrating in Japan in the 1930s, another form of democracy was still alive and well inside Komaba's Ichikō dormitories.

One could perhaps even go so far as to say that Ichikō's democracy was tied to a sort of individualism. Some students regularly attended class and studied until late at night. Others almost never went to class, preferring instead to read their favorite books during the day and have a good time in town until late at night. Sometimes a student would suddenly embark on a solitary trip and disappear for as long as a week or ten days. Others might become so engrossed in sports that they would not normally do anything else, except before the examination when they would study frantically and get good grades anyway. Some students took on an appearance of studied sloppiness, wearing tattered clothes and torn

2. *Education in Japan*, a publication in English prepared by the Japanese Ministry of Education in 1914 for the Panama-Pacific International Exposition, states, "the object of the Higher School is not to give a purely intellectual education . . . both mental and moral instruction must be given in the Higher School for the production of in all respects thoroughly-equipped men. The students of the Higher School being young men of the age of twenty or thereabouts, they are of an age very susceptible of moral influence, and consequently in each Higher School dormitories are provided where they are carefully shielded from evil and kept under strict control, great attention being paid to their moral and spiritual development" (74).

caps, while others were well-groomed in their starched uniforms. Even students living in the same room might differ in lifestyle and attire. There was a tendency to regard these differences as a matter of course and to accord them mutual and equal respect. Dormitory rules were leniently applied. For instance, even if one came back to the dormitory late at night, after the closing time, one could get in simply by climbing over the gate. Since such behavior was more or less openly condoned, in practice we were free to return any time we wanted.

The principle of self-government and the tendency to respect the individual did not, however, lead to a genuine appreciation of the idea of equality. On the contrary, there existed a grandiloquent elitist consciousness among the students, a vague belief that they and they alone were allowed prerogatives denied to the ordinary people. Since the Meiji period, Ichikō had been feeding the majority of its graduates into Tokyo Imperial University; graduates of the imperial university became government bureaucrats or technical experts and occupied positions of leadership in society. Students at Ichikō thought that even though the country might not actually be in their hands now, it would rightfully be so before long. The Hongō residents took an old melody as their dormitory song and continued to sing it in Komaba. In that famous song were the words "Gazing down at the crossroads of worldly prosperity."[3] With Japan's bitter war experience in China, rising commodity prices, and the onset of sufferings brought about by supply shortages, Tokyo at the end of the 1930s was far from being a crossroads of prosperity. But the significance of the lyrics does not lie in the reference to prosperity itself, but in the words "gazing *down* at" the city and its inhabitants. That is to say, the "equality" within that small community of students was founded on the premise of inequality within a larger social context. What that means is that the idea of equality had not been thoroughly applied. This failure also manifested itself in the direct borrowing of values from the surrounding society by the very group whose aspiration was to distinguish itself from its surroundings. Coexisting with the rationalism among its elite was an emphasis on a kind of spiritual fortitude or moral

3. The first stanza of the Ichikō dormitory song "Aa gyokuhai ni hana ukete" (Flowers in a jade cup) went as follows: "Standing tall atop Mukōgaoka Hill / We the stalwarts of the five dormitories / Our spirits high / Gazing down at the crossroads of worldly prosperity / As it indulges itself in dreams of peace / With flowers in a jade cup / And moonlight reflections on emerald wine" (as revised from Roden, *Schooldays in Imperial Japan*, 137).

thinking. Regulations applicable to all residents were determined rationally. But because of the elite's unique brand of spiritualism, rules and conventions applicable to only some residents, and particularly to the members of the athletics department, for example, were utterly irrational.

It was true that there was a time in the past when the interschool baseball competition between Ichikō and Sankō was regarded as the epitome of Japanese baseball.[4] Later on, it was the Waseda-Keiō game that enjoyed widespread popularity, and the Ichikō-Sankō showdown attracted only the attention of the students who were themselves involved. The same could be said of other sports competitions. In the late 1930s when I myself moved into the dormitory and became a member of the tennis team, the students there were more than just enthusiastic about the Ichikō-Sankō games; they absolutely went wild about them.

In order to win our game with Sankō that was scheduled in the fall, we started training from the beginning of the academic year in April. After classes were over at around four in the afternoon, we had to rush immediately to the tennis courts and begin our practice. Freshmen students were assigned to pick up the balls for the six upperclassmen who were undergoing rigorous training for the competition. Although the freshmen were not totally denied the opportunity to play themselves, they could do so only for a very short time during the three hours they spent on the court. But if I ever enjoyed playing tennis at Komaba, it was when I was a freshman. A year later when I myself became a member of the tennis team against Sankō, I came to realize that the kind of training where a few players monopolized the court while all the others picked up the balls was no fun at all. After two hours' practice, even the long spring day would turn into dusk, making tennis balls hard to see clearly. We would then each stand in front of the center net and practice running backwards as we tried to strike down the high overhead balls served by our partners from the other side. Even though it was getting rather dark, we could still see the ball quite clearly against the sky. I was already totally exhausted, and since this practice required a great deal of physical stamina, doing it over and over again twenty times or so would only make me trip over my own feet. Even now, I can still remember looking up at Komaba's evening sky in those spring days as I chased the little ball in the dark.

4. A reference to the Third Higher School located in Kyoto, amalgamated in 1949 into Kyoto University.

After coming back to the dormitory and taking a bath, we would have
our late dinner in the empty dining hall. The food was delicious! After
dinner, if I spent any time going over my textbooks to prepare for the
following day's classes, I had no more energy left to go for a play in town
or to look for the books I wanted to read. Although rainy days would
give us a chance to rest, if good weather continued for several weeks our
exhaustion would accumulate. I once suggested that instead of going on
with our practice when we were already tired, it would be more effective to take a break and continue after we got back our energy. But the
upper-class students who directed the tennis division absolutely refused
to set aside holidays from practice except when it rained. The rigorous
training was aimed not only at improving skills; it was considered a virtue
in itself and an opportunity to practice mental perseverance.

Technically speaking, Ichikō's tennis team at that time was not very
good. Nevertheless, there were indeed cases where mental perseverance
in the end helped score victories for us. One time the captain of our team,
known for his own unique style of playing, was competing against someone who was clearly a better player, both in terms of skill and physical
stamina. His adversary dominated the court from beginning to end, scor-
ing brilliantly with his powerful strikes, but it was our captain who won.
After that I had to admit that mental perseverance did have some effect.
At the same time, I also couldn't help wondering whether it was really
necessary to go to such lengths in order to win. We had succeeded in
knocking down a far superior adversary through our obstructionist techniques. It was not fair play.

The competition between Ichikō and Sankō took place in Tokyo and
Kyoto in alternate years. Residents from both schools organized their own
cheering teams independent of those from their own athletics depart-
ments, and they would go with their teams to Tokyo or Kyoto, as the case
might be, to root for them. They would shout out their dormitory songs,
hoot at the other team, beat their drums, heckle their opponents, and act
as though they were enjoying their harassing tactics. But when I was playing the game, neither drums nor jeers particularly bothered me. Rather,
the frenzied attention all these elite students paid to every little movement I made greatly satisfied my vanity. Nothing pleases the actor on
the stage more than an attentive and responsive audience. The rowdy
cheers from teams on both sides greatly encouraged my performance. If
I lost the game, it was because my competitor's skill was better, not because Sankō's cheering team succeeded in obstructing my play.

The excitement surrounding the game started well before the day of the actual event and reached its climax at the general assembly in which all residents convened to cheer the team. As their team representatives, the captains of the various sports divisions would rise and make their pledge as a gesture to the other students and their cheering teams. Their words were simple, something like "Our baseball team will definitely win!" or "Our tennis team will absolutely win!" They were uttered with great seriousness, and the other students would yell "All right!" and applaud.

Of course nobody could tell until the end of the game whether we would "definitely win" or not. It was a bad rhetorical habit—at least inappropriate—for such an assembly of "intellectual elites" to proclaim "We will definitely win!" when they should have said "We really want to win." That was what I said after attending such a general assembly for the first time. Then somebody explained to me, "It's not good enough to use such lukewarm words as 'We want to win.' What's important is the spirit of absolute victory." Hence the link between the notion of "spirit" and the idea of "absolute victory"—at the expense of rhetorical precision. The gathering at Ichikō's general assembly with its talk of "spirit" was certainly not a phenomenon isolated from the rest of Japanese society in the late 1930s.

The tennis team's practice schedules and a number of related rules were determined by the third-year students headed by the captain, not by all the team members as a whole. While the idea of self-government within the dormitory stemmed from the students' awareness of their privileged position vis-à-vis the outside world, the same idea failed to permeate the athletics department within the dormitory. On one hand, the students' academic life demanded rationalism; on the other hand, what shaped their daily life was an incredible emphasis on spiritualism. For instance, the tennis division banned cigarette smoking until our competition with Sankō was over, but rowdy singing along the corridor was tacitly approved even though it interfered with other people's sleep. It was not because cigarette smoking was believed to be more harmful than insufficient sleep before practice sessions. Rather, it was because anti-smoking was considered to be a virtue in itself while singing the dormitory song aloud was tantamount to a spirited evocation of the soul of Ichikō, which, presumably, was the loftiest manifestation of the very soul of Japan itself.

We could spend the whole night debating fiercely over something trivial and go on to emphasize action over words. Students respected their common pledge of "*Nō* Complaint"—*nō* being the English negative "no"—and they espoused the vaguely defined human and moral imperative "to act like an idiot."[5] We weren't sure what the precise meaning of acting like an idiot might be; the only sure thing was our conviction that we ourselves were *not* idiots. The more forthright among us even demanded that we "act like idiots once in a while." It never seemed to occur to anyone that we might very well have been idiots all along.

Among the freshmen in the tennis division was the son of an Osaka merchant and another from a wealthy Ashiya family. There were also people like me who were from Tokyo's middle or preparatory schools. The Osaka merchant's son was a skilled athlete. He could bounce from the ground, somersault in midair, and land on his feet. He'd had no experience with tennis in his middle school and still became a good player after only a year's practice. He never read anything other than his textbooks. Not only did he refuse to join our serious debates over trivial matters, he would make sarcastic and irreverent remarks about those who got carried away with their "spiritualism." Nobody's comments or advice had any effect on him. The rich man's son from Ashiya was a Christian; he observed the rules carefully, attended classes conscientiously, and abstained from both alcohol and cigarettes. He did frown on the arrogance of the Osaka merchant's son but thought it incumbent on himself as a Christian not to get into a quarrel even with those he found distasteful. But "the spirit of absolute victory" failed to inflame his passions, and he was not a good tennis player. The one who really held on to his conviction and thought that singing the dormitory song aloud would summon an upsurge of victorious spirit was a fellow from Tokyo. A young man with darkish complexion and big eyeballs, he realized his ideal of "studied sloppiness" even before a year was over, when his cap and uniform were reduced to dirty tatters. He was an incredibly clumsy tennis player. He was later put in charge of the affairs of the tennis division and devoted himself selflessly to the team members. Moreover, after the war when Ichikō was turned into Tokyo University's Faculty of Liberal Education, he became a counselor for student affairs. The Komaba he loved so much as a twenty-year-old turned out to be his workplace for a lifetime. I suppose the work of a student counselor demands a spirit of selfless dedication. As he himself believed, his life at

5. The original Japanese phrase *baka ni naru* means "to become a moron."

the tennis division probably provided a useful training ground for his future career.

In the tennis division, besides me there was another physician's son in my grade. Though we differed in many ways, we soon became close friends. He was conscientious about his studies, while I seldom attended class. He was fond of music, played the violin, and was a member of the school symphony orchestra. I continued to read literary works, befriended people outside the tennis division, and tried my hand at writing, naive though I was. He never broke any dormitory or athletic department rules or made any objection to them. I, on the other hand, often broke the rules or objected to them and found myself at the center of many disputes. But if there was something we had in common, perhaps it was our feeling that winning a competition was not a matter of any great significance in our lives. When he was done with his schoolwork and music, he might use his spare time for sports, but he would never sacrifice schoolwork or music for the sake of sports. As for me, once I decided, say, to idle away an afternoon without studying or working on my composition, I wouldn't want to sacrifice that time for anything else. Within a community where passions flamed with thoughts of absolute victory and self-sacrifice, we were more or less outsiders. Our difference was that he was good at using time and making astute compromises, while I was impulsive, often rebelling when my own interests were at stake, and had no tact in expressing my criticism. And so two years passed. When we were in our third year, we both left the tennis division.

By no means were the young people in the Ichikō dormitories from the same age group. I was nineteen when I entered higher school, but some of my classmates were close to thirty. Until that time I had never lived apart from my parents, a mere child compared to classmates who had already worked to support themselves or to friends who had cohabited with the opposite sex. While many of the dormitory's traditions struck me as being rather childish, I also felt my experience was nowhere near those of many of my fellow residents. Some of them were already masters in the art of drinking or flirting with waitresses. I, on the other hand, had never even tasted sake or gone into a restaurant alone.

Whenever an opportunity presented itself, residents would throw fraternizing parties called *komupa*, which might include sake.[6] If sake

6. More frequently called *konpa*, derived from the English word "company," and used by high school and university students. Roden (*Schooldays*

was served, it was customary for those who got drunk—or used the pretext of being drunk—to make a clean breast of their inner thoughts. Opinions they could express freely did not need a special occasion like this. The inner thoughts to be revealed consisted primarily of grievances or discontents they could scarcely utter in comfort with sober minds. They would say something like "Logically speaking, you may be right, but, hey, what harm is there in acting like an idiot once in a while?" In my two years with the tennis division, not even once did a decision represent majority opinion. The thinking was that persuasion could always change minority views, and that all members had to arrive at the same opinion at some point in time. Sometimes, sake and *komupa* became necessary in order to achieve consensus; even when efforts at persuasion proved wanting, sake and the ritual of "revealing inner thoughts" became indispensable mechanisms for people to vent bruised feelings. Reflecting on it after all these years, I suppose what all this means is that the student community at Komaba was, in this sense too, not atypical of a small Japanese social group. The institutionalization of the drinking party as a subtle means to convey intent is one of the great inventions of the Japanese people.

Overall, I found Komaba's lifestyle to be both impressive and repulsive; my sense of pride mingled with my realization of its absurdities. It was at Komaba's dormitory that I first learned about resignation, compromise, and subterfuge—all of them seem unavoidable in any kind of communal living. Within the group, I learned ways to defend myself, but I certainly did not learn to sacrifice for the group. Instead, I committed myself to justifying the idea of noncommitment to self-sacrifice.

---

in Imperial Japan, 110–11) describes such parties as follows: "They usually consisted of twenty or thirty students sitting around a table, nibbling on crackers, singing 'dormitory songs,' and listening to upperclassmen recite school folktales. It was not uncommon either for *konpa* merrymakers to cap off the evening with a round dance, or 'fire storm.' . . . The 'fire storm' was a spur-of-the-moment rite of exaltation. After igniting a small bonfire in the athletic field and stripping down to their waists (or underwear), participants danced arm in arm around the soaring flames in a state of 'fraternalizing ecstasy.'"

12   Self-Caricature

At the higher school in Komaba, the student dormitory was not the only place where its old customs were actively preserved; the "traditions" were faithfully observed inside the classrooms as well. Although students were not supposed to miss more than a third of a year's classes, teachers generally raised no objection if students answered roll calls for their absentee friends—we called it *daihen,* or "surrogate answering service." Students could decide for themselves whether they wanted to go to classes. And the teachers, for their part, did not have to compromise to please their students. They taught what they believed was worthwhile, and their assumption was that somehow students would absorb the preliminary knowledge about the subject entirely on their own. The physics teacher would not concern himself with the students' aptitude for mathematics, and the German teacher would immediately begin reading and translating the classics after just three months of elementary grammar. Pedagogically, their strategy was analogous to putting a child into a pool and expecting him to learn to swim all by himself.

At that time, Professor Iwamoto, a teacher of philosophy whom Natsume Sōseki likened in his novel to a "grand darkness," was using novels by the German romantics to teach us German.[1] He was a scrawny

1. Iwamoto Tei (1869–1941), known for giving his Ichikō students failing grades, studied philosophy at Tokyo Imperial University and wrote *Tetsugaku gairon* (General discussion of philosophy, 1944). • Natsume Sōseki (1867–1916), a preeminent novelist and literary theorist, a keen cultural critic, and an accomplished *kanshi* poet, whose novels ranged from light satirical narratives (*Wagahai wa neko de aru* [I am a cat, 1905–6] and *Botchan* [1906]) to introspective studies of the self and modern life (*Sorekara* [Since then, 1909], *Mon*

man with a hunched back, already quite advanced in age. When he walked up the stairs to the classroom on the second floor, he always looked as if he were slowly crawling his way up. Only red lips gave his deeply wrinkled face a liveliness and a strangely sensual impression. He would ask his students to translate a paragraph from a German novel and then correct their mistakes. "Now, that's not right," he would mumble in a hoarse voice. "What you have here is a description of the woman falling in love with the man. Understood?" Because that was all the explanation he was prepared to offer and because all we had to go on was three months of elementary grammar, naturally we could not understand why the passage meant what he said it did. Students were not allowed to ask questions in class, and more than half of us failed our examination.

Our teacher of German composition was Professor Petzold, a longtime resident of Japan known in his own country as a scholar of Buddhist sutras.[2] But we hardly understood anything he said, and, beyond that, we were simply incapable of writing anything that made any sense in German. Out of boredom, we actively engaged our surrogate answering service for his class, and even our stand-ins preferred to read other books under their desks. One time Professor Petzold came down from his podium, snatched the hidden book from one such student, waved it above his head, and shouted furiously. While we could see that a white-haired Westerner was raving with anger, we had absolutely no idea what he was saying. After listening more carefully to his unavailing attempt at communication, we realized that the old professor was speaking a mixture of English, German, and Japanese: "You are *nicht erai hito!*"—"You people are no good!" Professor Petzold spoke very little Japanese, and we, on the other hand, could understand hardly any

[The gate, 1910], *Kōjin* [The wayfarer, 1912–13], *Kokoro* [1914], *Michikusa* [Grass on the wayside, 1915], and the unfinished *Meian* [Light and darkness, 1916]). • Iwamoto was said to be a possible model for the middle-aged Hirota *sensei* in Sōseki's novel *Sanshirō* (1908), which portrays him as a sharp critic of traditional and contemporary culture, a learned and humble man who seeks neither fame nor wealth and is content to live in a "grand darkness."

2. Bruno Petzold (1873–1949) taught German at Ichikō from 1917 to 1943 and was offered a Tendai priesthood in his later years. Among his major works were *Buddhist Prophet Nichiren: A Lotus in the Sun* (Hokke Jānaru, 1978), *Die Quintessenz der T'ien-t'ai Lehre: eine komparative Untersuchung* (Wiesbaden: O. Harrassowitz, 1982), and *Goethe und der Mahayana Buddhismus* (Vienna, Octopus, 1982).

German. In addition, we had absolutely no interest in Buddhism. The barriers between us effectively blocked whatever potentially profound influence he might have had on us. I did not think of Professor Petzold again until more than twenty years later when I was explaining *Shōbō genzō bendōwa* in German to my students at a university in Munich.[3] If our encounter had taken place twenty years later, the two of us might have been able to have a good discussion on Japanese Buddhism, or we might even have developed a close friendship. But twenty years earlier my intellectual outlook was even less mature than that of the German students who were then listening attentively to my explication.

Professor Katayama Toshihiko, a poet, had chosen as his textbook the German translation of Bergson's *Introduction à la métaphysique*.[4] "This is just a translation, but the substance is really interesting," he said a little defensively. "If you should have any questions, I suggest that you refer to the French original." However, none of us who had had only three months of German could read French. Yet Professor Katayama was a thoughtful instructor, and the textbook was certainly interesting to the extent that I could understand it. When he explained Bergson and his ideas, Professor Katayama made references to numerous French and German poets and philosophers. Since most of their names were new to me, I had no idea how close or obscure their connections with Bergson were. But as these names were conveyed to us through his slightly reedy and agitated voice, they reverberated with an intoxicating charm, as if they were the names of faraway cities in utopian lands. The speaker's affection for his subject—if one could call it that—was compellingly contagious to his audience. Since the days of the Edo Confucianists with their profound admiration for the Chinese intelligentsia, I wonder if anybody

3. *Bendōwa* was a major work on Zen by Dōgen (1200–53), the mid-Kamakura monk who founded the Sōtō sect in Japan (see chapter 37, notes 12–13). • From May to July 1964 Katō taught at the University of Munich's East Asia Institute as a visiting professor; he was forty-five.
4. Katayama Toshihiko (1898–1961), poet, essayist, critic, and translator. Inspired first by Goethe, Rodin, and Maeterlinck and increasingly by Rolland, he translated his *Le Jeu de l'amour et de la mort* in 1926 and later visited Rolland in Switzerland. Returning to Japan, he published *Roman Roran* (Romain Rolland, 1937), *Kokoro no henreki* (Journeys of my heart, 1942), and a translation of Rilke's poems (*Riruke shishū*, 1942). After the war he supervised the publication of the collected works of Rolland while continuing to publish translations and critical works. His works are collected in *Katayama Toshihiko chosakushū*, 10 vols. (Misuzu shobō, 1971–72).

else had cherished, or honestly thought he did, the same deep-seated affection for literary figures from a foreign land. In his younger days Professor Katayama had studied in the West, and through his old acquaintance with the sculptor Takata Hiroatsu, he met Romain Rolland, someone he practically worshiped.[5] He was thoroughly familiar with the works of the poets around Rolland, not to mention Rolland's own works. He loved the tonality of Bonnard and the music of the German romantics and, like Rolland himself, abhorred all forms of militarism, including that of his own country.

Professor Katayama lived with his wife and two children in a one-story house in a residential area not far from Ogikubo Station on the Central Line. He spent his days buried in the mountain of books he had collected. One time I visited him at his Ogikubo home with my fellow students Harada Yoshito and Nakamura Shin'ichirō.[6] "Charles Vildrac was here once," Professor Katayama remarked at one point, as if he were relating a matter of great significance in his life. "In those days, there wasn't any other house in this area, and on their way here along the path in the wheat fields, Vildrac and Ozaki Kihachi could hear the trills of the larks.[7] That made Vildrac very happy, and he kept saying how this place could really

5. Takata Hiroatsu (1900–87), portrait sculptor and translator of Romain Rolland's works, stayed in France from 1931 to 1957 and befriended Alain, Rolland, and Vildrac. His critical works include *Furansu to Nihon to* (France and Japan, 1950) and *Verureenu to Rambō* (Valéry and Rimbaud, 1969). For Katō's moving reminiscence about him, see chapter 28.

6. Harada Yoshito (1918–60) graduated from the Department of German Literature at Tokyo Imperial University, taught at Ichikō from 1948 and at his alma mater from 1950, lectured on Japanese at Hamburg University (1954–56), and became the editor of *Hakobune* (The Ark), the literary journal for the Matinée Poétique group formed in 1942 by Katō, Nakamura Shin'ichirō, and Fukunaga Takehiko, and others (see chapter 18); Harada's works include *Gendai Doitsu bungakuron* (Contemporary German literature, 1949), *Doitsu bungaku nyūmon* (Introduction to German literature, 1952), and translations of Kafka's *The Trial* and *The Castle*, as well as Gottfried Benn's *Double Life*. • Nakamura Shin'ichirō (1918–97), novelist, poet, critic, and a prominent literary figure in postwar Japan, whose major works include novels (*Shi no kage no moto ni* [Under the shadow of death, 1947], *Kūchū teien* [Garden in midair, 1965], *Kumo no yukiki* [Movement of clouds, 1966], and *Kodoku* [Solitude, 1966]) and a critically acclaimed study of the late Tokugawa historian, Confucian scholar, and poet Rai San'yō entitled *Rai San'yō to sono jidai* (Rai San'yō and His Time, 1971).

7. Ozaki Kihachi (1892–1974), poet, essayist, translator. Closely connected with the Shirakaba (white birch) school, his art was influenced by Rolland, Vildrac, Hesse, Duhamel, and Rilke. His works are collected in *Ozaki Kihachi shibunshū* (Poetry and prose writings of Ozaki Kihachi, 10 vols. [Sōbunsha, 1958–75]).

be called the countryside." The house that had once stood alone in the wheat fields was by then buried among numerous other small houses in a heavily crowded area, so much so that it was no longer easy to find. Nevertheless, the master of this house was living in a world so far removed from its surroundings that one could perhaps still see it as a sort of solitary structure.

Professor Katayama once wrote about "stars exchanging whispers." The "stars" he referred to were men such as Novalis, Rilke, Nerval, and the old Aldous Huxley. Perhaps they also included Tagore and Vivekānanda as well. And from that distant world Vildrac descended to earth and landed at Ogikubo only once and never again. Romain Rolland himself, and Duhamel, Martinet, and René Arcos were just like stars sparkling in the infinite distance. Professor Katayama maintained almost no correspondence with them. The war came and went, and even after channels of communication between Japan and France were reopened, Professor Katayama never attempted to call on his old friends in the land he had once visited.

After the war I lived for a time in the home of the poet René Arcos.[8] "Katayama? Why, of course, I know him very well!" Arcos spoke with a slur, having had too much to drink as usual. "And I've met Takata once. But for some reason, I haven't heard from them since." At that time I did not tell Arcos that in a small house made of wood and paper in a place called Ogikubo in Japan, Katayama had been reading each and every one of his works. Had I done so, Arcos would have been moved to learn about a kindred spirit. But at the same time he would probably have asked me why Katayama had not written if that was indeed the case. It would then have taken me a long time to explain that it was *not in spite of* but precisely *because of* the absence of communication between the Japanese poet and his Parisian friend that Katayama was carefully reading every word his friend had written.

Professor Katayama's stars were naturally even farther away from me. I could not even imagine any relationship between their world and mine, a world consisting of Ogikubo's muddy streets, noodle stalls, and drunkards on the midnight Central Line. Yet I was filled with curiosity and probably intellectual vanity as well. As I looked back with deep mortification at the many long hours I had spent reading those ridiculous middle-school textbooks, I dreamed about embarking on a journey

8. See chapter 26.

to reach out for the world of the stars. As I could not read foreign language books speedily, I decided to read as many translations as I could, at a pace of one volume every three days so that I could finish a hundred volumes within a year. I then put my resolution into practice. Since then, I have acquired the bad habit of taking a book along everywhere I go, and I read whenever I have a little time on my hands. Years later, Arcos once asked me, "Do you have the habit of reading in bed?"

"Yes, I do."

"You should know that in bed, there are two things more important than reading: sleep and love . . ."

I agreed with what he said, though at that time there was no woman in his bed, or in mine.

Indiscriminate reading also leads to imprecise understanding. But my higher school gave me the opportunity to experience close reading in action. Professor Gomi, later the chair of Tokyo Imperial University's Department of Japanese Literature, was still a young man when he taught Japanese classics to Komaba's science students.[9] He endeavored to read the text as accurately as possible, not letting the shortest line or even a single word slip by easily. He had the overpowering dynamism and intensity befitting a young and brilliant scholar. Though I didn't become a specialist in Japanese linguistics or literature, the rigorous academic atmosphere that nurtured future scholars like the linguist Ōno Susumu and the literary scholar Koyama Hiroshi made a profound impression on me.[10] When they and Professor Gomi's other disciples gathered to form a reading circle on the *Man'yōshū*, I immediately joined. I had been familiar with the *Man'yōshū* since I was a child, but now these young disciples of Professor Gomi taught me for the first time the methodology of interpreting the work as precisely and accurately as possible.

9. Gomi Tomohide (1908–83) taught at Ichikō and then at Tokyo University from 1949 to 1966. His specialty was classical Japanese literature, the *Man'yōshū* in particular. Among his major works were *Kodai waka* (Ancient Japanese poems, 1951), *Man'yōshū no sakka to sakuhin* (Man'yō poets and their works, 1982) and *Man'yōshū kōgi* (Lectures on *Man'yōshū*, 3 vols., 1985–86).

10. Ōno Susumu (1919–) was a professor at Tōyō Eiwa Jogakuin University and a distinguished scholar of ancient Japanese etymology. Among his major works are *Jōdai kanazukai no kenkyū* (Study of ancient *kana* orthography, 1953), *Nihongo no kigen* (The origin of Japanese, 1957), and *Nihongo o sakanoboru* (Tracing the roots of Japanese, 1974). He was also an editor of Iwanami shoten's *Kogo jiten* (Dictionary of classical Japanese, 1974). • On Koyama Hiroshi, a distinguished scholar of *kyōgen*, see chapter 37 for more details.

My three years' experience in Komaba took in more than communal living in the dormitory and interactions with some of the teachers. I also frequented the Kabukiza and discovered the Tsukiji Little Theater.[11] It was the age of Uzaemon, Kikugorō, and Kichiemon at the Kabukiza.[12] As I stood in the gallery, I saw how a solitary dance by Kikugorō instantly transformed the huge, lifeless stage into an arena of heightened dramatic tension. The audience then was witnessing none other than the awesome display of a master's art. Uzaemon mesmerized me with his piquant trills, reaching all the way to where I stood in the gallery. And then there were Sukeroku, the gang of five thieves, Yūgiri Izaemon, and other memorable roles.[13] I had absolutely no sympathy for the samurai who sacrifices his own child for his lord in a kabuki play. I preferred protagonists like the vagabond gambler or the thief, amorous characters who are tough in

11. Situated in Tokyo's Ginza district, the Kabukiza ranks with Osaka's Shin Kabukiza as the two great kabuki theaters in eastern and western Japan, respectively. It was built in 1889 and rebuilt in 1951 after its damage by fire in 1921, by earthquake in 1923, and by the Tokyo air raids in 1945. • The Tsukiji Little Theater was built in 1924 by Hijikata Yoshi and Osanai Kaoru as the first modern theater for the performance of *shingeki*, or "modern drama," in Japan; in 1940 it became the People's New Theater (*Kokumin shingekijō*) and was destroyed during the war in 1945.

12. Ichimura Uzaemon XV (1874–1945) was a kabuki actor in the Taishō and early Shōwa period whose physical elegance and performing skills made him one of the most prominent *nimaime* (beau-part) actors in such roles as Sukeroku. He was best remembered for his roles in *kizewa-mono* (realist plays) with Onoe Baikō VI (1870–1934) in *onnagata*, or female roles. • Onoe Kikugorō VI (1885–1949) was a celebrated kabuki actor in a line of distinguished performers from the early eighteenth century. He and Nakamura Kichiemon I ushered in the Kikukichi age of kabuki performance; he founded the Nihon Haiyū gakkō (school for Japanese actors) in 1930 and was the first kabuki performer to receive posthumously a cultural medal from the Japanese government. • Nakamura Kichiemon I (1886–1954) was a major kabuki actor, especially noted for his roles as tragic characters in *jidaimono* plays and for joint performances with Kikugorō (*Kagatobi* [Firemen from Kaga] and *Terakoya* [Temple school]).

13. Sukeroku is either the belligerent hero or the common name of the play *Sukeroku yukari no Edozakura*, the only *sewamono* (contemporary play) of kabuki theater's Eighteen Famous Plays; in 1713 Ichikawa Danjūrō II first took the title role. • "The gang of five thieves" is a common name for the play *Aoto zōshihana no nishikie* (1862) by Kawatake Mokuami (1816–93), held to be among the most stylishly dazzling kabuki plays; like other *shiranami-mono* plays, it puts thieves in title roles. • Yūgiri Izaemon combines the names of a famous Osaka courtesan and her lover Fujiya Izaemon; they appear as heroine and hero in a number of Chikamatsu Monzaemon's kabuki and *jōruri* plays such as *Yūgiri nagori no shōgatsu* and *Yūgiri Awa no Naruto*.

brawls and somehow betray a latent rebelliousness against authority. Perhaps it was because I myself was inexperienced with women, helpless in brawls, and had never taken any action against authority. In any case, when I heard Uzaemon's rendition of Sukeroku's caustic dialogue, I felt a thrill run through my whole body, and I found myself literally breathless with excitement. Perhaps with the exception of Umewaka Manzaburō I's *nō* performance, I never experienced so directly such a powerful and sensual impact from any other dialogue uttered in Japanese.[14] In a way, it was comparable to my childhood fascination with Caruso's voice as it poured forth from Grandfather's old gramophone. What mattered was not the meaning of the dialogue, much less the plot, but the stirring dramatic effect manifesting itself through the actor's voice.

At the Tsukiji Little Theater, on the other hand, the movements and vocalization of the kabuki actor gave way to the substance of the dialogue and the personality, convictions, and psychology of the characters. *The Lower Depths, The Cherry Orchard, Northeasterly Winds, Land of Volcanic Ash . . .*[15] Anyone can easily find out the details about the *shingeki* theater during the late 1930s by referring to various source materials. Suffice it to say that during that time, the waves of militarism were gradually encroaching on the steps of the Tsukiji Little Theater. Inside, although the performers and their audience had not quite established a sense of solidarity among themselves, one could nevertheless sense a tacit understanding of their shared defiance of the tides of the time. To me, from the very outset, watching a play represented precisely the sharing of such an experience with the rest of the audience, people who otherwise were total strangers to me. From that time on, going to the theater has become one of my avocations, a part of my life. Later on I traveled to various Western countries and watched their plays. But that came about

---

14. Umewaka Manzaburō I (1868–1946), a *nō* performer of the Kanze school who played *shite* roles and rebuilt the Umewaka school in 1921 but returned to the Kanze school in 1933. On the disputes between these two schools see J. Thomas Rimer, ed., *The Blue-Eyed Tarōkaja: A Donald Keene Anthology* (New York: Columbia University Press, 1966), 234.

15. Among the plays performed at the Tsukiji Little Theater, along with those by Gorky and Chekhov, were *Hokutō no kaze* (Northeasterly winds) by Hisaita Eijirō (1898–1976)—a realist drama of the management dilemmas facing the president of a textile company (first performance, 1937)—and *Kazanbai chi* (Land of volcanic ash) by Kubo Sakae (1900–1958), an accomplished work of socialist realism (first performance, 1938); see David G. Goodman, *Land of Volcanic Ash* (Ithaca: Cornell East Asia Papers, 1986).

because I had already discovered the world of the theater in the Kabu-kiza and in the Tsukiji Little Theater, not because of any discovery in the West of what a play could accomplish.

What I discovered in the West was not the world of the theater, but the world of painting and sculpture, and quite possibly the world of architecture as well. At that time, my experience with Japanese art included only a few gardens in Kyoto. To begin with, I was not interested in the *fusuma-e* of the Kanō school, and the oil paintings exhibited at Ueno were no more than a display of imitations.[16] Japanese architects had yet to demonstrate their real creative talents, which did not blossom until the postwar period. And above all, there was nothing steadfastly ebullient in Tokyo culture during the interwar years to impel us toward an appreciation of the meaning of the formative arts. True, we did have the Katsura Detached Palace. But the discovery of the villa's significance in the 1930s came not from Tokyo culture but from its Western counterpart, which gave us Bauhaus and Bruno Taut.[17] I, on the other hand, was living under the canopy of Tokyo culture.

I was beginning to develop a great fascination for piano music— influenced less by Professor Katayama, a piano enthusiast, than by two classmates. They were the ones who initiated me into the music of the romantics. Often two or three of us would go to the concerts by Leonid Kreutzer, Hara Chieko, or Iguchi Motonari.[18] I remember how excited we were over Kusama Kazuko's (later Yasukawa Kazuko) stunningly

16. *Fusuma-e* is a generic term for paintings executed on Japanese-style sliding screens made of long, thin pieces of wood supporting paper or cloth mounted on both sides. • With official patronage, the Kanō school flourished from the Muromachi through the Momoyama to the Edo period; its major painters included Kanō Masanobu (1434–1530), Motonobu (1476–1559), Eitoku (1543–90), and Tanyū (1602–74).

17. Built around 1620 in Kyoto along the Katsura River as a villa for Hachi-jōnomiya Toshihito (1579–1629), a grandson of Emperor Ōgimachi, the Katsura Detached Palace exemplifies the *sukiya-zukuri* style with its three *shoin* (study) structures, landscape garden, and rustic tea houses dotted around the premises. Charles S. Terry writes that the palace's traditional Japanese architecture "has been widely admired by western architects, who find in its pristine lines, its openness and its lack of unnecessary adornment much that accords with the principles of 20th-century western architecture" (*Encyclopaedia Britannica* [1972], 12:950. • The German architect Bruno Taut (1880–1938) was highly impressed with Japanese architecture during a visit in 1933–36; his impressions of the villa are in *Houses and People of Japan* (Sanseidō, 1937).

18. Leonid Kreutzer (1884–1953), a German pianist and conductor who taught at the Tokyo Conservatory (later Tokyo University of Arts) from 1933

innovative style in her first concert performance immediately after her return from France.[19] Even after we returned to our dormitory, we rambled on until late at night, slurping noodles as we talked.

Sometimes, out of curiosity, we went to a special coffeeshop just to listen to music we had never heard before. There was a big gramophone and a large collection of phonograph records, and as long as we were willing to wait for our turn after making a request, we could listen to almost any song. There were probably only one or two such shops in Tokyo, and without them, the average student had very little chance of listening to so many different kinds of music. The atmosphere inside the coffeeshop was quite extraordinary. Amidst heavy cigarette smoke, some of the young patrons sitting on small chairs would listen with their eyes closed; others would stare abstractedly into the distance as they listened attentively to the music flowing from the gramophone. Almost nobody talked, and even the waitress who brought our coffee tiptoed quietly.

It is difficult for me to articulate how I felt about the music of the romantics, and about Chopin's piano compositions in particular. But this is certainly due not to any difficulty in recalling the past, but to the difficulty of putting into words an experience I can so vividly recall without doing it injustice. Art is not something words can explain; to me it explains language itself. With truly irresistible power, the music not only stirred but transcended my feelings. It elicited emotions beyond the destructive passion and rapture of Wagner's operas or the limpid exultation of Mozart's piano compositions; it represented something much closer to the heart, something with its own ambience of intimacy, like a private confession. It evoked wide-ranging psychological reactions from anticipation to agitation, from apprehension to passion, from sweet

---

to 1953. • Hara Chieko (1915–), who graduated in 1932 from the Conservatoire national de la musique in Paris and studied with Lazare Lévy, was runner-up in the third Chopin International Piano Competition in 1937 and the first Japanese pianist to gain an international reputation. • On Iguchi Motonari see chapter 4, note 6.

19. Yasukawa Kazuko (1922–96; maiden name, Kusama Kazuko), a graduate of the Conservatoire national de la musique in 1937 and a student of Lazare Lévy, won first prize at the International Piano Competition for Women in Paris (1937) and started performing in Japan in 1940. She became a professor at the Tokyo University of Arts in 1952 and won many medals and honors, including the Légion d'honneur.

yearnings to momentary euphoria, as it constantly transformed itself until it finally faded away.

In those days thoughts of death haunted me. In the middle of the night, I would suddenly be seized by the horrifying thought that I and everything around me would vanish without a trace. I would break into a cold sweat, unable to go back to sleep for a long time. This does not mean, however, that I recognized any positive purpose in being alive, and perhaps for that reason I developed an inexplicable attachment to life. And it was from the core of this attachment, or at least not far from it, that an infinitely poignant and delicate melody began to flow forth from the bass chord of its convolution. In any case, through Chopin and the romantics, music began to come into my life. And that was the beginning of my entirely new relationship with music.

As I think back on it, Tokyo in the interwar years was quite an amazing city. Everywhere one turned, one found foreign literature in Japanese translation and reprints of postimpressionist paintings or heard the instrumental music of the German romantics. These imports were enough to make one forget about traditional Japanese culture, but not enough to achieve any real understanding of Western culture. I read many translations of foreign literature; I became acquainted with the names of many French impressionist and postimpressionist painters; and I listened to flawed performances of the music of the romantics through somewhat defective audio equipment. Yet I did not even know that postimpressionist paintings were only a small part of the overall canvas of Western art, or that the works of the romantics hardly represented the totality of Western music. At the same time, I knew virtually nothing about Shintōism, Confucianism, or Buddhism. I was completely ignorant about the system of thinking that had long nourished the spiritual life of the Japanese people. Yet I continued to eat miso, rice, and tofu, the food that had sustained our ancestors. I continued to walk with my high boots or high clogs on the muddy streets long trodden by other Japanese. I abided by the long-cherished conventions of "respectable" behavior and had no close female friend at all. I had both lascivious fantasies and hopelessly romantic yearnings for women—and neither served any constructive purpose when I came face-to-face with a woman, even with a coffeeshop waitress. I was timid, but I had a strong sense of self-respect, and even when I wanted to take the initiative to talk to a woman, I had no idea how to proceed. Since women paid little attention to me, I arrived at an intense sense of inferiority. I was never really conscious of the fact that I myself represented a caricature of the cultural conditions of the time. I did notice, however vaguely, something in me that was not original, something only half-baked, something precarious. At the time, it was plainly impossible for me to think of ways to deal with these problems. Later on, the outside world provided me with ready answers. First, there was medicine, and second, the Pacific War. The study of medicine guaranteed the universality of knowledge; the Pacific War severed me from the dubious aspects of Japanese society. The only things left to discover were that society's more solid components.

13 Pastoral Song in the Highlands

Summer in the highlands begins with the cries of cuckoos. Since the summer I spent in Shinshū's Oiwake village during my final year at middle school, I've gotten used to hearing them every July. From the pine woods at the foothills of Mount Asama their calls floated through the clear air, now distant and now nearby, and somehow accentuated the area's natural tranquillity. The moment I arrived at the cottage in the woods, I forgot the bustling noise of Tokyo: the sweat and dirt during our tennis practice, the hustle and bustle at Shibuya Station, and the sun-baked room on the second floor at home. In the highlands, along with the cuckoos' cries were green grass and hiking trails, white birch trees in the soft breeze against the blue sky, and drifting mist streaming in and out through the thicket. And then there was the ever-changing face of Mount Asama and the purple Yatsugatake Range extending all the way to the distant western horizon.[1] A deep blue sky arched high above, decorated with magnificent columns of clouds during the day and with bright stars at night. Only a few visitors arrived to escape the heat before the end of July, and the nearby dormitory that opened for students in the summer was still closed. The oil shop and farmhouses with rooms for rent in the summer would turn busy in August, but just now it was still too early for them to be doing much business. Like the synchronized humming of musical instruments tuning up before an orchestral performance, the sounds of the cuckoos filled the air as I anticipated the arrival of Tokyoites who would soon turn the village into a bustling place.

1. A volcanic mountain range running north and south between Nagano and Yamanashi Prefectures.

Our Oiwake house was located just inside the woods from the Nakasendō toward Mount Asama. It had a beautiful view but no gas, no water, and no well. The head of a farming household who happened to be an acquaintance of ours agreed to deliver buckets of water from the well at a nearby temple, and we prepared our meals with firewood and charcoal in an earthen brazier. I suppose this lifestyle had some resemblance to what enthusiastic city dwellers would call camping in the wilderness. Father could not leave his medical practice in Tokyo during the summer, and Mother did not want to leave Father alone to endure the long, sweltering Tokyo summer. As a result, only Sister and I spent a good part of our summer vacation there.

Sister had by then graduated from Saint Maur Higher Girls' School and had been helping the family with housework. Mother had attended the same school, and it was there that she converted to Catholicism. That Sister did not do so too was probably due to the fact that the school had lost its former character. In Mother's day there were only four students in her class, including her. It was only natural to develop an intimate relationship with the foreign nuns who taught them. By the time Sister went there, the school had grown and the teacher-student relationship was no different from that in other schools. There was little contact between the nuns and the students. Religious instruction was limited, and no vocational training was offered. Furthermore, the teachers were not particularly enthusiastic about preparing their students for higher education. The aim of the girls' school was to prepare young girls from "decent families" for marriage, and by then the requirements for marriage no longer had anything to do with Christianity, but rather had to do with the values defined by the Japanese middle class. Young women's interests and general cultivation were to go toward educating their young; good manners and a "likable personality" were seen as positive attributes for successful social interactions; their ability to do housework must free the able bureaucrats and technicians of the Great Japanese Empire from all domestic anxieties. I suppose some of the students in a girls' high school were intelligent while others obtuse, and frequently they were both. Naturally, there were pretty ones and not-so-pretty ones. But Sister's classmates all seemed vibrant and cheerful. When she came home after her graduation ceremony, she told us how her classmates had all cried about having to bid farewell to their school.

"Oh, how foolish!" Father said after she had finished her story, "Did you cry too?"

"Well, I did. When everybody cried, I couldn't hold back my tears either. I suppose we just enjoyed being sentimental without really feeling sad."

Far from being foolish, Sister was probably a more dispassionate observer of her own character than Father was of his. In those days Father had become rather extreme in his aversion toward social interactions, and since Mother was by nature well disposed toward socializing and having a good time, there was always a difference of opinion, if not outright discord, between them. In addition, my preoccupation with idle literary matters and my lack of enthusiasm for schoolwork ran completely counter to Father's expectations, often leading to fierce arguments between us. Despite all that, our family atmosphere was neither gloomy nor tense because Sister was there. Her mere presence was enough to generate a harmonious atmosphere. Her judgment of others was often quite critical and astute. When she met some of my friends for the first time, she would just listen quietly to their remarks, and afterwards she would say, "I wonder how genuine he was. He seems to be the kind of person who likes to embellish his stories." I would take a long time to reach the same conclusion. Even when she had something harsh to say, she almost never assumed a combative posture. Mother, likewise, was sensitive to the feelings of other people. But she was also sensitive about her own and often quick to defend her beliefs. Only Sister had no liking for confrontations, and she would never measure human relationships in terms of winning or losing an argument. When it came to Father and me, we were simply too engrossed in our theoretical arguments to have even a fraction of Sister's and Mother's compassion for other people's feelings.

It was quite true that Sister's character and mine were different in almost every way. I was aggressive while she was not. I was uncompromising while she was generous. Many people detested and disliked me while, in all probability, no one detested Sister and hardly anyone disliked her. And yet we had similar tastes in a great many things. We liked the same food and the same music; we both enjoyed nature; and we both reacted the same way toward the same people, positively or negatively. Neither of us had any worldly experience, nor did we believe in any form of absolute authority. We were both morally conservative; we both spoke Tokyo's "up-town" dialect; and we both conformed to conventional norms of "decent" behavior. She had no boyfriend and I had no girlfriend. During the time when the two of us lived together in our house in the woods, we were just like good friends and never once did we have an occasion to argue. In her, I found all the elements of a kind and caring heart. She was cheerful, full of hope, and I could feel her trust and warmth for me. But surely even these qualities couldn't normally ward off minor arguments or conflicts from time to time. That we never had to go through such an experience was due to Sister's seemingly boundless generosity. At the Oiwake cottage, I was always the one making decisions. But by allowing me to do so, Sister set the course of our summer sojourns.

The beginning of August saw a convergence of students, teachers, and other summer vacationers into the area. Some stayed at the oil shop rebuilt after the fire on the other side of the Nakasendō, while others rented rooms at the main lodge, the *honjin*, a little farther away. In addition, many farmhouses also offered rooms for rent just in the summer. They still had the original names and structures that had been used during their heyday as lodging places along the Nakasendō before the opening of the Shin'etsu line. And enterprising monks from the local temple put up simple lodges on the temple grounds to house students, one in each room, and even offered their guests meals at the temple kitchen.

It was in one of these rooms that Assistant Professor Nakano Yoshio of the Department of English Literature at Tokyo Imperial University stayed one summer. I was not acquainted with Mr. Nakano at the time, but I had heard about him from a student who was his fellow boarder at the temple. "He has the best brains in the English department," the student reported. According to him, Mr. Nakano was then translating one of Swift's works.[2] An easygoing man, he would chat with the students during mealtimes at the temple kitchen. The student went on to say that Mr. Nakano had an awesome capacity for learning. His physical stamina, I learned, was also quite extraordinary. He would walk several miles to

2. Nakano Yoshio (1903–85), literary and social critic who taught Elizabethan drama and American literature at Tokyo University from 1935 to 1953 and at Stanford University from 1956 to 1957. His broad and precise knowledge of English literature has been compared to that of Natsume Sōseki, and his works reflect the range of his interests: *Arabia no Rorensu* (Lawrence of Arabia, 1940), *Okinawa mondai nijūnen* (Twenty years of the Okinawa question, co-authored, 1965), *Suwifuto kō* (Study of Swift, 1969), and *Eibungaku yobanashi* (Nightly chats on English literature, 1971), as well as translations of *The Merchant of Venice* (1939), *Gulliver's Travels* (1940), and Maugham's *The Moon and Sixpence* (1940), among others. His 3-vol. work *Roka Tokutomi Kenjirō* (1972–74), a meticulously researched biography of the modern novelist, set a new standard for the genre and won the Osaragi Jirō Prize in 1974.

the golf course in Karuizawa, stroll around it, and then walk back. If he found students playing baseball at the elementary school, he would take an active part in the game. Afterwards, while the students were having a drink and taking a rest, he would take a quick bath and then work until late at night. The student remarked that it was just impossible to keep up with him. I was absolutely amazed by the story. Soon afterwards at the tennis court by the station, I met this almost legendary figure.

We students would sometimes walk more than half a mile from our lodging for a game of softball tennis. If we had more than four players, the rest of us would sit under the trees and wait for the end of a game. Mr. Nakano was reading while waiting for his turn. "He's been reading on his way over here," the student said. By now I have totally forgotten what the name of the book was, but I remember it was a rather thick English novel. "Oh well, it wasn't that interesting a book," Mr. Nakano said nonchalantly. I knew all too well what an enormous amount of time it would take for me to read a foreign book because I was constantly consulting a dictionary. To discover that someone could read through a novel so effortlessly was quite an eye-opening experience for me. The thought ran through my mind: Indeed, it's not impossible to accomplish a feat like this! And here is a living example of somebody who can actually do it! If I can't do the same, how can I even *talk* about foreign literature? But it was only a thought. As it turned out, it would take me a long time to reach the point where I could actually read foreign novels with ease.

At that time Ozaki Yukiteru, the eldest son of Ozaki Gakudō, was living with his family like a cave dweller near Shinano Oiwake Station.[3] He dug a shallow vertical cave in the woods and built an octagon-shaped home there with Asama igneous rocks and cement. There was a well inside the premises and firewood stockpiled around the house. Throughout the entire year, they lived there without leaving for Tokyo. The Shinshū winter in the northern Saku area was severe.[4] And yet, the master of the house boasted, contrary to what one might think, it was rather warm liv-

3. Ozaki Yukiteru (1888–1964), a pioneer of Japanese aviation, was elected to the Upper House as an independent candidate in 1947 and was chairman of Japan Airlines and later of Hankyū Airlines. • Ozaki Gakudō was a pseudonym of Ozaki Yukio (1858–1954), a parliamentary politician whose unfailing support for party politics throughout the Meiji, Taishō, and early Shōwa period won him the reputation as "the god of constitutional government." He was governor of Tokyo from 1903 to 1912 and minister of justice in the second Okuma Shigenobu cabinet.
4. The Saku basin is situated in the eastern part of Nagano Prefecture.

ing inside a cave. This, I venture to say, was not necessarily the opinion of his wife, who had to do the cooking, nor perhaps of his twin boys, who had to walk for more than half a mile to get to their elementary school. Or for their eldest son, who had to commute to his middle school in Iwamurata on the Shin'etsu Main Line, which had no more than a few runs a day.[5] Only their daughter, about the same age as Sister, lived in Tokyo and came to see her parents during the summer vacation.

"We rarely get to see anybody else during the winter," Ozaki's wife said. "And, you know, it could easily be a week or so before we see another soul."

"Don't you see more bears than people?" I asked.

"No, we hardly see them," Mr. Ozaki remarked. "But we did find footprints even around the house. When winter comes and they can't find food in the mountains, they come down into the village. You can easily recognize them because their large footprints in the snow are different from those left by foxes and other animals."

I have no idea why Mr. Ozaki chose to retire into the mountains and live like a hermit. "Well, I like this place. City living is too much of a hassle." But people's opinions differ about what things constitute the hassles of city life. The master of the octagon-shaped house was certainly no misanthrope. On the contrary, he welcomed each and every one of the students who gathered around Oiwake. A cheerful man, he loved to talk, and his house was filled with an air of summery gaiety after a long wintry spell. But he rarely visited nearby Karuizawa, where Gakudō had his summer villa and where his half-sister, married to Viscount Sōma, and perhaps some other relatives of his as well, lived. Likewise, it appeared that they rarely came to Oiwake to visit Ozaki. Karuizawa was Tokyo's regional office in the summer, and to a virtual recluse like Ozaki, Tokyo had probably come to symbolize all the nuisance associated with the whole business of kinship fraternization.[6] What he did as a young man was fly newly imported airplanes; he became known as "the first civilian pilot of Japan." What he did while living in his octagonal house was, in his own words, "make discoveries." What else could he do, living in solitude in the mountains with snow all around him? At the time we first got acquainted, he was in the process of "discovering" a teapot that "could save the whole country as many as several tons of tea every

5. The old town of Iwamurata is now a part of the city of Saku.
6. Karuizawa was, and continues to be, a favorite summer resort for Tokyoites.

year." He said that this would also be an important discovery from the standpoint of national economy. That was during the end of the 1930s, a time when the Japanese economy was going at full speed toward building up a wartime infrastructure.

Mr. Ozaki was also a big enthusiast of softball tennis. Not only was he very good at the game, he taught his children how to play. His eldest son, already the captain of his middle school's tennis team, was my worthy opponent. On the Oiwake courts, the other regular student players included Mr. Ikawa, a future diplomat with a most witty mind, and Mr. Yamamoto Susumu, who later joined the economics division of the *Mainichi Shimbun* and became the editor of *The Economist*.[7] While we were waiting our turn, we would talk idly about an endless array of subjects. In summer under the dazzling afternoon sun, we could see the skirt of Mr. Ozaki's daughter fluttering in the wind and hear Sister's loud laughter and the sound of the racket hitting the tennis ball. It struck me that the Ozakis appeared to be living for precisely that single genial afternoon. The alluring daughter, the otherworldly father, and the sons so totally absorbed in their tennis game. For them, this was perhaps their most precious hour, and it was only on occasions like this that I got to meet them. The refreshing westerly winds soothed our sweaty bodies under the shade of the trees as the smoke from Mount Asama rose into the distant blue sky. Together we savored a moment of peace lingering on ever so precariously in the mountain village before the specter of an approaching storm. When the thunder and the rain suddenly came, we scooped up our things and ran up the slope of volcanic ash into Mr. Ozaki's house. There, a wood-burning stove dried our wet bodies and the warm tea took away our fatigue. As far as we were concerned, even the downpour, the thunder and the lightning which came and went with such sudden ferocity represented an integral part of the pleasure of living in the highlands. And the storm that hit us that day was not yet the real one.

When the Pacific War began, Mr. Ozaki's daughter married one of the Oiwake students and moved to Izu, and she never returned. There wasn't any obvious reason for me to have any regret over this, but I did

---

7. Yamamoto Susumu (1918–) is the author of *Tokyo–Washinton: Nihon no keizai gaikō* (Tokyo–Washington: Japan's economic diplomacy, 1961). • *The Economist* was founded in 1923 as a weekly and published by the *Mainichi Shimbun*.

feel one of my dreams was forever lost. Before long, when the tennis courts near Oiwake Station were turned into a vegetable field, the twin brothers, already grown, were being trained as pilots. The eldest son was drafted and sent to a battlefield somewhere. Mr. Ozaki continued his caveman's life with his wife, while Viscount Sōma, an early evacuee to this area, was, according to rumors, making jam with wild grapes he gathered in the Asama highlands. When the fighting became more fierce, I began to see Mr. Ozaki less and less.

It was more than a decade later and some time after the war that I met Mr. Ozaki again. He was living up a hill in Zushi.[8] At that time I learned that one of his twins, a mere youngster when I met him, was now a commercial pilot on overseas routes. As for his other two sons, Mr. Ozaki said nothing, and I, on my part, did not venture to ask. As before, Mr. Ozaki was cheerful and loved a good conversation, and in this sense he had not changed at all. This time, instead of softball tennis, he was interested in Western-style archery. "It's good for your health, and anyone can do it. Once I started doing it, I got hooked." Airplanes, softball tennis, a caveman's life, discoveries, and now Western archery. This was the son of a man who had single-handedly fought a lifelong battle for parliamentary democracy in Japan, and sure enough he had achieved something few men ever do. That was what I thought at the time. And he accomplished it without ever losing his simple and splendid faith that what he did could benefit others as well.

When I was living in Oiwake, I occasionally went to Komoro and Karuizawa, towns that served as fill-ins for Tokyo. Komoro was a rural town, and Karuizawa had a small shopping area with signboards in European languages and people coming and going in every direction: foreigners, rich people, and those who liked to pretend they were rich. I was fond of immersing myself in this sea of total strangers, something I could not do in Oiwake. The light rail service running from the station at Karuizawa to the Old Karuizawa Road had a charm reminiscent of an electric train in an amusement park. And as the train of the Shin'etsu line was negotiating its steep ascent from Komoro to Oiwake, I never grew tired of looking through the window at the ever-changing face of Mount Asama.

Sister and I lived in our Oiwake house until mid-September, when school began. From the end of August, people began to retreat from the

8. A coastal city on the Miura Peninsula in southeastern Kanagawa Prefecture.

summer resort like an ebb tide. More and more villas had their windows boarded up, and the dormitory lights at the girls' school, once visible through the shade of the trees in August, were also dark. The students' singing could no longer be heard, and a quiet tranquillity settled over the village lodges and farmhouses. As I was walking a friend to the station to send him off to Tokyo, I noticed that the tennis courts—bustling with activity just a few days ago—were now desolate. The days had grown shorter and the wooden fences around the station drew long shadows under the setting sun. At times like these we noticed the first red dragonflies dancing in the evening sky. "Autumn's here already," Sister remarked. I was reminded of the line "Adieu, vive clarté de nos étés trop courts!"[9] And I wondered if Sister was not thinking of returning to Tokyo. The thick tussocks of eulalia grass now stood taller than we did, and the evening breeze brought a sudden chill. The highland was at the height of its enigmatic charm when the lingering vestiges of summer were about to vanish altogether. Standing together like lovers, Sister and I looked at the autumn flowers blooming in profusion in the neglected fields and observed how the subtle variation of tones transformed Mount Asama's appearance in the crisp, clear air. When night came upon us, we heard across the distant valley the first gaspings of the steam locomotive as it gathered momentum for its uphill climb. In the silent dusk we could make out each change in the engine's noise as the train finally made its way up to the top of the hill and then the screech of the wheels as the train slowed to a stop at the station. In the vast expanse of space separating us from the train passengers, perhaps we were the only two people still awake. And without Sister's presence, I thought, I would be all alone in this world. I loved everything in the highlands, but I loved Sister even more.

The day after our return to Tokyo, we started going into town for movies and concerts and even for no particular reason at all. "The moment I thought you were home, you're out again all the time," Mother said. Yet Sister knew very well why I wanted so much to go out, and I knew that she knew. We wanted to register the end of our summer experience in Oiwake, and to do that we had to rediscover Tokyo over and over again. The lights of the Ginza reflecting on the rain-drenched side-

9. "Farewell, the brilliance of brief summers gone!" from *Les Fleurs du mal*'s "Chant d'automne" in *Charles Baudelaire: Selected Poems,* trans. Joanna Richardson (London: Penguin, 1987).

walks, the clouded glass windows of the coffeeshops, the faint fragrance of the sea carried by the southerly winds, the brick pavement from the concert hall to the Hibiya intersection, the reverberation of the music we had just heard, and the many different faces we saw on many different people. Those faces were never the same every autumn. At times they looked self-possessed, at times anxious. Sometimes they evoked a sense of nostalgia; at other times they looked hopelessly vulgar and idiotic. But they never looked gloomy or miserable. This yearly habit of mine, of rediscovering Tokyo after returning from Oiwake, continued for more than ten years and into the postwar era. When I broke it, the subsequent rediscovery of Tokyo came after my return from places much farther away.

14   A Microcosm

At the end of the 1930s the dormitories at the First Higher School represented a microcosm of Japanese society. The committee for the self-governing dormitories had some resemblance to an administrative organ. Only a few students were interested in its work, while the majority were apathetic. A democratic system in form and bureaucratic control in practice. Most of the residents were not isolated individuals, for they belonged to small communal groups typified by the Sports Division. Each group had a clear-cut hierarchy between the leaders and the rest of the members. In principle, the collective goals of the group took precedence over the self-interests of the individual. But very often these communal goals were only vaguely defined, making it difficult to even distinguish between means and ends.

Within the dormitory there existed something equivalent to a news agency and even a quasi-literary circle. A weekly newspaper was published and read by all residents, but it had only a limited number of contributors. An even smaller number of students wrote stories or essays for the *Alumni Magazine,* which was published several times a year. Although the magazine was distributed to students free of charge, its actual readership, in all probability, was small. One might say that the magazine was similar to a coterie journal run by the editors themselves with their close circle of friends.

At the beginning of my third year, I left the tennis division and became one of the editors of the magazine. From then on I got to know almost all the Komaba students who were either practicing writers or interested in becoming so. A few among them were Marxists who had survived the government's suppression. There was no longer any left-wing organization on campus, and I doubt if they belonged to any external organizations. They could perhaps be called isolated theorists. One of them held Tosaka Jun in high regard, was an enthusiastic reader of Ōmori Yoshitarō, and had a strong interest in Miki Kiyoshi.[1] But at the same time he thoroughly despised the entire Japanese literary world and the Kyoto school philosophers. Some students were drawn to more formal scholarship. A number of them tried to come to grips with the rather tedious concepts of German idealism, while others, as I mentioned earlier, tried to read the *Man'yōshū* in its original text. There was even a poet among us. A great admirer of Tachihara Michizō, Nakahara Chūya, and Miyazawa Kenji, he also read European and particularly French poetry at the turn of the century and wrote poems that succeeded only in baffling everyone.[2] One student revered Tokuda Shūsei as the premier novelist and tried his hand at the "naturalist I-

1. Tosaka Jun (1900–45) taught philosophy at Hōsei University (1931–35) and founded the Yuibutsuron Kenkyūkai (society for the study of materialism) in 1932 before a 1937 Home Ministry's order forbade him and other Marxist writers such as Nakano Shigeharu and Miyamoto Yuriko to publish; charged with infringement of the Peace Preservation Law in 1938, he died in a Nagano prison in 1945 (see his writings in *Tosaka Jun zenshū*, 5 vols. [Keisō shobō, 1966–67]). • Ōmori Yoshitarō (1898–1940) taught economics at Tokyo Imperial University, edited the influential Marxist journal *Rōnō* (Labor and farmers), and helped compile the complete works of Marx and Engels for Kaizōsha. • Miki Kiyoshi (1897–1945) taught philosophy at Hōsei University in the late 1920s after study in Germany and France (1922–25); a student of Nishida Kitarō and Martin Heidegger, in *Yuibutsu shikan to gendai no ishiki* (Historical materialism and contemporary consciousness, 1928) he related revolutionary Marxism to overcoming existential anxiety, but his part in the Konoe Fumimaro cabinet's Shōwa Kenkyūkai (Shōwa research association) of the late 1930s undercut his stature as spokesman for the intellectual left; a victim of the Peace Preservation Law, Miki died in prison in September 1945 (see *Miki Kiyoshi zenshū*, 19 vols. [Iwanami shoten, 1966–68]; and Miles Fletcher, "Intellectuals and Fascism in Early Shōwa Japan," *Journal of Asian Studies* 39, no. 1 [November 1979]: 39–63, esp. 48–52).
2. On Tachihara see chapter 9 text and note 18. • Nakahara Chūya (1907–37), a popular Shōwa poet influenced by Dadaism—and once called "Dada-san" by his literary friends—and by Baudelaire's and Rimbaud's symbolic poetry, was noted for his lyric evocation of the weariness of modern life; he wrote two major poetry collections (*Yagi no uta* [Goat's songs, 1934] and *Arishi hi no uta* [Songs of bygone days, 1938]). • Miyazawa Kenji (1896–1933), whose Buddhist and agrarian background and fertile imagination mark his collection of poetry (*Haru to Shura* [Spring and Asura, 1924]) and children's tales (*Chūmon no ōi ryōriten* [The restaurant of many orders, 1924]); see Sarah M. Strong, trans., *Night of the Milky Way Railway* (New York: M. E. Sharpe, 1991).

novel."[3] Another took Dazai Osamu as his model and abandoned himself to sake and women, or acted as if he did.[4] Occasionally, he would produce a piece based on his experience. One other student, an avid reader of Western novels, was also interested in the publications in both *Jimmin bunko* (The people's library) and *Bungakukai* (Literary world), sifting through them all to identify the ideal of the novel.[5]

I do not mean to suggest, however, that there were no crucial differences between the Komaba students and the Tokyo writers and critics. We were not professional writers, and we did not need to support wives and children by writing. Quite the contrary; our parents supported us. Our intellectual and literary contemplations were independent of any pragmatic consideration, and we had no misgivings about following wherever our interests might lead us. Our own experiences had taught us absolutely nothing about whatever significance there might be in the commodification of scholarship, the literary arts, and ideas. We were com-

3. Tokuda Shūsei (1871–1943), an imaginative naturalist writer noted for his stark realism in depicting shabby urban life in such works as *Tadare* (Fester, 1913), *Arakure* (Tempest, 1915), and his masterpiece, *Shukuzu* (Epitome, 1941). See Richard Torrance, *The Fiction of Tokuda Shūsei and the Emergence of Japan's New Middle Class* (Seattle: University of Washington Press, 1994).

4. Dazai Osamu (1909–48), a *Burai-ha* (scoundrel school) writer whose heavy drinking, flings with women, prewar flirtation with communism, and several attempts at suicide endeared him to many young readers living amidst the postwar moral crisis and social confusion. His best known works are two mid-length novels, *Shayō* (The setting sun, 1947) and *Ningen shikkaku* (No longer human, 1948), along with short stories.

5. The literary journal *Jimmin bunko* (1936–38), founded by Takeda Rintarō, stood against nationalist right-wing literary groups such as the Japan romanticists; besides Takeda, its contributors were Takami Jun, Honjō Mutsuo, Tamura Taijirō, Enchi Fumiko, and Tamiya Torahiko—Takami Jun called them "a rowdy group of young, anti-establishment writers," and Donald Keene labels the journal "one of the last bastions of liberal thought" of the time (*Dawn to the West: Japanese Literature in the Modern Era—Fiction* [New York: Henry Holt, 1984], 866). • *Bungakukai* (1933–44) began as an ambitious coterie journal of Kobayashi Hideo, Takeda Rintarō, Uno Kōji, Kawabata Yasunari, and Hirotsu Kazuo and grew into a literary who's who in Japan of the late 1930s (including Kawakami Tetsutarō, Funabashi Seiichi, Aono Suekichi, Kamei Katsuichirō, Nakamura Mitsuo, and Nakajima Kenzō); it published such outstanding works as Ishikawa Jun's antiwar story "Marusu no uta" (The song of Mars), Hōjō Tamio's haunting "Inochi no shoya" (The first night of life), and Kobayashi Hideo's acclaimed "Dosutoefusuki no seikatsu" (The life of Dostoyevsky) but came under the influences of jingoistic militarism and exclusive culturalism during the war (see note 12, below). It resumed publication in 1947 and continues to this day.

pletely ignorant about the commodification of the printed word, the ways it reached the masses through commercial newspapers and magazines, and then politics' intrusion into the picture. At the same time we were uninformed about the self-censorship of newspapers and magazines, changes in public taste, and the mass media's adjustments to such changes. Likewise, we were totally oblivious to the apprehensions pressing on writers whose livelihood was threatened when they did not flow with the currents of the time, and to the need they presumably felt to justify their position if they did. Our ignorance simply made us more conscious of their lack of moral integrity for allowing themselves to turn into willing conformists, and their inconsistencies when they tried to justify their actions. We were merciless critics, armed only with abstract notions of right and wrong.

At that time the government had concocted a numbingly large number of slogans in the name of *kokumin seishin sōdōin* (total mobilization of the national spirit).[6] One such example was Extravagance Is Our Enemy! "That's absurd!" a Marxist among us said. "Who can dispute the fact that Japan is a capitalist country supported and nurtured by low wages for its workers? How shameful to tell people on the verge of starvation that extravagance is the enemy!" And then there was this business of *Yamato-damashii* (the soul of Yamato), *bushidō* (the way of the samurai), *Hagakure*, and so on.[7] "Did those guys ever read Motoori Norinaga carefully?" a scholar among us said. "Don't forget that Norinaga identifies the essence of Japan with *mono no aware*. That's what you'd find in the world of romance in *The Tale of Genji*.[8] And 'the way

6. The movement was initiated by the first Konoe Fumimaro cabinet in 1937.

7. *Yamato-dashii* refers to the indigenous sensory perceptions, sentiments, and Japanese ways of thinking as distinct from continental influences; ultranationalist war propaganda made it an emotionally charged cliché to highlight the Japanese people's unique spirit by suggesting unhesitating self-sacrifice for the country's greater good. • *Hagakure*'s full title is *Hagakure kikigaki* (11 vols., 1716), ed. Tashiro Nobumoto, based on statements by the Nabeshima samurai Yamamoto Tsunetomo (1659–1719); before World War II this mid-Edo samurai manual was held up as a standard reference on the Japanese warrior's spirit.

8. Motoori Norinaga (1730–1801), the most influential Tokugawa nativist scholar of Japanese classics such as *Kojiki*, *Man'yōshū*, and *Genji monogatari*, whose *Kojikiden* (44 vols., 1790–1822), arguably his greatest work, is a monumental study of *Kojiki*'s formation and linguistic peculiarities, and whose prolific writings also include commentaries on classical poetry anthologies such as the *Kokinshū* [*Kokinshū tōkagami*, 1797–1816] and the *Shinkokinshū* [*Shinkokinshū mino no iezuto dō orisoe*, 1795–1797], poetry collections

of the samurai' was a concoction by Edo bureaucrats at a time when discipline among the samurai was getting out of hand. Surely, it *can't* represent the soul of Yamato when the only thing it reflects is just one aspect of Edo society."

Students who favored concrete action over theoretical argument would spend their time drinking and womanizing. They admired novels like *Yukiguni* (The snow country) and *Bokutō kidan* (A strange tale from east of the river), and they simply chose to ignore the militaristic rhetoric completely.[9] As for the slogan *hakkō ichiu* (the eight corners of the world under one roof), nobody quite understood what it meant, but somehow it was linked to the notion of "the divinity of the Japanese state" or the tradition of "the spiritual civilization of the East."[10] Such slogans struck us as nothing more than muddle-headed anachronisms.

Meanwhile, the world outside Komaba was witnessing the continuing suppression of the Marxists and the banishment of liberal scholars from their academic positions. Popular commentators were noisily

(*Suzunoyashū* [1798]), poetic treatises and linguistic studies (*Isonokami sasamegoto* [1816 and 1927] and *Kotoba no tama no o* [1785]); Motoori championed "indigenous" Japanese cultural sensibilities and forms against continental cultural influences (*kan'i*), a position challenged by another fellow nativist scholar and writer, Ueda Akinari (1734–1809); see Harry D. Harootunian, *Things Seen and Unseen: Discourse and Ideology in Tokugawa Nativism* (Chicago: University of Chicago Press, 1988). • In *The Tale of Genji* and other early classics, *aware* refers to an intense emotional or sensory experience evoked by external phenomena: "the pathos inherent in the beauty of the outer world, a beauty that is inexorably fated to disappear together with the observer" (Ivan Morris, *The World of the Shining Prince—Court Life in Ancient Japan* [London: Penguin, 1979], 208–9). See Motoori Norinaga on *mono no aware* in *Isonokami sasamegoto* and *Genji monogatari tama no ogushi* (1799).

9. Kawabata Yasunari's *Yukiguni* (1935–37, with sequel and revisions after World War II), considered one of the early Shōwa's finest novels, centers on a fleeting love affair in a rural hot spring resort; the novel's techniques and the dramatic relationship between the central characters have been compared to those of a *nō* play. • *Bokutō kidan* (1937; Eng. trans. by Edward G. Seidensticker, 1972) is among Nagai Kafū's (1879–1959) most celebrated novels of lyrical nostalgia for a vanishing cultural milieu; its enchanting *zuihitsu*-like story of a romantic encounter brings in the mannerisms and atmosphere of the Tamanoi redlight district and a thinly disguised Kafū as the novelist "I."

10. The expression *hakkō ichiu* from *Nihon shoki* (720) originally referred to the idea of Japan's internal unification under a central authority before becoming a militaristic slogan during the Pacific War to dramatize (and legitimate) Japan's overseas expansion. • Clichés of state divinity and spiritual civilization from the militarist era ascribe to Japan a unique national or cultural identity.

11. Or "Taikan shijin no goichininsha" (*Kogito* [July–August 1936]), an early

making cryptic proclamations about "the spirit of sacrifice for the country," "the gratuitousness of faith," or "the imperial poet laureate."[11] In slightly more dispassionate language with a slightly more plausible manner of discourse the Kyoto philosophers, the journal *Bungakukai*, and many literary figures talked about the lofty goals supposedly inherent in "the Great Japanese Empire's expedition against China." They also spoke about the desirability for us Japanese to create a culture that would transcend "modernity" now that modern Western civilization was reaching an impasse.[12] With the ever encroaching tide of militarism, a serious schism began to develop between the community inside the school dormitory and the world outside. And this difference exploded in angry words when Yokomitsu Riichi, a man regarded in those days as "the god of the novel," came to give a lecture at the First Higher School.[13]

Yokomitsu made his appearance on time in a large classroom that overflowed with students. With disheveled hair and a somewhat pale complexion, he said just a few words, then clamped his lips tightly and

essay by Yasuda Yojūrō (1910–81), the leading member of the Japan romanticist school. Along with the essay "Nihon no hashi" (*Bungakukai* [October 1936]), it helped launch Yasuda's career as a critic in the late 1930s (and see note 22, below).

12. Here Katō alludes to a controversial two-day symposium, "Kindai no chōkoku" (Overcoming modernity), sponsored by *Bungakukai* in July 1942 and the papers (published in the journal's September and October issues) from leading literary critics (Nakamura Mitsuo, Kawakami Tetsutarō, and Kobayashi Hideo), writers and artists (Hayashi Fusao, Kamei Katsuichirō, Moroi Saburō, and Tsumura Hideo), and other intellectuals (the Kyoto philosopher Nishitani Keiji, the Catholic theologian Yoshimitsu Yoshihiko). Only Nakamura Mitsuo's paper maintained that Japan's own pseudo-modern experience, not Western modernity, needed to be overcome. Debate over the symposium continued in the late 1950s (among critics such as Odagiri Hideo, Takeuchi Yoshimi, Ara Masahito, and Hashimoto Bunzō).

13. Yokomitsu Riichi (1898–1947), a major writer and critic of the 1920s experimental Shinkankaku-ha (new sensationalist school) who tried to recreate experience's incoherent and impressionistic effects, as opposed to the proletarian literary writers who stressed ideological content. The new tone and narrative style of "Kikai" [The machine, 1930] established his prominence; this work was followed by *Shanghai* (1928–31), an ambitious study of the 1920s city, and *Shin'en* (Sleeping garden, 1932), a psychological story of entangled love. His short postwar career was marked by severe criticism from the literary left of his "war responsibility" (see Dennis Keene, *Yokomitsu Riichi: Modernist* [New York: Columbia University Press, 1980]).

stared for a while at a corner of the ceiling before uttering a few more words. He did not rattle away whatever came to his mind with flowing eloquence, nor, on the other hand, was he aiming at any rhetorical effect with his manner of delivery. Yokomitsu had the appearance of an anguished poet as he tried on the spot to revive his memory while gathering his thoughts and searching for the right expressions. It was difficult to imagine any other speaker who could be less predisposed to frivolous improvisations and affected mannerisms. While I disagreed with many of the things he said, I was favorably impressed with his personality. A heated debate began when we moved to a roundtable discussion over some simple refreshments after the lecture. About fifteen students sat in a circle with Yokomitsu in the middle.

"Your novel *Ryoshū* (The melancholy journey) deals with the question of Western material civilization and Eastern spiritual civilization," one of us said. "Would you care to elaborate a little for us?"[14]

"Aren't they self-evident? Spiritual civilization is what exists in the hearts of the Japanese."

"By material civilization, do you mean science?"

"You might say that."

"Or is it technology?"

"That's right! It's about scientific technology."

"Now just a moment please! Aren't science and technology two different things?"

"No, they are closely related. I see them as one thing."

"But you can speak of a relationship precisely because you have two different things. And if you only have one thing, I don't think it makes any sense to speak of any relationship no matter how intimate or remote it may be."

"Now, you're getting too theoretical!"

"But science is about theories."

That's the way I remember the start of our discussion.

"I don't quite understand what you mean by science," another stu-

14. *Ryoshū* (1937–46), an unfinished novel inspired by Yokomitsu's 1936 journey in Europe, offers his vision of incompatibility between Japanese and Western civilizations, and hints at his allegiance to Japan's cultural traditions vis-à-vis the West and to certain ultranationalistic ideas of Japanism. Early postwar commentators were divided over its merits, but more recently Nishio Kanji has seen it as "a mirror reflecting the mental pathology of the Japanese in the early Shōwa period" (*"Ryoshū saikō," Bungakukai* [October 1983]).

dent said. "You have a short story in which the protagonist is a physicist, is that right? And there's a mathematical formula in the story. But if you don't have a proviso indicating what the letters in that formula stand for, the formula means nothing. Why didn't you . . . ?"

"I'm not a physicist." Yokomitsu cut him short. "That's a literary symbol."

But the student who started the question remained undaunted.

"But the formula as it stands has no meaning. I don't think you can say it's a symbol for science."

"That's why I called it a literary symbol."

"In that case, what in fact is it supposed to symbolize in a literary sense?"

"You boys can't expect to appreciate literature if all you care to do is to press your case with theories!"

"You may be right. In fact, you must be right. But, Mr. Yokomitsu, you equated material civilization with science. Since you brought up the subject of science, here's what I think. Forgive me for saying this, but based on what you said, I don't think you know a thing about what science is. Science is . . ."

"Once you bring up this subject, there's no end to the argument," someone interrupted. But the comment was not meant to rescue Yokomitsu from his predicament, only to pursue the question from a different perspective.

"Even if we leave aside the question of what science is, science clearly constitutes one aspect in the spiritual endeavors of humankind. If so, wouldn't it be a mistake to think of science and spiritual civilization as opposite categories?"

Very often Yokomitsu had no time to search for an answer because we had already started a debate among ourselves.

"I suppose what Mr. Yokomitsu means by material civilization is that science treats matter as its subject of inquiry."

"Now, just a second! Let me remind you that science is not just limited to the natural sciences!"

"You see, that's why the science Mr. Yokomitsu talks about is in fact the natural sciences. But the question is: the humanities are also well developed in the West, and they've come into this country too, right?"

"Whatever the case might be, it's odd to speak of Western material civilization as such."

"Instead of just going on and on about this subject, the right question to ask is how do we deal with Christianity when we speak of Western material civilization?"

"Absolutely. And then Platonism, Descartes . . . In other words, the claim that spiritual civilization exists only in the East goes against the facts. First of all, we need to know what material civilization means."

"When I speak of material civilization," Yokomitsu said, "what I mean is the proclivity toward materialism in modern times. Japan, too, has been infected with this poison of modernity. In order for us to live through this difficult time, I think that we as writers are called on to perform our duty to cleanse Japan from that poison. That, I tell you, is the real meaning of *misogi*.[15] The spirit of *misogi* is at the heart of our race. We are now witnessing the greatest epoch in time. *Now* is the time for us to return to the tradition of Japanese literature."

"What tradition are you talking about?" one student asked. Before Yokomitsu could give an answer, somebody else immediately jeered, "Edo's Bunka and Bunsei years!"[16] At this, Yokomitsu exploded in anger. Turning in the direction of the speaker, he shouted in a thunderous voice, "You people are absolutely hopeless for saying things like this!"

I was the one who had invited Yokomitsu to give his talk. With no moderator for the roundtable discussion, I was somewhat conscious of my role as its organizer and had remained silent until then. But Yokomitsu's outburst agitated me. Even though the phrase "Edo's Bunka and Bunsei years" was obviously intended as venomous sarcasm, at least its author didn't make his utterance behind the protective shield of political authority.[17] We students no longer felt comfortable in expressing our opinions in public outside the Komaba dormitory even when we had the opportunity. On the other hand, even if Yokomitsu himself wasn't trying to curry favor with the political

---

15. The traditional ritual of *misogi* purifies the body from sin or defilement with water by immersing it in the sea or a river. The early-eighth-century *Kojiki* mentions the purification ritual of Izanagi no mikoto; subsequent mentions of the ritual can be found in the *Man'yōshū*, the early-tenth-century *waka* poetry anthology *Kokinshū*, and the early-eleventh-century *Shūi wakashū*.

16. The Bunka period (1804–17); the Bunsei period (1818–29).

17. Because Edo secular culture blossomed in the first three decades of the nineteenth century—in the production of popular *gesaku* (playful compositions), painting, and theater—to suggest that its urban materialism and unabashed epicureanism represent Japan's spiritual purity makes a total mockery of Yokomitsu's view of Japan's traditional, *misogi*-sanitized culture.

establishment, his position was endorsed and welcomed by the authority of Japanese militarism. He might be able to cut short a debate by having an outburst, but we could not. A military man could silence his opposition by crying out, "Hold your tongue!" but a Diet member could not. To yell at an opponent who is not in a position to yell back is not fair. Regardless of what his private thoughts might have been, in effect Yokomitsu's behavior struck me as very little different from a high-handed act behind the cloak of political authority. How arrogant of him to tell us, "You people are hopeless!" I was too emotionally charged to appreciate Yokomitsu's unpretentiousness in allowing himself to get genuinely angry with mere students like us. Nor could I even begin to imagine that his wild rage at somebody's pointing out his weakness was perhaps in itself evidence of his own awareness of it.

"I'm afraid I don't agree," I said, trying for neutral restraint. "Literary and artistic tastes reached the height of refinement during the Bunka and the Bunsei years. And you were saying they don't represent the true Japanese tradition, am I right? But if you take the Genroku period, I don't think you'd get any better. Genroku style and mannerisms had nothing to do with *misogi*. The same is true if you go all the way back to Heian prose narratives and, indeed, to the *Man'yōshū*. So, what then is the Japanese literary tradition you talk about that has absolutely nothing to do with the *Man'yōshū* and *The Tale of Genji*, or with Saikaku and Chikamatsu?"[18]

"Mr. Yokomitsu, you said that Valéry was also practicing *misogi* in France. What do you mean by that?" another student asked.

"What I mean is that all enclosed meditations share the same spirit with *misogi*."[19]

18. Strictly speaking, the Genroku period dates from 1688 to 1704 but in narratives of Japanese cultural history it broadly refers to the period 1680–1709 under the rule of shogun Tsunayoshi, a golden period for Tokugawa culture (in painting, popular literature, and theater). • On Saikaku see chapter 9, note 16. • Chikamatsu Monzaemon (1653–1724), the Edo period's greatest playwright for the puppet theater (lovers' dramas, *Sonezaki shinjū* [The love suicides at Sonezaki, 1703] and *Shinjū ten no Amijima* [The love suicides at Amijima, 1721] and historical plays, *Kokusenya kassen* [The battles of Coxinga, 1715]) and author of kabuki plays (*Keisei Mibu dainembutsu* [Courtesans and the great recitation of the Buddha's name at the Mibu temple, 1702]); see Donald Keene, trans., *Major Plays of Chikamatsu* (New York: Columbia University Press, 1961).

19. The phrase "enclosed meditations" (*misshitsu no shisō* in the original)

"I don't really think so. You know, 'Le Cimetière marin' lies right in the open air."[20]

"But I'm referring to *Monsieur Teste*."[21]

"Oh, yes, indeed. But the work has nothing to do with *misogi*. Are you really serious when you talk about *misogi*?"

"What do you mean, 'Am I serious?'" Yokomitsu's voice began to tremble with anger.

"Because what you said makes so little sense. So I'm asking you if you're serious."

"All meticulous thinking pursued with great thoroughness shares something in common with *misogi*."

"That's nonsense! Let me remind you that *misogi* is not a thinking process but a ritual!"

"You people just want to bicker about words! You should be ashamed!"

"Not at all! Aren't you a writer yourself? You'd agree that a writer is a specialist with words, wouldn't you? If the best you can do with words is get yourself into trouble, that by itself is a fatal flaw on your part, isn't it?"

"I'm through with you people!" Yokomitsu roared with anger. "This is absolutely outrageous! I've never seen anything like this."

"I expect you would feel that way." I again joined in the discussion. "See, at Komaba everybody talks freely about what's on his mind. If I could just add something about *misogi*—so there's no misunderstanding about it—Valéry doesn't take up the idea; it's *The Golden Bough*. Rituals of purification and exorcism and things of that sort are in no way peculiar to Japan. They abound in primitive tribal religions. You see, in

---

comes from Valéry's *Soirée avec Monsieur Teste* (An evening with Monsieur Teste, 1896): "If this man had changed the object of his enclosed meditations, if he had turned the regulated power of his mind against the world, nothing would have resisted him" (quoted in Elizabeth Sewell, *Paul Valéry: The Mind in the Mirror* [New Haven: Yale University Press, 1952], 22).

20. Referring to Valéry's celebrated meditation at the graveyard by the sea (1920), the student comments on its "good ventilation" (*kaze tōshi wa yoi desu yo* [which I translate as "lies right in the open air"]).

21. Whether Valéry's protagonist in *La Soirée avec Monsieur Teste* is "the high priest of the idol of intellect," "a portrait of his intellectual robot," or an image of Mallarmé or Degas, he symbolizes "honest pursuit of knowledge and purity" by "being and seeing myself; seeing myself see myself" (Agnes Ethel MacKay, *The Universal Self: A Study of Paul Valéry* [Toronto: University of Toronto Press, 1961], 82–92).

order to understand Africa or 'Eastern spiritual civilization,' these religions are more telling than the rhetoric of 'loud weeping' of the Japan romanticists. Could we really 'transcend' Western modernity with 'loud weeping'? Today, a century and a half after the *Déclaration des droits de l'homme,* isn't it anachronistic to speak out for the idea of *misogi* and Japan as a divine nation?"[22]

Yokomitsu did not rise and leave in indignation. As long as he was still with us, we continued to go after him. Gradually Yokomitsu's words grew more guarded, his complexion ashen with anger. But because we knew his writings so well, we could anticipate what was on his mind and all together we spared no effort in smashing his ideas to smithereens one after another. No sooner had one of us stopped to catch his breath than someone else began.

We took up one point Yokomitsu had written about, "The West itself is aware of the impasse of its modernity."

"But does this make Japan the country to break that impasse?"

"And why not?"

"Because it's not Japan's impasse. Whether a modern Western society thousands of miles away finds itself in an impasse or not, Japan is not a modern society. It's simply out of place for us to lose any sleep over this kind of thing. The 1868 revolution was not the French Revo-

22. In *The Golden Bough,* the Scottish anthropologist James George Frazer (1854–1941) traces the development of the world's religions from their earliest forms. • The Japan romanticists (*Nihon rōmanha*), a very diverse literary group in the late 1930s, included Yasuda Yojūrō, Kamei Katsuichirō, Jinbo Kōtarō, Nakatani Takao, and later Dazai Osamu and Hagiwara Sakutarō, who collectively felt a sense of crisis regarding Japan's cultural identity and its problematic modernity; their advocacy of a new "romanticism" during a time of ideological conversion (*tenkō*) soon developed into a nativist interest in the Japanese classics and medieval Japanese aesthetics before the group was swept under the wings of fanatic ultranationalism. Their emotionally charged but often nebulous rhetoric included "loud weeping" (*dōkoku*), "our poignant aspiration" (*higan*), and "the idea of returning to the primitive origin of history written with the blood of race" (*minzoku to iu chi de kakareta rekishi no genshi ni sakanoboru gainen*). On the dynamics between the Nihon Rōman-ha and the Matinée Poétique group (discussed in chapter 18), consult Kamiya Tadataka's provocative *Yasuda Yojūrō ron* (On Yasuda Yojūrō [Kari shokan, 1979]), 26–33; see also Katō Shūichi, "Sensō to chishikijin," in *Chishikijin no seisei to yakuwari: Kindai Nihon shisōshi kōza,* vol. 4 (Chikuma shobō, 1959); and Kevin M. Doak, *Dreams of Difference: The Japan Romantic School and the Crisis of Modernity* (Berkeley: University of California Press, 1994).

lution. Now, mind you, the farm rent in this country is still paid in kind! Moreover, it takes up more than half the harvested crop. How on earth can anyone call it a modern land system? This is a country in which more than half the labor force is concentrated in the rural villages, and as long as Japan still keeps the feudal system of land ownership and goes on exploiting small farmers, I think it's meaningless to speak about 'modernity'—to say nothing of the totally ludicrous debate about whether we can transcend it."

"No, it's not ludicrous!" But despite Yokomitsu's protest, our group was no longer prepared to take it seriously. Instead, we rattled on about what was on our minds.

"Small farmers impoverished under the system of feudalistic exploitation became the source of cheap labor. Since Japanese capitalism took off from that springboard, naturally its domestic market is small. In essence, the *Dai Tōa kyōeiken* (Greater East Asia Co-Prosperity Sphere) is simply its logical conclusion in the form of continental expansion. The emancipation and independence of colonies? What a joke! I suppose the Japanese government might want to emancipate the British and American colonies, but it'd never think of emancipating its own. That is evident because they never even breathe a word about Korean independence. On the contrary, haven't we seen how Yanaihara Tadao got kicked out of the university just for criticizing the colonial policies in Taiwan and Korea?[23] And then they bring up this business about 'total mobilization of the national spirit.' Who is trying to mobilize the Japanese people and for what purpose? I don't know much about literature, but, Mr. Yokomitsu, I don't understand how our writers can talk about 'this great age' and things like that when they don't even have a firm grasp of the matter. What exactly is so 'great' about it anyway? If writers like you are being deceived, you can only blame your own stupidity. But if you aren't being deceived, then aren't you prostituting your own soul?"

At that time what we were doing, to follow Ōgai's phraseology, was simply fortifying ourselves by drawing our ammunition from Kafū when we cited the Bunka and Bunsei periods, from *The Golden Bough*

---

23. The liberal colonial economist Yanaihara Tadao (1893–1961) was forced to leave Tokyo Imperial University in 1938 for openly criticizing Japan's China policy but—after World War II—became its president. See Katō's reminiscences of Yanaihara as his teacher at Ichikō in chapter 10.

148   /   *A Microcosm*

when we dealt with the idea of *misogi,* and from the Kōza-ha when we offered our critique of the Greater East Asia Co-Prosperity Sphere and Japan's "sacred war."[24] On the other hand, Yokomitsu came to us empty-handed. His only ammunition was his literary fame and the current of the time unleashed by the authorities. Perhaps he did have something resembling a sense of conviction. But there is a difference between genuine belief and self-imposed faith. And I had no doubt that Yokomitsu himself could appreciate their difference more than anyone else.

For a long time I forgot about this encounter with Yokomitsu, my first and last with him. Then came Japan's defeat and the Occupation. Shortly after that, Yokomitsu passed away. His death was due to massive hemorrhage of his stomach ulcer. I was told that he had not sought medical attention, insisting that his illness could be cured not by science but by spirituality. When Nakajima Kenzō told me this story, I once again thought that Yokomitsu Riichi had paid the price for his wrong-headed philosophy, this time with his own life. Some illnesses can be cured by medicine, while others cannot. Nearly all stomach ulcers can be cured with proper medical care. At that time Nakajima half-jokingly said, "You guys killed Yokomitsu! After he was attacked by you people at Komaba, he seemed to have taken quite a knock. He wasn't the kind of man who

24. Mori Ōgai (1862–1922), novelist, critic, surgeon general of the Japanese army, and usually ranked with Natsume Sōseki and Shimazaki Tōson as one of Japan's three preeminent modern writers, translated German romantic poetry and introduced German aesthetics into Japan; Ōgai's short stories and other works include "Maihime" (The dancing girl, 1890), *Vita Sexualis* (1909), *Seinen* (Youth, 1910–11), *Gan* (The wild goose, 1911–13), *Shibue Chūsai* (1916), *Izawa Ranken* (1916), and *Hōjō Katei* (1917–20). Katō notes that "the variety of theme and range of contemporary characters treated in his short stories and novels will probably never be equalled in Japanese fiction" (*History of Japanese Literature,* 3:146). • Nagai Kafū, novelist, essayist, and an early advocate of naturalist literature in Japan, whose visit to France (June 1907—May 1908) began his lifelong admiration for French literature and culture and abhorrence of frivolous Japanese attempts at superficial Westernization; on Kafū's elegiac novel *Bokutō kidan* see note 9 above. • The Kōza-ha (lecture faction) was a group of early Shōwa Marxist economists and theoreticians who, contrary to its theoretical rival the Rōnō-ha (labor-farmer faction), characterized Japanese capitalism as one founded on a semi-feudalistic land system and identified the Meiji state as a political absolutism under the emperor-system (*tennōsei zettaishugi*). Chief members included Noro Eitarō, Yamada Moritarō, and Hirano Yoshitarō (and the Rōnō-ha's core members were Ōuchi Hyōe, Yamakawa Hitoshi, Inomata Tsunao, and Kushida Tamizō).

would easily pull in his horns, but let me tell you, he was pretty upset about it until his death."

"Is that so?" I said. "I didn't realize that."

"You fool! After you tore him apart like that, don't tell me you didn't realize it!"

But at the time we were only too preoccupied with our own defense, not so much against Yokomitsu as against the tide of the times. We could never have imagined that nameless students like ourselves could in any way deal a crushing blow to such a prominent "master." If we could indeed deliver such a blow, I suppose it was only because our opponent was someone who didn't need one. It seemed to me that Nakajima was tactfully making this point. To deal a crushing blow to someone who needed it was beyond our ability.[25]

Yokomitsu Riichi was an invited guest at Komaba. But the *Hitlerjugend* band came uninvited. Whereas we were prepared to engage in vigorous debates with our own guests, we simply ignored the uninvited ones. Clad in uniform and marching in synchronized steps, they would show up in regular ranks at Komaba's main entrance. They were still baby-faced teenagers with somewhat stern demeanor and, like puppets, had no expressions on their faces. On a number of occasions, the few students who happened to be there would stop and puff on their cigarettes as they watched the group march by. Others would turn around for a quick glance before walking past them through the campus gate. We refused to have anything to do with them. We still could not imagine that some of our own friends would soon be walking out of the main university gate at Hongō with rifles in their hands.

Those were the days when I spent many futile hours trying to write a novel. But my experience held no material relevant to what I thought a novel should be. I had never been romantically involved and hence I had never been betrayed in love. I had never experienced dire poverty, to say nothing of plunging myself into blood-boiling and heart-throbbing adventures. On the contrary, the things I had experienced and the things that had moved me seemed hardly material for a novel: books

25. Katō was one of many critics who tried immediately after the war to assess the war responsibility of Japanese literary intellectuals during the militarist era. See Katō's essay on Yokomitsu in *Bungaku jihyō* 6 (1946), along with ones by Odagiri Hideo and Obara Gen on Saitō Mokichi and Ishikawa Tatsuzō, respectively (Nakajima Kenzō, *Kaisō no sengo bungaku: Haisen kara rokujūnen anpo made* [Heibonsha, 1979], 216–17).

and music. And from the sidelines I watched a society racing blindly toward madness like an automobile about to overturn on a downhill run. I wondered what kind of destruction we would see and know after all the sound and fury had ended. Yet these thoughts had no apparent connection to literary matters. Meanwhile, trying to force myself to come up with something resembling a novel, I felt more and more keenly the considerable discrepancies between my own sensibilities and experiences and the fictional world I was trying to create.

15 Remembrances of the Good Old Days

Why did my mind just then bring back memories of Tokyo before the Pacific War? I wondered about it as I was lying on a lounge chair, looking at the clear summer sky stretching high above the tip of a white birch tree. I was in a university town in the United States, and near it was the Oakland pier where military supplies were being shipped off for the war in faraway Asia.

Nothing around me connected me to Tokyo or to my past. Perhaps only the sky above the white birch tree had some resemblance to the Shin-shū sky in the bygone days of the late thirties, the sky at which I never grew tired of gazing. Off in the blue distance a white trail of vapor from an airplane now invisible to the eye gleamed in the sun. Bombers taking off from a desolate Pacific island and appearing over the sky of Tokyo during the last year of the war . . . Until the very day the bombs were dropped over our heads, we never believed it could really happen.

Some years ago, the United States sent its troops to Korea and suffered considerable losses. Although it was not defeated, the sense of bitterness over not winning the war remained deep within the military and among the right wing. Later it manifested itself as antipathy toward the liberals' compromising foreign policies. Eventually it developed into the mentality of "teaching the Communists a lesson" and even led to a large-scale deployment of troops into Vietnam. An impassioned archbishop sent words of encouragement to the soldiers fighting a "holy war"; and with its overpowering weaponry, this huge army went ahead and occupied towns and strategic routes between them. Locally, the government created a puppet regime and spoke emphatically about the mass support it enjoyed; yet the resistance from the liberation front did not weaken even slightly. Thereupon it invented the theory about Hanoi's nefarious behavior, leading to the bombing of the Ho Chi Minh trail. When this action totally failed to slow the resistance forces, authorities said this time the real enemy was not Hanoi but what was behind it—China. On the one hand, the U.S. government emphasized its hope of achieving "eternal peace in the Orient," proclaiming its total lack of "territorial ambitions," and its only aim the creation of "a land of co-prosperity" for all countries involved. It also declared itself ready to enter into "peace negotiations" at any time. On the other hand, it noted its refusal to deal with the liberation front.

"The Wang regime," the "supply route to Chiang," and "refusal to deal with the Chiang Kai-shek regime."[1] Needless to say, Japan in the thirties was a different country from the United States today. Japan in those days was poor and inefficient; its military strength did not equal even a tiny fraction of what the United States has today. Instead of using its military budget for a grand-scale mobilization of scholars, Japan was a country dominated by military men who had the naïveté to ban school instruction in the "enemy's language." And like today's international censure of American involvement in Vietnam, public opinion at the time by and large concurred in condemning Japan's war in China. Surrounded by foes on all sides, the Japanese "imperial army" assumed an increasingly "determined" posture; Japanese "subjects" were increasingly moved to "loud weeping" over Japan's "poignant and historical aspirations of world proportions."

Did all these events represent a peculiarly Japanese phenomenon? I was living in France when the war in Algeria began. A sense of frustration over the war in Indochina lingered in the French army.[2] Furthermore, troops stationed in Algeria resented the apathy and war weariness among the French population at home. Thereupon the army decided to take matters into its own hands by expanding the local theater of war and by turning the situation into a fait accompli. There was even an attempted military coup d'état to seize political power. Although the rebellious sol-

1. Wang Jing-wei (1884–1944) defected from the Zhongqing national government and on March 30, 1940, became head of the "reorganized" national government at Nanjing, a puppet regime created by the Japanese invaders.
2. The war in Indochina lasted from 1946 to 1954, the same year that Algerian nationalists began their war of independence against France. A 1961 referendum for Algerian self-determination passed in both countries, and Algeria achieved independence in July 1962.

diers failed, they did force the government of the Fourth Republic to recognize various faits accomplis. I cannot remember how many times I heard the announcement "the Algerian uprising will be suppressed before long," or the promise "France will refuse to talk with the National Liberation Front." Until General de Gaulle finally saved the situation from further deterioration, certain political and military phenomena in France in the late fifties resembled those in the thirties in Japan, when the country sank deeper and deeper into the quagmire in China.

Of course, when I was living in Tokyo in the thirties, I could not know that one day France would be fighting in Algeria and the United States in Vietnam. What I knew, or more correctly, what I had heard about, was the France of the *front populaire* and the United States of the New Deal. *Là, tout n'est qu'ordre et beauté, luxe, calme et volupté.*[3] Yet all I could find around me in my country were supralogical fanaticism, chaos, poverty, clamorous agitations, and a total lack of intellectual freedom. To be sure, I was not entirely ignorant of the myths in *Nibelungenlied* or the noisy propaganda of *Blut und Boden* or the lack of intellectual freedom in the country that obliterated the writings of Heine and forced Thomas Mann into exile.[4] But like France and the United States, Germany was a far, faraway country.

What was worse, the fanatical Japanese "patriots" imbued every piece of their propaganda with a certain "Japanesque" quality. And so only the "divine and infallible" Japanese emperors were the descendants from the gods. In a country where "one does not raise one's voice in contention," we were told, there was no need for freedom of speech in the first place. Everyone in the world was to "look up in awe" at Mount Fuji; the imperial army was "invincible throughout the world." When the odds of victory were overwhelmingly against Japan, patriotic fervor found it imperative to characterize every Japanese item as "number one in the world." Quantitatively speaking, since Japan at that time had almost nothing that could be called "number one in the world," things that did not lend themselves to quantitative comparisons were deemed to be such. There you have the soul of Yamato, Japan's pristine traditions and cherished customs, the ideal of the family-state, the beauty of

3. The refrain in Baudelaire's "Invitation au voyage," in *Les Fleurs du mal* (1857): "There, all is loveliness and harmony / Enchantment, pleasure and serenity" (Richardson, trans., *Charles Baudelaire*, 103).
4. "Blood and earth" was a Nazi propaganda slogan.

the land and nature, and the two thousand six hundred years of imperial rule. Even in the case of historical chronology, the Japanese way of
dating was different from the convention the rest of the world used, making any comparison difficult. Propriety dictated that the unification of
Japan under the Jimmu emperor must *not* be several hundred years later
than the golden age of great thinker-philosophers and the "Hundred
Schools" of thought in ancient China or the rise of indigenous Buddhism
in northern India or the zenith of ancient philosophy around the
Mediterranean.[5] However nebulous the logic might be, Japan must
surely be as old as the creation of heaven and earth itself and "the num-
ber-one country in the world." We were so very often fed these ideas
that I became thoroughly disgusted with "things Japanese" and began
to idealize "things Western." Since at that time I had not seen the West,
idealizing it was easy.

The campaign for the "total mobilization of the national spirit" was
successful in the urban areas. Elementary school children would chant
"Stop *pāma'nento* your hair!" at young female passersby. When men
with an inferiority complex toward higher education found university
students reading foreign-language textbooks on the train, they would
yell, "Look! These people are reading the enemy's language during this
time of national emergency! How could you call yourselves Japanese!?"
The "enemy's language" was the collective name for all Western languages; the expression *pāma'nento* referred to the women's fashion of
perming their hair.[6] Because these things had not permeated into the
countryside and because farmers were more interested in their own villages and in their own fields than in themselves as Japanese subjects or
in any claims to "spirituality," the campaign for "spiritual mobilization"
did not succeed in rural areas.

But I lived in the city. Uniforms, directives, seven- and five-syllable
slogans, boorish attitudes, imprecise rhetoric, intrusion of privacy, hero
worship, supercilious demeanor, emphasis on our "Japanese" character.
My distaste for these things did not stem from my critical stance against
militarism. Rather, my distaste for them in the first place led me to be-

---

5. The Jimmu emperor was the first in the line, according to the *Nihon
shoki*. • The span of China's golden age of great thinkers from "a hundred
schools" included the Spring and Autumn period (770–403 B.C.; 772–481 B.C.
by another count) and the Warring States period (403–221 B.C.) and extended
into the Han dynasty.
6. Short for *pāma'nento uēbu* or "permanent wave."

come critical of militarism as well. Since my elementary school days, I had disliked uniforms and detested songs with seven- and five-syllable lyrics. Since my middle-school days, my inclination had been not for hero worship but for iconoclasm, not for grandiloquence of character but for the satirist's wit. I had never been conscious of myself as a Japanese from daybreak to nightfall, and I had never experienced the need to feel that way. The thought of intoxicating myself with some vague daydream while marching with others in uniform made me sick to my stomach. Likewise, I could not stand the absurdity of macho or comic acts performed at drinking parties where people burst into uproarious laughter for no apparent reason. The disgust I felt toward militarism came less from idealism than from rebellion against the onslaughts of the militaristic atmosphere around me.

Why then did I try to interpret and criticize the events occurring around me? For my personal safety, knowing how the authorities conducted the examination for conscripts would certainly be more pertinent than knowing the true implications of the Greater East Asia Co-Prosperity Sphere. For a sense of inner peace, preparing myself for the eventuality of death and, to that end, believing the rhetoric about Japan's "sacred war" would certainly be the more expedient thing to do. And until things actually turned critical, one could surely carry on with one's life without giving any thought to the war. Wine, women, poetry, music. . . .

Yet I was interested in probing further into the nature of this war. It was true that this interest did not come from a sense of social responsibility. In fact, I did not feel any sense of responsibility toward a society I could not influence. But of course my own powerlessness toward society did not translate into society's powerlessness toward me. There was no doubt in my mind that I would be dragged mercilessly into wherever society was heading, and I, for my part, wanted to understand the totality of the forces acting on me. My belief was that the war with China was morally evil, an act of aggression from the perspective of international law, and, as far as I could tell, slipshod planning from the standpoint of military strategy.

The dreams I had at that time were no longer the same as those in my childhood when I was suffering from a high fever. No longer was there the gigantic wheel threatening to crush me in its path, nor the eerie whirlpool sucking me into its unfathomable depths. Instead, I found myself encircled by a group of policemen. They could see through even my innermost secrets, and with thin smiles playing triumphantly around their lips, they seemed to be enjoying themselves before the impending torture. I knew escape was hopeless, and I confessed to the fallacy of my thinking and begged for mercy. While I was disgusted with myself for such behavior, I tried desperately to scramble out of my predicament. After I had abandoned all my ideas, I could almost feel in the back of my mind a comforting relief as if a heavy load had been taken off my shoulders. But after I woke up, my thinking remained unchanged.

I had no interest in what other people called "inside intelligence" or "special information," nor did I know any. I did not even know about the Nanjing Massacre until after the collapse of Japanese militarism in 1945. And I was ignorant not only about that, but about concentration camps as well, and Dresden, and the number of women, children, and noncombatants killed in Hiroshima. As a matter of fact, until I read a newspaper article recently, I knew almost nothing about the number of children killed in South Vietnam. "From 1961 to 1966, 250,000 children were killed by napalm bombs in South Vietnamese villages," the article reported; "750,000 people lost their limbs and suffered other injuries and burns" (the article was based on an investigative report on Vietnam by the director of a research institute for children at a Catholic school in the United States). The figures reported may not be entirely accurate, but I doubt they were deliberately inflated. Even if the number of children killed was not 250,000 but was instead 200,000 or 300,000, the significance of this matter remains unchanged. But there is nothing I can do about it. Why then am I concerned with what happened to these children in a faraway country, children I've never even met? I am unable to come up with a satisfactory answer myself.

The evening after I read that newspaper article, I had dinner at a Hungarian restaurant with an old friend of mine, an entrepreneur. We were in an ancient capital in central Europe. The wine was good, and a strolling musician played his violin well. My friend and I had not seen each other for quite some time, and we started talking about food and the recent fashion in underwear (the businessman's young wife was quite knowledgeable on the subject). After talking about these things for a while, I remarked, "Somehow, it appears the first sign of economic prosperity always manifests itself in our propensity for trivial matters." The statement was meant as self-mockery and a sarcastic jest, but the businessman's wife seemed to take it as serious criticism.

"What do you mean by that?" she asked without smiling.

"Well, here we are in the middle of the Vietnam War and we're talking about whether sleeves in today's fashion are longer or shorter by one centimeter. That's what I meant," I explained.

"What's wrong with that?" said the businessman.

"Do you know about the report that 250,000 children have been killed?"

"Oh! I don't believe that!"

"You can't just brush it aside so lightly," I said. "You probably don't know the first thing about the Vietnam War. You might have a vague notion about what one party in the conflict has to say about it, but you haven't even once read what the other side says. You haven't looked at the provisions of the Geneva Accords, nor at the official report of the International Control Commission. So you can't conclude that the things I said couldn't take place. You're proclaiming your disbelief without even looking at the basic facts. That's why your fellow countrymen could say they didn't know about the concentration camps and the gas chambers after the Nazis had killed as many as several million people. It's not that they didn't know about them; they simply didn't want to know. It's not that you don't believe what I said; you simply don't want to believe it."

"I don't want to know about these things. I just want to live and enjoy my life in peace," the businessman said. "Even if you know about them, what can you do?"

True, there is nothing I can do. To be sure, there are people who don't want to know because of their own powerlessness to effect any change, but there are also those who want to know in spite of it. I cannot logically argue that the former position is wrong. I only feel that I myself belong to the latter group. I am not saying that any particular logical deduction obligated me to feel concerned about the children in a faraway country. Very simply, I felt empathy for them, and my reactions, tangible or not, followed. 250,000 children dead . . . Whether or not I could do anything about it, at that time the fate of these children weighed heavily on my mind. I was completely helpless, yet I was angry about the situation, and I felt agitated because of it.

16   One Fine Day

One fine morning I was walking with my classmates across the Tokyo University campus from the Faculty of Medicine toward the university hospital, thinking about my next class and other matters.[1] Just then, one of the students began to read aloud from the extra edition of the newspaper he had gotten earlier at the Hongō-dōri. Immediately a swelling wave of emotion stirred the whole crowd. Nobody said anything; you might say our reaction defied verbal articulation and manifested itself spontaneously in something like a collective sigh. At that moment, we realized, we were coming face to face with the reality of the Pacific War.

I felt the world around me suddenly transform into a landscape I had never seen. For over a year the Medical Science building, the cluster of trees nearby, and my classmates' student uniforms had been familiar, everyday sights for me. But in the peaceful morning light of that balmy, early winter day, I had the odd but acute impression that I was looking at them for the very first time. The feeling I had was like being abruptly cut off from my familiar surroundings. But this is merely an artificial description. The sensation I had, like taste, is almost impossible to put into words, yet it was so vivid and distinct that if I should ever experience it again, I would most certainly know it immediately. In fact, after the war when Mother's life was slipping away, my surrounding land-

---

1. In April 1940 at the age of 21, Katō became a medical student. His text often refers to *Hongō no daigaku* (the university in Hongō), a description Japanese readers can readily identify as Tokyo University. My shift to the university's name is useful for non-Japanese readers but sacrifices its casual tone.

scape changed in exactly the same way. Likewise during a romantic encounter, I felt Tokyo was no longer the same city I knew.

Aside from my feelings, nothing I said or did was out of the ordinary. Even when I knew that the war had started, I acted as if nothing had happened and went on walking along with my classmates toward the university hospital. I was certainly not unaware of the fact that war clouds had been gathering, but I could not bring myself to believe that a war with England and the United States could actually take place. I could not believe that my own conclusion had become a reality, and the fact that it should take place on such a clear, winter morning made it even more incredible.

I went with my classmates inside the hospital and into a lecture hall. The lecture on diagnostics—I think that's what it was—began and ended at its usual hour. I listened to it blankly, not registering anything. I kept wondering whether our perfectly composed professor had learned about the report in the newspaper's extra edition, or whether he did not know anything about it and so behaved calmly as if nothing had taken place.

"What's going to happen, I wonder?" Mother said when I returned home.

"I don't think we have any chance of winning the war," I snapped.

"Really?"

"There's no other way to look at it."

"Your uncle did say the navy minister acted recklessly, and he was worried about the situation. Well, I suppose things might get pretty serious."

"No doubt about it."

"Mind you, don't talk about this sort of thing to anyone," Mother said.

Beginning with that evening, blackout was in effect in anticipation of air raids. But on that particular night I had a ticket to the Shimbashi Theater. It was having its last *bunraku* show of the year.

"Can't you stay home tonight?" Mother said. "There may not be any performance at all."

I knew very well that Mother was not worried about my wasting a trip to the theater. Still, I said, "I'll be back right away if the performance is canceled," and left home.

The subway was working as usual. When I got off at Ginza 4-chōme, the streets were almost dark. There were few pedestrians in front of the Shimbashi Theater; only the building itself stood in dead silence like a big black mass under the dim night sky. So the last show of the year had indeed been canceled, I thought. But just to make sure, I went up to the entrance and was surprised to find not only was it open, it even had a male receptionist on duty. Although I saw no other spectators anywhere, I handed over my ticket and went inside.

Since there were no other spectators on the second floor, I walked to the front and sat in the middle. When I looked down at the main floor, I could see only four or five men sitting here and there, and it didn't look like the performance was going to begin any time soon. Once again I thought perhaps the manager or somebody would come out to announce we could get a refund for our tickets.

Right at that moment, it happened. The *gidayū* and the samisen player made their appearance and took their seats. "The narrator today is . . ." And so the name was announced and the invigorating sound of the wooden clappers reverberated in the emptiness of the theater. The curtain was raised, and the puppets came to life with their movements. Immediately I was drawn into the world of the *gidayū* and the samisen. "And now, my dear Hanshichi-san . . ." And so the chant went.[2] It was, to be sure, an extraordinary spectacle. Seated in an inconspicuous spot, the chanter Ko'utsubo had transformed himself into an Edo townswoman of the distant past, his solitary figure twisting in every direction and his voice rising as he moaned, pleaded, and wept. I found myself in a world in which there were no longer any wars, blackouts, or agencies like the Cabinet Intelligence Bureau.[3] What stood in their place was a world of unrelenting resolve, a world in which a woman's lamentation over her love rose through every shade of its subtle nuance to the level of stylistic eloquence, a world of expression in which the sound of the samisen and Master Ko'utsubo's breath merged in exquisite unity. This very moment marked the beginning of its confrontation with another world existing outside the theater, a world erected on each and every facet of the ideology and the reality of militarist Japan. Instead of

2. The term *gidayū* usually refers to a celebrated *jōruri* reciter in Osaka, Takemoto Gidayū (1651–1714), but also applies to the recitation style he pioneered or to *jōruri* reciters in general. • "And now, my dear . . . ," O-sono's memorable line from the *bunraku* play *Hadesugata onnamaiginu* (1772), act "Sakaya no dan" (At the sake brewery), as she affectionately thinks of her husband, Hanshichi, who is about to commit love suicide with the dancer Sankatsu.

3. Toyotake Ko'utsubo dayū II (1878–1967 [received the title in 1909]; from 1947 Toyotake Yamashiro no Shōjō) was a leading chanter in the wartime and postwar *bunraku* theater and in 1955 was designated a "living national treasure"; he retired in 1959. • The bureau was created in December 1940 under the second Konoe cabinet for intelligence and propaganda functions as well as thought control in the press, publications, broadcasting, plays, and films.

asserting itself through the thick mantle of its audience, the *bunraku* theater met its challenge with sheer naked immediacy, with every element of its self-actualization and self-realizing legitimacy as an art form. With majestic grace and unyielding will, it stood tragically before its adversary. Was Master Ko'utsubo fighting this ferocious battle all by himself? I think not, for he had become the living embodiment of Edo culture in its entirety. The transformation of culture into the flesh. It manifested itself not in abstract words but as an immutable reality right before my very eyes. What more could anyone possibly need?

The bombs did not fall on our heads immediately. After the imperial proclamation of war, Tokyo was in a state of euphoria over the great success at Pearl Harbor and people went totally wild with joy.

"Oh! I feel so good! It makes me want to sing military songs," one university professor said. The United States Pacific fleet was totally destroyed. "How gratifying!" said the students. Famous *tanka* poets composed poems about Pearl Harbor in the newspapers, and other poets thanked heaven for giving them the good fortune of witnessing such a grand event in their lifetime.

During the following month learned men wrote journal articles about the shining future for the Great Japanese Empire, proclaiming *now* as the time to mark the "end of modernity" and open "the way for the Greater East Asian Co-Prosperity Sphere." Even my uncle, who as head of the Department of Naval Affairs had been critical about the opening of hostilities, now commented that the unanticipated military success at Pearl Harbor was "beyond dispute."

Needless to say, Tokyo was not the only capital where people were jumping up and down in euphoria on learning about Japan's attack on Pearl Harbor. Unbeknownst to me at the time, almost every other capital in the world, except perhaps Berlin, was jubilant at the news. Surely Moscow must have felt relieved at the accuracy of Sorge's intelligence when they learned that the Japanese forces were moving south instead of heading north.[4] London must also have been overjoyed at the Japanese operation because it virtually guaranteed the entry of the United States into the war. It was reported that when General de Gaulle learned

---

4. The Soviet spy Richard Sorge—as Roberta Wohlstetter notes—with "direct access to the Japanese Cabinet, had correctly predicted the southern move as early as July, 1941" (*Pearl Harbor: Warning and Decision* [Stanford: Stanford University Press, 1962], 392).

about the incident in his exile, he promptly remarked, "Now I know we're going to win the war." In the United States, at a conference of the Institute of Pacific Relations in Cleveland, the news of Japan's surprise attack reached the scholars just when they were in the middle of their discussion on how improbable it would be for Japan to go to war. They could not believe their ears. When they recovered from their shock, they decided to adjourn the meeting, feeling elated that Japan's action had "ensured the fall of fascism." The citizens of Tokyo were cheering among themselves because they had no idea that the rest of the world was also cheering over the same event.

In a somber mood, I watched them in their exultation. Never in my life have I felt more alienated from my fellow Tokyoites. When Tokyo was burning, I was at the side of those who had lost their homes in the fire, and my mind was totally preoccupied with treating the burned victims of incendiary bombs. After the war when I was living on the other side of the world from Tokyo, I felt a sense of closeness with a great many Tokyoites; and the longer I spent my wandering years abroad, the more I thought about the Tokyo within me. But I was not among those who cheered on the day Pearl Harbor was attacked. On that day, the closer I felt toward the Japan evoked by Master Ko'utsubo, the farther militarist Japan with its war euphoria retreated into the background. What the *tayū* chanted was not just a story from a time long past. He spoke only of the single irreplaceable world of my own, the very ephemeral world of all my love and affections, my happiness and sorrow.

Contrary to my expectations, no major changes occurred in our daily life in Tokyo during the early stages of the war. The British and American troops were even farther away from us than the war front in China. At that time I commuted to Tokyo University from our house in Akatsutsumi in Setagaya Ward. Earlier than that, Grandfather had mortgaged his Mitake-chō house along with his land in Shibuya as his business failed. After the foreclosure of his property, he moved into a small house in Meguro Ward; we, likewise, sold our Mitake-chō home and began living in a rented house in Akatsutsumi.

Since then, besides his army pension, Grandfather had supported himself by selling off things like furniture and other personal belongings. Meanwhile, he was quietly writing "a novel." "Instead of a novel, shouldn't it be called a record of your own amorous affairs?" Mother would tease him. I suppose Grandfather's intention was to find a way to preserve memories dear to him after everything had become a matter of the past.

In his "novel," there was no mention of how he made money or reference to wars. All it held was inconsequential, commonplace events, such as Mother's casual remarks when she sent him off at Tokyo Station on a short trip, the laughter of his grandchildren as he took them shopping, his old lady friends' compassion for him when he was down on his luck with his business, and their thoughtfulness for not making him conscious of their acts of kindness. As I followed Grandfather's rather awkward and old-fashioned prose, I knew exactly what had driven him to put down such matters in writing. It was the tenacious attachment to the past of someone who had throughout his life lived for the pleasures of the present. Soon afterwards, old Grandfather died in his small Meguro home.

Father did not resume his medical practice at our rental house in Akatsutsumi. He was working at the Sanitarium for Tuberculosis in Izu, living there by himself and seldom returning to Tokyo. Mother, Sister, and I sometimes went to visit him. There we could smell the fragrance of the sea and see the tangerine orchards covering the hillsides, and at night in bed, we could even hear the sound of the high waves. But there was no one to talk to besides my family, and every time I returned to Tokyo, I felt as if I had a new surge of energy. But even in Tokyo, there were fewer and fewer people I could talk to just as my need for companionship and communication grew stronger and stronger.

Although the Japanese army had been advancing like wildfire, it did not go beyond Hawaii. Now, instead of talking about "Expedition against America," "Victory," and the like, the government proclaimed that Japan was in an "absolutely invulnerable state." Yet the rhetoric before the war had been that "Japan should fight rather than just sit by idly and await annihilation." Just how the situation evolved from the dire possibility of national annihilation to being "absolutely invulnerable" was never satisfactorily explained. To be sure, Japan had acquired oil resources in the south, but natural resources were not the only element necessary for military preparedness. In terms of capital accumulation, technology, and labor force, surely the United States had a more advantageous position in the arms race. Psychosomatic claims about "the soul of Yamato" and America as "the country of effeminacy" were too tenuous to be worthy of any consideration. My thinking at the time was that the pronouncement of absolute invulnerability was most likely inaccurate and that in all probability Japan would be defeated.

Yet I was unable to predict when defeat would come. It would not be a hundred years away, nor would it be the next day. Such being the case, my judgment naturally had no direct bearing on my immediate actions. Thoughts of "absolute victory" or inevitable defeat had no effect on my daily routine of commuting to medical school, and still less on what I learned there. If I was thinking about hoarding goods or preparing for imminent evacuation, surely the essential consideration was not how long it would take for Japan to be defeated, but what commodities would be in short supply the next day or when Tokyo would be bombed. As a matter of fact, before long I began to see people around me doing things like hoarding canned food, cornering the war supplies market for profiteering, or busily preparing deft evacuations, as all the while the "spirit of absolute victory" inflamed their hearts. But I was not thinking of hoarding goods, making preparations for evacuation, or taking any concrete action at all. It was not because I lacked evidence for making the kind of judgment to spur me into action. It was because I was not thinking of taking any action in the first place that I felt comfortable about rendering my judgment irrelevant to my own actions. Once judgment was divorced from action, it was easy to renounce wishful thinking. As I witnessed the decline of my own family, I also anticipated the decline of the Japanese empire. In either case, I could think of no way to overcome it; the most I could do was understand how it came about.

While my thinking did not spur me into action, it did create a wall between me and my surroundings. In those days I felt like a tourist wandering the streets, as I could see more and more Tokyoites donning the "national uniform."[5] Both tourist and local resident look at the same landscape; but the former interprets it differently. Because of this, a tourist often becomes a source of irritation to local people, who are put off by his simplistic views. Tokyo had not yet fallen into ruin, but sometimes almost everything before my eyes took on the illusion of a desolate city in ruins, totally devastated by fire. And then suddenly, everything would begin to radiate a beauty I had never thought possible. Heaps of tangerines and apples piled up on the counter of the fruit store in front of Akamon (crimson gate), their colors, accentuated under the wintry afternoon sun, and the presentiment of their frostiness to the touch were enough to make me pause on the pavement.[6] Lines of ginkgo trees on the university campus, their fine mesh of leafless branches stretching out into the sky, and

5. A khaki-colored outfit similar to a military uniform worn by men after 1940.
6. Originally the property of the Maeda family of Kaga-han, the Akamon

the misty green of early spring. People with books or briefcases in hand coming in and out of the narrow office entryways on both sides of the corridor, the sunny yet solitary spot near Sanshirō Pond, and the evening sun illuminating the red-brick walls of the chemistry building. Nurses in white uniforms hurrying along the dim hospital corridor at dusk, the window lights at Hongō-dōri's bookstores and at The White Cross as evening approached.[7] And the owner of the secondhand bookstore crouching at the back of the store with a charcoal brazier by his side as he scrutinized his account book. All these images captivated me and moved me almost beyond words. For the first time, I really looked at the stone walls of the Imperial Palace and the glistening water of Chidorigafuchi.[8] And that was not all. I could feel all the hustle and bustle of Tokyo, its bumpy pavements, and sense the wind on my skin marking the change of seasons. I might survive, or more probably I would not. But as long as I was walking the streets, I wanted to make them my own.

Many years later I was walking on the stone pavement in a piazza in Florence, looking around at the Renaissance structures in the area, when it occurred to me that this could be my last visit there. On the other hand, the Florentines themselves must surely have been thinking about their own business transactions, their mayoral election, the price of wine, the good looks of the new priest, or the identity of the father of the child born to the girl next door, their emotions punctuated with every hope and regret, every joy and sorrow in their hearts. The only person enchanted by Renaissance stone pavements was me, the traveler, not the housewives who walked on them every day with their shopping baskets in hand. I discovered Tokyo when I was not actually living in it. Thomas Mann spoke of "another Germany," and the poet Katayama Toshihiko spoke of "another Japan." But that was not what I am talking about. From the very outset, my role was not that of an active participant but an observer. I myself might have thought that the war had revealed the naked core of the Great Japanese Empire, but perhaps what it did reveal was actually my own self.

---

is now on the Tokyo University campus and has become a popular symbol for the institution.

7. Officially called Ikutokuen Shinjiike, the Sanshirō Pond on the Tokyo University campus was named after Natsume Sōseki's novel *Sanshirō* (1908). • The White Cross, or Hakujūji, was a teahouse popular with students and faculty; it faced the university gate across from Hongō-dōri.

8. A particular part of the inner moat surrounding the Imperial Palace in Tokyo.

17 The French Literature Circle

At Tokyo Imperial University I attended classes not only in the Faculty of Medicine but also in the Faculty of Literature. I had studied English and German at school, and though I had also acquired some reading proficiency in French through self-study, I attended a French class designed for students with no special background. The lecturer Nakajima Kenzō explained rudimentary grammar as we read *Salomé*, and when we came across grammatical intricacies that defied easy explanation, he would make the students laugh by saying something like, "I don't quite understand them myself. You don't expect me to remember this stuff to this day, do you?"[1] Because the class was meant for students who were reading French for the first time, it was a little too easy for me.

I also attended, albeit irregularly, other classes offered by the Department of French Literature: "Nineteenth-Century Literary Thinking" by Professor Tatsuno, "A Study of Mallarmé" by Assistant Pro-

1. Nakajima Kenzō (1903–79), a critic and French scholar, who founded the journal *Furansu bungaku kenkyū* (Studies of French literature) and published translations and critical commentaries (including *Kaigi to shōchō* [Skepticism and symbolism, 1934], *Gendai bungeiron* [On contemporary literature, 1936], an attempt at literary criticism from the social and cultural perspective, and *Gendai sakka ron* [On contemporary writers, 1941], a study of Yokomitsu Riichi, Ibuse Masuji, and Takami Jun); his postwar activities included rebuilding the Japan PEN Club, establishing the Japan Comparative Literature Society (Nihon hikaku bungakukai, 1948) and the Japan-China Cultural Exchange Association (Nihon-Chūgoku bunka kōryū kyōkai, 1956), heading the central committee of the New Japan Literary Society (Shin Nihon bungakukai) in 1950 and publishing *Andore Jiidō shōgai to sakuhin* (The life and works of André Gide, 1951), *Shōwa jidai* (The Shōwa era, 1957), and *Gendai bunkaron* (On contemporary culture, 1966).

fessor Suzuki, reading classes on Maurice Scève and Montaigne by Assistant Professor Watanabe, and so on.[2] Professor Tatsuno's lectures,
delivered in his crisp Japanese, were a pleasure to the ear and easily allowed his personality to come through. I suppose that was why he was
so popular with the students—his lectures were always heavily attended. The "Study of Mallarmé" was exceptionally detailed. When I
was taking the course, part of our study of the poet's life dealt with the
amount of rent he paid in a certain year. When I expressed my amaze-
ment to Nakamura Shin'ichirō, then a student in the Department of
French Literature, he said, "Stop complaining! You guys should consider yourselves lucky. At least this year we're talking about Mallarmé.
It took us a whole year just to cover the period before his birth. One
whole year! Just think about that!" As for Professor Watanabe's reading class on sixteenth-century literature, for somebody like me who did
not even have a decent grasp of modern French, it was like returning
empty-handed from a mountain of treasure. Nevertheless, as long as
there was no scheduling conflict with my lectures at the medical school,
I would sit at the back of the classroom and listen to the exchanges between Professor Watanabe and those evidently more gifted students
such as Miyake Noriyoshi.[3]

Besides French literature, I also took Mr. Yoshimitsu Yoshihiko's lec-

2. Tatsuno Yutaka (1888–1964), the eldest son of the architect Tatsuno Kingo
(see chapter 3), was professor of modern French literature at Tokyo University
(1921–48). He worked with his colleague Suzuki Shintarō to establish French
literary studies in Japan, translated works of Molière, Beaumarchais, and Ros-
tand, and was an erudite man noted for his keen literary and artistic sensibilities and for his personal charm and wit; among his students were Watanabe
Kazuo, Kobayashi Hideo, Nakajima Kenzō, Miyoshi Tatsuji, and Nakamura Mitsuo. • Suzuki Shintarō (1895–1970), a leading Japanese scholar of French literature from the late 1930s into the postwar era, was known for his meticulous
study of French symbolic poets, particularly Mallarmé, and his translations of
Villon, Baudelaire, Verlaine, and Valéry. • Watanabe Kazuo (1901–75), a leading Japanese scholar of the French Renaissance who translated Rabelais's *Gar-
gantua et Pantagruel* (5 vols., 1943–65), published *Raburee kenkyū josetsu* (A
study of Rabelais, 1957) and *Furansu yumanisumu no seiritsu* (The formation
of French humanism, 1958), taught French literature at Tokyo University
(1942–62), and was a prominent intellectual figure of his generation whose cultural critique of Japanese society and uncompromising integrity during the war
in particular influenced his disciples, including Katō, Nakamura Shin'ichirō, Mori
Arimasa, and, from a younger generation, Ōe Kenzaburō.

3. Miyake Noriyoshi (1917–) became a linguist in French, a translator, and
a professor at Tokyo Metropolitan University and Gakushūin University.

tures on moral philosophy in the Faculty of Literature.[4] His articulate discourse had a different sort of eloquence from Professor Tatsuno's. For two hours he could go on and on without a moment's pause in incredibly long sentences. Whenever I came in a little late for class, I would find him in the middle of one of his long sentences that went for another several more minutes: "in the context of Barthesque, Brunnerian, and Gogartenian dialectic crisis theology, and in connection with the trembling soul of Saint John on the night he received God's grace, its repeated manifestation was seen."[5] Hearing only half of what he said, I had no way of telling who saw what. As a matter of fact, even if I had listened to it from the beginning, I would not have been able to understand what it meant at all. But after I read Yoshimitsu's major works and then Iwashita Sōichi's, I became interested in Catholic theology.[6] But at that time I was in no way prepared to embrace a religious faith. Like Western scholars of Japanese history with an interest in Buddhism, perhaps I was just intellectually interested in Catholicism when I first began to read French literature.

Even with my meager knowledge of Catholicism, I could immediately see French literature from a new light. Not only was its cogent order of rational thinking a virtual gem in itself, it seemed to me that its presence was more than sufficient to explain the origins of seventeenth-century rationalism. The ideas Péguy so passionately espoused—that evil represents the ultimate outcome of man's goodwill and that every new descent into the abyss of sin conversely enhances the possibility for one's salvation—struck me as some of the most profound and subtle observations on the dynamics of the human condition. Though they did not convince me, I thought that if faith had such a paradoxical structure

4. Yoshimitsu Yoshihiko (1904–45) taught at Tokyo's Sophia University and the Tokyo Catholic Seminary from 1931 and succeeded Iwashita Sōichi (see note 6) as the leading Japanese Catholic thinker. A translator of his teacher Jacques Maritain's *Art et scolastique,* he examined the contemporary relevance of Thomism, wrote on Dostoyevsky and Rilke, and influenced such Catholic writers as Endō Shūsaku. His works are collected in *Yoshimitsu Yoshihiko chosakushū* (Misuzu shobō, 1947–52).

5. Karl Barth (1886–1968), a Swiss Protestant theologian. • Emil Brunner (1889–1966), a Swiss Protestant theologian. • Friedrich Gogarten (1887–1967), a German Lutheran theologian.

6. Iwashita Sōichi (1889–1940), a Catholic priest and philosopher, student of Greek and medieval thought under Raphael Koeber at Tokyo Imperial University, and teacher at the Seventh Higher School who wrote *Shingaku nyūmon* (Introduction to theology) and *Shinkō no isan* (Legacy of faith).

at its core, those who professed it certainly had good reasons for doing so. For the first time I could see what Claudel in his plays and Mauriac in his novels were getting at. And there was no longer any doubt in my mind that all of Graham Greene's novels could have only a single theme—it alone embodied such a wide range of possibilities that even the lifelong efforts of one novelist would not exhaust it. What I knew about Catholicism also enlightened me about the Middle Ages. I had no knowledge of Western medieval history, but rather than imagine the Middle Ages as an era of darkness antithetical to the Renaissance, I chose to follow Etienne Gilson in thinking of it as a positive period that witnessed the profuse flowering of systems of values and ideas.

My association with Catholicism had begun with those Western nuns who scared me as a child. Later on, as a university student, I was attracted to contemporary Thomist and Catholic writers. During the interval, however, I had never been to a church, never attended a holy service, never listened to a sermon, and never talked to a priest. As a matter of fact, I could hardly ever perceive any church influence on the society around me in the first place. I had never personally experienced the enormous pressures from converts, religious orders, and the church in influencing elections, in swaying personnel decisions at universities, in inhibiting abortions and divorces, or in ruthlessly censuring the conduct of the girl next door. Perhaps I was having a Platonic love affair with Catholicism. But once you live with it under the same roof, human nature makes it impossible to keep matters of love and hate nice and clean.

In those days, the Department of French Literature had quite a gathering of men of character: Tatsuno Yutaka, Suzuki Shintarō, Nakajima Kenzō, Mori Arimasa, Miyake Noriyoshi.[7] But it was their casual conversations after the lectures rather than the lectures themselves that filled the air with a peculiar dynamism. It was completely different from the atmosphere at the medical school, where students had almost no chance to talk with their teachers outside the classroom. In addition, there was something about the French literature circle that sharply distinguished it from the external society I knew. Perhaps it was the fact that one could,

---

7. Mori Arimasa (1911–76), a philosopher and literary critic, taught French literature and philosophy at Tokyo University (1948–50), studied Descartes and Pascal, and wrote *Dekaruto no ningenzō* (Descartes's image of man, 1948), *Dosutoeefusukii oboegaki* (On Dostoyevsky, 1950), *Babiron no nagare no hotori nite* (On Babylon's riverbanks, 1957), and *Uchimura Kanzō* (1958). His collected works are *Mori Arimasa zenshū* (15 vols.; Chikuma shobō, 1978–82).

to a considerable degree, feel free to speak his mind on any subject without having to play the power game. Professor Tatsuno, with his dashing manner and open demeanor, would rattle on and on, inserting jokes that amused others as well as himself. In fact he was very perceptive about people's feelings, and his thoughtfulness was expressed with impeccable sensitivity. One was almost compelled to conclude that his penchant for telling jokes was his way of loosening up others who might otherwise be intimidated by his all too penetrating insights into every matter. Each time he saw me, he always asked, "How is your father?" Father had been his family's physician since his own father's generation and he never forgot to send Father his regards, even indirectly through me.

"There are many talents at the French department," he observed. "Like Watanabe, Mori, and Miyake. They are the best people we've had since the department first started. If there is anything I don't know, I ask Watanabe. He knows just about everything. Kobayashi [Hideo] is also quite brilliant . . . but not in the same way as Watanabe; he never comes to class and reads all day at home.[8] He takes books from my house and returns them smudged with cigarette ash. But he really studies hard. He didn't do well in exams because he never came to class. And then he had the nerve to ask me to pass him! He only brought along his graduation thesis and asked me to read it. When I did, I was just flabbergasted. That was a great piece of work! I gave it the best grade.[9] Watanabe, Kobayashi, and Mori . . . Mori likes to talk about Descartes and Pascal—and let me

8. Kobayashi Hideo (1902–83), generally regarded as the foremost modern Japanese literary critic, whose interests ranged broadly from Baudelaire, Rimbaud, Valéry, and other modern European and Japanese writers to the Japanese classics, Motoori Norinaga, historical meaning, Western music, painting, and the art of living; his works include *Bungei hyōron* (Literary criticism, 3 vols., 1931–34), *Watakushi-shōsetsu ron* (A discussion of the I-novel, 1935), *Dosutoefusukii no seikatsu* (The life of Dostoyevsky, 1939), and *Mujō to iu koto* (The notion of impermanence, 1946). See Paul Anderer, trans., *Literature of the Lost Home: Kobayashi Hideo—Literary Criticism 1924–39* (Stanford: Stanford University Press, 1995); Donald Keene, *Dawn to the West: Japanese Literature of the Modern Era, Poetry, Drama, Criticism* (New York: Henry Holt, 1984), 582–610; and Edward Seidensticker, "Kobayashi Hideo," in *Tradition and Modernization in Japanese Culture*, ed. Donald H. Shively (Princeton: Princeton University Press, 1971), 419–61.

9. Kobayashi graduated in March 1928 with a thesis on Rimbaud. His reflections on his student days under Professor Tatsuno are in "Tatsuno Yutaka Sa. E. Ra," in *Bungei Tokuhon Kobayashi Hideo* (Kawade shobō shinsha, 1983), 35. For Katō's recollections of Kobayashi, see chapter 37.

tell you, he's another great talent. We really need people like him in French Lit, though he sometimes baffles us with his difficult ideas."

Mr. Nakajima was always the one who brought the French literature circle news about the war. Wiping his face, he would rush into the room like a gust of wind and announce, "This is no time for just sitting around doing nothing! Something big has happened!"

"Oh my! So they really bombed the enemy warships into pieces and sank them," said Professor Suzuki.

"That's how they took over Hawaii."

At this boisterous scene, Professor Watanabe came in from his lecture, and then all of us went together to the White Cross tearoom on Hongō-dōri. Sometimes Assistant Professor Nakano Yoshio from English literature and Mr. Yoshimitsu Yoshihiko from ethics would join us.[10]

"Wouldn't it be fun to play golf in Hawaii?"

"Maybe. But the mainland is untouched. I tell you, the war is going to get nasty," said Professor Watanabe.

"Nah, we're absolutely invincible."

"Well, I hope so."

"Looks like Ka-chan is too pessimistic.[11] Cheer up!"

At this point, Professor Tatsuno said in a loud voice, "I am completely in favor of the Greater East Asia War! Provided . . . " After a short pause, he continued, "Provided that instead of sending promising young men to get killed, they draft people from their age upward. If they sent guys from the General Staff Headquarters or deadwood like me or Suzuki to the battlefield, I'd be completely in favor of a Greater East Asia War."

When the war first began, Professor Tatsuno was happy about Japan's big military victories. To him, Pearl Harbor was a "thrilling" performance, and "His Majesty the Emperor" a figure worthy of great respect. However, he could also see through the minds of the power-hungry military and the opportunists who were jumping on the bandwagon of militarism. And all of a sudden, he surprised everyone with his comments.

I also liked Lecturer Nakajima, never a devious man with dirty tricks up his sleeve. He treated a mere stripling like me as his equal. Never pretentious or deceptive, he was the kind of man who could immediately make one feel at ease. His interests covered nearly everything: contemporary music, assembling engines for self-powered bicycles, international

10. On Nakano Yoshio see chapter 13 text and note 2.
11. An affectionate reference to Kazuo, Watanabe's personal name.

affairs, recent developments in the Physiology Society. While he lectured on French symbolism at the university, he was also active in numerous committees and organizations. He'd be here one minute and gone the next, and then there he was again leisurely talking about something else. He was always on the run all over Tokyo and seemed to have an inexhaustible supply of energy; yet none of his many activities was undertaken out of self-interest. It might be difficult to tell what his current activity was, but I could very well appreciate why he was doing it. I was absolutely amazed at his indefatigable vitality, and I could feel a responsive chord with—how should I put it?—a certain quality in him.

But the person who had the greatest influence on me was unquestionably Assistant Professor Watanabe Kazuo, a man who seemed to have descended to wartime Japan from heaven. No sense of defiance against the realities of militarism he found around him caused Professor Watanabe to seek spiritual asylum in faraway France—he knew French culture much too well and he was too deeply involved with Japanese society for that. Instead, as he lived within Japanese society, where all the ugliness had been laid bare for everyone to see, he endeavored to determine what all this meant from a larger world perspective and from a broader historical context. He seemed to scrutinize himself and his surroundings both from the inside and from the outside, and even from the lofty heights of Sirius.[12] In this respect, he reminded me somewhat of the enlightened minds during the *bakumatsu* period. Recognizing the futility of expelling the "Western barbarians" and the anachronism of national seclusion, they realized that Japan's "backwardness" lay not only in the state of its technology but also in its traditional educational system and in the Japanese way of thinking itself. Thereupon, they proceeded to trace the historical roots of the problem. And if we had not had Professor Watanabe's indomitable spirit on our side, continually confronting madness and anachronism and identifying them as nothing less, I doubt very much if we could have survived all those long war years without losing our sanity.

Even though I wished to observe Japan's conditions from an external perspective, I had never been abroad and my knowledge of the outside

12. An allusion to Voltaire's 1752 satire *Micromégas*, whose eponymous protagonist travels from the star Sirius and makes observations on the earthlings. According to a private communication from Katō, Professor Watanabe was fond of referring to Voltaire's philosophic hero.

world was limited. At that time I had just begun to get acquainted with the works of French writers after World War I by checking out from the department's library issues of *Europe* and *Nouvelle Revue Française* published during the interwar years. For Professor Watanabe, the contemporary literature we spent our days reading was probably no more than one night's diversion from his study of sixteenth-century France. His work was not simply a thorough and meticulous study of that period. The sixteenth century was precisely the time of the Wars of Religion and the Inquisition, an age in which devotion to abstract systems of thought led increasingly to fanaticism. This development in turn led to the emergence of a number of humanists who spoke out fervently for religious toleration. In other words, these were not just historical events from a faraway foreign country; they were part too of the reality of Japan and the contemporary world around it. Through scrupulous handling of materials, the more one closes in on the realities of the past, the more one simultaneously discovers the present in the past and sees the past in the present. Professor Watanabe stood before us as the living embodiment of its truth. Yet this scholar in his awesome wisdom and sensitivity always managed to conceal his affinities with the *bakumatsu* samurai-thinkers behind a veil of subtle ironies and paradoxes, as if suggesting that cultured behavior called for understatement and self-restraint. Racine, for example, would have the death of his protagonist announced onstage but would never allow the sight of blood.

At the French department I also became friends with Mori Arimasa and Miyake Noriyoshi, both working as teaching assistants. In those days Mori was living in a room at the Hongō YMCA where he buried himself among books, cigarette stubs, dust, and unlaundered underwear and socks. In between reading Pascal in French or Calvin in Latin and playing Bach's organ pieces, he would converse eloquently, not only at the department but also at the coffeeshop named South American in front of the YMCA. Joining us there was another YMCA resident, the dramatist Kinoshita Junji, so I got to know him as well.[13] Miyake had a small,

13. Kinoshita Junji (1914–), a student of Victorian drama under Nakano Yoshio at Tokyo Imperial University and a preeminent dramatist of the postwar realist theater who writes in a new dramatic language and anchors his plays in a rich array of historical themes (*Fūrō* [Winds and waves, 1947], *Okinawa* [1963], and *Kami to hito to no aida* [Between God and man, 1972; Eng. trans. by Eric Gangloff, 1979]). His celebrated folklore play *Yūzuru* (Twilight crane, 1949; with Yamamoto Yasue in the leading role) earned him international recognition.

slender build and a pale complexion. He was never loud or excitable, but he had an incredible tolerance for sake. A man with a gentle heart and an interest in every conceivable subject, he also possessed an outstanding intellect and impressed us with his precise knowledge and his meticulous analytical skill. When we got into heated debate at the department, he would just listen quietly; but as soon as he said, "Now, on that point— just a second!" everyone would stop to reexamine his thoughts. Whether it was about an interpretation of French, a statistic, or a historical period, subsequent checking revealed that he was hardly ever wrong. He and Mori were no less stubborn or uncompromising than Professor Watanabe in their refusal to be deceived by war propaganda. Whenever I stepped into the French department from the medical school, I always felt I was entering a completely different world.

The progress of the war unfortunately demonstrated the accuracy of our views. The Allies, now joined by the United States, were pressing against the German army in Europe and were beginning to retrieve the Pacific islands that the Japanese army had once occupied. At the university, the time required for graduation was reduced—April graduation now took place the preceding September—and "student mobilization" was implemented. After my graduation from medical school, I began to work at the university hospital. But I continued going to the French department whenever I had a chance, and this continued for a long time, until the medical division itself was "evacuated" to another location. What drew me was no longer French literature but rather my need to talk to someone in the midst of the storm. As the country faced impending ruin, I increasingly felt that I myself was being driven into a tight corner.

At about that time Miyake and I were attending Professor Kanda's Latin reading class.[14] Besides us, there was only one other student. At a time when military drills and student mobilization were the order of the day, it was not surprising that few students were interested in the long and short vowels of a classical language. On campus or along Hongō-dōri, nearly everyone wore the "national uniform." Professor Kanda alone came to class in a British-made suit. He always put on that perfectly tai-

14. Kanda Tateo (1897–1986), a New Testament scholar who published the journal *Girishago seisho no kenkyū* (The study of the Bible in Greek) in 1934, and later was vice president of the Japan-British Society. His writings are collected in *Kanda Tateo chosakushū* (5 vols., 1976–81).

lored suit—provocative as it must have been to everyone's eyes—to go to his weekly lecture in Tokyo all the way from his home in Gotenba by train.[15] When the evacuation of Tokyoites to the countryside began and the trains became more crowded, Professor Kanda remarked, "People are getting in and out through the windows. When a train gets this crowded, it's impossible to even read a book. You can't get any work done this way." His voice was characteristically gentle and self-possessed.

We read first Cicero—the passage containing his famous line "O tempora, o mores!"—and then Virgil. On the day in June 1944 that we heard about the Allies' Normandy landing, Professor Kanda was reading Virgil as usual. When he finished translating Dido's lament over her love (pronouncing the name "Dī'dō," as the British do), he closed his book and was getting ready to leave. While he was doing that, he spoke softly, almost as a monologue. "Well then, with this, both our enemies and our friends are going to have a very difficult time." And then he got up and walked toward the door. He suddenly stopped, turned around in our direction, and said, "By our enemies, of course, I meant the Germans!" For a moment, we only looked at one another completely dumbfounded. When we recovered, Professor Kanda had already gone.

15. Gotenba is a city in the foothills of Mount Fuji in Shizuoka Prefecture.

18 The Spring of Youth

Soon after I entered the university I fell ill, first with pneumonia, then with moist pleurisy. Chemotherapy was not available at that time, and antibiotics had yet to be discovered. For a time my life hung in the balance, and during the ensuing recuperation period I listlessly spent my days in our rented house in Setagaya's Akatsutsumi area. During that time I realized how precious it was just to be alive, and things that might appear pitifully insignificant to others gave me irreplaceable joy. A simple cup of hot tea, the smell of paper from an old book, the sound of Mother and Sister talking downstairs, the melodies of a few familiar tunes, the clear bright rays of the sun on a wintry afternoon, the sensation of time serenely flowing by. At that time death meant nothing other than having such moments of joy snatched away from me. I looked at my skinny arms and legs, imagining how they would vanish without a trace in a conflagration, along with my consciousness of gazing at them. I began to abhor the very order of things that by its very nature was about to transform these visions into an inevitability. It was evil, unjust, and abominably irrational. I remembered the feverish nightmares in my childhood and the horror of near-suffocation as I was being sucked into the infinite depths of a gigantic whirlpool. I did not believe in any god; and even if there were one, I could not imagine he could be a god of justice. He might have created the world, but the world he created would soon go down in ruins. Perhaps we could be blessed with his grace, but grace was only bestowed in order to be taken away before long. That all forms of existence should reach their moment of death was the result of the world's internal structure, not the consequence of any external judgment. As long as a living thing exists, even though it might just be a flower in the wilderness, not even the creator himself can justify having it trampled underfoot. To be sure, not all living beings are necessarily virtuous. But since it is impossible to measure the value of existence, however insignificant it may be, one who destroys can only be evil.

Just as I had done in my sickly childhood days, I spent my long recuperation reading. My interest had long since shifted from the galactic universe and stories about prehistoric times to encounters with fair maidens and adventures in love. I became interested in literature, captivated as I was by Chikamatsu's *michiyuki* episodes in his double-suicide plays and by the modern and contemporary novels since Meiji.[1] But this sort of literature failed to fully satisfy my sense of curiosity. Not only was I intrigued by the subtlety of human emotions, I also began to develop an interest in the intellectual dimensions of history and society as well. Yet science does not concern itself with matters of imagination that defy verification. Chikamatsu sings the alluring sentimentality of love-suicides, but his works are almost devoid of intellectual content. When neither science nor Chikamatsu could satisfy my curiosity, what lured me to fill the void was Western literature.

For the first time I began to realize that there was another kind of literature different from the type represented by Chikamatsu's *sewamono*, or his "contemporary plays," one dealing with the sensory, emotional, and intellectual dimensions of experience as a whole, from Pascal to Gide, from Racine to Proust. In those days, "Le Cimetière marin" and *Introduction à la méthode de Léonard de Vinci* in particular were my sacred scriptures. Yet, just as the majority of Christians are almost totally uninformed about the historical background of the Bible, I had never seen the Mediterranean and I knew little or nothing about the Italian Renaissance. My linguistic ability was so terribly deficient that had I not by chance got hold of Gustave Cohen's meticulous commentaries, I might have given up all hope of reading "Le Cimetière marin."[2] As for *Introduction à la méthode de Léonard de Vinci*, there was a translation by Nakajima Kenzō and Satō Masaaki.[3] While a translation of "Le

1. For *michiyuki*, see note 9 below.
2. As in Cohen's "Essai d'explication du Cimetière marin," *Nouvelle Revue Française* (February 1929), which compares the poem to "a classical tragedy, not in five acts, but in four, a lyrical and dramatic dialogue between the three actors of Greek tragedy" (Agnes Ethel MacKay, *The Universal Self: A Study of Paul Valéry* [Toronto: University of Toronto Press, 1961], 172).
3. Satō Masaaki (1905–75), a graduate of Tokyo University and professor of

Cimetière marin" had indeed been published, inaccuracies appeared in almost every other line. I checked out Valéry's writings from the Department of French Literature and started reading them; but of course I could not understand everything and in fact understood very little. This also became evident some years later, when a French friend of mine helped me read *Eupalinos ou l'architecte*. But what interested me then was not Valéry's specific ideas or works. It was the totality of his sensual and intellectual world and the structure of that totality—or perhaps I should say its style—that offered me a revelation. To me, Valéry was not merely a poet, an aesthetician, a critic, a scientist, or even a philosopher, for his works help define one's attitude toward the totality of these varied intellectual endeavors. My encounter with Valéry's writings was such an invaluable experience that it no longer mattered to me whether or not others chose to call them literature.

A number of friends—birds of the same feather, perhaps—used to get together at my home in Akatsutsumi. Yamazaki Kōtarō and Nakamura Shin'ichirō, both French literature students, were doing a close reading of *A la recherche du temps perdu* and were trying to write their own novels. Fukunaga Takehiko must have already begun his translations of *Les Fleurs du mal* and *Le Spleen de Paris*. Kubota and Nakanishi, then attending the Law Faculty at Tokyo Imperial University, were engrossed in Mallarmé; and Harada Yoshito, a student in the Department of German Literature, was interested not only in German poetry and prose but also in the French symbolic poets.[4]

Although we indulged in idle talk most of the time, occasionally, as our *Man'yōshū* reading circle at the Komaba dormitory had done, we

---

French literature at Meiji University from 1949; besides translations, he wrote criticism on Baudelaire, Valéry, and Stendhal.

4. Fukunaga Takehiko (1918–79), novelist, critic, translator, and a core member of the Matinée Poétique group founded in fall 1942 by Katō, Nakamura Shin'ichirō, and Kubota Keisaku; though little known in the West, Fukunaga became a celebrated postwar novelist active from the 1950s to the early 1970s (*Fūdo* [Native earth, 1951], *Bōkyaku no kawa* [The river of lost memory, 1964], and *Shi no shima* [The island of death, 1966–71]) and wrote of his encounter with Baudelaire (*Bōdoreeru no sekai* [Kōdansha bungei bunko, 1989]). • Kubota Kaizō (pseudonym Keisaku, 1920–), short story writer and member of the Matinée Poétique group, translated Camus's *L'Etranger* and *L'Exil et le royaume* as well as the works of Paul Eluard and Julien Green. • Nakanishi's full name was Nakanishi Tetsukichi. • Harada Yoshito (1918–60), translator and critic; see chapter 12, note 6.

read *Duineser Elegien* by relying on Angelloz's French translation and *La Jeune Parque* with the help of Alain's annotations.[5] Problems any one of us encountered individually did not lend themselves to easy resolutions, even when we put our heads together. But as our group met regularly under such pretexts, we soon became very close friends.

That was not all. Like the Japanese in the past who were inspired by Chinese poetry to produce their own Japanese-style "Chinese" poetry, those of us reading Western poetry contemplated composing our own "original poems in translation," so to speak. The majority of the Japanese in the past also did not read Chinese poetry as works composed in authentic Chinese; they treated it as a sort of poetry in Japanese by reading it according to Japanese *kundoku* style. Likewise, we did not try to read Western poetry as works in a Western language, but instead we tried to transliterate it into Japanese ourselves without relying on the translations by others. Fukunaga, for example, did not take pleasure in reading *Les Fleurs du mal* in its French original; rather he derived from it the inspiration to create his own poetry in Japanese. In Kubota's case, he might have recognized in the verses of Catullus and Ronsard reflections of Japanese love poems from the time of the *Kokinshū*. Nakanishi was fond of the intellectual challenges posed by Mallarmé's sonnets, remarking that anything more simplistic than a world condensed in a poem was drab, like wine diluted with water.

Among those friends who were given to such fancies, Nakamura Shin'ichirō was both pragmatic and very knowledgeable about poetry and poets. One after another he presented us with an array of concrete suggestions. Since all of us were composing poems that had no chance of being published, Nakamura came up with the idea of having private recitals among ourselves. In a playful mood, we called the first of our poetry recitals a *matinée poétique*. The same name served for the title of a poetry collection we published jointly after the war, and that was how it came to be known to the general public.[6]

5. Alain's commentary on Valéry's work was dated 1936.
6. According to Nakamura Shin'ichirō, Fukunaga Takehiko took the name from the poetry recitals of Jacques Copeau's troupe before their performance—an intentionally flamboyant term of tacit defiance at a time when people using foreign expressions were labeled, contemptuously, *hikokumin*—"people unfit to be called loyal Japanese nationals"; see Nakamura's *Zōho sengo bungaku no kaisō* (Reminiscences of postwar literature, rev. ed. [Chikuma shobō, 1983]), 29–31 and his *Ai to bi to bungaku: Waga kaisō* (Love, beauty, and literature:

Nakamura seemed to have an awareness of himself as a professional writer, or at least as a future professional writer. A professional distinguishes himself from the amateurs by the training he undergoes, and in order to receive adequate training, one has to establish certain ground rules in conducting one's work. In Chinese poetry, there were already elaborate rules governing tonal variations in diction, and even in haiku there were seasonal themes. Besides *waka* and haiku, Japanese poetry ought to have fixed forms to be determined not only by syllable or line counts. The best thing would be to have stipulations governing rhyme as well. This theory, advanced by Kuki Shūzō earlier on, before the war, was convincing enough.[7] But Kuki's examples demonstrated only a part of such rhyming potentials. Nakamura argued that together we could explore the possibilities of rhymed verse in a broader context than what Kuki had attempted, and we became interested in this new experiment. After the war, when our poetry collection appeared in print, our critics contended that rhyming would not succeed in the case of Japanese; but compared to Kuki and Nakamura's theories, the basis of their argument was by far more superficial and naive. Neither Nakamura nor the rest of us were wrong in this respect.

The misfortune of the Matinée Poétique poets lies instead in the fact that our passions were consumed by the impossible task of employing contemporary Japanese as the raw material to approximate symbolic poetry, premised as it was on fin-de-siècle French. Since our focus in those days was not Kitahara Hakushū but Mallarmé, the only way to look at our enterprise was as a disaster that had struck where it should have. After this was all over, when I saw how *The Waste Land*, written by that awesome American-born Englishman, had driven so many young poets

---

my reminiscences [Iwanami shinsho, 1989]), 145; and his description of the group's activities in *Zōho*, 28–34, or Donald Keene, *Dawn to the West* (New York: Henry Holt, 1984), 1006–14. • *Machine Poetiku shishū* (The poetry collection of the Matinée Poétique group [Shinzenbi Sha, 1948]) was jointly published by Katō, Nakamura, and Fukunaga.

7. Kuki Shūzō (1888–1941), philosopher, professor at Kyoto Imperial University from 1935 to 1941, and author of *Iki no kōzō* (The structure of *iki*, 1930); see Leslie Pincus, *Authenticating Culture in Imperial Japan: Kuki Shūzō and the Rise of National Aesthetics* (Berkeley: University of California Press, 1996); and see Kuki's ideas about rhyming in "Nihonshi no ōin" (Rhyming in Japanese poetry), in *Bungeiron* (Treatise on art), published posthumously in 1941.

into a hopeless quandary, my mind often brought back memories of our own past. The issue from the outset was not rhyme but language. We thought we knew it all too well, but we most certainly did not.

By then, the war was encroaching on our doorsteps. Among my poet friends, Fukunaga ruined his health and soon ended up in a sanitarium for tuberculosis. Yamazaki left for Japanese-occupied French Indochina as an interpreter immediately after his graduation from the university. His destination was an ancient capital in central French Indochina where, he told us, there was a palace with an empress living in it. Even after the defeat, his return to Japan was delayed for a long time owing to suspicions over his alleged war crimes. Kubota was working in a bank and departed for its Shanghai branch office. He was married but left his wife behind in Tokyo. Harada and Nakanishi were drafted into the army. Harada soon became a trainee for the army cadre, and once he even appeared before us with his military sword.

"What a splendid soldier you make! You look just right for it!" Nakamura said.

"Don't be sarcastic! You don't even know how I feel," said Harada.

Even in my eyes, Harada's military uniform certainly looked fitting. Nakanishi, on the other hand, did not volunteer to become a cadre trainee. For a while his family did receive his letters from the army barracks; but before long, he wrote that he would be transferred by ship to the south. That was the last they heard from him. After the war Harada eventually returned to Japan, but Nakanishi did not. The ones who had not been drafted stayed behind in Tokyo, Nakamura at the French department, and myself at the university hospital.

Around that time one of Nakamura's relatives, the owner of an ironworks factory, was living in the city of Kawaguchi in Saitama Prefecture. Before his only son departed for the front, he held a send-off party at his house, inviting many young men of his son's age. Nakamura asked me to go along, and so I did. This metal-casting town, under subcontract from the military supplies industry, was bustling with activity. Around Kawaguchi alone its blast furnaces turned the dark night sky into a bright red despite the blackout restrictions. While sake was becoming a scarce commodity in Tokyo, it flowed freely at that party, and many of the young men there either got drunk or vomited from drinking too much. I suppose everyone there realized that he himself would be sent to the front before long and that Japan's defeat was drawing near.

"I'm going to survive, you'll see," a young man with a pale complexion and unsteady steps spoke to me, but I did not know who he was. "I'm going to join the army all right, but I'll do whatever it takes to survive. What good would it do if I die? And for what purpose? Tell me, for what? When you die, everything is finished. I'll be damned if I do." Another young man mumbled to me with a smile as if the matter did not concern him personally, "When do you think it's all going to end? I can still stay at the university for another six months. But I guess it won't end that soon. Well, I've been thinking of doing all the things I wanted to do during this time . . . Six months seems a long time, but once it's over, I guess you'll know how short it really is."

My own draft order might arrive the next day or it might not come at all. In any case, nothing was more oppressive than having to mix with these young draftees and listen to their moaning. The owner of the ironworks factory, however, did not mention anything about his son's departure for the front or about the war. Instead, he talked about songs performed at *nō* plays. He said that he and his old high school classmates such as Abe Yoshishige and Nogami Toyoichirō were going to invite masters from various schools to perform at the Nō Theater at Tokyo's Suidōbashi, and he asked me to come too.[8]

After watching the *bunraku* play on the day the war began, I had, for a while, abandoned the habit of going to the theater. But after the invitation from the owner of the Kawaguchi ironworks factory, I started going from time to time to the Nō Theater in Suidōbashi. Because of blackout regulations, the windows at the theater were heavily draped with black curtains, but inside a different world was at work. There, the beating of the drums and the sharp, piercing notes of the flute reverberating throughout the theater built up my anticipation for a figure from a distant world to appear at the end of the bridgeway. And again, the drums beat and the flute resounded. Just when I thought my heightened sense

8. Abe Yoshishige (1883–1966), critic, philosopher, and essayist; a scholar of Kant and Spinoza and a translator of Nietzsche and Merezhkovsky, Abe was a major intellectual figure of the Taishō philosophical generation and was minister of education under the Shidehara cabinet in 1946. • Nogami Toyoichirō (1883–1950), a disciple of Natsume Sōseki, scholar of English literature, and later the president of Hōsei University, who studied *nō* music and its theories in the latter part of his life; his works include *Nō: Kenkyū to hakken* (The study and discovery of *nō*, 1930) and studies on Zeami and Kan'ami, along with edited *nō* treatises and a six-volume collection of *nō* music (*Yōkyoku zenshū*, 1935–36). His wife was the eminent novelist Nogami Yaeko.

of anticipation was finally about to be answered with the rise of the curtain, it came down before I knew it. That incredible figure did not make his appearance on the stage; instead his full presence suddenly emerged right before our eyes beside a pine tree next to the bridgeway. From there Umewaka Manzaburō began to intone in his superb, gravelly voice, trembling with subtle evocativeness. Even though it was difficult to comprehend what he was vocalizing, I was immediately drawn into another world in which draft orders, food coupons, and national uniforms had all disappeared. Neither did *bushidō, Hagakure,* and even the samisen and the *michiyuki* scenes have any part to play in this world. Instead, there were only men and women suffering alone in hell for having loved or killed. Since hell is not a social issue, one *shite* alone would suffice.[9] And since everyone, regardless of personality, is capable of love and hate, I suppose that's why the *shite* wears a mask. By simply shading his eyes with one hand or taking a small step in his white *tabi* socks, an awesome *nō* actor could immediately transform the stage into the white sands of Suma washed by the waves or turn it into the village of Fukakusa, where the plumes of eulalia grass swayed in the autumn wind. No wonder there was no need for any stage prop except a polished floor and the front view of a single pine tree.

During the war, what I discovered at Suidōbashi's Nō Theater was not *nō* itself but what "drama" ultimately meant. By that, I do not necessarily have only Zeami's world in mind.[10] I discovered how absolutely exquisite an actor's human voice could be, how one slight movement could represent a thousand words, how pregnant the sense of anticipation and how intense and compact the element of time could become in-

---

9. *Michiyuki,* literally "traveling on the road," is a widely used dramatic convention in *gigaku, nō,* and *kyōgen* plays and enacts a journey to a certain destination, with accompanying music; in the puppet theater its most celebrated expression probably began with Chikamatsu Monzaemon's *sewa-jōruri* plays such as *Sonezaki shinjū* (The love suicides at Sonezaki, 1703), in which the lovers' last journey evokes the most poignant moment of their tragedy. Besides the *michiyuki* of ill-fated lovers, there are also those of parents and children and masters and servants. • *Shite* is the principal role in a *nō* play.

10. Zeami Motokiyo (1363?–1443?) of the Kanze school of *nō* wrote many of the 240 plays still performed today as well as more than 20 treatises, some highly sophisticated, on his aesthetic ideals about *nō* performance, including *yūgen* and *ran'i*. Katō later wrote an important essay on the dramatist entitled "Zeami no senjutsu mata wa Nōgakuron" (Zeami's strategy or a discussion of *nō*), now in *Shōwa bungaku zenshū* (Shōgakukan, 1989), 28:643–58.

side the theater. There and then I stood witness to the ultimate potential of an optimum performance as it manifested itself in the realm of
art. My experience, no doubt, was only accidental. But this accident aside,
the fact that I am Japanese had no relevance. Where a man was born and
where he grew up—that is to say where he first started—are what determine his nationality, not his final destination. As a matter of fact, later
in my life I had the opportunity to see first-rate performances in theaters in most parts of the world; but that was only after I had heard Umewaka Manzaburō's chanting and witnessed Kongō Iwao's dancing, certainly not the reverse.[11]

One after another, my friends went to war, and none of them came back
before it ended. There was only one exception. He was called into military service and went to China, developed an illness there, and was discharged soon after he was sent back to Japan for hospitalization. Before
being drafted, he used to live in Urawa with his elder sister, studied philosophy at Tokyo University, and discreetly tried his hand at writing poetry.[12] In the summer he would go to Shinshū. Looked at from afar, he
could be mistaken for an old man because of the way he strolled down
the Nakasendō in the evening wearing a casual kimono with a cane in
hand. A soft-spoken man of few words, he had very high standards when
it came to creative writing. He would dismiss mine with a laugh, saying,
"The stuff you people wrote is not worthy of reading." His sister, an instructor of civil law at a private university, was a cheerful, openhearted,
and brilliant woman. She loved talking and laughing, and when we found
ourselves in an argument, I was no match for her sharp mind. Both the
brother and the sister condemned militarism, firmly convinced that the
militarists were simply digging their own graves in starting a war with
Britain and the United States. After the brother was called into military
service, the sister continued to receive his letters, and I am sure she could
read much more between the lines. It was not difficult to imagine how
brutal life in the army would be for him. However, I did not ask her for
details. What I did hear quite unexpectedly one day was the news that he
had been sent back to a Japanese hospital due to his illness and was soon
discharged and returned to his Urawa home. In appearance, he seemed to
have changed very little from the time we last met before his departure.

11. Kongō Iwao (1886–1951) was the head of the Kongō school of professional *nō* actors and noted for his study of *nō* masks and costumes.
12. Urawa is a city in the southeastern part of Saitama Prefecture.

"All things considered, I'm glad you are all right. It must have been a difficult time for you," I said emotionally.

"It was not a matter of having a difficult time. Let's not talk about it. I don't want to think about it anymore," he said simply.

I did not know what had happened to him in China. To this day, I still do not, and I suppose I never will. But the man who returned from China was not the same man who went there. After a long while, it became increasingly clear even to me.

But Nakanishi died. The killing of a man who had wanted so much to live was something I could never accept in the course of the Pacific War as a whole. Of course Nakanishi was not the only person who wanted to live. But he was my friend. Compared with a friend's life, what could possibly be the worth of all the islands in the Pacific? I saw the oil-spilt ocean to the south, and I could picture the sun and blue sky he might have last seen with his eyes. In his last moment, perhaps his little sister's face floated across his mind, or perhaps it was his mother's, or the woman he might have loved, the work he might have accomplished, the poem he might have read, the music he might have heard. His life was just beginning, and he wanted so much to go on living! He did not volunteer his own death, nor did he choose to die because he was "deceived."[13] Ultimately, it was the same political authority—the one that had failed to deceive him—that drove him to his death with brute force. When I learned of his death, I was momentarily stunned, but when I became myself again, what I felt was not sadness but an irrepressible surge of anger. Even if I could condone everything else about the Pacific War, I could not condone Nakanishi's death. What had caused it was an irredeemable crime, and crime has to pay.

As time passed I found myself constantly haunted by another thought, the thought that there was no good reason why I should survive and Nakanishi should die. When we used to gather at his house and read *Duineser Elegien*, we shared our passions and hatreds, our appreciation and contempt for the same things. Likewise, we were ignorant of the world and both of us knew it. We believed our lives would last forever, and so we never thought it necessary to decide at that moment what we wanted to do in the future. We only felt within ourselves the need to be alive, hence our aspiration for life. If only our aspiration had not been so brutally shattered. This thought frequently crossed my mind after Naka-

13. That is, by the Japanese government's war propaganda.

nishi's death. If he had come back alive against all incredible odds, I wondered how he would have reacted toward the authority that had threatened to drive him to his death. If he had survived instead of me, what would he have wished to do? There is no doubt in my mind that the saying "To strike at injustice in the name of Heaven" is a meaningless statement. First, nobody knows what the will of Heaven might be. Second, even if we did know, nobody could properly claim to be acting in the name of Heaven. And yet one could infer what the fervent desires of a friend might be, and though one may not have the right to implement them on his behalf, it is certainly plausible to feel a nebulous and yet powerful temptation to do so. Later in life, when circumstances made me want to retreat and maintain my silence like a docile, harmless lamb, my mind would always bring back memories of Nakanishi.

When he was a higher school student, Nakanishi drafted a piece to satirize the trends of the time. I tried to have it published in the student newspaper. After the chief of the literary column had seen the galley proofs, he called me to his presence and asked me to delete the parts he considered "improper." "I tell you, if you publish this, the military police are going to come, and I'm not going to take any responsibility," was the way he put it. I explained to him that the parts in question were not "improper"; they were just a roundabout way of saying something already on everybody's mind. But the chief repeated his argument about the military police and refused to compromise, and Nakanishi, on his part, refused to have the passages deleted. In order to have the paper published, our only alternative was to take out the entire piece. Another article by Nakanishi appeared in the paper's next issue. This time the author did not sign his name as Nakanishi but as "Soramata Kakuzō."[14]

---

14. Phonetically, Nakanishi's pseudonym means something like "Just you wait and see! I will write again!"

19 Department of Internal Medicine

The Department of Internal Medicine at the Tokyo University Hospital rekindled my interest in the experimental sciences. When I joined the department as an unsalaried junior assistant, the nominal number of physicians there, including members of the new staff who had graduated in the same class as myself, was probably over fifty. Since most of them were drafted as military doctors immediately on graduation, in reality there were no more than twenty people remaining in the Medical Office—that was what we called the doctor's quarters at the hospital. There was one professor, one assistant professor, one lecturer, one director for outpatient services, and four or five assistants; the rest were junior assistants. I figured that should future circumstances require, I could at least support myself by working in a city hospital, though I did not have any concrete plans in mind. Since I did not know what the outcome of the war might be, there was very little I could do to plan for the future. While it was true that our family fortune was in decline, for the time being my livelihood was not in jeopardy even if I did not earn an income.

The world of the physician was nothing new to me. Since my childhood, I had been accustomed to the doctor's white lab coat, the medicine shelves, the smell of antiseptic solutions, and the cold sensation of the stethoscope on the skin. But that was not all. The very way of thinking that obligates one to draw conclusions only from proven facts and to question all unverifiable opinions was not something alien to me either. What I encountered when I first went into medicine—that is to say into the world of the experimental sciences—was not any new way of thinking but a self-awareness about an already familiar reasoning process and its thorough, empirical application through work in the laboratory.

Two senior colleagues of mine, both specialists in hematology, held very rigorous standards in this regard. They recognized only high professional competence and data obtained within a well-defined margin of error. Moreover, they would exercise utmost caution in making deductions from given facts. Dr. Nakao Kiku would say, "One cannot draw such a conclusion from these facts alone. The conclusion might be correct, but one can never be certain." And Dr. Miyoshi Kazuo would remark, "It is imperative that you yourself repeat the procedure to doublecheck. I don't care whose data they are, you'd be dead wrong to think you can base your conclusions on them." I learned the fundamentals of hematology from these two senior colleagues, particularly the morphology of blood and bone marrow cells.[1] After the war ended, I had many occasions to microscopically examine blood specimens for difficult diagnostic cases while working with specialists from the medical faculty of the University of Paris; but there was almost nothing about the morphology of blood cells that I had to learn anew.

Dr. Miyoshi brought one of the hospital beds into the night-duty room at the Medical Office so he could work until late at night and sleep over. Whenever I went into the laboratory after making my night rounds, the lights at his desk alone were still on. He would either be reading a pile of books and papers or arranging the specimens for examination under the microscope. Only on weekends would he return home to the Shōnan area, carrying a bundle of his laundry wrapped in a *furoshiki*.[2] How could a small, slender man like him possibly have so much energy? The only answer had to be the pleasure he derived from doing research and spending time in his laboratory.

Dr. Nakao was not only a hematologist. He also helped Assistant Professor Okinaka with his experiments on the autonomic nervous system and was very knowledgeable about internal medicine in general.[3] He

1. Among Dr. Nakao's publications was *Erythropoiesis: Proceedings of the Fourth International Conference on Erythropoiesis*, ed. Nakao Kiku et al. (Baltimore: University Park Press, 1975).

2. The Shōnan area, along the coast of Sagami Bay, in southern Kanagawa Prefecture.

3. Okinaka Shigeo (1902–92), an internist, neuroscientist, and professor at Tokyo University from 1943, later the director at Tokyo's Toranomon Hospital; he is known for his work on "the mechanism of body fluid regulation, clinopathological evaluations on cerebral vascular disturbances, and the autonomic nervous system of various visceral organs" (Nagatoya Yūji, *Kodansha Encyclopedia* 6:84).

could answer any questions I had, and he would listen attentively to my half-baked and biased ideas and fill in their inadequacies. He was also an astute observer of human character. Amidst the chaos in the immediate aftermath of Japan's defeat, he went to Hiroshima as a member of the joint Japanese-American investigation team to examine the effects of the atomic explosion. There, he could immediately read the minds of the Americans, to say nothing of his Japanese colleagues.

The number of physicians at the university hospital was getting smaller and smaller as a result of the wartime drafts, and the number of in-patients for each remaining doctor to care for grew from four to six, and then from six to eight. I was getting accustomed to my work at the hospital, but because both the number of patients under my care and my research work had increased, my return home to Setagaya from the hospital at night got later and later. Meanwhile, the hour-and-a-half one-way commute day after day had turned into something I could no longer afford. In the end I thought of following Dr. Miyoshi's example by staying overnight at the hospital.

I was not the only one doing that. At first, we would look for unoccupied rooms in the patients' ward to sleep in. Later, with Tokyo's deteriorating transportation situation, the Medical Office gave us tacit approval to stay in some of the rooms in the second-class patients' ward. We could have our meals at the hospital cafeteria, but we became hungry again late at night. The regular overnighters and the doctor on duty would gather at the Medical Office to parch soybeans and drink cheap tea, because even potatoes were becoming difficult to get, not to mention rice. Even so, because we could still conduct animal experiments, we used a big pot to cook and "feast" on rabbits or dogs—whatever we happened to kill. Somebody said that if we scooped away the froth from the dog meat boiling in the pot, it would taste something like horse meat. Late into the night we would gather around the dog pot and talk about our patients, our experiments, or miscellaneous events at the hospital, telling jokes and having a good laugh. Our conversations rarely touched on the war, but that does not mean we never talked about it.

One night we heard a report that the Americans had landed on yet another island occupied by the Japanese army. And, the report added, the Japanese forces "would decisively crush our enemies!"

"I'm afraid that's not going to happen. I think the Americans will once again end up occupying the island," I muttered.

Ordinarily, nobody would pay any attention to a comment like that, and our conversation would quickly turn to things about our daily life. But among those who gathered at our feast, a young doctor on duty that night seemed determined to take issue with what I said.

"What do you mean 'once again'?" he said in an unexpectedly impassioned voice.

"Well, this isn't the first time the Intelligence Bureau has told us Japan would decisively crush its enemies," I responded, hoping to end the discussion right there.

But he wouldn't give up.

"You should be ashamed of yourself for saying that the enemy will win in the end."

"Should I?" I said.

"Now don't be cute with me! Didn't you just say the Americans would once again occupy the island?"

"Indeed I did. And why should this make you so angry? Until now the Americans have succeeded every single time in occupying the Pacific islands after they land. So there's a greater probability of their succeeding this time than failing, is there not?"

"Not necessarily," the young doctor said.

"You're right. No one can say they'll definitely succeed. Nobody knows exactly what's going to happen tomorrow. But there are no grounds for us to speculate that the Americans will fail. On the other hand, there *is* abundant evidence pointing to the likelihood of their success."

"Where is your conviction for our absolute victory?"

"Whether I have it or not, this has nothing to do with conviction. It's a simple question of making an objective assessment of the situation."

"That's defeatism!" he yelled.

"Now just a minute!" I tried my best to suppress my emotions. "What I said was that the Japanese army on the island would probably be defeated, not that their defeat was desirable. Those are two completely different things. If I said Japanese defeat was desirable, it would constitute a betrayal of spirit, and I suppose you might call it defeatism. But no matter how much one may wish the Japanese army to win, that wish and one's judgment about the high probability of their defeat are entirely unrelated issues. If a doctor can't easily separate his desire to see his patient recover and his prognostic judgment, I don't see how you can practice medicine at all."

"But an illness is different from a war!" he protested.

"No, as far as my analogy is concerned, there isn't the slightest difference," I continued. "Of course I know very well that illnesses and wars are different. But certainly one cannot insist on a distinction between factual judgment and value judgment for one area and not for another. If you can't even conceptualize this simple idea, how can you engage in any serious scholarship? We are sick of hearing the army talk about convictions and defeatism. A university is a place for learning, and as far as learning is concerned, conviction is not worth a penny. Let's look at the facts. We don't know the strength of the American troops that landed, nor of the Japanese forces on the island. The only facts we have are that the American forces have landed on many small Pacific islands, and that until this day they've never failed to occupy them in the end. The question now is to determine on the basis of these facts alone whether success or failure is the more probable outcome of their landing. I never said the American forces *will* succeed. What I did say was that they probably will. So, what's wrong with my statement? If you want to argue that this assessment wouldn't please the Intelligence Bureau, that's a different matter. If that's what you wanted to say, why didn't you just say that in the first place? Just stop hiding behind the authority of the Intelligence Bureau and stop making false accusations! All this nonsense about defeatism and what not just makes me sick. How dare you say these things, with that intellect of yours."

"That's enough," somebody said, and I did not go on. The man who said it had been quietly listening to our exchange while sipping his "liquor," a mixture of medicinal alcohol and sugared water. I found it rather incredible that I let myself get so caught up in the heat of the moment, and then I realized that what prompted my agitation was not the young doctor but rather something else. Basically what I said was simply that things would take their own course irrespective of what one's intentions or feelings might be. There was no reason to get myself so upset over the whole thing. Perhaps I was thinking about the young men who had been sent to the island only to get themselves killed in this accursed war, and my anger was directed at the war propaganda and the society that willingly embraced it. I knew I, on the other hand, worked in the safe haven of the Medical Office, a realization that brought on pangs of guilt. Perhaps that was why I felt so much anger within me.

After I started turning a patient room into my living quarters, I also got better acquainted with the nurses. They worked their night shifts in pairs and stayed up all night long. One of the nurses on duty was kind enough to make me late night dinners with the rice and eggs she brought from home in the countryside. At the nurses' station, I watched with admiration as the young woman in white uniform went about preparing the food with brisk efficiency, using the gas and water originally meant for sterilization purposes.

The walls on all four sides of the room were covered with medicine cabinets, medical equipment, and piles of patients' charts, called *Karte*— in those days Japanese doctors used a lot of German or quasi-German terminology. The treatment charts for patients were written in chalk on the blackboard hanging on the wall. Also hanging there was a promotional calendar from a pharmaceutical company with large colored photographs of scenes like snow-capped Mount Fuji and cherry blossoms at the Heian Shrine, but no picture of the emperor or the empress or any popular movie star. Sometimes books like a nurse's manual or some women's magazines were left lying on the desk. At first glance the room might appear chaotic, but after a while one clearly sensed its underlying order. The disorderly appearance was not the result of negligence; rather, like a complex scheme, everything had a place and a specific role. There were always some little flowers carefully arranged in the vase on the table, and, amazingly, they would bring a soft touch to the entire scene.

When the food was ready, I finished it all. The young nurse almost never joined me at the late night dinners she herself had prepared. This came naturally to me because it followed the pattern of my family: Father and I did no housework whatsoever, leaving everything to Mother and Sister. Quite nonchalantly I accepted her kindness—what she did for me bordered on an act of devotion—but I had no idea what I could do for her in return.

Until then, I was convinced that no young woman could possibly have any reason to like me. Buttressing this belief was my less than attractive physical appearance and a demeanor that was anything but affable. I was myself aware of the distressing fact that I had nothing to appeal to a woman. Since my high school days I had watched with admiration and envy as my classmates smoothly went about flirting with the girls at the cafes. Rather than contriving to make myself attractive to girls, I learned to live without their attention. The nurse was the first woman I could regard as my girlfriend. She might not stand out in a crowd, but she was thoughtful, kind, and compassionate. Even though there wasn't really anything for us to talk about, we often found ourselves chatting after the patients had all fallen asleep.

She came from a seaside village on the western coast of the Bōsō peninsula, and I once visited her village a short time before the air raids on Tokyo began.[4] In those days, I hardly ever went out of the hospital other than to return to my home in Setagaya on weekends. On the train to the Bōsō peninsula I looked at the passengers around me with the curiosity of someone just back from a long trip. People in national uniform, people on shopping errands, people who looked preoccupied with their own affairs—I must have been the only person who was spending the weekend sightseeing by the sea. I suddenly came to an acute realization of myself as an outsider, as if the word "outsider" epitomized the totality of my relationship with society. But the nurse of course was no outsider. Every shop around the seaside village, every trail in the fields, every tree in the pine forest, and even the ocean breeze and the autumn sky knew her well. The person who had been living in the same world as I inside the Hongō hospital now became the one delicate thread connecting me to the alien surroundings outside. I wanted to know more about her in a world with just the two of us. But that world of course did not exist, and even if it did, it existed only for a very short time. The village by the sea, the pine trees, the sound of the waves, the fragrance of the sea, and my first girlfriend filled one day in my life with a sense of bliss but made no decisive change within me.

The first formation of bombers that appeared in the sky above Tokyo cut through the high clouds and headed toward the war plants in the suburbs. When it was reported around noon that bombers were approaching, we left the specimens and the microscopes on the table, went down into the hospital courtyard, and looked up at the clear wintry sky. The sparkling silvery bombers flew straight ahead, drawing long parallel vapor trails behind them. "What a beautiful sight indeed!" somebody uttered. Whenever our work was interrupted by sirens, we would mutter something like, "Are they coming back again? Not now, at our busy time!" Privately, I thought it would not be long before Tokyo itself would be attacked. This was just something I expected from the day the war began. Around me the citizens of Tokyo were a far cry from their ecstatic selves who had rejoiced over the victory at Pearl Harbor. They had grown weary of the war and seemed to realize for the first time that Japan had no chance of winning.

Even that did not help narrow the gap between me and my surroundings. There is a difference between perceiving the turning tide of

4. The Bōsō peninsula is in southern Chiba Prefecture.

war and arriving at the conclusion of imminent defeat from that perception. It was only after Tokyo had actually been bombed and after incendiary bombs had reduced one-third of the city to ashes in a single night that I truly developed a sense of camaraderie with the other people of Tokyo with whom I shared a collective fate. Tokyo Imperial University was located on the very edge of the destruction. Ueno Hirokōji and the area beyond were engulfed in flames, but not the streets on the side of the Hongō-dōri. Since the incendiary bombs did not fall on any wooden structures at the university, and since no bombs penetrated the roofs of the concrete buildings, the campus was spared from fire.

This fact we learned only after the planes had disappeared from the sky. As the bombers swooped down at a low altitude over Tokyo amidst the beams of searchlights and the frantic firing from anti-aircraft guns, all we could see was a sea of fire reflected across the sky over Ueno. Of course, we had no way of knowing what the scale of the air raid might be. Even though the university might have been spared by the incendiary bombs, I thought, there was probably little chance for survival if we were surrounded by fire on all sides. What should I do? There was nothing I could do. I thought about Mother and Sister. As our Setagaya home was in the suburbs, it was probably safe. If I were to perish like this, how absolutely ridiculous my death would be. I was not blaming anyone, nor was I even execrating the war. The fact of the matter was that under these circumstances, my life or death had already been determined by the Americans on a Pacific island. And the fact of my ignorance about their plans struck me as absolutely preposterous and made me furious. The patients in the hospital were quiet. I suppose they too were holding their breath and letting Heaven decide their fate. "Heaven"—that is to say the American war plans for that night—saved the university and the hospital. And then the bombers were gone, and a few hours later, I found myself living in a completely different world.

One after another, the burn victims were being carried into the hospital. Whatever few vacant rooms we had were quickly filled to capacity. As there was only a limited number of hospital beds, bedding was laid out on the floor along the corridor to accommodate the overflow of patients. All nurses and physicians from the Medical Office were mobilized, and we did the best we could in administering emergency treatment. Since severely burned victims suffered obstruction in their circulatory system, localized treatment alone was not sufficient. For several days every one of us worked so frantically that we practically forgot to eat or sleep. I continued to work for many more years in the hospital, but never again did I experience the same total immersion in my work or the same selfless camaraderie with my fellow workers. I could certainly identify with the victims being carried into the hospital—the old people, the children, the men, the women—people who had endured the same bombings and whose lives had likewise been driven to the verge of destruction. By helping one another, they compensated for the inadequate resources at the hospital. The work we were doing was precisely friends helping friends, ourselves included. I was a solitary being when the bombers were over my head, but I never experienced a greater sense of togetherness than in the few days after the bombers left.

After the air raid I continued to live in a second-class patient's room. Before I knew it, it had turned into my private quarters. Alone late at night I would lie on the iron-frame bed, reading literary works from faraway countries. Sometimes I listened to the few records I had on a small portable gramophone I had brought from home. A few books of poetry and a few recordings of music had already become something of a necessity for me regardless of where I might happen to live. No one outside the hospital ever came to visit me in that room—I was not there during the day, and venturing outside the hospital at night had become potentially dangerous because it was impossible to predict when or where there might be an air raid. Tokyo had turned into a devastated battlefield. My one and only visitor was Mr. Mori Arimasa, who was living at the Hongō YMCA. Behind the black curtains and the tightly closed door of my small room during blackout hours, we talked about things like the development of the war, the art of staying alive, and our precarious chances of survival. One night we were listening to César Franck's *Variations symphoniques*. Tokyo was no longer a city with anything beautiful to offer. But on that night the music was absolutely superb and I was deeply moved.

"That was almost angelic," I said.

"You're right," said Mr. Mori. "Almost seraphic."

20   August 15, 1945

During the last year of the war, in the spring of 1945, the Department of Internal Medicine at Tokyo University was "evacuated" to a sanitarium for tuberculosis in Ueda in the Shinshū area. The evacuation was neither planned by the university nor arranged by the Faculty of Medicine. What happened was that through the personal connections of the professors and the other medical staff, each unit moved its own equipment and physicians and even some of its in-patients from Tokyo to the faraway mountains. The new location naturally did not have adequate facilities or space to accommodate the entire internal medicine department; moreover, transportation by rail was extraordinarily arduous since the trains were crowded with factory evacuees and people made homeless by fire. Our unit's evacuation to Ueda involved just a few in-patients and barely a third of the Medical Office staff, but for me the relocation was a godsend.

I no longer had a home in Tokyo, since fire from the bombing had destroyed ours. Father, meanwhile, was living by himself in a sanitarium in Izu. Sister, who had married when the war began, was now the mother of two but had no idea when her husband would return from the Chinese front. For a while Mother took care of Sister and her two children, and together they tried to weather the war's final phase at the Oiwake house where we used to spend our summers. Leaving her children in Mother's care, Sister would go from one nearby village to another exchanging clothing for food, while Mother tried to grow potatoes and pumpkins in a tiny plot covered with volcanic ash. After our unit moved to Ueda, I received rice, miso, and potatoes from the farmers in return for my house calls, and during weekends I was able to bring them to Oiwake.

The highlands at the foothills of Mount Asama were not a good place for any prolonged sojourn when food was scarce. The winter was long and severe, the volcanic land was barren, and the local farmers were impoverished. That Tokyo's burned-out victims converged at places like Karuizawa, Chigataki, and Oiwake was not because they thought the local conditions were suitable for evacuees, but because they had nowhere else to go. These summer resorts were their only link to the countryside. The amount of food the local farmers could provide in exchange for clothing was limited to begin with—they were not willing to accept paper currency in which they no longer had any confidence. Besides, none of the evacuees had an unlimited supply of clothing for barter.

Professor Katayama Toshihiko had evacuated to Karuizawa's northern highlands and soon found himself unable to afford living there. He came down from the mountain and rented a room in a farmhouse in a village near the town of Komoro. Mr. Yamamuro Shizuka, who had earlier made his permanent home there, helped him find the place. Mr. Yamamuro was originally from Shinshū; but Professor Katayama was a Tosa man and a long-time Tokyo resident with no roots whatsoever in Shinshū.[1] All he had were some poetry collections in German and French, but hardly any of the woolen clothing the local people craved. In the springtime, when Professor Katayama came to visit me at my Oiwake home, young green leaves were sprouting profusely in the Japanese larch grove like a misty haze, and the chirping of small birds filled the woods. "This forest reminds me of the summer in Salzburg," Professor Katayama said suddenly. Just as I was worrying about my chances of surviving the summer, the poet Katayama probably had Mozart on his mind.

The family of one of Mother's old classmates had also evacuated to Oiwake. Their oldest daughter was married to the standard-bearer of the Imperial Guards. I heard that he was a student in the Army Academy, and this handsome young man would sometimes show up in the village. The head of their household was a retired soldier who was working as a secondary school principal. Food was never a problem for this family.

---

1. Yamamuro Shizuka (1906–), a noted scholar of Scandinavian literature and postwar literary critic who founded the literary journal *Hihyō* (Criticism) in 1936 with Hirano Ken and Honda Shūgo, published the journal *Kōgen* (Highland) with Katayama Toshihiko and Hori Tatsuo during the war, and was part of the group associated with the journal *Kindai bungaku* (Modern literature) in 1946; his major works are collected in *Yamamuro Shizuka chosakushū*, 6 vols. (Tōjūsha, 1972–73). • Tosa is the modern Kōchi Prefecture in Shikoku.

Another of Mother's classmates was married to a high-ranking executive of a large trading company and had two sons and two daughters. She sent her oldest daughter, married with children, to Oiwake as an evacuee. The daughter brought with her a lot of expensive clothes and was therefore in no fear of going hungry. Perhaps because of her lavish upbringing in the United States, she never stopped complaining about her impoverished livelihood in Oiwake. Despite Mother's annoyance at her self-centered behavior, Mother would respond to her desperate appeals for help by putting in a good word for her with the local people and giving her appropriate advice. "You see, we have been just fighting a losing war from the very beginning. I don't think it will last very long," Mother would say. "But when her husband comes back after the war, I think there's going to be trouble." When her husband did return to Japan as a civilian at the end of the war, she left him with the children and went off to the United States with a young soldier from the Occupation forces.

The young men in Oiwake were all gone. Even many of the young girls were drafted to work in war supplies plants that had relocated from Tokyo to nearby prefectures, creating a labor shortage afflicting the farming community. In spite of all this, the farmer who had been helping us each year with household chores looked at Sister's children and stated, "As long as I'm alive, I won't stand by idly and let these children die." He was already close to sixty, and his only son had gone to war, leaving him to work the fields with his daughter-in-law. When the daughter-in-law was out in the fields, her child was left to the care of Grandma, whose back was beginning to bend with age. Working the fields naturally took a toll on a sixty-year-old man. "All these big talks about Greater East Asia and stuff like that," the old man said. "I'm just a simple-minded fellow, but I don't know what they can accomplish just by talking big. Take the young people away and see what they've done. I'd say enough is enough and let's end the war."

For the time being, however, there was absolutely no indication that the war was about to end. After occupying Okinawa and reducing Tokyo and Osaka to ashes, the American forces continued to attack small and mid-sized cities from carrier-borne aircraft as well as by coastal bombardment from their fleet. Japan was virtually defenseless by then. In spite of that, the government still called for "a showdown on the Japanese mainland" and was talking, in all apparent seriousness, about such strategies as "combat with bamboo spears," "scorched-earth tactics," and "crushing the enemy at the shore." The big newspapers wrote about *ichioku gyokusai*—the honorable sacrifice of a hundred million lives—sang praises of "the soul of Yamato" as something that "thrives on great eternal principles," and argued emphatically how survival was unthinkable should we succumb to *kichiku Eibei*—the British and American beasts and demons.

At the sanitarium in Ueda, the head of medical affairs led us in anti-aircraft drills. Buckets of water were drawn from a cistern and relayed through a line of nurses to splash on the incendiary bombs. Besides water, sand was also made available. Some staff even came fully prepared with headbands and gaiters. But we did not have even one bomb shelter or a single water pump. With a wry smile, the hospital director watched as the head of medical affairs directed our drills.

"I wonder if the Americans would even bother to drop a bomb on this town," I said.

The hospital director chuckled and said, "If you talk like that, the people here will feel insulted. They think Ueda is the next target in Japan after Tokyo."

"If by any chance they do come, this town is going to be burned down."

"No doubt about it. But, you see, we live in a time when our government tells us to fight with bamboo spears against landing vessels. I suppose all conventional wisdom has been turned upside down."

"Do you think the government is really serious about it?"

"I surely hope not."

As we were talking in the director's room, we heard the nurses shouting loud instructions as they ran around the patients' ward, "All those who can walk, please go outside. All except those who are seriously ill."

Thereupon, the hospital director put out his cigarette in an ashtray, and as he slowly raised his stocky frame from his armchair, he winked at me and said, "Oh well, what the heck! The weather is good. Shall we go outside and enjoy it?"

From the end of July, when Japan announced that it would "ignore" the Potsdam Declaration and "bring the war to a successful conclusion," until the emperor's August 15 broadcast, I was in no mood to do anything except read the newspapers and listen to the radio, trying to infer from the slightest hints what the government's decision might be. Events were quickly unfolding—the atomic explosion in Hiroshima, the Soviet Union's entry into the war, and then another atomic explosion in Nagasaki. Japan was no longer in a position to postpone its decision, and the general perception was that in the next few days it had to make up its mind whether to surrender or fight to the death on its own soil. If it should surrender, the lives of those who were still alive would be spared; but if it chose to fight, the chances of survival were almost nonexistent.

But this was a country in which fanatical militarists filled every corner, from the center of political power all the way down to the smallest unit in a rural hospital, and it was difficult to imagine that the prospect of surrender would all of a sudden become a viable alternative. On the other hand, a showdown on the Japanese mainland was quite simply a ghastly suicidal act, an attempt by the authorities to take the entire Japanese people down with them to their graves. The idea was so utterly absurd that it was almost beyond contemplation.

As I had more private conversations with the hospital director, I noticed that people at the hospital seemed aware of an antiwar atmosphere between the two of us. But if Japan should decide to surrender, I no longer had to worry about this situation, and if it should decide to fight on, it was clearly meaningless to worry about anything at all. So we decided not to be bothered by what others might think, and they, on their part, seemed sufficiently apprehensive about the reality of defeat not to venture criticism of our attitude. Then finally, the decision to surrender came. But it was communicated to us subtly, like a reflection from a faint streak of light. The hospital director and I did not overlook the fact that from about August 10, instead of the usual rhetoric of "showdown," "honorable death," and "scorched-earth tactics," the newspapers started to emphasize the need to "protect and maintain the Japanese national polity." Needless to say, there was a powerful war faction; but there was no longer any reason to doubt that an influential peace faction had emerged within the high echelons of power. My hopes rose. When it was reported that there would be "an important radio announcement" on the fifteenth, I expected it was likely to be a surrender message.

At noon on August 15, the hospital director summoned everyone— physicians, nurses, staff members, and patients—to the cafeteria. All of us listened with breathless attention to the emperor's somewhat indistinct speech. After the announcement, the head of medical affairs let out a deep sigh, turned to the director, and asked, "What does this mean?"

"It means the war has ended," the director said simply.

Scores of nurses, all of them young women from the local area, laughed cheerfully and quickly dispersed into the patients' rooms just as they always did after lunch; for them, it was as if nothing special had happened. Despite all efforts at education, despite all kinds of propaganda, the war ultimately failed to permeate into the world of these young women. The head of medical staff along with many of the original and newly evacuated staff had dismal looks on their faces. But nobody cried.

When the director and I went into his office, I silently sipped the green tea he prepared, both of us absorbed in our own thoughts. Now my world was glowing with optimism, and even the summer clouds, the leaves on the white birch trees, the mountains, and the streets were filled with jubilation and radiant with hope. I had long hoped for this time to come, but I had little confidence that it ever would. The military boots that had trampled on all things beautiful, the authority that had made a travesty of all reason, and the militarism that had stifled all forms of freedom had now suddenly crumbled away like a nightmare—that was my thought at that time. Now I could live my new life, and if there was such a thing as the joy of living, now was the time for me to learn about it. I was so happy I felt like singing.

The atmosphere within the hospital changed abruptly after August 15. Before then, the head of medical affairs as well as many others would somehow try to avoid initiating a conversation with either the director or me. Yet beginning from August 16, an increasing number of people would engage the director in long conversations at his office for no particular reason.

"So I suppose this means that we are going to surrender."

"The army is not going to stomach this, is it?"

"I wonder what will happen to our future food supply."

"When they talk about occupation, does that mean American soldiers will land in Japan and come to this town too?" Since the director had had the audacity to speak critically about the war, when it ended he naturally became the only person who could explain everything!

"I suppose we have to think about returning to Hongō," I remarked to the professor of internal medicine.

"You must be joking! Nobody knows what's going to happen. It looks like we might have to evacuate quickly to an even more remote area."

"What needs to be evacuated?"

"Hey, this is no laughing matter! When the enemy comes, they're going to take everything away!"

"I don't think that's going to happen. In the first place, professor, haven't we been talking about America as a country of material abundance? The Americans don't have to pillage the kind of things we have in our Hongō labs. They already have them."

"That's not what war is all about. Women face the greatest danger. If we don't evacuate those who remain in Tokyo, there's no telling what's going to happen to them."

In Oiwake, the farmers gave drinking parties, killing the chickens they had carefully kept until then. The idea was to eat them before the American soldiers could snatch them away. The son-in-law of the retired soldier returned home in civilian clothes, and for a while his main job was chopping firewood for cooking. A uniformed officer on horseback made an unexpected appearance, drew his sword in front of the Nakasendō lodge, and proudly announced that if the occupation forces should come, he would slay them right before our eyes. The old man who came to draw water told us the story and said with a chuckle, "I wonder what he will do if they actually show up."

"Do I detect a note of sarcasm here?" Sister said.

"If he was really serious about killing the enemy, he wouldn't draw his sword in front of women and children!" the old man answered in a loud voice.

Professor Katayama, who had become emaciated with malnutrition, said excitedly, "Democracy has won. Now the world will be a better place." At that time, Nakamura Shin'ichirō and a medical school classmate of mine were also living in the Chigataki area. I also visited the actor Tsurumaru who used to be active in the Little Tsukiji Theater.

"The victory of democracy? Is that what he said? No such luck! The fact of the matter is that it was a war between imperialist powers and one side ended up winning. Period. Of course they have a clause about democratization in the Potsdam Declaration. But I'm sure the American Occupation forces will carefully preserve the Japanese ruling classes. You just wait and see."

I was not thinking in those terms. I thought the Occupation forces would disband the Japanese military, turn Japan into a thoroughly democratic nation, and rejuvenate Japan as a sizable market, even if economic aid had to be part of the package. At that time, I knew nothing about the Cold War, nor did I give any thought to the possible contradictions between thorough democratization (including dissolution of the *zaibatsu* conglomerates) and economic recovery. It was only some time after the war that I became aware of these issues.

Tsurumaru's beautiful daughter was also living in their Chigataki home. She was kind, cheerful, and intelligent, and, in my mind, the personification of the ideal young Japanese woman. But I didn't really know her nor did I have the opportunity to get better acquainted with her afterwards. Postwar Tokyo seemed to have swept away everything that existed before August 1945, even my vivid impressions of the little house in the Chigataki woods and the father and daughter who lived there.

We did not move the Department of Internal Medicine back to Tokyo until early September. At our Oiwake home, food was a constant source of anxiety, and I had to run about all over the area to secure it. The Shin'etsu line was crowded, or more precisely, it was so overwhelmed with discharged soldiers, shoppers, and people running around in search of their missing family members that passengers getting on and off the trains through the windows had become a common sight. I realized that for the time being it would be impossible for Mother and Sister to travel with the children, and so I went to Tokyo alone.

At Ueno Station I saw a city burned into a wasteland. I was myself surprised at how accurate my own predictions on December 8, 1941, had turned out to be. Where were the people who had greeted the war with loud triumphant cheers? Or, more important, where were those who had deceived them, driven them into the jaws of death, and babbled such cruel and delirious nonsense about "scorched-earth tactics" even when defeat was looming before their eyes? Where had those people gone? And where were those loyalist scholars, writers, and poets who had prostituted themselves before these figures of authority? Where were those literary men who had so devotedly engaged in both self and public deception and who even justified their contempt for human lives with pseudo-rationalizations such as "Dying is living" and "Scattering adrift like cherry blossoms represents the soul of Yamato"?

To me the ruined remains of Tokyo were not just the evidence of the city's burned-down structures; they were also the remains of all of Tokyo's lies and duplicities, anachronisms and megalomaniac delusions. The claim that "the Divine Wind will strike down enemy planes should they have the audacity to appear over the Imperial Palace" was a lie, or at least a fallacy. The piles of rubble were mute evidence demonstrating this fact beyond the slightest doubt to the entire Japanese people. When a lie has been exposed, it no longer means anything. The Tokyo now lying in utter ruin had nothing to touch the human heart—no ideas or words survived its blazing ordeal. What remained was just an infinite sense of emptiness for having accomplished nothing after mounting a colossal effort.

But it was no longer a world of lies and falsehoods. The wide evening sky and the summer grass thriving among the rubble were not fake; and as long as they were genuine, even the charred ruins shone with greater splendor than a palace concocted of lies. At that time, my heart was filled with hope. I had never felt more optimistic about Japan's future or more encouraged to rise to the occasion. Since I had yet to start doing any real work, there was nothing to dampen my high spirits. Since I was ignorant about Japan, there was nothing to inspire my pessimism. And since the ministers under the Tōjō cabinet had not yet reemerged as Japan's postwar leaders, there was, to be sure, hope as well. What was in short supply was food. But men do not live by bread alone.

Figure 1. Masuda Kumaroku, the author's maternal grandfather. Courtesy of the author.

Figure 2. The author with his family, April 1936. From left: his mother, Oriko; his father, Shin'ichi; the author; his sister, Hisako. Courtesy of the author.

Figure 3. The former Edo period *wakihonjin* at the old Nakasendō in Shinano Oiwake, Karuizawa-chō, Nagano Prefecture. Used as a lodging house under its former name, Aburaya, it was destroyed by fire in 1937. Courtesy of Tsuchiya Photography Shop, Karuizawa-chō, 1995.

Figure 4. The author with his family, 1942. His father is seated, the author is directly behind him, and his sister is at right. Courtesy of the author.

Figure 5.   The author (front row, third from left) with his fellow students of Tokyo Imperial University. Courtesy of the author.

Figure 6.   Yokomitsu Riichi, ca. 1942. Courtesy of Heibonsha.

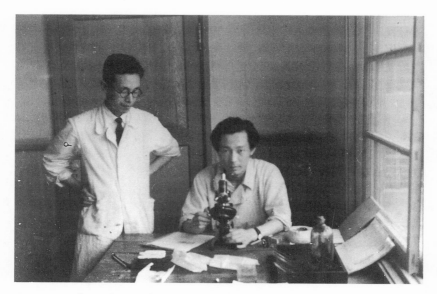

Figure 7.   The author (right) with his medical colleague Dr. Miyoshi Kazuo, Hiroshima, June 1947. Courtesy of the author.

Figure 8.   Ishikawa Jun, date unknown. Courtesy of Heibonsha.

Figure 9.   Hotta Yoshie (left) with the author, ca. 1950. Courtesy of Heibon-sha and the author.

Figure 10.   Kinoshita Junji (left) with the author in China, September 1977. Courtesy of the author.

Figure 11.   Maruyama Masao (left) with the author in Shinano Oiwake, Nagano Prefecture, ca. 1978. Courtesy of Heibonsha and the author.

Figure 12.   The author, late 1980s. Courtesy of the author.

Figure 13.   The author, mid-1990s. Courtesy of the author.

VOLUME TWO

21 Article of Faith

In September 1945 I again took up residence in the second-class patients' ward at the hospital in Hongō. During the day I examined patients and at night I worked in the laboratory with my microscope. Late into the night, after everyone had gone to sleep, I read whatever literary works I could lay my hands on, Japanese or non-Japanese. My status at the hospital was that of an assistant at the Faculty of Medicine, an unsalaried position. On weekends I went back home to Meguro Ward's Miyamae-chō by catching a connection on a crowded train from Ochanomizu.

Father had converted a room in the small house we rented in Miyamae-chō into a medical office, but he had very few patients. To make matters worse, Mother was not in the best of health, though she could still manage the daily chores for our small family. Sister had gotten married before the war and was by then a mother of two. She was living with her in-laws and waiting for her husband to return from the Chinese front. No one in our family died as a result of the war, but we lost whatever meager possessions we once had. We were at the mercy of high inflationary prices, and life after the war was hard. In the summer, when the water level of the open sewer ditch in front of our house dropped, columns of swarming mosquitoes plagued us. On the other hand, a prolonged period of rain caused flooding below our floor. On rainy days, even if the ditch did not overflow, the road beside it would turn into a muddy mire that was impossible to walk through in a dark night without stepping into muddy puddles. Whenever I thought about our family's plight, I realized I had no one but myself to rely on if we were to escape from the kind of existence we led in our Miyamae-chō neighborhood.

Grandmother, my aunt, and her daughter, that is to say my cousin, were living in a one-story house next door and were supporting themselves by selling off the property Grandfather had left. Grandfather, with his lifelong penchant for reckless extravagance, had squandered all the wealth accumulated by previous generations before he passed away during the war. Still, the remaining furniture, when sold to secondhand dealers, was enough to support the humble livelihood of the three women for a while. Mother lamented the fact that Grandmother, in order to survive, even had to resort to selling off Grandfather's personal belongings. But my aunt's oldest son, my elder cousin, was a research assistant at Tōhoku University and had no remittance to send home.[1] Other than Grandmother's old-age pension, their household had no income at all.

"I guess our family's decline has really hit rock bottom," I said.

"Well, I only wish Grandma realized that. But in any case, she's lived her life in luxury, and she doesn't even take care of housework herself."

The train from Hongō to Miyamae-chō took almost two hours one way, but the city buses converted from trucks discarded by the Occupation forces took less than an hour. While it only had uncomfortable plank seats, the bus dashed through the devastated city like a gust of wind. I was thrilled by the speedy ride, and I enjoyed looking at the street scenes through the window. In those days Tokyoites did not flaunt their social status or wealth at every opportunity. Men walking amid the ruins wore khaki-colored "national" clothes or military uniforms with the badges removed. Women wore *monpe* pantaloons or prewar-style "Western" clothes. Men who knew their way around were profiteering from black-market operations, and their idea of ultimate extravagance was having polished rice to eat and American cigarettes to smoke. Violent and thoughtless toward others, these men had no ideals or understanding of society as a whole. On the other hand, they were a lively crowd who had only themselves to rely on, and as such, they were far more honest than the arrogant and despicably obsequious men who hid behind the cloak of authority. Women who knew how to get around also knew how to make connections with the officers from the Occupation forces. When they boarded city buses wearing new clothes from the army PX, their happy faces always beamed with triumphant pride as if they were sitting on top of the world.

In the ruins of Tokyo, artificiality gave way to plain dealing, phony appearances to undisguised greed. Naked human desire, be it the passion

1. Tōhoku University is in Sendai in northeastern Honshū.

for food, material possessions, or sex, manifested itself with astonishing and unceremonious candidness. The Japanese government hit on the notion of *ichioku sōzange* (wholesale repentance for the entire hundred million Japanese people) and tried to sell the idea to the public, but nobody was prepared to repent and no one felt such a need. Indeed, repentance was the last thing on their minds; they were only too busy finding ways to keep up a livelihood that the present government could not guarantee—food rations alone weren't enough to ward off malnutrition.

This was a time when some people spoke of *sengo no kyodatsu jōtai* (the state of prostration after the war). But far from being perplexed by any "state of prostration," the Tokyoites I saw through the city bus window were filled with an indomitable vitality. Opinion leaders who once glorified the war might be in a state of prostration, but certainly not the black marketeers or the rice farmers who did well for themselves in the black market. The expression people came up with and loved to use was neither "repentance" (*zange*) nor "prostration" (*kyodatsu*) but rather *suto*—it means either "strike" or "strip tease." *Zene-suto* refers to the former, a workers' general strike, and *zen-suto* to the latter, stripping to the bare skin.[2] The word *suto* neatly epitomizes this postwar epoch for it exemplifies the struggles and self-indulgence of the Japanese people, both in organizations and as individuals.

I liked to ride the city bus as it sped across the ruined city, but on the train I sometimes got to see something different. Injured or sick veterans in dirty white coats would board the train at a station somewhere, make a round through the compartments, and change to a different train at the next station on the other side of the platform. During the short interval before the train reached the next station, the other passengers would pretend not to notice them by looking out the windows or engrossing themselves in their newspapers. Hardly anyone bothered to put change into the boxes held out by the soldiers. The passengers appeared unwilling to be reminded of an old wound, as if it had been some kind of mistake instead of the "sacred war" they greeted with so much enthusiasm on the day of Pearl Harbor.

On the other hand, there were many friendly faces among the passengers. On weekends, there were fathers traveling with their children and husbands with their wives. I had no doubt that in their respective families these men were caring fathers and loving husbands. How then

2. *Zen-suto* means "everything goes."

could one reconcile this thought with the probability that until yesterday these same men could have been killers on the Chinese continent? Had the character of the Japanese people changed? Or had only the immediate circumstances changed, making a repetition of the same behavior likely if the same conditions were to prevail again? Among the passengers, a middle-aged man was trying repeatedly to coax his unruly child, but in my eyes the face of this doting parent took on that inscrutable look of a hideous creature. The man who might have been yesterday's diabolical monster was today's good-natured human being and potentially tomorrow's diabolical monster all over again. Philosophers have expounded on the essential goodness or evil in human nature, but I cannot believe in either theory. Instead of debating the essential goodness or evil of man, I concluded that a more rewarding endeavor is to examine the history and structure of society as a whole that makes demons as well as angels out of a great many human beings. This was not an impulsive thought, for it determined the direction of my later thinking. Because no human being is evil, I am against the death penalty; and because war can turn any human being into a monster, I am against all wars.

On the train, most of the seated male passengers dozed with their knees spread wide apart. In order to get a seat, one literally had to shove others aside. That was why the seated passengers were all young men and not women or the elderly. One time a young soldier from the Occupation forces, noticing what was happening on the train, gestured to one of the men to give up his seat to a woman. The man grudgingly obeyed, but nobody was eager to occupy his seat. The soldier gestured to a woman to sit, but it took a while before she could understand what he meant. Even then, she looked first at the soldier and then at the man, and was still hesitant to make a move. Having already started his enterprise of switching passengers, the soldier could not very well throw up his hands and abandon it halfway. Finally, the woman looked blankly at the other passengers around her and mumbled, "I am so sorry," and sat down with a perplexed look on her face. The soldier, at last satisfied, got off at the next station.

The male passengers nearby, myself included on many occasions, started to reflect on what they had just witnessed. Their reactions ranged from irritation—"That troublemaker was poking his nose where he didn't belong!"—to somber realization—"We have no choice but to keep our mouth shut because we are a defeated nation." Meanwhile, the apparent look of embarrassment on the woman's face seemed to announce her role as just that of an unwilling party to the officious attention of the American soldier. On the other hand, she was not about to give up the seat she now occupied. That was how the American occupation of Japan began. In fact, the Japanese side did not use the term "occupation" but referred to the American forces as "stationary troops," just as it called Japan's surrender "termination of hostilities." In those days the Occupation forces apparently had little understanding of the Japanese people, and this lack of understanding was perpetuated by the Japanese, who, on demand, would rise from their seats without uttering a word.

At the beginning of the Occupation, I felt that my earlier predictions had been gradually turning into reality. I had not anticipated the concrete form of Japan's surrender but had expected the defeat itself. My prediction was based, negatively speaking, on my belief that popular claims about Japan's strengths and America's weaknesses were fantasy pure and simple. Positively speaking, I believed that from the outset the war represented a contest between the forces of democracy and the forces of fascism. I viewed world history as a gradual but sure progression from the integration of church and state to their separation and to religious freedom, from irrational spiritualism to rationalism, from ineffectually integrated communities to highly efficient organizations, from feudal agrarian societies to industrialized capitalist societies, from subservience toward authority to autonomous individualism, and from an insistence on sex and class distinctions to an emphasis on equality among human beings. As I assessed it, Japanese fascism represented nothing more than a desperate attempt on Japan's part to reaffirm the backwardness of its own society. In a global confrontation between fascism and democracy, rooted as they were in the forces of backwardness and progression respectively, only history could predict the outcome. The wheel of history does not turn backwards. That was my article of faith. It informed my predictions, and when they turned out to be accurate, my conviction was strengthened.

Generally speaking, it goes without saying that the accuracy of one's prediction does not necessarily validate the premise of such a prediction. But the issue here was not the certitude of knowledge but a sense of moral purpose. There can be no escape from the scrupulous net of Heaven's justice.

The logical conclusion from this line of thinking was that the Occupation authorities would eradicate the forces of militarism and "impose" democracy on Japan. The Japanese people could be expected, for the first time, to enjoy human rights and freedom of speech. The development of world history seemed to lend support to the prediction that a backward-looking society would henceforth evolve in a progressive direction. This projection appeared to be further substantiated by the rapid succession of announcements and directives that began to pour forth from the general headquarters of the Occupation forces. The anticipation that the Occupation forces would protect the people's rights as a means to achieve thorough democratization proved to be more accurate than the prediction by those who feared the worst possible rampage and plunder by the "British and American devils" after their armies had occupied Japan. The anticipation that American capitalism had little interest in destroying Japan as a potential market proved to be more realistic than the prediction that the foreigners would devastate the whole country and leave. The communiqués of the Occupation forces explained Japanese militarism in terms of Japan's feudalistic land ownership system with its high levies on the tenant farmers, giving rise to an impoverished agrarian sector and a cheap labor supply for the factories. They pointed to Japan's small domestic market, which subsequently encouraged its radical expansion into overseas markets. This in turn led to the resistance from countries with high labor costs and hence the rise of militarism within Japan to crush that resistance. I gathered that this was their line of argument, and I was surprised at how very closely it corresponded to ours.[3] I myself believed that I had a fairly accurate understanding of the war and our adversary, that is to say, the Occupation forces. This belief consolidated my conviction in the theoretical framework of my understanding—though my understanding did not really have the kind of systematic or coherent constructs to deserve the name of theory. If one could call the nebulously formulated system in this belief "ideology," then I was far from being "skeptical of all ideologies"; in fact at no other time in my life have I been a firmer believer in the power of ideology.

There was more to it than that. During the war I could find numerous examples around me that exemplified Japan's "backwardness." Yet I had no knowledge about the *realities* of Western "progress"; all I knew were Western *ideals* that I had learned from books, and the rest was my imagination. I knew about the Bill of Rights but nothing about police actions in the West. I knew in essence the workings of a democracy, but almost nothing about the behavioral patterns of state authority toward domestic and foreign affairs. I knew the principle of sexual equality as

3. Katō very likely refers to his close circle of friends.

stipulated in civil law, but I was totally ignorant of any concrete examples of real sexual discrimination. I could scarcely avoid thinking of Japanese society as the epitome of all "backwardness" or identifying "progress" with my imaginary West. And where, for example, would the other Asian countries fit into my scheme? The truth of the matter is that they did not even cross my mind!

Of course, my guiding principles were not only related to matters of war and the Occupation. What other principles did I cherish as I stood face to face with postwar society? And what other experiences did I have, or rather, not have?

I did not hold any religious faith. I did not find arguments for the existence of a god convincing, nor did I think it possible to prove the nonexistence of a god. Nevertheless, I had a persistent interest in the different ramifications of these two premises, on the individual level as well as on the societal and cultural levels as a whole.

Epistemologically, I was a skeptic but, for all practical purposes, not a faithful one. For example, unless I had a great deal of time at my disposal, I would not give any thought to whether the noodles in front of me actually existed, or how I was made aware of their existence through my sensory faculties. Just by thinking about them, I found it difficult to arrive at the objectivity of the noodles on the basis of my subjective consciousness and equally difficult to arrive at the transcendence of my epistemological subjectivity on the basis of the objectivity of the noodles. Hence I ventured to go no further than that. I concluded only, for example, that the opposing positions of historical materialism and subjectivism had exactly the same standing.

When it came to moral principles, I ultimately recognized none as absolute. One could perhaps compare moral codes to the eternity of the starry skies, but there discussion would turn on abstract canons of morality in general, not their substantive stipulations. Concrete moral values can only be relative, subject to the specificity of time, society, and the particular circumstances of the individual involved. This moral relativism often turned me into an iconoclast in my thinking, because I refused to acknowledge as absolute the values that society and tradition were trying to mold into precisely this. Yet the same relativism also turned me, in practice, into a conservative, because if new and old values were similarly relative to one another, I felt no absolute need to replace the old with the new. In real life, I was, generally speaking, a law-abiding person with no particular wish to inflict harm on either people or animals.

But then I was not much of a dispenser of good fortune. I suppose I could be considered a dutiful son to my parents, and I loved my sister dearly. I abided by all these conventions as long as they did not seriously conflict with my own interests. I applied myself reasonably hard to my chosen profession; I looked at world and national affairs with only detached interest; and I tried to live a calm and peaceful life.

Psychologically, I had always lacked self-confidence. Perhaps that was why I hoped I could at least become an independent thinker, serving no other master but myself. I was not like the brave soldier who could defy the perils of the battlefield, and I never tried to become one. I did not aspire to greatness, and I did not believe I had the talents necessary to contrive a master plan in pursuit of any great ambition. Of course I wanted to have a reasonable standard of living, but I had little desire for extravagance. I disliked being ordered around, and I had no desire to lead others by the nose. I could be disagreeable and stubborn, just as I was as a child, and to others I might often appear combative. While I was not entirely unaware of my own traits, I was not terribly bothered by what other people might think. Above all, I was full of curiosity, and I wished to know everything that was happening in the world. As a matter of fact, many things were happening or about to happen in the world where I lived.

While I had no chronic illnesses, occasional malnutrition had contributed to my skinny physique and slight build, a far cry from the all-muscle macho type. I consoled myself by thinking that no man, however strong, could be a match for a bull. To begin with, "he-man" or "masculine" attributes never interested me a great deal.

In both the psychological and physical senses, I had little experience with sex. I seldom had contacts with women other than Mother and Sister, and even when such contacts did take place, I was enormously shy. I had never stepped into a *zen-suto* joint or found any private pleasure in pornography, not because of lack of interest but, I suppose, because of inertia. Tokyo, despite its devastation, was filled with vibrant young women with cheerful laughter, sparkling eyes, and streaming black hair. Watching them gave me tremendous pleasure, but initiating a conversation was too much of a bother. And sleeping with them was not within my immediate thoughts.

Armed with a few ideas but totally "inexperienced," I began my journey into postwar Japanese society. And so, along the way, it seemed only natural to encounter worldly, "experienced" types and discover the infinite strengths and weaknesses of ideas.

22 Hiroshima

Not a single living tree remained in Hiroshima. The wasteland extended as far as the eye could see, its flat surface crisscrossed by intersecting roads and waterways. A few stone buildings were still standing, but their windows were broken, their walls half-destroyed, and, as one approached, blue sky could be seen on the other side. None of the remaining houses was fit for human habitation. Yet in this scorched wilderness, there were always wandering souls haunting the landscape like shadows: disoriented men in national uniforms with faces covered with dirt; children whose scarred faces twitched with spasms of pain; hairless women walking under the sun like frightened animals, their faces covered with a *furoshiki*. Hospitals in the suburbs sufficiently far from the center of explosion to have escaped destruction were still packed with patients suffering from continuous high fever, swollen gums, and wounds oozing pus. Only two months ago, they had been citizens of Hiroshima, and now they were the survivors.

The city of Hiroshima had been there until the morning of August 6, 1945, a castle town still untouched by the bombings. Several tens of thousands of families lived there, each with its own share of joy and sorrow, hope and remorse. That morning, in an instant, the whole city vanished. More than half of the citizens living around the city center were either crushed under the collapsed houses or drowned in the waterways into which they threw themselves or instantly killed by the blast. Survivors tried to escape to the suburbs amidst the black smoke covering the sky and the flames scorching the earth, but some collapsed on the way and others died just as they had made their way to safety. Those who survived the ordeal and thought they had narrowly escaped the jaws of death were celebrating their good fortune with relatives in the countryside, but within a mere three or four weeks their hair began to fall out and their noses and mouths began to bleed. Soon they developed a high fever and died before any medical attention could be administered. Two months later those who did manage to survive were numb from the shock of losing their close family members, and they themselves became fearful of the effects of radiation from the atomic explosion. Like unwanted animals, they wandered aimlessly in the scorched wilderness. These former citizens of Hiroshima were no longer the same human beings; their former identities had vanished as though they had never existed.

Those who had gone through such an experience were reluctant to talk about it. The only thing they were prepared to say was, "We got nuked, that's what we call it here.[1] We just feel more dead than alive."

I had never before felt such an infinitely insurmountable distance separating me from another person. A huge, dark mass of experience was locked inside their hearts, and if they themselves could not articulate it, how could I possibly understand what it meant? It was something beyond comprehension—no sooner had some meaning been extracted from the experience than the substance of that meaning began to evaporate. And yet as long as one came face to face with it, the weight of the experience irresistibly defined the totality of one's being. This was an experience I had never had before. But I witnessed those who had. Whenever I heard people talk about Hiroshima, no matter how convincing their words might be, I always had a feeling of something not quite right. A voice inside me would say, What you said is true, but it's not the whole story. This applies even to the phrase "No More Hiroshima." When I saw Hiroshima, I was not thinking at all about the future of nuclear weapons. Later, I did think about nuclear weapons, but I was always reminded of the vast gulf between my own thoughts and the experience that inspired such a muted silence in the people of Hiroshima.

But the immediate silence between the patient and the doctor had to be broken. I had to turn their individual experiences into observable categories by extrapolating the significance of what they could articulate.

"Where were you at that time?" I asked.

"My sister's husband had already gone to the front, so I was at my sister's place . . ."

---

1. The local people, especially children, used the expression *pikadon: pika* refers to the bright light and *don* the sound of the atomic explosion.

"Could you tell me where your sister's house was on this map? So it was about three kilometers from the center of the explosion. Now, it was a wooden house, wasn't it? And what direction were you facing inside the house?"

As far as the patient was concerned, it was obvious that these questions were at best inconsequential. Indeed, I felt that bombarding Hiroshima victims with these questions bordered on the barbaric. Whether the house was made of wood or anything else, the patient's life was forever changed as a result of the death of her sister's child and the blindness of her sister. On the one hand was a core of experience to which no verbal articulation could do justice, and on the other, a string of facts totally unrelated to the life of the person concerned. And yet in order to comprehend the world, it is necessary to translate into words not life's decisive experiences—these defy articulation—but bare facts. If Hiroshima taught me anything at all, it was the lesson of how vehemently incompatible and unbearably agonizing such a contrast could become for the observer. For me, it came down to a choice between quietly returning to Tokyo or remaining in Hiroshima to observe my "cases." What I saw before me were not "medical cases" but real human beings, and yet I could say or do nothing for them. Besides, I had no reason to prolong my stay there in the first place. But I stayed. By so doing, I could devote myself to my laboratory work, treating human beings as medical cases. The victim's distance from the center of the explosion, whether he or she was under any cover, the nature of the cover if any, the loss of hair and other symptoms deemed typical for victims of atomic radiation, particularly the findings in the victim's hemogram, and most importantly, the results from the bone marrow sample. My mind was so preoccupied with such matters that I scarcely gave any thought to the war, to its moral ramifications, or to the effects of nuclear weapons on human beings. Samples of bone marrow were relevant to my Hiroshima medical cases; the effects of nuclear weapons were relevant to the people of Hiroshima. During my two months in Hiroshima, I thought less about the atomic bomb than at any other time thereafter.

At that time I was a Japanese participant in the Joint Investigative Team on the Impact of the Atomic Bomb. The team had been sent to Hiroshima jointly by the medical faculty of Tokyo Imperial University and the American contingent of army doctors. Professor Tsuzuki from the Department of Surgery, the organizer of the Japanese team, consulted

Dr. Nakao, a hematologist.[2] Even before that, samples of bone marrow had been sent from hospitals in Hiroshima to Dr. Nakao, and I too had examined those samples. Our findings were that they resembled the effects of aplastic anemia as cited to date, suggesting drastic changes in the victims' bone marrow. What had happened there? We had already discussed the matter, and we wanted very much to know more about those bone marrow samples. So when Dr. Nakao asked me if I wanted go to Hiroshima with him, I accepted his offer without the slightest hesitation.

Even before the joint investigative team left for Hiroshima, specialists from the American side showed up at our Internal Medicine Division to examine Dr. Nakao's medical cases. They came every day to make handwritten records of the patients' medical histories and to scrutinize with us the bone marrow samples under the microscope. Once they sat down in front of the microscope, Dr. Nakao's ability was immediately apparent. When young American doctors encountered difficulties in classifying cells they saw under the microscope, they sought Dr. Nakao's help. In expressing their appreciation for Dr. Nakao, their manners were invariably courteous and not the least impertinent. But communication between us was close to impossible.

"Hey! Go find out what they want!" Dr. Nakao turned to my desk and yelled. "Earlier on, they seemed to be asking me for something, but I had no idea what it was."

As I approached the Americans, they looked relieved at the arrival of opportune help and rapidly repeated their question. But I too could not understand what they were saying. Baffled, they looked at each other. Then one of them took great pains to repeat the same question slowly. When it finally dawned on me that they were in fact asking where the toilet was, we all burst out laughing.

"Why didn't they just ask in plain English?" Dr. Nakao said. "We can't understand them when they speak in this roundabout way."

This was my first encounter with foreigners since my high school days with our German teacher. This time, it took place when the Occupying forces were coming into contact with the occupied Japanese people, and our business revolved around technical problems in the highly specialized area of hematology. In other matters, Professor Tsuzuki was the one who negotiated with the American side. He explained to us that the goal

2. Tsuzuki Masao (1892–1961), a specialist in thoracic surgery who taught at both Tokyo Imperial University and the Naval Training Hospital.

of the joint investigative team was purely academic, and he laid out our concrete itinerary to Hiroshima. Later, an American transport plane brought us and our medical equipment, food, and transport vehicles from Tachikawa to Hiroshima.

My first and last "contact" with the Occupation forces—perhaps "contact" is too strong a word here—surprised me at every turn. Inside the transport plane we took from Tachikawa was a huge nude picture of what the Americans called a pinup girl, and sitting in front of it were young baby-faced soldiers with rifles in hand. If it were the Japanese army, I don't suppose such a picture could be publicly displayed inside a military plane, though surely no soldier could be uninterested in naked women. The official stance of the Japanese army was one of stoic spiritualism, of great significance in combat situations.

Heading the American team was an army doctor, Colonel M, a professor at the University of Southern California who had many famous patients in his private practice in Beverly Hills. He spoke some French and from time to time would make wisecracks. Once he pointed to a formation of bombers over the sky of Hiroshima and said, "They destroyed the Nazis." I didn't know about Germany at that time, or how many tens of thousands of people had been killed during the blanket bombing of Dresden. I was just wondering if there had been pinup pictures inside the B-25 bombers at that time as well. Besides Colonel M, Lieutenant Colonel L, a very fine pathologist from Yale University, was likewise not originally an army doctor. They joined the army after the war began, were given their respective ranks, and were able to apply their abilities as specialists in their fields. I could not help remembering the time when Assistant Professor Okinaka, a scholar respected by the medical school as a whole, was drafted toward the end of the war as a soldier-nurse.[3] "Well, a soldier-nurse is someone who does things like sweeping the hospital corridors," someone in the medical office said. "Don't tell me some army doctor trained by Mr. Okinaka could order him to do that!"

One fine autumn day Colonel M and I were traveling in his jeep from Hiroshima to the naval hospital in Iwakuni. It had been a long time since I smelled refreshing sea air instead of the drugs in my laboratory. Not far from the shore above the deep blue waters of the Inland Sea, the remains of a Japanese warship sunk during the bombing lay exposed to the sun. On the road, I saw soldiers from the Occupation forces

3. See chapter 19, note 3.

trying to hitch rides from passing vehicles. All the vehicles on the road—automobiles, trucks, and jeeps—belonged to the U. S. Army, and I couldn't see even a cart that belonged to the local people. At one point, Colonel M stopped his jeep in front of two young soldiers and asked where they were heading. The soldiers stood up straight, raised their hands in salute, and answered, "The service club." "Well then, get into the back seats!" All along the way until the soldiers got off, the colonel, in high spirits, cracked jokes and engaged in idle conversation with a receptive audience. "I wonder how many Japanese girls there are in the service club?" And so the conversation went. I was wondering whether a Japanese colonel might not also have taken his soldiers in his own vehicle to a "service club" in some occupied territory. After our passengers got off, the colonel whistled a tune from *Madama Butterfly*. As I listened, I realized I couldn't bring myself to share in the cheerful mood.

"Prostitution isn't a cheerful business," I muttered. That was not necessarily all I had in mind.

"But, hey, that's life!" Colonel M replied in French, his voice cheerful as ever.

Lieutenant Colonel L was preoccupied with his pathological examinations and had little contact with us since our work was clinical diagnosis. The majority of the Japanese team members went out every day to the local hospitals to examine patients. Besides Lieutenant Colonel L and Dr. Ishii working in the pathology laboratories, the only people who stayed in the rural army hospital—which provided us with our examination room as well as our lodging—were Dr. Nakao and four or five clinical staff. Inside the hospital, hardly anyone from the Japanese team talked about the war. Scarcely anyone expressed his views on the subject of the Americans' dropping the atomic bomb, and only Colonel M on the American side and Professor Tsuzuki on the Japanese side occasionally talked about the war in general terms.

One day Colonel M went into the diagnostic room and, without saying a word, wrote in big letters on the blackboard, "People who live in houses made of paper and wood should not throw stones at others," and left. "So he's saying it was stupid of us to start the war, I suppose. The guy is making fools out of us," somebody mumbled. But the matter went no further than that. As always, Professor Tsuzuki chatted with the Americans in his fluent English, and one time he said, "The war's ended, you see, and now we're cooperating with you and our joint investigation team's going well. But, mind you, in the next war, we're going to win."

Clearly, Professor Tsuzuki meant that as a joke, but the Americans reacted rather strongly. First Lieutenant L, originally from Yale Medical School like Lieutenant Colonel L, was listening to Professor Tsuzuki with us. Because we worked in the same examination room every day, I was beginning to develop a friendship with this young American physician. No sooner had Professor Tsuzuki left the room than L said, with a somewhat agitated look on his face, "Did you hear what he just said? What kind of joke is that? And we're right in the middle of a tragedy in Hiroshima!" I had to agree that in October 1945, when cities throughout Japan had been burned to rubble and when the Japanese people could barely escape starvation on the supply of American food, the words "the next war" did have a strange ring to my ears as well.

Sometime later when I alone was with First Lieutenant L in a room in a mountain lodge, he said, "Do you think Professor Tsuzuki is a militarist?"

"Professor Tsuzuki was also a surgeon vice admiral in the navy. Do you think there was a military officer in the Japanese imperial forces who *wasn't* a militarist?" That conversation took place when the two of us were out on a trip all by ourselves.

As Dr. Nakao and I were studying blood and bone marrow samples in Hiroshima, we came to the conclusion that we should go beyond the examination of the breakdown of hematogenous tissues caused by radiation and also observe the recovery of those tissues. In order to do this, we had to follow up on our patients after their release. But once they left their hospitals near Hiroshima, patients in recuperation were scattered throughout the nearby villages. There seemed to be no other way to gather our data than to mark down on a map beforehand the known addresses of some of our former patients and then make a round of follow-up calls in a jeep with all the equipment on board. I discussed this idea with Dr. Nakao, and since I couldn't carry it out alone, I also talked with First Lieutenant L. He very much agreed with me and said he would explain our plans to Lieutenant Colonel L and request a jeep and a week's leave. We had been living almost exclusively in the examination room for more than a month now, and admittedly, we also wanted to breathe the air outside. When we received approval, First Lieutenant L said, "Lieutenant Colonel L is a workaholic. But I've been working very hard and I suppose that's why he gave us his approval this time."

"Dr. Nakao is also a workaholic," I said. "Although we're no match for him, we've been working hard too, and we definitely need some diversion."

The two of us prepared the equipment for the examinations, collected the maps, loaded up our spare fuel and food supply, and had a jeep ready in a great hurry. As we were about to depart, he brought a rifle along. While he was putting it under the rear seats, he said in a seeming effort to justify his action, "I know I don't need it, but the rules say we have to do this in an occupied territory."

During the journey we lost our way sometimes at night, got caught in heavy rain on a mountain road, or were forced to make detours around destroyed bridges. On a few occasions, with no place to stay overnight, we had to negotiate with the local police. Still, we enjoyed the journey while visiting our patients from one village to the next. Riding in a jeep from the Occupation forces, we never encountered antipathy or hostility anywhere. Instead, we were sometimes met with kindness and an occasional following, and in most instances people greeted us with curiosity. The war had not brought any destruction to the mountain villages, and the Occupation forces had not yet penetrated that far. During the journey, I was very keenly aware of myself as neither a local person nor a member of the Occupation forces, but as an observer of an encounter between the local people and a physician from the Occupation forces. Although I clearly realized that the local people regarded me sitting inside the jeep as someone from the Occupation forces, I realized even more acutely that I was not.

The journey brought L and me closer together, and our conversations often went beyond the technical areas of medicine. Though my English was as inadequate as before, little by little I felt more comfortable with it and I could more or less understand what L was saying. As we rode along he asked me questions about the local customs, and I offered my explanations, duly simplified according to my ability to articulate them.

"What's that large building over there?"

"That's a temple."

"Considering how poor Japanese villages are, why don't they build schools and factories instead of large temples?"

"Next to the temple, the school is the largest structure. Even if there had been factories, they would've been destroyed in the bombings."

But of course we also talked about democracy as a universal ideal. We agreed that it was essentially realized in the United States.

"Was the democratic ideal widely recognized in imperial Japan?"

"No, the idea was prohibited in imperial Japan, and only very few people believed in it."

"Were you one of those few people during the war?"

"Yes."

"If so, weren't you a traitor to the Japanese empire?"

All of a sudden, the word "traitor" struck like an arrow, piercing me, and I winced but recovered myself quickly.

"What is imperial Japan?" I remember myself saying. "It consisted of the government and the people. And if a government betrays its people, the only thing a person can do is oppose the government, or at least not support it, if he doesn't want to betray his own people. Now you just said the government of imperial Japan during the war was not democratic. An undemocratic government by definition betrays the basic and legitimate rights of the people. And so if a man is loyal to the government, he becomes a traitor to the people, and if he's loyal to the people, he's a traitor to the government. I was only trying to be loyal to the people of Japan."

"I see," L muttered. Then he remained silent as if trying to catch his own train of thought.

That was the last time I met L. I wonder if he would still agree with my arguments today. By now, I can perhaps articulate my thoughts a little more effectively. The issue itself, however, has nothing to do with the art of articulation.[4]

Returning from Hiroshima, I felt exhausted. And for a long time afterwards I did not think about the city.

4. Katō met L again for the first time since 1945 in Los Angeles in November 1991 during his trip to the United States as a commentator on a PBS *Frontline* program about the role of Japanese business in that country (see Katō's essay "Kokyū wasureubeki," in *Katō Shūichi chosakushū*, 22:243–46).

23   1946

Most of the young men who gathered in a drinking party in the blacked-out city of Kawaguchi toward the end of the war to send their friends off to the front did manage to survive and return to the gutted ruins of Tokyo. And by the time they themselves were drafted, no vessels were left to transport them to the battlefields in the South Pacific. They were expected to strap their bodies to gasoline bombs and throw themselves at the enemy's tanks in the "battle of Japan"—but in the end the battle never took place. These young men did not know war; they knew only how senseless life was in the army. They had no experience at killing Chinese; their only experience was their expectation of getting killed. They had not lived for the future, but they felt the need to define the present and the future for themselves.

When these young men gathered once again in occupied Tokyo, they founded a coterie magazine called *Sedai* (Generation). Among them were Hidaka Hiroshi, later to become an economist, and Nakamura Minoru, a poet and the author of an epochal book on Miyazawa Kenji. In the same magazine I serialized a number of essays later published in *1946: Bungakuteki kōsatsu* (1946: a literary inquiry), a book I coauthored with two novelists, Fukunaga Takehiko and Nakamura Shin'ichirō.[1] In that book,

1. *Sedai* (July 1946–December 1952, in 17 vols.) was one of the first significant postwar literary journals. • Hidaka Hiroshi (1923–) studied philosophy at Tokyo University, taught Marxist economics at Hōsei University from 1954, and wrote on *Das Kapital* and on economic theories; under the pseudonym Hamada Shin'ichi, he wrote literary criticism, especially on Yoshiyuki Junnosuke. • Nakamura Minoru (1927–), whose 1955 study of Miyazawa Kenji (and its expanded editions) was a landmark in Japanese postwar scholarship and later

the two novelists contemplated the future of the novel. With what struck me as a skillful combination of two perspectives, Nakamura emphasized the idea that the novel as understood by the prewar Tokyo literary establishment was in fact nothing more than a peculiar representation of the form. If one assumes that *The Tale of Genji* and *A la recherche du temps perdu* represented the typical forms of the novel, the *watakushi-shōsetsu* (the Japanese I-novel) since the advent of naturalism can scarcely be described as a novel at all. And if one traces the history of the novel in England and France since the eighteenth century, with its progressive development of techniques, the realm of the novel has obviously expanded. In this day and age, is it not an appalling anachronism, he argues, to adhere stubbornly to the naturalist style of depicting every minor detail about a third-person character? After pondering these issues, they began their inquiry into the newest techniques of the novel. For example, Fukunaga wrote about William Faulkner's artistic devices, and Nakamura spoke of the necessity for new narrative techniques and went on to explain how they worked. Now that I think about it, Nakamura Shin'ichirō was a literary specialist even before he was widely known as a writer, and Fukunaga Takehiko was a professional novelist before he began to make his living as one.

During the war I was more interested in reading the collections of the *Shinkokinshū* poets than contemporary novels. As far as I was concerned, literature, more than anything else, meant the *Sankashū, Shūi gusō,* and the *Kinkaishū,* works that transcend time and strike a chord in the depths of my soul.[2] I wrote essays on Teika and Sanetomo, but what enabled

---

triggered a debate (the *Ame ni mo makezu* controversy) with the critic and philosopher Tanikawa Tetsuzō, also a Miyazawa scholar; he also wrote on the contemporary poet Nakahara Chūya (*Kotobanaki uta—Nakahara Chūya ron* [Songs without words: a study of Nakahara Chūya, 1973]). • *1946: Bungakuteki kōsatsu,* published in 1947, helped launch Katō's career within the Japanese literary world.

2. An early Kamakura imperial anthology, the 20-vol. *Shinkokinshū* (New poetry collection of ancient and contemporary times) holds 1,978 *waka* poems from 101 poets compiled by Fujiwara Teika, Fujiwara Ariie, Minamoto Michitomo, and the priest Jakuren at the order of the retired emperor Gotoba, also himself a compiler. • *Sankashū* (The mountain hut collection) is a 3-vol. collection of unknown date of poems by Saigyō (1118–90), a late Heian and early Kamakura poet and priest. • *Shūi gusō* (Meager gleanings) (1216–33) is a collection of poems by Fujiwara Teika (1162–1241), an early Kamakura poet and critic and generally regarded as one of Japan's greatest poets. • *Kinkaishū* is a poetry anthology of Minamoto Sanetomo (1192–1219), the third shogun of the Kamakura *bakufu,* who was assassinated at the age of 27.

me to do so were the collapse of militarism and the recognition of freedom of the press. I also wrote about my experiences after gaining my freedom of expression. In other words, I was speaking my mind about the laudable postwar democratic ideal and the absolutely ludicrous war propaganda we had been fed during the war years.

What precisely was the similarity among the three of us? Perhaps it was our common resolve to bring our private and long-cherished thoughts out into the public forum. And for me, that public forum was represented by the scorched wasteland, the wasteland where philosophers of the Kyoto school, Japan romanticists, Takamura Kōtarō, and Mushanokōji Saneatsu had all crumbled away in the wake of the bombings.[3] The only literary figures who seemed to have survived intact were Nagai Kafū, the chronicler of *Risai nichiroku* (Diary of war sufferings), and Ishikawa Jun, the author of "Mujintō" (The everlasting light).[4] It never

3. Katō argues that the Kyoto school philosophers such as Tanabe Hajime (1885–1962) used such expedient constructs as "the philosophy of world history" to justify the war ("Sensō to chishikijin" [1959], in *Chishikijin no seisei to yakuwari, Kindai Nihon shisōshi kōza* [Chikuma shobō, 1972], 4:325–61, esp. 345–48). On the Japan romanticists, see chapter 14, note 22. • Takamura Kōtarō (1883–1956), a sculptor and poet best known for his collection *Dōtei* (Journey, 1914) and his love poems collected in *Chieko shō* (Selected works on Chieko, 1941; as ed. Kusano Shimpei, 1956) who was president of the Poets' Division of the Patriotic Literary Association in 1942 and, after the war, was charged by the critic Odagiri Hideo for his war responsibility; on Takamura during the war, see Yoshimoto Takaaki, *Takamura Kōtarō: Zōho ketteiban* (Shunjūsha, 1973), 95–140. • Mushanokōji Saneatsu (1885–1976), a leading novelist of the prewar Shirakaba-ha (white birch school) who allowed himself to align with Japan's war efforts (see his *Dai Tōa sensō shikan* [Personal views on the great East Asian war, 1942]) and later stated he was "deceived" (*damasarete ita*) during the war, to which Katō replied: "Perhaps he was. But what that actually means is that he himself wanted to be deceived. Our question is not who was deceived, but why one wished to be deceived; not who was not deceived, but why one did not wish to be deceived" ("Sensō to chishikijin," 327). Katō's essay remains an astute assessment of the role of Shōwa writers and intellectuals during the Pacific War.

4. Kafū's *Risai nichiroku* was his diary for 1945 and part of his massive 42-year diary *Danchōtei nichijō* (Chronicle from the house of heartrending grief) from September 16, 1917, to April 29, 1959; it records the Tokyo air raids and the destruction of his house, the Henkikan (house for the eccentric), along with "ten thousand volumes" of his beloved books on the night of March 10; he refused to read any Japanese books—he read only works in French—an act Katō interpreted as Kafū's resistance to fascism and to Japan: see Katō's "Sensō to chishikijin," 352, 360, his more extensive discussion in "Kafū to iu genshō" (Kafū as a phenomenon, *Sekai*, June–August 1960), and Edward Seidensticker,

even crossed my mind that somewhere else, some other people might also privately entertain ideas similar to ours. But though Tokyo lay in ruins, it was by no means a totally barren landscape.

As I mentioned earlier, I continued to live in the second-class patients' ward at Tokyo University Hospital and went back to my house in Meguro Ward only on weekends. One day a nurse came in to tell me the unusual news that I had a visitor. As I opened the door and stepped out into the corridor, still dark in the daytime, I saw a stoutly built stranger standing straight and looking at me without a word. After I invited him into my room and offered him the only chair, I climbed up and sat on my bunk. Then my taciturn visitor finally opened his mouth and quietly uttered a single word: "Kibachi."

"Kibachi?" If he was a salesman trying to peddle a new drug, he should visit me at the medical office instead of coming over here out of the blue and asking to see me by name. I wondered if "Kibachi" could be the name of some sort of secret organization. What on earth was the language he was speaking and what did the word mean?

"I came to see you about Kibachi." My visitor paid no attention whatsoever to my mounting suspicions and spoke with imperturbable composure. "I really want you to do something for it."

That was Noma Hiroshi.[5] He went on to explain to me that *kibachi*, a Japanese word meaning "yellow wasp," was the name of a new literary journal, though the tone of his voice seemed to suggest that the name did not matter one way or the other. He said that the most compelling thing for writers to do then was to start new literary journals from the standpoint of pacifism and respect for human rights.

Kafū the Scribbler (Stanford: Stanford University Press, 1965). • "Mujintō" (*Bungei shunjū* [July 1946])—the everlasting and ever-expanding light of the Buddhist law—comes from a series of wartime and early postwar works suggesting Ishikawa's resistance to the militarist period and his desire to keep alive his inner sense of freedom and independence. Katō ranked Ishikawa and Nakano Shigeharu as the two finest writers of postwar Japan (see the memorial issue on Ishikawa, *Subaru* 4 [1988]: 58; and "Sensō to chishikijin," 360–61 n.21).

5. Noma Hiroshi (1915–91), a prominent postwar writer, the author of youthful reminiscences of wartime student activities at Kyoto University (*Kurai e* [Dark painting, first published in *Kibachi*, 1946]), a massive 5-vol. social novel (*Seinen no wa* [The cycle of youth, 1947–50, 1962–71], on the leaders of the burakumin liberation movement), and a scathing study of the corruption and brutality of Japanese military life (*Shinkū chitai* [The vacuum zone, 1952]).

In order to raise questions about a speaker's comments, one has to wait until he finishes talking. Meanwhile, the author of *Shinkū chitai* (The vacuum zone) was speaking at a painfully slow speed. His talk seemed endless, and when it finally did come to an end I was almost under the illusion that I had become his convert.

At that point Noma Hiroshi remarked, "It's not going to do any good to keep on writing the same kind of novels as before!" Nakamura Shin'ichirō had said the same thing. To be sure, their messages were very different in substance; but I had an unmistakable feeling that what I was witnessing was none other than the dawn of the age of postwar literature.[6]

In those days Hanada Kiyoteru was in charge of the journal *Sōgō bunka* (Culture in synthesis), and all kinds of people would gather at his editorial office. Occasionally they would engage in high-spirited discussions that energized the atmosphere of the office. During the war Hanada wrote *Fukkōki no seishin* (The Renaissance spirit), in which he discusses Eastern and Western classics from all ages and along the way castigates Japanese militarism with admirable dexterity.[7] I knew nothing about his work during the war, and when I read it for the first time after the war ended, I was greatly astounded by his talents. As we became more closely acquainted, I was all the more impressed by his awesome presence. With bright piercing eyes and long hair flowing like a stallion's mane to the nape of his neck, he would utter words loaded with

6. At Noma's request, Katō wrote the essay "Hyūmanizumu to shakaishugi" (Humanism and socialism), *Kibachi* 3 (October 1946). He was then twenty-seven.

7. Hanada Kiyoteru (1909–74), a Marxist critic, novelist, playwright, member of the Kindai bungaku (modern literature) coterie, and editor of *Shin Nihon bungaku* (New Japanese literature) from 1952 to July 1954. His colleague and critic Sasaki Kiichi aptly summarizes Hanada's postwar leitmotiv as an attempt "to rescue the subjective praxis of art from the trap of formal logic and to unify dialectically the political avant-garde with the artistic avant-garde" (*Nihon kindai bungaku daijiten* [Kōdansha, 1984], 1187). • *Sōgō bunka* (July 1947–January 1949) was founded by the first generation of prominent postwar intellectuals (Katō, Hanada, Sasaki Kiichi, Noma Hiroshi, and the poet Sekine Hiroshi) to create "synthesized art" (*sōgō geijutsu*) by probing the relations between politics, science, and art. • Hanada's classic *Fukkōki no seishin* (1946), 21 essays written between 1941 and 1946, ostensibly address the European Renaissance but take up the universal question of an intellectual's role in society and during cultural transformation; his discussions of Dante, Machiavelli, da Vinci, and Luther to Cervantes, Swift, Goethe, and van Gogh employ an array of similes and metaphors, devices he describes as "the weapons of the suppressed."

such profound implications and insights that one could hardly fathom them, and indeed they often went beyond my comprehension. Meanwhile the poet Sekine Hiroshi was talking enthusiastically about "the energies of the masses," while the physicist Watanabe Satoshi was touting the "republican system" as if he had total faith in it. Miyagi Otoya astonished me by declaring that if only psychology, his specialty, became a little more sophisticated, literature would be reduced to a superfluity.[8] I protested and challenged his views, and the arguments went back and forth. Since I was ignorant about psychology and Mr. Miyagi's knowledge about literature was almost nil, mutual communication was doomed from the start. Another psychologist, Minami Hiroshi, conducted himself with an air of detachment and seemed to enjoy directing witticisms at himself and the people around him.[9] "The Japanese are so fond of ideologies! That's why they'll never get tired of debating on and on forever."

It was also around this time that I became acquainted with the Kindai Bungaku (modern literature) critics. Their magazine [*Kindai bungaku*] often carried debates on the subject of "politics vis-à-vis literature," and the Kindai Bungaku members maintained that literature should not be turned into a handmaiden of political ideologies.[10] I surmised that they

8. Sekine Hiroshi (1920–94), a poet, critic, and chief editor of *Sōgō bunka*. • Watanabe Satoshi (1910–93), a founder of the Nijisseiki kenkyūjo (research institute for the twentieth century) in 1946 with Shimizu Ikutarō and the influential journal *Shisō no kagaku* (Scientific discourse), known for his liberal wartime stance and critique of Marxism in *Genshitō sengen* (Declaration of an atomic physicist, 1946). • Miyagi Otoya (1908–), a prominent psychologist and son of a Protestant priest, was a Marxist during his days at Kyoto University who later used Freudian ideas to reinterpret Marxism after the purge of Stalin and also criticized Japanese Marxism's feudal character and passivity toward political authority ("Hōkenteki Marukusushugi," *Shisaku* [1948]). He later taught at the Tokyo University of Technology (1949–68) and wrote *Yume* (Dreams, 1953), *Seikaku* (Personality, 1960), and *Shinshinrigaku nyūmon* (Introduction to new psychology, 1981).

9. Minami Hiroshi (1914–), a distinguished Cornell-educated social psychologist known for his study of the Japanese personality and his historical analysis of *Nihonjinron*, or discourse on the Japanese character; his major works include *Nihonjin no shinri* (1953; trans., *Psychology of the Japanese People* [Honolulu: East-West Center, 1970]) and *Nihonjinron no keifu* (The genealogy of the discourse on the Japanese character [1980]).

10. The Kindai Bungaku coterie and its magazine of the same name (January 1946–August 1964) were highly significant in shaping postwar Japanese literature into the mid-1950s and beyond. The common war experience, sympathy with Marxism, and broad knowledge of Western literature helped its

were opposed to treating literature as a tool for political revolution in the way left-wing literature had been treated in the past. It was only natural for those who had devoted themselves so selflessly to the proletarian literary movement in the 1930s and suffered repeated hardships as a result of thinking in those terms. Because I myself had not experienced such anguish, for me the word "politics" first conjured up images of the strategies of the Occupation forces and of the conservative Japanese government rather than the Japanese Communist Party, which was, after all, a minority opposition party. On hearing the words "politics vis-à-vis literature," I didn't have the thinking or rhetorical habit to associate them instantly with the idea of "the revolutionary movement and literature." Now when I reflect on it, I realize that the Kindai Bungaku critics treated me with great generosity and kindness. But we did have a problem in communication.[11]

With the collapse of militarism, people began to emerge everywhere from the ruins of Tokyo, forming congenial groups and speaking out on issues they hadn't dared mention before. I most certainly didn't find myself in a "state of prostration"; what I saw was an age filled with great expectations. For the first time—and probably the last—I felt events

---

founding members—Honda Shūgo, Hirano Ken, Ara Masahito, Sasaki Kiichi, Yamamuro Shizuka, Odagiri Hideo, and Haniya Yutaka (who published his monumental metaphysical novel *Shirei* [Departed souls] in its first issues)— redefine the relationship between politics and literary imagination, between the individual and organizational collectivism, and reassess major prewar writers and the modern Japanese novel. Katō became a Kindai Bungaku member in July 1947 along with Nakamura Shin'ichirō and Fukunaga Takehiko. • The postwar "politics vis-à-vis literature" debate revived attempts since mid-Meiji to define the political and aesthetic dimensions of modern Japanese literature and set writers and critics who believed in the sociopolitical imperatives of literature as defined by Communist political agenda against those who upheld its artistic autonomy against intrusive politics; for more details see chapter 34, note 3.

11. The Matinée Poétique writers and the Kindai Bungaku critics were of roughly the same generation and agreed on the primacy of art over politics and the dignity of the individual over the collectivist impulse but not on all issues: Katō and Ara Masahito, for example, differed significantly in their ideas of the subjective self and their assessment of the Japanese literary tradition, as they did in personality and in war experiences. Nakamura Shin'ichirō in his memoirs *Sengo bungaku no kaisō* (Reminiscing about postwar literature) laments the failure to create a sense of solidarity with the Kindai Bungaku critics; see the summary on the subject in Matsubara Shin'ichi, Isoda Kōichi, and Akiyama Shun, *Zōho Kaitei Sengo Nihonbungakushi/nenpyō* (History and chronology of postwar Japanese literature, rev. ed. [Kōdansha, 1985]), 94–98.

were moving in my direction. I found many new friends, but at the same time I also discovered the difficulty of articulating ideas among ourselves. It was Japan in the immediate aftermath of the war, not Europe years later, that made me conscious of the problems involved in communication between those who speak different languages.

At the time when nameless young men like us were publishing coterie magazines and speaking our minds, a number of novelists living in Kamakura pooled their own resources and founded a publishing firm called Kamakura Bunko (Kamakura books). It published a literary monthly called *Ningen* (Humanity).[12] Its chief editor, Kimura Tokuzō, had read *1946: A Literary Inquiry*, and on one occasion he asked the three of us to contribute to his magazine. "Because this is your first time writing for us, I won't be able to pay you much," Mr. Kimura said. "As for subject matter, you're free to write anything you please." Before that time, I had never received manuscript fees. Thanks to Mr. Kimura's kindness and his magazine, I thus began my vocation as a writer.[13] Mr. Kimura knew the marketplace we called the *bundan* (literary world) inside out. He knew exactly whether the mix of a certain editor and a particular writer would set up a seller's or a buyer's market. And he impressed me as an editor who hoped to infuse his journal with idealistic literary spirit. Usui Yoshimi, the chief editor of the magazine *Tenbō* (Perspective), and Yoshino Genzaburō, the chief editor of *Sekai* (The world), shared this idealism.[14] This was a time when we were living on

12. Kamakura Bunko began as a lending library and became a publisher after the war. Its founders were Kume Masao, Kawabata Yasunari, and Takami Jun. • *Ningen* was published from January 1946 to August 1951.

13. Katō received his first manuscript fees for contributing the essay "Shinkō no seiki to shichinin no senkusha" (The century of faith and seven precursors) to *Ningen* in July 1947.

14. Usui Yoshimi (1905–87), a critic and novelist who wrote on Saitō Mokichi, Nakano Shigeharu, Hori Tatsuo, Shiga Naoya, and Mishima Yukio in *Ningen to bungaku* (Man and literature, 1957) and modern literary debates in *Kindai bungaku ronsō* (1956); his ambitious long novel *Azumino* (1965–74), set in his native Nagano Prefecture and Tokyo, won the Tenth Tanizaki Jun'ichirō Literary Prize. • *Tenbō* (January 1946–September 1951, and October 1964–August 1978 under Okayama Takeshi as chief editor), founded by Karaki Junzō, Nakamura Mitsuo, and Usui, was to be "a magazine we ourselves would like to read," and it serialized such major postwar works as Miyamoto Yuriko's *Dōhyō* (Guideposts), Ōoka Shōhei's *Nobi* (Fires on the plain), and Shiina Rinzō's *Shin'ya no shuen* (Midnight feast). • Yoshino Genzaburō (1899–1981), a critic and translator, who created the Iwanami shinsho (Iwanami new book) series at Iwanami shoten in

meager rations of food and clothing; the black market was thriving, and the red flags of the "rice movement" fluttered along the streets. Yet an indomitable spirit of idealism flourished in Tokyo. In *Ningen* I began to serialize *Aru hareta hi ni* (One fine day), a novel based on my experience during the war.[15]

While it was still an unsalaried position, I continued to work as a physician. In the first place, I had been working too long to get out of the habit; second, medicine itself was endlessly fascinating to me; and third, I thought I could still make a living practicing medicine should money become a problem in the future. The need for money, however, never arose. After I started to publish in *Ningen*, I could somehow make ends meet by accepting requests from newspapers and journals for manuscripts. And so I continued to live a life in which writing was my occupation and medicine my avocation, not the reverse.

In those days, I was often keenly aware of the conspicuous "backwardness" of Japan vis-à-vis the West. In my specialized area of hematology, Japan had made very little progress during the war, but meanwhile in the West pioneering work had been accomplished. We already knew about this through our contact with American scholars in Hiroshima. But the Western sources we had in our university library only went up to the late 1930s—giving us no way to learn about the details of Western progress. I discussed the matter with Dr. Nakao, and through the good offices of First Lieutenant L, we got a special pass to go inside Tsukiji's St. Luke's Hospital, at that time requisitioned by the Occupation forces.

At the hospital gate, we saw a posted bill that read "Those who enter without permission will be shot." After showing our pass to the armed guards, we were allowed to walk through the hospital corridor with the American doctors and nurses and into the library. There I avidly read the new American medical journals. Until the late 1930s, the field of hematology, developed primarily in Germany and Austria, had dealt with

---

1938 and was chief editor of *Sekai* from 1946 to 1965; on his role as spokesman for postwar democratic thought see Suzuki Tadashi, *Senchū to sengo seishin* (Keisō shobō, 1983), 3–27. • *Sekai* (January 1946–) remains one of the most influential and widely read journals among the Japanese intelligentsia today.

15. The novel, which began Katō's career as a novelist (serialized in *Ningen* [January–August 1949]), is set in Karuizawa and Tokyo during the air raids and its protagonist is a young physician, the author's alter ego.

the microscopic morphology of hemocyte and hematogenous tissues, an area we knew very well. But during the war, by focusing on the study of blood transfusion, researchers had made progress in figuring out the thitherto highly obscure mechanism of blood coagulation. The electrophoresis of blood plasma protein had come to be widely practiced. What had until then been nearly independent studies of areas such as morphology, serology (the observation of antigens and the reaction of antibodies inside a test tube), and the chemical analysis of blood constituents had now become mutually relevant. To us, this meant the discovery of new methodologies and, for all practical purposes, the emergence of a new area of study. When we saw the specialized journals on hematology from America in the St. Luke's Hospital library, we became keenly aware of our ignorance about what had happened outside Japan, how the world had changed as a consequence, and how serious our "backwardness" was. It almost reminded me of the bygone days of *Rangaku kotohajime* (The beginning of Dutch learning).[16] If my work in hematology had any significance to speak of, it was perhaps in my assistance of Nakao Kiku and Miyoshi Kazuo, the two scholars who, after the war in their poorly equipped study, devoted their energies so totally to redeeming Japan's backwardness. Late one winter night in his makeshift study built in the corridor of the university hospital, Dr. Miyoshi rubbed his freezing hands over a small electric heater under his table as he put together perhaps one of Japan's first devices for the electrophoresis of blood plasma protein. "Until we have the equipment, I'm afraid we can't have any clinical study," said Dr. Miyoshi. "But this freezing temperature is unbearable." The only warm place in winter was the library at St. Luke's Hospital.

I felt that Japan's backwardness was not limited only to the field of hematology. During the war, while many Japanese writers ingratiated themselves with the militarist authorities, sang praises of fascism, and allowed literature to degenerate into a total wasteland, many French poets were waging their resistance against Germany's national socialism, denouncing fascism, and breathing new life into literature by champi-

16. *Rangaku kotohajime,* completed in 1815 and published in 1869, was a 2-vol. memoir by the physician and scholar Sugita Gempaku (1733–1817) on the development of *Rangaku* (Dutch learning) from mid-Edo translations and interpretations that marked a systematic Japanese effort to learn Western medicine, astronomy, geography, physics, chemistry, and the military sciences.

oning the cause of human freedom and dignity. I learned from the book exhibition at the l'Institut franco-japonais about how poets who fell silent before the war quickly returned to their vibrant selves and how new writers, unknown before the war, were now competing with one another. That was an unprecedented and inspiring development. No one could deny the spiritual backwardness among Japanese literary intellectuals. The fact that Japanese writers could not produce a literature of resistance against fascism was, of course, due to the absence of any popular antifascist feelings around them, just as the complete reverse was true in France. The differences between our writers and their French counterparts, I thought, must ultimately mean the difference between the premodern and the modern mentality—between the idea of the Japanese people as "subjects" and the French people as "citizens," between the Japanese Imperial Rescript on Education and the French Déclaration des droits de l'homme, and between the Japanese notion of the way of the Shintō gods and Descartes's spirit of rationalism.[17] But my way of thinking oversimplified the facts: the Pétain government was a puppet regime created by a foreign power, while the Tōjō government was not. And insofar as my thinking was premised on the French national sentiment, something I knew practically nothing about, my thinking was also inaccurate.

One time Nakamura Shin'ichirō and I visited Professor Takeyama Michio in Kamakura.[18] Every now and then when our conversation turned to the backwardness of the Japanese masses, Professor Takeyama with his keen insight immediately saw through such flaws in my argument. Outside the window of the Takeyama residence, the pine forest rustled in the ocean breeze. Clad in his informal kimono, Professor Takeyama would calmly puff away on his cigarette as he listened to what I, in my youthful rashness, had to say on the subject. Then he said, "But the

17. From 1890 to its annulment by the Diet in June 1948, the conservative Meiji Imperial Rescript on Education established the absolute standards of national morality and defined the fundamental principles of education. Occasional later efforts by conservative politicians and intellectuals to "reevaluate" it testify to its resilient spirit.

18. Takeyama Michio (1903–84), a critic, scholar of German literature, and novelist (*Biruma no tategoto* [Harp of Burma, 1947–48; Eng. trans. by Howard Hibbett, 1966], a novel about Japanese wartime experience in Burma), also wrote studies on the origins of ideology in Japan and Germany, the role of modernity in war, ancient Japanese art, and the political situations in Nazi Germany and the Communist-bloc countries in Europe.

masses are the same everywhere! They are all stupid enough to be duped by stupid propaganda. I have seen enough of that in Germany. It was by no means true only in Japan. . . ." Until that time, I had never seen Europe, and I had never spoken any of their languages. I had read a few books, but Professor Takeyama must have read and known at least ten times as much as I did. I was by no means convinced by his ideas, but I could not refute his arguments. Are the masses the same everywhere? Later, after living in Europe myself, I came to agree substantially with the professor. But at the same time, I was also able to see through the flaws in his argument. I wasn't mistaken about Japan's backwardness; I exaggerated it.

My reading of French Résistance literature not only strengthened my conviction about Japan's backwardness, it also forced me to realize how immature my understanding of French literature had been. For instance, I had read through the bulk of François Mauriac's writings, but my understanding in no way prepared me to imagine that one day this Catholic writer would join hands with the Communists and throw himself into the network of Résistance writers. And even though I was not entirely ignorant of the works of Louis Aragon and Drieu La Rochelle, the images I formed of these writers put me at a loss to explain the source of Aragon's movingly beautiful poetry written during the occupation of France, or the motives for Drieu La Rochelle's collaboration with the Germans and his suicide at the time of France's liberation. In other words, it was obvious that something was missing either from my reading or from my perception of French writers. Also, while Jean-Paul Sartre and Albert Camus had taken the world by storm with their dramatic emergence after the war, it was difficult to grasp the core of their writings without altering the way one normally perceived and read literature. I realized how backward Japan was in terms of its intellectual discipline. The question went beyond novelistic techniques. It was necessary to make a fresh start on more fundamental issues. I was young; I felt that there was nothing I couldn't do, and I thought I had all the time in the world to assemble my tools before I started to work. Instead of justifying Japan's backwardness and more so my own backwardness, I thought the new age for our recovery was opened infinitely into the future. The only person who questioned whether Japan and the Japanese had really changed was my teacher Watanabe Kazuo. As a few of us gathered and talked about new currents of thought overseas and our reform ideals—come to think of it, these two things had been inseparably intertwined since Meiji, or rather, since the days of the Japanese missions to the capital of T'ang China—Professor Watanabe said, "Shall we listen to some music?"[19] The song that poured forth from the gramophone blared, "We'll return with our victories, you'll see! / After we have pledged this heroic vow and gone to the battlefield overseas."

"Isn't it a good idea to listen to this kind of song from time to time, just to help us remember the past . . ."

And sure enough, throughout the twenty years after the war, that song kept on reverberating inside my ears. But there were also times when we needed to let our angry screams drown out its noise.

19. From 630 to 894, Japanese envoys made sixteen overseas missions to Chang-an, the capital of the T'ang dynasty; the Buddhist monks and students who accompanied them were instrumental in introducing continental culture to Japan.

24   Gardens in Kyoto

Because of *her*, I often went to Kyoto. I thought I was in love. Perhaps I was thinking that being in love and thinking I was in love were, ultimately, one and the same thing. And if the phrase "to be in love" means anything at all, I thought it meant the degree to which I could act in the interest of the person I loved.

She spoke the Kyoto dialect with a soft, delicate voice as if she were singing a song. Even the most mundane words came out of her lips with an indescribable charm. For a Tokyoite like me, there was an exotic air to her speech, and yet at the same time I felt the reassurance of a familiar intimacy. It was not that I thought the Kyoto dialect was particularly beautiful; I just knew how incomparably beautiful it could be. I told her I had never heard a more tender language. Her bright, clear eyes smiling, she said she could be hopelessly stubborn all the same. Perhaps she was only stubborn toward those who believed women were not supposed to be stubborn. It was only fair to say that it was virtually impossible to convince her of anything without first starting a debate. Though born and raised in Kyoto, she seldom went into the city. Her late husband, a Buddhist scholar who seemed to have immersed himself in the study of consciousness, had died when he was still young. She herself did not really have any serious interest in Buddhism. She led a quiet life taking care of their only child, an elementary school student who attended a neighborhood school. In her dimly lit house the whiteness of her face seemed to glow in the shadowy darkness.

Before I knew it, I had formed a habit of strolling the streets of Kyoto alone or paying solitary visits to old temples whenever an occasion presented itself. In those days, complete tranquillity could always be found in any of the old temple gardens in Kyoto. In early winter, the stones in Ryōanji's rock garden cast long shadows under the afternoon sun. In the spring, the moss at Saihōji, moistened by the rain, appeared radiant here and there under rays of sun filtering through the trees for nobody else but me to see.[1] This was the same Kyoto that had existed in the Muromachi period, a city free of tourists and the noise of automobiles. This was also a city whose many temples and their gardens were completely forgotten by contemporary Japan. In those days, Tokyo was so busy translating, interpreting, and discussing Western ideas that almost no one seemed to be interested in looking back on the ancient civilizations of East Asia. In Kanda's secondhand bookstores, classical Chinese works were dirt cheap, and the tables of contents of magazines or the titles of new books seldom made mention of ancient Japanese art. You might say that I took advantage of this period to purchase classical Chinese works with what little money I had, to visit old temples, and to enjoy the designs of the remaining medieval gardens.

And then one autumn afternoon in the garden of a Zen temple, I had quite an extraordinary experience. Its design was nothing unusual—just a small garden unpretentiously taking advantage of Kyoto's Eastern Hills as its distant background and with a "dry landscape garden" layout in the foreground.[2] But the garden's complexion never stopped changing with every passing moment. No sooner had the afternoon sun cast bright rays on the fall colors of the Eastern Hills than clouds suddenly veiled it, instantaneously turning the dry garden an ashy gray. Just a hint of the sun reemerging quickly gave way to droplets of silvery rain coming down noiselessly on the white sands, rejuvenating the moss-covered rocks on the stone pavement with a lustrous luminescence. I was gazing at one garden and more than one garden. Expressions of joy and sadness, gaiety and grief flashed one after the other across the landscape,

1. The famed rock garden of the Zen temple Ryōanji, said to have been designed by the late Muromachi painter and *renga* (linked-verse) poet Sōami (Shinsō [?]–1525), consists only of white sand, stones, and pebbles and creates impressions described as islands on an ocean, or tigers crossing a river. • Saihōji's garden, known for the beauty of its moss, was designed in the early Muromachi period.

2. Kyoto's Higashiyama with its graceful contour is often regarded as representative of the natural beauty of the city. • The *karesansui* design typically uses pebbles, sand, and rocks to represent mountains and rivers; its greatest popularity was in the Muromachi period.

each changing movement merging exquisitely into what could only be described as a restrained stylistic unity that transcended the garden's particular appearance at any one moment. To be sure, I was just a beginner when it came to Japanese gardens, and what I was experiencing must have been something akin to curiosity. Nonetheless, at that moment and quite without any presentiment, I could feel with incredible certitude a world more intimate than anything I had previously thought possible. It must have been due to my unequivocal understanding of that world and to the unmistakable fact that something in me was a part of that world. By being away from my native Tokyo, I encountered an authentic entity, an authentic relationship linking my external and internal selves. Kyoto is the other hometown I discovered when I was away from my own. Could I have been reading in Kyoto every imaginable movement and expression of a single woman? No, I don't suppose that was the case; what I was looking at was probably the reflection of that world within a woman.

From that time, I developed an interest, beyond Japanese gardens, in Buddhist sculptures and painting. I also wrote many essays, not only on Japanese art, but also on matters that bore no direct relationship at all to Japanese art. I began by writing "Nihon no niwa" (Japanese gardens), and fifteen years later, I wrote "Shisendō shi" (Account of the Hall of Poetry Immortals).[3] I did not learn about the value of Japanese art from what I saw in the West. On the contrary, it was only after I saw in an autumn afternoon the effects of the setting sun on the slopes of Kyoto's Eastern Hills and the rain falling on the white sands in the dry landscape garden that I began to develop an interest in observing the West.

During the screening test for my application to study abroad, my interviewer asked me in French, "What sort of French writers are you especially fond of?" My struggles to provide an appropriate answer to that question came from the fact that I had not gotten used to speaking French. My astonishment at the question, however, had nothing to do with the language. It was true that I had read some French writers, but until then I had never asked myself that question before. Or rather, I had not read any writers in such a way that would allow me to give a

---

3. "Nihon no niwa," in *Shōwa bungaku zenshū*, 28:584–97. • "Shisendō shi," in ibid., 28:541–53. See its English version in J. Thomas Rimer, Jonathan Chaves, et al., *Shisendō: Hall of the Poetry Immortals* (New York: Weatherhill, 1991).

prompt and confident answer to that question. And surely, to decide whom I was "especially fond of" was not a point one could address properly on the spot. And before I contemplated the issue at all, first there must be an unwavering commitment of love and attachment to the subject matter—like the kind of authentic relationship between the object and me as I stood face to face with the garden in Kyoto. To articulate that relationship, I had to return to Japanese poetry from the days of the *Kokinshū*, to the flowing accent in the speech of the one woman I knew, and to the evening sky over Dōgenzaka from my window on the second floor of my Shibuya home during my childhood—endless thoughts that flowed from memories going back half my life. When it came to Western literature, it was true that my appreciation of certain aspects of it was sufficiently solid that I did not find my grasp of it to be elusive. But I had never felt that my understanding was as authentic as the experience I had when I stood before the garden in Kyoto. It was only after I saw the garden that I became aware of this. Western culture and classical Japanese culture—how were they different to me? I felt at that time that it would be dishonest of me to go any further without answering that question. I was not thinking that I could find the answer by going to the West. But then there was no reason to postpone my trip either.

I mentioned earlier that Mother was not in the best of health. She had a heart disease, and occasionally she also exhibited the complex symptoms of autonomic ataxia. These conditions had continued for a long time, and in the end she developed stomach cancer. Her operation at the Tokyo University Hospital went well despite her heart condition. But at that time, it was impossible to tell whether metastasis had taken place. If it had not, and because Mother was still young, she could live a long life; otherwise, she had only several months to live and there was nothing medicine could do for her. After discussing the matter with Father, we decided to tell her that her operation revealed no cancer. For a physician, that was just a matter of conventional wisdom.[4] After she returned home to our rental house in Meguro Ward on her discharge from

4. For Japanese physicians, the issue of giving cancer patients the facts about their medical history remains controversial: only 29.5 percent of Japanese physicians in a 1995 study told their cancer patients about their diagnosis, and over 80 percent in northern Europe and the United States did (*Kawahoku shimpō*, September 10, 1995). A 1993 survey by the Ministry of Public Welfare reported that only 18 percent of patients who died of cancer had learned about their illness (*Yomiuri Shimbun*, September 7, 1993).

the hospital, her postoperative recovery went better than we had expected. But talking face to face with her about her illness was an agonizing experience for me.

"There were signs of stomach ulcer. Because that might turn into stomach cancer, they removed it just to be on the safe side," I said.

"If that's all there is to it, it looks like I'll recover soon."

"Oh, sure. You'll recover."

As I was speaking to Mother, I thought about the possibility of metastasis. I was the only person who knew she might have only a short time to live.

On her sickbed, Mother composed Japanese poems in her notebook, saying it was like writing a diary. One poem said that she would have no regrets even if she were to die, now that her children were all grown. Another said she had no worries about her daughter because everybody liked her amiable character. On the other hand, other poems revealed her anxiety over her son's future because of his fiery temperament. Mother loved to travel, but she had seldom had an opportunity to do so. She loved to socialize, but we seldom had guests. She was fond of good food, but now her only nourishment came from a liquid diet and injections. Even in her condition, she still chatted with my aunt who lived next door and with my sister, who came to visit every day. Her optimism and cheerfulness never left her until the very end.

I told jokes to entertain the people in Mother's sickroom, and meanwhile I was reminded of Hiroshima. Just as the victims had rejoiced over their survival, a few weeks later symptoms of atomic radiation began to appear. At the height of their jubilation for having so narrowly escaped the clutch of death, the effects of atomic radiation struck them down like a second bomb when they least suspected it. I wanted to do everything I could for Mother as long as she was alive. But by that time all I could do was pray.

But Mother's condition began to deteriorate even before she had fully recovered from her operation. It was no longer possible to hold out any hope for her. There had been a metastasis and its symptoms had appeared. The patient was beyond help. When she told me her pain was getting worse, I could find no words to say. I tried to do as much as possible to alleviate Mother's sufferings and at the same time to prolong her life, totally exhausted by the impossible task of reconciling these inherently conflicting goals. Witnessing the agony I could not bear to witness, my mind was confused. In consultation with Father, I could only barely decide on the immediate course of action, but I could not bring myself to think about anything else.

Many weeks like that went by, and when Mother died after suffering the worst, I felt that everything inside me had turned into a void.[5] I registered neither joy nor grief; my only sensation was profound fatigue. For a while I was totally stupefied. That the funeral left virtually no impression on me must reflect the fact that I had lost interest in all the things around me. It was true that after a short while I returned to my work at the university hospital, but I cannot remember how I felt or what I did with any clarity either. My only clear recollections were images of Mother's face and words that surfaced erratically in my memory whenever I was alone at night. Then came the truly unbearable feeling of losing them all forever. The source of infinite love had vanished from my world, and I could no longer concern myself with what would become of it. In the brightness of day, the ordinary everyday scene around the open ditch near our house would suddenly lose its color and turn into an unfamiliar and totally alien scene. My past was buried inside of me, and it alone had the feel of reality. Outside, there was nothing but a dream.

With the passage of time, I was able to reflect more calmly on Mother's death. For the first time, I was assailed by an intense feeling of remorse. I wished I could have done this or that, and the list was endless. Even though some of the things would have been impossible for me to do, I thought repeatedly that at least I could have accomplished some of the others if only I had summoned my will to do so. I came to hate and loathe myself. But that was not all. Meanwhile, I also began to think of my own life in terms of an early and a later half, with Mother's death as the line of demarcation. When I realized that the center of gravity, if you will, of my world in these two phases had shifted, the thought surprised me, because until then I had not been dependent on Mother; rather it was she who had been dependent on me. But after I lost her, I soon became acutely aware of the fact that I was drifting away from a world in which I had been blessed with unconditional trust and love, to another in which I could hardly expect to enjoy the same again. I realized that I had to seek and create for myself another source of trust and love. The woman in Kyoto did not change this fact in the least.

A Catholic priest had been called to Mother's deathbed, and he ad-

5. She died on May 30, 1949.

ministered the appropriate rites. I thought Mother might have believed in Catholicism. As a matter of fact, that was why I, a non-Catholic, also agreed to the idea of summoning a priest. But there was a reason why I said Mother "might" have been a convert instead of simply saying she "was" one. First of all, I suppose the substance of "religious belief" itself is difficult to understand in isolation from one's religious experience. And besides, even though Mother might think she believed in God, it seemed to me the nature of this god had turned into something very different from the god she had been taught about at her Catholic school when she was young.

"I only wish you two would become converts," she once said jokingly. "So when we die, we can meet in Heaven."

"But we don't know if we can go to Heaven or not," Sister replied.

"I think anyone with a good heart will go to Heaven," Mother said.

What she said seemed not to be very different from the idea that anyone kind in heart and righteous in deed can go to Heaven, regardless of whether he or she was a convert. In fact, when it became apparent that both Sister and I would not become Catholic converts, Mother became more inclined to think in those terms. Because she firmly believed in the good nature of children—and as far as she herself was concerned, it was not unreasonable that she should have felt that way—she seemed unable to bring herself to believe that a righteous god would impose punishment on one's good intentions. She once said, "I think there's something strange in what the priest preaches. If everything on earth is explained away as God's will, then the death of children would also be His will. . . ." Then she went on to say, "There are many types of priests, and there are some who don't think very deeply." Unless there was some special occasion, she did not visit her church, and only rarely did she go on Sunday. "More than these perfunctory conventions, I think it's what you feel inside that really matters."

One might say Father had succeeded in convincing Mother to act this way, but he failed to convince her of atheism. I myself did not see any need for the latter, and I found it unfortunate that I could not share Mother's faith. Even many years after Mother's death, when I sometimes thought about my own death, I would imagine, for no reason at all, that I would die of cancer. Moreover, I even thought that if there was such a thing as Heaven, that was where Mother would certainly be, and perhaps I could see her there once again.

Mother was not pleased about my trips to Kyoto, though marriage was on my mind. Yet my desire to see the West also intensified after Mother's death. This was a time when the medical school at the university was beginning to send students to study in the United States. If I had been given the opportunity to go at that time, I would probably have ended up becoming a natural scientist, devoting myself to research in a laboratory at some American university and playing a hard game of tennis in my spare time. I had already obtained my degree in Tokyo and I was sufficiently interested in my specialized field to want to work at some well-equipped research facility.[6] But I myself did not seek after such an opportunity, and it, on its part, never knocked at my door. What I had longed for was a chance to go and live for a while in France, the country whose literature I had been reading, even if I were to do no medical research there.

Such an opportunity was not easy to come by while Japan was under the Occupation. The first postwar recruitment for French government-sponsored students was not open to the public; applicants were nominated. One of the people selected to go was Assistant Professor Mori Arimasa of the Department of French Literature, and his experience in France changed his life thereafter. The second round of recruitment was open to the public. I took the examination but was not selected as a scholarship recipient, though I passed as a "half-scholarship student." What this meant was that if I could afford my own two-way transportation and living expenses, the French government would waive my tuition and offer other conveniences like giving me a visa to stay in France. In those days the Japanese government did not even have the authority to issue passports, and leaving the country was next to impossible for ordinary Japanese citizens even if they could support themselves. In this respect, the status of a "half-scholarship student" was crucial because it eliminated that difficulty. My problem was whether or not I could come up with the necessary funds. I worked around the clock doing translations to earn my travel expenses, and I planned to live on my manuscript fees as a correspondent in France for some local newspapers in Japan.

If the woman in Kyoto had at that time strongly objected to my plans of going abroad, I probably would not have left. If so, my life thereafter would most certainly have been very different. But she raised no objections. Not only did she make no attempt to stop me; she did not even

6. Katō received his M.D. from Tokyo University in February 1950 at the age of thirty-one.

utter a single word of protest about my trip. I was left with a sort of un-fulfilled expectation, but on the other hand my heart was even more deeply moved. I told her that my trip would only be for a year, and I promised to write regularly. I also told her that anytime she needed me, I would always be prepared to return.

"Let's think about getting married after I come back."

"Yes, when you do. . . ." she replied.

In Tokyo, I had just begun my career as a writer. And in Kyoto, little by little, I was also beginning to see the delicate relationship between my long-beloved Japanese poetry on the one hand, and the Japanese cultural landscape on the other. It was true that I hoped to see the West with my own eyes, but I most certainly did not want to leave Japan behind. I did not have the slightest intention of disrupting my life and work for more than a year, and I seriously meant every word I said to her at the time. I never dreamed that I would live in Europe for any substantial length of time, let alone that those years of my sojourn would change me so fundamentally.

I returned to the gardens in Kyoto many years later. But I did not return to the woman whom I had thought I loved so much.

25   The Second Beginning

In the fall of 1945 I started my journey into postwar Japanese society, and in the fall of 1951, I departed for the West as an observer. That turned out to be the second beginning of my life. My intent then was to find out for myself as much as possible what "the West"—as we knew it in Japanese society, and hence "the West" in me—was all about in its authentic context. But of course things did not always turn out the way I planned, and "the West" turned out to be something more than just an object of observation.

The trip from Tokyo by air did not take long. When I saw the city lights of Paris for the first time through the car window after leaving Orly airport, I was reminded of the street lights I saw as our car was heading toward Haneda. It was not easy to convince myself that I had in fact traveled this far. "That's the Seine," said one of my friends who had been good enough to pick me up at the airport. They were Mori Arimasa, who had come a year earlier, and Miyake Noriyoshi, who had arrived just a month before I did. But instead of thinking about the Seine, I was meditating vaguely about the enormous distance I had traveled.

Of course I had not forgotten my two-day trip as the plane went through the southern route. The noise of mah-jongg tiles showering down from the windows on both sides of Hong Kong's narrow streets, the dense rain forests of Southeast Asia extending into the infinite distance, the Karachi airport in the middle of the night, the white deserts of Syria, the Dead Sea, the unfamiliar mannerisms of men and women with sunglasses at Beirut airport in the morning, the gemlike Prussian blue waters of the Mediterranean, the rosy peaks of the Matterhorn under the evening sun. . . . These distinct but mutually exclusive images filled my mind. I knew there had to be some significance in each and every one of these images. But when exposed to them all at once, it was plainly impossible to reflect on what they might mean as a whole.

Instead, I was thinking more about the one single consistent experience I had had from the time I boarded my plane at Haneda until my arrival in Paris, the experience of being in a world in which the Japanese language could no longer serve to convey intent. It is true that in Hiroshima I spoke English with the American doctors. But that was simply an exercise of periodically translating my ideas into English in an otherwise authentic Japanese setting; the totality of my milieu was not sustained through the medium of the English language. On the plane, I had already begun to feel that if I had to express every thought I had in a foreign language, it would inevitably affect the substance of my thinking as well. I knew I could get by if I simply translated my thoughts from Japanese whenever the need arose, but surely that would not allow me to achieve any understanding of the world around me from within. To interpret the world in which I had become a willing participant meant that in the process I myself would have to change, or that world would cease to be comprehensible. In this sense, the new world I was entering was fundamentally different from the one I had known. As I was looking at the distant lights from the plane's tiny window when it began its takeoff from the runway of Haneda airport, I could feel a rift separating the worlds inside and outside the airplane. At that time, and all at once, the distance separating me from Tokyo grew so enormous that even when I arrived in Paris, finished the entry formalities, and left by car, I did not feel that the discrepancy had grown any greater.

In Paris, I first lived in the university area in the fourteenth arrondissement. Many countries had built dormitories here for their own students, one of which was Japan House, in one of whose rooms I took up residence. In those days, the number of Japanese students in Paris was still small, and two-thirds of the students in Japan House were not Japanese. We had to walk quite a distance to the central cafeteria for our three meals, and since this was the place where foreign students from the other dormitories also congregated, I soon had friends among students outside Japan House as well. But those were only superficial friendships. The language barrier was part of the reason. Besides, there was also a feeling that something was lacking between us. With Miyake, a fellow resident of Japan House, and Mori, who boarded in the downtown area, we could speak Japanese. Even if my French had been completely proficient, it would have been hard to expect the same degree of intellectual stimulation from foreign students in their late teens or early twenties.

But of course there were exceptions. Soon after I took up residence at Japan House, I got to know a philosophy student from Brittany. He was fond of the old buildings on the île St-Louis and the prose of Saint-Simon. He listened to Debussy and read Nietzsche, and despite his youth he already seemed to have acquired an air of solitary dignity.

"I think there's an aristocratic element in the character of French culture," he once said.

"At the same time it also had a popular tradition, exemplified by the storming of the Bastille," I remarked then.

Our debate continued like this well into the night. Each room in our dormitory had only a bed, a table, and a chair, with neither sheets on the bed nor a single painting on the walls. On the table there was nothing but a pile of books, a bottle of wine, and an ashtray filled with stubs of Gauloises.

At that time, I did not intentionally provoke him into an argument. I was interested in his way of thinking, and I was only trying to make him clarify his position by playing the devil's advocate. And in order to do that, I had to defend the position I had taken. As a result, I ended up speaking in French the whole night long, trying to adapt to the rhetoric my opponent used so effectively and apply it to my own arguments by manipulating a still unfamiliar language. At the beginning, it was an exceedingly painstaking exercise. But once I grew accustomed to it, the task was less strenuous. I didn't learn to speak French before I got into debates; it was rather because I already found myself embroiled in debates that I somehow learned to express my ideas, however terribly clumsy my French was. I was myself conscious of that, and I also knew what it meant. The distance between me and my outside world very quickly diminished.

What I acquired from my friendship with the young man from Brittany was not just the habit of getting into debates. As soon as I began to speak French, I found out that I had never properly read French writings. My friend was good enough to read carefully to me Valéry's *Eupalinos et l'architecte*, a work written in the form of a dialogue. Why did the author use this particular expression and not another in this particular context, and why did he choose to say something in this particular way and not in another? For questions like these, a French-Japanese dictionary was just about useless. In Tokyo I had read Valéry's work with considerable care with the aid of French-Japanese dictionaries and its English translation, and I thought I understood it well. But what I had in fact understood was just the plot. In Tokyo, I thought that I could read and understand Valéry and that speaking French was hard. In the university district of Paris, I began to realize that speaking French was not that hard, but reading Valéry was no easy task.

My friend repeatedly asked me the following question about Japan: "In Japanese writings, is there such a thing that could properly be called style in the French sense of the word?"

"Perhaps not in exactly the same sense. But there is something equivalent to it."

But my answer did not satisfy him. At that point, we had to take up the intricate question of how to define the idea of style in Japanese.[1] One of his young friends had started to write a novel, but he said that he had no desire to experiment with any ungainly works until he himself could be fully satisfied with his own writing style. That attitude often reminded me of my own experience when I was about twenty. My knowledge of Russian novelists, French poets, and German philosophers was probably much broader than his, but my ties with the Japanese language and the Japanese classics were apparently not as deep-seated as those that connected this French youth to his mother tongue and its national classics. My own literary cultivation was broadly international but shallow; his ran deeply into the fabric of his own national history. Our contrast left a strong impression in me. Many years later, when I wrote about Japan's "hybrid culture" and emphasized the possibilities latent in the Japanese cultural environment, I was reminded of the experience I had had in the Parisian university district. I described a broadly based, cosmopolitan literacy as "hybrid," and a profound, depth-oriented literacy as "authentic." I argued that it was no longer possible for contemporary Japanese to choose freely between these two categories and that accordingly their only option was to seek out the positive qualities in the "hybrid" form.

In the university district, I was also acquainted with a black American painter. She was taller than I was and had a well-proportioned and

1. More than three decades later, Katō and the literary critic Maeda Ai coedited *Buntai* (Literary style), vol. 16 in Iwanami shoten's *Nihon kindai shisō taikei* series; see Katō's accompanying essay ("Meiji shoki no buntai," 16:449–81) on the literary style of the early Meiji period.

really attractive figure. She was working in oils at an art school, and one time she showed me one of her works and asked me to give her my honest opinion about it and about her future prospects as a painter.

"I don't know about the future," I replied. "But as far as this painting is concerned, it's not an accomplished work yet, only an amateur's."

"I can tell this myself," she said frankly.

"But I like your works."

It was true that I liked the painting she showed me, but more than that I was fond of her. In our excitement after visiting an art exhibition, we would sit down in a nearby café and have long talks about paintings, painters, America, and France. As we were watching the busy stream of pedestrians at the place d'Alma, she said, "I don't want to go back to America." Another time, she said, "In Paris, since everybody speaks English, I can never learn to speak French."

"You must be joking. In their tenacity for their mother tongue, the French have few equals, don't you think?"

"But aren't we speaking English right now?" At this, we laughed together for no particular reason.

She also introduced me to a young black man she called her cousin. And she sometimes brought along a German painter who was making his living as a guide for foreigners at the Louvre. Once they dropped in on me at Japan House with another young American. "I brought him along because he said he has something to ask you," she said. The American's question was so utterly out of the ordinary that at first I wondered if he was joking. But he was dead serious.

"Do you think that religion, or faith if you will, is absolutely necessary in life?"

"Generally speaking, I'd say no," I replied.

"But for me. . . ." he went on.

"Well, I suppose it depends on the individual," I repeated myself. There was little else I could say.

"What kind of people do you think need it?"

"Now just a second. The very question about need may be immaterial," I said. "Even if someone answers yes, it doesn't mean he's got a religious faith. And even if someone answers no, I suppose those who choose to have faith will."

The American, a mechanical engineer I was told, listened intently without saying a word. I decided to change the subject.

"Religious faith is like love. You don't fall in love because it's necessary. Even if there is no such need, you fall in love when the moment comes."

"Now I'm thinking about what love is," he answered.

With a grin, the German painter muttered as if talking to himself, "In this time and age, I suppose only Americans are capable of asking what love is!"

The American engineer then proceeded to explain that there were three types of love—spiritual love, physical love, and a blend of the two. The first type was more easily said than practiced, the second was unseemly, and therefore it was the third type . . . Americans in Paris, and this engineer in particular, seemed to have descended to earth from a distant star somewhere. They were incredibly good-natured, they told jokes at the most incredible moments, and they were incredibly blockheaded in appreciating jokes. And they became my friends. Years later when I met them again in America, one of them cursed social injustice in America, another felt contented for having found common bonds between Paris and New York City, yet another had managed to fit in so well with his surroundings that he no longer betrayed even the slightest trace of his former incredible self. And all of them extended to me their warm friendship and went out of their way to make a foreign traveler like me feel at home.

In those days, only a few Japanese lived in Paris. The embassy had not yet been established, but Mr. Hagiwara, later the Japanese ambassador, was already at the office which served as the forerunner to the embassy. A tall man of slender build, Ambassador Hagiwara was fluent in both English and French, was fond of the theater, and when at leisure he conversed very perceptively about literary matters.[2] And then there was the sculptor Takata Hiroatsu, who had left Japan at a young age and made his home in France even during the war years. I was greatly indebted to him, a subject I would surely return to later. Paris also provided me with the opportunity to meet Asabuki Tomiko.[3] A resident in Paris before

2. Hagiwara Tōru (1906–79). A graduate of Tokyo University, Hagiwara was head of the Japan Liaison Office in Paris in 1950 and Japanese minister to France in 1952. Before serving as ambassador to France in 1961, he had been Japanese ambassador to Switzerland and Canada.

3. On Asabuki Tomiko see chapter 26, note 6; and on Takata Hiroatsu, chapter 12, note 5.

the war, she returned earlier than anyone else after it ended and took up residence at the house of the poet René Arcos. After I left Japan House, I too began to live in the Arcos residence.

During the time when I was living in Japan House, I attended the Faculty of Medicine at the University of Paris.[4] The faculty chair, an old man with a head of white hair, made his rounds along with his attending staff, just as we had done at the university hospital in Tokyo. In more than a few instances, the conversation at the patients' ward turned to national or international issues. One day he suddenly turned to me and asked, "Do you think the American army in Korea is using germ warfare?" The Korean War was at its height at that time, and when I replied that I didn't know, the professor asserted, "I think they might just be doing that." One time when a young female outpatient appeared naked before him, he said something like, "Wow! What a spectacular pair of breasts!" This kind of wisecrack would be difficult to imagine in Tokyo. But as far as the practice of medicine was concerned, one would not expect to find fundamental differences between Tokyo and Paris, and in fact I could safely say there weren't any. To be sure, the manner of discourse at conferences was not the same; the composition of the research staff was different; and perhaps there was a certain peculiarly French proclivity in choosing research topics. But these were not fundamental issues.

The fundamental differences between Tokyo and Paris, I felt, lay outside the hospital and the research laboratory. The massive, solid stone buildings on both sides of the streets gave the impression that the whole city of Paris was a piece of elaborate sculpture. The stone structures accentuated the green of the trees lining both sides of the streets. To me, even the thin slice of gray sky squeezed in between buildings had a different appeal, and indeed a stronger appeal, than the wide open sky of Tokyo. During the days when I was living at Japan House, I loved to walk the streets of Paris. There I found a space completely different from what I had known before, and its spatial order never for a moment ceased to fascinate me. Why, for no practical reason, was I so fond of strolling along the streets of Paris? Reflecting on it now, I find it hard to explain. Certainly it was not from any interest on my part in city planning, nor was it the result of curiosity about celebrated spots or places of historic interest. I didn't even bother to see the tomb of Napoleon. Whether Victor Hugo had lived in the place des Vosges or Delacroix

4. Katō studied at the Institut Curie within the Institut Pasteur.

in Furstenberg did not change the significance of those squares as far as I was concerned.

I suppose the only explanation I can give is that in Paris I was looking at the externalized core of a culture, an entity that had become objectified to allow appreciation through our sensory perception. That cultural core has remained essentially intact from perhaps around the twelfth century until this day, linking the past to the present with its strong, unmistakable bonds. This does not only mean that the buildings dating back to the twelfth century are still standing in the center of Paris along with the representative structures of the succeeding eras. What it also means is that the impression I got from the church designs of the twelfth and thirteenth centuries was not totally divorced from my impression of Paris on the banks of the Seine. In both instances, I perceived the strong will that had externalized an impulse from within the framework of a sensory order. This was something I had never experienced in Tokyo. As I walked along the streets of Paris, I felt as if I were being drawn into a world of unfathomable depths. What was happening to me? I could not help thinking that, more than my work at the laboratory, my more urgent and immediate task was to delve to the bottom of this mystery.

I did not travel all the way to Paris in order to meet other Japanese. But once I was there, meeting fellow countrymen whom I probably never would have met in Tokyo turned out to be a pleasurable experience. Among the residents in Japan House in particular were many people who were quite accomplished in their professions. I went to concerts with a composer, and I learned about the "splendor" of the mathematical system from a mathematician. But perhaps what we all had in common was our habit of comparing Tokyo and Paris at every turn. It was because we didn't know any country other than France when we made comparisons with Japan. But surely it was also because we didn't have the kind of concrete examples that would have kept us from making easy generalizations about France. Economically, we all depended one way or another on our connections with Japan. Physiologically, I suppose every one of us craved female companionship. I was no exception. Soon I felt the need to leave Japan House.

26   The Poet's House

Around the time of the First World War, a group of young men under the influence of Romain Rolland rented a building in an old monastery and set up a commune for artists. Known as the Abbaye de Créteil group, its central figures appear to have been the novelist Georges Duhamel, the dramatist Charles Vildrac, and the poet René Arcos. Duhamel was later elected to the Académie française, and Vildrac's plays were later included in the repertory of the national theaters. Arcos produced several modest volumes of poetry and ran his own small publication firm.[1] After the Second World War, he lived quietly on the rue de l'amiral Mouchez in the thirteenth arrondissement. He was married and had one son, in whose future he apparently placed great expectations. But soon after his son's marriage, Arcos's beautiful wife—I had seen her photograph on the desk—died of cancer, only to be followed by his son's death as a result of a brain tumor. Thereafter all that was left of the family were the aged Arcos and Michèle, his son's young widow. It was during this time that I went to Paris.

His house, a rare two-story wooden structure in the city, was built a small distance from the street. The first floor consisted of a large study, a dining room, and an adjoining living room. A narrow staircase led up to the three bedrooms on the second floor. The walls of the study were lined with leather-bound works of French writers from all ages, with a

---

1. Among René Arcos's publications were *Le sang des autres: poèmes, 1914–1917* (Geneva: A. Kundig, 1919); *Autrui* (Paris: F. Rieder, 1926); *Le bien commun, récits,* with woodcuts by Frans Masereel (Geneva: Editions du Sablier, 1919); and *Romain Rolland* (Paris: Mercure de France, 1950).

few French translations of modern foreign writers among them. On the walls of the living room were paintings by Vlaminck, Modigliani, and the young Marie Laurencin, as well as sketches and woodcuts by Jean Cocteau and Frans Masereel; the rest of the space was filled with ceramics, bronzes, and old furniture. The family's history over the years spoke from every nook and corner of the room. The study was as unlike an efficiently managed office as one could possibly imagine, but here Arcos would sink his body into the armchair in front of a large table and read the manuscripts and documents related to his publication business. Working in the living room at a typewriter on a small table, Michèle, young and agile, would assist him in writing letters, answering the phone, and the like. Their work also included copyright negotiations regarding the writings of Romain Rolland, and it appeared that they had to communicate all over the world with the publishers of his translations. "I have yet to receive any copyright fees from Japanese publishers," Arcos once grumbled. The letters from abroad were written mostly in English or French, and in rare cases I would translate letters in German for them. Michèle called Arcos by his pet name of *petit père*. When she hummed some melody while preparing food in the kitchen, Arcos would say something like, "Listen! A thrush is singing in the house!"

The poet, already in his late sixties, was no longer argumentative, but the two of them were constantly engaged in debates.

"A white woman walking together with a black guy, now that's not a pretty sight."

"What's wrong with a black man?"

"I didn't say there was anything *wrong* with him."

"Then why did you object?"

"On the street they just appear unsightly."

"But that's preposterous, *petit père!* There are many good-looking blacks, you know."

"Ha!"

"And racial discrimination doesn't fit Romain Rolland's disciple!"

"You impudent little devil!"

Despite his words, Arcos evidently enjoyed the arguments. The lack of a bitter aftertaste at the end of a long, impassioned altercation probably came from the fact that the center of the controversy did not impinge on matters of personal interest. But as soon as the conversation shifted to another topic, Michèle's machine-gun barrage would quickly change into amiable and compassionate chitchat with *petit père*. From my standpoint, I could only marvel at their exchanges. The habit of deriving pleasure from an argument without hurting each other's feelings was not something I had ever experienced in Tokyo. And other than in Paris, I don't recall ever having experienced anything like it in any foreign city later in my life, at least not to the same degree. Uttering the literal translations of "Pas du tout! Ce que tu as dit n'est pas du tout vrai!" in other languages would upset not only the Japanese but a lot of other people as well. Under similar circumstances, an Englishman would probably say something like, "Oh well, perhaps we don't quite see eye to eye," and a Japanese would probably say, "You certainly have a point there. You are quite right in saying so, but . . ."

After I left Japan House at the students' colony, I moved into one of the bedrooms on the second floor of Arcos's house. There was a bed, a table, some chairs, and a small bookshelf. When I opened the window facing the courtyard, I could see a piece of gray sky squeezed between the roofs of surrounding buildings. Down below was a thick growth of lilac, and when May arrived the fragrance of the flowers would reach all the way to the window.

I prepared my own meals in the room, by which I don't mean doing my own cooking but rather simply filling my stomach with ready-made food and washing it down with wine and coffee. Normally, I went out once a day to some cheap restaurant, and in the early fifties you could get a rather substantial meal in such a place for 200 to 300 francs, and the food was splendid. When a Japanese traveler asked me whether I missed miso soup after living abroad for so long, I knew what his implications were. Accordingly, my tacit agreement to his question was prompted not by any actual yearning on my part for miso soup, but by my reluctance to subject my Japanese identity to any skeptical scrutiny. I was reminded of Kobori Enshū's design of ponds and streams when I looked at Le Nôtre's garden constructions;[2] but drinking a nameless red wine in a cheap Parisian restaurant never brought back memories of the taste of sake at a Tsukiji sushi joint, nor did having a breakfast of *café*

---

2. Kobori Enshū (1579–1647), one of the most accomplished garden designers of the early Edo period and the founder of the Enshū school of tea ceremony. • André Le Nôtre (1613–1700), French landscape architect during the reign of Louis XIV.

au lait and *tartine* (buttered bread) remind me of miso soup. As far as food was concerned, I was satisfied from the outset with even the most modest meal the French had at the time.

On the other hand, mending holes in my socks was quite a feat. Because I liked to walk around the city, my socks would be worn out in no time. Yet my way of mending a hole would only end up shortening the sock somewhat. Should another hole develop, my sock would become even shorter after the new repair. I would get a new pair only if my socks had become ridiculously short. That was how tight my money was.

I frequently spent my dinner hours chatting with Arcos downstairs. At that time of the day, Michèle was often out somewhere, but the old man very seldom went out. The cease-fire negotiations in Korea had been dragging on for a long time and the Cold War was at its height. During that time Arcos had a habit of saying, "The Americans are such fools." One time I said, "The Americans are not fools; they just started off from a wrong premise." And we had an argument.

"What premise might that be?"

"The premise that Communists are evil monsters."

"Well, that very premise proves the Americans are fools."

"A wrong premise is not necessarily based on stupidity."

"If that is so, what then is it based on?"

"I think it's based on the fact that most Americans have never even seen the face of a live Communist."

"Even Dulles?"

"He doesn't question the accuracy of his premise. He accepts a given premise, and as long as he believes it, his policy is a rational one. The rationality of his policy is not evidence of foolishness but of intelligence."

"There is a town called Arcos de la Frontera in Spain. I know Spain quite well, and for some reason the Spanish bulls are like the Americans in a way. Once you show them a piece of red cloth, they instantly get excited and lose their senses. . . ."

At that time, the colonial war was still going on between France and Indochina, and for Arcos that was a "dirty war." He would refer to Foreign Minister Georges Bidault as "Bidaultche," a name worthy only of contempt. Already close to his seventies, the poet had a habit of talking about contemporary world affairs rather than reminiscing about his good old days. And of course current affairs were not the only thing he talked about.

"You believe in God?" he once asked a woman who came to his house every now and then. "Where is God anyway? In Heaven? That would be down under from the standpoint of the folks in Tokyo." Another time he remarked, "I'd rather celebrate the sin of nonpregnancy than the virtue of virgin birth." And when he handed me a specially ordered leather-bound volume of poems, he said, "Go on, touch it! Feels like the softness of a woman's thighs, doesn't it?"

Romain Rolland had most certainly left his mark on this man. If Rolland could be regarded as a humanitarian, an internationalist, and a progressive irrespective of his interest in music, glass pyrography, and mysticism, the poet Arcos was more unambiguously a humanitarian, an internationalist, and a progressive without embracing any serious contradictions, if you will, within himself.[3] Though his world was by far more circumscribed, his genuine sincerity left no place in it for any falsehood or hypocrisy. Even in his old age, it truly pained his heart to see how nationalists were being killed in faraway Asia—something I am afraid only a true poet could feel. A poet can also be a newspaper reporter or a political scientist (and of course Arcos was neither). Yet no newspaper reporter's knowledge or political scientist's methodology can turn them into poets.

I had developed a casual habit of exchanging jokes with Arcos, but linguistically that was not always easy. Before dinner, Arcos would go to Café Coupole in Montparnasse to have a drink of Pernod, and at dinner he would have wine, only to be followed by cognac or calvados. In the evening hours, his speech was no longer clear. Gradually I began to develop a strong affection for this old poet who no longer wrote any poems. I was fond of his jokes, and even though his arguments might be flawed or too simplistic, his motives would almost always strike a responsive chord in me.

Every now and then I would invite Michèle out for the evening. We would have dinner somewhere, go to a concert or watch a play. Young and full of curiosity, Michèle seemed interested in everything that was happening in Paris and around the world. I, on my part, was extraordinarily curious to see what might happen if I turned my world thitherto based on the linguistic "propositions" of Japanese (to borrow Wittgenstein's terminology) to one based on those of French.[4] Michèle

3. In a private communication, Katō explained that he was contrasting Rolland's sociopolitical commitments and his aesthetic and religious interests.
4. In *Tractatus Logico-philosophicus* (1921), the Austrian-British philosopher

and I never ran out of topics in our conversation; indeed we could never finish our discussion on any single topic to our satisfaction. Perhaps this had something to do with the fact that I never tried to interpret Japan for her and she never tried to explain France to me. You could say that we both tried earnestly to articulate not mutually exclusive but shared experiences—the play we just saw, the conduct of *petit père* that particular morning, John Foster Dulles's announcement as reported in the papers, or the lighted tower of St-Germain-des-Près visible from where we sat at an open-air café. Michèle was reading a wide range of contemporary literature in French and Italian. She was deeply impressed by García Lorca, the productions by the junior Pitoëff of Chekhov, and the plays at the T.N.P. led by Jean Vilar.[5] She preferred Bach and Mozart to the romantics, the frescoes of Giotto and Uccello to the works completed at the height of the Italian Renaissance, and Romanesque churches to Gothic architecture and sculpture.

Later in this book I will have an occasion to talk about my own interest in French medieval art in those days. But speaking of plays, I was beginning to revive my old theater-going habit from my days at the *nō* theater during the war. During this period I saw so many Western plays from Pirandello on that I was beginning to get a little tired of going to the theater. Sometimes I went alone, of course, but most of the time I went with Michèle or her good friend Asabuki Tomiko.[6] My recollections of the theater cannot be dissociated from my memories of these two lovely ladies. Once we stepped out of the playhouse, one of them would rattle away her comments like a machine gun, while the other

---

Ludwig Wittgenstein (1889–1951) maintains that meaning in language is possible only through "propositions" defined as depictable facts or "pictures" of "atomic facts" that make up the world.

5. Federico García Lorca (1898–1936), eminent Spanish poet and dramatist known for his dramatic *Gypsy Ballads* (1928), his association with the theater of La Barraca, and his premature death at the hands of an armed Fascist group at the outbreak of the Spanish civil war. • Pitoëff was the son of actors Ludmilla and Georges Pitoëff; during the 1930s the senior Pitoëff was a prominent director in the French theater, along with Louis Jouvet, Charles Dullin, and Gaston Baty. • The Théâtre national populaire was founded by Jean Vilar in 1951.

6. Asabuki Tomiko (1917–), a noted translator of French literature including Françoise Sagan's *Bonjour tristesse* and Simone de Beauvoir's 4-vol. autobiography beginning with *Mémoires d'une jeune fille rangée*; her other work includes essays (*Pari no otokotachi* [Men of Paris, 1965]) and an autobiographical novel (*Ai no mukōgawa* [The other side of love, 1977]).

would refer to her deep impressions in Japanese, providing in turn the excitement of brisk, clear-cut analysis and the delight of experiencing an emotional realm beyond what words could convey.

I think contemporary plays in Paris appealed to me for several reasons. First, I had reached a point where I felt virtually no linguistic barrier watching a foreign play in French translation (for instance, those by Chekhov). Though I still encountered a great many linguistic obstacles with contemporary French plays, they weren't serious enough to frustrate my enjoyment of their substance. But when it came to classical plays with dialogues uttered in verse, I could hardly understand them. Michèle was excited after watching Gérard Philipe's interpretation of Le Cid. "How fabulous!" But I found myself unable to follow his extraordinarily rapid speech. For the time being, I realized that if I were to enjoy a French play, I could go only to a contemporary one. But that was not the only reason.

The second reason was that the Parisian theaters represented, I felt, a merging of the prewar Tsukiji Little Theater and the wartime nō theater. A modern play addresses the modern times on the stage with its own style; its appeal consists of the substance of its material as well as the manner in which the actors deliver their lines. Takizawa Osamu, for example, could with exquisite skill execute his lines in subtle alignment with what was happening on the stage, and although one could not tell exactly what Umewaka Manzaburō was uttering, the intonation of his speech alone held an indescribably magical appeal.[7] However, Takizawa's exquisite skill and Umewaka's magical appeal belonged to two completely different worlds. But in Paris, I was able to observe the fusing of these two elements within a single world.

Third, this was the time when Anouilh wrote L'Alouette, when some of Giraudoux's works were posthumously staged for the first time, and when Sartre wrote Le Diable et le bon dieu and Kean; Bertolt Brecht was at the height of his popularity, and Samuel Beckett was beginning to

7. Takizawa Osamu (1906–), one of the most accomplished actors in the Shingeki theater. Among his highly praised prewar roles were the tragic protagonist Aoyama Hanzō in Shimazaki Tōson's Yoake mae (Before the dawn) and the hero Amemiya in Kubo Sakae's Kazanbai chi (Land of volcanic ash); in the postwar era he founded several major troupes and took the leading roles in such plays as Death of a Salesman. • On Umewaka Manzaburō see chapter 12, note 14, as well as chapter 18.

make a name for himself. Truly many things were happening at the theater in Paris.

Yet when I wrote earlier of getting "a little tired of going to the theater," it wasn't just a figure of speech. Having watched contemporary plays in Paris for two years, I began to feel I had seen all the really interesting ones. More accurately put, the novelty in the new plays did little more than embellish their superficial appearance, and in the final analysis, I felt that the structure of their dramatic tension was essentially the same. And then *for the first time,* I began to develop a greater interest in classical than in contemporary plays. I am not suggesting that I knew a great many classical plays, since my subsequent stay in Paris was not an extended one. But when I saw Jean Vilar's production of *Dom Juan,* I was totally mesmerized by the performance, and I thought that it epitomized the pinnacle of fulfillment a play could afford its audience. My own inadequacy delayed my discovery of Molière's appeal for over two years since I started going to the theater! And it was only after I saw Gérard Philipe playing *Richard II* that I realized for the first time that Shakespeare was a great playwright! (I decided then to go to England, and, as a matter of fact, I soon put my resolution into practice.)

My thinking about the theater continued to evolve. No longer was I interested in the modern versions of Greek drama adapted by Giraudoux and adorned with Cocteau's brilliant dialogues; I became interested in the classical plays themselves. Men like Sophocles and Euripides invented the dramatic situation itself, and their successors merely provided footnotes of psychological depiction, interpretation, and the background of the time, all of which are not beyond our imagination without these appendages. It seemed difficult for the modern playwrights to create new dramatic situations to rival those of the Greek tragedians. When I was in Tokyo, I was impressed with Anouilh's *Antigone,* but Sophocles' original, even in a translated version, was by far a more magnificent and a more humanistic work, and it easily overshadowed Anouilh's efforts. But these differences were not only limited to plays. I would say that this was also the time when I first began to appreciate the substantive significance of "Greek civilization."

Spending an evening a week with Michèle had enlarged my social circle. I met several of her friends, including a young technician from Tunisia, an American scholar of French literature, and a young member of the French Communist party. But I did not develop a close friendship with any one of them. Perhaps the young Communist party member might have turned out to be an interesting person if we had been able to continue our friendship. But he never spoke clearly and I could not understand most of what he was saying. Michèle was also a close friend of the famous sociologist Georges Friedman. At a cocktail party Michèle held, I heard Friedman talk about Chaplin's *Limelight*.

"What do you think? A masterpiece, isn't it? Certainly one of the greatest artists alive today." But the institution of the cocktail party hardly made it possible for me to find out his reasons for saying so, just as it was impossible to know why someone might oppose or be in favor of nuclear weapons.

During the spring and autumn seasons, Michèle sometimes took solitary trips to Italy and Spain. She always remembered to write me a postcard at her destination. The postcards were carefully chosen, and for a while I never got tired of looking at them as they sat on my desk. She would scribble only a few almost unintelligible lines as if she were sending off a telegram, but they did vividly convey what impressed her at the time. "Córdoba. Wonderful city with a relentless sun. Stone pavements with medieval fountains everywhere."

While I was setting out to discover Europe, one might say that Michèle was continuing with her own discoveries. Before she had married Arcos's son, not only was she unfamiliar with Europe, but she didn't even seem to know Paris well. I was told that her father—the owner of a factory with several hundred workers in Lille during the prewar days—forbade his children to talk with the family chauffeur and declared that children of good upbringing should not set foot on the places de la République and Bastille. But the war smashed the anachronistic attitudes of the upper bourgeoisie. And in that sense, Arcos's thinking was not bourgeois. When I first met Michèle, she felt herself liberal enough to laugh at the middle-class prejudices of her late father and her sister who had emigrated to the United States. She knew there was a larger world and she wanted to know more. That impulse defined a phase of her life, and I suppose she realized it herself at that time. Flamboyant and cheerful, she was also strikingly beautiful. Her movements and expressions were as lively as one could imagine, but at the same time she also possessed a delicate sensitivity. Until then I had never met a more free-spirited young woman in terms of her interest toward general human affairs not immediate to her own. I found her absolutely enchanting. I also admired her femininity for not flaunting it through the pretentiousness of her speech.

Soon afterwards, Michèle left Paris to marry a young Italian who, I was told, was working for a trade union in Rome. In her place, Michèle's mother, a widow who lived alone, became a regular visitor to Arcos's house. When she came, she would water the garden plants, tell the cleaning woman what to do, prepare meals for herself and Arcos, and have long conversations by the window with the neighbor's cat. I heard that she had once been a singer, and occasionally she would sing fragments of opera arias in the kitchen. As for me, I continued to live in the second-floor bedroom as before. I got up late in the morning, went to the hospital, had a simple lunch outside, and sometimes returned late at night and sometimes not at all. Whenever I came back, I continued my habit of chatting with Arcos downstairs. But since Michèle was no longer there, Arcos was consuming more Pernod, and so my conversation with him at night was a rather strenuous business. When he said to me, "Good night! I'll go upstairs to rest. See you tomorrow," the part "See you tomorrow" was uttered in Italian. Perhaps old memories of his visit to Italy and his thoughts of Michèle now living there combined to produce that effect.

Many years later, after I had left France, Michèle moved to the suburbs of Paris with her husband and two children. She was very enthusiastic about her children's education (I came back to visit Paris every now and then, and each time I would call on her). Her husband was a busy marketing agent for Italian products in France, and on the side he was trying to learn Chinese. His motivation came from his strong empathy with the history of the Chinese Communist party, and together we talked about the Chinese revolution.

"Our thinking as parents is too radically different from the conventional norm," Michèle once remarked. "Perhaps it's unfortunate for children to be raised with such ideas. But I also don't think it's right to squeeze them into the conformist mold. What do you think?"

I replied at that time that it probably depended on the intellect and fortitude of the child. If he was an average child, it might be advisable for him to learn to compromise. However, if the child had the capacity to persevere in his minority position, the sooner he learned about the truth the better.

Some years later Michèle's family moved from the suburbs into the city, and they settled into a place not far from the rue de l'amiral

Mouchez. And since the children had already grown up, Michèle began working again at a publishing firm as she had been doing at the time I first met her. When she left Paris for Rome to get married, Arcos told me repeatedly, "Michèle is going to come back soon."

"Why?"

"You asked why? Because those who grew up and have lived in Paris cannot live anywhere else!"

Arcos was right. But when she actually returned to Paris, the old poet was no longer there.

27 Southern France

The old poet no longer liked to take solitary trips. But if I would go along with him, he said he would leave Paris early in the summer to attend an International PEN Club conference to be held in Nice in southern France. I had never visited that part of the country, nor had I attended any international conference before. So we took off on an express train from the Gare de Lyon.

The relentless southern sun gave the Mediterranean Sea beyond the promenade des Anglais a dazzling glitter.[1] A few Japanese writers had already arrived for the conference, affording me the rare pleasure of speaking with them in my native tongue. The stoutly built Tamura Tai-jirō, constantly wiping off his perspiration, grumbled and wondered why the waiter always brought him something other than the shaved ice he had repeatedly ordered. I came to the rescue of this best-selling writer of *Gate of the Flesh* and placed the order for him.[2] And he, on his part, seemed to truly enjoy what I had ordered. The kimono-clad Hiraba-yashi Taiko told me that she was amazed at what was actually going on

---

1. The promenade des Anglais, the four-mile-long embankment along the Mediterranean, was constructed between 1822 and 1824.
2. *Nikutai no mon* (1947), a midlength novel by Tamura Taijirō (1911–83) about young prostitutes struggling to live amidst the turmoil of postwar Tokyo; with his previous work *Nikutai no akuma* (Evil of the flesh, 1946), a love story between a Chinese Communist intellectual and a Japanese army officer, it brought Tamura popular success as a *nikutai sakka* (writer of the flesh). His other major works include *Shunfuden* (Biography of a prostitute, 1947), *Senjō no kao* (Face in the battlefield, 1958), and *Inago* (Locust, 1965).

at the conference.[3] Meetings were held in the mornings, and the afternoons were mostly for touring or going to the mountains. Hirabayashi had expected the participants to engage a little more seriously in discussion, and she was disappointed. Furthermore, she couldn't tolerate the sight of a fellow guest, a representative from a certain country who brought a woman into his hotel room and had no apparent intention of coming out to attend the conference. I was impressed by her sharp observations.

At the conference, French writers were having a good time making eloquent speeches. This was especially true of Jules Romains, a member of the Académie française and a latecomer to the conference, a man who exhibited unparalleled skill and talent in delivering absolutely vacuous speeches in splendid French. I could only describe his performance as quite a spectacle. Even at the end of his speech, when he was surrounded by a large crowd of men and women, he continued to indulge in his brilliant act as the master novelist with all the pomp of theatricality.

"Let me introduce you to him. He is an old friend of mine," my companion Arcos said.

More accurately, perhaps Arcos should have said, "He *was* a friend." A friend, I would think, is not somebody you have to approach just to shake his hand; he himself would leave the crowd to come to greet you on his own initiative. Writers, writers-to-be, and other literary aspirants filled the same room, each babbling away about whatever was on his or her mind. It was a boisterous scene, and the air was thick with the odors of tobacco, perfume, and people.

But in Nice I also met Frans Masereel. The Flemish artist did not look a bit old and, like a character in his own woodcut prints, seemed to transcend his age and possibly his time as well. His tall frame clad in plain

3. As a young girl, Hirabayashi Taiko (1905–72) avidly read Russian literature, Zola's *Germinal,* and early Japanese proletarian literature. She and her anarchist lover were forced into exile in Manchuria and Korea before she published her first major story, *Azakeru* (Mockery, 1926), a gloomy account of the parasitic life of an anarchist. "Seryōshitsu nite" (In the treatment room, 1927), a powerful semiautobiographical story about an anarchist's wife and the death of her newborn baby in a colonial Manchurian hospital, established Hirabayashi's fame as a rising proletarian writer, and a series of autobiographical works ("Hitori yuku" [Walking alone, 1946], "Kō iu onna" [This kind of woman, 1946], and "Watashi wa ikiru" [I will live, 1947]) continued it. Around the time of the Korean War, Hirabayashi changed to an anti-Communist position, producing such works as *Sabaku no hana* (Flower in a desert, 1955–57).

clothes and his white hair streaming in the sea breeze, he walked buoy-antly by himself in the springy, long strides of an athlete. The interna-tional conference, the plush buildings on the boulevard des Anglais, the gaudily dressed women equally eager to show off their skin, the writ-ers babbling away for lack of anything substantive to say—all these seemed to evaporate into thin air around him. Only one white path lay straight ahead of him. "What a nice breeze! I like to walk with the wind blowing in my face," he said in a low, deep voice.

Masereel himself lived high up in a building overlooking Nice's *vieux port*, its old harbor. The building had no elevator, and the staircase squeaked under one's feet. Every wall in his small apartment was cov-ered with bookshelves, and a few of his unfinished oil paintings rested on easels. Leaning out of an open window, one could see the old harbor with the masts of its many fishing boats and, beyond the breakwater, the glistening Mediterranean. Aged buildings with yellow walls lined the old harbor's waterfront, and their narrow sidewalk was busy with streams of laborers and women carrying shopping baskets. It was here that the town came alive. "I almost never go to the promenade des Anglais," he said. "I went this time only because of you."

At the old harbor, some fishermen and laborers still in their working clothes were drinking in the tavern. They all knew Masereel, and when he came in, they greeted him with their eyes or with a hello. He shook hands with some of them, patted an old man on the shoulder, exchanged a few words, and made them laugh with his jokes. There he was no longer alone. I loved everything about this small harbor town—the sun-weath-ered faces of the men, the deep wrinkles across the old women's fore-heads, the taste of salt and the odor of petroleum that hung in the air, the tables and crudely made chairs at the tavern.

"Well then, I'll see you tomorrow," Masereel said.

He was doing a landscape, in oils. "Abstract paintings are such a waste of time. Don't you think it's a beautiful world we live in?"

And Paris had nothing that interested him. "The city has become harder and harder to live in. It's all so shallow and superficial."

He told me that occasionally he would go to Germany for an exhibi-tion; otherwise he had no desire to go anywhere. But he was by no means "retired." Not only did he continue with his work, he also had a strong interest in world affairs. And he was far from being a misanthrope. He was fond of the town and its people, and the words he uttered were filled with genuine warmth.

"How's Katayama doing?" he suddenly asked as we were taking a walk in town. He was referring to the young Katayama Toshihiko he had met twenty years earlier.[4] Back then, Masereel was a close friend of Romain Rolland's. What in fact had transpired in those days among Rolland and his circle of friends? Years later, the poet Katayama would describe their association as one of "spiritual communion," "a gathering of stars in the sky." But I didn't quite know what to make of it when I heard such an explanation, expressed as it was in those terms, and I doubt if anybody would. But if what Katayama said was just a figure of speech, surely Masereel would not, twenty years later, suddenly remember this young man from Japan, someone who could barely even speak French.

"In all these years, Katayama never wrote to me, not even once," Masereel said.

I imagine the explanation was that, for Katayama, their encounter two decades earlier was not just an ordinary meeting but an event of extraordinary significance, something that had exerted a decisive impact on him. His silence could not have been the result of his forgetfulness. On the contrary, he had so much respect for his friends that he must have searched in vain for a topic in the world around him worthy of writing about. I remembered how even during the war years the poet would open up Masereel's woodcut collections, how he would curse Japanese militarism and criticize the ultranationalist excesses of his country, and how proudly he always reminisced about his meeting with Romain Rolland and Mahatma Gandhi in the distant Swiss mountains on that bygone day. It was his friends in France who had given him the strength to spend a life in solitude for twenty long years in Tokyo. And because of this, he was unable to bring himself to communicate with them in writing or come to visit them in France after the war ended. I knew only too well why Masereel's friend never wrote, and consequently I could not articulate the reason to him. After returning to Japan I, too, never wrote him.

I do not mean to suggest, however, that I did not enjoy the gathering at the International PEN Club. On one occasion, the mayor of Nice invited us to a garden party on a small hill with a panoramic view of the sea and the city. The many flower beds, the fountains, and the landscaped footpaths were all gracefully illuminated; on the tables in the open air

4. For Katayama and his relationship with Romain Rolland and his circle of writers and poets, see chapter 12 and its note 4.

were wines and all sorts of delicacies to suit every taste. I was impressed with the extravagant display and bored by the conversation around the table. Part of it was that, as a passive participant listening to their conversation, it was hard to understand the exchanges between the foreign guests as the wine began to take effect on them. Even if I had understood what they were saying, as someone who lived outside their circle, I wouldn't have been interested in their gossip about their colleagues or inside talk about their publishers. And so after a little while, I left Arcos behind with his wineglass and his French friends and took a walk in the garden. At that time, standing by himself on the balcony and gazing at the city lights was a British novelist who later became a friend of mine.

"What a pretty sight!" I said.

"Prettier than the faces of our fellow writers, to be sure."

His words reminded me of a line by Morgenstern, which I repeated: "Denn er denkt die Alpen sich als einen Würfel aus Touristen, Kühen und Steinen."[5]

"What was he referring to?"

"Switzerland."

"Do you like it?"

"It's a beautiful country," I repeated Arcos's words in French. "But unfortunately, it's inhabited by the Swiss!"

"I think Switzerland is not beautiful but clean," he remarked. "I'd gladly trade all of Switzerland for a small Italian town."

He said that he often visited Italy, spoke the language easily, and had many Italian friends.

"But southern France is also pretty."

"Except the resort cities on the coast, that is."

"No, except the promenade des Anglais, you should say!"

He burst into loud laughter and then suggested that we talk a little about Japan.

Meanwhile a young woman approached us.

"What are you gentlemen doing here," she said abruptly in English, "hiding in a place like this?"

"We're doing nothing of the sort."

"Oh, excuse me. But what were you talking about? The West or the East?"

5. From Christian Morgenstern's "Alpinismus I" in *Alle Galgenlieder* (The gallows songs, 1905).

"About neither, really," the British novelist responded, "We were just talking about sightseeing."

"Oh, I got so tired," she muttered.

"Of what?"

Without first answering the question, she let out a peal of laughter, then stopped abruptly, and began in a provocative tone, "Writers, of course! It's totally ludicrous. And they call this a conference? Nobody has said anything on any subject! What a sham! Nothing's on display except vanity! But so many of these writers have the cheek to show up in gatherings like this, from morning to night."

"Well, did you expect anything else? If you don't like it, you shouldn't have come in the first place."

"You're right. Perhaps I shouldn't have come at all," she repeated those words in an unexpectedly low and almost subdued voice as if she were talking to herself. But she did not stop there.

"This country is now fighting a war in Indochina. People die every day. Under these circumstances, how can people hold a conference like this? Nobody spoke a word about the war. All we heard were lofty and empty words. If that's literature, then I'd say literature is deception and a bunch of lies. This is why the Anglo-Saxons are so insufferable."

"But it's the French who are fighting the war, not the Anglo-Saxons," I said.

"Oh, they're just the same," she asserted. Her big eyes sparkled in the night as she made almost incoherent statements. On the other hand, what she said was not entirely untrue. Meanwhile, somebody walking by called out to the British novelist, and he took the opportunity to leave the scene. Suddenly I was reminded of what had happened that afternoon.

It was at a casino on the beach at Juan-les-Pins. I was on the deck, watching the performance of water-skiers with well-groomed middle-aged men and women. The other end of the deck appeared to be built in such a way that one could practically go into the water from there. A young woman who had just got out of the water walked right by me. Her face looked vaguely familiar, but I could not remember exactly where I had met her. So that was it. The wet swimming suit clung tightly to her body, showing every curve of her figure. Droplets of water on her taut thighs were glistening in the sun.

She was Irish and was living in London. She seemed to be connected with the British PEN Club through her work, but it didn't matter to me one way or the other, at least not as much as her wet thighs.

"You're Japanese, aren't you?" she said. "I cannot understand your people. Why don't they resist the occupation by the United States?"

And then all of a sudden she asked me what my profession was, whether I was a novelist or a poet.

"If you're healthy, I'm a writer. But if you're feeling under the weather, I'm a doctor," I answered.

"I like the way you put it," she said.

"Would you like to come by my room tonight?" I asked her.

"Because I am a patient?"

"No, because you're healthy."

"Well, we'll see," she said, again letting out a loud laugh.

We left the garden party, went down the hill, and picked up a taxi in town. Meanwhile, she repeatedly said in her strongly accented French, "This is a sad country. I don't know what I'm doing." When the taxi stopped in front of my hotel, I once again invited her in. But nothing would convince her to get out of the cab.

I have never again seen this Irish woman since our fortuitous encounter. When I left Nice at the end of the conference, everything faded into the remote past. She became no more than a faint shadow amidst the intense and cluttered realities hovering in the world around me, even though her shadow had for a while held me captive. I repeated to myself a Provençal proverb I read on the wall of a Nice restaurant: *L'amour fa passa lou tem, Lou tem fa passa l'amour.* But we didn't even have love.

I parted with Arcos at Nice's train station and took a trip by myself around southern France. The eloquent speeches and extravagant banquets in Nice soon gave way to van Gogh's sun and the wide open sky, to hills covered with vineyards and white walls surrounding towns on hilltops. Resting under a shady tree, I could feel an invigorating breeze running through my entire body. This was a world luxuriantly radiant with bright colors and well-defined forms. Red rooftops, yellow walls, green thickets, white stones, paths in the fields running straight into the distance, and hills whose contours cut sharply into the deep blue sky. The gray skies of northern France were nowhere to be seen; there were no subtle plays of light or images of thickets appearing and disappearing amid drifting mists. Nowhere could one experience the refined neutral color tone or the elusive images levitating ever so enigmatically along the Yamatoji in my faraway homeland.[6] Everything down to the finest detail was clearly defined and relentlessly delineated; a world made up of primary colors resolutely resistant to the most minuscule intrusion of alien hues. I could hardly imagine anything in this milieu that would resonate with the feelings of bitterness, anxiety, hope, or remorse buried deeply within my breast.

Stretching out my tired legs on the grass under the shady tree, I looked at the Pont du Gard aqueduct built by the ancient Romans. The magnificent structure cut across a deep valley, its multilayered arcades soaring into the sky. Come to think of it, few spectacles could possibly have been more incongruous with the scene painted since the *Shinkokinshū*— or should I say since the *Kokinshū*—where images of "spring night dreams" and "trailing clouds parted by a mountain peak" have become so imperceptibly fused into our consciousness.[7]

Irrespective of what an onlooker might think, the waterway built by the Romans had been there for more than two millennia. Its existence was that of an external form totally independent of my internal thoughts and feelings. Furthermore, I would venture to say that it was independent of whatever sentiments its builders might have cherished, and that it forms a part of the sensory order of the external world—for the external world, in the final analysis, is a datum of our senses. Under the bright, clear sky of southern France, even art had ceased to be expressions of "innermost sentiments" or "feelings," let alone manifestations of "personality" or confessions of "personal experiences." It became none other than a sense of order actualized in the realm of the external world, from the multilayered *arcade* to the structure of polyphony, from Pont du Gard to the ceramic plates of the painter of Vallauris.[8] If Picasso had indeed indulged in toying with chance as he painted his pictures on ceramic plates, surely he was not dallying with his own capricious mood but with the unpredictable elements that invariably intrude into the process of pottery making. I wonder if the artist's own caprice has ever

6. Yamatoji is an ancient and poetic name for the road between Kyoto and today's Nara Prefecture through Fushimi and Kizu.
7. The original poem by Fujiwara Teika in the *Shinkokinshū* reads as follows: "The floating bridge of / my spring night dreams / has collapsed. / The sky with trailing clouds / parted by a mountain peak" (quoted in Katō's *History of Japanese Literature*); Katō comments, "The 'floating bridge of dreams' is taken from the *Genji monogatari* and the image of the clouds drifting apart is a subtle expression of the sweet sorrow of lovers parting" (1:244).
8. A reference to Picasso.

been accorded its rightful place in the world of art since the construction of Pont du Gard. For a long time, I vaguely entertained such thoughts in solitude. Later, these contemplations led to a sort of chain reaction in me and inspired many other ideas.

While traveling alone, I very rarely spoke with anyone, and I felt quite contented with the situation. In Nice, I had been talking for an entire week from dawn to dusk and I became more fed up with my own chattering than with that of others. All day long, I roamed about wherever I happened to be, and at night I rested my totally exhausted body in cheap lodging places. I must have looked rather sullen during the day, for I was quietly draining away my energy in meeting the dire challenges from a sensory world so diametrically different from the one in which I grew up.

28   Medieval Europe

From the very first day they landed at a European port, Japanese travelers to the West in the late 1920s and early 1930s were most surely overwhelmed by the enormous differences between Europe and Japan— differences in their cities' appearance, in clothes, food, and accommodation as well as in everyday customs and manners. Buildings in Tokyo in those days were low structures mostly made of wood; most of the roads were unpaved, and the city streetcars moved slowly within the bounds of the metropolitan loop line. A woman dressed in Western clothing was a rare sight, and the men, after returning home from work at their companies or government offices, would change into their *dotera*, sit cross-legged, and drink sake served by their wives. Indoor heating left much to be desired, and in the winter the room temperature would approach freezing. Differences between the sexes were institutionalized through inequalities in educational opportunities and voting rights, in salary scales and civil law status. And the state did not even bother to pretend that national sovereignty belonged to the people.

When a man born and raised in such a society was thrown all of a sudden into the middle of Paris, he would naturally find it difficult to escape the impression that everything there was different from Tokyo. Everyone's first thoughts were not about the similarities between these two cultures but about their differences. Despite the great changes that had taken place in Japan during their absence, poets returning to Japan from Paris would compare Japanese society with the France they remembered during the interwar years and continue to rediscover fundamental and insurmountable differences. On the other hand, artists who stayed on in France would keep comparing Tokyo as they remembered it from the days after World War I with the Parisian society around them, only to reinforce their first impressions about the miseries they found in one and the greatness of the other.

During the first half of the 1950s, however, a Tokyoite residing in Paris would not have experienced any serious discrepancies between the two cities, at least in daily life. It was not in France that I first saw the subway; only the system in Paris was a little more convenient than the one I used to take in Tokyo. I was not surprised by any fundamental institutional differences; all I noticed were certain variations in the way similar systems worked. Coffee was no exotic drink, and sleeping in a bunk was something I had gotten used to from my days at the Tokyo University Hospital. My first impressions were not about the differences between Japan and France but their similarities.

Furthermore, at that time I was working every day in a laboratory for the natural sciences, a discipline whose methodology and empirical findings are universal and transcend national boundaries. I was not examining any intricate and profound questions such as whether the emperor-system was circulating in the blood of the Japanese people, or whether the spirit of rationalism was flowing in the veins of the French. My research was about the effects of a specific serological environment on the behavior of human white blood cells in general. First impressions about everyday life can surely be reaffirmed, even on the intellectual level, through a habit of scientific thinking. I started off with the premise that things in both countries essentially worked the same way and concluded that any fundamental differences lay first in their language and, in the final analysis, in their history dating as far back as the medieval period.

I mentioned language just now. By the time I was quite comfortable using French in everyday situations, I became even more acutely aware of the differences between French and Japanese. These differences were so fundamental that if French were to become an integral part of my daily living, I felt it would inevitably draw me deeper and deeper into a mental construct intricately different from the world of Japanese. It often made me shudder to think of the possibility of entering deeply into that world.

The medieval presence in Paris astonished me. That was the only thing I had not anticipated while I was in Tokyo. I had expected the Eiffel Tower to rise above the clouds, and surely it did. But until I saw Paris with my own eyes, I could never have imagined that Notre-Dame and the significance of the medieval style would loom in such prominence over the city as a whole. Moreover, it was not just a matter of architecture. I soon came to realize the similarities between the continuity in French culture from the medieval age to the present day and its Japanese parallel from the Kamakura period. By that I do not mean similarities in their feudal systems. To discern the aesthetic sensibilities of the Heian aristocracy, imagination alone would not suffice; knowledge derived from scholarship was also indispensable. There is no way of knowing what sort of melody the heroes in *The Tale of Genji* were playing on their flutes. There is a discontinuity between Heian aristocratic culture and contemporary Japan. But the same kind of discontinuity does not exist after the Kamakura period. The flute on the *nō* stage presumably produces the same notes today as it did during the Muromachi period, and their effects on us are presumably the same as those felt by the people of that period. We can imagine what their sensibilities were because medieval culture has continued to develop into the present time.

As far as contemporary Europe is concerned, Greco-Roman civilization was rediscovered after it had ceased to exist. Medieval civilization, on the other hand, has continued to survive in cities and is alive within the people. We have no way of knowing the tunes to which Sappho sang her poems. But inside the churches dating back to the Middle Ages, we can still hear medieval music, from Gregorian chant to the works of Palestrina. But no one around us believes in the Greek gods anymore. While the Parthenon appeals to us aesthetically, I seriously doubt that the temple as it stands today would similarly appeal to the ancient Greeks who decorated their marble structures with rich, brilliant colors. Yet the religious faith of those who built the medieval churches is still alive today, and if its architecture, sculptures and the luminous stained glass are beautiful to us, they must have been equally beautiful to the people who created them. People's thinking changed with time, and so, presumably, did their sensibilities. But these changes took place in an evolving continuum and their transformation is not interrupted by any discontinuity. If we were to trace the origin of contemporary Western civilization, I felt, we would invariably arrive at the Middle Ages. That was an enormously overpowering impression, but I remember no one ever talked about it in Tokyo.

At that time the sculptor Takata Hiroatsu had already spent half his life in France, and whenever we met—and we always met at a café in Montparnasse or in Quartier Latin—he would say, "Every time I look at a twelfth-century sculpture, I feel devastated." A white-haired man with a boyish face, Takata would talk on and on for hours, sometimes contentiously and sometimes modestly, using his unique Japanese studded with literal translations from French. "You know, he *is* a good man. But his work? *Zéro.* Japanese intellectuals are . . ."[1] Whether his views were about France or Japan, politics or art, they represented a blend of his broad knowledge, wild generalizations, and really sharp intuition; he drew his unfettered inspirations from between the superficial and the deep-seated strata of his experience. Today, I cannot remember anything he said. But there is something about the artist that I will never forget, something that poured forth with overwhelming vitality from his diminutive frame.

I believe that Mr. Takata, in his total being as man and artist, was consistently making one quintessential statement—that culture is a "construct," that a "construct" represents the manifestation of a spirit, and that a spirit can achieve self-realization through, and only through, self-manifestation. My indebtedness to Takata Hiroatsu was not a matter of his telling me where I could find such and such a masterpiece of medieval architecture or sculpture. For that, a travel guide like the *Guide bleu* could provide more detailed information than Takata's recollections. Rather, I came to my own conclusive understanding about the inseparable relationship between the world of the formative arts and culture as a whole, and Takata bore witness to that understanding in his flesh, so to speak. What the Japanese sculptor Takata Hiroatsu discovered during his long years working in Paris was not the least different, for example, from what the central European poet Rilke discovered while working as the sculptor Rodin's secretary.[2] Rilke discovered his "thing." I wonder if a discovery like his can be made anywhere. Even if the answer is yes, it's not important. Takata loved France. Love breeds endless misconceptions, but it also leads to understanding that would otherwise be impossible to achieve.

I discovered medieval art in France, or, more precisely, I discovered what art itself meant to me through medieval art. Since then, the world

---

1. The word Takata used is *chiseijin,* or *homo sapiens,* rather than the conventional term for an intellectual, *chishikijin,* though presumably he was referring to the latter.

2. Rilke came to appreciate Rodin's comparison of an artist's work to "the only satisfactory mode of religious activity." See Victor Lange's entry on Rilke in *Columbia Dictionary of Modern European Literature,* 667; and Rilke's *August Rodin* (1903).

of the formative arts has become an indispensable part of my overall universe. Why did this happen in France and not in Japan? Surely, one reason was that I had the good fortune of not having much money to spend while I was traveling in the West. Otherwise, like many other travelers, I would probably have been interested only in the things money could buy—famous hotels, sumptuous food, demimondaines, souvenirs, oil paintings in art galleries. But having barely enough money for a roof over my head and food to fill my stomach, I could direct my interest to things I didn't have to pay for—social and political conditions, the French language, love, art museums, and churches. Beyond that, I saw in France a society in which art in its various historical forms was intimately integrated as a significant part of its overall intellectual makeup.

I had noticed earlier that the image of Japanese gardens in Kyoto could hardly be separated from the world of lyric poetry after the *Shinkokinshū*. But whatever subject in contemporary culture I might contemplate, I didn't have the habit of constantly going back to the Hōryūji, the *emaki* scrolls, or to Sōtatsu and Kōrin.[3] When I heard how very often the French make references to "the angel's smile at the cathedral of Reims" or the "spirituality" of Avignon's *pietà*, I couldn't help feeling that the relationship between their culture and their formative

3. The Hōryūji temple in Nara Prefecture is one of Japan's most celebrated architectural showpieces and holds invaluable Buddhist sculptures and other national treasures; one theory dates it from 607, making some of its Asuka-style wooden structures the oldest in the world. • The illustrated *emaki* scrolls often use *kotobagaki*, or calligraphic narratives, to elucidate scenes from classical literature, Buddhist tales, or biographical accounts of famous monks; the tradition began in eighth-century China and developed in Heian Japan through the Kamakura, Muromachi, and into the premodern era. • Tawaraya Sōtatsu (dates unknown), early Edo period painter whose bold colors, vibrant imagination, and versatile lines rejuvenated the tradition of *yamato-e* painting. One of his most famous works is *Fūjin-raijin-zu byōbu*, with impressive images of the wind god and the thunder god against the gold-leafed background of a wide folding screen; another masterpiece, *Matsushima-zu* (Waves of Matsushima), is in Washington, D.C.'s Freer Gallery. • Ogata Kōrin (1658–1716), a successor of Sōtatsu's style and one of the most celebrated Edo painters; his influence reached European artists overseas. His best-known painting of natural objects is perhaps *Kōhakubai-zu byōbu* (Red and white plum trees) on folding screens, in the Atami MOA Art Museum. In chapter 37 Katō mentions Terada Tōru's reaction to the painting; see note 11 there, and see also Harold P. Stern, *Rimpa: Masterworks of the Japanese Decorative School* (New York: Japan Society, 1971).

arts was different from ours. It didn't necessarily mean that Japanese art was skimpy whereas the reverse was true in France but rather that historical art occupied a different position—in terms of its prominence and role—within their respective intellectual milieus as a whole. Once the world of art came to assume a special meaning for me, it was only natural that the object of my future interest would not necessarily be French art alone. In fact, I was interested above all in thinking about the intimate and indeed, inseparable, relationship between the history of Japanese art and the spiritual history of Japan—going beyond mere contemplation of the natural surroundings of Japanese gardens or the background of lyric poetry into much broader and much more fundamental issues. But these reflections took place almost a decade after my first stay in France.

When contemplating French art before I came to the West, my immediate association was with nineteenth-century paintings (if I'd been born, say, in Chicago instead of Tokyo, I suppose it would not have made any difference). But after living in France, I came to appreciate the far greater impact of twelfth- and thirteenth-century architecture, sculpture, and stained glass designs. That was nothing unusual, just common knowledge. The Gothic style that developed in northern France spread throughout Europe and became the dominant form for several centuries. If Italy is the country that best represents the Renaissance, France is the country that epitomizes the medieval Gothic style.

My initial interest in medieval art was not based on any such considerations in art history. Rather, it was because I could see medieval architecture right before my eyes, and it caught my fancy. I liked the old stones and the colors on their rough surfaces. They were sometimes light and sometimes dark, or gray, or yellow, or roseate. I also liked the kaleidoscopic variations in which the heavy stones come to terms with the soft, vertical lines ascending to the sky. At times the weightiness of the stones deemphasizes the impact of form, at times the exquisite delicacy of form diffuses the gravity of the material, and yet in other instances, the perfect equilibrium of form and material produces a perfect harmony.

I also loved to watch the interplay of light and shadow created by the tall towers and the flying buttresses. A tower sometimes appears like a narrow auger rising above the distant horizon against the evening twilight. Sometimes, it soars dauntlessly into the sky amid a snowstorm;

and yet at other times it appears to be sprinkling soft musical notes from the church bells into the clear blue sky. On the outside of churches there are stone statues of the saints and on the inside, stained glass. The expressions on the saints' faces betray the intensity of their inner spirituality. With the exception of the sculptured heads of Buddhist deities from the Northern Wei period, I know of no other works in sculpture that could delineate with such flawless precision what might well be described as spiritual profundity.[4] The faces of the angels often radiate an indescribable tenderness. I had never before seen such an enrapturing sweetness that transcends the realm of the senses.

And of course the stained glass provides the only colors in the monochrome world of the church and produces a direct, sensual elegance. From the windows set in the churches' high ceilings, they seem to shine like a myriad of jewels. From the windows nearby, dramatic scenes in all sorts of human postures depicted in strong pulsating lines come alive. All of these images enchanted me, and before long I became enormously fascinated by the astonishing diversity of character among the churches built in the same Gothic style.

Medieval art spreads all over Europe. And if one looks beyond the Gothic structures to include Romanesque architecture and sculpture, its magnitude becomes even more formidable. To satisfy my curiosity, I traveled widely in France. I also realized that if circumstances allowed, I should go beyond its borders. I hoped to give my observations a degree of coherence by limiting them to medieval art. But I doubt very much if I succeeded. I felt that the area to cover was infinite and my fascination boundless, and if I were to become really serious about my enterprise, I could easily ruin what I had been working for so far in my life. I told myself that I must seize the right opportunity and get out of it.

Beyond the strong impressions individual art objects left on me, my reasonably judicious observations of medieval art left me with a propensity for tracing the historical development of specific styles in art. During the process, I noticed the imprecise use of language in narratives

4. Strong Buddhist influences in the Northern Wei dynasty (386–534), despite massive Sinification efforts, especially during the reign of Hsiao Wen Ti (471–99), contributed to making this period one of the great ages of Chinese Buddhist sculpture, exemplified by the famous shrines and colossal Buddhist figure sculptures at Yünkang along with the images at Lungmen (see Michael Sullivan, *The Arts of China* [Berkeley: University of California Press, 1984], 104–14).

about styles in sculpture and grew skeptical about whether stylistic changes in medieval sculpture could be delineated as a linear development at all, even with more precise language. I had no time then to meticulously examine these questions and consider every significant piece of work in medieval sculpture. Later on, I was able to reexamine these same questions with regard to almost all the major works of Japanese Buddhist sculpture from the Asuka to the early Kamakura period.[5] I might not have been able to accomplish this task if I hadn't roamed about the French countryside, waiting for buses, traveling on foot under the blazing sun, or making my rounds visiting solitary churches until sunset.

I liked traveling alone, hopping from one cheap lodging place to another. One time I missed the bus that came only once a day, and I had to wait until the next day to visit the only other church not too far away from where I was. Another time I lost my way and wandered into a desolate place late at night with no one to greet me except a suspicious policeman. On my return from a long trip, the first scenes of Paris coming into view through my train window invariably evoked in me the same emotions I had experienced when I first saw the area around Ueno on the Shin'etsu line on my return to Tokyo from Shinano Oiwake at summer's end. It was a nostalgic emotion of homecoming, a sense of relief for having returned to the good old city, a feeling of going back to a regular routine. I had never felt more strongly that I was a resident of Paris and not just a temporary visitor. There is no place like home. Yet living represents the interplay of accumulated experiences, sometimes with past experiences reinforcing those in the present, and sometimes with the present reviving memories of a long-forgotten past; and to live is to be able to sense this entire process as a tangible continuity. But is there a reality beyond this perception of continuity? When I thought of "last year," its substance no longer had any bearing on events in Japan. And with the passage of time, "last year" soon turns into "the year before last," and then "the year before the year before last." In the can-

5. The Asuka period in Japanese art history, roughly 593–645 [or 671, or 710]; the Kamakura period, 1185 [or 1192]–1333. Katō's study on this subject is best represented by his major essay "Butsuzō no yōshiki" (Styles of Buddhist sculpture), in *Shōwa bungaku zenshū*, 28:598–621; in it he attempts a redefinition of "realism" as it relates to narratives on the history of sculpture. See also his essays on the same and related subjects in *Form, Style, Tradition*, trans. John Bester (Berkeley: University of California Press, 1971).

vas of my past, my experiences in Paris came to assume a greater immediacy just as those in Tokyo were relegated further and further into the background.

I got off the train easily, not having lots of baggage to worry about. I would buy some cigarettes at the stand in front of the train station, have some coffee, read about the change of cabinet in the paper, or give a friend a call. And when I felt it was time, I would get up from my seat and catch the right bus home.

29 Communication from Home

Correspondence was not the only form of communication from home. An endless stream of travelers from Japan descended on Paris—distant relatives, middle-school classmates, friends of a friend—all of them wanting me to "show them around." "Are there any interesting places to go?" my uncle, a vice president of a large company, asked me the same question. In those days, despite strict control over access to foreign currency, Japanese travelers seemed to have more money than they could spend. I had never been to any first-class restaurants in Tokyo, and thanks to them, I became familiar with a number of such places in Paris.

Besides acting as a tourist guide, I also agreed on occasions to work as an interpreter at week-long conferences. For instance, when a French labor union held a reception for Japanese officials from Sōhyō, they had to recruit a Japanese interpreter in Paris.[1] The hourly pay was not that good, but I was interested in the French labor movement. And the work itself was quite interesting.

C.G.T. officials gave a systematic presentation of their organization and their thinking.[2] "All medical and other expenses resulting from

1. Sōhyō (*Nihon rōdō kumiai sōhyō gikai*), at the time Japan's largest national organization of labor unions, began in July 1950 with an official membership of 3.77 million. It took a more radical leftist position after 1951, against the background of the Korean War and changing U.S.-Japan relations under the security treaty. From the mid-1950s it had a close, though controversial, relationship with the Japanese Socialist Party and in 1989 became part of the Japan Trade Union Confederation (*Nihon rōdō kumiai sōrengōkai*).
2. C.G.T., the Confédération générale du travail (general confederation of labor), formed in 1895, is the largest labor union and has close ties to the French Communist party.

injuries incurred during working hours have to be paid in full by the company."

"Does that include accidents caused by the carelessness of the worker himself?" one of the Japanese visitors asked.

"Absolutely."

"But what happens if a train operator dozes off at work and suffers an injury?"

"Of course that too is the responsibility of the company."

At that, a commotion overtook the Japanese side.

"I'm not sure how that argument holds up. Now we are talking about someone who clearly dozed off and hurt himself. If you include a case like that . . . ?"

A debate ensued among the Japanese themselves. The French, anxious to know what was going on, looked at me with inquisitive eyes. I had to say something.

"The Japanese are now deliberating the reasons why the company should bear the responsibility for accidents when they are caused by their employees dozing off," I told them.

The French response came as swiftly as an arrow. "Who wants to doze off at work? It's the company that creates the kind of working conditions that make people doze off. And for that reason, all responsibilities for all such accidents have to be borne by the company."

"Well, I'm not so sure. . . ." the Japanese side muttered.

"I'd say if you can get people to accept that kind of logic, then there's no problem."

"That's why. . . ."

"What a surprise this is!"

It was not that I did not understand how they felt, but to translate such sentiments into French was beyond my skill as an interpreter.

Among the French labor union officials, one of them was a middle-aged man with a scar on his forehead. When we asked him how he got it, he said nonchalantly that it resulted from torture by the SS. He told us that he had been arrested in occupied France and that he had "smashed up the heads of two guards" and escaped.

"I don't like Moscow. It's too different from Paris," he told us. "When I came to Vienna, I felt so relieved. Perhaps because it resembled Paris." He was a Communist, to be sure, but I thought he was first and foremost a Frenchman.

I also worked as an interpreter for the Japanese delegation to an international conference held in Switzerland for government representatives. Consisting of about a dozen Japanese Diet members, the group met with the speaker of the Parliament and the president and toured the mountains by mountain trolley. The group bought several dozen watches per person and surprised the salesgirls by declaring that they would buy up all the postcards in the shop. Some of them did attend the conference itself, if only erratically. In their less enthusiastic moments, only two attended, and one dozed off during the conference. When he opened his eyes and tried to adjust his earphone, I asked, "Do you want me to interpret?" From the earphone, only the English and French versions could be heard.

"Nope, no need for that," he said. "Everyone is just talking about things like freedom or democracy. Basically everything I know."

But even in a social gathering like this conference, representatives from postcolonial countries raised sharp criticisms against imperialism. In contrast to their often denunciatory tone, representatives from Western Europe were put on the defensive, and their arguments sounded almost vindicatory. This sharp contrast very tellingly reflected the international atmosphere and tendencies for a time during the postwar period. And I doubt if those were "just things he already knew."

Mr. H, an upper-house member of the Fourth Republic, requested a meeting with two representatives from the Japanese Socialist Party and asked them a series of questions on Japanese foreign policy. They had to do with Japanese policy toward China, Japan's relationship with Taiwan, the division of Korea, nuclear weapons, and the Japan-U.S. Security Treaty.

"Of course the Japanese Socialist Party is opposed to the Japan-U.S. Security Treaty. We are also engaged in the struggle against military bases. Please tell him that."

"What are the reasons for your opposition?" H asked.

"The Japanese Constitution stipulates that we relinquish our military weapons. So they're against the Constitution."

"That's your legal basis. What then is your political basis?"

"We don't want to get involved in wars. We wish only for peace."

"By that, do you mean that military alliances in general are dangerous, or the Japan-U.S. Security Treaty in particular is dangerous?"

"What a finicky question! I don't know what answer to give to that." The two Japanese looked at each other and then said, "In any case, the decision is based on the principle of our party. We cannot answer every single question about why we do this or that. When we said that we are opposed to nuclear weapons, why, he immediately demanded the reason. Why don't you just tell him that it's Hiroshima's earnest prayer. He'll understand that!"

"I wonder if the guy is really against nuclear weapons," said the other Japanese.

"Why don't you ask him that?" I suggested.

H gave a logical and coherent answer. According to him, if France were to develop its own nuclear weapons, it would cost too much economically. Socially, it would only aggravate the lack of highly skilled technicians in other areas. Militarily, it was difficult to retaliate with nuclear weapons. Politically, it would only exacerbate the Cold War and give rise to the vicious cycle of more military expansion and greater tension. . . . By now I cannot remember everything H said. What I do remember is the extraordinary gap between the Frenchman's discourse and the Japanese notion of "earnest prayer." Not only did that gap perplex me as an interpreter, it also compelled me, as a Japanese, to reflect on many things.

Through my work as an interpreter, I got to meet many people in Paris, and I also learned about certain facets of the Japanese people unbeknownst to me when I was in Tokyo. But these were not necessarily the result of my work as an interpreter alone. Although I was engaged in medical research in Paris, I was not a physician by profession. Occasionally, however, when my countrymen fell ill in this foreign land and wanted to consult a Japanese doctor through the introduction of a mutual acquaintance, I would usually comply with their wishes as long as no great obstacles stood in my way.

One time, I learned from a telephone call from Takata Hiroatsu that Shiga Naoya and Umehara Ryūzaburō had been involved in a traffic accident in the suburbs of Paris.[3] It happened the day following their arrival in Paris after their trip through Italy. Fortunately, they did not suf-

3. Shiga Naoya (1883–1971), an accomplished short-story writer, leading member of the influential literary group Shirakaba-ha (white birch school) in the 1910s and the early 1920s, and prewar I-novelist whose only long and still much discussed novel *An'ya kōro* (Dark night's passing, 1921–37; Eng. trans. Edwin McClellan, 1976) depicts a young artist's quest for inner peace and a place in the world beyond. • Umehara Ryūzaburō (1888–1986), a distinguished painter of Western-style works closely associated in his early career with Shiga Naoya and the journal *Shirakaba;* he incorporated the techniques and traditional expressions of *yamato-e* with the styles of *nanga* and Ogata Kōrin.

fer any serious injuries. Mr. Umehara said that he had just a few scratches on his forehead, and he looked fine. Mr. Shiga did appear to be exhausted, but from a medical point of view, he had nothing to worry about. Mr. Takata and I visited them at their hotel. I explained their situation to them and suggested that they get some rest. I also told them that I would be happy to help in whatever way I could and left them with my telephone number.

That was the first time I had met Mr. Umehara. As for Shiga Naoya, though it was the first time I had ever spoken with him, I had seen him many times at the Nō Theater at Suidōbashi during the war. He always carried himself with an air of transcendental grace. His countenance, his white hair, and his poise had not changed in the slightest after all these years. Only a few days after the accident, we found ourselves talking together as we took a stroll down the Champs-Elysées under the strong afternoon sun.

"Mantegna was really interesting," Shiga said. "You know about his painting of Christ? I was thinking of writing about it in my story."

After leaving Japan, he first went to Greece and Egypt before traveling from northern Italy down to the south (Mantegna's painting of Christ can be found in a gallery in Milan).[4] By the time he arrived in Rome, he was physically exhausted. On top of that, he had been looking at so many paintings "skyward" that his eyes were "turbid with tears," and he no longer seemed to have "much interest in looking at the works by men like Raphael." That reaction coincided exactly with my long-held image of Shiga Naoya based on his bearing and his works—a man of keen sensibility, a literary solipsist with a precise sense of language and a thorough self-centeredness. His mild manners had no trace of arrogance or pretentiousness, and with his dignified presence, he merged splendidly with the surroundings of the Champs-Elysées. I suppose a man whose presence of mind could not be swayed even by the weight of the Italian Renaissance surely would not have been struck with wonderment by a place like the Champs-Elysées. Taking no notice of his surroundings, Shiga continued his leisurely talk. "I feel fine now. Seems just a matter of exhaustion. But the most interesting thing I saw was Mantegna's image of Christ."

Once I was also asked by the Paris bureau chief of the Japan Broad-

4. Mantegna's painting *The Dead Christ* (1506) is in Milan's Brera Art Gallery.

casting Corporation to go to a hotel near the place de la Concorde to pay a visit to an announcer who had fallen ill during his trip. He had gone all the way to Helsinki for a live broadcast of the Olympics and had fallen ill there. Even before his departure, it seemed that he had not felt well, but he forced himself to go anyway. After the conclusion of the Olympic games, he came to Paris with his friends from the media, only to find himself too sick to move. When I went to see him, he looked better than I had expected and he was overjoyed to see a Japanese physician. That alone, I thought, was worth my trip.

"She has really been taking good care of me," he gestured toward a young nurse with his eyes while trying to get up from his bed, "but after all we can't communicate in words. It makes me so happy to be able to ask for your help in Japanese."

He told me that ever since leaving Japan, all he had thought about was how to return home at the earliest possible moment. "Don't you think it's funny? If only I could sleep on a tatami mat one more time, I wouldn't mind dying for it."

When he finished talking, I checked his blood pressure and concluded that it was totally out of the question to send him back to Japan. I suggested that he be immediately given the best possible medical attention at a well-equipped hospital, and even with that I was not sure his life could be saved. "If only I could sleep on a tatami mat one more time, I wouldn't mind dying for it." Beyond bringing myself to give short responses, it became almost unbearable for me to continue our conversation. After promising to come the next day, I rose from my seat and asked the nurse to come outside with me. In a soft voice, she anxiously inquired after his condition. I briefly explained what his situation was.

"We have to take him to the hospital as soon as possible. I'll talk with the bureau chief and make the necessary arrangements. But a coma brought on by uremia could occur at any time. It may happen tonight. I want you to be prepared for it."

"Because I don't understand what he says, I'm afraid there are many things I can't do," she said at that time. "Although I'm not very experienced, I'll follow your instructions and try to do my best."

Only three days later and soon after the ill-fated announcer had been transferred to a hospital, he fell into a coma and died without ever regaining consciousness.

There was little I could do in his room before his transfer to the hospital. To give the kind, conscientious nurse a little break, I sometimes invited her out for coffee nearby. In those hectic hours, we quickly became good friends. Perhaps it was because we were both foreigners in France and because we both developed a bond with the same patient, however briefly it might be. She was from Denmark, and while she wasn't accustomed to speaking French, her English was fluent.

"What will you do after this patient?" I asked her.

"Well, I suppose I'll take care of another patient."

"Where?"

"Most likely in Paris, but I don't know for sure."

Somewhere in my heart, I wished that she would be working in Paris. And then one day, when she suddenly asked me, "What do you think of Dr. Schweitzer?" I was somewhat stunned. "I think he is a modern-day saint," she said.

"I don't believe anybody is a saint," I responded.

"It's strange that a person like you would say that."

"A person like me? But you don't know me."

"Oh yes, I do," she said with a smile.

"Hmm, I wonder about that." I was trying to tease her, but I had something else on my mind.

"I think somebody has to help the doctor with his work," she said.

His hospital in the African jungle was recruiting nurses, and she had applied. It looked like Dr. Schweitzer himself would come to Paris to take her back with him to his hospital. It would be a two-year contract, and she felt that nothing would give her more emotional satisfaction than working at his hospital. As she was telling me all this with shining eyes, she looked vibrant and beautiful. That beauty almost perplexed me. I could not even begin to tell how much more precious this young woman before me was over any African hospital or any "saint." I was impressed with her beauty and I felt affectionate toward her. My only regret was that she would be leaving, for whatever reason, for a land far away. "What an unlucky fellow you are," I thought to myself. "When it comes to someone who matters, I have to compete with Dr. Schweitzer of all people!" But at that point, it was obvious that nobody could have prevented her from going.

However, a few months after she left for Africa, she sent me a long letter. From it, I could well surmise why she had not written right after her arrival, what had happened in the last several months, how her thoughts and mood had changed during the time, and why she had come to write this long letter. It began with "I remember our long conversation in Paris and that's why I am writing this letter. You are the one who can best understand what I mean." The old Dr. Schweitzer she had met in Paris was like a kind grandfatherly figure. But after arriving at the hospital in the jungle, she hardly had any chance of seeing him anymore. The doctor was so busy that he seldom had the time even to show up at the patients' ward. He had an endless stream of visitors, and in fact a group of Americans was just then making a film, to which the doctor was devoting all of his time and energy. Because of Dr. Schweitzer's opposition, the hospital had not yet acquired any X-ray equipment, and the other doctors working there were not necessarily happy about the situation. But by then she had gotten used to the tropical climate and the day-to-day routine of her hospital work. There was no mention of the word "disappointment" anywhere in her letter. But the reason she had gone to Africa with all her burning passion was to help a saint in his noble enterprise, surely not "to get used to the day-to-day work routine."

And finally an unfortunate incident had occurred. "He was really a nice young man, and if you had met him, I'm sure you would have liked him as well," she wrote. The young man, full of idealism, was working without pay in the construction of a hospital extension. But for whatever reason, in the middle of his work, the young man was driven out by Dr. Schweitzer. He had no other place to go. "I tried to comfort him, but he had already lost all hope. My best efforts proved useless, and he ended up committing suicide. I can't believe such a tragedy could happen."

I mentioned earlier that from the outset I myself professed no faith in any "saint," although I had faith in the young woman who had put her faith in "the saint." I respected her inner beauty. It was many years later that I wrote about this event in a short story called "The Great Humanitarian."[5] Perhaps my words failed to adequately convey my intent, and an immediate reaction came from a totally unexpected source. I learned from someone, an old and trusted friend, that one of my former teachers was furious after reading my work. I do not, however, have the habit of responding to secondhand criticism. With the death of my former teacher, my opportunity to respond to him directly was forever lost.

But if I had had the opportunity, how would I have pleaded my case? I don't suppose I would have. Instead, I probably would have said that if we were to discuss a hospital in Africa, we would first need to inquire

---

5. "Jindō no eiyū," first published in *Bungei* (September 1955), is in *Katō Shūichi chosakushū*, 13:219–55.

about the opinions of the Africans themselves, and in fact I had met and spoken to a number of them regarding this matter. I probably would also have said that before a citizen of a colonial empire could be transmuted into a "saint" for managing a hospital in its colony, we would need to know exactly what he thought about colonial imperialism itself. And because colonial imperialism by its very nature is founded on a system of hypocrisy, I probably would also have asked how it is possible to separate individual acts of goodwill from that system without challenging the system itself.

Back then in Paris, I was not incapable of raising such arguments. Yet I did not mention them to the young woman about to leave for Africa, for I did not feel it was necessary. I absolutely refused to hurt the heart of a woman I probably loved in exchange for the reputation and authority of a legendary figure.

30   Two Women

In those days, there was virtually no mention of Japan in the French press. Nor was there much chance for me to talk about Japan with the French. Our everyday conversation was not about the kabuki theater or about the Yoshida cabinet; it was, or, rather, it could only be, about the Théâtre national populaire or Mendès-France.[1] Perhaps the only exception was Robert Guillain, who, as *Le Monde's* special correspondent to the Far East, had been traveling back and forth between Tokyo and Paris since the prewar days. This was what he told me: "You ask me what the French public know about Japan? All right, let me tell you. Before I left for Japan, my mother always asked me: 'Can you eat fish in Japan?' I told her over and over again that she had to be kidding, that Japan has ten times as many varieties of fish as France. And then two or three years later when I was about to depart for Japan again, she asked me the same question. It's just hopeless."

That was the time when the French army was still fighting a war in Indochina, when cease-fire negotiations in Korea had dragged on at Panmunjom, and some years before Japan's economic recovery was to become the center of international attention.[2] Among my friends, the left-

---

1. Prime Minister Yoshida Shigeru (1878–1967) organized five separate cabinets from 1946 to 1954. • Pierre Mendès-France (1907–82) was prime minister of France from June 1954 to February 1955.
2. The Vietnamese struggle for independence continued until 1954, with the French defeat at Dien Bien Phu. The country was divided at the 17th parallel into North and South Vietnam at the conference in Geneva. • Negotiations at Panmunjom began in July 1951 but dragged on for two years until an armistice was signed on July 27, 1953.

ists were perhaps the only people besides the veteran Guillain who had some interest in postwar Japan, even though they might not have any concrete knowledge about the country. From the left wing's point of view, it was a matter of great concern to know where and what kind of resistance John Foster Dulles's anti-Communist crusaders were facing in the world, and I suppose in that specific context, the conditions in Japan also warranted their attention. This was especially true after May 1, 1952.[3] On that day the Japanese masses burned American cars in the square in front of the Imperial Palace, and for the first time after the war they ascended to the world stage. "How would the Japanese people express their will next time? What opportunities would native Japanese capitalists seize to regain the Chinese market?" Intellectuals of the French left seemed to have no doubt about their premise that the Japanese people were against the U.S. remilitarization policy for Japan and that Japanese capitalism could not possibly be satisfied to trade with Taiwan alone.

One time, I tried to explain to a Communist friend of mine that Japan's internal affairs were not that simple. She could not be easily persuaded and said that to pressure Japan into remilitarization less than ten years after demilitarizing the country was tantamount to making a mockery of the Japanese people.

"There's no way they can be satisfied with the situation," she said.

"But on the other hand, the Japanese economy did improve as a result of Korea's special procurement demands."

"I think the ones who've profited from the war were the capitalists and not the people."

"But by keeping businesses from going under, the workers too will be saved."

"That's only a secondary phenomenon. I don't think it changes the essence of the matter."

"But the masses don't concern themselves with the essence of things.

---

3. On May Day 1952 in the square before the Imperial Palace, protesters (variously reported as 6,000 up to 30,000) against the Japan-U.S. Security Treaty and the San Francisco Peace Treaty (1951) gathered—despite government obstruction of the square against a district court's order granting permission for such use—and clashed with armed Japanese police. The incident resulted in 2 deaths, more than 1,000 casualties, and the arrest of over 1,200 people. After 20 years of litigation, in November 1972 the Tokyo Supreme Court found 16 protesters guilty but threw out the primary charge of trying to instigate a riot. See Okamoto Mitsuo, *Meedee jiken* (The May-day incident [Shiraishi shoten, 1977]).

Even if in fact it's a secondary phenomenon, they'd only react to direct consequences, whether favorably or unfavorably."

"Well, psychological reactions are just a variable," she said. "The essence of the matter determines the latent discontent of the people. Whether or not the discontent manifests itself depends on the situation at the time."

"That's why I say the situation at the time isn't as simple as you think."

"Perhaps you're right. But the interests of American imperialism can never coincide with those of the Japanese people."

As a matter of fact, there was no reason to expect that they would even coincide with those of Japanese native capitalism in the first place, and so I supposed the Japanese government would someday consider expanding trade with China against American pressure.

"Japan has to import raw materials and export manufactured products. As a market for Japanese products, China is more important than the industrialized countries in the West. The Japanese economy cannot continue to prosper without China," she remarked.

I, too, agreed that this might be true in the long run. But in the short run, again one could not make this simplistic assertion because there were other factors to consider. And we talked about this matter as well.

She was a Jew with Romanian roots. Small-framed and slim with a darkish complexion, she had eyes that always shone with a glowing vitality. There was a nonchalant air about her; the color of her clothes, their rough texture, and even their cut matched and so suited her small frame, her black hair, and her expressive gestures that the impression she gave could almost be described as one of refinement. She was married, but I had no idea what her husband did for a living.

"Now, this doesn't concern you, does it?"

"I am surprised that you can come out so often on Sundays!" I said.

"I come out because I can. No need for you to worry about it."

She herself was a schoolteacher. And a passionate admirer of Stalin.

"What do you think of Picasso's portrait?"

This was the time when the French Communist Party was fiercely criticizing Picasso's portrait for desecrating Stalin's aura of authority. I was reminded of the words of Picasso himself: "Whether a society is capitalist or socialist, there is no difference in the way the shoemaker hammers in his nails."[4]

4. When Stalin died in 1953, Louis Aragon, editor of *Les Lettres françaises,*

"If it makes no difference to him whose portrait he paints, there was no need for him to do Stalin's. To us, Stalin has a special significance. And to deliberately desecrate that significance . . ."

But our opinions on Stalin and at least on the nature of Soviet power were not as radically different as our opinions about Picasso. In those days, if one were to believe western European "Soviet specialists," Stalin would have become critically ill once every year—in fact they said he had, on various occasions, been on the verge of death. If the dictator died, confusion and disintegration would inevitably follow within the Soviet system. However, year after year Stalin did not die, and the Soviet system of course did not disintegrate even after Stalin's death. I had no faith in the opinions of "Soviet specialists" in the Western press. With regard to their writings about the concentration camps and the secret police, she asserted without reservation that "those are merely propaganda from reactionary newspapers." I thought they might or might not be so, and the reason I stated was that I had yet to see the Soviet Union with my own eyes, and I had no firsthand information myself.

"The German-Soviet Non-Aggression Pact was just a means of self-defense by the socialist regime in response to its betrayal at the Munich Agreement. What do you think the Soviet Union *should* have done if they hadn't made the non-aggression pact with Germany?" she asked.

What should it have done? I, naturally, did not have the answer.

"Finland? If the Soviets had waited, the German army would have gone into it first.[5] The war had already begun, you know—the war Stalin didn't start."

I had to agree with her point that since 1917 it was western European imperialism that had sent its army into Soviet territory, and that the Soviet Union had never started a war.

---

asked a somewhat reluctant Picasso to do a portrait of him. The plain, rather lifeless, and unflattering image Picasso sketched from an early photograph triggered the fury of the French Communist Party, by whom Stalin was still revered; one English critic (Timothy Hilton, *Picasso* [London: Thames and Hudson, 1975], 265) calls the work "surprisingly clumsy, even amateurish." See also Patrick O'Brian, *Pablo Ruiz Picasso: A Biography* (New York: G. P. Putnam's Sons, 1976), 412–13.

5. After the Finnish government refused Stalin's demands in October 1939 for a strategic area of the Karelian Isthmus and the lease of the Hanko Peninsula, the Soviet Union invaded Finland on November 30, 1939 and set up a puppet government two days later.

"Remember, the Soviet declaration of war on Japan was *after,* not be-fore, the declaration of war on the Soviet Union by Japan's ally," she said emphatically. Perhaps our difference was just that she took a very clear-cut, definitive stand on issues, whereas I was skeptical and would not unequivocally agree with any position.

I probably looked younger than my age. There was in fact almost no age difference between us, but she seemed to think I was ten years younger. This sort of thing did not happen to me alone; many Japanese men had the same experience with Westerners. Be that as it may, I had never been denied entry to a movie theater because of being mistaken for a minor. And yet even a decade later, when I was lecturing at a uni-versity abroad, I was mistaken for a student quite a few times.

I also noticed that I could very well pass as a Chinese, an Indochinese, or a member of the "yellow race" from central Asia. It was not just the Westerners; even the Asian peoples themselves seemed to think of me that way. To jump a little ahead in the sequence of events, many years later when I went to the central Asian city of Tashkent, somebody asked me the way in the local Uzbek language. At that time I knew how to say "I can't speak Russian" in Russian, but I didn't know how to say "I can't speak Uzbek" in the Uzbek language.

Still more so in the West, Asians are very often lumped together and known collectively as Chinese. In the back streets of Rome, children would gather around me shouting "Chinese! Chinese!" scrutinizing me as I scrutinized their city. In Paris I was an Indochinese, because at that time Paris had many foreign students from French-controlled Indochina. Once I was accosted by a middle-aged man at a subway station.

"What are you doing in Paris?"

"I'm studying medicine." I gave him a short answer.

"When do you plan to go back home?" the man was a little drunk. I didn't pay attention to him.

"So you don't want to go back at a time when your people are suf-fering, is that it? Don't you know they're the true patriots? Don't you feel ashamed to be living in France?"

Meanwhile, the man's speech became more and more eloquent. "Your people are fighting a war, but Bao Dai is having a good time in southern France.[6] He is nothing but a tool of colonialism. What are you doing in

6. Bao Dai (Nguyen Vinh Thuy, 1913–97), the last emperor of Vietnam's Nguyen dynasty, until 1945, when he abdicated as Ho Chi Minh rose to power;

France when your country is fighting for its independence?" And quite naturally, the man's compelling lecture came to an end when I called his attention to the fact that I was a Japanese.

Racial prejudice did not cause me any unpleasant experiences, at least not in my daily life. But the Romanian Jew often talked about racial discrimination.

"Why do you think they dropped the atomic bomb on Hiroshima? I tell you, it was because the people living there were Asians."

"The fact that they were Asians might have had something to do with it," I corrected her statement.

"You said racial prejudice is not prevalent in Paris? How can you say that? Don't you think that few places could be worse in terms of racial discrimination?" she said.

Racial prejudice, she maintained, did not take the form of Asians being refused housing. It became apparent when, say, a man and a woman got a little more intimate. She made it sound as if it was only because of her that we were still friends, whereas other women would probably not have bothered. The impression I got from her was not a pleasant one. I do not get down on my knees to beg for anyone's friendship—at least that was something I did not want to do.

My friendship with her did not last long. One day she told me that she wanted to talk in a quiet place such as in my room. At that time I was staying at a small place in the city. I showed her in, leaving the door half open, and helped her take off her raincoat. Outside, there was a misty drizzle. She sat down in an armchair and surveyed the room with her eyes. "Hmm, nice and clean," she muttered meaninglessly. Then she got up, closed the door, and locked it. I was silent.

"You're a doctor, aren't you?" she said, and without waiting for my answer, she asked me to examine her, saying that she was not feeling well.

I explained to her that I could not do that because I was not a practicing physician and that I also did not have the necessary equipment with me. But I added that I would be happy to hear her out and offer some advice.

"You don't need the tools to find out," she said. To be sure, she looked pale and tired.

---

in 1949 the French restored him as a puppet emperor. After a referendum in 1955 abolished the monarchy, he lived in exile on the French Riviera, earning a reputation as a playboy.

"Let me be the judge of that after I get all the details. Now, please tell me what's wrong."

All she gave me, however, was a discursive and ambiguous account about her stomach and intestines not feeling well, and she had no specific symptoms that might suggest an illness. When I asked her for more details, she repeated peevishly, "Aren't you going to examine me?" Then she suddenly rose from the chair, took off her blouse, and lay on the bed. Under her black undergarment was her slender upper body, her chest moving quietly up and down with her breathing. In order to begin my examination, I would have to lean over her. I realized that my "examination" was not going to end there. In the small room, the distance separating the bed and my chair was just three steps. Should I maintain that distance or should I cross it? For a moment I could not make up my mind.

Then I said, "I don't think you need to be examined."

"You are a strange man!" she said in a voice calmer than I had expected. "So what should I do? Please tell me what treatment I'll need."

But she herself must have realized that there was no longer any point in talking about it. She turned up the collar of her raincoat, and as she was about to step out onto the sidewalk into the misty rain, she said, "Au revoir!" as if nothing had happened. But both of us clearly knew that it was going to be our last good-bye.

Chicago in North America has a "black belt," an exclusively black community. The northern part of Paris, on the other hand, has a "red belt" where a majority of the residents vote for the Communist Party. One Sunday morning, I visited the town of St-Denis in that area, not with the female Stalinist but with a bourgeois woman, the proprietor of an art gallery in Paris. Our plan was to go to Chantilly in her Buick and stop by the Romanesque church in St-Denis on our way. We would then go through Senlis to look at some Gothic structures on our way back.

It might be an exaggeration to say that I had always been dumbfounded by her Buick; but its enormous size did strike me as being rather ludicrous. Moreover, in those days American cars were like birds incapable of flight despite their wings.[7] As her car entered the town of St-Denis,

7. In this literary allusion Katō paraphrases from a famous envoi (*hanka*) to the long poem (*chōka*) "Hinkyū mondō ka" (Dialogue on poverty) by Yamanoue no Okura, a major Man'yō poet known for his concern about life's hard-

we saw the graffiti U.S. GO HOME painted in white on the pavements and on walls.

"Do you think the Communists did that?" Looking at her beautiful profile, I tried to get her to talk about what was on my mind.

"I suppose they're the ones who painted it, but the sentiment goes beyond the Communists," she gave me an unexpected answer as she was looking for a place to park. But surely, many of the business clients at her gallery were Americans.

"I heard that somebody wrote on the door of a wine shop in the Champs-Elysées. . . ." I said. It was something I had just read some where. Anticipating what I was going to say, she laughed. "Saying U.S. DON'T GO HOME right? Well, there are certainly people who feel that way as well. But, you know, there are things money can't buy."

The workers there were standing and talking to one another on the church pavement or basking in the sun. When we got out of the car, I felt all at once that their eyes were riveted on us. What hotshots were going to get out from that ridiculously huge car? Instead of American tourists, out came a French woman and a mean-looking Oriental man. Now what sort of relationship could they possibly have . . .

Undisturbed, she went on looking at the church. The workers were looking at her looking at something that did not interest them, while I was looking at the workers themselves, realizing that there was a big gap between us. It reminded me of the days when children had followed me like phantoms along the village paths in Saitama Prefecture.[8] As a child, I felt at the time the insurmountable distance separating us. Had I not changed in all these years? Was I always the third party, always the observer no matter where I might be?

The gap between me and her circle of friends in Paris was also quite considerable. I was bored after spending hours with formally behaved, overbearing, unfeeling, and frivolous men and women who never seemed to run out of conversation topics, and I became irritated at myself for having wasted my time. When she was with these people, she had no interest in me. With them she was on her home turf, as it were, always energetic, chatty, and cheerful. Before whatever friend she was speaking with could finish what he or she was saying, she was already

---

ships: *Tobitachikanetsu tori ni shi araneba* (But I cannot take flight, not being a bird with wings).

8. See chapter 2.

seeking out the next person to socialize with. She was friendly to everyone, but there was also no question that she was only half-heartedly interested in what anyone had to say.

"Oh, I'm so tired! I guess that's part of my job."

I thought she had to be joking. If that was a necessary part of her business, why did she always have to involve me in it? But when I was with
her alone, she was almost like a different person—quiet, sensitive, and
considerate. She had gotten married young and had separated from her
husband, and she said she hardly ever thought of him. I was never bored
when I was alone with her. But I was not sure why she kept on seeing
me, and this uncertainty constantly perplexed me. In her house in Passy,
she had a remarkable collection of Paul Klee. In fact, I had first gotten to
know her when I went to see her collection through the introduction of
a third party. During my subsequent visits to her house, however, I was
never able to feel at home. Her house was too large, and there were too
many things commemorating a life in which I had played no part.

"It has nothing to do with the fact that you are Japanese. I never feel
bored when I am talking to you," she remarked.

"You're not going to say that the majority of crimes in Paris are committed by Algerians, are you?"

"But according to the statistics . . ."

"You French are no different from us," I continued. "No different
from the Japanese who compiled the crime statistics for Korean residents
in Japan. It was not because Koreans had committed crimes that such
statistics existed; it was because such statistics had to be compiled that
the crimes were committed."

"You're being a little harsh today, aren't you?" she said quietly.

"What is harsh is not me but the reality of the situation," I replied.

For her, the "dirty war" in Indochina served only to exacerbate corruption and decadence within France. On the other hand, she was no fan
of Mendès-France's.[9] She found it "surprising that a wonderful actor
like Gérard Philipe could be a Communist," though she did recognize
the Communists' role during the French resistance. "In fact, it's important not to forget that the French resistance movement did not really
take place until after the landing in Normandy," she said. "Until then,

9. Mendès-France, a longtime harsh critic of French policy toward Indochina and North Africa, ended French involvement in Indochina during his
administration.

there were many who admired the Germans. Not all those who claimed to be resistance fighters while pillaging the countryside deserve to be called heroes, don't you agree?" At times like these, she possessed an air of transcendental objectivity. Perhaps that kind of objectivity is a luxury the privileged class alone could afford to dispense once in a while.

That day in the forest in Chantilly, the yellowing leaves glowed in the golden rays of the afternoon sun. As we strolled in the woods, I saw in her eyes a reflection of the high autumn sky and the quiet movement of the white clouds. I was completely entranced, body and mind, except for one thought: a time like this could not last. As a matter of fact, not only did this turn out as I expected, she made absolutely no attempt to repeat the experience with me. The night I spent in her bedroom in Passy, the taste of the *calvados* we had that evening, along with the image of the forest in Chantilly, lived on in me for a long time as if it had happened only yesterday. But it did not happen a second time. Did the fact that she had satisfied her curiosity make her act in such a way? Or was it because she had too many other diversions? Or could it be the result of some sort of self-imposed discipline in order to preserve our friendship into the future? My doubts lingered on. And the more wearisome I became over my doubts, the more I would try to explain everything away to suit my own convenience. After our visit to Chantilly, she said, "I envy your work as a doctor. At least you seem to have a goal in your life."

We were good friends. How could it have turned out otherwise, as long as two human beings were as fond as we were of Paul Klee's wit and humor, his delicate movement of lines, his delightful changes of tonality, and the feel of his works to the senses? To become true lovers, however, I suppose we were neither sufficiently blind nor sufficiently dreamy about our future.

31   Winter Journey

From my window seat on the Orient Express, I looked out into the distance at the snowy mountains of Switzerland as they began to sparkle in the rays of the morning sun. The heating in the compartment was working all too efficiently, and after my departure from Paris the afternoon before I had not been able to get a good night's sleep. Thoughts about the past and the future meandered through my mind. What an endless journey—this line from a song reverberated in my thoughts. The train was heading toward central Europe and would eventually take me to Vienna under the quadripartite Allied occupation. A young woman I met in Florence was there, waiting for me.

I was overwhelmed by the Italian Renaissance. Its impact on me hardly approximated anything a "sightseeing tour" might suggest. I could never have imagined the scale of its coloration or the allure of the marbles, nor dreamed of the extraordinary energy and talents they brought together to fully and richly realize the potential of the human senses. It is said that modern Europe began with the Italian Renaissance. Until one sees Venice and Florence with one's own eyes, that is just an empty statement. Even the collection of Italian paintings in the Louvre fails to do justice to the Renaissance in the profundity of its significance and the depth of its experience. Although Italy certainly did not alter my thinking, every observation I made about European culture helped define, directly or indirectly, the substance of my essential vocabulary. My own taste did not change because of that; I still preferred the fifteenth century to the height of the Renaissance in the sixteenth century, and more than the fifteenth century I cherished the age of Giotto. But my experience in Italy had absolutely no relevance to my personal preferences. Once he visited Florence, the American Bernard Berenson became so captivated that he spent the rest of his life there.[1]

From an art museum to a church, from a church to another art museum, from a room filled with the works of Fra Angelico to the next with the paintings of Lorenzo Lotto, I kept on walking as if I had been possessed. And there I saw a young woman who was walking on the same road and at the same pace as I was—a living, breathing woman among all the numerous others carved in marble. At that moment I was seized by a strong impulse to escape from the past capsulated within the art museums and into the bustling present under the sun on the streets filled with the aroma of coffee. I invited her to go up the hillside of the Boboli Gardens, which afforded a panoramic view of Florence from the top. The dark brown tower of the Palazzo Vecchio and the green dome of Santa Maria del Fiore soared skyward above layers of roofs, and the Arno River flowed below us.

"How long will you be staying in Florence?"

"Until tomorrow," she replied.

"Where will you go from here?"

"Venice."

"Would you like to go to Rome with me?" I said.

"I've just been to Rome."

"What about staying one more day and going to Siena?"

"Siena isn't on my itinerary."

"But I bet it'd be interesting. You won't regret it."

Petite and with the appearance of a student, she had with her a small camera, one that was certainly cheaper than those carried so proudly by Japanese tourists. On the hilltop, the chestnut-colored hair on her forehead fluttered in the wind.

"Do you like Strauss?" she asked suddenly.

We were both speaking in awkward English. She couldn't speak French, and I couldn't speak German.

"Well, I've listened to waltzes."

She laughed and said, "I meant Richard Strauss."

I could remember the tunes from Italian operas Grandfather had

1. Bernard Berenson (1865–1959), a scholar and art critic of Italian Renaissance art who studied languages and literatures at Harvard, shifting to art history after his visit to Italy. He became a foremost authority on Italian Renaissance artists and bequeathed I Tatti, his eighteenth-century villa outside Florence, to Harvard; it became the Center for Italian Renaissance Culture.

hummed when I was a child, and in the Parisian *opéra comique* I had heard what Nagai Kafū once called "Carmen's famous melodies." But in the long interim, I had not attended any opera performance. She said that whenever she came across art that moved her, she would recall her experience with Strauss's operas.

Once the train crossed the Austrian border, an officer from the British Occupation Army came on board to check our passports and baggage. That was quickly accomplished. Outside the window, the magnificent Swiss mountains began to give way to a subtly different landscape. The steep mountain slope was closing in on the railroad tracks. Scenes of snow-covered coniferous forests, brooks, bridges, and scattered farmhouses flashed outside the window and immediately receded into the background—images of remote, rustic mountain villages that would attract neither mountaineers nor tourists. Enchanted by the scenery, I drew my face toward the window with inquisitive eyes. Several passengers had gotten off the train in Switzerland, and the only people remaining in the eight-person compartment were a young couple clasped in an embrace in the seats opposite, and me.

Siena was wonderful. We had a late lunch on a balcony where we could see the Piazza del Campo's stone-paved streets and fountain as well as the surrounding medieval architecture. (We looked for the cheapest item on the menu to order, but the high cover charge, together with the tax and the tips, ran our bill to twice the price on the menu. Moreover, there was not enough food. Fortunately, she had brought along some dried sausage, which we sliced and ate with a small knife.)

Time stood still for us as we strolled through the old city. At the outskirts of town, a solitary church stood in the evening dusk. Deep inside the dark interior of its spacious main structure, a woman in black was kneeling in prayer alone with her child. A priest who happened to be passing by said in Italian, "This is a place for prayers, not for pleasure"— or so we thought. (She said in perfectly fluent Italian, "Excuse me, but could you tell me where the train station is?" But we couldn't really figure out his reply. I always had a feeling that I understood Italian when it was spoken to me, but afterwards I realized that I had absolutely no idea about what had been said.)

The autumn days were short, and by the time we got on the train to go back to Florence, the hills and plains of Tuscany were already enveloped in darkness. We could hear some Italians singing in chorus from another compartment, and the sound of their voices blended with the sound of the train's wheels. I ran my fingers through her soft, silky hair as I thought how we might never see each other again once our train arrived at its destination. The past we had shared—the afternoon on the hills of Florence and the day in Siena—was enough to convince us that we would not want to say farewell just like that, but not long enough to make us want to give up Rome or Venice on our itineraries. I was not thinking about the future then; I was simply totally immersed in the sensual realm of the present. The faint sensation on my fingertips permeated my entire body, and the only way I could describe that experience was to say that our hearts were one.

The extraordinarily long train of the Orient Express began its run on the plain, and the powdery snow drew oblique lines as it fell on the surface of the window. Now in the seats opposite mine, a man was explaining to a woman in French, "Now we're entering the Russian sector. The British are easy to deal with. Not so the Russians. You can never tell how long you have to wait at the border." His manner of speech suggested that he was quite familiar with the territory. His somewhat blunt statements, I suppose, might be attributed to the fact that he was from an occupying country. The woman was listening in silence. "The Russian officers speak only Russian," the man added.

After returning to Paris, I sent a postcard to the young woman I had met in Italy. When she wrote back and asked if I wanted to see Vienna, my curiosity was aroused—both about her and about the city. I was reminded of a motion picture Tōwa Company imported into Japan in the 1930s. In it, townswomen were dancing to waltz music with their skirts whirling like circles. A young maiden was singing "Das ist nur einmal, das kommt nicht wieder" (it comes only once and never again)[2]—the song became a hit in Tokyo—as she rode alone in a carriage speeding through the town late at night. I wanted to see the city with my own eyes.

I was also somewhat interested in comparing the occupation of Berlin with that of Vienna. At that time, tension had arisen in Berlin, while in Vienna the Russian and the Western occupation forces were able to coexist with few reports of conflicts. But getting there was certainly not easy. The whole country was divided up and occupied by four nations with only the capital, Vienna, under their joint administration. I applied for visas in Paris, but since the British, American, French, and Russian

2. From the theme song of Erik Charell's film *Der Kongress tanzt*. See chapter 9, note 4.

occupation authorities all issued visas separately, the application procedure was not only tedious, the time it took was totally unpredictable. By the time I finally received all the necessary papers, it was already toward the end of the year. But since I had no serious obligations in Paris, I made a reservation on the Orient Express and, with a small amount of baggage, boarded the train at the Gare du Nord shortly before Christmas. December was a busy month in Paris; the vitality of the city could be felt in the air. In my heart, I bade farewell to Paris, but when the train started to move, my thoughts were no longer with it.

Just when I thought the train had been traveling for quite a while through the British sector, it suddenly came to a halt. There was neither a train station nor a town nearby. The conductor came around and pulled down the window shades. "There are soldiers holding automatic rifles on both sides," the man sitting opposite me said in an explanatory tone, half for the benefit of his female companion and half for me. A little later two Russian soldiers came into the compartment. That was my first time face to face with soldiers from the Red Army. Both of them were young with plain rustic features, and neither allowed any expression to show on his face. Without uttering a word, they took the passports from the man and woman sitting opposite me, looked over the pages, and returned them, again in silence. Their manners were by no means rude, but one could not quite describe them as just being businesslike—though they undoubtedly meant to conduct themselves that way. There was something strangely awkward about their demeanor.

When I handed them my passport, they examined its pages but did not return it to me right away, as they had done with the couple. Meanwhile, there was a long pause with nobody speaking a word, and then a longer pause. I told myself that there could not be anything wrong with my passport. Then, quite suddenly, one of the soldiers looked up from the passport and began to say something in Russian.

"He's asking about your nationality," the man sitting across from me explained in French.

"I'm Japanese," I said in French, but the soldiers did not understand.

Then I remembered that the local language was German, and so I repeated myself in that language. Yet the soldier holding my passport and the other one standing silently next to him showed absolutely no reaction on their faces. "Japanese," the Frenchman said in Russian, and the soldiers began to thumb through the pages of my passport again.

I felt a little anxious, but more than that I was also beginning to get irritated by the absurdity of the whole thing. A passport is not an encyclopedia. There was not much written in it, and if one could not figure it out in three minutes, one certainly couldn't do so in three hours. Five minutes passed, then ten minutes. Finally the soldier handed back my passport in silence and walked out of the compartment. I felt relieved, but I had already broken into a sweat.

The French couple got off the train at the next stop. In their place, an elderly officer from the Red Army came in and took the window seat facing me. Suddenly I felt hungry, so I bought a hot sausage at the station, added some mustard, and ate it. Then I took out a Gauloise, taking my time smoking it as I opened the German grammar book I had bought in Paris. Even after all these years, German grammar still reminded me of the days when I had first started learning German at the First Higher School in Komaba and the dormitory life there. Part of the melody of its popular dormitory song revived in my mind, but I had forgotten almost all of its lyrics.

Sitting motionless like an Egyptian statue, the officer opposite me kept looking out the window at the incessant snowfall—that was all one could see. The train was approaching Vienna. There I was, a total stranger; the only person I knew was one young woman. The country's language was alien to my ears, and I could not even begin to imagine what its customs were like. I even found it difficult to believe that a large metropolis was soon to emerge from this endless stretch of snow. *Ikyō, dépaysement, ikusanka, au bout du monde* . . .[3] I was trying to approximate a psychological state of mind suggested by a mixture of all these Japanese and French expressions. When I found myself in an environment alien to my familiar daily routines, that would be a time for self-discovery. What lay in the depths of my emotional life? What, ultimately, were my aspirations? What would I be willing to sacrifice? And what could I expect to accomplish?

She met me at the station and, now that she was in a city she knew so well, she appeared to be even more self-confident than she had been in Italy. She had arranged for a place for me to stay in a convenient part of the old city, and on our way there from the Westbahnhof, she gave me a brief description of the city's geography. She mentioned many unfamiliar proper names I didn't quite grasp, but I can still remember the

3. *Ikyō* is a somewhat poetic term for "a foreign land"; *ikusanka* means roughly "far, far away from home."

names of places such as Stalin Square and the Brücke der Roten Armee (Red Army bridge). Later, I noticed that while these names did appear on city trams or on maps, no Viennese referred to them as such, preferring their old names of Schwarzenbergplatz and Reichsbrücke. (Still later, when the occupation ended, these artificially imposed names disappeared the day after the foreign troops left Vienna and were openly replaced by their original names, just as one would expect.) The structural damage to the city caused by the bombings was not as severe as I had imagined. To be sure, many buildings, most notably the Vienna State Opera House, could no longer be used, but not many places had been reduced to rubble.[4] The supply of goods was plentiful in the stores, and the city finally seemed to be on its way to recovery from the war devastation. Armed Red Army soldiers standing in pairs appeared like shadows amid the blowing storm, only to disappear the next moment in the drifting snow.

Since its regular house could no longer be used, the national opera company performed at the Theater an der Wien instead. It was there that we listened to Wagner and Alban Berg. The makeshift theater was nothing elaborate, but it had good music and a passionately enthusiastic audience. Perhaps one could even go so far as to say that music gave the Viennese something to live for. To be sure, life was hard. But precisely because of that, rather than in spite of it, opera music was not just a source of pleasure but something central to their emotional life. That evening before our excitement subsided, we came out of the theater and found that darkness had taken over the streets. Only the words "Soviet Intelligence Headquarters" shone brightly in red against the dark night sky.

During my stay in Vienna, we took a stroll around the city, visited an art museum to see Brueghel, and then walked into a large, old-fashioned café to warm our frozen hands and feet. There were only a few other customers; everything was quiet, with only an elderly waiter sitting idly in a corner staring in our direction. Afterwards, we took the city tram, passed in front of the working-class quarters of Karl Marx Hof—its name, in commemoration of so-called Austro-Marxism after World War I, survived the annexation by Germany and the war—and arrived at the

4. The Vienna State Opera House was rebuilt and reopened in 1955 after its near destruction during an Allied bombing. Vienna suffered fifty-three Allied bombings as well as shelling from the Germans and Russians, with several thousand fatalities, more than a quarter of a million people homeless, and the destruction of a reported 20 percent of all houses.

wine-producing town of Grinzig. Buildings there had low roofs, and the windows were scraped out from the thick walls at a level just above the accumulated snow on the pavement. The clouded-up double-pane windows, the yellowish glow of lights, the clamor and the melody of the violin just faintly audible from the outside . . . Under the street lamp's cone-shaped light, glistening powdery snow from an unremitting snowfall streamed along with the wind in an uninterrupted dance. I had never before seen—and never saw again—a more lovely town in the snow. A glass of white wine and a young woman had turned my world into a realm of infinite beauty.

I took her home late every night. Even after the key turned in the lock, the large, heavy door of her house needed a hard push before it would yield with a little squeak. Again we kissed, made plans for the next day, and said good-bye.

I stayed in Vienna for a week, and then I extended my visit for another week. But I knew I could not stay there forever. I went back to the Westbahnhof and took the Orient Express back to Paris. She did not say a word when she came to see me off; she just stood under the train window, her big eyes moistened with tears. As the train started to glide quietly away, she turned and walked away in the opposite direction, never stopping or looking back. As I leaned out at the window and saw her walk away, I realized for the first time that I was in love with her.

That for me was a new experience. I thought about her day and night—the shine in her eyes, the touch of her hair, the delicate variation in the intonation of her speech, the sun in Tuscany, the snowstorm by the Danube. Remembrance now brought back memories that seemed endless. While the past was interrupted at Vienna's Westbahnhof, by no means was it to end there, because it was to be connected with everything in the future that the power of my imagination could summon. I was myself taken by surprise that one young woman—an outsider— had come into the center of my world, a development that inevitably would lead to a change in its order. This had never before happened in my life. Now I could understand very clearly that I had not been in love with the woman in Kyoto; I had merely thought I was in love with her, or perhaps I had just wished I could love her. Where would this new experience lead me? In any case, my only thought then was how to seize the next opportunity to go to Vienna again.

The opportunity came with the arrival of spring. In Paris, representatives from Japan to an international conference to be convened in Vienna were looking for an interpreter to go with them. The official languages at the conference were English and French, and the itinerary included a tour of West German cities. Since by then I also knew some German, I took the job and this time arrived in Vienna from Berlin on a passenger plane.

Stadtpark in May came alive with a profusion of flowering plants, and the Vienna woods were putting on fresh green colors. In front of the baroque Schönbrunn palace, Mozart's songs and orchestral music filled the evening sky with an air of elegant optimism. We were in the midst of happiness, and we were resolved that our happiness was not to end there. Yet we had no concrete plans, just a vague notion about a future that was sure to visit us. For this reason, I was not worried about any real difficulties or impending obstacles coming our way.

At that time I was staying at Vienna's Hotel Sacher where remnants of the extravagance of a fallen empire were still evident—thick carpets, antique furniture, old paintings, gilding on the ceilings, window frames, and doors. In the restaurant on the lower floor, an elderly woman was sipping coffee all by herself, a touring American couple was examining a spread-out map, and a distinguished-looking elderly man was reading his newspaper with a magnifying glass in hand.

One morning I ordered my breakfast there, picked up a newspaper furnished for its patrons, and learned for the first time about riots in Berlin.[5] It was reported that citizens on both sides of the city had pulled down and torn up a red flag in the eastern sector. As for the number of participants in this "anti-Communist" riot, the figure reported in the European edition of the *Herald Tribune* turned out to be several times higher than that in the *Times* of London.

5. On June 17, 1953, Soviet tanks suppressed a general strike by the citizens of East Berlin and imposed martial law that lasted until July 12.

32 Music

One night in a snowstorm I was listening to *Tristan und Isolde* at the Theater an der Wien and was so totally entranced by it that I became oblivious of myself. For me, that was a completely new experience.

I had imagined that opera, as a form of entertainment, comprised two elements: a lifeless, mundane melodrama accompanied by good singing. The relationship between the two, I thought, could not be nearly as close as that between a kabuki play and samisen music. That night, for the first time, I realized how utterly ignorant I had been. I discovered Wagner. There I found expressions of tumultuous emotions that almost defied description, expressions charged with such intensity that they had no conceivable equal in music or, indeed, in any other form of art. It struck me that their musical representation of irrationality, destructiveness, and coerciveness not only precisely and quintessentially defines Wagner; it also characterizes German romanticism as a whole, recapitulated as it is in his music. It represents the core of Strindberg's plays or the dark, uncanny passions (or tenacity of purpose) in Munch's paintings, along with their curious sense of raw immediacy and internal tumult.

Up to that time, my attention to German culture had been drawn not to the subtlety of its sensibilities or to the pragmatism in its way of thinking, but to the precision and rationality in its systems of thought. When I was working as a specialist in internal medicine, there was no other contemporary textbook in the world as systematic and comprehensive as Müller's *Handbuch*.[1] And in terms of the massive extermination of

---

1. Johannes Peter Müller (1801–58), a German physician, comparative anatomist, pioneer of experimental physiology, and author of *Handbuch der*

human beings outside the battlefield, perhaps few examples in history can parallel the systematic and highly organized act at Auschwitz. But beyond this highly organized, systematic, and rational aspect of German culture, it has another facet that manifests itself with such extraordinary vibrancy, so pregnant with tempestuous passions, that one cannot help but be lured into a state of *Rausch*, to use an indigenous German word.[2] After listening to Wagner, I realized for the first time the utter irresistibility that is its intoxicating appeal. If such a cultural duality exists in Germany, how are the two aspects interrelated? For a long time, incoherent thoughts about this errant question would continue to stir in my mind.

Tristan und Isolde did not simply provoke my half-whimsical thoughts about northern European culture. More significantly, by adding a new element of "rapture" to my experience, it changed the internal order of my world. Until then, I had never gotten drunk. At least I had never experienced self-oblivion in a state of euphoria, nor had I ever wanted to. Whether wine elicits tears or grief, it simply brings about the kind of psychological and physiological state that no voluntary action can induce.[3] In a crowd, it's relatively easy to get a feeling of intoxicated elation by embracing strangers, synchronizing footsteps, and singing or howling together. Yet I never appreciated that kind of instantaneous intoxication. When I looked at the pictures of Hitler and his gang in the mass gatherings they organized in the 1930s, I thought that I too might have become euphoric had I joined their ranks wearing their uniform, but the thought nauseated me. In the fifties when I saw men and women in a southern German beer hall drinking, singing, and swaying their bodies arm in arm, it gave me the shivers just to imagine the stupidity of participating in their activity. If I didn't want to join in, my only other alternative was to leave. Outside the beer hall, there was a town near the Alpine mountains and the night air carried with it a faint scent of flowers. I needed the liberty to think as my will dictated—that much was essential for me.

Physiologie des Menschen (1833–40); according to George W. Corner, it was "a standard textbook for two generations" (*Encyclopedia Americana* [1976], 19:556).

2. *Rausch* means intoxication, delirium, or frenzy.

3. Here Katō cites the title of a Koga Masao song, "Sake wa namida ka tameiki ka," popular in Japan in the early 1930s. See chapter 4, note 1 for more details.

The psychological state I called "rapture" does not mean, of course, simply "lack of consciousness of self." To reach that state no special circumstances are necessary. I can achieve it, for example, by simply trying to overtake the car ahead while driving. I am conscious only of the speeds and the positions of the cars and the conditions necessary to overtake the car ahead—certainly not the subject, myself, who's doing the overtaking. Or say I'm concentrating on solving a problem in my elementary geometry examination. What's in my consciousness is the triangle and not "I." Lack of consciousness of self is not an exceptional condition at all; it is the most commonplace state of our daily life.

But when I am in a state of rapture, as happens sometimes, I am oblivious not merely of myself but of everything except the agent of my rapture. Moreover, as long as the state of rapture continues, I wish I could remain in that state forever. In such moments, I am both passive (in terms of emotion) and active (in terms of value orientation). But when I try to overtake a car or solve a problem in an examination, all I am doing is directing my active attention to the object, lest it be unsafe to pass or impossible to solve the problem within the allotted time. In a state of rapture, no real action or precise thinking is possible. And yet it is only in such a condition that values become absolute and totally internalized. While I myself did not actively seek after such a condition, something from the outside seized me and enticed me into that experience. What then were those agents? Surely, they were not grandiose ideals about humanity, or religion, or even literature. In the sense I described, I think only the woman I love and music could have such a power to captivate me. They both came into my life at about the same time, taking me unawares and seizing me by force. At that time, there was nothing more valuable in the world to me. Not only was I oblivious of myself, I was oblivious of the whole world. That was how Wagner's music struck me at one time.

Until then, music had never affected me like that. When I was a child, I listened to Mother playing the melancholy and monotonous tunes of "Rokudan" on her koto, notes that filled our large, dim house in Shibuya's Konnō-chō like a perfumed mist in the air.[4] But instead of making me forget everything, they only reminded me of everything and

---

4. "Rokudan" is a representative solo koto piece composed by Yatsuhashi Kengyō (1614–85), the father of popular koto music and the pioneer of the Yatsuhashi school.

evoked all sorts of fantasies. I was moved by Yamada Kōsaku's "Kara-tachi no hana" (Wild orange blossoms) and "Kono michi" (This trail), and I also very much enjoyed the so-called *kayōkyoku*, popular songs such as "Akagi no komori-uta" (Lullaby of Akagi) and "Kare susuki" (Withered eulalia).[5] Once, while practicing on his *shakuhachi*, Father said he couldn't understand the mentality of those who enjoyed such silly songs, but Mother responded by saying that preference in music had nothing to do with the mind. At that time, I couldn't quite figure out what the lyrics of the popular songs really meant, but the melodies impressed me beyond words.

Nevertheless, this state of contentment did not last long. Once I realized what the lyrics meant, I got tired of them. Far from being evocative, their sentimental melodies now turned into a source of irritation. Songs I once loved so much now gave me the shivers. Perhaps one reason was that just when I was trying to cultivate some peace of mind—and unfortunately I needed to try that quite often—all too often such songs forced themselves on me. On my return voyage to Japan after my long stay in Europe, I heard such popular songs for the first time in several years. The ship was a Japanese freighter, and Japanese food, Japanese conversation—indeed everything Japanese—brought a sense of nostalgia. But I just could not stand the songs. There was a loudspeaker in my cabin, and when the central control was turned on, these popular songs, with their characteristic nasal crooning, automatically filled every room on the ship. I asked that the loudspeaker in my room be turned off, only to be told that they did not have individual controls. I then implored them to at least turn down the volume, but to no avail. The songs invaded my room throughout the day, and there were two more weeks to go before the ship arrived at a Japanese port. So I smashed the loud-speaker and spent my time reading Ronsard's poetry instead. The reading was boring, but it was not as unpleasant as the popular songs. Even today when I hear such songs on the streets of Tokyo, I recall my cabin with the broken loudspeaker, the undulating horizon of the South China

5. On Yamada Kōsaku's "Karatachi no hana" (1924) see chapter 4, note 1; the trifoliate orange plant's white flowers bloom in late spring. • For "Kono michi," also with lyrics by Kitahara Hakushū, Katō cites its first line, "Kono michi wa itsuka kita michi" (This trail we once trod). • The lullaby (1934), by Takeoka Nobuyuki, was made popular by the singer Shōji Tarō (1898–1972). • On "Kare susuki" see chapter 4, note 1.

Sea outside my circular window, and a few lines of poetry by a sixteenth-century poet from a foreign land.

A melody or a piece of music often evokes memories of the specific time and place I heard it. For instance, the flute on the nō stage would remind me of Suidōbashi's Nō Theater during the war, César Franck's *Variations symphoniques* of the second-class patients' ward at the Tokyo University Hospital, Bach's *Well-Tempered Clavier* of Hongō's Nishi-katamachi, and Chopin's ballads of the summer in Shinano Oiwake. Among the works of Stravinsky, *The Soldier's Tale* would always bring back memories of the Redoutensaal in Vienna, and *Oedipus Rex* of the Palais de Chaillot and the place de Trocadéro in Paris, or the composer Bekku Sadao.[6] *Figaro* and Vienna, *Così fan tutte* and Salzburg . . . To be sure, all of these connections were coincidental. Yet I often felt there was a certain correlation between the land and the music. I have seen *Der Rosenkavalier* many times in Vienna, an opera so beautiful that no words can do it justice, and every time I saw it I was convinced that it was impossible to talk about the beauty of the female voice without bringing Richard Strauss into the picture.

Even so, when I saw the same opera in London, it was a little different. During the intermission at Covent Garden, a distinguished-looking man turned to me and asked, "What do you think of that?" By "that," I wondered whether he meant the music itself or the orchestra's performance. If he meant the former, the subject struck me as a little too grandiloquent to raise during the intermission of the opera. But the orchestra's performance was not so exceptional that one would be inspired to start a conversation with the next man. "Well, I thought it was quite good, but . . . ," I stammered out something. But without waiting for me to finish, he snapped, "I've never seen anything so obscene! Absolutely outrageous!"

Later, when *Der Rosenkavalier* was performed in Tokyo, I was totally amazed to learn that it was sponsored or recommended by the Japanese Ministry of Education. Even if one does not go so far as to describe the play as "obscene," surely one can't regard it as something beneficial to

6. Bekku Sadao (1922–), a graduate of Tokyo University in aesthetics, studied music in Paris from 1950 to 1954 and later taught at Chūō University; he composed symphonies (*Kangengaku no tame no futatsu no inori* [Two prayers for orchestral music]) and an opera based on three kyōgen plays called *Sannin no onnatachi no monogatari* (The story of three women, 1964, revised in 1986).

the moral education of the Japanese empire's young men and women. If the Ministry of Education had indeed opened up as far as that, I thought, it would not be long before *Lady Chatterley's Lover* could serve as an English textbook in our schools.[7]

But when I saw the performance, it was as healthy as an athletic meet—cheerful, innocent, and full of youthful vigor. Nothing in it offered even the slightest hint about the dark shadow lurking behind the love affair of a middle-aged woman with her young lover, or the pathetic predicament of an old man out to get a young girl with his mind running wild with erotic fantasies. Of course that was not Richard Strauss, and perhaps it could not even be called music. I could only marvel how a place like Tokyo, with its youthfulness and vitality, finally succeeded in transforming even an opera like dear old *Der Rosenkavalier,* the last glory of the fallen central European empire with its perverted world mixed with irony and cynicism, into a vivacious and morally correct play. Outside the theater, crowds of young people were walking on the street and saying, "Hey, man, you know . . ." Automobiles raced frantically in all directions as if they had all gone mad, and the words "Great Divine Prosperity to Japan" floated across the air polluted with exhaust fumes.[8]

I never got into the habit of comparing Japan and Europe at every turn, because I think such comparisons are not very rewarding either in the practical or in the theoretical sense. But when *Der Rosenkavalier* was performed in Tokyo, it inevitably reminded me of a baroque city in a faraway land. According to the dictionary, the word "baroque" was originally a Portuguese word referring to pearls of irregular shape. During the prosperous days in the past, people in this old city seemed to prefer somewhat irregular-shaped pearls to the perfectly rounded ones, thinking that the former afforded greater sophistication. *Tristan und Isolde*

7. In a notorious postwar censorship case in 1950, the government prosecuted the distinguished critic and novelist Itō Sei (1905–69) for his translation of an "obscene" work, *Lady Chatterley's Lover* (Koyama shoten, 1950). Itō lost his case in 1957, despite the support of other prominent writers and psychologists. In 1980 the Supreme Court reversed the verdict, more than a decade after Itō's death.

8. The setting of *Der Rosenkavalier* is aristocratic Vienna around 1740, during the early reign of Empress Maria Theresa. • Apparently for sarcastic effect, Katō's words call on the phrase *Jimmu keiki,* literally "the greatest prosperity since the time of the Jimmu emperor" (Japan's first emperor, who ascended the throne in 660 B.C. [*Nihon shoki,* 720]).

is a love song. *Der Rosenkavalier,* on the other hand, is a song reminiscing about a bygone love and a parody of a love song. How fitting it was to hear it in a large metropolis of a small country so full of recollections about the old empire and so cynical and ambivalent about its own present.

It might be an exaggeration to say that I grew up watching Japanese puppet plays and listening to the *gidayū* narrators, but since my student days I have been fond of the harmony produced between the *gidayū* recitations and the sound of the samisen. The Western equivalent of *gidayū* is what the French call a *chanson.* If one listens only to the melody without the lyrics, it is not particularly interesting. But the lyrics are often quite clever, and the music often goes well with the words. It is almost like a narrative. In the case of *Die Winterreise,* knowing the words certainly makes it more interesting, but even without them the music itself can be enjoyable. Yet without the words, Juliette Gréco's narrative is meaningless. The only difference is that the Western version of *gidayū* is more abstract and addresses more universal themes than those in Japanese puppet plays. "Je hais le dimanche!" All those "Sundays" she refers to can surely be found in any city in the world.

I was fond of music, at least of some of the pieces I happened to hear. Not only did I enjoy it, but music has come to occupy a special position in the body of my collective experience, one I could not easily replace. The significance of its position contrasted markedly with my lack of training and knowledge about the subject. Nevertheless, I did become acquainted with a number of composers and learned about their thoughts on music. Their ideas were not incomprehensible to me—at least that was how I felt most of the time. Ogura Rō would talk only about ideas he had thoroughly considered, and when he spoke he was marvelously articulate.[9] Few people I know either inside or outside of Japan can approach his lucidity, precision, and single-mindedness—for only a single-minded artist can do his work—in addressing the artist's creative process and the gist of the complex questions involved. "It won't do you much good to aim at effect, don't you think?" Zeami also said the same thing in the old days. Ogura said it not because he had read Zeami but because

9. Ogura Rō (1916–), a prize-winning composer and the author of *Gendai ongaku o kataru* (On contemporary music [Iwanami shinsho, 1970]). Katō's essay on Ogura, "Ogura Rō mata wa ongaku no gendai" (Ogura Rō or contemporary music) is in *Katō Shūichi chosakushū,* 11:339–60.

he had contemplated his art in the same way Zeami had contemplated his. If one were to elaborate fully on the significance of his words, it could easily take more than a hundred pages.

Yoshida Hidekazu has also become a long-time friend of mine.[10] A generous man with broad erudition and precise knowledge about music, he would gently correct my mistakes when I made naive remarks, make up for my inadequacies, and turn my inconsequential ideas into something that makes sense. And he was good enough to talk to me about a subject he knew so thoroughly that he must have felt wearied in the process. He also knows much about art other than music, and he can freely talk about all kinds of issues at various levels of abstraction, in Japanese, German, or English. I can scarcely think of a better person with whom to have an enjoyable and a uniquely witty conversation.

Another person who enjoyed a good conversation was Mrs. I, a professor at the Conservatoire de Musique in Paris and a violin teacher in Tokyo. Politics, society, customs, and people—whatever the subject might be she would talk volubly, like a rapid-fire machine gun. Her views were explicit and emphatic, revealing distinct traits of her personality. I greatly enjoyed her way of coming up with quick and clear-cut answers to complex issues. But when our conversation turned occasionally to music, her manners would undergo a complete change regardless of how trivial the issue might be. Suddenly her voice softened; she became contemplative as she sought the right words, which she would then utter slowly and prudently. I respected her attitude. At that moment, the artist was no longer articulating her personal views but the facts and the truths alone. Any observer could tell how totally serious and engaged she was.

I am not fond of sentimental music. Chikamatsu's *michiyuki* is not sentimental; it is suffused only with the love the man and woman have for each other in their hearts. The only experience in my life comparable to the euphoric rapture a certain kind of music evoked in me is having a woman I love in my arms. Whether the embrace is long or short is just a relative matter; that it must end at some point in time is just a reality of the human condition. Music has a beginning and an end. An individual life, social institutions, and history itself also have their be-

10. Yoshida Hidekazu (1913–), a celebrated music critic, founder and director of Nijisseiki ongaku kenkyūjo (Research institute for twentieth-century music) and head of the Mito Art Tower (see his 10-vol. collected work *Yoshida Hidekazu zenshū* [Hakusuisha, 1975–76]).

ginnings and their ends. If there is a meaning somewhere to it at all, that meaning must be appreciated in the present. No amount of treasure equals a moment of togetherness with one's love. Within the world of art, I found its equivalent in music. Did my experience in music teach me that, or did that turn music into such an experience for me? I cannot tell.

33 The Other Side of the Channel

It was sunset on a windy day. I still cannot forget the moment when I first saw across the rough foamy sea the white cliffs of Dover tinged with a rosy flush. The ship's rolling motion had turned some passengers pale, forcing them to double over. As I gazed at the white cliffs gradually coming my way, I was excited about the fact that I was finally able to see that island country with my own eyes. For over twenty years, I had heard and read about and envisioned in my own mind its history and culture, and I had never believed that I would one day set foot on its soil.

England reminded me of Tokyo in my childhood days. Paris or, I should say, any city in continental Europe, bore little resemblance to Tokyo. But the brick structures in some parts of London seemed indistinguishable from the Mitsubishi Building in Tokyo's Marunouchi district. At the counters of cafeterias everywhere they sold doughnuts like the ones I used to crave as a child. The area around Paddington Station, with its littered streets, soot and smoke, prostitutes, vagabonds, and hustle and bustle, reminded me of the neighborhood around Ueno Station. And in the many secondhand bookstores along Charing Cross Road, everything from the proprietors' facial expressions to the habit of standup reading brought back memories of the Kanda district. Large leather armchairs that I saw inside office buildings reminded me of the one in the Western-style room in Grandfather's house, and the hot-water bottle my friend kept for each of his family members was the same kind we used when we were still living in Shibuya. An unheated bedroom in the winter was something I had practically forgotten while living in France. And then there were the things that might not be exclusively British but were a part of my childhood, like afternoon tea and a game of bridge.

The custom of afternoon tea must have been something Mother learned from the English nuns at her girls' school, and the game of bridge was most probably something my uncle, a naval officer, brought back from his studies in England and then popularized among our relatives. The headmaster at our Shibuya middle school loved to quote "the British prime minister Gladstone" whenever he lectured to his students at the assembly hall. Although practically anybody anywhere could have thought of those ideas, his quotations were never from a Japanese prime minister, a French poet, or a German philosopher.

My knowledge of continental European culture was acquired through reading German and French literary works and medical books over a long period of time. Iwanami Books, Maruzen, and Nankōdō, the Imperial University's French literature department and the Medical School Library.[1] I learned the names of different human body parts and every illness in German, but I had no idea, for example, what to call an ordinary piece of tableware in that language. I read Mallarmé and the poets around him, but I never imagined what the social institution known as the café was really like.

"England," on the other hand—even though it might have been just a faded shadow of the Victorian era—was always floating in the air of my childhood as far back as I could remember, long before I could read or study. Fragments of things British in no coherent order surrounded me, so to speak, and during that time I never found any systematic way of dealing with them—things ranging from Grandfather's breakfast and furniture to Mother's "afternoon tea," from my uncle's "bridge" to my headmaster's Gladstone. But as soon as I stepped on British soil, I became keenly aware of the fact that these things together formed a tightly knit whole. I also came to realize very clearly that customs I had not previously associated with Britain had actually been imported from that

1. In 1927 Iwanami Shigeo began Iwanami bunko's pocket-sized paperbacks of Japanese and international classics in literature, philosophy, and social and natural sciences that still educate and enlighten Japanese readers; other major publishers such as Kōdansha, Kadokawa shoten, Shinchōsha, and Chikuma shobō now have comparable series. • Maruzen is a Tokyo bookseller and office-goods supplier (founded 1869) noted for its import of foreign publications for Japan's serious reading public; members of "the Maruzen generations" included prominent writers and critics (Uchida Roan and Tayama Katai in the Meiji era to Akutagawa Ryūnosuke in the Taishō and early Shōwa periods). • Nankōdō (founded 1879) publishes books and journals in the medical sciences.

country. The only exception was perhaps the English language we learned at our middle school. Contrary to our long-held belief that it was the native tongue of the British, it was in fact mostly a Japanese product. While the British could understand what I was saying, much of what they said was incomprehensible to me. I am afraid the responsibility did not rest entirely with the school; I too was responsible in no small degree. But this state of affairs arose at least in part from the way our English textbooks were compiled, with extraordinary emphasis on the technicalities of the language but almost total disregard for practical usage or the essence of English literature.

I learned to enjoy English literature not through my Tokyo middle school but from Herbert Norman, the Canadian diplomat who committed suicide in Cairo after the military intervention over the Suez Canal. A historian known for his works such as *Japan's Emergence as a Modern State* and "Andō Shōeki and the Anatomy of Japanese Feudalism," Norman was born in Japan and educated in Britain, read Japanese and Latin, was well versed in Roman history and widely read in English literature.[2] He once said, "I think classical Chinese is a good language for translating Latin prose and poetry. It is succinct and semantically condensed."

2. Egerton Herbert Norman (1909–57), born in Karuizawa of Canadian missionary parents, studied European history at the University of Toronto and at Cambridge, and East Asian history at Harvard and Columbia; he joined the Canadian diplomatic service in 1939, served as a language officer in Japan until 1942, and died in Cairo on April 4, 1957. On his life and his suicide (attributed partly to investigations into alleged left-wing connections and his criticism of Occupation policy) see Cyril H. Powles's entry on Norman in *Kodansha Encyclopedia of Japan*; Roger Bowen, *Innocence Is Not Enough: The Life and Death of Herbert Norman* (Vancouver: Douglas and McIntyre, 1986); and Roger Bowen, ed., *E. H. Norman: His Life and Scholarship* (Toronto: University of Toronto Press, 1984). Katō's essay "E. H. Nōman—sono ichimen" (E. H. Norman—one aspect of him, *Shisō*, special ed., *Hābāto Nōman shigo nijūnen* [Twenty years after Herbert Norman's death] [April 1977]) is in *Katō Shūichi chosakushū*, 15: 271–77. • The British, French, and Israeli intervention in October 1956, precipitated by Gamal Abdel Nasser's nationalization of the Suez Canal Company in July, ended in December at the direction of the United Nations. • On Norman's works, *Japan's Emergence* (1940) was a pioneering and influential study of the dynamics of the Meiji Restoration and its aftermath (reprinted in John W. Dower, ed., *Origins of the Modern Japanese State* [New York: Pantheon, 1975]); "Anatomy of Japanese Feudalism" (*Transactions of the Asiatic Society of Japan*, 3d s., 2 [1949]: 1–321) presented a detailed study of Andō Shōeki (1703?–62), an innovative mid-Edo thinker-physician.

I met Norman frequently when he was representing Canada at a UNESCO conference in Paris. That was before he went to Cairo as the Canadian ambassador. Perhaps his job as a UNESCO representative afforded some free time, or rather I suppose he could afford to create some free time for himself in his position. I had the general impression that a large part of a diplomat's work, or at least his major concern, consisted of attending cocktail parties. But one day Norman said nonchalantly, "Today I've nothing more than a cocktail party, so I don't need to be in Paris."

And on that autumn day we went to the private residence of a secretary at the British Embassy. I have completely forgotten by now where in the suburbs of Paris it was located or whether another diplomat, a classmate of Norman's at the university in Britain, was from New Zealand or Australia. All I can remember is how amazed I was to learn that, of the three diplomats gathered there, one was a specialist in Japanese history, another was translating thirteenth-century Persian poetry, and the third was editing the collected works of a nineteenth-century Russian playwright to be published by Oxford University Press. That left me with a strong impression. They were certainly exceptional even among diplomats from the Commonwealth countries. Years later when I was traveling in Hong Kong with my friend the sociologist R. P. Dore, I was reminded of these three men I had met in the suburbs of Paris.[3] In Hong Kong an acquaintance I had met in London, a young British diplomat named H, was living by himself. When we went to visit him, we saw in his small room a volume of Lao Tzu lying open on the table, and a book of Bartók's music left opened at the piano. After we talked for a while in his room, he took us to a Chinese restaurant. There was not a single foreign patron, and H chatted away cheerfully in Cantonese with the Chinese waiter and other patrons as if he were speaking his mother tongue. Since I already knew back in London that his Japanese and French had absolutely no foreign accent, I could only marvel at his fluency in Cantonese. But something else was in store for me. "My Cantonese is not that good," H said with a smile. "The language I feel most comfort-

---

3. Ronald P. Dore, a prominent British sociologist on Japan, wrote *City Life in Japan: A Study of a Tokyo Ward* (Berkeley: University of California Press, 1958) and *Land Reform in Japan* (London: Oxford University Press, 1959) and edited *Aspects of Social Change in Modern Japan* (Princeton: Princeton University Press, 1967).

able speaking is probably Malay." He told me that he had visited old vil-
lagers in the Malay hinterland to gather materials on local folklore.

"I was there for a long time," he said.

"If I'm not mistaken, you also speak Arabic, don't you?" Dore asked.

"Oh well, just enough to get by in ordinary daily conversation," that
amazing Englishman answered.

At that time it again occurred to me that the extraordinary dilettan-
tism of the men produced by the old colonial empire characteristically
went beyond mere avocation into areas that nobody could imagine.

Norman's Japanese and French were not fluent, and my English was
rudimentary. However, we could communicate in any one of these three
languages.

"It would be a good idea if you'd read *Abinger Harvest*. I'm sure you'd
like it."

And sure enough, I did like it. Afterwards, I started to read as many
of E. M. Forster's works as I could get hold of.[4] I also learned from Norman the alluring charm in the prose of the so-called Bloomsbury Group
and John Aubrey. Indeed, unfolding before me was a world different from
that of French literature. It was a world difficult to define and still is. But
if there is a certain affection within me for English culture, it certainly
has something to do with—how should I put it?—perhaps an intellectual form of *wabi* in their prose. The essence of *wabi*, in works like *Nambōroku*, eschews the ostentatious extravagance of the stately mansion
in favor of the simplicity of the thatched hut by the seashore as the highest form of beauty.[5] And a certain type of modern English writer, when
naming their works, would not bother with grandiose titles and pick
names such as *Abinger Harvest* or *The Common Reader*.[6] I like that
frame of mind. As a matter of fact, Norman shared it to some degree. In

4. Essays in Forster's *Abinger Harvest* (1936), written over three decades,
include "Notes on the English Character," "The Birth of an Empire," "The Early
Novels of Virginia Woolf," and "Adrift in India" (Abinger is the name of a village in Surrey). See also Katō's essay "E. M. Fōsuta to hūmanizumu" (E. M. Forster
and humanism), *Sekai* (February 1959).

5. *Nambōroku*, a 7-vol. work (1593) by the Momoyama-period Zen monk
Nambō Sōkei (dates unknown) on the art of tea he learned from his teacher Sen
no Rikyū (1522–91) and on Rikyū's life, though one theory ascribes it to the
elder councillor of Fukuoka *han* Tachibana Jitsuzan, whose text is the source of
current editions.

6. Virginia Woolf's first *Common Reader* appeared in 1925, the second in
1932.

addition to his subtle intellectual refinement, he was extraordinarily sensitive to the feelings of others with whom he was conversing.

The last meeting I had with Norman was a totally accidental encounter on a street corner in Paris. We stood and talked for a long time in the middle of the night. Our conversation included Senator McCarthy's House Un-American Activities Committee, then running amok in the United States. At that time, for reasons I still do not quite understand to this day, Norman began to talk about the sensitive relationship he found himself in within the Canadian Foreign Ministry, going so far as naming names. And he added, half-jokingly, something to the effect that he wished he could resign from the Foreign Ministry at an opportune time and go to a university on the Canadian Pacific coast where he could devote himself to the study of Japanese history. In an encounter between the two of us for the first time after quite a while, or as a piece of conversation on the street in the dead of night, I couldn't help having the impression that his remarks were rather odd. This mystifying impression remained with me for a long time. Nevertheless, Norman did not take his retreat into the university and continued with his diplomat's work until his death in Cairo. At that time, I could not even dream that one day I would myself find refuge at that university on the Pacific coast and spend some leisurely days there.[7]

Since I had very little money to spend after I landed in England, I had a hard time finding a cheap rooming house. Finally I found one in Earl's Court. Rent was to be paid on a weekly basis, and breakfast and dinner were provided. The eating hours were fixed, and even if one was late for just a minute, the door to the dining hall was closed and no one got in. The room was small, and with the addition of a chair, a desk, and an iron-frame bed, there was not much space left. The bed had a unique design, the kind that could scarcely be found in any cheap hotels in Paris. It stood high off the floor and was so small that one could hardly turn over. Moreover, thanks to its meticulous design, the middle of the bed rose in a semi-cylindrical shape. Even if one could actually fall asleep on the thing, it would surely be a miracle if one did not tumble out of it.

7. Katō taught at the University of British Columbia in Vancouver from September 1960 to August 1969, before becoming professor and director of the East Asian Institute at the Free University of Berlin in September 1969 at the age of 50. During his tenure at UBC he wrote *A Sheep's Song,* first serialized between 1966 and 1967.

There was a small gas heater in the room. Primed with a shilling, it gave off heat—but only for a fixed time. When the time ran out, it shut itself off automatically. If that happened in the middle of the night and if one was out of shillings, the only thing one could do was to endure the severe cold. Sixpence would not buy half the time. It was then that I discovered that the British shilling and the French franc, while different in weight, had exactly the same size and thickness (since one shilling was worth five yen and one franc only eighty *sen*, it also served as an economic solution).[8] And so I carried a lot of francs in my pocket.

People from various countries gathered at the rooming house, turning it into something of a racial exposition. The owner was from central Europe, and the room maid was Irish. Among the residents were a young worker from India, a jobless man from Ceylon, a black man from some African country, a couple from Germany, a female student from France, a middle-aged English working woman, and another young man with refined features who might have come from India. Nobody had any idea what he was doing for a living, but that was only because he did not understand any English.

The man from Ceylon had with him many ivory elephants in various sizes, and he made his living by peddling them to any willing buyer. He caught me one time and, with a very earnest look on his face, said he had something interesting to tell me. "If it's about your elephants, I can't afford it," I responded. Oh no, he explained, he wasn't going to ask me to buy his elephants. With excitement in his voice, he whispered to me that he had just discovered he could spend a night with a dancer from such and such cabaret for the price of just one of his small elephants.

"Oh, is that right? Good for you. But I'm not going to buy your elephants just so you can have your dancer."

"That's okay. The owner of this place already bought one. But can you imagine how cheap it is . . ." And on he talked with unabating enthusiasm.

The female student from France was not there pursuing her studies but looking for a job—at least that was what she said. She would always get a call in the morning, and very often she would be out for the entire day.

8. There were 100 *sen* in a yen.

As long as the rent was paid, the owner would not even make a fuss about night visitors. Every weekend, a pretty woman would come to visit the Indian, the one with a job. I had talked with the Indian at the dining room, and I knew a little bit about the woman as well. As a matter of fact, when I first decided to come to England, it was not only because I wanted to see the country I had heard so much about since my childhood. The real reason was that I could not forget the young woman from Vienna. She had found a job in London, working in an office in the City. The pretty blond woman who came to visit the Indian was also an Austrian and a good friend of hers. In time I learned that the Indian did not have much money but did have a wife back home, and that his female friend had been working as a live-in maid for a wealthy English family since she left her country. Her job was demanding and she could not get out of the house often, but until she could speak better English it was difficult for her to change her job. Living in a big city in a foreign country, she had few friends, and she apparently thought it was difficult for her to sever her relationship with the Indian.

One night after dinner, the Indian told me that he wanted my advice on certain things. The young woman had demanded that he give her a straight answer whether he had any intention of marrying her, and he asked me what he should do. When I said, "I don't think you can do that," all at once he looked relieved.

"I don't even know her that well. I can't make that kind of commitment."

"If that's the case, you should tell her that," I said. "Even if it means that you two are through, perhaps it's better to end the relationship now before you have a baby on your hands."

The last sentence seemed to have quite an effect on him. He soon disappeared from the rooming house and went somewhere else.

The young woman from Vienna was working in a small investment firm for a small salary. We would meet in town, but finding a place for dinner was just as hard as in Paris or Vienna in those days. Restaurants that seemed to serve good food were too expensive, and in a cheap one we did not mind the food as much as its boisterous atmosphere, which did not really permit any relaxed conversation. The room she rented was small, and mine was even smaller. She did have a distant relative she called an "aunt," who for a long time had been working as a cook and a housekeeper at a rich man's house in Chelsea. When the owner was away, the aunt would often entertain her own acquaintances, including myself, through the back door. She practically worshiped the master of the house and, speaking in a strange language mixed with English and German expressions, would tell us in great detail about his daily activities in a tone ranging from praise to marvel. During his absence, she would treat us to a sumptuous dinner. The house was not that large, but the furniture was all antique. There were silver tableware and candelabra, a Renaissance marble statue and medieval wood sculpture. In the library, old editions of classical and English literature, history, and travelogues filled the shelves. Through the French windows in the living room, one could see in between the trees on the riverbank the masts of sailboats going up and down the Thames. I heard that every year the owner of the house would go hunting for chamois in places as far away as the Pyrenees or the mountains of Turkey.

Without ever meeting the owner, I had lavish meals at his house, took leisurely baths, and occasionally spent a night there and left the next morning. Waiting for the bus at Chelsea's riverbank, I would often hum the tune of the thief's song in *The Three-Penny Opera.* But of course, I am sure the owner must have known very well what his cook did while he was away. Like Japanese companies giving their employees "bonuses" equivalent to as much as several months' pay instead of a routine salary raise, I suppose the owner, having weighed the situation, decided that her habit of entertaining guests was a safety device working to his advantage.

My accommodation at Earl's Court was not always satisfactory. I began thinking that instead of living in a small room with board, it probably would not cost me much more to rent a slightly larger room without board. But I was not successful in finding such a place, though the experience taught me about another aspect of English society. First, I looked through the ads for room rentals posted in front of shops. If the cost, the location, and the other conditions seemed agreeable, I would call them up from a nearby public telephone. But roughly a quarter of these ads carried a provision saying "For Whites Only" or "People of Colour Need Not Apply." Even when I called places without such provisions, they would ask for my nationality once they heard my accent. When I told them I was Japanese, they would immediately hang up or sometimes say that their room had been rented just a moment ago. When I was living in Paris, I was naturally conscious most of the time of the fact that I was a foreigner. But seldom was I conscious of myself as a "person of colour," or of the Japanese as former enemies in the eyes of the French. However, room hunting in London made me think of myself as nonwhite, and the drunks in England reminded me that the Japanese were once their "enemy."

"Are you Japanese?" a drunk asked me.

"That's right."

"The Japanese gave me a terrible time in Malaya."

"I'm sorry to hear that." That was all I could say by way of carrying on a conversation.

This sort of experience was not exactly pleasant for me. Nevertheless, as far as this notion of "people of colour" is concerned, I have never once felt angry at the prejudice exhibited by the other party. Perhaps the anachronism of that attitude is too ludicrous to evoke any anger in me. For it seems to me that to emphasize the distinction between whites and nonwhites and, furthermore, to underscore their confrontation, is far less damaging to nonwhites than to whites. They are the minority of the world's population, and on the stage of world history there is nothing more foolish than to emphasize confrontation with the majority.

Yet racial prejudice cannot always be gotten rid of with this kind of reasoning alone. As a matter of fact, when I returned to Japan from Europe and saw for the first time how mannequins in department stores were made to look like Westerners, I was shocked. It was not just limited to the ones wearing Western clothes; even those in kimono no longer had black hair or black eyes like those of Japanese women! Was this not evidence of the fact that the patrons of department stores, in other words the overwhelming majority of Japanese women, felt that Western women were more beautiful than they were? I have never thought that Western women in general are prettier than their Japanese counterparts. It is true that the physique of Western males is better, but I myself have little interest in this matter. Since childhood, I've known that many of my countrymen have better looks and physique than I do. Neither my body nor my appearance can be improved anyway, so instead of concerning myself with them and developing an inferiority complex, I decided that good mental health meant not bothering myself with these matters. For a long time, this attitude has been second nature to me. Whether somebody has long or short legs does not affect me emotionally, and as far as I am concerned, skin color doesn't matter either. If I cared about the way I looked and believed it was outstanding for a Japanese but not for a Westerner, I too might end up either rejecting Western aesthetic values (or standards) or idolizing the Westerners and dyeing my hair another color. But on this matter I've always been a bystander, someone who doesn't have the time to get all worked up to begin with. As for other matters, almost all arguments about the superiority or inferiority of races essentially exhibit nothing but the ignorance of their advocates. And unfortunately, ignorance has often been the force that drives the wheel of history.

34 Hypocrisy

The art historian S lived just outside Oxford in a farmhouse he was re-modeling and commuted to work at the university art museum in his own small automobile of indeterminate age. That car did not inspire much confidence that it could move but, once the engine got going, generated an incredible array of complex noises from every part of its body and put-putted along the country roads between the fields and the woods. The two-story home was being not only remodeled but enlarged, with S himself laying the bricks. Once every two years he writes a book on Chinese or Japanese art; once every four to five years he builds a new house with his own hands. Years later when I met him in North America, he was telling me his fourth house was about to be completed. The farmhouse he was remodeling in Oxford's suburbs was probably his second one. The walls in the add-on room had not yet been painted, and plain wood panels were fitted into the windows to prevent the cold air from coming in. The fire was blazing vigorously in the large fireplace, and the flames cast quivering shadows over objects in the dimly lit room. The outside was very quiet, but the chill grew more and more severe as the night dragged on. I was seated facing the fireplace, but my back felt the cold all down the spine.

"It seems to me the British value the psychological effects of heating over its physical effectiveness," I said.

"Are you cold?"

"No. I never get tired of watching a fire burning. We Japanese are used to sitting in airy houses made of wood and paper, even in the middle of winter. We watch the red-hot charcoal fire as we savor its psychological and poetic effects—from *The Pillow Book* to the *Seven Collections* of the Bashō school."[1]

We then began to talk about the earl of Rochester's sensuous poetry, Bartók's music, and the musical traditions of central Europe. Mrs. S had played a string instrument in a chamber orchestra, but now with a small child to take care of, she said it was close to impossible for her to reconcile a musician's life with the demands of her family.

S was talking about parliamentary democracy in Japan. "On one hand, you have a radical left wing, and on the other you have a right wing, which, I'm afraid, is no different from what it used to be in prewar days. Wouldn't parliamentary democracy be crushed by forces from both sides?" I remember replying at the time that if democracy were to be crushed, it wouldn't be from both sides. Where would Japan's "reverse course" beginning with the onset of the Korean War lead us? To be sure, the left wing was now stronger than in prewar days, but in many ways it was even weaker in comparison with German democracy under the Weimar Republic. And the force that crushed German democracy didn't come from both the left and the right; it came from the right organized by Hitler.

I also visited a novelist I had met at the conference in southern France at his country home. There were quite a few bedrooms on the second floor of his large house, and the living room, the dining room, and the study were on the ground level. Still, the novelist had built a small shed among the fruit trees in his garden as his workplace. "No matter what my family does, they won't bother me here." But there were only three people in his family, including himself. His wife, an instructor in Italian at a university in London, was even taller than her husband and was also around forty. She spoke with coherence and consistency, and in her presence even the novelist appeared somehow like an adolescent student. Their young son was studying classical languages, had impeccable manners, and was very courteous to their family guest.

---

1. *Makura no sōshi* (Pillow book), a collection of private reflections, reminiscences, and diary-like entries by Sei Shōnagon (written ca. 1000 A.D.), like the contemporary *Tale of Genji*, has long been cherished as a paragon of classical Japanese aesthetic sensibilities. • The Bashō school's *Shichibushū* (compiled ca. 1733) are *haikai* poetry collections: *Fuyu no hi* (Winter day, 1684), *Haru no hi* (Spring day, 1686), *Arano* (The wild fields, 1689), *Hisago* (The gourd, 1690), *Sarumino* (The monkey's straw raincoat, 1691), *Sumidawara* (Sack of charcoal, 1694), and *Zoku Sarumino* (Sequel to the monkey's straw raincoat, 1698).

"Next year, he'll probably go to public school," his mother said. That's the kind of school to which only the rich send their children.

"In theory, everybody can go," the novelist remarked. "But in reality you won't find kids from working-class families because it costs too much."

"It's not just a matter of money. It also depends on the kind of education parents expect their children to have," his wife said. "In any case, as far as education in the classical languages is concerned, that's the only course to take."

Outside the large window in the living room was a meadow with white birch trees planted on its slope. From the dense fog drifting across the meadow, a grazing horse appeared like a shadow and came close to the window. "We're good friends. Other horses never come near the window," the novelist said. It was a young, white horse. Suddenly, I was reminded of my grandfather who went to Australia to procure military horses during World War I, and the pictures of horses hanging over the fireplace in his house. Though I had had no association with horses in any way since that time, the novelist's words "We're good friends" were filled with genuine affection, and for some reason I was moved.

While living in England and during subsequent visits there, I developed a number of close friendships, not just with the art historian and the novelist, but also with a neurologist, a historian, a sociologist, and an actor. I noticed that most of them preferred living in the countryside. This choice, it occurred to me, had something in common with that of the Edo poets and scholars who aspired to a leisurely life in the fields and mountains after they resigned from their official posts. Such was the ideal of *seikō udoku*—work in the fields when the sun shines, read at home when it rains. But unlike the Edo Confucian scholars, the English also read their newspapers. Beyond differences in their professions and specializations, every one of my close friends in England shared an interest in domestic and international affairs, each person holding to his or her own views. This was something not often seen in Tokyo, at least not to the same degree. The literati after Edo didn't bother themselves with national or international affairs, preferring instead to engage in the elegant tradition of chitchat about abstract matters of artistic taste.[2] Any

2. The literati's tradition of "elegant chitchat" (*qing-tan; seidan* in Japanese) began after the Later Han dynasty, in the early third century, and reached the height of its popularity in the Six Dynasties (222–589). A sense of alienation

discussion of mundane affairs was anathema. Even if they touched on worldly matters from time to time or talked about the subtleties of a woman's sensibilities, any attempt to analyze international affairs was unbearably bad taste. The traditional dichotomy was one between elegance and worldliness, with politics belonging to the latter category. If one has to come up with a close Western equivalent, I suppose it would be the duality of spiritual culture and material civilization the Germans speak about. In that formulation, politics belongs to the realm of "civilization" and not "culture." Realpolitik refers to the arena in which the concerns of spirituality or idealism are irrelevant. But in the British view, the lack of direct links between politics and spirituality or between reality and ideal did not imply a total disjunction.

It was true that I had had many occasions in Tokyo to learn about the political views of the left. *Seiji to bungaku* (politics vis-à-vis literature).[3] But the notion of "politics" here was not what the British meant by the term. Rather, it appeared to refer to political ideology or, more specifically, to Marxism. I would argue that in Tokyo, it was not because we were interested in politics that we discussed the relationship between politics and literature. It was because we had so little interest in political matters that, instead of talking about politics and literature, we debated on the relationship between political ideology and literature. Calling political ideology "politics" was just a bad rhetorical habit. That was something I often thought about when I was in England. To live in England meant that I had to think in English, and thinking in English made it

---

and personal vulnerability in an often treacherous political climate inspired the escapist impulse central to the *qing-tan* mentality; its ostensible unworldliness, heightened by wine, music, and Taoist and Buddhist discourse, often masked its more pragmatic design as a precarious art of political survival.

3. The postwar *seiji to bungaku* debate set the Kindai bungaku (modern literature) critics, most notably Ara Masahito and Hirano Ken, against the orthodox leftist Shin Nihon bungakukai (new Japanese literature association) group represented by Nakano Shigeharu (on Nakano, see postscript, note 11). The radical leftist critics and their more "liberal" counterparts disagreed about the relation between artistic imagination or the self's "subjectivity" and literature's political imperatives as set out by the Japanese Communist Party; the controversy later included issues ranging from writers' war responsibility to prewar ideological conversion. For at least a decade after 1945, no other literary controversy so defined the character and dynamics of postwar Japanese literature. See Victor Koschmann, *Revolution and Subjectivity in Postwar Japan* (Chicago: University of Chicago Press, 1996).

imperative to translate into English long-familiar Japanese concepts. And naturally, translations also helped to clarify the semantics of the Japanese language.

In some ways, the conversations I had in Paris were not unlike those in Tokyo. We talked about man the rebel, the organization and the individual, revolution and reformism, mass movements and ideology, communism and humanity, and so on.[4] Ultimately, we were generally concerned with what was right and, consequently, what we thought was desirable. But it seemed to me that the British did not have a habit of thinking in terms of what was desirable but rather what they could accomplish within a given situation. "About the only thing the Japanese government could do was delay Japan's remilitarization," they would say. "Isn't that what the Yoshida cabinet has been trying to do all along?" But when I witnessed how the former invader of the Chinese continent was entering into a military alliance against the government that represented the Chinese people instead of concluding a peace treaty with them, I thought the whole business was an outrageous moral disgrace.

What I learned in England was not to treat morality and politics as separate categories, but to see how they were interrelated. Around that time, I already harbored some doubts myself about tackling political issues from a purely moral perspective. From my point of view Japanese militarism was injustice itself. Yet given our hindsight about the course of the Cold War, it was no longer possible to see the Pacific War *only* in terms of a struggle between democracy and fascism. On the other hand, if we think of all wars simply as manifestations of power politics, the injustice perpetuated by Japanese imperialism would appear to be at worst just a matter of degree. My question was also connected with the issue Albert Camus tried to address in *L'Homme révolté*. A human being who aspires to freedom always rebels against authority. Since authority represents an organized entity, the rebellion against it, too, has to be organized in order to become effective. But Camus was saying that once it becomes organized, the organization of the rebels itself would end up crushing the freedom of the individual, and he went on to discuss complex issues ranging from artistic freedom to the organization of the Com-

---

4. *Kyōsanshugiteki ningen*, the Japanese title (1952) of Louis Aragon's *Homme communiste* (1946), is also the title of two books by the cultural critic Hayashi Tatsuo (1896–1984) and the Kindai bungaku critic Odagiri Hideo (1916–), both dated 1951.

munist party and its relationship to social justice.[5] And so one could say that the crux of his argument has to do with the correlation between moral values and power politics.

Because these issues were close to my heart, I was practically stunned when I read in a weekly magazine a review of Camus's book by Richard Crossman of the Labour Party.[6] Crossman wrote that he had no idea what had driven Camus to paint such a gloomy picture in his political discourse in *L'Homme révolté*. Demands for social justice—the organization of a Communist party—the suppression of individual freedom—injustice—that was Camus's line of argument and it showed nothing but the author's ignorance of European political history. Look at the history of the Fabian Society and the British Labour Party. Look at the social policies of the Scandinavian countries. Crossman went on to argue that there were many other ways to rise up to the call for social justice besides organizing a Communist party and bringing about a Communist revolution.

When I was reading his critical remarks, I could not help recalling what Dr. Miyoshi Kazuo had told me in the research laboratory at Tokyo University's Medical School. He said, "One cannot accomplish much if one does not ask the right questions. And when no solution is possible, then one has to scrutinize the questions themselves." When the subject was politics, I came to realize that perhaps the questions Crossman raised were more pertinent than Camus's. Instead of asking how absolute moral values could be reconciled with the entrenched realities of power politics, one should instead ask what concrete avenues were available to realize relative values in a political reality not dictated by power relationships alone. To the question, Are you in favor of communism? I would

5. In *L'Homme révolté* (The rebel, 1951)—a subject Katō refers to in his Parisian conversations—Albert Camus rejected both Christianity and communism, causing an open break with Sartre in 1952, as he set out an allegory of revolution within a new Promethean fable: "Proclaiming his hatred of the gods and his love of man, [Prometheus] turns disdainfully away from Zeus toward the mortals to lead them in an assault against the sky . . . [and] Prometheus, alone, has become god and reigns over the solitude of men. . . . [But] he is no longer Prometheus, he is Caesar" (*L'Homme révolté*, quoted in Germaine Brée, *Camus* [New York: Harcourt, Brace and World, 1964], 218–19).

6. Richard Howard Stafford Crossman (1907–74), a fellow and tutor in philosophy at Oxford (1930–37) and editor (1970–72) of the *New Statesman*, a leading socialist weekly; in Harold Wilson's Labour cabinet he served as Minister of Housing (1964–66) and leader of the Commons (1966–68).

answer in the negative if I were an Englishman, but in the positive if I were a Chinese. To the question, Are you in favor of social democracy? I would say yes if I were a Swede, but no if I were a Cuban. I came to realize the futility of arriving at an answer without qualifications and to appreciate the fact that answers are meaningful only when they come with reservations. This way of thinking has since determined my attitude toward political issues. My subsequent involvement with politics was extremely limited. All I did was simply follow other political pundits and proclaim why I felt policy A was more desirable than policy B. Most of my ideas have not been realized, but that never made me feel the need to alter my views or to become disillusioned with politics.

I suppose what I acquired in England was not any specific way of thinking about politics but, rather, an attitude toward it, one that would not directly associate moral sentiments with political contemplations. It seemed to me that this attitude was indispensable if the fundamental alliance between political and moral considerations was to be maintained. Needless to say, the British differ greatly among themselves in their way of thinking. But there seemed to be a unique style in their manner of discourse, a delicate balance between a sense of intellectual objectivity and a tendency toward moral self-restraint. It was highly questionable whether British foreign policy was more "hypocritical" than those of other countries. Even if it were, I think one could hardly expect more from a nation's foreign policy. Without the recognition of "virtue," surely there is also no need for "hypocrisy." Hitler's political actions were not hypocritical. And if one is totally convinced of one's own righteousness and the other side's evil, there is also no place for hypocrisy. One could argue that Dulles the anti-Communist crusader might be blind, but he was not a hypocrite.

After several months in England, my financial circumstances were increasingly desperate. But in London, I could think of no immediate means of coming up with the money I needed. I thought about returning to Paris, realizing that there I might be able to support myself, though not two of us. At the time she and I bid farewell in Florence, I also thought it would be the end for us. As I had when I saw her walking away from my train window at Vienna's Westbahnhof. I could not allow the same thing to go on endlessly. Before leaving England, I had to make up my mind what to do. Either we were going to work out a suitable plan to live together in the future or, if that proved impossible, we had to accept our last chance together as what it really was. The woman waiting for my return in Kyoto had not uttered a word of protest when I was about to leave for Europe. If she had done so emphatically, I probably would not have gone at all. I had no desire to exploit another person's kindness by turning it against her, still more so when she was too far away to defend her own position. And so I decided that before leaving England, I would travel to Edinburgh, touring medieval churches along the way, and make the trip my last chance together with the woman I loved.

It was our first long journey in Britain. The owner of every inn we went to would look at us suspiciously and declare, "No unmarried couple can stay in one room."

"We aren't asking for one room. We're asking you if you have two," I responded angrily. "What a hypocritical custom!" I muttered.

"But this sort of thing could happen elsewhere, not just in Britain," she noted.

It would not happen in Japan. All one does is write "Additional person" in the hotel register and that's the end of it. Moreover, for example on the subject of abortion, one does not have to pay a ridiculously large sum of money and put oneself at risk with a quack; if necessary it can be performed at a well-equipped hospital at a low cost. And divorce also can be accomplished at any time as long as there is agreement between the couple. That even matters like those cannot easily be done in many European countries results from excessive interference by church authorities into people's private life. "I want to go and see Japan," she remarked.

On reflection, I think that for a long time Christianity to me had been part of the history of a distant land associated with Aristotelian theology and the spirit of capitalism. To be sure, when Dulles talked about punitive expeditions against "Godless countries," he reminded me of the Crusades and the burning of heretics at the stake in the old days; but these thoughts, too, had nothing directly to do with my everyday life. In Japan, I had never found myself in any trouble because of a church. Japan's Christian converts are a powerless group, and they are in the minority. They do not meddle in elections or infiltrate the upper echelons of political power, and they do not interfere in any way with the manners and customs of the Japanese people or with their private life. Ever since the Edo period and under militarist Japan, the party that has initiated regulatory controls over public morality has not been the church, not even the Buddhist temple, but always state authority itself.

If Christianity and the Christian church were evaluated not on the basis of their relationship with Aristotle's heritage or with the capitalist spirit but on their impact on how people fill in their hotel register and on matters of pregnancy and divorce, one would naturally come to a different conclusion. It was not just in the past that the Western church killed Galileo. Even today with its enormous influence, there is no telling how many unfortunate young women have been driven to suicide or how many couples have been chained to their hell of mutual hatred. I remember one time in Paris talking to a small child next door. Still walking in uncertain steps, he was just beginning to talk.

"You shouldn't do such a naughty thing," I said.

Looking a little scared, the child stared at me with wide-open eyes and nodded.

"You shouldn't do naughty things even if your mother isn't looking."

"I won't even if she doesn't see me," the child said.

"Why?"

"Because the good God is watching me!"

"Even outside your house?"

"Inside, outside, all the time."

"Where is God when he is watching you?"

Without the slightest hesitation, the child raised his little arm above his head and said with a serious look on his face, "High up there."

I smiled. The child, too, broke into a smile, his face filled with a joy no words could possibly describe.

"And do you believe in God?" she asked me once.

"No, I don't. But I have nothing against others who do."

"What if a convert asked you to believe as he does?"

"I'd tell him to leave me alone. That's all."

"Just what I thought you'd say," she said.

In Edinburgh many people gathered for the music festival. The illuminated old castle town on the hill formed a sharp profile against the night sky. In the distance we could hear bagpipes from a Scottish military band. We couldn't get tickets for the opera, but we walked around the city, went to a concert and a play, and looked at a Cézanne exhibition with works selected from British and American collections. In terms of its quantity and quality, the chronological categorization, and the lighting effects, it was a superb exhibition. I thought I understood for the first time the significance of Cézanne as a phenomenon, and I was excited by my new discovery. In the history of modern Western painting, first there was Giotto and then, I learned, Cézanne.

"It makes me sad to think our trip's coming to an end," she remarked.

London, the tube, the City's gray walls, the cockney accent, the old charwomen going to work in the offices early in the morning, the Sundays on the banks of Chelsea, "the aunt's" neuralgia and her "Oh I *bin alt*, you know . . ."

"Remember to write when you get to Paris," she said.

"Of course," I said.

"Once a week."

"Of course," I repeated. But what was running through my mind was that once I crossed the Channel, it was a different world. Could "I" possibly exist at all independent of my surroundings? What exactly *was* this "I" anyway? Was there a greater hypocrisy than to imagine I would never change? And since I had left Japan, wasn't it true that even the part in me I believed to be the least susceptible to change *had* changed? If I really intended never to see her again, I knew I should not write.

I left England soon after my return from Scotland. On the train I heard French spoken for the first time after a long while, and through the train window my eyes caught the changing scenery of Normandy. In the limpid air each leaf on the trees glistened under the rays of the early autumn sun like a crisply pronounced syllable. France had not changed. The young woman from whom I had parted was never away from my mind. But my letter to London remained unwritten for a long time.

35   Farewell

After returning from England, I obtained the foreigner's work permit I had applied for a year earlier. I had just about forgotten the whole thing. With the permit, I should be able to solve all my economic problems at one stroke. At the time of my application, I already held a position at a national research institute. And if I went back to work there, I had every reason to believe that I could support myself in France.

Until then, I had been earning my living by sending manuscripts to Japanese newspapers and, if necessary, working as an interpreter to tide me over any emergency needs. As my stay in Europe stretched on, I grew less interested in writing short articles about everyday experiences. Similarly, witnessing again and again the same phenomenon of how extraordinarily difficult communication was between the Japanese and Westerners, I lost all curiosity about the job of interpretation. But that was only part of the story. I also realized that whether I worked for the newspapers or for the travelers, as long as my business dealings were with the Japanese, my exposure to life in the West could only be one-sided. If my economic infrastructure was so entwined with the fabric of Japanese society, it would be difficult, if not impossible, to understand the superstructure of a foreign society from within. As long as I was living in France, I wanted a local job commensurate with my professional credentials.

My professional training was in internal medicine, especially clinical care and research in hematology. This specialized work could only be found in large hospitals or research institutes, and such establishments in Paris were all state-operated. Working for a private enterprise, in certain circumstances I might have been able to arrange an advance on an unofficial monthly salary—but this was not possible in a national institute. That was why I had to apply for an official permit at the Labor Bureau for Foreigners as soon as I got the job.

In France in those days, a Japanese applying for something as simple as a one-year student visa had to go through a rather arduous application process. When it came to the application for a work permit, the process was even more complicated. I had to appear at the government office many times, and it took a long time to obtain the certification from the research institute and prepare the documents for the police. After keeping me waiting for some time, a policeman took out a thick file of documents and began to turn them over in front of me.

"I see, looks like you've been to southern France last year," he said.

"Yes, I have."

He then enunciated my exact travel dates (which I myself had forgotten), and when he said, "You also stayed in Avignon," I was amazed. "And then you went to Aix-en-Provence."

"Was there anything wrong with that?"

"No, as long as you haven't done anything improper," the man muttered haughtily.

That reminded me of the time when a plainclothes policeman stopped me on a street. I was walking alone on a boulevard near the Arc de Triomphe holding two or three newspapers I had bought at a subway exit.

"Monsieur!" somebody behind me suddenly called out. As I turned around, I saw a stranger walking quickly in my direction. He simply flashed his policeman's I.D.—I suppose that's what it was—and said only one word, "Identification." With a contemptuous demeanor, he practically snatched my residence papers and passport away from me and examined them for a while before thrusting them back at me all without even the courtesy of uttering a single cordial remark. I suppose when government bureaucrats like him play with their young children at home, they, too, can be good fathers. And whenever I had to deal with the police, I always thought that perhaps my less than distinguished looks were to blame.

The trouble with the application process went beyond the ridiculously long hours I spent with the police. To begin with, the regulations clearly stated that foreigners were permitted to work only in jobs for which replacement by French workers was deemed difficult. With the exception of manual labor, roadwork, housework and the like, jobs for which France at long last was beginning to feel the pinch, I could not imagine such positions even existed. In fact, as rumor went, among the few hundred Japanese residents in France at that time, those who had work permits and were officially employed at French enterprises or organizations were the exceptions among exceptions. To be sure, these people did have unusual skills difficult for the French to replace. One such individual was a high-ranking judo expert working as an instructor for the police. Another was the singer Ishii Yoshiko, who sang Japanese songs at a Montmartre vaudeville.[1] Another person made his living at a chicken farm by instantly identifying the sex of the chickens to be hatched simply by holding freshly laid eggs in his palm.

And here was I, with a weak constitution and no liking for physical combat. I inclined toward effeminate intellectual pursuits and never managed to acquire any rank in the martial arts. Furthermore, I was not endowed with a beautiful voice and cannot even imagine myself singing songs from any country in front of an audience. As for telling the sex of an egg, even if I had a whole day to examine it in my hands, I still wouldn't have even the foggiest idea, to say nothing of making instant and accurate identification. The only special skill I had, if one could call it that, was at accurately identifying the type of human blood cells after briefly examining them under an oil-immersion microscope. This, of course, was something French specialists could do as well. About the only thing I could say was that because there were not many such specialists around, immediate replacement of my services by a French national could, in certain situations, be deemed "difficult." So even though I took the trouble to go through with the application, I could by no means be optimistic about the outcome.

Before permission was finally granted—before I knew what my prospects of making a living in France were—I continued to live my life without thinking about it. As long as I had gone through all the necessary steps, worrying about the same thing over and over again would only be a waste of time. Furthermore, I had not yet made up my mind whether to live in France for any substantial period of time. If I should decide to stay, I hoped circumstances would permit me to do so. But deciding on how long to stay was a completely different matter.

When I saw Paris for the first time, I thought big cities everywhere were

---

1. Ishii Yoshiko (1922–), a graduate of Tokyo Music School, first sang pop American songs and switched to *chansons* after she went to Paris in 1952. In 1961 she began a music agency to train singers such as Kishi Yōko and Katō Tokiko; she returned to her singing career in August 1975.

essentially the same and after a year's stay I'd simply return to Tokyo. After a while, I came to appreciate a sense of depth in French culture, and I realized that a year's stay was just a preparatory phase before I could even begin to fathom it. Without the slightest hesitation I extended my sojourn. Toward the end of my second year, I began to feel that the depth of French culture was infinite and, once I ventured into it, I'd fall into an abyss so deep that finally there'd be no way out. The thought threw me into a dizzy spell almost like a frightful shiver. A culture permeates all one's senses. Encountering a different culture and simply observing it, one can always return to one's old nest with all senses intact. Malinowski's experience with the Trobriand Islands is one such example.[2]

But if the second culture ceases to be merely an object of observation and affects the observer himself to the extent that it changes his basic makeup, the process is irreversible and gives rise to a situation where there can be no turning back. Koizumi Yakumo, a long-time resident in Matsue, is one such example.[3] Lafcadio Hearn at that time was not merely observing Japanese society as an object; he immersed himself in Japanese culture and became Koizumi Yakumo. Genuine immersion in the new culture banishes, at least in part, the culture indigenously acquired. I wonder if the process did not send shivers of apprehension through Koizumi Yakumo too. I often felt that an extension of my sojourn in France was, quite naturally, tantamount to an extension of my absence from Japan, and if I had any desire to pack up and go at all, I should do so before I found myself too deeply involved in the whole affair.

By then, the French language, my relationship with the French people, their customs, their manners, and the seasons of the land had al-

2. Bronislaw Kasper Malinowski (1884–1942), an eminent Polish-born British social anthropologist whose analysis of four years of fieldwork in the Trobriand Islands and northwest Melanesia (1914–18) set new standards in field research. He was the first professor of social anthropology at the London School of Economics and also taught at Yale. Among his major works were *Sex and Repression in Savage Society* (1927), *A Scientific Theory of Culture* (1944), and *Freedom and Civilization* (1960).

3. Koizumi Yakumo, the Japanese name of Lafcadio Hearn (1850–1904), the best-known early interpreter of Japanese culture and folklore for Western readers, who went to Japan in 1890 as a correspondent for *Harper's New Monthly* (including fifteen months in the ancient provincial city of Matsue on the Sea of Japan coast), became a naturalized Japanese subject in 1896, and taught English literature at Tokyo Imperial University (1896 to 1903). His works include *Glimpses of Unfamiliar Japan* (1894), *A Japanese Miscellany* (1901), and *Japan: An Attempt at an Interpretation* (1904).

ready permeated into my inner self, forming layers of interacting experiences, and were about to create a new part of me. When I said, "This winter is really cold," the statement no longer evoked memories of the winter in Tokyo last year or the one the year before that; I was thinking about the winter in Paris. It was different from a traveler's impression of a cold Parisian winter. Past experiences determine the significance of those of the present: the kind of winter in which gray skies stretched across the space between the stone walls, when unremitting rain mixed with ice dampened the pavements, when the warm glow filtering through the café's clouded windows in an early evening enticed the hearts of the passers-by. After several months with almost no sun, suddenly spring arrived with its blue skies and young leaves on the tree-lined streets, dazzling the eye with their infinite brilliance and freshness. In order to savor "the warm breezes on the first day of spring," one needs to entertain vivid memories of "the frozen waters once soaking through the sleeves."[4] The coming of early spring can only be appreciated in the same place one has spent the winter. And that is not all.

At first, my vocabulary in French was nowhere near my vocabulary in Japanese. But increasingly I learned the names of things in French before I knew how to say them in Japanese: vegetables I had never eaten in Japan, systems and institutions I had never come across, philosophical concepts I had never utilized. Each and every one of these items was closely connected with my everyday life and thoughts. Of course, with the aid of a dictionary, I could translate these expressions into Japanese. I could say something like, "I took a stroll along 'a thoroughfare lined with a kind of chestnut tree,' ate 'a kind of shrimp' and 'a variety of pear grown in the West,' went to see a play in a 'theater supported by government subsidies,' and thought about 'a dominant idea running through the entirety of the play.'" But I could not think like that! And if the topic moved from chestnut trees or pears to democracy and existence, surely I could not say something like "a type of democracy" or "a Western kind of existence." Translation does not solve the real problems. To think in two different languages inevitably means to think, to a larger or lesser

---

4. A famous "spring" poem by Ki no Tsurayuki (ca. 872–945) in *Kokinshū*: "On this first spring day / might warm breezes be melting / the frozen waters / I scooped up, cupping my hands / and letting my sleeves soak through?" (*Kokin Wakashū*, trans. Helen Craig McCullough [Stanford: Stanford University Press, 1985], 14).

degree, about two different things. If the same person has to think about two different things at the same time, I am afraid his mind may not last very long. I was just beginning to try to think in French. If I were to take this route, I felt I still had a long way to go, and, inevitably, the more committed I became, the further I would be from the Japanese way of thinking. It would take considerable resolve to take the plunge.

And I also remembered the saying "Long absent, soon forgotten." Nothing could hurt the good fellowship I had with my Japanese friends more than staying away from Japan. Besides my friends, there was also my sense of bonding with certain parts of Japanese society over the last thirty years of my life. That bonding had nothing to do with race or nationality; it came from the fact that we had lived through the same age together. To say we would still be living in the same age if they were in Tokyo and I remained in Paris was accurate only in a highly abstract sense. No tangible historical time can be severed from a specific cultural space. Be it a research institute in Paris, a drainage ditch in the Tokyo suburbs, an investment firm's office in London, or a tent in the Syrian desert, each of these places exists in its own temporal sequence. The material distinction between two experiences surely must lie in the distance within their temporal space and not in the time that transcends space or in the distance that transcends time. To live in a specific place implies the choice of a specific time sequence in which and in which alone all concrete experiences take place. I became more keenly aware of this than ever. I did not want to leave Europe, but I wanted very much to live in Japan. This had absolutely nothing to do with any sentimental nostalgia. Should I return or should I not? If I should, I kept reminding myself that I had to return soon.

On the other hand, I did not like to give things up half way. So far as I had become an interested observer of France, I also wanted very much to see with my own eyes what had inspired my curiosity in the first place. One could visit Paris in the winter just once and have all kinds of impressions about it, saying things like "The winter in Paris is really cold." Such impressions cannot be the starting point for any proper assessment of the situation. There are two preconditions. First, statistics on winter temperatures for the last several decades, the kind of information that can be obtained in Tokyo. Second, past winter experiences, the kind that have been internalized to form a part of one's own makeup, the kind one achieves only by living in the place. What then is the relationship between these two preconditions? Without experiencing the latter to the fullest extent, I couldn't possibly answer the question. Perhaps parallel lines will always be parallel lines, but yet they might intersect at some point. If they do, the question of where I happen to live perhaps no longer makes any fundamental difference to me. But that was not what I expected, nor did I have any presentiment about it. And it was impossible to predict how much time it would take to reach into the depths of layers on layers of experience. Thinking of returning to Japan only served to defeat my purpose. There was not much I could do other than continue to live in Paris as if I might spend the rest of my life there.

While I deliberated, new developments in my personal relationship somehow made the decision for me. I was mulling over an end to the relationship with the young woman in London, and for a time I did not send her any letters. Thinking it was odd, she took a leave from work and suddenly appeared at my Paris residence. I was reading in bed and went to the door, still in my pajamas, opened the door a crack, and there she was quietly standing in the corridor in an overcoat with turned-up collar and a small bag.

"I didn't think you'd leave my letters unanswered, so I thought you might have left Paris already," she said.

The moment I heard her voice and touched her soft hair, I changed the decision I had made in England or, rather, realized I hadn't really made up my mind in the first place. All other considerations no longer meant anything compared to the time we spent together.

"I don't think you can live with that Japanese woman," she said. And sure enough, I could not even imagine it.

"In that case, rather than give up the idea of you and me together and make three people miserable, shouldn't we at least try to make two people happy together?"

Her reckoning did not entirely convince me, but I had already decided not to leave her again. I had already started thinking ahead and realized it was unfair to keep the woman in faraway Kyoto waiting forever for my return. To tell her about my change of heart in the form of a letter would hardly be respectful. I had to meet her and explain before I could say good-bye, and to do that I had to return to Japan. The foreigner's work permit came too late for me. I decided to leave early.

It occurred to me, after I made the decision, it might be a good idea to take her along to revisit southern France before I left this country where I'd been living so long. When we'd gone to Scotland, I thought it would be our last trip. Now I thought, in a sense, this would be our first trip together. It was just a matter of time before she would come to Japan one day, and we would most certainly be doing some traveling there as well. And in all probability, we would return to Europe via places like Hong Kong and India. My head was filled with all these thoughts, and I kept talking about them endlessly.

The express train to Marseilles was terribly crowded, but that did not have the slightest effect on my high spirits. Someone said that rain comes only three days a year on the coast with the perpetually azure sky, but when we got there a late autumn rain was pouring, and waves were raging in the ashen gray sea. Even that failed to dampen our spirits at all. To young lovers and elderly people, every day is precious regardless of the weather and the surroundings. For the former the future seems endlessly long, and for the latter the future is all too short. When we went out to the coast of St-Raphaël, we were the only people there besides the elderly. During intervals between the rain, we went swimming or rowing. The room by the seaside was decorated with old-fashioned furniture, with the windows on one side facing the sea and on the other opening onto a small Italian-style garden. There we spent our time late into the night listening to the sound of the waves.

"I've wanted to go see Japan ever since I was just a child," she said, "and I didn't even have a reason."

She did not seem to know anything about Japan. I was moved by her courage, or perhaps I should say by the way she came to that decision and the manner in which she took responsibility for her own life. She had not been encouraged by her parents to go, nor did she discuss her plans with her friends. On the contrary, should she decide to go, she surely would go alone despite opposition from her parents and misgivings from her friends.

At the end of the trip, we no longer had any doubts that we would spend our lives together. She left for London and would wait for my letters there. I remained in Paris and made preparations to return to Japan. Because I had already spent all my traveling expenses, those preparations were not as smooth as one might think. But more than that, my heart was confused. I could imagine what the meeting in Kyoto would be like, knowing I had scarcely anything to say in defense of my selfishness. But those thoughts did not change my mind. I knew I was not leaving Europe for good but was simply interrupting my stay because of an urgent need to be in Japan for a time. She later became my wife, and after that I often lived in Europe.

36 Japan as Seen from the Outside

I had not set foot on Japanese soil in three years. When the full view of the northern Kyushu coast came into sight from the ship's deck as it passed through the Kammon Straits, I saw Japan from the outside for the first time, and probably the last.[1] (Later on, I left Japan on many occasions, but on my subsequent returns, the distinction between Japan from the outside and the inside no longer held the decisive impact it once had on me.)

It took over six weeks for the freighter to travel from Marseilles to the Kammon Straits. The journey was analogous to a process in which European forms—languages, architectural styles, manners, and customs—gradually gave way to the growing intensity and distinctiveness with which the natural and cultural diversities of a different world manifested themselves, a world called, for lack of a better term, "Asia." In Cairo, one could still communicate in English and French and read the street signs and even the newspapers in these two languages. The air was dry, and off southern France or northern Africa, the Mediterranean Sea glittered with the same deep blue color.

As soon as the ship crossed the Indian Ocean and entered into the Strait of Malacca, however, everything began to change. The air turned humid, and even the color of the sea appeared to be different. At the coastal areas, thick tropical forests encroached on the water's edge. At the harbor, while the ship was loading and unloading, I went ashore to

1. The Kammon Straits (also known as the Shimonoseki Straits) separates the western tip of Honshu at the city of Shimonoseki and the northeastern tip of Kyushu at Moji harbor in the city of Kitakyūshū.

357

look at the dense forests, the Chinese settlement, and the indigenous villages. I also saw the port of Singapore, the cranes, and the skyscrapers. The scene was not any different from any Western port, but here alone it stood out from its surroundings like a totally alien entity, as if it had nothing at all to do with the local climate or people. Here, English was nothing more than a tool for commerce. In Hong Kong, numerous Chinese were working at the port loading and unloading cargoes, and in the city's bookstores people were standing in front of the bookshelves reading Chinese books imported from the mainland. In Manila, the authorities allowed the ship to enter port, but Japanese passengers were not permitted to go ashore. In Pusan, not only did the authorities prohibit Japanese passengers from going ashore, but the ship was stuck at the port for as long as a week because of an ongoing longshoremen's strike.

"We lose about one million yen every day we are stuck here," lamented the captain.

"Is this some form of anti-Japanese harassment?"

"No, I guess the delay will also prevent the American ship from unloading."

That American ship had entered the harbor with a full load and could now be seen departing with its red belly exposed above the water. When it came to this part of the world, not even a shadow of Europe remained. What reigned supreme here was the United States, or, more precisely, the U.S. military itself along with jeeps, prostitutes, and cigarettes sold in the black market.

"Look! Half the city is in darkness," the captain said. "Each half takes a turn getting electricity from the generators on the American ships pulled alongside the pier."

The wintry South China Sea was rough, and waves raged high on the Genkai Sea.[2] But the Kammon Straits remained unruffled, and a whitish morning mist hovered over the distant sea. The northern Kyushu coast appeared through the openings in the morning haze like a print in light ink. Soon, columns of smoke from the factories became visible from the coast, and the oil storage facilities glistened in a silvery radiance in the morning sun. As the ship passed by a small island, one could even see the crooked pine trees and the tile-roofed houses.

2. On the traditional route from northern Kyushu to continental Asia, the Genkainada (sometimes known as Kyūshūnada) is north of Fukuoka and Saga Prefectures and is known for its high waves during the winter.

This was the Japan I had not seen in three years, a world delineated not in the colors of an oil painting but in shades of ink from a brush painting, not from a geometric perspective but from a depth perception created by the morning mist. Surely, Watsuji Tetsurō likewise must have seen the same scene.[3] However, his ideas about *fūdo* (cultural physiography), the conclusion he drew from it, were a mistaken view. If the seas or the mountains had never been veiled in a haze, perhaps the genre of monochrome ink painting would not have existed. But Watsuji's idea that *fūdo* and the haze had given birth to the monochrome ink painting was most certainly incorrect. What created it, I thought, was the inhabitants' order of life as it evolved on the Japanese archipelago over many centuries—the tile-roofed houses, the shades of ink in a monochrome painting, and the harmony between its lines, the subtleties and complexities of its lifestyle and its internal consistency. Regardless of what it might actually be, Japan first appeared before my eyes not as a natural environment but as a manifestation of the history of its inhabitants, not in the form of deserts or dense forests or rocky hills, but, most assuredly and above anything else, as a tangible social entity. I saw Japan as a phenomenon. My perception of Japan had come with such thoroughness that I doubt if I would ever waver from it (and from that standpoint, I have produced a number of essays).

The six-week journey by sea was enough to highlight for me Japan's position within Asia. Nowhere else in Asia could I find scenes similar to the northern Kyushu coast or the Kobe harbor. Whether they might be

3. Watsuji Tetsurō (1889–1960), whose travels to and from Germany (1927–28) inspired his still controversial *Fūdo—Ningengakuteki kōsatsu* (1935; Eng. trans. *A Climate* [1961]), which divided societies into three physiographic categories (monsoon, desert, and pastoral), arguing that each environment gave rise to distinct behavioral and cultural patterns among its inhabitants—for example, the receptiveness (*juyōsei*) and submissiveness (*ninjūsei*) supposedly inherent in the Japanese character reflected monsoon-type society; after studying philosophy at Tokyo Imperial University, Watsuji turned from literature to study Nietzsche, Schopenhauer, Kierkegaard, and Buddhism, as well as ancient Japanese cultural history. • One student of traditional Chinese painters' treatment of perspective suggests that they deliberately avoided it: "Scientific perspective involves a view from a determined position, and includes only what can be seen from that single point. While this satisfies the logical Western mind, it is not enough for the Chinese painter. . . . [What he] records is not a single visual confrontation, but an accumulation of experience touched off perhaps by one moment's exaltation before the beauty of nature" (Michael Sullivan, *The Arts of China*, rev. ed. [Berkeley: University of California Press, 1979], 163–64).

factories, cranes, or hospitals, "modern" facilities built not by foreigners for their own benefit but by local people for their own purposes appeared for the first time in Japan after I left Marseilles. In that sense, Kobe was a lot like Marseilles and completely different from Singapore or Hong Kong. I suppose that's why, superficially, the city lights of Singapore or Hong Kong, when viewed from a ship's deck after dark, reminded me much more of Marseilles than of Kobe. I needed to reexamine this nebulous idea of "Asia," and the thought kept running through my mind even while I was going through customs after landing at Kobe.

I left my belongings in Kobe and went immediately to Kyoto. The woman who had been waiting for me had said she could not come to meet me in Kobe due to her child's illness. I explained the reason for my return and told her repeatedly that the only thing left for us to do was to say good-bye. But she could hardly believe my words.

"How can you say such a thing after I waited for you for so long?"

I was disgusted with myself for having to repeat the same thing again. I realized that I was destroying the emotional life of another human being.

"You're such a fool! The same thing will only happen again."

She was probably right, but whether the same thing would happen in the future did not matter to me at all.

"If you're displeased with me, just tell me what it is!" she demanded.

But that was not the issue. For a long time I had thought that I loved her, but when I really fell deeply in love with another woman, I realized that her relationship with me was something different.

"I'm not the least displeased with you or anything like that. If there are any flaws between us, I'm the only one who more than deserves the blame," I said.

That was the way I truly felt. When I acted, or rather had to act—in the full knowledge that I was making her life miserable because of something she had no responsibility for—naturally there was nothing I could possibly say to her. I kept talking, though I realized how meaningless my words were and I felt totally exhausted. I left her while I was in an abstracted state of mind. We would never see each other again, and I no longer had the energy to even think about her. I was totally preoccupied with my own feelings. But at the same time, I was also looking at myself as if I were a third person. What was this "I"? What was the makeup of a man who left a woman only to head toward another? If my relationship with these two women were to be obliterated, I couldn't help feeling, there'd be nothing left in me but a pervasive feeling of emptiness.

I did not return to Tokyo at once. Instead, I wandered around Kyoto visiting old temples and gardens. I realized that once I began to work as a physician in Tokyo, I would simply become too preoccupied to think about myself. What I needed was self-rediscovery, not self-obliteration, and for that purpose, I needed some time for myself alone. I did feel like having someone to talk to but couldn't think of anything to talk about. Alone in the evening, I took a walk around the busy amusement quarters. There were only Japanese around me, all with the same black hair, forming an endless wave streaming along the sidewalk to unknown destinations—an extraordinary and incredible scene. Even compared with the situation three years ago, they were now much better dressed, and the many young people in the crowd looked healthy, with bright, cheerful faces. What relationship did these people have with the wars that had just ended in Korea and in Indochina, I thought, and Pusan and Paris came back to mind. In Japan, they might or might not have reacted to the conflicts, and that was a Japan I did not know.

But the old Kyoto was always there. Into Shisendō's frigid interior came the crisp and high-pitched sound of bamboo pipes hitting against the rocks to chase away the deer. The curved eaves atop the temple gate of the Daitokuji, the morning frost columns on the grounds of the Yasaka Shrine, the white walls and the setting sun at Ninnaji. Nowhere did I encounter any tourists. Although some men and women gathered at the Rokuharamitsuji, they were Buddhist worshipers, not sightseers.[4] Everything in the ancient capital quietly permeated every part of my

4. Shisendō, built in 1641 by the poet Ishikawa Jōzan (1583–1672) as his secluded residence, is noted for its garden and the display of Jōzan's calligraphy with poetry and images of thirty-six *shisen*, or "poet-geniuses," such as Li Po and Tu Fu (see Katō's essay "Shisendō shi" [Account of the hall of poetry immortals, in *Katō Shūichi chosakushū*, 13:261–92] and chapter 24, note 3). And in "Gendai Nihon bungaku no jōkyō—seikatsu no geijutsuka to geijutsu no seikatsuka" (The state of contemporary Japanese literature: the artification of life and the domestication of art, in ibid., 6: 21–40), Katō underscores the dramatic contrast in attitudes toward art and life between Jōzan and the modern I-novelists. • The Daitokuji's original structure was founded in 1324 and soon became the greatest temple in northern Kyoto; the head temple of the Rinzai sect's Daitokuji branch, it is known for its architectural grandeur and medieval art, as well as the Zen garden (designed by Sōami) in Daisen-in, a subordinate temple. • The famous vermilion Yasaka main shrine was built in 1654 and hosts the Gion Festival every July and the Okera Festival on New Year's Day. • Ninnaji,

362 / *Japan as Seen from the Outside*

body along with the severe chill of winter. Until then, there had been one place I would always visit after taking a solitary stroll in Kyoto and its suburbs, one place where I could always enjoy a relaxed, light-hearted chat over a cup of tea. The very presence of one single woman born and bred in this city had summed up my entire experience of the day, giving it a focus and embodying it in her diminutive frame, her unaffected movements, and the expressions in her eyes. I used to have that feeling even when I was standing by myself looking at the Buddhist statues. But now, that inkling had gone. The only living person who represented the essence of everything I knew about Kyoto was no longer there for me, and Kyoto itself was no longer the city I once knew so intimately. I followed the paths and the stepping-stones I had walked on countless times, but I was looking at a city I had never seen. What lay before my eyes was only a culture and its forms, that was all. Kyoto now appeared before me in just the same way Florence once had.

Not a soul could be seen on Jingoji's extensive grounds. Assailed by piercing northerly winds, I could feel the numbing pain at my fingertips and my ears as I stood for a long time face to face with the five images of the Ākāśagarbha bodhisattva.[5] In the dim light, the gilded wooden statues sat erect in a motionless posture, eyes shining with penetrating intensity. They did not simply represent the bodhisattva's manifestation into this world or an evocation of his infinite compassion; there was something about their heightened sensual impact that completely captivated the onlooker. Buddhist statues in the Tempyō era were nothing of the sort.[6] Just as great changes took place in north-

---

built in 888, is the head temple of the Shingon sect's Omuro branch. • Rokuharamitsuji was founded in 963 as Saikōji and noted for its many works of Heian and Kamakura sculpture.

5. Jingoji is a special head temple of the Shingon sect's Tōji branch and dates from 824; Kūkai (774–835), founder of the Shingon sect, turned the Jingoji into a seminary, and the temple enjoyed a period of prosperity under his disciple Shinzei as abbot. • The bodhisattva's five images, the statues of the Godai kokūzō (void store) bosatsu—a national treasure and a masterpiece of early Heian Buddhist sculpture—were created by Shinzei around 847 (*Sandai jitsuroku* and *Jingoji ryakuki*, cited in Kurata Bunsaku, *Mikkyō jiin to Jōgan chōkoku, Genshoku Nihon no bijutsu* 5 [Shōgakukan, 1976], 75–76, and *Mikkyō jiten: zen* [Kyoto: Hōzōkan, 1975], 217).

6. With reference to Japanese art history, the Tempyō era (729–749, during the reign of Emperor Shōmu) also refers broadly to some eighty years during the late Nara period (710–94).

ern France from the end of the eleventh to the beginning of the twelfth
century, surely something happened in Japan in the ninth century.[7]
Not that early Heian Buddhist statues bear a certain resemblance to
early Gothic sculpture: they certainly do not. But both transformations,
once begun, gave rise to artistic forms that inevitably dominate and
have lasting effects on the subsequent development in their respective
cultures. A comparison between Japan and Europe on that subject would
make an enormously fascinating study. At that moment, I was literally breathless with excitement as I gazed transfixed at the statues of
the bodhisattva.

Nothing can be more foolish than to suggest that someone with a
connoisseur's eye for Western art would, on reexamination, dismiss
ancient Japanese art as trivial and inferior. What strikes one as trivial
is the Tōshōgū, not the Katsura Detached Palace.[8] Far from being trivial, in terms of the parity between spirituality and sensuality, the harmony between form and material, and the coordination between imposing splendor and the sense of movement, Japanese Buddhist
sculpture magnificently rivals its Gothic counterpart. The issue here
is not one of style but of quality, and the questions involved are so inexhaustible that they cannot fail to inspire interest. Later on, I began
to write about Japanese art, but it has nothing whatsoever to do with
patriotism. To this day, my profound admiration for the Yakushiji trinity has been inspired by the same affection I cherish for the Buddhist

7. In Katō's discussion of the ninth century (*Nihon bungakushi josetsu: Jō,*
in *History of Japanese Literature,* 1:91), he identifies it as "a period in which
imported Chinese civilization was gradually digested and submitted to a native
transformation. . . . Of the patterns and tendencies which emerged in the ninth
century in such fields as politics, economics, society, language and aesthetics,
some were preserved to the end of the Heian period, others survived to the beginning or end of the Tokugawa period and some, particularly in the nature of
politics and the written and spoken Japanese language, are still making their presence felt today."

8. Tōshōgū, built in 1617 as a mausoleum for Tokugawa Ieyasu in Nikkō,
exhibits flamboyant and ostentatious embellishment: "the buildings remain an
almost complete antithesis of the simplicity and taste that are usually counted
among the characteristics of Japanese architecture" (Charles S. Terry, in *Encyclopaedia Britannica* [1972], 12:951). For Katō's assessment of its artworks see
"Nikkō Tōshōgū," in *Katō Shūichi chosakushū,* 12:221–37; his more recent essay describes its structures as "an artistic Disneyland" that elaborately but in-
coherently reproduced architectural or design motifs from various periods (see
"Tōshōgū saiken," in *Gendai Nihon shichū* [Heibonsha, 1987], 244–49). • On
the Katsura Detached Palace see chapter 12, note 17.

images of the Northern Wei period and the figures of angels at the cathedral of Reims.[9]

Shortly after returning to Tokyo, I went back to work at the Tokyo University Hospital in Hongō. Once I went for a few drinks with my colleague Dr. Miyoshi in a sukiyaki restaurant and heard him sing "Otomi-san" when he was drunk.[10] The song had swept the country while I was gone. "I wonder if there's any Japanese man who hasn't heard it," Mr. Miyoshi said. I also met my old friends Nakamura Shin'ichiro and Harada Yoshito, and through them, I learned about the popularity of the serialized television drama Kimi no na wa (And what's your name?).[11] "Essentially what you have is a story line about romances breaking up in various places over Japan, so the play can continue forever. Not what you'd call a drama," Nakamura said. "But, this aside, if you don't know about it, you might become something of a moron for having lived too long in the West." Harada once taught Japanese as a lecturer in a university in Hamburg. I had met him there as well as in Paris. He returned to Tokyo earlier than I did and was then teaching German at the Komaba campus of Tokyo University. "I suppose you can call them reactions to the postwar reforms. But I think such retrogressive tendencies are emerging in various facets of life," he remarked. This was something we had also talked about in Europe.

I rented a room in my sister's house in Setagaya's Kaminoge and commuted from there to the hospital in Hongō. Work at the hospital was practically nonexistent, and soon I accepted a position working alternate afternoons at the medical office of a mining company at its Nihonbashi headquarters. From the medical standpoint, the job was not an interesting one, but the monthly salary was sufficient to support me.

I also went to lecture once a week in the faculty of literature at a private university. Ostensibly, my lectures were on French literature.

9. The three principal Buddhist deities worshiped at Nara's Yakushiji, the head temple of the Hossō sect, are the Yakushi Nyorai (Bhaiṣajyaguru), the Nikkō Bosatsu (Sūryaprabha) on his left, and the Gakkō Bosatsu (Candraprabha) on his right. • On the Northern Wei period see chapter 28, note 4.

10. "Otomi-san" (1954) by Watakuchi Masanobu, with lyrics by Yamazaki Tadashi hinting at a wounded past and a self-abandoning present.

11. A serial melodrama by Kikuta Kazuo (1908–73) for NHK television and radio broadcast from 1952 to 1954 that began with the famous romantic encounter on Tokyo's Sukiyabashi during the great air raid in early 1945; it became a successful motion picture, directed by Oba Hideo, in 1953. For a critical review, see Uriu Tadao, *Nihon no eiga* (Iwanami shinsho, 1956), 87–92.

But when I tried to give my students instruction in French, they rather preferred the illusion of studying French literature than learning something substantive. My income was barely enough to cover my traveling expenses. I began to think that although Japanese and French societies appeared to be similar, there were also significant differences. "Oh, that's only natural!" Professor Watanabe Kazuo said. "Everybody here has worked awfully hard for no good reason. Now this is what makes Japan such a marvelous country!"

The company was mining coal in Kyushu. But business had fallen on hard times. At the company's social club, the personnel chief who oversaw the medical office at the company's headquarters boasted that it had every kind of wine in the world.

"I wish someone would just do us a favor and start a war somewhere," he went on. "You know, our business had the best time ever during the Korean War. Oh, those were the good old days."

"You mean the company can't make a profit without a war?"

"That's right."

"Now, that sounds just like the official line from the left," I said.

But the quip eluded the personnel chief.

"Trade unions are here for no good. The whole idea was forced down our throats by the Americans and is so incompatible with the reality in Japan. Let me tell you, it's because of them that we're in such bad shape. Hey, how about another drink?"

I decided to go to the mountains of Kyushu to have a look for myself. The company made the necessary arrangements for me. Since the young staff at the labor affairs section knew the trade union officials well, they gave me a letter of recommendation to take along. I thought that in order to get a good personal perspective on what happened there, I had to listen to both sides and assess the situation from both angles. Once I got there, the company arranged for me to see the mountain during the day, but at night we had banquets continuing into the late hours. I could not help feeling that the company was trying to prevent me from getting to know the trade union people.

"You just can't talk with these people, you know," the on-site personnel section chief said as he put his arm around a geisha. "I've tried many times to negotiate with them. But you know what? I really wanted to spill their guts even if we had to go down together."

If that was his attitude, no wonder he couldn't communicate with the union. But I didn't need him to tell me whether I could or couldn't talk with them. When I declined to attend the second banquet, his response was "Now, doctor, don't tell me you only fool around in secret!" I told him I had not come all the way to Kyushu just to look at geishas. The union, on the other hand, treated me cordially.

The two sides disputed over everything. Take the conveyor belt controversy. From the company's point of view, the facility made the operation much easier for the workers. The union regarded it as a device to speed up operation and drive the miners to work nonstop. The replacement of wooden mine posts by steel structures was, according to the company, a measure to prevent cave-ins and to drastically improve safety. But the union said that it did little to guarantee safety in the mines, where the greatest danger came from gas explosions. As to why the workers lived under such impoverished conditions, the company's explanation was that the workers themselves allowed drinking to wear down their bodies and they relied on loan sharks after squandering their money. The union, on the other hand, argued that the company's indifference to the workers' safety put them in imminent danger every day and made drinking their only solace in life.

Each side presented more and more witnesses, and it seemed that the more detailed their arguments got, the more fundamentally unbridgeable their respective positions became. Which side was right? It struck me that it was impossible for any third party to offer an objective assessment as long as he had no on-site experience himself. The problem here was not lack of information, as it was when the question of whether planes had been flying outside the Berlin air corridors arose: there was no information other than the opposing views from the governments concerned, thus making any judgment from a third party impossible. In contrast, there is an avalanche of information on the French Revolution. And yet the choice to curse or praise the revolution ultimately depends on what one's own position is. Taking the middle ground between two extremes, needless to say, is not terribly meaningful. In fact, an objective judgment by a third party is impossible. One cannot simply argue that an event like the French Revolution was neither good nor bad or shrug off its consequences as being neither harmful nor desirable. There was no question that the conveyor belt had radically changed the nature of work in the mines, and the workers could not possibly have been totally neutral about it.

During the Pacific War, by distancing myself intellectually from the conflict, I came away with the experience that one's objective judgment could turn out to be quite accurate. But in the coal mines in Kyushu, I encountered a situation where making objective decisions became virtually impossible. Under such circumstances, I suppose one could abstain from judgment. In Kyushu, I was neither arbitrator nor judge. But what is one to do if abstention becomes impossible? What will I do if I am required to decide on an issue on which any objective—that is to say, scientific—evaluation proves impossible?

Thinking about the matter in Kyushu, I concluded that my basis for judgment had to be my own experience inside the mine shaft, however brief a time I spent there. I remember the tiny slice of blue sky I saw beyond the exit every time I made my way out of the dark, dangerous shaft. And the people who, seeing just such a tiny slice of blue sky every day, had nothing else to summon forth all the joys buried deep within their hearts. That was the only kind of life they had, the only way they could feel. Whether or not they were drunk, whether or not their arguments made any sense, who were we living every day under the blue sky to repudiate their words? I thought at the time that until we could explain objectively that they were wrong, everything they said was right. It is not always possible for a bystander to pass judgment. And for this reason, there is always a time when a bystander should cease to be one.

37   Enlightenment through Empirical Experience

I wrote a novel called *Unmei* (Destiny) based partly on my experience in the West and partly on my imagination, and another called *Jinkōsai* (Festival of the gods), an embellished account of what I saw in northern Kyushu.[1] While I was writing the second novel, I also became interested in the local dialect, which I started to learn from a friend native to the area. After I finished writing the dialogue in dialect, my friend corrected it. I had long thought that Tokyo's spoken language was rather lively, but its inconsistency of form was problematic and so I came up with the idea of writing the dialogue in the local dialect in hopes of remedying the situation somewhat. But perhaps it only makes the novel more difficult to read.

During that time, I wrote many essays for journals and newspapers, primarily on ways of interpreting Japanese culture. Living in the West altered the way I looked at Western culture, which in turn compelled me to change the ways I had looked at Japanese culture. One idea I mulled over was that since modern Japanese culture represents a mixture of long-cherished indigenous traditions and Western learning, arts, and technology, it cannot be transformed into a purely Japanese or a purely Western product, nor is there such a need. There was nothing new in thinking that modern Japanese culture was in this sense a "hybrid culture." But in terms of its potential, a hybrid isn't necessarily inferior to its purely authentic counterparts, and we need to just roll up our sleeves and do the best we can with what we already have. At least for me, this

---

1. *Unmei* was published in May 1956 and *Jinkōsai* in March 1959, both by Kōdansha.

state of mind was something nobody else had talked about.[2] To develop it into a coherent body of ideas, beyond the specificity of time and space, I had to identify examples that brought together the ability to assimilate alien cultures and the capacity for cultural creativity. Then I had to explore the general dynamics behind such cases. I was not at a total loss as to where such examples could be found, but I did not have the luxury of time to investigate and examine foreign cases to my own satisfaction. I simply wrote short essays in a hurry and published broad outlines of my ideas in journals.

My other thought was related to modern Japanese history. According to a popular theory, Japanese culture after the Meiji Restoration represented a "discontinuity" with its earlier traditions; I too had once accepted this view without really thinking through the issue. After my experience in the West, I could no longer think of the cultural relationship between the pre- and post-Meiji periods in any area of endeavor in terms of a "discontinuity." Besides oil paintings we also had Japanese-style paintings; besides Western-style orchestral music, traditional musical instruments, scales, and techniques of vocalization were widely practiced. And in the world of post-Meiji lyric poetry, the tradition of classical Japanese poetry still played a significant role; and the contemporary novel and *zuihitsu* most certainly cannot be considered as having been uprooted from the Edo *yomihon, kibyōshi,* and *haibun* traditions and the like.[3]

2. See his essays, "Nihon bunka no zasshusei" (The hybrid nature of Japanese culture, *Shisō*, June 1955) and "Zasshuteki Nihon bunka no kadai" (Question about Japan's hybrid culture, *Chūō kōron*, July 1955), in *Katō Shūichi chosakushū*, 7:5–46.

3. The *zuihitsu* (random essay, lit. "following the brush") dates from Sei Shōnagon's *Makura no sōshi* in the late tenth century; distinguished modern and contemporary writers of *zuihitsu* include Shimazaki Tōson, Nagai Kafū, Terada Torahiko, Tanizaki Jun'ichirō, Nakano Shigeharu, Yasuoka Shōtarō, and Kushida Magoichi (and other political/literary figures such as Nakae Chōmin and Sakai Toshihiko). • Edo *yomihon* fiction began in mid-eighteenth-century Osaka and was strongly influenced by traditional Chinese fiction, meant to be read as a text, and with relatively few illustrations; its representative writers include Ueda Akinari, Santō Kyōden, and Takizawa Bakin. • *Kibyōshi* (lit. yellow covers) was late eighteenth- and early nineteenth-century popular illustrated fiction meant for mature audiences—sarcastic, frivolous, and later even didactic; its major writers include Santō Kyōden and Koikawa Harumachi. • *Haibun* were prose writings by haiku poets whose best-known examples include Matsuo Bashō's *Oku no hosomichi* (The narrow road through the provinces, 1702), Yokoi Yayū's *Uzuragoromo* (Patchwork cloak, 1787–1823), and Kobayashi Issa's *Ora ga haru* (The year of my life, 1819).

Though I had written about these ideas, I was unable to examine specific writers and their works in detail to substantiate my views. I do not think that my ideas were incorrect. However, my writings were like skeletons without the flesh. The more I wrote at the request of journals and magazines, the less time I had to adequately examine the facts, leaving me no choice but to merely describe my impressions and opinions before I could complete my preparatory work. Working full-time as a physician, I was in the hospital and could not be reached at home during the day. Telephone calls from my editors would come to my residence even at night, and I had to interrupt my meal or dash out in the middle of my bath to answer them. There were times when an editor would come over on a weekend and wait in a room until I finished writing the manuscript he requested. Sometimes, I was up all night trying to meet the deadlines; at other times I would write short manuscripts on the commuter train to and from the hospital. While I still managed to continue my work as a physician, so many things required my immediate attention that I could no longer even think of reading a book. In Paris not only did I have time for reading, the theater, and art museums; I even had the luxury of admiring the trees on the riverbanks and the rows of houses glowing in the setting sun.

My hectic life as a literary journeyman, however, had given me the opportunity to get to know people in the same trade. The language they spoke differed strikingly from the familiar everyday conversation among ordinary people. Perhaps one could describe theirs as a sort of telepathic communication, for merely a few words could instantaneously convey with dramatic effectiveness their subtle "feelings." They shared a unique lexicon framed within a specific context. Consequently, if one could not fully appreciate what its implications were, at times it would be totally impossible to surmise what they were actually talking about. Somebody might say, "There is no bigger fool than that fellow. See what a splendid thing he's done!" and everyone would understand and join in a hearty laugh. I could not help remembering the time when I found myself in a Parisian vaudeville theater listening to an anecdote, conscious of myself as a foreigner, a man out of place. On one occasion, the editor of a literary journal went so far as to ask me, "Could you address the aspect of Sōseki as a moralist from the standpoint of an actualized problem consciousness?"[4] Though I responded in all plausible seriousness,

4. The Japanese reads "Sōseki no morarisuto to shite no men o akuchuaru

in fact I didn't really understand what he was saying. On those occasions I felt somewhat irritated and also lonely for being left out in the cold. Nothing hurts what sociologists call one's sense of belonging more than the inability to communicate within the group.

On the other hand, these problems in communication also helped arouse my curiosity. "Oh my! What you gentlemen are talking about is really beyond me!" a bar hostess remarked. While I felt the same way, I enjoyed socializing with novelists, literary critics, and editors. "I'll tell you," one of them said. "Science is *not* going to help you appreciate literature." What he really meant was, "You're a physician, a practitioner of the medical sciences. Therefore, literature isn't something you can understand." But he and others like him had very little idea of what science was all about. And there was another fellow, an admirer of "science," who merrily proclaimed, "According to quantum theory, an elementary particle is a particle in wave motion. With that, the validity of dialectics is scientifically proven." But why should I spoil the occasion when somebody was having such a good time? And so their conversation, be it on "science" or on "literature," ran on smoothly.

Small though my social circle was, it held many charismatic personalities. I don't believe I have encountered as many people with such refinement of character and sensitivity in any other society than in Tokyo's so-called *bundan*, our "literary world." The late Takami Jun was such an individual.[5] Moreover, what could only be described as an inner warmth animated his personality. The reason I enjoyed our friendship had absolutely nothing to do with my curiosity. It came from my respect for his extraordinary character.

Takami-san—that was what I called him—and some of us once held

---

na mondai ishiki kara toriagete . . ." On Natsume Sōseki see chapter 12, note 1.

5. Dominating the prewar career of Takami Jun (1907–65) was a series of attempts to come to terms with his "abandonment" of Marxism in 1933 under official pressure. In his classic *Kokyū wasureubeki* (Auld lang syne, 1935–36) he describes the suicidal decadence and political impotence of a generation of former left-wing intellectuals; in *Ikanaru hoshi no moto ni* (Under what star? 1939–40) he depicts wartime dancers and entertainers in Tokyo's popular Asakusa district, a work so successful that Nakajima Kenzō spoke of "the Takami Jun era." His major postwar works include *Iya na kanji* (Feelings of disgust, 1960–63), an ambitious historical novel about an anarchist active in Japan, Korea, and China, and *Shōwa bungaku seisuishi* (The rise and fall of Shōwa literature, 1952–57), an informative literary history.

a reception at a Shinjuku bar for a guest from afar. Among those present were Matsuoka Yōko, then the executive director of the Japan PEN Club, and Asabuki Tomiko, who was known for her translations of female French writers.[6] In her introduction of Takami-san, Ms. Matsuoka remarked that he was one of the most celebrated contemporary novelists. No sooner had she finished than our attentive guest from France turned to Takami-san and asked, "What kind of novels do you write? What are your themes and how do you treat them?" Considering the circumstances, it was a natural question for a Frenchman to raise but an altogether awkward thing to ask in a gathering of Japanese writers.

"Ha! You really put me on the spot here," Takami-san said. "It's not easy to explain one's own works."

And so I took the liberty of speaking for him. Takami-san might have thought I had misinterpreted his works in my impromptu commentary. In fact, I think he must have. But when I finished, he was in a very cheerful mood and said, "Come on, let's have another drink. Now, I seem to know what I have been writing all along," a comment that made everybody laugh. And there was not the slightest hint of sarcasm in what he said.

In addition to the charismatic personalities among my circle of friends, the precision of their knowledge often struck me with awe. Among my old friends were the French linguist Miyake Noriyoshi and the music critic Yoshida Hidekazu.[7] They could answer almost any question about French linguistics, or Eastern and Western music of all ages, including the background. In those days I frequently went to the Mitsukoshi Theater, where members of the Nomura family gave bimonthly kyōgen performances. There I would always meet my old friends Kubota Kaizō and Koyama Hiroshi.[8] After the performance we would have

6. Matsuoka Yōko (1916–79), journalist and executive director of the Japan PEN Club in 1956 and most noted for her social commentaries and her active role in the women's movement. • On Asabuki Tomiko see chapter 26, note 6.

7. See chapter 17 for Katō's reminiscences of Miyake while they were fellow students at Tokyo University. • On Yoshida Hidekazu see chapter 32, note 10.

8. Kubota Kaizō is the pen name of Kubota Keisaku (1920–), short-story writer, literary critic, and translator of contemporary French literature; see chapter 18 on his association with Katō dating from the days of Matinée Poétique. • Koyama Hiroshi (1921–), a distinguished scholar of nō and kyōgen; among his edited works are two volumes apiece on kyōgen in the Nihon koten bungaku taikei series (1960–61) and on yōkyoku in Nihon koten bungaku zenshū (1973–75); he taught at Tokyo University from 1959–81 and was head of the National Institute of Japanese Literature (Kokubungaku kenkyū shiryōkan) in Tokyo.

dinner somewhere nearby and talk about *kyōgen,* or to put it more accurately, Koyama would answer our questions on the subject. As far as *kyōgen* was concerned, the only questions Koyama could not immediately answer were precisely those nobody in the academic world of the time could elucidate.

My association with these friends amply heightened my awareness of my own shallow knowledge on literature and matters of literary taste, as well as on any subject within the broad spectrum of the humanistic sciences. The same thing could be said of my later friendship with novelists and literary critics. Each and every one of them took long years to cultivate the truly solid foundation of his erudition. For example, Kobayashi Hideo would not speak about Mozart's music without scrupulously listening to his compositions, or comment on Tessai's scroll paintings without meticulously observing the master's art.[9] Ishikawa Jun is thoroughly familiar with *nanga* and has absorbed Edo literature into his own flesh and blood.[10] His ability, with a sake cup in hand, to impress and awe every one of the listeners around him with the sophistication and eloquence of his delivery came from the extraordinary insights he had accumulated. Once I also heard Terada Tōru speak in a symposium about Kōrin's painting *Red and White Plum Trees.* "Every time I look

9. Kobayashi Hideo (1902–83) wrote a 1946 work on Mozart and one on the master painter Tomioka Tessai (1836–1924) in 1948; he was an editor of *Tessai* (1957). See also chapter 17, note 8.

10. Ishikawa Jun (1899–1987), one of the most prominent contemporary Japanese novelists known for his polished neoclassicist style and extraordinary erudition in both modern French literature (esp. Gide, Claudel, and France) and the classical Chinese and Japanese traditions. In Katō's view, Ishikawa more profoundly epitomized the literary tradition of the Edo intelligentsia (*bunjin*) and their literary sensibilities than any other writer of his generation after Mori Ōgai and Nagai Kafū (*Subaru* 4 [1988]: 58); among his best-known and acclaimed works are *Fugen* (1936; *The Bodhisattva: A Novel,* trans. William J. Tyler [New York: Columbia University Press, 1990]), "Marusu no uta" (The song of Mars, 1938), *Shion monogatari* (The story of asters, 1956), and *Shifuku sennen* (Thousand years of consummate bliss, 1965–66). On his story "Mujintō" see chapter 23, note 4. • *Nanga* (southern paintings), inspired by China's Southern-school style of literati painting (*wen-ren* painting; in Japanese *bunjinga*), flourished after the mid-Edo period with artists like Ike-no-Taiga (1723–76), Yosa Buson (1716–83), and Uragami Gyokudō (1745–1820) in contemplative and poetic landscapes in ink or light colors with soft brushes. See Katō's essay "*Nanga daitai* ni tsuite" (On Ishikawa's *General principles of nanga, Asahi Jānaru,* April 5, 1959); and Ishikawa Jun's *Nanga daitai* (General principles of *nanga,* 1959), which praises Buson's work in particular.

at it, the roots seem to be floating in the river."[11] In this symposium sponsored by a journal, we were supposed to talk about "the traditions of Japanese culture." But unless a commentator is able to scrutinize Kō-rin's folding screens as Terada did, any words he utters on cultural traditions only ring hollow.

Listening to Terada reminded me of Dr. Miyoshi of the Tokyo University Hospital. I once told him that I thought an infection had occurred because there was an elevated white-blood-cell count. "Who did the blood count?" was his immediate response. "You'd better do the counting again yourself to make sure before jumping to conclusions." Dr. Miyoshi would never make any deductions based on information about which he had the slightest doubt, not even for something as rudimentary to a physician's trade as a white-blood-cell count. How then could one seriously talk about the Rimpa school or ink paintings without even having properly examined the works themselves? When it comes to Dō-gen or Hakuseki, how reliable could one's casual thoughts be without reading through their entire collected works?[12] And if one excludes the

---

11. Terada Tōru (1915–95), an erudite literary critic who took up Stendhal, Balzac, Chekhov, Tolstoy, Valéry, and Camus, as well as *The Tale of Genji*, Izumi Shikibu, and Dōgen, Japanese medieval painting, philosophy, and major modern Japanese writers—the critic Kanno Akimasa compares Terada's critical commentaries to spiritual dialogues; among his major works are *Terada Tōru bungaku ronshū* [Collection of the literary commentaries of Terada Tōru, 1951], *Gendai Nihon sakka kenkyū* [Study of contemporary Japanese writers, 1954], and *Waga chūsei* [My medieval period, 1967]. • Kōrin's painting of plum trees, on a pair of two-panel folding screens with gold-leaf background, is dominated by the almost menacing image of a river in black and gold that swirls and dramatically expands across the scene in bold contrast to the poetic elegance of the red and white plum blossoms. See Yamane Yūzō, "Kōrin no shōgai to geijutsu," in *Kōrin to Sōtatsu, Genshoku Nihon no bijutsu* (Shōgakukan, 1976), 14:237–39; and the commentary in *Rimpa Bijutsukan: Kōrin to Kamigata Rimpa* (Shūeisha, 1993), 2:55.

12. Dōgen (1200–53), the founder of Sōtō Zen Buddhism and one of the greatest religious minds in Japan, wrote *Fukan zazengi* (General views on the rites of zazen, 1227) and *Shōbō genzō* (The eye treasury of the true dharma, 95 vols., 1811), which holds his teachings from 1231–53 and *kōans* and anecdotes from daily life (see Katō's comments in the next note). • Arai Hakuseki (1657–1725), mid-Edo historian, renowned *kanshi* poet, linguist, political adviser to the shoguns Tokugawa Ienobu and Ietsugu, and one of the most celebrated intellectual figures of his age whose *Seiyō kibun* (News about the West, 1715) demonstrates his interest in the world outside Japan, while his historical writings (*Koshitsū* [Comprehensive survey of ancient history, 1716] and *Dokushi yoron* [Random comments on history, 1712]) exhibit extraordinary intellectual

Rimpa school and ink paintings or dismisses Dōgen and Hakuseki, how substantive can one's notion of traditional culture be? Acquiring critical intelligence through empirical learning became something of a habit to me in the course of my medical research. And if I were to apply it thoroughly in the realm of literature and aesthetics, the only way was to take my time savoring paintings and books. I could never have this luxury if I continued to work at the hospital and stay up all night writing my manuscripts. It was not despite but precisely because of the long years I had spent in medical research that I began to think about leaving the profession.

Yet being overburdened with work was not the only factor that prompted me to abandon medicine. Medical research had also entered into a period of extreme specialization. After immersing myself in work, at the end of the year I frequently felt I had accomplished nothing. I had no recollection of how the seasons had changed or how things had happened around me. During that time, I did not know life outside my research laboratory. My memory drew a total blank on those years, and all I had to show for them was a research paper in my name. Was that a fair exchange? A year's time constituted a part of my life; an article constituted a part of the total structure of universal knowledge. For two things that belonged to two entirely different schemes of things, comparison was impossible. Nevertheless, I was not satisfied with the bargain. Perhaps the fact that my research work was in the natural sciences had nothing to do with it. But in a field that had become so exceedingly specialized, it was simply impossible for me to bridge the gap between my personal life and the substance of my research. Being totally committed to writing poetry, I suppose, is different from being totally committed to scholarly research; the poetry of Li Po and Tu Fu must have been the very substance of their lives. Perhaps what I needed was poetry in my life.

And that was not all. I also wanted to know what was happening in

independence and objectivity. His work most widely known in the West is his autobiography *Oritaku shiba no ki* (Told round a brushwood fire, 1716; Eng. trans. 1979), "the first Japanese autobiography in the prose terms known in the West" (*Princeton Companion to Classical Japanese Literature*, 142). See Katō's long article "Arai Hakuseki no sekai," in *Katō Shūichi chosakushū*, 3:225–94; and Kate Wildman Nakai, *Shogunal Politics: Arai Hakuseki and the Premises of Tokugawa Rule* (Cambridge, Mass.: Harvard University Press, 1988).

society around me. During the Pacific War, Japanese government propaganda failed to cast its spell on me even though I was living in Japan.
This was not because I knew what was in fact taking place, but because
the propaganda itself was so filled with contradictions that one could easily see through its folly even without specific knowledge. My assessment
of the general course of the war had turned out to be fairly accurate, not
because I knew what the real situation was, but because I believed, from
the course of modern history, that those who tried to turn back the clock
of history would only end up destroying themselves. Heaven's vengeance
is slow but sure. But in the final analysis, my belief was a value judgment, not a deduction from facts. While the premise on which I based
my value judgment did not conflict with the facts as I knew them, my
knowledge of the facts was extremely limited. Reflecting on the matter,
I couldn't but feel there was just an equal chance that my predictions
could have turned out to be incorrect. I did not want the same thing to
happen again. There will always be a limit to the information accessible
to an ordinary citizen about important national or international issues.
In spite of that, in order to assess current situations and their future development as a whole, one can only establish a premise of thinking that,
to a greater or lesser extent, correlates with one's value judgment. But
I wanted to work on a more meticulous premise based on more facts than
I had had during the last war. In order to do that, I desperately needed
more time, even if it meant that I had to draw myself away from my literary interests.

I was fortunate to survive the Pacific War. But I witnessed how my
native city was reduced to ashes overnight, how devastated people were,
how communication broke down even between former colleagues, and
how the resentful voices from starving people filled the streets. Many
young people died every day, and among them were two of my close
friends. All these events had a determining impact on my life. Furthermore, they did not come about because of any natural calamity or any
twist of fate, but precisely because of a series of political decisions. One
of my old friends who used to share many thoughts with me during the
war was sent to the Chinese front, became sick, and returned home.
When we met in Tokyo after the war, he said, "Let's not talk any more
about politics. I just want to be left alone in my corner and live my life
quietly."

"But what dragged you out from your corner was the war, and a war
is a political phenomenon," I remarked.

"But the war has ended."

"Political phenomena will never end."

"But there is nothing I can do."

"Even if there is nothing we can do," I said at the time, "I want to scrutinize a phenomenon that had or may again have a decisive influence on my life. It's the same as a man's desire to know who committed adultery with his wife even if there is nothing he can do about it."

"I just don't want to know about it," he said.

"Well, I don't suppose that's because you feel helpless to do anything. You first started out not wanting to know, and then you rationalize yourself by saying there's nothing you can do."

"You may be right. Shall we just leave it at that?"

"But that's a curious logic. You said you wanted to live a quiet life. But the condition for living a quiet life, more than your wife's behavior, depends on the policies our government adopts. And you said you don't want to know about it."

"The happiest man is somebody who doesn't know anything," he muttered.

I could appreciate his feelings. The scars of war must run deeper than anything I could ever imagine. I suppose that was because I could not even begin to imagine the kind of experience he had gone through. At this point, there was nothing else to say. As for me, however, I was determined to find out the conditions defining my being as long as it was not physically impossible to do so. History, culture, politics . . . the only way for me to impart any personal relevance to these categories was for me to acquaint myself with them.

I did not turn away from being a specialist in hematology to being a specialist in literature. I did not change the field of my specialization; I obliterated the very idea. Privately, I aspired to becoming a specialist without a specialization. Since then I have written about Takeuchi Yoshimi, about the Japan-U.S. Security Treaty as well as *The Tale of Genji* picture scrolls; I have also written on modern Japanese intellectual history and modern European thought; and in universities I have talked about *Shōbō genzō* and *Kyōunshū*.[13] These topics were not requests

13. Takeuchi Yoshimi (1910–77), an influential cultural critic noted particularly for his study and translation of Lu Xun (1881–1936) and cultural comparison of the modern Chinese experience to what he perceived to be Japan's illusory modernity and slave mentality vis-à-vis the West; see his "Chūgoku no kindai to Nihon no kindai" (The modernity of China and Japan, 1948); Katō's

from outside sources but my own choices for various occasions, and for me they are not unrelated issues. Their relationship with one another was not apparent to me at first, and I only gradually came to appreciate it later on.

It was not easy for me to leave the medical profession. But the opportunity presented itself when I decided to go to a writers' conference to be held in central Asia. The mining company that employed me allowed me a maximum of one month's leave by entrusting my work at the medical office to another doctor. What I needed was three months. I resigned from my position and departed on my trip, and never again did I return to the medical profession.

---

article "Takeuchi Yoshimi no hihyō sōchi" (The critical apparatus of Takeuchi Yoshimi) is in *Katō Shūichi chosakushū*, 7:268–87; and his more recent assessment in English is "Mechanisms of Ideas: Society, Intellectuals, and Literature in the Postwar Period in Japan," in *Legacies and Ambiguities: Postwar Fiction and Culture in West Germany and Japan*, ed. Ernestine Schlant and J. Thomas Rimer (Washington, D.C.: Woodrow Wilson Center Press, 1991), 256–58. Takeuchi resigned his professorship at Tokyo Metropolitan University in 1960 to protest the forced ratification of the Japan-U.S. Security Treaty, saying that "the only point of contention is a choice between democracy and dictatorship." • On the security treaty see the discussion in chapter 40. • On the *Genji* scrolls see Katō's essays "Nihon no bigaku" and "*Genji monogatari emaki* ni tsuite," in *Katō Shūichi chosakushū*, 12:5–33 and 179–88, respectively. • On *Shōbō genzō*, a vast theoretical tract in Japanese by Dōgen that is the fundamental scripture of the Sōtō sect, see Katō's assessment: "one of the prose masterpieces of thirteenth-century Japan" because Dōgen "[opens] up a whole new world through his polished use of the possibilities of the Japanese language" (*History of Japanese Literature*, 1:233–34). • *Kyōunshū* (Collection of the wild clouds, date unknown; Eng. trans. Sonja Arntzen, 1973) holds 1,060 poems attributed to the fiercely independent-minded mid-Muromachi poet and Zen priest Ikkyū Sōjun (1394–1481); Katō divides them into three categories: ones on Rinzai Zen doctrine, others on the era's faults, and love poems; he writes, "In the *Kyōunshū* Zen and love are one and the same thing. . . . In the age of the secularization of Zen, only Ikkyū created a unique and original poetic world by giving flesh to a foreign ideology" (*History of Japanese Literature*, 1:290 and 293). See also his engaging article, "Ikkyū to iu genshō," in *Shōwa bungaku zenshū*, 28:622–42.

38 The Asian-African Writers' Conference

The Second Asian-African Writers' Conference was held in October 1958 in Tashkent in Central Asia. The first conference in New Delhi was attended by Hotta Yoshie on behalf of Japan.[1] At the second conference Itō Sei led the Japanese team made up of a few "representative" Japanese writers.[2] I joined its International Planning Committee one month before the conference convened.

Beyond my official business at the conference, I had hoped to see Central Asia and the Soviet Union for myself. For this reason, the opportunity to stay for some time alone in Tashkent suited my purpose much better than participating as a group member. With my personal belongings in a small bag and two or three books, I departed from Haneda on an Air India flight. I was scheduled to change planes at Calcutta to go on to New Delhi, where I would change planes again to go on to Tashkent. My travel agency in Tokyo told me that because I was just passing through India, in all probability I would not need an entry visa. On my arrival in Calcutta, however, an airport official examined my passport and announced in his strongly accented English that I could not get into India.

1. Appearing in the many memorable novels by Hotta Yoshie (1918–98), who attended the first conference in 1956, are portraits of a Japanese reporter drawn into the Korean War and its ugly political consequences in *Hiroba no kotoku* (Loneliness in the square, 1951; Akutagawa Prize, 1952), a Chinese intellectual in wartime China before the Nanjing Massacre in *Jikan* (*Time*, 1953), and the Shimabara Uprising in the early Edo period in his historical novel *Uminari no soko kara* (From beneath the roaring sea, 1960–61); more recent works include *Wakaki hi no shijintachi no shōzō* (Portraits of poets as young men, 1966–68) and a renowned biography of Goya (1973–76).

2. Critic, novelist, and poet, Itō Sei (1905–69) caricatured the modern Japanese

"I don't want to get into India. I'm just a transit passenger."

"Being a transit passenger means you are going into India."

Around that time I got a feeling I had finally embarked on my journey into "Asia." Officials in full uniform, half-naked men standing or sitting everywhere, curious American tourists looking over their surroundings, the killing heat, the languid ceiling fans, and the questioning that went on for over an hour with frequent interruptions. Essentially, what the officials seemed to be saying was this: my Tokyo-Calcutta and New Delhi-Tashkent routes were international flights while the Calcutta-New Delhi segment was domestic. To change planes for a domestic flight, a passenger was required to go through the country's entry formalities. Without a visa it was impossible to do so.

"We'll keep your passport until you leave India. You are not permitted to go out of the airport."

In any case, I managed to change to a domestic flight and arrived in New Delhi in the evening. A few hours of questioning followed before I could obtain a permit to go into town and find a place to stay for the night until my flight's departure for Tashkent the next day. When I finally managed to reach a hotel, it was already very late at night. The receptionist said, almost triumphantly, that I could not stay there. The room charge had to be paid in advance and, without my passport, he said, he could not accept my traveler's checks.

"Is there a money exchange shop around here?"

"It's closed at this hour."

"Can I pay you when the shop opens tomorrow?"

"We don't accept guests without advance payment."

Totally exhausted and not knowing what to do, I found myself cursing "Asia-Africa" and myself. My wretchedness must have been written all over my face. When a group of high-spirited, young Indonesian officers marched into the hotel, one of them approached me and asked

---

literary intellectual, a man who "does not commit suicide nor become a revolutionary" in his innovative novel of style, *Narumi Senkichi* (1946–48), and analyzed the narrative dynamics of the *watakushi-shōsetsu* vis-à-vis the modern European novel in his classic and controversial *Shōsetsu no hōhō* (The technique of the novel, 1948). He also traced Meiji literary history in *Nihon bundanshi* (The history of the Japanese literary world, 1952–69; 18 vols.) and translated Joyce's *Ulysses* and Lawrence's *Lady Chatterley's Lover* (see chapter 32, note 7).

sympathetically, "What's the matter?" I briefly explained to him my circumstances, and he was kind enough to pay for my room for the night
in Indian currency, saying, "We should help one another in times of trouble." That was how I was rescued from my helpless predicament by an
officer of Sukarno's army.

When I went into my room, I found that the large air conditioner was
not functioning at all even though the control was pointing to the "on"
position. It was unbearably hot inside. I opened the window, only to discover that the midnight air coming into the room was even warmer than
that in the room itself. I randomly turned the control of the air conditioner, but nothing worked. Ready to give up, I switched it to the "off"
position. Amazingly, the machine made a noise and started to work,
quickly cooling off the room. What a country! And what a paradoxical
machine!

On the plane to Tashkent the next morning, a sense of emancipation overtook me as I watched the green fields of Punjab recede farther and farther into the distance. The sky was clear, and the large plane
with only a few passengers was comfort itself. Soon it passed over
northern Pakistan's mountain ranges before the landscape merged into
the rocky hills of Afghanistan. As the plane flew past the mountain-
tops and went farther into the continental interior, there were fewer
and fewer signs of water or trees, and human habitation became more
sporadic. Nothing but overlapping layers of rocks stretched as far as
the eye could see.

And at the fringe of this unforgiving Central Asian landscape where
nomads roamed in antiquity, and indeed at this very extremity of history itself, the modern city of Tashkent suddenly loomed before my eyes.
The airport was lined with passenger jets (in the autumn of 1958, the
only country in the world scheduling regular flights with jet planes was
the Soviet Union). Tashkent had compulsory education, hospitals, telephone service, and journalism—essentially everything Tokyo had. My
first impression of a socialist country, after coming from India, was how
similar everything was to Europe.

Of course it did not take me long to realize that Tashkent was not
Moscow, and that Central Asia was just the borderland of the Soviet
Union. I soon gave up my unduly ambitious plan of traveling around
the Soviet Union. Instead, I decided as much as possible to get a close
look at its peripheral region, namely the Republic of Uzbekistan, and at
a later date to visit Yugoslavia (Croatia) on the periphery of the social-

ist sphere of influence. If things worked out, I also wanted to see the realities of the local Communist administration in a nonsocialist country
such as in the state of Kerala in India.[3]

I am not fond of experiences drawn at random. If I considered the Soviet Union on the basis of my travel experiences, it would be just coincidence that set me down primarily in Tashkent and not Moscow. But if
the purpose of my trip was to compare the peripheral regions of socialist countries, Tashkent was the only natural choice. At any rate, I later
translated my thought into action, and I wrote *Travels in Uzbekistan,
Croatia, and Kerala* after I returned to Japan.[4] Though it was not widely
read, among my other works, this compact little volume contains relatively more information and more leads to my thinking. When I thought
about socialist societies later on, I always started with the experiences it
described.

"Representative" members of the planning committee and executive
officials of the conference stayed in a house with an old-fashioned gate
in the middle of an orchard surrounded by fields in the suburbs of
Tashkent. My large room on the second floor had a high ceiling and came
with a bed, a desk, some chairs, and a large heating fixture in one corner. Whenever I opened the window, the chirping of tiny birds gathering around a thicket in the garden would fill the room. Every morning
when I went downstairs to the washroom to shave, I would meet some
of my fellow guests. There I learned how to say "Good morning! Did
you sleep well last night?" in Russian.

I suppose the building must have once been a villa belonging to a big
landlord or an aristocrat. Sometime after the revolution, it assumed the
name "Village Home" and had been used by the Union of Soviet Writers as a workplace for novelists or as a guest house for foreigners. On
its large premises were several other buildings, one of which was used
as our dining hall.

At the time of my arrival the planning committee's representatives
consisted of two people each from India and China, one person each from
Mongolia, Thailand, and Burma. Later we were joined by a young writer

3. Kerala is on the extreme southwestern coast of India and borders on the
Arabian Sea. Its residents are among the most highly educated in India and
elected a Communist ministry in 1957 (an anti-Communist administration followed in 1960, and another Communist ministry in 1967).

4. Published in August 1959 by Iwanami shoten. A related article, "Ajia Afu-
rika sakka kaigi kara kaette," was published in *Bungaku* (April 1959).

from Cameroon and somebody who apparently was the Algerian representative. The executive officers of the conference consisted of a secretary from Moscow's Union of Soviet Writers along with three interpreters. Among the interpreters, the more elderly woman spoke English, and of the two other young women, the one with a small build, named M, spoke English, and the other one, nicknamed "the frog," spoke French. The interpreter for the Chinese participants was a Chinese student studying at the University of Moscow, an intelligent and cheerful young man who immediately became everybody's favorite.

Our daily routine was to ride in separate cars sent round to pick us up in the morning to go from Village Home to the conference hall in the city. Our meeting lasted for about three hours. Then we returned to Village Home for lunch. In the afternoon, sometimes we went back to the conference hall for more deliberations, but sometimes we took a break from our business to visit collective farms or small factories in the vicinity. The leisurely one month at Village Home was the most peaceful rural life I ever had the pleasure of spending.

The work of the planning committee consisted of such bureaucratic trivia as making room assignments and special food arrangements and so on. I was asked—first in Russian, then in English, and finally in French—whether there ought to be any special considerations in preparing the food for the Japanese participants. I said no. The translations involved several languages, but the matter was settled in no time. However, for the Indian participants, the answer would depend on which writers were coming and on the specific time and circumstances for each and every participant. A foreigner might be struck by the sheer strangeness of it all, but the matter was quite complex. In order to understand the significance of food choices, one has to trace back their historical roots and to appreciate the regional and climatic factors involved. And so, the representative from India spoke endlessly, first about his own experience and then about his analysis of Indian culture. The issue was just what food to serve, but his lecture in English had to be translated first into Russian and then into French, and before he could continue he had to wait for his interpreters to finish. The young man from Cameroon sitting next to me grew impatient and said, "This is why I can't stand Asians! There's not a trace of *esprit cartésien* in them!"

It was agreed that the details of the conference's daily schedules and programs were to be determined among the leading members after the arrival of the representatives from various countries. When it came to which countries and who to invite, the question became a little more complicated. Clearly, Israel was part of the Asian-African region, and it would seem odd not to invite them. But the presence of even one Israeli writer in a conference, we heard, would preclude the participation of representatives from the Arab countries. What were we to do? On most of the issues involved, I myself had no particular opinion one way or the other.

But controversies unrelated to the planning of the conference had also arisen. At that time, a provisional government of Algeria had formed in Cairo, and somebody suggested that an announcement be made in the name of the Planning Committee of the Asian-African Writers' Conference in full support of that government.[5] Our views were divided, and I opposed the idea. My reason was that the planning committee was charged only with the responsibility of making logistic preparations for the conference. As for supporting the provisional Algerian government, I argued that if necessary a resolution could be adopted at the conference. In the end, no announcement was made.

Meanwhile, China was shelling the island of Quemoy near the mainland coast in the Taiwan Strait. The two Chinese representatives on the planning committee might have a detached air about them, but they were in fact very courteous and serious-minded. Through an English interpreter, I talked with these two writers about the Taiwan situation.

"To which country do you think Taiwan belongs?" they asked me.

"It is a part of China, of course."

"You are right. And now it's under American occupation."

"In principle, I think the American troops should withdraw from Taiwan."

"I cannot agree with you more."

"But I don't think the Americans *are* going to withdraw," I said.

"You're wrong in thinking that," they remarked.

I turned to my interpreter and said, "Please ask them why they think I'm wrong."

The interpreter spoke in Chinese with the two writers for a while before he turned to me and said, "It's because you haven't gone into the people yet."

"But I was talking about the future prospect of an international situation."

"Have you ever worked among laborers and peasants?"

5. It was formed in September 1958.

"No, I haven't."

"That's why there are things you don't understand."

I could not judge the extent to which the interpreter's English had adequately conveyed the nuances of the original. Yet as far as the English translation was concerned, he almost never used such expressions as "in my opinion" or "my personal view is." The language was terse and the tone unequivocally definitive.

The Chinese representatives proposed that the planning committee make an announcement demanding the immediate withdrawal of American troops from Taiwan. I opposed the motion. My first reason was that such an action was beyond the responsibility of the planning committee, as it had been in the case of supporting the provisional government of Algeria. Second, regardless of what my capacity as the Japanese representative might mean or what my own personal views might be on the matter, I could not "represent" Tokyo's writers in signing an announcement when it was apparent that an overwhelming majority of them would not endorse it. And third, speaking from my personal view, as a matter of principle (and as an ultimate objective), I would like to see the withdrawal of American troops from Taiwan, but it was not my desire to demand an immediate withdrawal at that moment in 1958 (it would have been totally futile to do so). My opposition received the support of some influential people, and the announcement was dropped.

I wanted to find out as much as I could about the situation in the Uzbekistan Republic. The people had been establishing farms and creating industries out of the wilderness of Central Asia; they had conquered illiteracy, epidemics, and hunger—great achievements that could almost be described as miraculous. I wanted to know how these great enterprises came about and particularly what effects the new policies had on this land after the campaign to denounce Stalin. But it was not always easy to find out. We were invited as guests to an elaborate banquet at a collective farm, but a banquet is not always the appropriate place to ask direct questions and get straight answers. It took me a long time consulting my dictionary just to read the headings of Russian economic statistics. When my stay became more protracted, I also wanted to know something about what was happening in other parts of the world. Because we could not read Russian newspapers, the young man from Cameroon and I expressed our desire to get newspapers in English and French—the daily *Le Monde* and the weekly *New Statesman*. We were told that our wish would be relayed to Moscow, and so we waited. When papers did arrive, they were only the official publications of the British and French Communist parties. In the end, I had no way of knowing whether, for example, China was still shelling its offshore island, and if so, to what extent.

I do not mean to suggest that my life in this rural community was boring. We had meetings in the morning and local field trips in the afternoon. We had things to read, people to talk with, and occasionally interviews by local newspaper reporters and a special correspondent from a Moscow broadcasting station. Also, the playwright Simonov was staying in Tashkent, and from time to time he would come to visit the Village Home. In the evenings, we had movies in the hall on the ground floor, and there I watched *And Quiet Flows the Don* and *The Idiot*.[6] M was good enough to sit next to me and whisper the gist of the dialogue in English into my ear.

"What do you think of these films?"

"I think they're wonderful!"

"I think so too. If only you knew how long it has taken us to make them!" she muttered.

I wanted to learn Russian, but I was too busy to have the time for it. Or perhaps I should say that life there in the countryside had too many distractions.

In front of Village Home a road lined with poplar trees extended all the way into the fields beyond, its treetops reaching high into the dark blue evening sky. After dinner I enjoyed taking a walk there with M and Frog.

"Ah, there goes another day!" M said.

"But the day is still young." Frog was a tall and robust young woman, smartly dressed and cheerful.

"Now that's a foolish thing to say," M replied in French. And then she continued in English, "There's an end to everything. To these wonderful and peaceful days too. Some day life here in this village home will come

6. Konstantin Mikhailovich Simonov (1915–79) wrote war plays (*Paren iz nashego goroda* [Lad from our town, 1941] and *Tak i budet* [So be it, 1944]), on the defense of Stalingrad (1945), autobiographical war poems, and other plays (*Russkiy vopros* [The Russian question, 1946]). • *And Quiet Flows the Don*, based on Mikhail A. Sholokhov's classic novel of the Soviet revolution, *Tikhiy Don* (4 vols., 1928–40), hailed as "the supreme portrayal of Cossack life" (Jean-Albert Bédé and William B. Edgerton, eds., *Columbia Dictionary of Modern European Literature* [New York: Columbia University Press, 1980], 739); and *The Idiot*, based on Dostoyevsky's 1869 novel.

to an end, and we will return to Moscow. I wonder if you've felt this way. Whenever you see something really beautiful, you always get a feeling it's going to end very soon. Perhaps it's odd for me to feel like this."

From the tree-lined road we turned into a small path in the fields. There was a stream, and where we least expected it we found a little bridge, some shrubbery, a lawn, and an orchard with crumbling hedges. Above us was the wide, crystal-clear sky.

"This is the place I like," M said.

The gentle breeze gliding across the field brought back memories of the summer evenings in Shinshū's Asama foothills. Like M, I was very fond of this place, but I could not explain why in particular. Perhaps there was something of a communion of minds between us. She was not only sensitive but smart, so there was no need for me to lie. Even if I had, she would have seen through me in no time. Meanwhile, Frog was cheerfully humming some melody. Together we talked about all kinds of things—war, ancient Egyptian sculpture, the heart of the Japanese, the never-ending conference, the bureaucrats, and socialism. We had more than enough topics to engage our conversation every day for a month. During this time none of the things M said, not a single word, was difficult for me to understand. And of course I learned a great deal from her about Soviet society. But this aside, it must be a truly extraordinary experience anywhere and any time during one's life to meet another human being and be able to share the other's feelings and thoughts to this extent. And, I keenly felt, the beginning of the writer's conference would mark the end of my life at Village Home and I would probably never again have the opportunity to take another delightful evening stroll with her. For a conference is merely a place for the exchange of proclamations, not for the meeting of souls. I had never heard her sing. But every time she helped me pronounce "What do you call this?" in Russian, her voice was imbued with a sweet tenderness no words could possibly describe.

Then came the conference. Many people were gathered in a newly constructed residence; a great many words were exchanged and a great many speeches were made. And behind the stage long discussions went on regarding the conference proceedings. And then the conference came to an end and people started going their separate ways. M's husband S had come to the conference while it was still in session, and together we visited the old capital of Tbilisi in the Caucasus; from there we flew to Moscow and traveled to Leningrad and back. It was at the beginning of November, and Leningrad and the banks of the Neva were enveloped in a snowstorm.

The blue sky and the poplar-lined streets of Tashkent now seemed to have receded into infinity like a distant dream. Did I spend a few years or just a few days at Village Home? It was no longer possible to measure the time that had drifted away.

I did not return to Tokyo at the end of the year but instead spent Christmas in Vienna. From there I visited Yugoslavia and went on to India via Greece. When I went through India on my way to Tashkent, my only contact was with officials there. On my return trip, I visited an Indian friend I met at the Asian-African Writers' Conference, and I was able to catch a glimpse of the country, as it were, from the inside.

India left me with an exceptionally strong impression. It added a third dimension of experience totally different from my perception of the world based so far on Europe and Japan (it was not until later that I saw for myself the realities in North America). Nearly every issue facing the underdeveloped regions reached dramatic intensity in India, and I suppose nearly every question facing India also applied to other underdeveloped regions in general. Explosive population growth, sluggish agricultural production, widespread poverty and illiteracy, estrangement of the educated minority from the rest of the population, economic dependence on the developed countries, cultural dependence on its own past, separatist regionalism, absence of a common language, a parliamentary democracy existing only in name . . . Later on, whenever I heard such phrases as "underdeveloped countries," "the Third World," or "Asia, Africa, and Latin America," what invariably came to mind first was the overwhelming sight of massive starvation and pervasive poverty among people everywhere—at the roadside of bustling amusement quarters, inside the entrances to government buildings, and in villages in faraway mountains. While the Indians I saw might be just skin and bones, their facial features radiated a dignified elegance. It is foolish to preach the abstract idea of freedom to someone with an empty stomach. But it is even more foolish to think one can make a hungry man happy simply by throwing crumbs of bread at his feet.

39 Death

A friend of mine died. Shortly after that, I began to lose my grip on what people around him might be thinking about his death. People came together, tears were shed, funeral arrangements were discussed, gossip was exchanged, and then a stubborn silence took over. His mother said, "Ever since my son got married, I seemed to have lost him completely." His mother-in-law remarked, "He never gave any thought to money. If only he could have been a little more concerned about his family." And a close friend of his muttered to no one in particular, "I am so very angry with him because he chose to suffer alone without ever sharing his anguish with us." Another friend declared that under the circumstances someone was needed to head a funeral committee and then went on to argue fervently about who would or would not be a good candidate for the job. I had a feeling that I was being dragged onto the stage in the middle of a play whose plot I did not know, trying in vain to search for my role among strangers. Yet the people around me at the time were all old friends or else friends of my friends. I could not expect to find a more congenial group.

The man who died—I wonder if I really knew him. When I heard he was not feeling well, I wanted to find out over the telephone what his real condition was. For one thing, we had not met for quite some time, and besides, I had not visited him for years. In those days, the many commitments I had with various journals and magazines always kept me preoccupied. I almost felt that being busy with work was proof of my being alive.

When I asked him how he felt, he replied casually, "Oh, it's nothing," and then a little nervously, he asked, "Who told you about my condition?"

"That's not the issue," I said. "Never mind that and tell me how you feel. What is bothering you?"

"Oh, just a little stomachache, as usual. Nothing to worry about. I've had it before once in a while."

"Can I see you tomorrow at your place?"

"There is no need for that. I'll be all right."

"Why don't you let me talk to you about it?"

"It's nothing, really."

"Why don't you let me make sure everything is all right?"

"I know you're busy, and besides . . ."

"No, I'm not," I replied. "Not to the extent that I can't visit an old friend and talk about things at our leisure." I said I would come over to see him at his house the following afternoon and hung up before he could respond.

The square in front of the Central Line station seemed a little different every time I went there after varying intervals of time. New shops were now opened, construction work for large buildings had been making some headway, and the location of the bus stops had also been changed from the right to the left of the square. I stood there for a while to gather my vague recollections of the geography of the area. Walking through a narrow shopping arcade where pedestrians moved along literally shoulder to shoulder, I headed toward the residential area with rows of single-story houses, all with a similar appearance. One of them was his residence. His wife came out to greet me at the vestibule, saying, "Thank you for always being so kind to us." Come to think of it, I was ten times more indebted for what he had done for me than the other way round. But I didn't say anything.

He was wearing a *dotera* and his complexion was a little pale. What hadn't changed was his long hair and his characteristic smile. He didn't really want to talk about his illness, but at my insistence he started to tell me about it in a disinterested tone, as if he were talking about someone else. Just by listening to him, I could tell things were quite serious.

"No matter what I say, he just refuses to go to a doctor," his wife said as she looked at me.

"Would you get some tea for us please?" he said to her.

"A really stubborn man," she said as she rose and went to another room.

"How about it? Shall we take a look?" I tried a nonchalant tone, realizing that I was coming to the important business.

He was not the kind of man to be taken in by the tone of what people said. With a clear voice and without changing his expression, he said, "I don't think that's necessary. Let's talk about something else. After all, we haven't seen each other for quite a while." But I persisted. I told him since I already knew what he had to say about his illness, it was a good idea for me to examine him. After that, we'd decide what to do next. Otherwise, it'd just amount to making a superficial diagnosis. Meanwhile, I thought that his condition might already have deteriorated beyond treatment. After I examined him, I became all the more suspicious that this might indeed be the case.

"I don't think you need to worry," I said, "but you need to be examined at a good hospital to confirm the diagnosis. The examination isn't going to take long, so I think it's better if you check into a hospital. You can't have that kind of examination as an outpatient."

He seemed a little stunned by my obstinacy and agreed to be hospitalized. But for the moment he had a mountain of work to do; besides, he also had teaching commitments at the university. He promised me that after he had taken care of these things, by next weekend, he would do everything I said.

"No, I think the earlier you have it done the better."

"But I am *not* a child either, you know!" he spoke sharply as if he wanted to cut short our conversation.

"Let me decide what's good for your health!" I yelled back at him. "I'm a doctor."

"But this is my body."

"When I said the earlier the better, I'm not telling you to forget about your work and your responsibilities. What I mean is after you have given it some thought, the earlier you do that the better. If possible, tomorrow." He checked into a hospital the next day.

When I met several of his friends in the hospital corridor, one of them, a Catholic convert, suggested that should his illness prove incurable, it might be better to tell him the truth. Everybody else there opposed the idea, but I didn't have a particular opinion one way or the other. What is a friend if one cannot even trust his words unless one sees the proof? It was difficult for me to lie to his face when I knew he trusted me completely—even though the lie was in his own best interest. Moreover, we knew at that time that nothing could possibly save him. There was no reason to doubt the accuracy of the diagnosis, which meant no one could reasonably hold out any hope for him. In the patient's room, he said, "Look how skinny I've become." His voice was weak, but as always he was more concerned about other people around him than his own well-being. "Thank you all for taking the trouble to come. I know you're all so busy. If I get better, there's work waiting to be done." I simply could not bring myself to tell him that there was no hope that he would ever get better again.

Soon after he passed away, a thought kept recurring in my mind that he himself might have wished to die. That does not mean that he wanted to commit suicide. After discussing the matter with his attending physician at the hospital, we had decided not to reveal to him what he had, a decision we kept, I believe, until the end. I thought that he, on his part, was rather high-spirited about returning to work again. But perhaps he was only saying it out of consideration for us, his friends who would like to see him live. I had a lingering suspicion that he had earlier already sensed that his illness would eventually kill him, and that he had waited quietly until his condition deteriorated beyond repair. Maybe he was not prepared to die each time the illness had assaulted his body. Maybe he was torn between his fear and his wish for death at the same time. Earlier, he had told me, "I may not have the right to do other things, but even a man like me should at least be given the right to die if I wish to." His voice struck me not so much as subdued as unrestrainedly impassioned. I wondered what he meant by doing "other things," and I did not venture to ask. If he could tell me, he would do so without my inquiring. But he didn't say another word. I had known him for twenty years, but at that time I felt that a very substantial part of him still eluded my understanding.

What does it mean when two human beings "understand" each other? I suppose it means that they can sometimes appreciate each other's "feelings." But no one can predict something as volatile as one's own "feelings." Ultimately, I wonder how much I did really understand the man beyond his persona as it is manifested in his works.

In a sense, we had traveled along the same path for twenty years. Both of us had always tried to reach a higher standard for ourselves and to understand the world and other people around us. As we broadened our perspectives, we both endeavored to explore the correlation between independent facts and experiences. Along the way, I scribbled down my thoughts, while he, for the most part, gathered his experiences and internalized them. But our differences were not significant. He had not done any work worthy of its name, and I, on my part, had not accomplished any either. And yet meanwhile, I must say I had an inkling within me that I was about to come to a turning point in my journey. I had begun to detect a certain correlation between a great many things, and this discovery went hand in hand with my awareness of my own position on various issues. I was coming to see that wherever I might be and whatever I might be doing, I would always be my own self. I felt that the time had come for me to start my real work. It was true for me, and I believed it was true for him as well. What could be more cruel than to succumb to illness at this juncture? I did not know what kind of work he could have accomplished in the future, but in any case, I had great faith in its quality. Here we are not talking about the death of someone who had not done any preliminary work, nor about the death of a man of accomplishment of some sort. Here was a man who had died before he could begin his work after he had finally completed all his preparations.

Once a female friend of mine remarked that he was an oddball, a very strange man. She did not elaborate, and I had not heard anything about him from her since. But on one occasion, for some reason I mentioned her to him. It was during one afternoon at a coffeeshop in Nihonbashi. Around us men and women taking a break from the office talked and laughed merrily among themselves. I had just returned from Europe, and he also must have come back recently to Japan. We talked about many things, and naturally, Europe was one of them. He remembered the time he met her there, and I suppose that was why I mentioned her. His reaction surprised me. "Let's drop the topic." His voice, almost shouting with anger, had an intensity I had never experienced. Since then, we had never talked about her. My imagination, however, helped to concoct what might have happened.

He met her in Europe and fell in love with her (if a man had never been deeply infatuated with a woman, surely he would not suddenly get so agitated at the mere mention of her name). However, he had no intention of leaving his family in Tokyo (I cannot tell why, but I would guess it was due primarily to his strong sense of responsibility). Not knowing what to do—if such were not the case, few men would act like "an oddball" and be "very strange"—he must have thought of a last resort. He would look after his family in Tokyo, and she would live alone. What happens when a man and a woman in love decide on their own to give up their hopes of living together and bear the pain of separation? The bonds between their hearts would only grow stronger with time until a consummate friendship developed between them. This friendship would no doubt help both of them in their work and enrich each other's humanity. This must have been his impossible dream.

Perhaps the story I imagined was not what really happened. But after his death, I came close to believing that he had once loved passionately, that the love agonized him and made him concoct impossible dreams, and that the discrepancy between his dreams and reality caused him profound torment. His short life was not spent in lukewarm indifference. There was no question in my mind that he, in his own special way, lived every minute of it with all the enthusiasm and energy he could muster.

Once, after visiting him at the hospital, I headed for Hongō on some business. Overcome by the thought of death and a wretched sense of powerlessness, I walked mechanically on the quiet Hongō-dōri without taking any interest in the things around me. When I reached the main entrance to the university, I suddenly encountered a group of students coming out of the main gate carrying signboards saying "Opposition to the Japan-U.S. Security Treaty!" As their loose formation quietly passed the university gate, they began to walk toward the Hongō 3-chōme area. I knew where they were heading from there. However strange it might seem, they reminded me of the scene toward the end of the war during the student mobilizations. With rifles on their shoulders, they walked out the same university gate on their way to the front—young men who were about to lose their lives at sea or in some dense forests far away from home, from their lovers, and from their families. As I watched students pass the main gate, I could not bring myself to leave the scene. Perhaps a number of them—who knows how many?—were about to be butchered by the police of the Kishi government and would never return.[1] Yet I could not join their ranks or prevent the sacrifice of their blood. What powerlessness! And what wretchedness! All I could do was to speak in a weak voice. Just as I was helpless against cancer, I was completely powerless in the past against the authority that had sent students to the battlefield and was now grinding students under the boot of brute force. Was I destined to end up a bystander just as I had grown up one? That was the gloomy feeling I had deep in my heart.[2]

1. Chapter 40 takes up the demonstrations against the treaty's ratification in 1960.
2. Katō's reminiscence about this particular episode in 1960 resonates with a literary ghost of the not-so-distant past: Nagai Kafū's short piece "Hanabi"

He was truly a hard worker. While teaching at a national university, he also served as a lecturer at a private university. While working as a literary critic for journals and newspapers, he also produced remarkably precise translations of difficult works. Moreover, he also read widely and meticulously on Japanese and foreign literatures. To do all that, a man would have to work ceaselessly day and night. He himself must have felt the drive to accomplish all that. But another important factor was that he was simply not the kind of man to turn down other people's requests easily. A lot of his work was done for the benefit of others, and I only wished he had lived long enough to do his work for himself. Whenever I put down my thoughts in writing, I knew I could always count on him to appreciate their worth. While others might misunderstand what I wrote, I felt certain I had at least one reader who never would. Once, for instance, I introduced the poet Gottfried Benn to Japanese readers and talked about the significance of his intellectual drama to us.[3] A year later, he produced a scrupulous translation of Benn's *Doppelleben* entitled *Nijū seikatsu*. I could not begin to imagine the amount of preparation and effort he put into that translation. Nor could I begin to articulate what a great loss his death was to me.

One time, after visiting him at the hospital, I rode in a car with two other old friends who had come to visit, a man and a woman.

"Is there any hope he could be cured?" the man asked.

"I don't think so," I replied at that time.

(Fireworks, 1919), in which he confesses to a debilitating powerlessness at the sight of political prisoners accused of conspiring to assassinate the Meiji emperor in the Kōtoku Shūsui Incident (1910–11). Beyond the superficial similarities of their reactions lie more fundamental questions about the modern Japanese literary intellectual's role in broad social and political discourse. On Kafū's piece see Moriyama Shigeo, *Taigyaku jiken: Bungaku sakka ron* (San'ichi shobō, 1980), 113–30, esp. 113–15; and, in English, Jay Rubin, *Injurious to Public Morals: Writers and the Meiji State* (Seattle: University of Washington Press, 1984), 190–93; and Katō, "Japanese Writers and Modernization," in *Changing Japanese Attitudes Toward Modernization*, ed. Marius B. Jansen (Princeton: Princeton University Press, 1972), 425–45, esp. 430–31.

3. A reference to his "Gottofurīto Ben to gendai Doitsu no seishin" (Gottfried Benn and the contemporary German spirit, *Sekai*, July 1957), in *Katō Shūichi chosakushū*, 2:198–225. For English versions of Benn's works, known for their resistance to translations, see J. M. Ritchie, *Gottfried Benn: The Unreconstructed Expressionist* (1972) and E. B. Aston, ed., *Primal Vision: Selected Writings of Gottfried Benn* (1958). *Doppelleben* (Double life, 1950) is the title of his autobiography.

"How long will he live? I think we also need to think about what's going to happen next."

"I don't know, but probably not more than a month," I said—but couldn't bring myself to talk about "what's going to happen next."

The woman, whom I had not seen for many long years, was still every bit her old self. As I listened quietly, I was struck with the impression that her short exchanges with my other friend were filled with an undertone of utter helplessness over the imminent and irreclaimable loss of a friend. She had known him since his younger days when the world was opening up before his eyes with all kinds of possibilities, a time when he, on his part, was prepared to greet each and every one of them with ardent enthusiasm. There were no tears in her eyes, but her reminiscence of him—so I thought—brought a beautiful twinkle into them.

After his return from Europe, he must have tried as much as possible to commit himself to his wife and children. Yet his love and hate must also have been directed elsewhere. I suppose the farther away the object of his passions had moved, the more intensely personal his own internal drama became, and the more difficult it was for him to justify his own agony.

"Do you think it's good to be alive under any circumstances, no matter how much sacrifice one has to make?" he once asked me. "Now, don't get me wrong. I'm not speaking about myself, but just as a general question." But of course, I knew it was not a general question. Yet I could not come up with an answer.

I did not understand him then, and perhaps I still do not. The only thing I do understand is the bond that existed between us. This became increasingly apparent to me after his death. Our bond was as authentic and tangible as a piece of rock. What more can one expect from life? I sit writing this piece now, in a country he barely knew. My quiet little room is bright and warm, and there on the table lies a book he wrote. Outside the window is a melancholy autumn and a gray sky. How I wish he could suddenly knock at the door and come into the room, saying, "Hey! It's been a long time! Looks like you're doing all right here!" But I knew it was an impossible illusion; I could never see him again. I am deeply chagrined by the thought. I do not want to talk with him—I only want to see his long hair and his pale complexion once more. Can anything be more absurd than not being able to do even that or something as simple as give him a call? But this anything, however absurd, is possible. Not only is it possible, it is now a reality, an irrevocable, unfathomable, and totally incomprehensible reality.

Shortly after he died, I left Tokyo again. It was true that I was encouraged by the popular movement against the Japan-U.S. Security Treaty that summer. But his death had changed something in me. Until then I had been very particular about where I lived and worked, but after he died this became a secondary concern only. I realized that wherever I went, I could do whatever I was capable of doing. When a new position became available on the other side of the Pacific, I accepted it and departed from Haneda Airport alone. From the window of my plane, I looked at the lights of Tokyo as they quickly receded into the distance and soon disappeared into the deep darkness of the ocean. I wasn't the least sentimental, or the least regretful.

40 Unfinished Judgment

Negotiations for the revision of the Japan-U.S. Security Treaty had be-gun as early as 1959. For a long time their substance was not accessible to the Japanese people. In the autumn of the same year, as the public grew more or less aware of what was going on, an opposition movement developed at the grass-roots level. In January 1960 representatives of the Japanese government went to the United States for the formal sign-ing of the new security treaty. With the public disclosure of its terms, active discussions in Japan over its pros and cons added new momentum to the opposition movement. In the spring of the same year, unanimous newspapers' public opinion polls showed more people in Japan against the ratification of the new treaty than those in favor.

The first major difference between the old and the new treaties had to do with the circumstances surrounding the formal signing of the treaty. The old treaty, the brainchild of the United States, was part of a package with the peace treaty, and it was signed by Japanese represen-tatives at a time when the country was still under occupation.[1] At that time Japan in effect had no other choice. Moreover, the Korean War had just ended and U.S.-Soviet relations were exceptionally tense. The new security treaty, negotiated at a time when there were finally some visi-ble signs of "thawing" in U.S.-Soviet relations after top-level talks in the autumn of 1959, was a military alliance pursued by the indepen-dent Japanese government on its own initiative.

The second major difference had to do with the terms of the treaty

1. The first Japan-U.S. Security Treaty and the Treaty of Peace with Japan were signed in San Francisco on September 8, 1951.

themselves. The new treaty revised the unlimited term of the old treaty to ten years, formally stipulated the United States' obligation in the defense of Japan, and had an additional provision that any movement of American troops stationed in Japan required "prior consultation" with the Japanese government. And Japan promised to further strengthen its "self-defense capabilities."

The third difference involved the "administrative agreement" about U.S. military bases. The new administrative agreement recognized greater Japanese authority in an attempt to bring it up to par with the convention established by the North Atlantic Treaty Organization.

The Japanese government primarily emphasized the second and third points and maintained that the new treaty was more advantageous to Japan than the old. The opposition, on the other hand, regarded the first point as being the fundamental issue and insisted that it was undesirable for Japan to take the initiative in plunging the country into a military alliance. One could come up with four main reasons why they held such a position. First, entering into a military alliance was unconstitutional (or at least counter to the spirit of Article 9 of the constitution).[2] Second, such an act would increase tension in the Far East (leading to the vicious cycle of generating tension, then military expansion, yet further tension, and further military expansion). Third, Japan might be embroiled in a military conflict because it involved the United States. Fourth, strengthening the military held a potential threat to the future of Japanese democracy.

I personally hoped to see the abolition rather than the revision of the security treaty. Therefore I followed the lead of like-minded senior colleagues and friends and, along with several experts, took part in a symposium to voice our criticism of the government's policy. The result was published in the journal *Sekai* under the title "Futatabi Anpo kaitei ni tsuite" (Once again on the security treaty's revision).[3] After that, I also

2. Article 9 of the 1947 constitution reads, "[Japan will] forever renounce war as a sovereign right of the nation and the threat or the use of force as means of settling international disputes"; it stipulates that Japan will not maintain land, sea, or air forces and other forms of military capabilities.

3. *Sekai*, February 1960. Katō and twenty-one others looked at hypothetical scenarios of international threats to Japan's security and stated that in the world context of the time, the best national defense for Japan was "demilitarized neutrality" (*hibusō chūritsu*), a position that liberal intellectuals and the Japan Socialist Party had taken as far back as 1950; see *Sekai*, March 1950, for the declaration by the Peace Discussion Group (Heiwa mondai danwakai).

met and debated with those who favored its revision. My conversation with Foreign Minister Fujiyama Aiichirō was published in *Chūō Kōron*, and another conversation with Hayashi Kentarō at the Conference on the Freedom of Cultural Expression appeared in the *Asahi Shimbun*.[4]

I also took part in a televised symposium to express my views. But the proponents of treaty revision had not bothered to read the published essay from the first symposium carefully enough to dispute its main arguments. Consequently, during the public discussion there was not much we could do except restate the same ideas, in less polished terms. Putting together cogent arguments to sustain a political opinion not only involves lengthy explications, but the discourse cannot always be as captivating as a crude allegory. Few bother to follow it. And yet oversimplification often leads to imprecise arguments. An effective presentation in front of a general audience requires the proper division of labor among like-minded people. It occurred to me at the time that I had to find a suitable role to play.

I am not suggesting there was unanimous opposition to the government from the spring to the early summer of 1960. Public opinion in Japan was divided over the pros and cons of the security treaty. The majority of the Japanese people who opposed the government did so not because of the treaty's terms but because of the way it had been ratified. The treaty had to do with Japan's foreign relations; the way it was ratified had to do with the workings of democracy within the country. The unprecedented mass mobilization into a struggle against the security treaty (*Anpo tōsō*) was a domestic phenomenon. Since Japanese public opinion was divided over the ratification of the new security treaty, the Japanese people and the opposition parties demanded that the Kishi cabinet dissolve the Diet and let the voices of the Japanese people be heard. As everybody knew at that time, the ruling party had an absolute majority of seats in the Lower House. Yet during the general election that decided the apportionment of seats, the controversy over the security

4. Fujiyama Aiichirō (1897–1985), president of the Japan Chamber of Commerce and Industry (Nisshō) in 1941 and a wartime director of the Imperial Rule Assistance Association, who became foreign minister in Kishi Nobusuke's first (1957–58) and second (1958–60) cabinets. • Hayashi Kentarō (1913–), a historian of modern Germany and former president of Tokyo University (1973–77), who set up the Japan Culture Forum with Takeyama Michio and Kōsaka Masaaki (1958) and then became director of the Japan Foundation (1980) and a Liberal Democratic member of the Upper House (1983–89).

treaty had not been a contentious issue. Moreover, as the substance of the new security treaty became common knowledge, it was increasingly apparent that the distribution of Diet seats did not reflect the realities of public opinion on the matter. The decision to ratify the treaty, once made, would not be easy to modify and would bind the Japanese people for at least the next ten years. And to make such a decision without due respect for the will of the majority of the Japanese people could only be described as an act against democratic principle. The demand for the dissolution of the Diet largely followed this reasoning. But on May 19, 1960, the government and the ruling party ordered the police to come into the Lower House and remove opposition Diet members who were staging a sit-in protest. The government and the ruling party then prolonged the Diet's session and passed the new security treaty in the middle of the night without the presence of the opposition Diet members. This action in turn provoked a popular protest movement that developed into the largest of its kind in modern Japanese history.

The U.S. president, who was visiting America's satellite countries around Asia, had to cancel his plans to visit Japan. The Kishi cabinet was toppled and had to be replaced by the Ikeda cabinet.[5] Nonetheless, the new security treaty was ratified and the conservative party that had unilaterally forced its passage again won an overwhelming majority of votes in the general election in the fall.

The president's cancellation of his visit to Japan surely convinced at least some quarters in the United States that a considerable discrepancy might exist between the pronouncements of the Japanese government and the feelings of the Japanese people. Yet newspapers in the United States went on declaring that Tokyo's disturbances were simply the result of "the instigation of a number of Communists." As the Americans were still ardent believers in the almighty and omnipresent Communists, they seemed to imagine that a mere handful of "Communists" could, at the snap of their fingers, mobilize millions of people anywhere in the world to demonstrate on the streets.

European newspapers, and the British and French ones in particular,

---

5. Massive student demonstrations in Tokyo forced President Dwight D. Eisenhower to cancel his visit to Japan, and Prime Minister Kishi Nobusuke resigned in July 1960 (his cabinets had lasted from February 1957 to July 1960). Prime Minister Ikeda Hayato (1899–1965) formed a new cabinet. See George R. Packard III, *Protest in Tokyo: The Security Treaty Crisis of 1960* (Princeton: Princeton University Press, 1966).

were not as pharisaic as their American counterparts. They read the popular movement in Japan, an event that managed to turn away the president of the United States, as a reflection of "the will of the Japanese people not to submit tamely to their nation's satellite status" since the Occupation. Perhaps this interpretation represented an inference from their own feelings about the United States.

I had a dialogue with Maruyama Masao for the *Mainichi Gurafu* as we looked back on the struggles against the security treaty.[6] At that time, Maruyama said something to the effect that, first, the people, whether they were ordinary citizens, laborers, or students, had not been mobilized under the direction of any organization; rather, they spontaneously rose up in protest, and the organizers subsequently followed their lead. Second, their behavior was not due to their anti-American feelings or even to their opposition to the establishment that had presented them with a new security treaty. It was due primarily to their opposition to the way the government had rammed the treaty through the Diet. Third, this very fact marked the transition of Japanese democracy from its inception as a postwar institution to a political movement. It signified, according to him, a stage in the development of democracy into a truly functioning institution. I agreed with Maruyama's views.

While I was opposed to the ratification of the security treaty, I did not feel frustrated when it was passed despite the massive opposition movement. Many who later confessed their frustrations were those who had worked actively within political organizations. Perhaps it was only natural that I should feel the way I did, since I had taken no action except to make my opposing views public. But beyond that, it was my assessment from the very beginning that even an optimistic projection would give the popular movement only a fifty-fifty chance of blocking the ratification of the treaty itself. My interpretation of the event was that

6. Maruyama Masao (1914–96), a prominent scholar of Japanese intellectual history and professor of political thought at Tokyo University from 1940–71, was actively involved in the political turmoil of 1960 with such figures as Takeuchi Yoshimi. Among Maruyama's best-known works in the West are *Thought and Behavior in Modern Japanese Politics* (London: Oxford University Press, 1963) and *Studies in the Intellectual History of Tokugawa Japan* (Princeton: Princeton University Press, 1974); he and Katō coedited *Honyaku no shisō* (The ideology of translation), vol. 15 of *Kindai Nihon shisō taikei* (Iwanami shoten, 1991). See Rikki Kersten, *Democracy in Postwar Japan: Maruyama Masao and the Search for Autonomy* (London: Routledge, 1996).

it had already achieved a not insignificant two-fold objective. Even though it might have failed to block the treaty's ratification, the movement clearly demonstrated to the rest of the world that a great many Japanese citizens in no way welcomed the presence of Occupation troops in Japan. Domestically, the movement served as a warning to the government and to the ruling party about how the people could react if the former did not respect basic democratic principles.

In retrospect, it was not the opposition parties and citizens' organizations but those in power who had learned many a good lesson from the experience during the early summer of 1960. The Ikeda cabinet adopted a "low profile," meaning that the government avoided provocative actions and paid very careful attention to the reactions of public opinion while gingerly implementing specific policies in small, incremental steps. This posture went hand in hand with its talk about "doubling the income level," meaning that in ten years' time, discounting the effects of inflation, personal income among the Japanese people would statistically double its current level.

Meanwhile, it went about expanding the police force that was deemed effective in suppressing student demonstrations on the streets or sit-in protests. In order to control opposition views against the military alliance with the United States, the government proceeded, short of taking any overtly atrocious tactics, to keep left-wing intellectuals from gaining access to public broadcasting facilities. These government policies, based on the valuable lessons its officials had learned, did not all became evident in the fall of 1960. But when the general election in the fall did not produce any significant change in the number of conservative seats in the Diet, there was little doubt about what the future course of Japanese politics would be in the next few years.

The year of the revision of the security treaty had allowed me to develop some new friendships. But at the same time, although it might be an exaggeration for me to say that it had also taken some friends away from me, it had at least caused us to drift further apart. Communication with some had become even easier than before, while with others it became even more difficult. And this was not necessarily the result of our agreement with or opposition to the treaty alone.

I frequently recalled the conversations I had had during the Pacific War. Still a student in those days, I had never stated my views in a public forum. Even in our private conversations, the proponents of the war, backed by the political authority, were free to speak their minds without any apprehension as to who might be listening in around them. On the other hand, those who opposed the war, fearful of the authorities, had to avoid using so many taboo expressions that they were rendered half-paralyzed in their attempt to substantiate their ideas. It was not a debate on an equal footing. To be sure, in 1960 we were broadly guaranteed freedom of speech to an extent inconceivable during the war years. But in open debates, I don't think the defenders and the opponents of government policies were standing on equal ground. The party that wanted to have the treaty ratified was the political establishment of the Japanese state itself, and, if that wasn't enough, it had the backing of the most powerful political establishment in the world. To espouse the cause of the security treaty in Tokyo—or to condemn it in Beijing—was the easy and safe course of action to take and certainly the expedient thing to do to secure the future of one's career. I don't mean to suggest, of course, that everyone in favor of the security treaty in Tokyo necessarily made such calculations. Nevertheless, it does seem to me that a debater who identifies with the interests of the power establishment runs a greater risk of intellectual corruption. Fairness goes out the window in a discourse when one party has the backing of an awesome power establishment while the other side has only reason as its champion. Ignorance of this fact constitutes intellectual depravation; knowing the fact without being sensitive to it constitutes moral decadence.

"The students are no good, and the policemen who beat them up are also no good. Violence is wrong."

"The Socialist Party staging their sit-in is no good, and the Liberal-Democratic Party bringing in the police is also no good. Politics is dirty."

Decadence in discourse typically manifests itself when proper discussions about the specificities of politics, war, peace, and violence insidiously hide within proclamations of broad generalizations.

I wonder what karma might have driven me, while being a Japanese citizen, to so persistently oppose the policies of the Japanese government as far back as I can remember. Already in 1941, I could not bring myself to support the war of the Tōjō cabinet. When one of his cabinet ministers reemerged twenty years later and tried to forge a new military alliance, I again could not support his policy.[7] I doubt if my opposition

---

7. Katō refers to Kishi Nobusuke (1896–1987), who was minister of commerce and industry (1941) and minister of internal affairs (1943) under the Tōjō cabinet, arrested after the war as a suspected class-A war criminal but released

comes from any fanatical predisposition on my part or to any defiant spirit raging in my bones. On self-reflection, I would venture to say that my temperament was as gentle as that of a sheep, and indeed that was the year in which I was born. I do not even like to raise my voice or shout during a conversation. While I might resign myself to the blame of being old-fashioned and temporizing, I don't think I could fairly be criticized for being stubbornly uncompromising or unduly radical. Nor did any moral position compel me to entertain any unsuppressible patriotic passion. From the outset, I held no absolute values on moral issues, to say nothing of political matters. Rather than create a new security treaty, my view was that a better policy would be to work toward its nullification. And yet I didn't think that the latter course was absolutely correct or feel that the world would come to an end with the conclusion of the new security treaty. When freedom of speech did not exist, I remained silent; when it did exist, I made my views known. I never had enough faith in political morality to plunge myself into any political movement at the risk of my own life. But I place even less faith in the value of personal advancement, fortune, or glory. That was all.

I wonder how much more satisfaction I would have felt if my books had sold a little more, or if I had become a little richer or a little more famous. Surely, it couldn't even begin to compare to a sense of moral gratification or intellectual fulfillment, however relative the former and however incomplete the latter may be. In the final analysis, my continued opposition to government policy at any one time was based on my own moral sense. This moral sense was certainly not something derived from any unequivocal conviction, but it was the best justifiable position I could arrive at on the basis of all the evidence available to me. Perhaps it also had something to do with the fact that I had lost some of my friends during the war. The value of their lives was immeasurable, and their deaths irrevocable. But war is a political act, and the significance of any political act can only be relative. My mind is always haunted by the impropriety of employing irrevocable and absolute means to coerce others into making inestimable sacrifices for a goal that can only be relative.

---

in 1948, reemerging as a hawkish pro-American conservative to become president of the Liberal Democratic Party in 1955 and prime minister in 1957. See *Kishi Nobusuke kaikoroku* (The memoirs of Kishi Nobusuke [Kōsaidō shuppan, 1983]).

One could never exhaust one's means to avoid a war. To determine the most effective means to accomplish this goal is not a question of morality but of judgment and reasoning. Perhaps there is no definitive answer to that question. And yet when the time comes, with what little information to rely on and what meager abilities I possess, I myself have to give a tentative answer . . .

The signing of the new security treaty reminded me of the Anglo-Japanese Alliance.[8] Look for the big tree when you seek shelter, as the saying goes (at the time of the Anglo-Japanese Alliance, the British navy ruled the seven seas). Japan quietly cultivated its strength and managed to stand alone, but later it picked a wrong path. Now that Japan had achieved economic prosperity while relying on the military power of the United States, what future course would it take? In any event, with the new security treaty, the Japanese government made its choice. With that, a postwar epoch came to an end. That was something I keenly felt. At the same time I also had a strong feeling that this point in postwar society also marked a watershed in my own life.

When I think about it, I realize that I spent my earlier years largely within the confines of my own world rather than out exploring my surroundings. This tendency became all the more pronounced during the war. But in the fifteen years that followed, I did very much the opposite. Nevertheless, the experiences I acquired and the many observations I made over those years seemed mutually independent of each other, and the correlation between them was not always clear to me. As I began to perceive, little by little, what they meant to each other, I felt the need to probe more deeply into the matter, to discover the mutual links between experiences, and to incorporate independent observations into the totality of my world. Increasingly this desire grew stronger in me. To think rather than to observe, to read rather than to write, and to at least learn something about my own self. As I looked back on my past, I also thought about my future. The prospect of leaving Tokyo for a while to live in seclusion in the mountains was alluring, but given the economic situation of my family this aspiration could hardly be fulfilled.[9] The only al-

8. The Anglo-Japanese Alliance was formed in January 1902 in preparation for a probable Russo-Japanese confrontation in Manchuria, twice revised, in August 1905 and July 1911, with changing political objectives, and abrogated at the Washington Conference of 1921–22.

9. "Random thoughts of a mountain recluse" became Katō's syndicated

ternative for me was to seek employment in a far-off location. I did not necessarily wish to live abroad then, but from time to time positions were available for me outside Japan.

In the year 1960, my life in postwar Tokyo came to a conclusion; 1960 was also the starting point of my life ahead. But of course that conclusion was only tentative. As far as my work was concerned, I had completed certain preliminary preparations and was about to get down to the real work. As for my life, I no longer sought after something new in a different lifestyle; I was thinking only of getting the most out of what I already had. The months and years linking 1960 to the present have come and gone. Perhaps one day the time will come for me to reminisce about those passing years. But it is not now. My judgment on myself is still pending.

---

literary column in the evening edition of *Asahi Shimbun* (July 1980–May 1984); some forty essays for the column are in *Sanchūjin kanwa: zōho* (Random thoughts of a mountain recluse, enlarged ed. [Asahi shimbunsha, 1987]).

Epilogue

Ever since the fall of militarism and the revival of freedom of speech in Japan, I have made writing my vocation. During these twenty years, I have written virtually nothing about my private life. That I should suddenly feel inspired at this time to look back on the first half of my life and to piece together my reminiscences was the result not necessarily of irrepressible nostalgia about my past, but of my realization that my personal experiences were in some ways comparable to those of an average contemporary Japanese.

I am of average height and build, neither wealthy nor poor. My linguistic and intellectual makeup is an even mixture of Japanese and Western components. As far as religion goes, I believe in neither Shintoism nor Buddhism. I have never entertained any high political ambitions, and when it comes to matters of morality, I am a relativist. Racial prejudices I have almost none. I take great pleasure in art, though I have not felt compelled to pick up my own brush or play a musical instrument. What are the conditions that have given rise to such a Japanese? In this book, I attempt to address this question by using myself as an example.

The book is entitled *A Sheep's Song* partly because I was born in the year of the sheep and partly because the sheep's gentle and docile nature is not entirely alien to my own.

A Sheep's Song was first serialized in the *Asahi Jānaru* from October 1966 to March 1967, and its sequel from July to December 1967. To avoid causing trouble to anyone, I have not used the names of those who are still living and have exercised some restraint in my narrative.

On the occasion of this publication in the Iwanami New Books Series, I have deleted repetitions and corrected infelicities. That I have been able to do this was due largely to the encouragement and advice from Mr. Ebihara Mitsuyoshi of Iwanami Publishing House. To him I wish to express my gratitude once again.

Early summer of 1968, Tokyo

Author's Postscript
to the English Edition

AND SO LIFE GOES ON

The narrative of *A Sheep's Song* ends with the year 1960. In the thirty-five years since then, many changes have taken place in the world and in Japan. During these years I lived in Japan half the time and spent the rest abroad. I had the good fortune to meet a number of people who have since become very dear to me, but I also had to part with others who are irreplaceable in my heart. Their friendships brought stimulation not only to the intellect but also to the senses, and together, I have been blessed with moments of unimaginable joy. Needless to say, I have also had my share of frustrations and disappointments, but I think that my way of life remained fundamentally unchanged. Perhaps it did so because I was unable to change it, or perhaps it was because I had little desire to do so. I continued to earn my living as a writer and as a lecturer in universities at various places. I spent a lot of time traveling and reading, and I continued to enjoy the camaraderie my friends provided me. When the occasions presented themselves, I would listen to music, look at paintings, and watch plays and films. And so life goes on.

One of the books I wrote during this period was *A History of Japanese Literature,* in which I tried to trace the intrinsic and extrinsic determinants on the development of Japanese literature and elucidate the characteristics of the Japanese mind.[1] To that end, I felt the need to advance a broader definition of "literature" (*bungaku*) and to discuss writers and writings that literary histories had rarely taken seriously. Another thing on my mind was the comparative angle between Japanese literature and the Chinese classics on the one hand and modern West-

---

1. Original title: *Nihon bungakushi josetsu.*

ern literature on the other. To accomplish that, I tried to present my narrative as lucidly as possible by using critical criteria with the broadest universal application. Fortunately, the book has a wide readership in Japan, and through its translation into six foreign languages (English, French, German, Italian, Chinese, and Korean), it has also become accessible to the non-Japanese audience.

I also wrote a number of books and articles on the plastic arts, and some of these works are known outside Japan in English translations. Additionally, I compiled and wrote poetry collections and published a collection of short stories, but they did not attract much attention. Besides that, I wrote articles for a column in the *Asahi Shimbun* once a month in which I expressed my views and impressions on the political, social, and cultural affairs of the time. My column was under the collective title "Random Talks of a Mountain Recluse," and later its name was changed to "Untempered Utterances."[2]

I taught at three universities: the University of British Columbia, the Free University of Berlin, and Sophia University. Because I spent most of the time as a visiting professor at various universities in different countries, I had little involvement with university administration. My primary duty was to interact with students in the classroom. In most instances, my lectures had to do with Japanese thought and culture under the rubric of area studies. The only exception was a series of five lectures I gave at Princeton University under the title "The United States as Seen by a Japanese."

Those were the things I did. On the other hand, I did not acquire any wealth to speak of. I was satisfied with my modest living, sustained as it was by the income from writing and teaching. I had little desire for more. I also did not get myself involved in politics. I did not belong to any political party or political organization. I did vote in elections, but I took no part in election campaigns, nor did I participate in mass movements or street demonstrations. It was not because I thought active political participation was meaningless, but because such activities did not agree with my temperament.

As a man without wealth, power, or organizational affiliation, I have always lived as a private citizen on the fringes of Japanese society. Chance and circumstances contributed to this state of affairs, but I also con-

2. *Sanchūjin kanwa*, now collected in *Katō Shūichi chosakushū*, 21, and *Sekiyō mōgo*, in vols. 21 and 22.

sciously chose to take this position. Likewise, a combination of circumstances and inclination explained the time in Japan or abroad after the war. It goes without saying that my life abroad was that of a marginal existence. And the many long years I spent outside Japan clearly contributed to my inevitable disengagement from the center of social influence in that country. If living on the periphery of society deprives one of social influence, it can also afford the greatest degree of spiritual freedom. There is a certain advantage to observe, to analyze, and to discern the totality of our condition from the periphery as opposed to the maelstrom of activity. In retrospect, perhaps I was more interested in achieving an understanding of my social, cultural, and political environment than in transforming it. I was not always successful in my attempts. For instance, I was right in my prediction on the day of Japan's attack on Pearl Harbor that Japanese militarism would be defeated, but I was incorrect in my understanding of postwar Japan and failed to predict the course of its subsequent economic development. I was not surprised when two or three East European countries I knew to some extent broke away from Soviet domination, but I never expected the disintegration of the Soviet Union itself. After it happened, I recognized my total unfamiliarity with the Soviet Union.

Awareness of my own ignorance did not, however, dilute my strong sense of curiosity, nor did it cause me to waver in my conviction of an intrinsic order of causality embedded in the ebb and flow of historical events. While I do not discount the accidental element in historical processes, I still believe in our ability to comprehend their dynamics. My primary intellectual interest, regardless of where in the world I happen to be, has always been Japanese history and society. They are the very entities that had the most profound effects on my total makeup. How did Japan and its culture evolve and where are they heading? These were the questions that occupied my thoughts. I might have been in a Zen garden in Kyoto or inside a conference room in Tokyo. Or at home in Vancouver as I watched ships going in and out of the harbor on their trans-Pacific journeys, or in a Berlin tearoom as I listened to students arguing with impassioned ambiguity about the revolution, or in Venice as I reminisced about the trip of the young Japanese delegates in the late sixteenth century on the canals just outside my classroom window.[3]

3. In 1582 the "Christian" daimyos of Ōtomo, Ōmura, and Arima in Kyushu sent a delegation of young men to visit the papal states. They left Nagasaki in

And time went by with increasing relentlessness. Perhaps the protagonist of Richard Strauss's *Der Rosenkavalier* is right when she says that
time is an extraordinary thing. Once conscious of its passage, one will be
left without a capacity to sense anything else. Several decades flashed by
after the completion of *A Sheep's Song*. And occasionally, time came to
a halt. I suppose such moments marked the turning points in my history.
The experiences these nodular markings represent are what engage my
act of reminiscing here. I have little to say about old age, nor do I intend
to mention each and every reminiscence that happens to cross my mind;
for I still wish to look ahead, to the things I plan or aspire to do.

DISCOVERIES OF NORTH AMERICA

In 1960, fifteen years after the war, I set foot on the soil of North America for the first time in my life. On the invitation from the University
of British Columbia to join its faculty, I went alone to take up my position that autumn. My initial status was that of an assistant professor;
later I became an associate professor, and shortly afterwards a full professor. In the Fine Arts Department, I lectured on "Introduction to Oriental Art," and in the Department of Asian Studies, on "Japanese Literature in Translation." I established my residence in a student dormitory
before Professor Bill Holland was kind enough to make available to me
a room in his house. Bill was the former executive director of the Institute of Pacific Relations, based in New York. After the institute was forced
to close down as a result of McCarthyism, he sought refuge in Canada
and became the head of UBC's Asian studies program. At the same time,
he also became the editor of the journal *Pacific Affairs*, then published
through UBC Press instead of in New York.

From my room on the second floor of his house I looked down a small
hill toward the harbor and the mountain range on the other side, as ships
loaded with Canadian wheat passed through the straits on their way to
China. This was the time when the United States adopted a contain-
ment policy toward China, and the ships seemed to symbolize the delicate differences between the U.S. and Canada with respect to their
China policies.

February 1582, reached Rome in March 1585, and had an audience with the pope
before returning to Japan in 1590. See *Dai Nihon shiryō Tenshō ken'ō shisetsu
kankei shiryō*, ed. Tokyo daigaku shiryō hensanjo (1959), *Bekkan* 2.

Bill Holland knew practically every senior Asian scholar working at North American universities. One could find newly published books on area studies on every bookshelf in his house, and there was always a pile of newspapers and journals from the United States on his desk. The newspapers and journals in particular greatly stimulated my intellectual curiosity, but I couldn't even skim through all of them. For relaxation after dinner, Bill himself would watch Hollywood Westerns on TV without the sound while listening to Brahms's symphonies on his stereo and browsing through the *New York Times*, all at the same time. And the spectacle struck me as a spontaneous coalescence of American popular culture, the "American dream"—though a Western movie actor had not yet become an American president—modern journalism, and the legacies of nineteenth-century Western European culture.

Besides Bill Holland, there was quite an assembly of interesting people at the University of British Columbia. B. C. Binning, who single-handedly ran the Fine Arts Department, was a well-known artist in Canada and lived in the woods of West Vancouver with his elegant wife. Gentle and self-effacing, he loved the sea, the sailboats, and England, and was fond of talking about Cézanne, Tomioka Tessai, and Beckmann.[4] When Binning visited Japan, I took him to Takarazuka's Seichōji Temple, where the head priest, Sakamoto Kōjō, was Tessai's disciple during the master's later years. Bert—that was what I called Binning—later invited Mr. Sakamoto to Vancouver and organized the first Tessai exhibition outside of Japan. "Tessai is like Cézanne," he used to say. "Their art represented the culmination of tradition and heralded the advent of modernity."

Among the faculty in the Department of Sociology was Kasper Naegeli. A Viennese who had coauthored a book with Parsons, he sought political asylum in Canada during the Nazi years. One time, on seeing some books I was reading in my office, he muttered, "Now you can find everything in there." If I remember correctly, the books he saw were Heidegger's *Sein und Zeit*, Karl Kraus's *Die letzten Tage der Menschheit*, and Christian Morgenstern's poetry collection *Galgenlieder*. Perhaps these books brought back memories of his distant homeland. His air un-

---

4. Tomioka Tessai (1836–1924), a celebrated and imaginative Japanese-style painter known for his vivacious sense of color and bold execution, drew his inspiration from *yamato-e, nanga*, and other Ming and Qing genres, taught at the Kyoto School of Art (1894–1904), and became a member of the Imperial Academy of Art in 1919.

mistakably reminded me of a typical Western European intellectual of a certain era. His acute sense of history, his deep interest in every aspect of culture, his cultivated habits as a polyglot, along with his ever-present sense of temperate skepticism toward himself and the world . . . Reminiscent of the nimbus of a Buddhist statue, the aura Naegeli exuded was that of an ancient capital on an old continent.

One time we had Kasper as our house guest. At one point, my companion, herself a Viennese, started to talk about "Herr Karl," a performance by a well-known actor in a Vienna political cabaret at the time. The story was an autobiographical narrative triumphantly recounting the life of a petty bourgeois named Karl who managed to live through Nazi Germany's annexation of Austria, the country's defeat, and its postwar turmoil, thanks to his skills at unbridled opportunism. Told in a seemingly endless monologue in the local Viennese dialect, the story as a whole emerged as a relentlessly trenchant satire. Kasper said he wanted to listen to the story on the LP we had. I was interested to see his reactions to the monologue, which I could only half-understand. As he listened, his expressions grew increasingly somber, even anguished. Then at last he said in English, "Let's stop it! I can't stand it any more." His suicide occurred shortly after that.

Of course, what killed him was not a single LP. But for a long time I regretted my role in bringing back to his memory the Austria of Herr Karl. I asked several of his close friends at the university what could have been the reason for his suicide, and yet no one there seemed to have even the faintest clue.

The Chinese historian Bing-ti Ho was a member of the Asian Studies faculty. A graduate of Beijing University, he came to Canada in the wake of the Chinese Revolution of 1949. Although he became a naturalized Canadian citizen, his allegiance to China was still quite extraordinary. While he opposed the Communist government on the mainland, he took great personal pride in the success of China's atomic experiment under the same regime. Each day he would write with his brush a few lines from the Chinese classics, saying that his skills in calligraphy would deteriorate if he did not observe this daily routine. He was very knowledgeable about the Confucian classics, and whenever I asked him the source of a quotation from such texts, he could tell me without a moment's hesitation.

One time I invited him for lunch at the faculty club. "I never have lunch there," he said. "I usually go home and prepare some simple Chinese dishes. There isn't any food in this country worthy of the name cuisine." When I asked him how good the food was at Beijing University, he said with perfect composure that he had never eaten at the university dining room, even during his student days there. "My lunch was always delivered to me from home" was his reply.

"Every day?" I asked.

"That's right. Every day."

"Who prepared it for you?"

"I had a cook at home, and I also had someone deliver the food to me at the university," he answered as if that was the most natural thing in the world.

And so, at Bill Holland's house I managed to get acquainted with his guests such as the ones I have described. The person who came most often was a petite Irish-American woman called M, an editorial assistant of *Pacific Affairs* who came from New York with Bill. With rich facial expressions and rarely shy, after a few drinks of her favorite whisky she would confront everyone head-on with a harangue of caustic words and excoriate all dissenting opinions in an endless string of curses. Some of them were unique. Speaking of the history of British imperialist oppression in Ireland, she would say, "You Anglo-Saxons! Do you know how much blood you have on your hands!" Bill, who must have heard her remark dozens of times, would say something like, "Come on, M, that was in the past!" On rare occasions, she would even direct her curses at me, whereupon Bill, with a wry smile, would remind her of my nationality.

With her, I visited Mexico for the first time, and I was fascinated by the country. Through her work at the Institute of Pacific Relations, she came to know Frederick Vanderbilt Field, and we spent half a day at his house. Well known in the United States for a time as the "American millionaire Communist," Field was married then to a beautiful Mexican dancer and lived in the suburbs of Mexico City, engrossing himself in pre-Columbian archeology. Details about his life are available from his work *From Right to Left: An Autobiography* (Lawrence Hill, 1983).

I cannot quite remember the immediate circumstances now, but in Mexico City I also had the pleasure of meeting Sano Seki. When he showed me around his newly created theater, he stood onstage and, with no one in the audience except me in the front row, proceeded to give an impassioned recital of Ibsen as if it were the first opening performance. Rather than a mere presentation for a lone spectator, his mind must have supplied the vision of a full house. I could never forget this legendary figure from the history of modern Japanese proletarian drama. Active in Japan in the late 1920s, he spent most of the 1930s in the Soviet Union as a political refugee and sought asylum in Mexico in 1939 after Stalin's purge. Since then he had established his drama school and begun his important contributions to the Mexican theater. There was no question in my mind that his theater, along with his plays, was the culmination of his career and the pinnacle of his life. Perhaps Sano had never allowed himself as much hope and optimism as when he stood before me in Mexico City in the early 1960s. When I returned to Mexico later as a visiting professor at the Colegio de México, Sano was no longer with us.[5]

My first impressions of Mexico were of course not limited to my experiences with the two exiles I met. With its roots in pre-Columbian civilization, the country's culture—and in particular its architecture and sculpture—was far more refined, more regionally varied, and more magnificent than that of indigenous American Indians north of Mexico. In the realm of the formative arts, I came to realize that Mexico is not simply a region or a country; rather, it represents quite another world altogether. Moreover, the Mexican character manifested itself not only in its past but also in numerous forms in the present—in its sense of color and in its expressions of violence, in its capacity for deep compassion, its poverty, its nationalism, and the cosmopolitan character of its upper classes. I also became acutely aware of how dramatically different the United States appeared when observed from Mexico or from its other neighbor, Canada. From the north it seemed so close, but so infinitely far away from the south.

What was happening in the United States? In November 1963 at the University of British Columbia, I learned about the assassination of John F. Kennedy. On that day many teachers and students at UBC, myself included, decided to cancel our classes. As we all know, after the Kennedy assassination the American government decided to escalate the Vietnam War. Meanwhile, domestic antiwar activities were also gathering momentum. Eventually, on March 31, 1968, while I was with a number of university colleagues at a friend's house in Vancouver, we heard the tel-

---

5. Sano Seki (1905–66) organized Teatro de las Artes in Mexico City in 1939 and after 1945 directed plays ranging from *King Lear* to *A Streetcar Named Desire*. See Tsurumi Shunsuke (Sano's cousin), *Nihonjin to wa nan darōka* (Shōbunsha, 1996), 399–410.

evised speech by President Johnson in which he announced the termination of American bombardment of North Vietnam and his decision not to run in the next presidential election.

The "anti-Communist" war in Vietnam reminded me of the "sacred war" brought about by the militarist government of Japan. First you have the establishment of a local puppet regime, followed by the claim that there were only a few "anti-Japanese Chinese" (or Vietcong in the former case). Then came repeated proclamation that fighting was localized and the American version that "victory is just around the corner," the gradual escalation of the theater of war, and the sending of troops, resulting in the increase in the number of "anti-Japanese Chinese" (or Vietcong) and the phantasm of the Great East Asia Co-prosperity Sphere (or domino theory). . . . But at the same time, I was also struck by the remarkable differences between Japan during the Fifteen-year War and the United States during the Vietnam War. The Japanese bureaucratic machinery under the emperor-system effectively crushed any hopes for antiwar movements. Even criticism of Japan's war policy was almost nonexistent during the late 1930s. On the other hand, freedom of speech and of public assembly existed in the United States. The impact of antiwar activities, beginning first in the universities, started to be felt in the churches and in certain sectors of the financial establishment, as well as among ordinary citizens outside academia. These forces, combined with their influence on the television media and Walter Cronkite, brought about a change in the government policy. While Japan had no effective mechanism for changes in national policy before its surrender, the power of public opinion in the United States provided that possibility. It led me to ponder the factors that gave rise to these differences between the two countries.

1968

During the 1960s I customarily stayed in Vancouver from September of each year to the following April. During these eight months in Canada I gave lectures at the university and read mostly Japanese classical works in the university library, which happened to contain part of the George Sansom and E. H. Norman collections. I wrote *A History of Japanese Literature* as well as *Essays on Art.*[6] I traveled frequently to the United

6. *Geijutsu ronshū* (Iwanami shoten, 1967).

States, giving lectures, visiting art museums, and participating in Japan-related conferences. During the four and a half months of summer break beginning in May, I lived either in Tokyo or Vienna or sometimes in both places. I maintained a small residence in both cities, and from Vienna I could easily visit other European countries.

The United States I saw in 1968 was San Francisco and the Bay Area in April and New England and Chicago in November. By then, anti-Vietnam War demonstrations seemed to have flared up everywhere in that country. Their effects were felt on Canadian university campuses as well. In Japan, the Beiheiren, a citizen's movement with the slogan "Peace to Vietnam," was active in organizing public rallies and in offering assistance to American army deserters.

American supporters of the Vietnam War insisted that the conflict was caused by North Vietnam's "aggression" against the south, an action seen as a manifestation of China's "expansionism." So went the domino theory according to which other Asian countries were supposed to fall one after another under Communist control should South Vietnam first turn red. It struck me that this view and all its interpretations were a concoction spun out of fantasy without due recognition to the realities of local history and Vietnamese nationalism. What could have given rise to a theory so far removed from reality? Just as many antiwar advocates in the United States pointed out, it was not merely an accidental error in judgment but a way of thinking intimately connected with the ideological framework of Cold War logic. Among American scholars, particularly political scientists and Asian area specialists, the views of "concerned scholars" could also be heard.

At the University of British Columbia, I had the occasion to participate in an antiwar teach-in. At a gathering of mostly students mixed with their instructors, a series of antiwar speeches were made by historians, professors of English literature, and mathematicians, all nonspecialists in American politics. Then a professor of political science stood up and said that the former speakers had no idea how American foreign policy decisions were made. In his view as a specialist in the field, the war was not simply a unilateral decision by President Johnson but the result of a complex interaction of forces consisting of the internal power politics of the United States Congress, the bureaucracy, the military, and a large number of other pressure groups. He went on to say that ignorance of this fact would render any opposition against the war ineffectual.

While I believed he was right, I also thought that the more convincing a political scientist was in explaining the realities of a situation, the more he would find himself inclined to support the status quo. To explain how the status quo has come into being is almost tantamount to demonstrating how preexisting conditions have led to the formation of the status quo as a natural progression of events. And if the given conditions cannot be altered, it also becomes impossible to change the inescapable consequence. All this means that it is meaningless to oppose the status quo because it is the predetermined consequence of such conditions.

But when we are speaking about an extremely complex phenomenon such as war, references to its inevitability are no more than just a superficial facade. Strict adherence to the laws of causality cannot explain a phenomenon when a myriad of factors come into play. To oppose a war is not a matter of scientific interpretation but a question about basic human values. We cannot tolerate children dying every day under the bomb. This is not the conclusion but the beginning of any discussion.

I went on a journey in 1968. I visited my friends during the early spring in California and spent two months during the early summer in Japan, a month and a half during midsummer in Europe, and the late autumn on the east coast of the United States and Canada. In Japan the policy of high economic growth pushed ahead by the Satō cabinet, the successor to the Ikeda administration, was starting to change the everyday life of the Japanese people. It witnessed, in material terms, the emergence of an affluent consumer society represented by the so-called age of the three Cs—car, cooler, and color television. Psychologically, it gave rise to a sense of complacency among most Japanese and political conservatism. It was said that the Japanese people as a whole were being transformed into the middle class.

On the other hand, Japanese university students continued to be critical of the structural realities of high economic growth itself and "collusion" among the universities, the financial world, and the conservative political establishment. Their protest took the form of confining their instructors inside their offices, occupying university buildings, and blockading lecture halls. Student activists at Tokyo University occupied Yasuda Hall at the center of the Hongō campus, an event that led to their confrontation with the Japanese riot police in January 1969. I did not have any direct dealings with the students during my two-month stay in Tokyo; the first time I met with student activists during the 1968 student movement was not in Tokyo but in Berlin in the following year.

In mid-July, I went to Europe via Moscow. For the Parisians at that time, the May revolution was still very fresh in their memory, and every conversation I had with my friends inevitably returned to that subject. They instantly recalled the huge gatherings of students and citizens of Paris that buried the boulevard St-Michel. They also vividly remembered Jean-Louis Barrault's speech at the citizens' meeting at the Odéon, the tear gas thrown by the police, Cohn-Bendit, and the prudent reactions of the Renault factory workers. The graffiti on the walls of university buildings were still visible with the words "Imagination au Pouvoir!" "Changez la Vie!" It must have been a time of uncertain hopes, a time filled with a sense of emancipation and vivacious visions about the future. At the same time, the events of May also seemed to evoke images of a festival just the day before, of a legend buried in the great distant past. When I met Sartre, he told me that whatever real possibility he had felt for a revolution and a commune disappeared after the first week of events.

During this time, my colleague at the University of British Columbia B. C. Binning and his wife were spending their summer vacation in England. My wife and I met them in Vienna and together we decided to journey around Alexander Dubček's Czechoslovakia in my small Volkswagen. In January 1968 Dubček had succeeded his country's Stalinist predecessor as national party chief and subsequently sought to liberalize the socialist regime by instituting thorough administrative as well as organizational reforms within the Communist party. This was the Prague Spring of 1968. Come to think of it now, I think it is fair to say that Dubček's initiatives preceded Gorbachev's perestroika by twenty years.

And he was a very popular leader. At a small town near the Austrian border, I saw perhaps twenty to thirty townspeople in groups of three to five standing on the roadside watching a car slowly passing them by. Some of them were waving at the vehicle. Who could be the passenger inside? There was no motorcade in front or behind that particular car, and not a single policemanlike figure anywhere in sight. It was Dubček. Could any other East European leader travel freely like an individual citizen without being surrounded by police and security guards or having secret police positioned at various destination points? What was happening in Czechoslovakia then, in terms of the relationship between the socialist leadership and the people, was unprecedented. There was no doubt of the country's long search for political liberalization and of the people's overwhelming support for Dubček's administration, which brought it about. If the Chinese peasants had not supported Mao Tse-

tung while he was fighting the Kuomintang with his People's Liberation Army, the victory of the 1949 Chinese Revolution would have been
inconceivable. Mao was not an elected leader. Dubček, too, was not elected
by popular vote in 1968, and yet he could move about freely in his country without armored protection.

Compared with Austria, Czechoslovakia then was not as prosperous.
But it was not poor; goods and commodities were plentiful and I saw no
lines in front of food stores. There were many black marketeers trading
in foreign currencies, and even at my hot-spring lodge in the Slovakian
mountains such individuals came up to foreigners and tried to buy dol-
lars at the black-market price. Obviously, economic problems in the country still remained to be solved, but the severity of these problems eluded
the casual traveler.

During my journey, whenever I had an opportunity I would ask local people in provincial towns what they thought about liberalization.
None of us spoke Czech, Slovak, or Russian, and we had no interpreter
with us. But some townspeople we met spoke simple English or German. One man said that it was wonderful to have political liberalization,
but he wondered how long it could last. An elderly woman was more
pessimistic and said in rather fluent German that she did not believe the
process would continue much longer. "Liberalization is going too fast,"
she asserted. "They'd never allow it." And it was not difficult to guess
whom she meant by "they."

Totally contrary to this gloomy outlook in the provinces was the optimism among the Prague intellectuals. I met a number of newspaper
reporters, writers, editors of literary journals, and other intellectuals, and
their predominant sentiments were almost euphoric. Finally, the freedom of speech had returned, I was told. Censorship had disappeared, and
now they could criticize socialism as well as capitalism not only in their
journals but even in newspapers and on radio and television. They could
now freely visit cities in the Western bloc; and Prague, they said, was
now a European city again just like London and Paris. "Our spiritual
horizon has opened up," an editor who had just returned from Paris
spoke rapidly in French as he offered me French wine and cheese. "Our
journal serves not only Europe but the whole world. We welcome manuscripts from the United States or from Japan. We don't want any left-
wing dogmatism or anti-Communist propaganda, but as long as the writings are based on a free, critical spirit, we welcome any variety of views
on any subject." I promised them that after my return to Vienna, I would

think of something to write about. "We don't have any deadlines or length limitations. Any subject you care to write about is okay," the editor continued.

How long would the spring in Prague last? When I asked them about the possibility of Soviet intervention, all the Prague intellectuals I met answered in the same way. "We have absolutely no worry about that. Why? The answer is simple. There's no reason for them to intervene. Dubček is a socialist, and so are we. We are neither anti-Soviet nor anti-socialism. All we're trying to do is overcome Stalinism and build a free, humanistic, and true socialist society. We cannot imagine that a socialist country like the Soviet Union would come and crush our hopes. It just won't happen."

Perhaps they are right, I thought to myself. Dubček was trying to rekindle the last hopes of socialism that Stalin had killed. While it has been my habit not to cherish any absolute faith in anything, I realized that our different thinking on this matter reflected the fact that it was they, not I, who were the citizens of Prague. This was the time when they needed hope more than anything else.

And hope was contagious. As I was driving on the motorway on my return trip to Austria, I was lost in thought, pondering the possibility of living in Vienna for a while and traveling back and forth between Vienna and Prague.

Several days after my trip to Czechoslovakia, I went to Salzburg for the music festival. There I found myself immersed in an intimately familiar environment—the Vienna Philharmonic and Mozart, German spoken with an Austrian accent, terraces of coffee houses overlooking swiftly flowing streams, lights scattering on the icy surface of night streets, and old castles on hilltops illuminated against a dark sky. On August 20, I heard Christa Ludwig singing *Fidelio* conducted by Karl Böhm. This was a world infinitely removed from the student movements in Tokyo, the May revolution in Paris, or even the milieu of the Prague Spring. Which of these worlds held a greater sense of reality?

In the pension where I was staying, a simple breakfast was served to the guests down in a room on the first floor with five or six small tables. As I had no particular plans until the evening on the following day after *Fidelio*, I got up late and went downstairs for a leisurely cup of coffee. And I learned from the pension's proprietor that the Soviet army had entered Prague. His message immediately transformed Salzburg into an unreal world, and the Prague I had visited just ten days before along with every fragment of my experiences there came alive vividly in my mind—the faces of the people waving to Dubček's car, the eyes of the old woman asserting that Prague's spring would never be allowed to continue, the conversation in the editor's office so filled with hopes and dreams, the taste of French cheese blended with the aroma of freedom. . . . Soviet tanks had entered the city limits last night, declaring their mission to "rescue our ally from national crisis." My immediate priority was to find out as much as possible about what was happening in Prague and what was about to take place.

Quickly, I changed my plans for Salzburg, though the music festival did appear to continue into the end of August as if nothing had happened. I loaded my bags into my Volkswagen and left for Vienna the same afternoon. Back home in Vienna, I could leave my television on and have easy access to newspapers from various countries. I could also consult some of my many friends who knew about the internal situation of the Soviet Union and Eastern Europe. Driving on the Salzburg-Vienna West-autobahn, I saw quite a number of small cars with Czechoslovakian plates. It seemed safe to assume that many of these Czechs had come with their families to visit the Western bloc during the summer vacation without any premonition that troops from the Soviet Union and the Warsaw Pact would intervene in their country's affairs. With the situation changing so traumatically, were they now returning hastily to Czechoslovakia? Or were they thinking of seeking political refuge elsewhere, realizing how difficult it would be for them to leave the country again once they returned?

In Budapest in 1956, Soviet tanks had opened fire on the armed insurrectionists, but the same did not happen in Prague in 1968. The Czechoslovakian army was not mobilized, and the people did not stage an armed resistance. Instead the citizens of Prague changed all the road signs to make them point toward Moscow. Young Soviet soldiers had come expecting to protect the citizens of Prague from "anti-revolutionaries," but the latter were nowhere to be found. Instead, when these young Soviets found themselves and their tanks surrounded by the protesting citizens who demanded their withdrawal, they scarcely knew what to do.

That night the news broadcast on Vienna television was suddenly interrupted by a somewhat indistinct half-length image of a man. Facing the camera with a sad expression and speaking clearly in German, he was making repeated appeals to the citizens of Vienna. "The television station in Prague has now been occupied," he said, "and we are broadcasting this message to the citizens of Vienna from a secret location. The Soviet troops certainly did not come to Prague at the invitation of our government as they claim. They are here in spite of the will of our government and all the people in Prague. Dear citizens of Vienna, please relate this message to the rest of the world. I will continue to speak out, and when my face disappears from the screen and my voice can no longer be heard, it means they have found out about this location and have come to stop us. I don't know how much time we still have, but we will go on as long as we can . . ."

Those might not have been his exact words, but who could forget their message? I knew then what forces stood in the streets of Prague. On one side was an army of overwhelming power with nothing legitimate to say, and on the other a powerfully persuasive and deeply humanistic vision filled with wisdom and hope for a better society. In Prague in August 1968, the war against Soviet tanks was waged with words. I took that as the title of a book I later wrote.[7]

BERLIN, NEW HAVEN, CHINA

In the fall of 1969 I was invited to be a professor at the Free University of Berlin and to head its East Asian Research Institute.[8] The university had officially hired me, but it was the students there who had chosen me for the position. It was a time of great student activism, and in Berlin reforms in university governance had already been put into effect. As a result, university policy—including personnel matters—was to be decided by committees with equal representation from three groups, namely professors, students, and assistants and other clerical staff. Student decisions thus carried considerable weight. Moreover, students were also able to boycott classes not to their liking.[9]

7. *Kotoba to sensha* (Words and tanks) (Chikuma shobō, 1969).
8. That is, the Freie Universität, Berlin, and the Ostasiatisches Seminar.
9. Student activism and reforms (*Drittelparität*) began in 1967 in Berlin, then in Frankfurt and Marburg—"as a movement against an outmoded university system and the heavy authoritarianism of senior teachers"—before it spread to other parts of Europe: "Maoist and other groups, in fierce rivalry, roamed the faculties breaking up lectures, sometimes locking professors into their rooms or scuffling with the police, while students boycotts led to many seminars and courses being cancelled, especially in the social sciences" (John Ardagh, *Germany and the Germans: An Anatomy of Society Today* [New York: Harper and Row, 1987], 423, 213).

Day after day, I met with students either at the institute or at restaurants surrounded by woods in the Dahlem district, an affluent residential area in which the university is situated. There we discussed the methodology and the content of our instruction. The students were consistently critical of the kind of learning based on what they called "bourgeois positivism." For example, did elementary Japanese language instruction fit that description? According to a student activist, the answer depended on whether those on the receiving end were sufficiently imbued with "revolutionary ideology." Thus, before newcomers to such courses began to read Japanese, they must first study revolutionary ideology! While discussion with students on the appropriate ways of instruction went on, the teaching itself did not begin until later.

In those days, the Berlin Wall divided the city into two parts. To get to the East sector from where I lived in the West, I had to pass through Checkpoint Charlie. On the western side, two or three soldiers from the British, American, or French forces were standing with a bored look on their faces and letting people pass even without inspecting their identification papers. Then the visitor came to the checkpoint in East Berlin. There, the inspection was meticulous and took a long time before anyone was let go. The procedure became even more tedious if one had to pass through East Germany by car in order to go to Western Europe from West Berlin. I myself often used the British, French, or American airlines for that purpose; Lufthansa still did not have flights connecting West Germany and West Berlin. Isolated in Eastern Europe, West Berlin was no longer a manufacturing center. But the impact of West Germany's consumer society was quite evident there—one could find ample supply of all kinds of consumer goods, from ordinary everyday products to luxury items.

The cultural activities in this part of the city were lively, thanks to its preferential economic status and, surely, to its own cultural traditions since the nineteenth century. Students from various parts of West Germany came to its universities; one reason, I suppose, was that young people who established their residence in Berlin were exempt from compulsory military service. The Berlin Philharmonic Orchestra held regular performances at concert halls with splendid acoustics; in opera houses one could hear world-class singers throughout the year. Berlin perhaps had more theaters than any other West German city, with troupes from Hamburg and Munich performing their most famous plays. Moreover, one could also go to Brecht's Berliner Ensemble in East Berlin and watch the performance of Frau Weigel, as long as one remembered to return to Checkpoint Charlie before midnight.[10]

I lived in a prewar building in the middle of the city. The ceiling in my room was incredibly high, an effect driven home more dramatically as I looked down from a ladder when I climbed up to hang my window curtains. And because my house was situated at the intersection between Kantstrasse and Leibnizstrasse, whenever I was asked where I lived, I often replied, "At the place where epistemology and ontology meet." The opera house was only a very short distance away, and the theaters, too, were also not very far off. I met with my students at the institute in Dahlem during the daytime, and at night I often enjoyed going to concerts and plays. While I had no interest in watching German-dubbed American movies in the cinema, I often enjoyed watching East European films from my television at home. It was in Berlin that I first encountered Hungarian and Czechoslovakian films that in those days could rarely been seen in Tokyo or in Western Europe.

The heroes among my students were men like Ho Chi Minh, Che Guevara, and Mao Tse-tung. Their common characteristics were their status as leaders against imperialist colonialism and the fact that their geographical centers of activity were too far away from Berlin to allow my students intimate knowledge about the background of their words and actions. The gods certainly do not live in the next city block, but way up in the skies. In their conversations, my students often quoted Benjamin, Adorno, and Marcuse as well as Frantz Fanon and even more historically remote figures such as Rosa Luxemburg, but very rarely Marx or Engels. It was true that the pronouncements of my students lacked logical precision or any realistic program for political action, but there was a consistent undertone of anti-authoritarian sentiment. I found these conversations quite interesting.

And yet it was not easy to come to an agreement in my deliberations with student activists over the interpretation and application of the new regulations on university policy. Our views differed sharply when a number of students asked if they could jointly present their graduation thesis (a work equivalent to a master's thesis at an American university). As a piece of joint endeavor, there would be no clear indication as to the extent of each individual's contribution to the work. As a result,

10. Helene Weigel took over control of Berliner Ensemble after her husband's death in 1956 (see Ardagh, *Germany and the Germans*, 364–65).

it would be impossible to judge the degree of knowledge or competence of each participant. But the degree was to be granted not to the students as a group but to each and every individual. I therefore indicated to them that I could not accept their suggestion because I found it unreasonable. They in turn told me that my arguments betrayed individualistic thinking reflective of the competitive nature of bourgeois society and that I failed to appreciate the solidarity among my students. But I refused their proposal on the grounds that it would be irresponsible of me as a university instructor to approve the granting of a degree when no sufficient basis for such recognition existed. My student representative then replied that students on their part would refuse to take classes from an "authoritarian professor" such as I. That they were at total liberty to do.

As a matter of principle I neither refuse those who choose to come nor attempt to detain those who wish to leave. I enjoy speaking to those who wish to listen, but I have little desire to waste my limited time with those who have no desire to stay. I came to Berlin because I was so invited, and I had no intention whatsoever of overstaying my welcome. It was then that I decided to leave the city.

I visited New Haven in New England in 1974. The autumn was beautiful, but the little town had nothing that characterized Berlin—no art museums, theaters, opera houses, no Herbert von Karajan, not even a place where one could have a good glass of draft beer. The streets were not named after men like Kant or Leibniz; instead they were called First Street, Second Street, and so on. There was no Checkpoint Charlie to pass through on my way to New York for plays. But the town has a splendid university, and I lectured on Japanese history and Japanese literature for Yale's graduate students. As far as Japanese studies was concerned, Yale during the 1970s had everything the Free University of Berlin didn't.

First, my university colleagues. As far as Japanese studies was concerned, I had experienced very little intellectual stimulation from the scholars I met in Berlin, but at Yale there was my old friend the historian John W. Hall. Along with Professor Marius B. Jansen at Princeton, he was one of the central figures who espoused the "modernization theory" for Japan not long after the war. He was the person who invited me to Yale, and while there I often worked in his office. On many occasions, I also met Professor Edwin McClellan, a specialist on modern Japanese literature. Regrettably, I think extremely few readers these days, inside or outside Japan, can match his critical judgment when it comes to assessing the quality of Japanese prose. One time he asked me for the names of living Japanese writers whose prose I evaluated most highly. With little hesitation, I mentioned two names: Ishikawa Jun and Nakano Shigeharu. "I agree completely," he said. "But I would like to add Ibuse Masuji's name to the list."[11]

When I was at Yale, the scholar of psychoanalysis Robert Lifton, well known in Japan for his investigation of Hiroshima survivors, was with the Yale Medical School. He was interested in developing general psychological theories regarding attitudes toward death encompassing the experiences of survivors. Together, we organized a seminar on modern Japanese attitudes toward life and death, with equal enrollment from students in the medical school and graduate Japanese studies. The ensuing discussions with our students, always quite lively, greatly stimulated the instructors themselves as well. Michael Reich, a graduate student and the coordinator for the seminar, worked on writing up the contents, and the three of us published through Yale University Press *Six Lives Six Deaths: Portraits from Modern Japan*. A two-volume Japanese version, entitled *Nihonjin no shiseikan* and translated by Yajima Midori, was also published in the Iwanami shinsho series.[12]

Active interactions existed between American universities. While I was teaching at Yale, I became acquainted with a number of sociologists and Japan specialists from other universities as well. The intellectual

11. On Ishikawa Jun see chapter 37, note 10. • Nakano Shigeharu (1902–79), a leading prewar proletarian theorist and the movement's most celebrated literary figure, founded the New Japan Literary Society (Shin Nihon bungakukai) after 1945 and had a central role in the postwar democratic literary movement; his works include poetry (*Nakano Shigeharu shishū* [Collection of the poetry of Nakano Shigeharu, 1935]) and novels (*Uta no wakare* [Farewell to poetry, 1939], *Nashi no hana* [Pear blossoms, 1957–58], and *Kō otsu hei tei* [ABCD, 1965–69]); on his prewar career see Miriam Silverberg, *Changing Song: The Marxist Manifestos of Nakano Shigeharu* (Princeton: Princeton University Press, 1990). • Ibuse Masuji (1898–1993), novelist, short-story writer, and essayist, whose works include *Yofuke to ume no hana* (Midnight and plum blossoms, 1930), "Yōhai taichō" (The worshiping captain, 1950), *Chinpindō shujin* (Master of the curio shop, 1959), and *Kuroi ame* (Black rain, 1966); see Anthony V. Liman, *A Critical Study of the Literary Style of Ibuse Masuji* (Lewiston: E. Mellen Press, 1992).

12. In 1979. The three authors offer case studies of six well known modern Japanese men: Nogi Maresuke, Mori Ōgai, Nakae Chōmin, Kawakami Hajime, Masamune Hakuchō, and Mishima Yukio. • Its Japanese version was published in 1977.

stimulation I got from them was not inconsiderable, but at this point I would not go into this subject.

Second, the students I had. They no longer spoke about things like "revolution," "the military-industrial complex," or "bourgeois positivism," nor were they particularly passionate about antiwar movements or university reforms. In 1975 when Saigon was captured by the Communists and when the last Americans were returning home from Vietnam, I commented on these matters with some of my students at the university cafeteria. Their reaction made it abundantly clear that they were interested not in talking about the righteousness of the anti-Vietnam War movements in the 1960s but in dropping the subject.

Generally speaking, the students were quite knowledgeable and their analytical ability was rather good in their specialized field. In the foreign universities where I have taught, only Yale's history graduate students were able to give commentaries in Japanese on the original texts by Japanese historians we were reading—or those at Beijing University. The differences between the students I met in Berlin and those in New Haven were quite considerable. But I was in Berlin in the late sixties, and in New Haven in the mid-seventies. During those five years, everywhere in Europe and in the United States, as well as in Japan, another crop of students had emerged. Instead of criticizing and negating the system, they were now seeking to explore the various mechanisms within the system itself. As a matter of fact, twenty years later, when I returned to the Free University of Berlin for one semester of lectures, the students in Berlin had a different outlook altogether.

The Yale students were generous to me even outside the classroom. Far from insisting on unpleasant confrontations, they offered me great assistance. This continued after their graduation and into their professional careers. Those who became university professors, lawyers, and diplomats assisted me in my academic work or accommodated me in their various capacities. When I was in New Haven, I rented a house with Michael Reich, then a graduate student in Political Science and later a professor at the Harvard School of Public Health. As there was no furniture in the house, we rented secondhand items from the local Salvation Army. For transportation, I relied on his car; while some of its windows could not be rolled up, the engine was still working. He was the coordinator and the organizer of my joint seminar with Professor Lifton; at the same time, he was also my student, friend, roommate, chauffeur, English teacher, as well as my valued guide to certain facets of American society.

The third difference had to do with the easy availability of source materials. The university's main library had all the Japanese materials I wanted. Moreover, the library was right next to my department building and it was open until late into the night. Whether inside or outside Japan, I have never experienced such convenience in gaining access to source materials.

That is why I said earlier that the university in the rather solitary town of New Haven was so wonderful. I spent two years there, often spending my weekends in New York and on rare occasions in Cambridge. During our holidays and with Michael Reich, I also had the opportunity to visit the South, which reminded me of Japan. I found it strange that there had been so few comparative studies of postwar Japan's society and culture and those of the American South, though I myself was unable to look into the subject.

During the years I lived in Berlin in the early 1970s, followed by my stay in New Haven, I did return to Japan from time to time. And in the autumn of 1971 I was invited by my old friend Nakajima Kenzō to visit China with the Association for Japan-China Cultural Exchange.[13] I had no idea why Mr. Nakajima invited me to go along. I had never visited that country, and before our departure he told me how splendid a country China was and added, "It's totally impossible to imagine its splendor without going and seeing it for yourself." Then he added, "You and your Western fixations, you always jabber away. But China is a serious country, and if I were you I'd be more circumspect."

That year, 1971, witnessed the China-U.S. rapprochement. In early July President Nixon's Assistant for National Security Affairs, Henry Kissinger, had met with Premier Zhou En-lai in Beijing, while in China itself Zhou and the People's Liberation Army must already have taken measures to bring the Cultural Revolution to an end. But what I saw gave me the impression that China was still in the maelstrom of the Cultural Revolution. The "Gang of Four," as the group would be referred to later, was still in complete control. The Red Guards filled the streets, and the people were brandishing their little red books. Mr. Nakajima was right; it was certainly wise to be prudent.

In late September, after I walked across the border from Hong Kong into China, I was in a totally different world. There were no advertise-

13. See chapter 17 on Katō's friendship with Nakajima at Tokyo Imperial University.

ments, no exhaust fumes from automobiles, no noise pollution, and no skyscrapers. Instead, what I saw was a serene world with wide open blue sky, clean streets, and weeping willow trees with branches swaying in the wind. Without exception, men and women wore the light gray "people's uniform" that did little to underscore differences of figure, social status, or even age. I didn't come across many corpulent people or many who were skinny as a result of malnutrition. The first people I spoke with through the aid of an interpreter were the train service personnel, the *fumuyuan,* who served us tea on our journey to Guangzhou. In all my train trips in other countries, I had never encountered a service personnel so flawlessly clean and attentive. I wondered what made them so and was told that their job was "to offer their services to the people by following the teachings of Chairman Mao."

"What about it? Aren't you impressed with China?" Mr. Nakajima said.

"Mmm . . . ," I replied vaguely.

I was in China only a few hours. My first impression was that everything I saw was different from my previous experiences. It struck me that the organization of Chinese society was based on a different grammar from those of all other societies I knew. I had no idea how that grammar worked, and I started to become curious.

After we reached our hotel in Guangzhou, we were given our own little red books, *Quotations from Chairman Mao* edited by Lin Biao, and we were told to bring them along when we left our hotel to visit the people's commune, for example. These pamphlets reminded me of the Michelin travel guides but, heeding the advice of the leader of our party, Mr. Nakajima, I kept my mouth shut on this frivolous thought.

We were also given volumes of *Important Documents of the Great Proletarian Cultural Revolution,* which contained many speeches by comrade Lin Biao. Lin ended all of them by giving three cheers to the paramount Chinese leader: "Long live Chairman Mao!" I understand that there was such a thing as giving three cheers, but I commented to someone in our party that chanting "Long live ten thousand years! Ten thousand years! Ten thousand upon ten thousand years!" was a little excessive. Because of that, someone in our party seemed to think of me as being anti-Chinese. In any case, at the time when we were in China Lin Biao had already died. But it was not until the next spring when it was officially announced that Lin, having failed in his military coup d'état against Chairman Mao, had died in Mongolia in August the year before.

After my return from China, I published my impressions in Japanese newspapers and journals. These writings were collected in a book called *Chūgoku ōkan* and subsequently translated into English under the title *The Japan-China Phenomenon* (London: Paul Norbury Publications, 1974).[14] The opinions of reviewers inside Japan and abroad were split between those who thought I was being too positive and those who thought I was too negative about China during the Cultural Revolution. Since my first trip to China, I have visited the country repeatedly, once every few years, sometimes as a member of Japan's delegation from the Association for Japan-China Cultural Exchange, sometimes as a private individual, and at one time as a visiting professor under the auspices of Beijing University. Essentially, classical China to a Japanese is comparable to classical Greece to a Westerner; it is impossible to separate Japanese history from Chinese continental civilization and make sense of the former. And my travels to China have become a regular event until this day.

During the first half of the 1970s, I lived primarily in foreign countries and returned from time to time to Japan as a visitor. From the latter half of the same decade, I lived primarily in Japan and made frequent trips abroad. In Japan from 1975, I became a teacher at Tokyo's Sophia University lecturing on Japanese intellectual history, and there I met a number of very enthusiastic students. Three among them later became teachers at Japanese universities and another two at American universities. One of the latter is Chia-ning Chang, who translated *A Sheep's Song* into English. I also began to write for the literary column in the *Asahi Shimbun*, where I often published my views on current affairs. Meanwhile, I managed to finish the latter half of my book *Nihon bungakushi josetsu*, and Chikuma shobō published the first volume in 1975, followed by the second in 1980.

THE END OF THE JOURNEY

After that, I made my home in Tokyo and traveled abroad frequently. Writing was my primary vocation, and since that activity amounts to a sort of manual labor, I could in principle do this kind of work wherever I might happen to live in the world. My secondary occupation was that of a university professor, and when invited I could take off as a visiting professor to various institutions around the world. And thus I spent an

14. The original book was published by Chūō kōron sha, 1972.

academic year each in Geneva and Venice and half a year each in Cambridge, Zurich, and Berlin after the German unification. I also spent some time in Providence on the east coast and Davis on the west coast of the United States, teaching at Brown University and the University of California—and in Mexico City, at the Colegio de México. I also lectured for a period ranging from a few weeks to several months in places such as Beijing and Princeton.

Since invitations from foreign universities came at their own discretion, I often lived in cities and towns where I just happened to work. These places or the universities or sometimes both often struck me as intellectually engaging and sometimes sensually enchanting as well. The crocus flowers in Cambridge announcing the coming of early spring, fragmentary conversations at high table, students coming and going on their bicycles, and the wonderful and ever seductive bookstores. And then there were images of the Venetian winter, of steam whistles piercing the fog, snow falling on the canals, labyrinthlike alleyways, gondola crossings, the now burned-down opera house La Fenice, the city of Tintoretto with its carnivals and marble sculptures. These were the cities where I spent my days and met various people. Even today I still fondly remember many of my acquaintances, people who have become or might have become, if fate had appropriately intervened, close friends of mine.

I suppose I could attribute my reason for residing abroad to my strong curiosity about foreign environments. 1919 was the year in which I was born. But if my birth year had been 1819, how would my experiences have turned out? The question invites a historical retrospective. On the other hand, Tokyo was where I was born and raised. But if the city in question had been Beijing or Mexico City instead of Tokyo, what would I have seen, how would I have felt, and what would have inspired my thoughts? These questions invite a journey into the unknown. Life is filled with accidents. Our physiological makeup is accidentally determined by the composition of our DNA. But our external conditions—which turn into our flesh and blood and give definitive form to our very being—consist particularly of the time and place of our birth. No one can dictate the particular circumstances of these conditions or do anything to transcend them. But at least on the intellectual level, whether we accomplish it by virtue of our historical knowledge or by our choice of our living environment, we can challenge the peculiarities of our given conditions and establish our own spiritual freedom.

"I wonder when it all began, as I found myself carried away by the wind trailing the thin clouds, hopelessly infatuated with thoughts of wandering." Bashō wrote these words at the beginning of his *Narrow Road through the Provinces*, but he did not offer an explanation for his wanderlust. Yet for a poet sensitive enough to the flow of historical time to speak about notions of immutability and temporality, I strongly suspect that the motive lay in an attempt to free himself from the peculiarities of his spatial environment, convinced as he was of the transience of temporal living. He was an indefatigable traveler, and the impressions he gathered on his trips are condensed in his haiku compositions. "Hopelessly infatuated with thoughts of wandering." Perhaps the same can be said of my own wanderlust. Not only did I often change my domicile inside and outside Japan, I often embarked on various journeys.

For all these years, I visited France many times and stayed in locales in virtually every part of the country. Sometimes my purpose was to participate in conferences, sometimes to give lectures at universities, but for most of the time I went to visit friends. The sites include an isolated village in Bretagne where the Nabi painters used to live and where remnants of Celtic culture still remain today. And one friend lived in a pine forest in the depopulated department of Landes, the setting of one of François Mauriac's novels. Another friend lived in the foothills of the Jura range near the Swiss border and commuted to Lyons and Paris for work. Yet another lived in a remodeled farmhouse on a small hill deep in the massif Central so that he could devote himself to writing. My sojourns brought me into contact with the nature, customs, and traditional culture of places far removed from metropolitan areas. I also learned about how they were being preserved as well as the state of their deterioration. Industrial consumerism first transformed the cities, as it did Paris in the sixties. Increasingly, the charms of the good old days could be found only in the countryside.

When I was living in Cambridge, I once drove around England when friends from France came to visit; and when I was making my home in Geneva, I visited various places in Italy with my Japanese friends. I enjoyed these trips enormously, but they rarely reminded me of faraway Japan. On the other hand, I must admit that my experiences did inspire all sorts of musings on my part as I compared the various local customs with those in Japan. My plans to embark on a trip to the South when I was living in New England grew from my conscious desire to broaden my focus for comparing U.S. and Japanese societies. And sure enough, I discovered that many of the things that have traditionally been pointed out as well-defined contrasts between the United States and Japan were themselves characteristic differences between the American Northeast and the South. What I saw in the South—its lingering memories of defeat in the Civil War, its emphasis on family roots and the prestige of the family name, its tenacious hold on the land and the effects of such tenacity on the region's social mobility—pointed to the coexistence of a highly industrialized society with the fundamental values of a historically agricultural setting. It seemed to me that the historical differences between the American Northeast and Japan also helped to explain the similarities between the American South and my country.

My immediate impressions after crossing the U.S.-Mexico border were unlike my discovery of the American South. There I found a world totally different from Japan and the United States. Even the differences between the United States and Canada now seemed negligible, to say nothing of regional disparities between north and south. Japan retreated so far into the distant background that any attempt at comparison seemed impossible. There I learned about the coexistence of many cultures and the multifarious ways of interpreting the world depending on just where one happened to stand. The specter of violence as well as expressions of human compassion filled the rhythms of daily living, dominated by the realities of extreme wealth on the one hand and dire poverty on the other. The poor congregated in huge slums at the outskirts of the city, while the rich fortified themselves behind high walls, punctuated only by well-hidden entrances to their large estates.

Three different kinds of commodity prices appeared to be at work at the same time. The incredibly low fares for public transportation seemed to be socialist-inspired. Free market forces, on the other hand, clearly dictated the price for hotel accommodation according to its particular class, while taxi fares relied on a precapitalistic relationship between the driver and his passenger. The World's Soccer Games happened to take place in Mexico City while I was living there. Despite the fact that I spoke almost no Spanish, my mere mention of the word "soccer" on my taxi ride often sent the driver into an endless discourse on the strengths and weaknesses of the Mexican national team—at least that was what I thought he said—until we reached my destination. And as long as my hand gestured my agreement with his views from time to time, I could get away with paying only half what he normally charged.

There would really be no end to talking about my impressions of Mexico if I were to delve into the subject in any depth. All I can say is that I tried my best to understand how the Mexicans behaved within their society, how these patterns related to the country's long historical past, and how they differed from those of the Japanese. I was also trying my best to appreciate the richness of Mexican culture that has managed to survive despite the worst destructive impulses of the Spaniards.

Also in the early spring of 1988, under the auspices of the Japan Foundation, I was able to undertake a lecture tour through the socialist bloc in Europe—beginning with Moscow and Warsaw through Prague and Budapest and ending with Bucharest under Ceaucescu. It was my second visit to Prague after the spring of 1968; as for Budapest, I think it was my third visit. My dialogue with a number of Moscow's intellectuals was free-flowing and very stimulating intellectually; and in Warsaw and Budapest I had various informative conversations with my friends and their families. But in Prague and Bucharest, I got the impression that the custom of engaging a foreign visitor in any substantive conversation had not been a common practice. In Prague, I spoke in English on matters concerning Japan that my audience wanted to know, though today I can scarcely remember what the exact subject was. The Prague audience appeared to listen attentively but made absolutely no reaction after my talk. In Bucharest, I spoke in Japanese through an interpreter and met a similar response from the audience. I then asked to meet and speak with university students, a request finally granted under the conditions of specific time limits and the accompaniment of an interpreter. Afterwards, in a small room with a self-proclaimed interpreter and three or four male students, I said I had no need for an interpreter and proceeded to talk with the students in French. Although their French was not fluent, it was evident that they understood my questions and tried to articulate their thoughts, intensely curious as they were about the views of a visitor from a faraway land who had suddenly shown up before them.

What did I learn from my short visits to these East European countries? I learned almost nothing about what was happening at the time. I had only two observations. First, the general economic conditions were poor, and in Bucharest they were exceptionally bad. The other was that the strong resentment against Soviet domination had permeated widely into the masses. I had been aware of such popular feelings in Poland and Hungary. Not only did my trip confirm these impressions, there was no reason to believe that the same could not be said of Czechoslovakia and

Romania as well. It was a year and a half later that the Berlin Wall came down.

The traveler, free from the cultural specificity of his own historical environment, is concerned only with the immediacy of the present; neither the past nor the future seem to exist.[15] The movement in space effectively suspends the continuity of historical time. That is probably why a traveler is always sensitive to the irrevocable uniqueness of experience at any given moment. Perhaps it was for this reason—of course there might have been economic factors as well—that Bashō was so fond of traveling. In *waka* reminiscences and premonitions may be superimposed on immediate experiences; haiku, on the other hand, invariably seizes the fleeting moment of the present.

I recall the Marschallin's lines near the end of act one in *Der Rosenkavalier*, when she has made up her mind to leave her young lover. There she expresses the state of mind of a middle-aged woman seized with the premonition of her declining years. The arias, along with the lines of the contessa in *Le nozze di Figaro* ("Dove sono"), are absolutely superb and probably matched by none other. "Die Zeit, die ist ein sonderbar Ding. . . . Wenn man so hinlebt, ist sie rein gar nichts. Aber dann auf einmal, da spürt man nichts als sie." True, the sentiment has to do with age, but it is more than that. Experiencing foreign cultures always cuts across specific time barriers, which in turn sharpens one's awareness of time.[16]

One time after saying good-bye to a friend, I was traveling on a northbound train from New York City. The late evening had already cast a darkening shadow on the thickets outside. As I looked out vacantly from my window seat, the distant treetops of an expansive wooded area suddenly began to turn bright crimson in the evening sun. I stared at this fleeting spectacle, with layerings of flaming red projecting on the expanse of darkening hues. At the same time, my memory presented an image of the friend I'd just left, an image so vivid it seemed she stood right before my eyes. At that moment, I was clearly aware of her immediate presence, and yet at the same time I knew it would last

15. I partly summarize and partly translate a portion of the relevant paragraph.
16. In the Japanese postscript of *A Sheep's Song* (*Katō Shūichi chosakushū*, vol. 23), this paragraph from the manuscript was edited out, but I retain it to convey the original narrative's spontaneous movement.

no more than a split second. An evanescent, irreplaceable experience never to be repeated. And the intensity of this experience only deepened with passing time.

It was an autumn in Nara inside the temple garden of Shin-Yakushiji where the *hagi* flowers, blooming in great profusion, greeted the soft rays of the afternoon sun under a clear sky.[17] The place was quiet and had no other visitors. There within its spatial cosmos, I once experienced a self-contained present with neither past nor future. Even the images of the Twelve Divine Generals of the Tempyō period I'd just looked at seemed to retreat into the distant background, to say nothing of the totality of the world I had known. It was at that moment and within that space that I seemed to live in eternity.

And there were other places at other times: along the waterways in Hawaii, on the footpath through the bamboo grove in Kyoto's Giōji Temple, in the wheat fields and woods of the île de France . . . But here I'd rather not dwell on my private affairs. I continued to travel, to think, and to write, and my daily life scarcely adds up to anything out of the ordinary. In between these activities, my love and affection found their objects in a few individuals, and I came to recognize in no uncertain terms the possibility of experiences that transcend history and society. Of course, I am not talking about the Zen notion of disentangling oneself from the bondage of worldly matters, nor do such experiences have anything to do with overcoming the human condition of "existence within the world."[18] And yet these experiences will not be buried under the flow of history or overwhelmed by the onslaughts of societal forces.

Now my journey is coming to an end. Regardless of what my own sentiments and thoughts may be, history marches on into an unknown future. The last decade of the twentieth century saw the disintegration of the Soviet Union and began the process of changing the post-1945 world overshadowed by the Cold War to a new order dominated by the world's only superpower. I had thought it was only a matter of time for Eastern Europe's socialist bloc to rid itself of Soviet domination, but I had not anticipated the collapse of the Soviet Union itself. I have no idea where the future will lead us. Returning to the subject of Japan, my firm belief on

17. *Hagi,* Japanese bush clover.
18. In the margin of the original manuscript Katō sent me, he wrote the German phrase *In-der-Welt-Sein.*

the day of Pearl Harbor was that its eventual defeat was merely a matter of course, but during the days of the Occupation I failed to imagine that the country would one day become an economic giant. I have no idea how this country will continue to survive into the future. I can only turn to myself and mutter the lines, "There are more things in heaven and earth . . . than are dreamt of in your philosophy."

Katō Shūichi
Early 1997, Tokyo

Index of Author's Works

Ajia kenchiku no genzai (Asian architecture today), coauthored, xxxiv
"Amerika inshōki" (Impressions of America), xxiv
"Amerika ni manabi risei o motomeru tame no hōhō josetsu" (Methodology for acquiring the American sense of reason), xvii–xviii
"Amerika 1964," xxv
"Andore Jīdo to bungei hihyō no mondai" (André Gide and the question of literary criticism), xviii
"Ankoku o hirake!" (Lift the curtain of darkness!), xvii
"Anpo jōyaku to chishikijin" (The Japan-U.S. Security Treaty and intellectuals), xxiv
Arai Hakuseki, coannotated, xxviii
"Arai Hakuseki no sekai" (The world of Arai Hakuseki), xxix
"Aruban Beruku *Votsekku*" (Alban Berg's *Wozzeck* [by Georg Büchner]), xxi
Aru hareta hi ni (One fine day), serialized, xviii, 240
"Aru kansō: Seiyō kenbutsu tochū de kangaeta Nihon bungaku no koto" (Some reflections on Japanese literature during my journey in the West), xxi
Aru ryokōsha no shisō: Seiyō

kenbutsu shimatsuki (A traveler's thoughts: An account of my journey to the West), xxi
"Aspects de la littérature japonaise contemporaine," xxv
Atama no kaiten o yoku suru dokusho-jutsu (Reading strategies for quick thinking), xxiv

"Beichū sekkin–kansō mittsu" (The U.S.-China rapprochement: Three thoughts), xxvii
"Beikoku saihō" (Revisiting the United States), xxvi
"Ein Beitrag zur Methodologie der japanischen Literaturgeschichte," xxvii
"Berunāru Byuffe to wareware no jidai" (Bernard Buffet and our time), xxiv
"Betonamu sensō to heiwa" (Vietnam: War and peace), xxviii
"Betonamu sensō to Nihon" (The Vietnam War and Japan), xxv
"Betonamu to Zen to Anpo ni tsuite" (On Vietnam, Zen, and the Japan-U.S. Security Treaty), xxvi
"Bōdoreeru ni kansuru kōgi sōan" (Lecture draft on Baudelaire), xviii
Bosch's *Enfants de l'absurde* (Warera fujōri no ko), translation, xxii

General Index

Compositor:	Integrated Composition Systems
Text:	10/13 Aldus
Display:	Aldus
Printer and binder:	Maple-Vail Manufacturing Group